Miracle on Luckie Street

from Homeless Drug Addict to Multimillionaire — His Personal Turnaround

Bob Williamson

Miracle on Luckie Street

This book is a true account of Bob Williamson's life; however names and locations of other characters and events in this book have been changed where necessary in order to protect their identities. Any similarity to persons living or dead is coincidental and not intended by the author.

Library of Congress Cataloging-in-Publication Data is available upon request

Williamson, Bob, 1946-
Miracle on Luckie Street / Bob Williamson

ISBN 978-0-9829764-0-1 *(Hardcover)*

Printed in the United States of America

First Edition

Book Design by Cuneo Creative, *Tallahassee, Florida*

www.MiracleonLuckieStreet.com

Dedicated to Teresa,
my wife and best friend of 39 years,
who faithfully stood by me and
loved me unconditionally
in spite of my inner demons.

Chapter One

A prescription bottle with 15 Desoxyn pills is sitting on the worn-out wooden kitchen table in front of me. A syringe lies next to the pill bottle and beside it sits a fully loaded .357 Magnum pistol. Tap water covers the pills and has saturated, dissolved, and absorbed the medication out of them, transforming the water from clear to a deep amber color. The golden liquid residue in the bottle is as close as you can get to pure pharmaceutical grade methamphetamine.

It's past midnight and the small dingy apartment that I'm staying in is faintly lit with a soft yellow lamp. New Orleans is known for its large cockroaches, and a big one with long antennae is working its way down the wall, casting an eerie-looking shadow on the faded wallpaper. The filthy apartment is in complete disarray, littered with dirty dishes, trash, and boxes of half-eaten food. Empty beer cans, wine bottles, and dirty ashtrays are strewn throughout.

My long disheveled hair is partially covering my gaunt face and beneath it you can barely see my Fu Manchu mustache and long sideburns. My hollow eyes appear dark and sunken. I prefer the darkness of night and rarely see the light of day; consequently I look pale and colorless, as if I were already dead. It's ironic that my appearance is reminiscent of a dead person because I view myself as being among the walking dead.

I'm strung out from constant drug use, not eating, and rarely sleeping. I've dropped about 70 pounds and am so scrawny as to appear skeletal. I look much older than my 23 years.

Being a speed freak does that to you.

My eyes are cold, unfeeling, piercing, and filled with hate. I'm told that when I look at you my eyes scare you. To that I say, "Good!" People would be well advised to be afraid. The police are quick to point out that few criminals are more callous, dangerous, or unpredictable than a paranoid speed freak, especially one who carries a loaded .357 Magnum everywhere he goes. Extended meth use can cause severe paranoid delusions. Speed freaks have no conscience, are suspicious of everyone, can turn psychopathic in an instant, and will violently try to defend themselves from all perceived or real threats. Paranoid delusions are hallucinogenic in nature and appear as very real, eminent threats to a speed freak's life and can make them violent and unpredictable. I should know because I've been there and done that.

I roll a piece of cotton between my fingers to resemble a little ball about the size of an English pea and drop it into the liquid meth inside the bottle. Next I pick up the syringe and put the tip of the needle down into the center of the piece of cotton, which is already saturated; the cotton will act as a crude filter as I draw the golden liquid through it and into the syringe. I fill the syringe about a third of the way; it's a large dose, but I've used much more.

I recently was in the hospital for overdosing on meth and stayed in recovery for several months. During this time my tolerance changed for the better. So right now it doesn't take as much meth to attain the level of Nirvana that my dark side desires. Repeated use will change all of that, and soon it will take more and more to achieve less and less of a high. It's the cycle of increasing doses that is the addict's retribution.

I carefully squeeze the plunger until some of the yellow liquid squirts out; this ensures that no air remains in the syringe. Next I place a belt around my arm and tighten it to expose my veins. I hold it as snug as I can with my teeth, but I can feel them move when I bite into the leather. My gums are infected and my teeth have begun to loosen and deteriorate due to my constant drug use and years of neglect.

I carefully examine my arm, looking for a suitable entry point. A neat row of red scabbed-over needle marks—"tracks"—follow each vein like a colony of red ants marching up and down both of my arms and my wrists. I've been mainlining so long that my veins are as tough as dried leather from repeated injections, and it's not easy to find a clean injection point. I don't like shooting up in my legs, but lately have been experimenting with it, because soon I'll burn out the rest of my veins and I'll have no other choice.

I finally select a point that looks suitable and thump the vein several times to make it swell. I inject the needle into it by lightly tapping the topside of the syringe with my finger. *Tap. Tap. Tap.* I finally feel the needle overcome the stubborn vein as it suddenly breaks through and slides in.

I cautiously adjust the needle by moving it forward ever so slightly, being careful to hold the syringe in a near horizontal position. That way it stays within the middle of the vein. Once inside, the vein offers little resistance and the needle slides easily. Next I hold it in place as I lightly pull back on the plunger a little with my finger. Red blood comes swirling into the syringe and a faint smile crosses my face as I see the red cumulus cloud of blood slowly billowing its way into the golden liquid inside the syringe. Addicts call this "registering." It ensures that the needle is inside the vein and signals when it's safe to inject.

If I inject it without the needle being in the center of the vein, or inject too fast, the meth will blow out of the vein and will burn its way under the skin surrounding the injection point. A blowout hurts like hell, swells badly, easily becomes infected, and remains sore for weeks.

Worst of all, there is no high with a blowout.

Now that I'm in the vein and registered, I release the belt and slowly push the plunger forward with my index finger. My dark side is eagerly anticipating his fix.

With his serpent eyes gleaming, he's excitedly licking his evil lips in anticipation. When the plunger is pushed all the way forward, I immediately remove the syringe and drop it on the table. I quickly put my thumb in place over the injection point and apply pressure to avoid any meth from escaping and to stop the bleeding.

Instantaneously I feel the meth rushing up my neck. It takes my breath away. It slams into my brain, causing my head to slump back from the impact of the collision. I limply drop my hand from my arm, and once my thumb is removed I dazedly watch as a little stream of blood begins to trickle down my arm. I'm plummeting into paradise. My dark side is gleefully chanting and wildly dancing to pounding drums, frenetically running around and around in tight little circles back and forth and throughout my brain. The noise is so intense that I feel it, instead of hear it, and it grows louder and louder and louder. It's deafening. And I love the rush.

I'm zooming now and feel as though I'm the master of the universe.

After the initial rush subsides I settle into a mind-racing frenzy that will sufficiently anesthetize me for at least a couple of hours. I stand up and go to the kitchen sink and run some rusty water into a dirty-looking glass with a layer of red wine stuck to its bottom. I use it to clean my syringe—sucking water in, squirting it back out at the kitchen window, and then repeating several times. I briefly wonder about the sanity of my sterilization procedure, but quickly come to the conclusion that I really don't give a shit.

Furniture is scarce in this crummy apartment. The few items that are in it are dirty and dilapidated, like the tattered couch in the corner that's so filthy I won't even sit on it, but there is a record player. A Jimi Hendrix Experience album is loudly playing on it and the music is blasting its rhythm within my head.

The band is now softly secreting soothing blues background music while Hendrix defiantly proclaims,

> *White-collared conservatives flashing down the street,*
> *Pointing their plastic finger at me.*
> *They're hoping soon my kind will drop and die,*
> *But I'm gonna wave my freak flag high . . . HIGH!*

I join in chanting, "*Wave on, wave on.*"

Now Jimi says and I join in again,

> *I'm the one that's gonna have to die*
> *When it's time for me to die*
> *So let ME live, MY life, the way I want to!*

The guitar is wildly screaming, the bass is vibrating, and the drums are hammering as I wrap my syringe and the remaining Desoxyn inside a washcloth. I stash it underneath a loose board that I pried up underneath the kitchen sink.

Desoxyn is a federally regulated diet medication and I wrote a prescription for it earlier. Another speed freak that I know has an overweight girlfriend and she took it into a drugstore and had it filled late this afternoon. I wrote the prescription for a 30-day supply and they took half and I took half. I have several prescription pads from different doctors that have been stolen by various acquaintances, and I can write one as well as the best doctor in New Orleans. I stashed my extra scrip pads under the board too. I replace the board and I'm ready to boogie.

I put my .357 in its holster and secure the holster clip inside my pants in the small of my back. Then I put on my coat and head out into the dark night. I head for a rough bar that I hang out in, called the Seven Seas. It's off the beaten trail, located toward the upper end of the French Quarter adjacent to the French market, and most of the people there are locals.

I walk only a couple of blocks down the dark street when I encounter a skinny little guy who looks to be about five foot six inches tall and probably 19 years old. From the way he's dressed, he doesn't appear to be a street person from the Quarter. He looks more like some poor white trash hick who just wandered out of his trailer park. He's wearing jeans, cowboy boots, and a sleeveless white T-shirt. I can't see him all that well on the dimly lit street, but I can easily see the knife in his hand glinting in what little light there is.

"Gimme your wallet *asshole.*"

I say, "Okay man, take it easy."

I'm not afraid of this little punk. No, it's more like I'm enraged that he would attempt to rob me on my own turf. I own these dark streets and he has no business being here. If there are any armed robberies to be committed on this street, it will be me doing them and not this hillbilly. I reach behind me as if I'm going for my wallet and instead come out with my chrome-plated .357. It clicks loudly as I cock it and swing it around in front of his face. I point it right between his eyes and say, "Did you say something? . . . *Asshole!*"

His cocky short-man swagger and tough-guy demeanor vanish. He appears to be physically sagging at the shoulders now and is trying to back up, all the while submissively pleading, "Please man, I'm sorry."

I slowly advance toward him as he stumbles slightly as he backs up. Without a word I motion to the knife with my pistol.

He drops it and it clatters to the street. He's standing there holding his hands in the air, looking scared shitless. I snarl at him, raising my voice louder with each word that I utter, "Now gimme *YOUR* wallet *ASSHOLE*"

"Okay, okay, please don't shoot."

He's holding up his hand and nervously waving his palm back and forth between his face and the barrel, as though vainly attempting to ward off a bullet and protect himself. Yeah right, like his pissy-ass hand might somehow stop a .357 Magnum bullet from blowing right through it and on through his face, removing the back of his skull and splattering his brains all over the place in the process.

He reaches behind with one hand to grab his wallet and nervously hands it to me; his hands are shaking badly and he's still feebly holding them up in front of his face. He's now crying and sobbing like a baby. Who can blame him? He's looking down the evil end of my cocked .357 Magnum chrome-plated revolver, and I'm *pissed.*

I look at him with raging contempt and glance inside his wallet. He has only one dollar in it, and for some reason this loser having only one dollar sets me off and makes me even more furious. I jerk his one friggin' dollar out and stuff it in my shirt pocket and then angrily sling his empty wallet on the street.

The meth has fuel-injected both my brain and my heart beyond their upper limits. My mind is blazing at blistering speed and my heart is wildly beating. I'm clocking record RPMs now. I'm so mad I can hardly think. My mouth is dry, my eyes are wild and dilated, and my dark side is screaming, screaming, screaming:

Shoot that son of a bitch!

What are you waiting for?

Shoot that son of a bitch!

SHOOT!

I scream, "*Is that all you got?* ***ONE LOUSY DOLLAR!***

"*Is that all you got? You asshole!*

"*You think you're some kind of bad ass with that knife?* ***DO YOU?***

"*You want to rob ME?* ***DO YOU?***

"*You cocksucker. I'll blow your damned head off.*" He's terrified as he looks down the barrel pointed between his eyes. As I slowly continue advancing toward him, he begins to fervently cry. He's sobbing, intensely pleading for his life,

"*Please don't kill me! Oh please, please don't kill me!*"

He's out of control now crying and sobbing with a pitiful tortured, agonized, pleading voice, "*I'm sorry! I'm sorry!*"

Mournfully now, grief-stricken, resigned, subdued, softly begging, "*Please don't kill me mister! Please! Please! Don't shoot . . . I'm so sorry!*"

My brain is redlining as it races toward the finish line. I grab him by his hair with my free hand and shove his head tightly against the doorsill. I ram the cocked .357 between his eyes and shove it against his skull as hard as I physically can. I'm pushing the barrel against his forehead with all my might, putting the entire weight of my body behind it. My teeth clench tightly and my face twists with blinding hate and furious demonic rage.

I'm insane!

My dark side is screaming, "*SHOOT. SHOOT. SHOOT THE SON-OF-A-BITCH! SHOOT HIM!*"

My meth-inflamed mind is now a violent furious uncontrolled red-hot fireball. Suddenly it leaps from my mind and a flash of red-orange flame lights up the dark street.

BOOM!

Chapter Two

The would-be mugger's body lies in a heap as I quickly walk toward Decatur Street. I'm careful to stay in the dark shadows where I can't be seen. It's not unusual to hear an occasional gunshot in this section of the French Quarter, but this was a .357 Magnum and when it went off it sounded as loud as a cannon. My ears are still ringing a clear, high-pitched, continuous and unrelenting sound that is grating into my mind. *Eeeeeeeeeeeee . . .*

I doubt any tourists will be in this dark and dangerous section of the Quarter so late at night. If any do accidentally stumble in here, it will be because they're so drunk that they're lost. I'm not concerned about drunken tourists fingering me: There are no streetlights and drunks don't remember anything.

I know that none of the residents will come outside to see what's going on either. The street-wise residents of the French Quarter know without having to be told to mind their own business. The last thing anyone will do when he hears a gunshot is go sticking his head outside to see what's going on so he can take a bullet in his head too. At night everyone's blinds are always drawn and their shutters are always shut. No, they will not do anything that stupid, and they won't dare to call a cop either. No one will want to be involved. Better not to see, hear, or know anything. It's healthier that way.

I'm more worried that maybe a cop is somewhere in the vicinity and heard the loud *BOOM* of the gun. If so he'll be coming soon to check it out. So far anyway, I'm in luck. I don't hear any sirens or see anyone on the empty streets. I continue walking and it's eerily quiet except for a lone dog that is barking a couple of streets over. The streets are inky dark—just the way I like them. I silently glide through the shadows like a dangerous man-eating shark that has just devoured its prey in a bloodied frenzy and who's slowly drifting back down to its lair in the solitary deep.

I pass by Jackson Square and reach Decatur Street without incident. I still haven't seen anyone. I dart across Decatur and immediately hook a right and head for the ferry on Canal Street. I continue to stay in the dark shadows and don't see a soul as I make the long walk.

I'm in luck, as the ferry is on this side of the river and is boarding. I walk onto the deck and sit by myself on a wooden bench, smoking a cigarette. My foot is nervously dancing up and down, keeping time with the hammering drums in my head. The speed that controls my nervous system has me grinding my teeth and repeatedly clinching and reclinching them.

And I can't get that Hendrix song out of my head. It's playing over and over in my mind. Damn Hendrix is good on his guitar. I think maybe he's the best guitar player ever.

The ferry across the Mississippi River holds only a couple of cars, ready to go into Algiers. The captain gives a couple of loud blasts with the foghorn, and black water swirls as the ferry leaves the dock and starts moving. I can smell the river, and its distinctive muddy scent can almost be tasted: I think of it like the intense flavor of some New Orleans chef's roux. I've always liked that river smell—it reminds me of low tide at the ocean. Some say it stinks like a sewer, but I like it.

I enjoy riding the ferry at night. I never get off on the other side. I just like to get loaded and ride it back and forth, sometimes all night long by myself. I love the river—it's a mighty force, powerful, and mysterious, and the humid warm blackness that blankets me seems peaceful and tranquil. I feel safe on the ferry.

When I see that we are halfway across, I stand up and head for the darkness of the passageway that leads to the ferry's front. I'm on the opposite side of where the few ferry passengers left their cars and they're congregating and loudly talking and laughing. They have no doubt been to the Quarter partying. They're all sloshed to the max with booze and are having a grand old time. One lady with bleached-blonde hair and a scarlet dress keeps laughing and laughing, but her annoying laughter reminds me of a cackling hen that has just laid an egg. I'm betting she gets laid tonight herself. They're all oblivious to me and that's a good thing.

I'm now in the complete darkness. No one can see me in my position in the shadows. I take my beloved revolver out of its holster and give it a farewell kiss. It has served me well, but now it must descend to the depths of the river and become forever lost in the mud, where its beautiful chrome finish will never be seen again. I toss it far out into the black water and then follow with the holster. Then I take the would-be mugger's knife that I collected off the street and throw it over too. He won't need that anymore. Finally, as if to put a period on the end of the sentence to end this saga, I flip my cigarette overboard too.

Done!

I lean on the rail, gazing across the black water of the river. It's an awesome sight, with the twinkling lights of New Orleans reflecting on the water and shining back at me like sparkling diamonds scattered on black velvet. The encounter with the mugger was too close for comfort. My dark side had very nearly convinced me to shoot that poor bastard right between the eyes. The one tiny sliver of good that remained buried deep within my black soul—my mother used to refer to it as my "angel of light"—appeared for the first time in a very long time and at the last second had convinced me to let him live.

It was a classic battle to the end. My dark side was screaming in a rage to *kill him, kill him, kill him*, and my angel of light was begging me to let him live and telling me, *Don't be stupid Bob. Don't be stupid! Let it go Bob. Let it go!* It was the fierce battle of good versus evil that has gone on within me all my life. Those battles usually have been won by my dark side.

I wanted to shoot him. Every ounce of my fiber wanted me to shoot that bastard and teach him a lesson. Instead, at the last conceivable second, I moved the gun barrel slightly to the right and held the gun close beside his ear and pulled the trigger. The bullet tore into the wooden door frame beside his face and not into his skull. There is no doubt that the blast from it ruptured his eardrum. I then viciously slammed his head into the large wooden door frame, banging the back of his head on it as hard as I could; once, twice, and then one more time, savagely hard. He slid down to the street like a piece of cooked spaghetti, unconscious.

Tell the scorekeeper to make a note. My angel of light, my lost and forgotten good side, finally won a battle. That son of a bitch would-be mugger does not know how lucky he is. He should be kissing my angel of light's shining feet for saving his worthless punk-ass life. My dark side is pissed that I didn't kill him, but I'm relieved.

The ferry is slowly working its way towards Algiers and I light up another cigarette. As I stand there staring at the black water, I think about a guy I know; I've been thinking a lot about him lately. His name is Ronnie and he served four years in the notorious Angola State Penitentiary. They just paroled him. He scares the shit out of me with stories about that place. Angola is named after a place in Africa where slaves came from, and it's located on a former 8,000-acre plantation in Louisiana full of gators and snakes.

Angola is also known as the Bloodiest Prison in the South due to the large number of inmate-on-inmate attacks within its walls. Ronnie is a survivor and he has a wicked-looking scar that runs all the way from the top of his chest down to his groin—it's from an attack by another inmate who had a grudge to settle.

The guy that knifed him claimed that Ronnie had stolen a pack of cigarettes from him—a fact that he denies. Ronnie was attacked in the shower and was gutted like a pig with a homemade shiv that sliced its way through his body like a razor. It took him to the very brink of death and he was in recovery for almost a year.

I'm creeped out listening to him describe the brutality of the sociopathic guards—many should be serving time in Angola themselves—and the inmates and their brutality and sexual perversions, and the hard work chopping cotton all day in the hot sun while guards sit atop horses with shotguns, just itching for some poor bastard to make a run for it.

If I don't change my ways soon, a damn gun is going to land me a murder one or armed-robbery charge and put me in Angola too. I'm at a point where my dark side is too influential and my angel of light is all but nonexistent. I'm oozing evil from every pore and it's dripping from my fingertips. I don't want to end up in Angola and I don't want someone to spin the bottle back toward me like I just did to that poor hick bastard. That's why I threw away my gun.

I think I'm too far gone and fear that there's no hope. I wonder if I could ever be normal. I don't think so. I think it's time for me to end the madness. I've been thinking about suicide a lot lately.

Chapter Three

It's lightly raining and it's a nasty, ugly day. I'm walking down Royal Street in the French Quarter in New Orleans, returning to the apartment. Even though there's no sun, I'm wearing dark black sunglasses. I cautiously approach the site of the shooting incident last night. I'm ready to turn down a side street and disappear in a flash if I see the first sign of a cop. I breathe a sigh of relief as I see that the street is completely empty.

I continue walking, and when I pass the exact location where it occurred, the only indicator of what happened is a splintered door casing where the .357 Magnum bullet tore into it. The trailer trash kid is gone.

I'm relieved that no police tape cordons off the area, signaling a crime-scene investigation. It's not uncommon to see crime scenes sealed off in the Quarter. I'd been wondering how badly that little redneck had been hurt. As hard as I banged his head against that door I might have killed him; I'm glad I didn't.

A sardonic smile comes to my face as I remember savagely and repeatedly slamming his head into the door frame. I wonder if he has a headache today. I emit a wicked little chuckle as I think about shooting that gun right next to his ear. I bet that scared the living shit out of him. I can just see him spending the rest of his miserable life saying, "Huh? Come again? Eh? What was that? Could you please speak a little louder?"

It serves that sawed-off son of a bitch right. Who the hell does he think he is trying to rob ME? He got what he deserved and is lucky I didn't kill him. He needs to go back home to his trailer park before someone does kill him. He chose the wrong person at the wrong time in the wrong neighborhood.

I keep walking toward my apartment. The streets in the French Quarter are especially nasty dirty when they're wet, and they're always wet from the daily dousing of afternoon tropical rain showers or from the street-cleaning machines that spray water every morning. The whirling brushes spin the nasty, dirty water around in the nasty, dirty, fine black dirt that covers the streets and creates even nastier dirty wet streets. They don't clean anything and the streets are always covered with black ooze. My tan leather Hushpuppy shoes are now coated with black slime.

I've been up all night and through midmorning. After the ferry returned to the New Orleans side, I walked to the Seven Seas and spent my time drinking and mingling with other street people. I managed to score a free hit of speed from a guy that I know, and we shot up together in his place not far from the Seven Seas. It kept me hopping all through the wee early-morning hours, right up until now. My mind is still buzzing, but my body has just about exceeded its exhaustive limits and I have the shakes. Sleep is out of the question, but I desperately need to lie down and rest for an hour or more in order to prevent physical collapse. I can't remember when I last ate, but the mere thought of food repulses me.

After some rest, I'll geez up another hit of speed and continue on this run. I barely know the guy who has been letting me crash at his apartment for the past few days. I hope he's not there, because I don't want to share my drugs with him.

My thoughts are interrupted by someone calling me from across the street. "Hey Bob! *BOB!*"

I turn around to see who it is and it's Lenny. I met him through my old girlfriend Debbie, who went to school with him. One time Lenny, Debbie, and I all got wired up on speed for an entire weekend and had a hell of a good time. Lenny and I have been tight ever since, and whenever I have them to spare, I sell tabs of speed to him.

Lenny doesn't use the needle yet. He's a weekend-warrior wannabe hippie who works at a body shop during the week and always has plenty of money. I like to hang out with him because he always pays for everything. He drops tabs of speed and drinks alcohol with reckless abandon every weekend. That's how I started. Drinking and dropping is a good combination and yields an excellent high, but it's nothing compared with the rush of the needle. If Lenny ever tried it, even one time, he'd never go back and would be forever hooked—just like me and a million other lost souls.

I turn around and smile, "Yo Lenny, how you doin' man?"

He has a dark look on his face and says, "Dude you're in *big* trouble. The cops are looking for you."

"*What?*" My mood instantly changes and now I'm on full paranoid alert. My mind instantly goes to that little trailer-trash redneck, and I wonder if maybe I did kill him after all. I quickly glance around the street looking for cops. I nervously raise my voice, "What are you talking about Lenny? *What's going on?*"

Lenny pulls out a 4 × 6 black-and-white police mug shot with two photos of me displayed side by side. In one photo I'm facing forward and in the other I'm facing sideways. This is a copy of the mug shot photos that the cops took when they arrested me for possession of heroin and hauled me off to Parrish Prison a few months back. Lenny turns it over and on the back it has printed:

Wanted for numerous narcotics violations, including felonious forgery of medical documents and other charges.

Considered to be armed and dangerous.

The hair stands up on my neck. "Where did you get this? 'Armed and dangerous.' Where did they come up with that shit?" My heart feels like it's going to explode and once again I cast a paranoid look behind me.

"Did Mike give you this?"

"Yeah, Mike said you better get the hell out of town fast. The cops are passing these out everywhere. They're sweeping the Quarter right now looking for you. I've been trying to find you all morning man. Here take this."

Lenny shoves the mug shot into my hand as if he couldn't wait a second longer to move it out of his possession. Lenny's roommate Mike is a New Orleans cop. He's in his early 20s too. Lenny and Mike went to school together through every grade from kindergarten through high school and are still the best of friends. In fact they're roommates. Mike's a cool guy and he feeds me good information from time to time. New Orleans is known for corrupt cops and Mike is a good example of one. His loyalty goes to the highest bidder and he's on the take to several pimps, fences, small-time drug dealers, and petty criminals on his beat. He makes good money at it.

Mike also has part ownership in a small drugstore on St. Charles Avenue. I've heard that the mafia owns the other part and it's a thriving portal to obtaining illegal pharmaceutical drugs. I don't know whether that mafia stuff is true or not and don't want to know. Mike's smart, he's careful and selective, and he won't sell to just anyone. I got in with him through Lenny and he told me that he'd kill me if I ever snitched on him.

I believe him.

It's not uncommon for people on the street to become snitches. The cops bust you and then use you to rat out your friends up the ladder. If you don't cooperate, they send you to Angola prison, where you'll become someone's bitch.

I occasionally buy blue morphine tabs from Mike's drugstore. I buy 250 tabs at a time and pay $7 a tab for them. I resell them to my connection for $30 to $40 bucks a tab, depending on the current supply of heroin (or smack, as it's known on the street). When times are lean, I can sell them for top dollar. When times are fat and there's lots of heroin on the street, buying and reselling them isn't worth the risk and I usually don't even try. My price is higher than smack, but heroin is always cut several times. My stuff costs more but is pharmaceutical-grade pure blue morphine. The junkies can divide the tabs into four equal pieces and each piece will support three hits. One tab will satisfy four junkies for a day.

I sell only to dealers, and my connections all have to buy a minimum of 50 tabs. This reduces my risk of multiple sales. The dealers deal the blues by the individual tab or a couple at a time to their slimeball users, who in turn sell to their connections by the quarter tab. All the dealers end up getting their dope free, and the street junkies pay for everyone's habit by stealing and fencing anything they can put their hands on.

I don't like junkies and I don't like street dealers. Even though I have a reputation as being a bad ass speed freak with a gun, they'd snitch me out in a half second to stay out of jail.

It's a risky business, but the connection with Mike has proved to be too good to pass up. Aside from making some good cash, blues come in handy for my own habit in providing a good way for me to come down after zipping along at the speed of light for 3 or 4 days. No matter how wired up and sleepless I might be, blues flat knock me out. And they have the added bonus of giving me a hell of a rush.

I asked, "Can you give me a ride out of town Lenny?"

"No man, I'm walking myself." I knew that was a lie. Lenny always has wheels. I don't blame him. If the cops catch me in the car with him, he'll be under scrutiny from now on; and no one in our world wants that kind of heat.

"You have any money you can lend me?"

"Sorry Bob, I'm flat broke." I know that is a lie too. Lenny always has money. I almost press the issue, but then I think about the effort and the risk that he just took to tip me off, and I think better of it.

"I'm completely busted too, I got one lousy nickel to my name and I just found that. All right man, I gotta go!"

"I hate you gotta go Bob. Where you going?"

"I have no idea. Anywhere but here." Even if I knew I would never tell him or anyone where I was going. One thing I've learned is that I can't trust anyone. I wonder again who the snitch might be and what he (or she) told the cops.

"I'll see you man. *Thanks* Lenny, I owe you. Tell Mike thanks for me."

"You got it Bob. Good luck my man."

Damn it! I'm only a block from where I've been staying and when I unlock the gate and step inside the courtyard, I run all the way up the rickety wooden stairs to the apartment, taking two steps at a time. I pack in less than a minute. Into a dirty blue pillowcase go all my possessions, which consist of one change of clothes, shaving gear, a tube of toothpaste, and a toothbrush. It will now serve as my suitcase. I think about my stash hidden under the sink, and then I think about Angola and I think better of it. I need to get gone *right now!*

I run back down the stairs, this time taking three steps at a time. I figure that by now the cops probably already know where I'm crashing, and as soon as they can obtain a search warrant they'll be looking here first. *Damned snitches.* I wonder who it is. I'll kill that son of a bitch if I find out.

I run through the courtyard and reach the gate leading out to the street. Anxiously peering through the bars of a small opening, I scan up one side of the street and down the other, tensely looking for cops or anyone who looks like a cop. Other than a couple of tourists who look like they're shopping, I don't see anyone.

I quickly open the door and cross the street. I try to walk as slowly as my panicked mind will allow. Stay low, stay calm. I tuck my blue pillowcase containing my stuff further inside my corduroy coat so as not to draw attention to it. I try to look normal, but I'm extremely paranoid and apprehensive. Visions of the Angola State Penitentiary keep appearing in my mind. I feel eyes on every corner looking at me and I have a bad, bad feeling that I'm being followed. But I'm afraid to look back; I feel like screaming. I wish I had my gun back.

I walk a couple of streets and am absolutely mortified when I see a cop car coming. *Shit! Shit! Shit!* My mind is racing. I'm terrified but I need to act normal. Don't panic!

If he stops, should I just give it up? Raise my hands and surrender? My dark side hisses, *Hell no, you ain't going down without a fight man. Make a run for it. If you're shot in the back, so be it.*

He's right! I'm not going to Angola!

Okay, stay cool now, he's almost beside me. I'm very close to having a heart attack and hyperventilating, but somehow manage to maintain my steady walk—not too fast and not too slow. As he slowly passes me, I nonchalantly keep my head down, looking at the street as though I'm preoccupied in deep thought. The police car seems to be going in slow motion, one frame at a time. The pressure inside my mind is building like a huge volcano ready to erupt. It's about to blow my mind and I want to scream. The cop continues slowly driving down the street and passes me by.

I'm thinking, *Don't stop! Please don't stop.* I have an urge to take off running and it's all I can do to continue my slow pace. My heart is pounding so hard it feels like it's going to burst through my chest.

After what seems like an agonizingly endless amount of time, I finally reach the street corner. I glance back as I turn onto the side street, and see that the cop is about half a block down the street and still slowly cruising along. After I turn the corner, I can't stand it another second—now that I'm out of his sight I race down the street as though demons released from hell are viciously snapping at my heels.

I quickly cover the three streets to Bourbon Street at a full run. As I approach crowded Bourbon, I slow back down again to a brisk walk. I'm nervously looking around and my stomach is in a knot. I feel like puking and I'm gasping for breath. I'm not used to physical exercise and I feel nauseous and have sharp chest pains.

When I hit Bourbon Street I breathe a sigh of relief. Here I can easily blend with the crowd. Even though it's early and has begun to intermittently rain a light drizzle, the usual combination of drunken tourists, prostitutes, pickpockets, and street people milling around now packs Bourbon Street. The scene reminds me of frenzied ants emerging from an ant pile that someone stepped on. No one seems to be going anywhere in particular; they just seem to be meandering back and forth. They go in one direction and then for no apparent reason turn and go another, only to return to where they were before. They all seem to be looking for something that they don't seem capable of finding.

Blues and jazz music are drifting out of the titty bars that line both sides of the street. The thick, humid air reeks of stale beer and the street is already littered with empty cups and beer cans. Later on there will be so many of them littering the crowded streets that tourists will have nowhere to walk but on top of them.

Hawkers are yelling at everyone who passes by. They hope to lure people inside by swinging open the doors and offering a free peek at some topless pig doing the bump and grind.

The stripper's job is to keep customers buying overpriced, watered-down drinks for as long as possible. She's good at it. She'll strip to nothing but a G-string and glitter-covered nipples, and then swing her naked body around a pole and simulate grinding sex as music thumps in the background. All the while she'll stare directly into your eyes with a seductive sexy look and a smile that can only mean that she wants to screw you just as soon as she's off work.

More than enough guys buy into the fantasy to make it a profitable con, and they'll stay right there until they're flat broke or too drunk to care anymore. Then they'll stagger off into the night.

I recognize a guy I know who's hawking, and he calls out to me. I pretend not to hear him and keep walking. I don't see any cops and easily lose myself in the crowd. I follow Bourbon Street toward Esplanade. When I reach St. Ann, I cut left over to North Rampart and wait for a bus at a covered bus stop.

It has begun to rain again, only this time harder. I turn up my collar as I check my pocket for the nickel that I found. A bus ride costs a nickel in New Orleans and that is exactly what I found lying in the street earlier—one lousy nickel. This must be my lucky day, because aside from that five cents, I'm flat broke.

A city bus pulls up and I hop on board. I tell the driver where I want to end up and he tells me where to get off and how to manage the transfers. When I take a seat on the bus, I notice a newspaper folded open to the want-ad section. I disinterestedly scan through it and notice an ad for a night school in Atlanta that offers computer training. I don't really understand what computers are, but I've heard a little about them and think it might be something to look into. Maybe I should sign up for that class and start over again. I was thinking of maybe going to California, but Atlanta will work. I tear the ad out and put it in my pocket. There just might be hope for me yet.

I think about my mother and her crazy notion about the angel of light on my shoulder that always looks out for me. I wonder if that son of a bitch left the nickel lying on the street for me to catch a bus. Maybe he's also the one who left this want ad for me. Maybe he's encouraging me to go back to school.

My dark side takes over and tells me that he doesn't know why I tore that damned ad out. Deep down I know there really isn't any hope for someone like me. I'm not going to school. I won't get a job or kick the drug habit or do anything other than put a needle in my arm at every opportunity.

He reminds me that I'm penniless, homeless, hopelessly addicted to drugs and alcohol; that I have a criminal record, was kicked out of the military, and am wanted by the police on felony charges right this moment; that my parents and brother long ago gave up on me; and that I have no friends (unless you want to call a handful of criminals that want something from me friends).

I've tried before but always go back to drugs, usually on the very first day—that's what happened the day I was released from prison. I have tracks everywhere and have already worn out every major vein in both arms. I've even tried to shoot between my toes, which incidentally hurts like hell. I have needle marks there too. I take drugs now just to achieve some sense of normalcy. Without them I'm climbing the walls. I can't live without them and that'll never change.

My dark side hisses, *If you can't take it anymore, then why not quit whining about it and just end it all? You should just blow your damned head off and be a man for once.*

Maybe I will . . . maybe I will. I'm dead serious. I want to change my life or I want to end it. I'm sick of living on the streets and I don't want to be paranoid all the time. I'm like the ocean's waves that constantly, endlessly churn back and forth, never resting for a moment. There is no stability in my life. I never rest. The only constant for me is fear.

I fear all kinds of things. Most of all I fear being locked up in Angola State Prison with dangerous men. But I also fear being shot in the back of the head or in the face because of some drug deal that went bad. I fear that the many armed robberies that I have been committing lately will go bad and result in my being shot, stabbed, or beaten to death. I fear OD'ing from a hotshot of bad dope dealt to me by someone who has a grudge. I've seen it happen to others. I fear that it's only a matter of time until I kill someone and get caught. I fear freaking out on drugs and staying hopelessly insane forever. I fear. I fear. I fear!

Somehow I'm able to maneuver my way to the outskirts of New Orleans, changing buses three times. After I step off the bus on the outskirts of New Orleans, I go inside a convenience store and ask the guy behind the counter, "You got a black marker I can use for a minute?"

He nods and pushes a marker across the counter toward me without saying a word.

I had torn off a big piece of cardboard from a box that I found in the dumpster beside the store. I write in big letters:

ATLANTA GA.
DAD'S FUNERAL

I roll the marker back to the guy behind the counter and walk out to Highway 90. I hold up my sign and stick out my thumb.

Chapter Four

I came up with this scam several years ago. As far as I know, my dad still lives in Columbus, Mississippi, and is very much alive and in good health. The sign not only will easily garner me a ride, but more often than not will help me con the driver out of money too. Softhearted suckers love a sob story and I'm the master hard-luck storyteller. The only thing better for catching rides than this sign is hitchhiking with a good-looking girl—and right now I'm fresh out of girlfriends.

Almost immediately an 18-wheeler pulls up. I climb up and open the door and the trucker says, "Goin' to Atlanta?"

I respond, "Yes sir!"

"Well this is your lucky day 'cause that's where I'm headin' too."

"Cool!" I toss my sign on the side of the road, climb into the big rig, and slam the door shut. As we pick up speed heading away from New Orleans toward Atlanta, I look in the big rearview mirror and see the skyline of the "Big Easy" disappearing behind us. I breathe a sigh of relief.

That was entirely too close . . .

The truck driver is a big burly man with a shaved head. He makes up for his baldness with a long full beard that is jet black. He has on blue jeans with a chrome chain attached to his belt loop and a black Harley Davidson T-shirt, which reveals bulging biceps completely covered in tattoos. He's wearing a gaudy gold bracelet and gold necklace with a big garish medallion hanging from it. He constantly smiles, which reveals really bad, crooked teeth. He glances at me from underneath his bushy eyebrows with piercing brown eyes that almost look black and says, "Lost your dad, huh?"

"Yeah." I try to look pitiful.

He says, "Lost mine a few years back too. What happened?"

"Heart attack."

He looks at me and somberly says, "Life is short man. Did he live in Atlanta?"

I nod and look down, trying my best to appear to be going to tears. I want to look as though I can't bear to talk about it anymore. I really don't feel like talking and just want a ride out of town. I don't want a bunch of moronic conversation.

The trucker nods as though he understands my "grief" and we ride along in silence. I settle in and shut my eyes and actually drift off for a few minutes of fitful sleep. I'm exhausted and it's coming down hard on me.

The instant I wake up and open my eyes the truck driver says, "You hungry?"

I rub my eyes as I try to gather my thoughts and say, "Naw, you go ahead. I'm dead broke. I lost my job on the oil rigs and have been out of work for about a month now. I hurt my back on the job and got laid up and couldn't make the crew boat just one time and they fired me and hired another guy and gave him my job. Just like that, I don't have a job anymore. Can you believe that shit?"

I'm amazed at how easily I can lie and how believable this crap sounds. I hope it'll work and he'll give me some cash.

Taking the bait the trucker exclaims, "Those *assholes!*"

I say, "Yeah, caught me by surprise, but maybe I'll find something in Atlanta after my dad's funeral. You go ahead though. I'll just wait outside until you're through."

I'm thinking, *Yeah right, I know damn well that this sucker will never let me sit out here and starve while he sits in there and eats.*

Right on cue he says, "I didn't ask if you had any money. I asked if you were hungry. It's on me buddy."

"Gosh, are you sure?" I can just see my dark side laughing his ass off at my acting skills.

"Damn right I'm sure. What's your name anyway?"

"Bob Johnson," I tell him, using one of my favorite aliases. "What's yours?"

"Just call me Bud. I'm pulling in here, Bob. I need fuel too." He starts pulling into a truck stop just over the Alabama line. It's beginning to get late and is already dark.

"Thanks Bud!"

"No problem kid. I wish I could do more, but I'm tapped out myself. Been drunk in New Orleans shacked up with a whore for nearly a week. Spent all my money but what little I had stashed in my truck for emergencies, and that's barely enough to get me back to Atlanta. I'm hoping I can get a draw there, or I'm gonna be in a world of hurt myself. I got enough to buy us both a big hamburger steak and some fries tonight though."

"Awesome Bud. I'll pay you back when I'm back on my feet."

"Bullshit you will. It's the least I can do for someone who just lost his father and his job."

"Thanks man I really appreciate it. I owe you big time."

"You don't owe me shit, Bob! Let's get something to eat."

As we walk across the parking lot together he says, "Damned, rotten booze and rotten women," and starts rubbing his hand on his forehead with one hand as though his bald head is hurting. Then he grabs his crotch with the other hand and winces as if he's in pain there too. But then he belly-laughs so loudly that people turn and look at him to see what's going on.

Then he winks at me and laughs, "Now that's a hell of a combination isn't it son? HAW, HAW, HAW!"

I laugh.

I can't take Bud up on eating the steak and fries—they're way too heavy for my ailing stomach at this point. My system is beginning to go into withdrawal and I'm nauseous and don't feel worth a shit. I settle for a few sips of mushroom soup, a couple of Saltine crackers, and a Coke.

We head back onto the road and talk for a while, and then out of sheer exhaustion I manage to sleep a little. When I awaken it's 10 a.m. and we're approaching Atlanta on Interstate 20. I can see the high rises of the downtown area. That will soon be my new home.

Street people nearly always go to the bus station downtown when we head into a new city. There I will find others who share my dark disorders and I can find out the things that I need to know. Someone will no doubt also be there in the shadows anxious to sell me drugs, but I'm determined now to avoid them and make my angel of light proud.

Bud needs to go toward Marietta, Georgia, to his terminal, which he says is way up on the north side of Atlanta. I tell him that I'd appreciate it if he could just drop me off on the side of the road near any exit that would lead into the downtown area. I could call someone to come and pick me up and take me to the funeral home.

"I'll do better than that Bob. I'll take you downtown."

"Naw man, you can't take this big rig through downtown Atlanta. Bud, just drop me off on the side of the road and I'll walk."

"The hell you say. I can take this rig anywhere I want. Just watch this old dog show you a few tricks."

Bud turns off on an exit that takes us right to downtown Atlanta. We are of course the only 18-wheeler downtown, and people are actually stopping on the street and staring at the bizarre sight of this huge rig traversing the narrow city streets of Atlanta. I laugh and say, "Man you're one crazy dude. You've lost all sanity."

He says, "I never had any! That's exactly what all my ex-wives keep telling me. Any place in particular you heading?"

I can't believe my luck because I see the bus station right down the block from where we are. I say, "This'll be fine right here, Bud."

"Hey Bob, it's been nice getting to know you man." His tone turns serious for a moment. "Hang tough at your old man's funeral son. I love you man."

I solemnly nod to him, as I pretend to tear up. I dab at my eye with the back of my hand and we firmly shake hands. "I will Bud. Thanks again. I might have missed the funeral if it hadn't been for you. I *really* appreciate it man."

I think the tears are a nice touch and my dark side agrees.

"Good luck Bob!"

"Yo, same to you Bud. Later."

I climb down and wave goodbye. Crazy Bud lets off on his air brakes and the big rig immediately makes a loud hissing and squealing noise and his diesel engine rattles loudly as he powers up and begins to lurch the giant rig forward through the narrow streets of downtown Atlanta.

Now, as if his rig is not already creating enough of a stir, Bud has rolled his window down and is yelling and leering at a hooker standing on the corner. He's grinning and waving to her like some deranged mental patient. She smiles and waves back and lifts her short skirt up about a foot exposing her black panties and motions him over.

That ignites old Bud like pouring lighter fluid on a charcoal pit. He's really going now. He's hollering at the top of his lungs and jumping up and down in his seat and sticking out his tongue and wiggling it at her. Now he's imitating a hound dog on the trail emitting bloodcurdling howls: *OW, OW, OW, OW, OW, OOW. OWWWWWW*. He looks back at me maniacally, grinning like a lunatic.

I'm standing there laughing, shaking all over from deep within my belly and watching the show. I salute him like a soldier. Bud's really a funny and good-hearted guy. Yes he's a stupid idiot, but he's a good-hearted stupid idiot.

Just then I happen to look up at the street sign and it says, "Luckie Street." A good omen. No doubt a very good omen. Just what I need: some good luck for a change.

I head down the street toward the bus station and still have a big smile on my face. I immediately see what I'm looking for, a street person about my age with hair down to his shoulders just hanging on the corner. He looks like he's up to no good. Great, just the person I want to talk to.

"Hey man, they got a blood bank anywhere close?"

He points across the street and I see it. "Damn, if it'd been a snake it would have bit me. Thanks. How much they pay for blood?"

"Seven bucks. You just get into town?"

"Yep, just pulled in. Where you staying?"

He points again, only this time on the opposite side of the street to an old brick building several stories high. "Been staying at the YMCA. It's a dump, but only five bucks a night." He takes a drag on his cigarette. I point toward the cigarette and say, "Got any more of those?" He reaches in his shirt pocket and shakes a Winston out of his pack. I grab it and say, "Light?"

"Damn son, all you got is the habit?" He pulls a lighter out of his pocket and gives me a light.

I take a deep drag and then exhale and say, "I'm busted man. I just got out of jail and I'm flat broke."

"Been there, done that."

I ask, "Got any spare change?"

"No, but the daily workforce is right down the street. Be there early and you got a shot at going out. They pay cash daily—$15 a day. No way to miss it. Every wino who isn't too drunk to stand out there will be there."

I notice that his eyes have pinpoint pupils. That means one thing: He's a heroin addict and has hit up recently. He ought to wear sunglasses like I do so no one can tell. Damned junkie. I don't want to be around him. "Thanks again man."

"No problem. See you around."

There's almost always a bond of some type between street people, and there's limited cooperation of sorts, but I'm not sucked into getting too close to a junkie. In order to get high, a junkie would sell his or her little sister, mother, and favorite Aunt Claire in a package deal to a pervert knowing damn well that he's going to chop them into little pieces after ravaging them like an animal. The junkie wouldn't think twice about throwing his own soul into the pot if the perv would add an additional hit or two. My experience with them (and I've had plenty) has been that there is absolutely nothing they won't do to feed the demons within that are raging. Nothing!

I'm mostly a loner. I've learned to never get too close to anyone on the street (not just junkies). I put my trust in one thing and one thing only, and that's me. I've seen the blood, the violence, and the death firsthand. No one gives a damn if a street person winds up dead, *especially* the cops. *Good riddance* is their attitude. If you survive, you have to keep your wits about you, because no one has your back.

I cross the street and go into the blood bank. I approach the woman at the counter and ask, "Can I sell some blood?"

A fat surly-looking bitch with uncombed gray hair looks over her dirty glasses at me with disgust. She curtly nods and tells me to take a seat and wait. She rattles around pretending she's looking for something and deliberately waits until I walk all the way over to my brown folding chair and sit down. Then she says, "Okay," and impatiently taps the counter with her grubby fingernail and nods to a clipboard with a form that was already on it. In a hateful tone she snaps, "Fill this out."

I glare at her as I stand back up and stalk over to snatch the clipboard off the counter so I can take it back to sit in my folding chair while I fill it out.

I use my alias Bob Johnson for the name and just make up an address. I check off "No" to all the questions about diseases that I have had, sign it, and give it back to her. She doesn't even look up to acknowledge me. I sit back down.

In a minute a nurse comes in and picks up the clipboard and, barely glancing at it, motions for me to lie down on a bed. She noticeably frowns when she sees the tracks on my arms, but is not deterred. After tying me off with a rubber tube, she deftly puts the needle in my arm and amazingly registers on her first try. She releases the rubber tie and dark purple blood starts slowly flowing into and filling up a clear plastic bag while I squeeze a rubber ball. I'm thinking, *I'm impressed*. I would like for her to hit me up sometime. As professional as she is, she could find a good vein in record time.

In a few minutes, she finishes and removes the bag of blood and then gives me a cup of orange juice. She tells me to drink it and lie there for a few minutes. I feel sorry for the poor son of a bitch who receives that blood. No telling what kind of diseases I might have. And one thing's for sure: That bag of blood is "high" test.

In a few minutes the surly bitch says in an obnoxiously rude tone, *"Here! You're done!"*

She shoves seven dirty wrinkled dollar bills at me and makes it a point to give me one last look of contempt, emphasizing that she thinks I'm just another piece of dog shit fouling her office. I've had just about enough of this bitch. My dark side glowers, thinking that I should put my .357 Magnum to her head to see if that would wipe the smirk off this ugly whore's fat face. I'd like to see her rude ass begging, sobbing, and crying for her worthless fat-ass life right before I bust a cap in her fat ear. Maybe she'd treat people who come in here with a little dignity and respect if that happened.

That would all be well and good, except for one thing, I don't have my .357 chrome Magnum anymore.

I cross the street again and take a room at the YMCA for $5. Then with the remaining blood money I buy a pack of cigarettes, a Coke, some peanut-filled crackers, and a candy bar.

My room is on the fourth floor and it's nasty dirty. This place is little more than a flophouse. I lie down on my filthy bed for a couple of hours and restlessly try to nap. My stomach is rolling and I'm sweating profusely. I have the dry heaves and can't get comfortable. I'm chain-smoking cigarettes in between bouts of retching. I need to take a leak, and when I go to the community bathroom I notice that all the windows are open. I step up to the urinal and then I see why. A queer is two rooms down from the bathroom watching men go to the bathroom through his open window. He's watching me with sick perverted eyes as I urinate, and he's smiling. I give him the finger and zip up my pants.

I go back to my room and grab my pillowcase and dig out my one change of clothes and toiletry items. I return to the shower and manage to take a shower in the end stall where the queer's prying eyes cannot watch me. The shower feels refreshing and my long hair is no longer greasy. I brush my teeth and even shave. I feel clean for the first time in a week.

I head for the street. It's night now and I'm definitely more comfortable in the dark shadows. I walk outside and see street people hanging out in front of the bus station. They're loudly talking and occasionally laughing and hanging out in front of the Y. Some are sitting on the steps drinking cheap wine from bottles hidden by brown paper bags. Others are staggering around trying to bum smokes or drinks or money from anyone that passes. One guy is pissing on the street.

I spot a street dealer and I immediately want to get high, but I resist trying to make contact. I know I can talk him out of a free sample by telling him I just got into town and will soon be his best customer, but instead I go back inside.

I go back to my room and soon I'm climbing the walls. It goes on for most of the night. I'm fortunate that I haven't been using as regularly since I got out of prison. I went off drugs cold turkey in prison and thought I would die.

As time goes on the mental craving and the incessant voice of my dark side urging me to go onto the street and score is almost too much to bear. I'm still sick as hell, but can't puke. I have the dry heaves again. I'm nervous, sweating profusely, and have diarrhea. I go to the bathroom and the queer is still at his post leering at me. I give him the finger again and he just stares.

Finally it's dawn and I'm hungry. I hit the street and see about 20 winos already lining up. I go over and stand around too. I talk to no one. A stocky man with a flattop crew cut comes out of the little brick building and says he needs three guys. We all raise our hands. I'm skinny as a rail, but still bigger than most, and look like less of a reprobate than the drunken winos standing around in a stupor. I'm the first guy he picks. Two more take the nod and we load up in the back of his pickup truck and drive to a construction site.

An old home has been demolished and we are standing beside a huge pile of used bricks. We're all given hatchets and told to use the hatchets to chip away and remove the mortar from the bricks and then stack them neatly on pallets. They're going to reuse them on another project. The short stocky man shows us how to do it.

It's hard work and I'm not used to any work, much less hard work. I'm tempted to just quit and find someone to mug. My only work lately has been bartending (if you want to call it work stealing drinks and getting drunk all night). I'm hungry but have no lunch or money left to buy anything; not even a candy bar. My blue shirt is soaking wet with an inordinate amount of sweat, partially from the humidity and hot Georgia sun and partially because I still have remnants of drugs and alcohol in my system. I do have a pack of cigarettes that I stole off the counter from the clerk at the Y and I smoke one right after the other, holding them in my mouth as I chop at the stubborn dried mortar on the bricks, squinting as the smoke seems to follow and get into my eyes no matter how much I twist my head away from it.

The other two guys are older than me, perhaps in their 40s or 50s, and appear to be in far worse physical condition. I'm convinced that they may die at any minute. They drink water constantly and one has unending diarrhea and stays in the portable bathroom most of the day. Both of them stink like hell and probably haven't had a bath in a month. Their hair is nasty greasy and unkempt, and their teeth look like they're germ-infested and are overlaid with greenish yellow scum. I wonder if I'll end up like them in another 20 years. I laugh. I bet I won't make it to age 25.

It's a long, grueling day and by now I'm starving. Finally the short stocky man comes over and yells out, "Quittin' time." He hauls us back downtown in the back of his pickup truck. We're all paid $15 cash and are told that if we want to keep working, to be there first thing in the morning. I say, "I'll be here." The others don't say anything; I assume they won't work again until every penny of the $15 is gone.

I go to a dumpy-looking restaurant near the Y and buy some greasy chili, a grilled cheese, and a Coke. While my food is being prepared, I pick up a newspaper and look at the want ads for a boardinghouse and jobs. I find a couple of boardinghouses that look affordable and tear out the ads. I'll stay at the YMCA flophouse again tonight, but I want to get the hell out of there as soon as I can. The place is crawling with queers, dopeheads, winos, and other human garbage.

When I walk out to the street, I see two guys beating the hell out of another guy. I keep walking—it's none of my business. I go back to my room and repeat the previous restless night. I'm sorely tempted to use my brick-cleaning money to score some dope to ease my pain. But I resist and succeed. The next morning I clean bricks again, but this time when the truck comes around at lunch time, I have money. I buy a soggy sandwich, Snickers candy bar, and a Coke. The sandwich is too gross to eat, but the candy bar and Coke go down well. Two new guys are there today and they reek of alcohol; I assume the guys from yesterday are dead drunk and passed out someplace where other winos will strip them clean of any remaining brick-cleaning money.

After work I board a city bus with my blue pillowcase and ride it to a boardinghouse that has an opening. It's situated near downtown. They serve two meals a day—breakfast and dinner. My room is a little doghouse-looking affair on the second floor—actually it's a dormer with a window that juts out over the roof. It's designed for looks, but every square inch of this home is utilized. My space is smaller than a jail cell and there is barely enough room for the cot that is my bed. It's hot as hell with no air-conditioning, and the window faces the hot Georgia setting sun, which heats it up even worse. The bathroom is down the hall and 14 people share it. I can wash clothes in the house, but there's no dryer; it's broken. What a shithole; but it's just $15 bucks per week including meals.

After about a week of cleaning bricks, I'm appointed foreman and I get $5 extra a day as a working supervisor to the winos. I can ride up front with the stocky man now instead of in the back. I still don't know his name. It's probably worth five extra bucks a day for the short stocky man not to have to smell and supervise those stinking-ass winos all day.

The hard work and absence of drugs has been good for me, in that I have gained a little appetite and even put back on some weight. I actually have some color from the blazing Georgia sun and don't have the look of death. My mind is still jumbled up like a jigsaw puzzle strewn across a room. I have trouble making even the simplest of decisions. Sometimes it actually brings tears to my eyes because I just don't know what I should do and I can't think straight. I don't know if it's a result of the drug use or sleep deprivation. I rarely sleep much more than a few minutes at a time and hardly ever more than a couple of hours a night. Mostly I just nervously toss and turn and my mind races. I yearn for drugs virtually all the time. It's maddening.

I'm trying to find a real job. I've saved up enough cash to buy a decent pair of blue jeans, another couple of shirts, and some new shoes. I had my hair cut really short and I'm trying my best to look straight. I shaved my mustache and sideburns and I'm very serious about making a final run at becoming clean and staying that way. If I fail this time, I've made my decision. There will be no going back. I will definitely kill myself.

CHAPTER FIVE

I scour the want ads and finally find a factory opening on the outskirts of Atlanta. They want someone with drafting experience to be trained to design sprockets and gears. I took engineering drawing in school and figure I can bullshit my way through the interview process and easily snag this job.

I take a bus out to the suburbs and apply for the job and then lie like hell about everything. The man interviewing me seems to like me and without so much as a reference check, or even an application to fill out, I'm hired right on the spot. It pays only $300 a month but that's a hell of a lot better than cleaning bricks in the hot sun alongside winos.

I start my new job the next day. I have my own desk in a nice air-conditioned office, and my job is easy. I perform a few simpleton calculations to determine the necessary dimensions for the shop drawings, which the factory workers use to cut out blank metal disks. The disks are machined into sprockets and gears that range in size from huge to very tiny. I'm told that they are sold all over the world.

After a few weeks I'm bored shitless. Management has told me that they're amazed at how quickly I've learned my job. I'm amazed that they're amazed. The way I see it, any dumb ass could easily do it. By now I've fallen into a routine and it's boring as hell. I'm working every day and I'm making steady money and I suppose this is the way normal, "straight" people are supposed to live. I wonder if this is all there is to being a straight person. If so, I can't see myself making it. A life in the suburbs working at Martin Sprocket and Gear and mindlessly doing this job day in and day out would be worse than death. I think I might rather be dead.

Adding to my death wish is my craving for drugs. It has become an all-consuming fire that is raging out of control in my brain practically 24/7. My thoughts are almost entirely consumed by my burning lust for a hit. At night I think about hitting up and I rub my arms; when I look in the mirror I have a crazy look in my eyes.

I crave drugs. I long for drugs. I ache for drugs.

My intense yearning to get high is unbearable, impossible to resist. I'm becoming quite mad. I can think of nothing else. Words are not adequate to describe how much I want it.

I could've scored drugs at least a thousand times by now and have steadily resisted. But I'm getting weaker. I can't hold out much longer. I'm losing the war for my soul.

I see people who are stoned in the bars, at the Laundromat, at the liquor store, at restaurants, and on the street—everywhere I frequent. I see the gleam in their eyes and know what's going on in their heads, and I envy them. I want to fly high too. I miss drugs.

There's nothing else for me. I feel so alone and hurting. There's something vital that's always missing in my life. Deep down I know that the drugs will not fill that void even if I succumb to their call, but I want them just the same.

I'm entirely devoid of love. I don't have any hope: not for ever being normal, or ever being loved, or ever being capable of loving anyone else. I see no future for me. I don't have anyone—no friends, no close family, no one.

I'm always afraid and looking over my shoulder. I live with a feeling of dread, as though I'm waiting for the guillotine to fall and chop my head. I'm convinced that I will not live to see my 30th birthday, and that's fine with me. I prefer death to what I have. I'm tortured, miserable, and filled with hate. I hate all of society. I especially hate any and all authority. I hate God (if there even is one). I hate myself with a special intensity. *I hate! I hate! I hate!*

My dark side is putting up 10 to 1 odds that I don't make it another month. He'll probably win because I've already started planning my suicide.

First I'll eat 200 tabs of a powerful barbiturate, such as Seconal, Nembutal, or perhaps Quaaludes. Now that I think about it, ludes would indeed be very nice. I'll quickly slug down handfuls of them at a time and wash them down with a chilled bottle of Lambrusco wine. Next I'll immediately shoot up a hotshot of heroin. The hotshot will be more difficult to obtain because it'll require uncut and pure heroin, or as pure as I can find. I can overcome that obstacle with the one thing that all dealers desire: money. I'll put my order in ahead of time and pay extra for it.

When I shoot up a massive dose of pure heroin, it will give me one hell of a rush and then immediately I'll go to the nod and from there to unconsciousness and violent seizures. And then I'll be prostrate on the floor, where I will more than likely vomit. I might drown in my own vomit like Jimi Hendrix did, or maybe my heart will just stop. Either way I won't feel a thing because that hotshot of uncut heroin will kill me within minutes without undue suffering. And if not, the ludes will. They're my insurance.

I smile to myself. I think the chilled wine is a nice touch. I could just as easily take the pills with water, but I don't like the taste of water and I very much like the taste of Lambrusco.

Tonight I'm heading to a familiar bar. My biggest expense is my bar tab and I get drunk every night. Getting drunk is not the same as getting high on drugs, but it helps, and I have to have something. It's not without its downside. I've had a wicked temper for as long as I remember and have been trying to control it, but it's nearly impossible to control the rage when alcohol is smearing my mind. I'm being reckless and taking a big chance drinking so much night after night, because alcohol makes me mean.

Unlike when I'm high on drugs, I want to fight when I'm drunk. I'm not a happy drunk; I'm a mean drunk. I've learned that I can't drink tequila or any hard liquor that is clear, like gin or vodka, because my mind can just snap without warning. I don't see it coming and rarely remember what happened the next day. When I'm drinking heavily, someone will look at me wrong, or pop off, or otherwise piss me off, and instantly I'll be in a fight. And when I fight, I fight to the bitter end—until the last dog dies and one of us is no longer moving. That usually means jail for me (or the hospital), and if they run my prints I'm gone.

Bye-bye.

I go to a bar not too far from my new boardinghouse. I'm having a few beers and talking to the barmaid. I've been coming here for the past several nights. The barmaid's name is Sallie. She has a really bad case of acne and is as ugly as an iguana, but will soon be off work. And then a good-looking little beauty named Brandy will take over as barmaid for the rest of the night. I'm hoping that tonight just might be the night that I score with her. Finally Brandy arrives and she looks especially beautiful tonight. She has long blonde hair, blue eyes, naturally red lips, and a ravishing smile complete with super-white teeth. I want some of that, plain and simple.

When she checks in, Sallie closes out her register and Brandy takes over. Sallie says her ride isn't here yet and comes around and sits next to me. Brandy gives her a draft beer and the three of us sit there making small talk with occasional laughter.

The next thing I know some guy comes up from behind and grabs Sallie's long hair and snatches her backward off her bar stool. As she's falling, he hits her hard in the nose with his fist and knocks her to the floor, where she flops around like a ragdoll.

He yells at her, "You bitch, *git out to the damn car.*"

Then he angrily turns to me and points his finger in my face almost touching my nose and says, "And you, you son of a bitch. If I ever catch you talking to my wife again, *I'll beat the shit out of you!*"

My dark side does not like it when anyone points a finger in my face or yells at me or hits women or, most of all, threatens me. There's no hesitation. A hot explosion of white rage goes off in my head, and then I'm ballistic. I hit him as hard as I can on the forehead with my half-full Budweiser bottle, breaking it in half on his head. He slumps to the floor like he's just been shot between the eyes by my old gun. I jump on top of him and start stabbing him in his face with the broken part of the bottle that remains. I stab him a half dozen or more times until the broken bottle breaks further, leaving shards of glass in his face and deep cuts in my hand.

I stand up grimacing in pain. My hand hurts like hell. I pull a piece of glass out of it and futilely try to stop the bleeding by holding it tightly. All the while I'm stomping his face into the floor as hard as I can. He's now squealing like a pig. I keep stomping and stomping his head. He's no longer squealing, but I don't stop stomping. Brandy is screaming, begging me to stop. "Stop, Bob! You're gonna kill him! Stop! *Please STOP Bob!*"

Stomp! Stomp! Stomp!

I hear a siren and finally I stop. Brandy called the cops. I'm breathing hard and involuntarily shuddering all over, heaving my chest up and down as I try to regain control from the rage of my dark side. Brandy hands me a towel for my bleeding hand.

She's scared shitless and crying. Sallie has managed to stagger to her feet and is wobbling over toward us. She has bright-red blood all over her white shirt and is sobbing and crying and a gusher of blood is streaming out of her nose and down her face. She's rubbed blood all over her face trying to stop the bleeding. Brandy hurries and gives her a towel with ice in it and tries to clean up her face. Her nose looks crooked and is badly broken and has already begun to swell as if she had been stung between the eyes by a wasp.

The guy on the floor isn't moving. I wonder if I've killed him. He looks dead, and I'm afraid. I breathe a sigh of relief as I hear him begin to softly moan and slowly roll back and forth on the floor in the pool of red blood that is streaming out of his face and head.

My dark side doesn't want it to end. He excitedly exclaims, *Look, look he's still moving. Finish him! Stomp him some more! Kill that son of a bitch!*

I want out of here, but just as I start toward the door, two cops come inside. They see the guy writhing around on the floor and they see me standing there with blood all over me. The bigger of the two has mean eyes. He immediately grabs me with one hand to my throat and shoves me hard against the bar, bending me in half and nearly breaking my back. The cop is huge, with muscular arms, and he's tightly holding my throat with one hand and wielding a billy club high in the other, ready to start clubbing me senseless if I so much as act as if I want to resist.

He has a sadistic look of rage on his face and is daring me to give him some excuse, any excuse, to beat me senseless so he can obtain his release. I've seen that look in the mirror. He has a dark side too.

Brandy is screaming at him from behind the bar and she's vainly trying to push the muscular cop's arm away from my neck, shrieking, "Let him go! Let him go!"

Sallie is joining in now, telling the cops that I was minding my own business and the other guy attacked her first and then me. She sobs, "I'm married to that prick! He started it. He's drunk. Arrest him! This guy was just trying to protect me and himself. Look what that asshole did to my nose."

The cop looks at her bloody nose and reluctantly lets me go. He gives me a shove anyway just for the hell of it, or maybe he did it to try to impress Brandy.

The other cop radios for an ambulance for the guy on the floor. After learning that he'd just hit a woman in the nose, the cops don't seem concerned about him in the least. He's a woman-beating coward and got what was coming to him. After they sew his ass up, they'll take him to county lockup; and when the cons in there find out what he's in for, they'll likely beat the shit out of him again for being a cowardly woman beater. It's a strange code of justice: The law of the underworld punishes woman beaters on the inside.

The cop glances down at my hand and gruffly asks, "You want me to have someone take a look at that hand?"

I say, "No it's not that bad. Can I go now?"

"Yeah, get your ass out of here."

I head for the door, nodding to Brandy as I leave. She looks distressed and manages a weak smile. I don't need to be told twice and I ain't hanging around for small talk. I walk out the door and into the night.

Another close call. Had I been booked and my fingerprints run, I would soon be on my way back to New Orleans and Angola. I have to be more careful.

My dark side is oblivious to any consequences and is gleefully, hysterically laughing. *Did you hear that punk ass squealing like a pig?*

I grin.

I should have killed that son of a bitch . . .

Chapter Six

It's the weekend following my fight, and I'm sitting in a crowded little bar named the Store smack dab in the center of Atlanta on Spring Street. The din of chattering people fills the air and music jumps from the jukebox, and the whole place is thick with the aroma of cigarette smoke and spilled beer. I like it here. I'm in the right place. It's a popular nightspot, which means I should be able to find some suitable girl I can have sex with.

I start thinking about tonight. I don't look like the same person that I was in New Orleans. My hair is short, I'm clean shaven, and I'm dressed like a straight person; for all practical purposes I look like a college boy. That's exactly the persona I want to project. I've always been charismatic. And when I want to be, I can be charming. I usually shower attention on women to get what I want. I can take on a personality totally unlike me as easy as putting on a coat. It's like a game to me and I rarely lose the game. I con, manipulate, and fool even the very best of them. If I make up my mind to go after something, I almost always get it.

I've always been particular when it comes to women. I like blondes, am partial to blue eyes, and I especially like beautiful women. I don't like street women. I like women who are clean and wholesome. I don't use prostitutes. They are nasty dirty and disgust me. I've never had sex with a prostitute and never will. I don't frequent titty bars; and strippers disgust me too—most of them are lesbians. I don't like to look at pornography. It bores me. Unlike the overwhelming majority of street people, I've never had a venereal disease, because I'm particular about the woman I have sex with.

I don't like sluts either: They're too easy and I don't respect them. I enjoy the game of seduction as much as the sex. I'm turned on knowing that a beautiful, nice girl wants to have sex with me just as badly as I want to have sex with her. I especially like it if she knows that she shouldn't do it, but is ready and willing to break the rules and mores of society to do it anyway. It's the ultimate win for me, with or without the culmination of actually performing sex. I suppose it's more about the psychological stimulus of being sexually desired than the physical stimulus that turns me on. But I take them both.

Still, I much prefer drugs to sex. I wasn't always that way, and at one point chasing sex pretty much dominated my thinking. But after I began shooting up drugs, I found that it's much better than sex. There's no comparison really. Now that

I'm not shooting up drugs, I've gone full circle and have renewed my interest in sex.

All this talk about sex has stirred my dark side up. I need to find someone to love. I'm nursing a beer and leveling my absolute coolest "Mr. Cool" stare at a blonde sitting two bar stools over with a couple of other girls. Ah . . . she is looking at me and smiling. She's saying something to her two friends, and now they're all looking at me. There are smiles all around and they're giggling. The blonde is easily the best-looking one.

Come to me my little chickadee. What a lovely smile you have—you will be mine tonight.

I continue to stare at her. Yes, I'm sure of myself. Yes, I'm confident and even arrogant. Why not? I'm Mr. Cool!

I've used the charming Mr. Cool persona with good success many times in the past, particularly in my post-high school days. Mr. Cool is ruggedly handsome, on the wild side, and a little reckless and rebellious—but only to an extent; he's not too scary or a drug-head loser, but mischievous, tempting, and alluring. No mention of drugs or darkness ever come out of Mr. Cool's mouth. You'll never know his past or learn his dark secrets. He's intelligent, engaging, witty, clever, interesting and entertaining, and his likable, devilish charm seems to melt girls right out of their pants.

I received the nickname "Mr. Cool" when I played high school football in Mississippi. In between morning and afternoon practice sessions, we'd escape the noonday heat by killing time at our quarterback's house, and calling girls. Everyone on the team had the hots for Barbara Beatty. She was the odds-on favorite for homecoming queen and every guy's absolute dream. My teammates could jar your teeth and knock your jock off on the football field, but not a single one of them had enough courage to call her.

My family had moved around the world like gypsies all my life, dutifully following my father, first in his military and then in his personal career. I had changed schools often, and in fact this was the third high school I'd attended and one thing was sure—by now, I wasn't shy and I wasn't timid.

I told them to give me the phone. When Barbara answered, I immediately told her she had beautiful eyes and particularly beautiful lips. I could actually hear her smiling through the phone as she asked,

"Who is this?"

Ignoring her, I said she was perhaps the most beautiful girl I'd ever seen. She immediately asked again,

"Who *is* this?"

I ignored her again and resumed the conversation by saying that her long blonde hair looked as soft and thick as a lion's mane and that I wanted to run my fingers through it.

By this time my teammates were hysterical, rolling on the floor like a bunch of excited wild-eyed five-year-olds, pounding their fists on the floor and kicking their legs wildly in the air.

"Who *are* you?"

I winked at the guys and suavely said, "This is *Mr.* Cool."

I had to cover the receiver to muffle my teammates' roar. I continued charming her for another 30 minutes, but all my devilish charisma and wit were for naught as she said she was going steady and couldn't date me. But the name Mr. Cool stuck. Word traveled fast and each story was exaggerated, and soon girls were lining up like lemmings to meet me. They desired a taste of the wild, the reckless, and the naughty. My dark side was smiling from ear to ear and ready to accommodate.

I smile at the blonde on the bar stool again, and she smiles back. That is all I need. I grab my beer and confidently walk over and strike up a conversation.

"How're you doing?"

"Just fine."

The music is thumping, thumping, thumping from the jukebox.

"You like Creedence?"

"Of course," she says.

"Want to dance?"

"Of course!"

We dance on the small dance floor and then have a beer, and then dance some more and have another beer. I'm a good dancer, and I can see that she's impressed. It's a skill that comes in handy when you're trying to pick up women. In between dances we make small talk, and I have another beer. (She says she's reached her limit.) I softly tell her she has the most beautiful green eyes I've ever seen. Stunning, actually.

She smiles broadly and exaggerates batting her eyelashes at me as though she were some beautiful movie star. I laugh. I take a swig of beer and then another. I tell her she has the most incredible lips I've ever seen. She closes her eyes, licks her lips, and puckers them up, once again in an exaggerated movie star fashion, only this time I reach over and kiss her.

She opens her eyes in surprise—she wasn't expecting that, and she recoils momentarily. I give her a big boyish smile to reassure her, and her momentary look of alarm disappears. She closes her eyes again and puts her hand on the back of my neck and guides my lips to hers.

Just as things are starting to heat up, one of her friends appears. I give her an annoyed stare. Her demeanor reminds me of some pushy Neanderthal prison guard.

"Come on, Teresa," she says in an irritating, nasal voice. "We need to get going or we'll be late for the party."

I perk up. "Party? I love parties. Can I come along?"

Teresa frowns and says, "No."

I look hurt. I reach for my beer.

Teresa tries to explain: "I have a boyfriend, and he'll be there."

I look surprised. "Where's my damn beer?"

"He's in the Army and is getting ready to ship out to Germany for a two-year tour."

She continues, "I'm going to break up with him tonight. We haven't been getting along, and I think he's expecting it, but I want to let him down gently. If you come along, there might be trouble. I don't want any fights breaking out."

I try to reason with her. I lie and say I won't cause any problem with her boyfriend. She must be intuitive enough to see through that. She reaches in her pocketbook and takes out a pen and paper, and then writes her name and number on it and presses it into my hand. "Call me!" she says.

I watch as she gathers her purse and moves toward the door. I'm disappointed and mad, but I know this isn't over. I'll call her tomorrow.

I'm betting that my blonde beauty will be unable to resist looking back at me just one more time before she leaves. I watch her as she hurries to catch up with her friends. Come on . . . come on . . . turn around . . . turn around. Just as she reaches the door, she turns around and looks back at me. She hesitates. Now she's making her way back across the crowded bar. She reaches up on her tiptoes and puts her arms around my neck and kisses me goodbye. We hug. She tries to pull away, but I won't let her. I hug her harder, pressing her breasts tightly against my body. She recoils and pushes decisively against me to move away, telling me she has to go. I reluctantly release her. And just like that she's gone.

Back on the bar stool I lick my lips, still tasting her. The one that got away . . . *Damn it!*

I half-heartedly glance around for a suitable replacement, but my mood has irrevocably turned and I'm really not into this whole scene anymore. I'm brooding now and my plastic Mr. Cool smile is gone. My dark side has regained his rightful possession of me. The blonde and hundreds of girls before her are fools. They think I'm handsome, captivating, funny, the life of the party, and perhaps the coolest guy they've ever met, but I use them, dump them, and then move on. That's how I think. That's how I roll. There's something very wrong, disturbing, dark, sinister, mean, nasty, totally evil about me.

I can keep it well hidden when I want something. And mainly what I want is drugs, sex, alcohol, or money. In order to get them, the charismatic and fun-loving Mr. Cool takes over. He can charm a snake. In fact, my dark side is a serpent, a dangerous evil snake dripping with poison. And my dark side is filled with hate. I drunkenly glower. I'm mean. I'm twisted. I like to fight, hurt, and destroy. I like getting high. I use drugs and alcohol to survive. Enough of either will do.

I drink another beer and then another and another and another. The entertaining Mr. Cool is completely gone now. I look straight ahead and talk to no one. I just keep drinking and drinking until my mind is numb enough to call it a night. I walk outside into the misting rain. *Damn! What a miserable night.*

One thing I failed to mention: While I was trying to mesmerize the blonde, I couldn't invite her over for a nightcap even if I wanted to. If I did, she'd freak out when she met my boardinghouse roommates. Of the 14 of us living in that dump, one's a ward of the state and is stone-cold crazy as a loon. She runs around all night muttering strange things. She has weird-looking eyes and long, frizzy hair and no matter when I come in she's roaming the halls talking to herself. There are three or four construction workers who travel back and forth to their homes in North Carolina. The rest, including me, are assorted scumbags either in love with the bottle or the needle.

Mr. Cool bragged about his new car to the blonde, but of course he lied about that. It's borrowed. I don't own a car and haven't even driven one much in the past several years. I have one sibling, an older brother named Jim. Last week I hitchhiked up to his home in Kingsport, Tennessee, and convinced him to loan me one of his cars so I could drive back and forth to my new job without riding the bus. I told him that the job I have doesn't pay much, just $300 bucks a month, which it doesn't, and it's entry-level. But at least it's a job—my first in years.

I've burned Jim before, and at first he was reluctant to let me borrow his car. But I poured on my boyish charm, told him that I was drug-free and sober, and that I was going to straighten out my life once and for all. I told him, "Just look at me, my hair's short, I'm clean shaven, and my clothes are clean."

I did look better than I had in a long time, and Jim desperately wanted to see me straighten myself out, so he finally agreed and I drove off in his shiny, maroon 1969 Malibu.

Mr. Cool looked good in his new ride.

I'm not very familiar with Atlanta, but I know that after coming out of the bar I don't have to drive far to reach the boardinghouse. That's a good thing because I'm drunk. I stagger to the car, trying to remember exactly how to get home. I think I need to head down West Peachtree, and then turn right onto Peachtree Street, and then go another few blocks before making a left on Peachtree Circle, or is it Peachtree Avenue? Why the hell does every street in this city have to be named Peachtree? Don't they know there are drunks out here trying to find their way home?

I start the car and drive. It's very dark, misting rain, and looks a little foggy. I turn on the windshield wipers and strain to see the road. Vainly, I try to rub the windshield clean. I wonder why there aren't more streetlights.

As if on cue, my old friend Jimi Hendrix comes on the radio, ironically singing:

Rainy day, rain all day
Ain't no use in gettin' uptight
Just let it groove its own way
Let it drain your worries away yeah

I move my head with the music, pat the dash in time to the beat,and join in:

Lay back and groove on a rainy day HEY
Lay back and dream on a rainy day

I approach a slight incline . . .

WHAM!

Sudden . . . loud . . . deafening . . . sickening . . .

Total blackness.

CHAPTER SEVEN

Somehow, in spite of the pitch-black darkness, I can plainly make out the twisted wreckage of my brother's car. The entire front end has been crushed, presumably by the tremendous impact of a head-on collision, and the twisted metal is just inches from my face. I see the car engine. It's been shoved all the way up in front of my lap.

It's quiet to the point of being eerie, and wisps of steam and smoke are rising around me. It seems like a drug-induced dream. But I know it's real because excruciating pain is coming from the area of my right leg with a sickening vengeance. I look down and see that my leg is facing the wrong way. My body is facing forward and my right leg is behind me in the backseat, and a large mass of bone is bulging through my pants near my upper thigh. My foot is facing down at an odd angle instead of up as it should be.

Overhead is the blood-spattered windshield, with a hole in it the same size as my head. The steering wheel is gone, probably snapped off by the force of my chest slamming against it. My chest hurts like hell and I'm having trouble breathing. Sharp pain shoots through my left shoulder. Dislocated, I can tell. The impact has bent the driver's side door nearly in two and left it hanging by its hinges. Blood is freely flowing down my head and neck. It feels like thick, warm bathwater. I can taste it.

Noises. A face is peering through the shattered window. The window covered with raindrops. Black dark outside. A flashlight in my eyes. Someone, I think, telling me to stay calm. I do not respond.

Total blackness . . .

A siren wailing . . . An engine gunning . . . Movement.

I'm lying flat on my back in what must be an ambulance. I hurt so badly I feel like puking.

I open my eyes. Everything is extremely bright. Brilliant white light. Someone dressed in white is hovering over me, frantically doing something to me. Bright-red blood spraying everywhere. My blood! It smells peculiar, like freshly plowed dirt maybe.

Am I tripping on LSD?

Excruciating pain. I'm going to be sick. I need to vomit, but I can't. I need to scream, but I can't.

Blackness.

A woman screaming, screaming, screaming, almost in perfect time to the *wah-*

wah-wah of the siren. My head is spinning. Car wreck. Serious. Shit! I must be dying. I brace myself.

I'm ready for this. Death will be better than my crappy life. I've often said I wish I'd been born dead. But I always thought I'd kill myself with an overdose of drugs and drift away into darkness—or just put the .357 to my head and pull the trigger. Not this.

Blackness.

"Stay with me! STAY WITH ME!"

NO!

The guy in white is yelling in my face, working on me, blood spattering his clothes in neat patterns. Christ, if he knew me he wouldn't be wasting his time. Let me die.

My mind is racing like an iridescent red meteor blazing through the night with a million stars twinkling against a black curtain. It's beautiful. I've figured it out! Those are my million thoughts arching through my mind. The black is the evil that permeates me. The iridescent meteor is my life expiring.

Despite the pain and chaos, I'm surprised at how I'm able to think like this and be aware. I've read that soldiers describe combat like this, talking of things slowing down, of becoming detached, and that's how I feel. My scrambled brain is processing those million thoughts, and I'm waiting for what comes next. Will death hurt? Will there be something on the other side? Is there a hell? I have no use for God or Satan. Judging from my crappy life, if there is a God, He must be mean, and I want nothing to do with Him, other than perhaps asking Him why the hell He's so mean. In New Orleans, I dabbled in black magic and Satan worship. But it wasn't worth crap either. I don't need any of it. I'm not afraid to die. I've been alone my whole life and I'll die alone and I'll face whatever is coming alone. God, devil. Good, evil. Heaven, hell. I don't give a damn one way or the other. Just let it happen.

Intense pain. Leg throbbing. Chest heaving. Blood spurting . . .

Bring it on!

Darkness.

I'm drifting in a troubled sea like a piece of wood banging and banging against the shoreline with the tide. Mercifully the pain is subsiding. I begin drifting, drifting, out into a serene black sea. The painful banging has given way to the calm of the blackness. This is better . . .

Someone screaming.

Screaming.

I'm reluctant to come back. I want to keep drifting in the quiet, painless calm of the serene black sea. But a girl is screaming, and then another. Where is that coming from? There must have been other people in the accident. We're all in this ambulance. Why can't they shut up! Why can't they accept their fate like I have and just die?

The guy in white is covered in blood. He's frantically trying to stop my bleeding. He's telling me to stay with him. He's giving me a shot. I hope to hell it's morphine.

I try to tell him I don't want to stay with him. I want to go back to the serene black sea where there is no pain. I want quiet. I want peace. I want the tranquillity of the darkness. I want to drift.

The few people who know me won't be surprised to hear of my demise and most will no doubt mutter that the world and I are better off because of it.

What will they put on my tombstone?

I have a suggestion.

Danger! Polluted! Use caution! Human waste!

Merciful blackness.

WHAP!

WHAP!

WHAP!

WAKE UP!

My face stings. Someone is . . . slapping me? I try to look around. I'm no longer in an ambulance—I'm on a stretcher in a hospital and a nurse is yelling something about my next of kin and that I'm seriously hurt.

No shit! Who is this?

I reason that if I give her this information I'll die, so I say nothing. I don't want to die anymore. I'm just 23 years old. It's too difficult. I just want to make the pain stop. And to puke.

WHAP!

WHAP!

"Who is your next of kin? ANSWER ME!"

WHAP!

WHAP!

I will die if I tell her, and I don't want to die now. But I must make the slapping stop. So I blurt it out: my father's name and where I think he lives. But it's been years. That's it . . .

Now I die. What a violent way to die.

Darkness. Drifting. Rest.

Just what I'd hoped for.

CHAPTER EIGHT

***Atlanta* — Robert Lynn Williamson, 23, died May 5, 1970, at Grady Memorial Hospital, of injuries sustained in a car accident.**

Bob was born in Shreveport, Louisiana, on November 27, 1946, to Benjamin L. and Peggy J. Williamson. He graduated from New Hope High School in Columbus, Mississippi, and five weeks ago obtained a job at Martin Sprocket and Gear Co. after he moved to Atlanta from New Orleans.

Bob is survived by his mom and dad, Peggy Jean and Benjamin Lee Williamson of Columbus, Mississippi; his brother, James Lee Williamson of Kingsport, Tennessee; and his son James Michael Williamson of Columbus, Mississippi.

His mother is a successful cotton buyer; his dad is a retired Air Force major and currently manages the Columbus Air Force Base Federal Credit Union; his brother is a national sales representative with Abbott Laboratories.

Memorial services will take place at 11 a.m., Saturday, May 8, at Columbus Funeral Home, in Columbus, Mississippi. The Rev. Gene Smith will conduct the ceremony. There will be no visitation. Bob's ashes will be privately placed.

The family suggests that memorials in Bob's name be directed to the charity of your choice.

Short and sweet—that's my obituary. There isn't much anyone can say about me that's fit to print. I can read between the lines for you if you please. As it says, my name was Robert Lynn Williamson. I was born in Shreveport, Louisiana in 1946. I was a military brat and attended so many schools (19 in all) that I don't even remember them all. I graduated from New Hope High School in Mississippi at age 17.

At the time of the accident I'd been in Atlanta for only a few weeks and had just started a low-paying, entry-level job. I'm survived by a son, James Michael Williamson, but there isn't any mention of his mother because we were divorced 11 months after we were married. I hadn't seen my son in a couple of years because my ex-wife had me arrested the last time I tried.

I was just 23 when I met my untimely, violent death. There won't be any visitation because, aside from my immediate family, no one would come. A memorial service is scheduled for Saturday, but no one will attend that either. I don't have any friends.

The obituary has nice things to say about my family. I'm survived by my father and mother and one sibling, an older brother—Jim. My father's name is listed as Benjamin Lee. That's not his real name. His real name is B.L. Williamson Jr. Those initials were given to him by his dad, who never got any formal education. Dad has been called B.L. his entire life, and that's what's on his birth certificate. My mother combines the initials and refers to him as Bill. But the military didn't like using initials instead of names, because initials didn't fit the various forms in its system. It caused so many problems, in fact, that eventually he was forced to pick a first and middle name. He chose Benjamin Lee. I don't know why.

My father is a retired Air Force major. He currently manages the federal credit union at Columbus Air Force Base. Dad was one of 11 brothers and sisters raised on a Mississippi cotton farm during the Great Depression. He used to chop cotton in the broiling sun for 50 cents a day. He left the family farm at 17 and went into the Army-Air Corps. That is what it used to be called before the two services branched off and separated. He was always in the Air Force side of it. Being in the service provided his first exposure to electricity, running water, and indoor toilets. He used to tell us that his early life on the farm was "rough as a cob." I visited the old homestead once and discovered they actually used corncobs instead of toilet paper in the outhouse. I assume that's the source of the saying.

Dad worked his way up through the military ranks and later went to school at night and obtained an associate degree in psychology and a teacher's certificate, which he never used. He describes himself as a plodder—steady and sure, not a quick thinker but a practical thinker with common sense, ultraconservative, not a risk taker, not creative, just steady and sure. He was a perfect fit for the military. He was exceedingly loyal to his superiors and followed orders to the letter. He has a need to be told what to do and my mother serves that purpose in our household. In 1948 he applied for and received a rare commission as a second lieutenant. This was due in part to his distinguishing himself during training bombardier pilots. Eventually he retired as a major and then went on to manage the federal credit union at the Columbus base, which is very large.

He is successful.

My mother's childhood did not allow her to go beyond a high school education. Her mother died when she was just eight years old, and her father had to move around the country looking for a job anywhere he could find one. They were in Texas when it was going through some of its toughest days during the Dust Bowl. Her dad eventually became a long-distance truck driver.

After her mother's death, she and her 10-year-old sister, Betty, went from relative to relative, and her early years were filled with instability and hardship. She met my dad right after she graduated from high school; she was 17 and he was 21. They married not long afterward. She has a great sense of humor, and she's beautiful. She's extremely bright, having read thousands of books, and unlike my father is a fast and creative thinker. My father worships her. She worked as a bank cashier for many years, but eventually secured a good job as a cotton buyer and now works for a rich old man who lives in Columbus. He adores her.

She is successful.

My brother, Jim, is one of Abbott Laboratories' top salespeople. He sells all kinds of pharmaceutical supplies to hospitals. He's two years older than me and has been idolized by my parents since birth. Unlike me, Jim is everything they wanted in a child—and was spoiled as a result. My dad describes Jim as a plodder like himself and his father before him—steady and sure, a Williamson through and through. That is one reason he idolizes him. My dad never thought I had the traits of a Williamson. He told me that I took after his mother's side of the family, the Coons. They weren't plodders, nor were they steady and sure. They were intellectuals. In his mind, they were too intelligent for their own good, which made them aristocratic.

My brother graduated from Mississippi State University. He was a chemistry major, and my father gave him the sparkling new maroon Malibu—the one I wrecked—as his graduation present. He recently married a nice-looking young girl from New Orleans. He lives in Tennessee, where he works his three-state sales territory on behalf of Abbott. He is one of their top sales producers and has won several trips and awards.

He is successful.

That's my full obituary. Short, and come to think of it, not so sweet.

I was unsuccessful.

Chapter Nine

Am I dead? Is this what death is like? I feel as though I'm drifting on a calm serene black sea, and I feel a slight cool breeze. I'm far removed from any consciousness of life as I've known it. Total blackness, and yet here I am. I never envisioned death to be like this. I can sense that I don't have a body anymore, and my mind has been totally encapsulated and tightly wound inside a cocoon with a million black strands of darkness binding me in place. I am exceedingly comfortable, but I'm not going anywhere. As far as I can tell, there is nowhere to go anyway, and I have no means of going. No legs. No arms. No body.

Just my mind really. Or I wonder if I'm a spirit, or maybe a soul. Whatever it is, I'm confined to a cocoon of darkness; but strangely I'm vibrantly *alive.* This is really far out.

My dark side is absent and I have the impression that my angel of light is now running things. I've begun a review of my life, and it's intriguing. I'm not merely viewing it as if it were on a movie screen; instead I'm actually reliving it—but only to a degree. I'm there, but I'm not there. I'm here tightly encapsulated in my cocoon as a detached, interested observer who is not allowed to speak. But I can see, hear, smell, and feel my life being vibrantly relived.

I'm a small child again. It's really almost too weird for me to comprehend, but I'm fascinated by it all . . .

Tap. Tap. Tap.

Bam! Bam! Bam!

BAM! BAM! BAM!

Hammering noises and then loud laughter. Dad looks up from his morning paper and asks Mom what the commotion is all about. She's curious, too, so they walk out into the bright sunlight. Mom is dressed in navy blue shorts and a freshly pressed yellow cotton blouse. She's barefoot and beautiful and every hair is perfectly in place. She always looks impeccable, but is losing the battle to keep my brother and me looking as freshly pressed and sparkling clean as she is. Dad's not much better and is wearing what he always wears at home: brown khaki pants, black socks, brown lace-up shoes, and a white sleeveless jersey-style undershirt that reveals his big lily-white, freckled shoulders. His hair is greased up with hair cream and is combed straight back. He and my mother hold hands as they walk around back to investigate the ruckus in the backyard.

It's a Saturday morning, and it's already hot and steamy. Not a cloud is in the deep-blue tropical sky. I'm barely five years old, and my buzzed hair is as blonde as the white-sand beach not far from our home. I have on shorts, but go shirtless and barefoot. I'm standing in the manicured grass of our backyard in front of a shed surrounded by banana trees and other tropical foliage. I'm proudly admiring my handiwork. A hammer is dangling from my hand.

We live on Okinawa, and our house here is not far from the Air Force base where my father is stationed. It's 1951, six years after the end of World War II, and the Japanese are being very accommodating to the military personnel occupying their country. My father is a second lieutenant, and the Air Force has provided modest living quarters reserved for officers with families. Our home is really just a glorified tin hut and looks like a gigantic galvanized drainage pipe that has been cut in half and covered with tin roofing. The hut has a wooden floor and is about 30 feet long and perhaps eight feet high. It has doors and a couple of tiny windows cut into each end. Two small fans labor constantly to move the humid air around. These typhoon-resistant buildings are called Quonset huts, and they're quite common in Okinawa and on military bases in general.

We have two Japanese maids to help with the housecleaning and laundry, and also a Japanese houseboy named Gaboon. All are provided free of charge by the Japanese government, I suppose, as some sort of retribution for Japan's poor behavior at Pearl Harbor and elsewhere during the war.

Gaboon is a very slight man—he's not even five feet tall. He loves tending our little yard and small garden. He invariably wears a large coolie-style straw hat. He smiles constantly, creating quite the contrast between his white teeth and his aged brown face. He lovingly cares for the brilliant exotic flowers that bloom year-round in this lush tropical environment.

One of Gaboon's primary assignments is to keep an eye on my brother Jim and me, and whenever we're outside he's always right there with us. Gaboon genuinely loves us, and so do the Japanese housemaids. They tend to us as though we're their own children. In fact, when we were eventually transferred back to the States, the housemaids were so distraught they wept, and I remember one of them crying so hysterically that her nose started to bleed. When it was time to go, she grabbed my brother and wouldn't let him go. She was so upset that she screamed maniacally and sobbed as she tightly held on, not wanting to give him up. My father had to pry her arms apart to release Jim from her hysterical grip.

As my parents reach the backyard, it's readily apparent to them that Gaboon is the source of the laughter. His head is tilted back and his slanted eyes are tight slits as he laughs heartily. Tears are streaming down his weathered face, one hand is holding his stomach, and the other hand is pointing toward my handiwork.

Mom stares in disbelief. Her face grows ashen. She screams, ***"BILL!"***

Dad has a sick, concerned look on his face.

They're no longer holding hands.

I have nailed my pet rabbit, Bugs, to the shed. I've driven a large nail through his little neck. Bright-red blood is streaming down the white fur, and Bugs is quivering slightly. His pink eyes are already beginning to glaze, and are blankly staring off into space.

Gaboon senses this might not be as funny to my mom and dad as it is to him. I don't know why Gaboon thought it was so funny for me to nail my pet rabbit to a shed and thereby condemn him to die a slow and painful death. Perhaps it's because his Asian culture is not as sensitive to animals or death as Western cultures are. Maybe he's like the Roman populace of years gone by who reveled at gladiators being torn apart by each other and by wild animals, or perhaps it's some other reason that only he understands. Whatever his reasoning, he has stopped laughing and is standing silent with his head and eyes lowered. His large coolie hat conveniently hides his face. Bugs makes one final kick and then dies.

Mom turns and runs back inside the house and is violently sick.

Just then, I notice my brother Jim standing there. He's dressed like me: shorts, no shirt, and no shoes. His hair is buzzed too, but he's black headed. He has a quizzical look on his face and is stoically staring at Bugs with his black, penetrating eyes. Dad notices him and says, "Jim, go inside the house with your mother."

Jim shoots me a look of disgust and then runs inside. I hear the screen door slam behind him.

Dad's practiced military gaze is sweeping from me to the rabbit to Gaboon. His steely-blue eyes settle on Gaboon, and they suddenly turn fierce and glowing, like twin furnaces. His face is twisted in an animal-like rage. Despite being a short man, just five-foot-eight, he's built like a gorilla. He's rock solid and stout. He has a large chest, legs that are like oak trees, and huge wrists, forearms, and biceps. I notice that his big hands are balled into tight fists.

"What happened here?" he roughly demands.

Gaboon is trembling and barely able to stammer out in broken English, "I no see, I no see." He blurts out that he heard some noises, came to check on me, and discovered this.

Now my father slowly turns his glowering rage toward me. He's madder than I've ever seen him. His face is red. I'm slowly backing up, trembling. I have seen that look before, and a fierce whipping always follows. He stares at me as though loathing my very existence, seemingly forgetting I'm only five.

I'm scared. I start crying. I don't realize what I've done. I'm just five years old. I have no concept of life or death or pain or suffering—these terms are not even in my vocabulary. Bugs was my pet rabbit. I'm sobbing now. I'm scared. I'm just five years old.

I had this hammer, and I . . . I don't know . . .

I flinch when he screams again, *"What is wrong with you?"*

CHAPTER TEN

I'd nearly forgotten the rabbit incident. It seemed so real as I relived it from my cocoon. I'm now watching with concerted interest to see what happens next. Incident after incident in my life is replaying itself for me.

I'm seven years old now and we live in a small home in Fairfield, California, just outside of Travis Air Force Base, where my dad works. Jim and I are enrolled in our third school in as many years. We've been going to our new school about a month now and it's close enough that we can walk back and forth. We arrive home before Mom gets off work and are by ourselves for a couple of hours. Dad is usually due home around six.

One day, my mother arrives home from work and she's tired from a long day of being on her feet at the bank, and now she wants to change into something more comfortable. She walks down the hall toward her bedroom in the back of the house and as she passes the open door to the bathroom happens to glance inside. She sees a big mess.

There are hundreds and hundreds of soap chips and soap shavings strewn all over the sink and floor, and even in the bathtub of the hall bathroom. One of my mother's kitchen knives sits on top of the back of the toilet. Someone has carved a bar of soap into a myriad of pieces and left a huge mess for her to clean up. Mom is obsessive-compulsive about keeping her house spotless, and this isn't going to be tolerated.

She yells at us to come in. When we arrive she's standing at the bathroom door with her hands on her hips, eyes ablaze. She asks, "Who made this mess?"

My brother looks at her and says, "It was Bob."

I look at her and say, "It was Jim."

One of us is lying. She asks again, a little more emphatically. "Who did this?"

Jim points at me and I point at him.

My mother doesn't like to administer corporal punishment—not because she doesn't believe in it, but because she's not very good at it. She's a small, delicate woman and we're tough, gritty kids. When she applies corporal punishment, it's hilariously funny to watch the spectacle. Her blows are largely misses and when she does land one, it's so anemic that it doesn't hurt. To add to her frustration, Mom is uncoordinated; and while she tries to flail away at us with a belt, we dance around and away from her, avoiding her blows. Invariably she hits herself. She hits herself almost as often as she lands a blow on one of us. Neither Jim nor I fear her spankings in the least and sometimes we even laugh at her when she tries to give us one.

Mom sees our nonchalant, bored expressions as we listen to her rant on about the soap-chip mess. She says that our smug attitudes and smirks will soon change because Dad will be home shortly.

She's right. The smiles disappear and the smug looks are gone. They're instantly replaced by anxiety, fear, and apprehension. My dad's whippings are no laughing matter. In about three seconds, she can easily have him stoked into a roaring fiery rage. When he whips us, we remember it. I've been there before.

Jim tells me that I'd better tell her that I did it. I retort that *he'd* better tell her that *he* did it. He hits me with his fist in my stomach and I retaliate by hitting him in the mouth with my fist. We start wildly throwing punches at each other and Jim rushes me and tackles me as I pound him with my fists on his back. He forces me to the floor and we wrestle and fight for advantage. My mother is slapping us and screaming at us to stop fighting. She finally manages to separate us, breaking a fingernail in the process.

She tells Jim to go to the living room and me to go to my bedroom and wait for our father to come home. We sullenly glare at each other as we reluctantly obey and start making our way in opposite directions down the hall.

There's nothing worse than knowing I'm going to get a whipping and having to wait for it. I'd much prefer to get it over with. I look out my bedroom window for about the fifth time trying to see if Dad is home yet. I dread hearing him drive up. By now Mom has changed into comfortable clothes and is preparing dinner.

Finally I hear Dad drive up. He no more than slightly opens the front door and immediately I hear the sharp, angry *flip, flip, flipping* sound of her shoes as she angrily crosses the room. She meets Dad in the same manner that she met us, with hands on her hips and hazel eyes ablaze. She tells him that we made a huge mess in the bathroom and left it for her to clean up, that we each blamed the other for making the mess, and then we got into a fight and she broke her fingernail trying to break it up.

"*Get in here!*"

My brother and I timidly enter the hall in front of the bathroom where my mom and dad are now standing. My eyes are wide and I'm scared. Dad has a dark look on his face and is angry. He asks through clenched teeth, "Who did it?"

I nervously point at Jim and he points at me. Dad orders us to follow him into the living room and removes his belt. He gives us one last opportunity and asks again,

"Who did it?"

No change in our response. Round one is ugly. Dad harshly grabs me by the wrist and begins furiously whipping my legs and butt with his belt with intense fury. We go around and around the living room in a tight circle. Dad lashes me time after time and his narrow leather belt is landing solid blow after blow. I'm screaming and crying, hurting from the pain.

Jim is next and his whipping is equally intense. We're both crying and sobbing now.

He stands towering over us, holding the belt tightly in his hand, his face flushed red.

"Who did it?"

I point at Jim and he points at me. Round two makes round one seem like a fun day at the beach. This time it's vicious! Dad is in a rage and this time it lasts longer than the first. Finally, mercifully, he quits swinging. We are standing there quivering, crying, and sobbing. The pain is throbbing. Deep-red welts are forming.

Dad's face is now nearly purple with rage. He screams. He is out of control.

"Who did it?"

I stubbornly point at Jim and he stubbornly points at me.

Round three.

My turn first. *Whap! Whap! Whap! Whap! Whap! Whap! Whap!*

Now Jim's turn. *Whap! Whap! Whap! Whap! Whap! Whap! Whap!*

The veins are protruding from my father's neck. He looks deranged. He appears ready to explode. He maniacally roars at the top of his lungs,

"WHO DID IT?"

I raise my hand.

My father looks at my sobbing, trembling brother and tells him that he's sorry. I'm incredulous as I watch him hold out his hand to Jim and with a sheepish embarrassed look on his face, offer to shake hands. Jim reaches up and shakes his hand. He's just been beaten within an inch of his life and was innocent of any wrongdoing, and now my dad is shaking hands with him in order to make things right.

It's comical to me as a detached onlooker to see him shaking hands with someone he's just savagely beaten, but as an engaged participant I'm not even tempted to laugh. Mom grabs Jim and hugs him and tries to console him. She's crying with him, feeling his pain, sorry now that she stirred Dad up. Her regret is limited to Jim though; she gives me a dirty look as though she abhors me for what I've done.

Dad is now turning his gaze and full attention back to me and I try to brace myself. I'm scared. He still has his belt in his hand. I'm really scared. He yells,

"Why?"

I blurt out in my childlike sobs, "I tried to carve a puppy out of a bar of soap. I kept shaving more and more off each side and never could make it look like a puppy. Finally I gave up and went to my room and forgot about cleaning up the mess."

Dad screams, "*You idiot.* I mean why did you *lie* about it?"

I don't know how to answer him. I don't know why I lied. I'm looking down and searching my child's mind for an answer. I'm seven years old and that question is just too deep for me. I don't have a clue why I lied. I honestly don't know. I don't know how to answer, and I just stand there looking down racking my brain for an answer. I'm nervous and trembling now. I don't know what he wants me to say. I'm more afraid now than before. I just stare at the floor and desperately try to think of something to say.

I flinch when he unexpectedly screams, "*What is wrong with you?*"

CHAPTER ELEVEN

My tightly wound black cocoon floats on a serene black sea surrounded by blackness. I'm indistinguishable inside this black ink where I reside, and I'm amazed at the minute detail and clarity of the replay of my life that I'm watching. Not a single moment is being omitted, including events that I'd long since forgotten. I'm seeing a firsthand rerun and *everything* is here, down to the tiniest detail.

While my entire life scrolls by minute by minute, second by second, certain events do seem to be more conspicuous than others. It's not as though I'm spending an undue amount of time reviewing these particular events, but nonetheless they stand out as if they were somehow being emphasized, perhaps by the angel of light. It's almost as though I'm being instructed, without verbal communication, to take note of these precise incidents.

About one week has passed since the soap-carving incident and things have slowly improved to the point where both my mom and dad have forgotten about it and quit mentioning it. Jim on the other hand is still mad and not talking to me.

It's late afternoon and Mom is preparing dinner. She's a great cook and is preparing one of my favorite meals, spaghetti and meat sauce. I smell it and follow it all the way from my room down the hall and into the kitchen like I'm following the Pied Piper. Mom's standing by the sink and preparing a salad to go with the spaghetti.

"Mmm . . . Something smells yummy."

She looks down at me and pats me on the head and smiles her beautiful, radiant smile. "You love your spaghetti, don't you? Dad will be home soon and then we'll eat."

"I can't wait, I'm starving. I made a 100 on my English test today."

"That's wonderful. What are you doing about those U's in conduct? Are you getting along better with your classmates now?"

I frown, "Mom, I already told you that I got that bad grade because an older kid was picking on me. He pushed me down and I stood up and hit him back. The teacher saw me and told me that I shouldn't be fighting on the playground. What am I supposed to do when someone pushes me down? She made me write 500 times that I will not fight on the playground and she gave me a 'U' on my report card. Nothing happened to that older kid. It isn't fair. He started it."

"Your brother gets all E's on his report card and you should too. You should try harder to get along and make friends and not be fighting in school, Bob. You have to make an effort to get along with your classmates like Jim does. Now go wash your hands and get ready for supper. Dad will be here any minute."

I start walking down the hall to the bathroom to wash my hands for supper.

Thud!

I fall like a felled tree crashing to the forest floor. Jim was not about to let me get away with causing that undeserved beating from Dad. He waited a full week and then, when I was least expecting it, sneaked up behind me and swung a large encyclopedia with both his hands and hit me squarely in the back of the head with all his might.

I'm knocked nearly unconscious from the solid blow of the large book. I'm dazed and my head is hurting. I can't focus my eyes or see clearly. Jim throws the encyclopedia to the floor and is standing there with both fists balled up and black eyes blazing. He's ready for full combat. My brain is scrambled, but I rise to my feet and scream at him at the top of my lungs, "You chicken-shit bastard!"

I need say no more. He instantly attacks!

He comes after me with fists flying and we are instantly engaged in a fistfight of major consequence. The vicious blow to the back of my head has taken its toll and he's landing blow after blow to my face in rapid succession. In my addled condition, I'm simply no match for him. I can't defend myself and I'm badly losing the fight.

Finally Mom, who has heard all this from the kitchen, comes running into the hall and is angrily trying to separate us. She succeeds in pulling Jim off me and demands to know what happened.

Jim quickly tells her that I called him a "chicken-shit bastard." I can taste blood and wipe at the inside of my lip where Jim's fist has cut it. I'm mad and yell at her that Jim sneaked up behind me and hit me on the back of the head with an encyclopedia for no reason.

He tells her, "That's a lie. Bob walked down the hall and when he passed me he pushed me and told me to get out of his way. Then he called me that bad name and I hit him."

Perhaps my recent lie about the soap-chip mess clouds her objectivity and she believes Jim instead of me, or maybe she considers the loud cusswords she clearly overheard to be the greater evil, or maybe she just likes Jim more than me. Whatever the motivation, I now become the object of her wrath. She roughly grabs me by my arm and drags me into her bedroom.

We sit down on the edge of her bed.

"Bob you simply can't use language like that and you can't keep starting fights. I'm sick and tired of your bad behavior!"

"But Mom, Jim hit me from behind with a book for no reason. I'm telling the truth Mom."

"He says you started it by pushing him and no matter who started it, there is no excuse for using bad language like that."

I raise my voice. "It isn't fair. Why aren't you saying anything to Jim for hitting me for no reason?"

She sighs real deep and says, "That's what you always say Bob, just like on your report card and when you carved up the soap. Do you remember that? You don't know how to tell the truth."

I say, "But Mom, I'm telling the truth this time."

"Bob there's an angel, an angel of light, that sits on your left shoulder and watches everything you do. He wants to protect you and help you do good things. A red devil—your dark side—sits on your right shoulder and watches everything you do too. He wants you to be bad and do naughty things, like fight and say cusswords, that will get you into trouble. Your problem is that you only want to listen to your dark side and that's why you are always in trouble. You need to be a good boy and listen to your angel of light."

I raise my voice even louder now. "But Mom, he hit me in the back of the head for no reason. What was I supposed to do?"

She's frustrated and angry now, and abruptly stands up and drags me by the arm down the hall and into the bathroom. She picks up a used bar of soap off the sink and runs some water on it; and then she jams it into my mouth and starts washing my mouth out with the soap bar. It tastes terrible and I'm sputtering and spitting the foul-tasting soap into the bathtub as she vigorously rubs it into and all around my mouth until my mouth and face are thoroughly lathered with the slimy mess. My mouth has been cut by Jim's fist, and blood is intermingling with the soap, turning the lather a pinkish color.

She angrily says, "You want to cuss? Then maybe you need your mouth washed out with soap to make it clean." Then she rubs it even more vigorously. When she's finished, she tells me not to ever cuss again. She heatedly tells me to clean off my mouth and clean up the mess and says, "And you can just forget about having dinner too."

She leaves and heads toward the kitchen adding, "Dad will be home any minute."

The soap in my mouth tastes awful and it's all over my face and burning my eyes. I'm crying and looking for a washcloth when I hear something. I turn around and see Jim standing at the door pointing and derisively laughing at me.

My dark side isn't on my right shoulder now: He's in my mind. He's roaring, screaming, angrily shrieking at the top of his lungs, and his howls are reverberating throughout my brain as he screams at Jim,

"You son of a bitch, you.

"You chicken-shit bastard!

"You'll pay for this Jim!

"One day soon. You'll pay!"

Chapter Twelve

I'm like an aborigine lost in my dreamtime. The years of my existence from beginning to end are recurring at the speed of light, but I'm strangely capable of keeping up and have not missed a half second.

I'm still silently drifting on the serene black sea, and it's calm and peaceful. My tight cocoon of darkness is providing a safe, warm, and comfortable abode. I'd long since forgotten about these childhood events. My dark side has been strangely quieted and—I suppose—is enjoying the deep, because he's gone. It's just me and the quiet reflections and the eerie feeling that my angel of light is running this show.

I don't know how I know this, but I'm now convinced that the angel of light brought the chaos and anarchy of my downward spiraling life to their abrupt and final conclusion in that car wreck that night. I also have the impression that the angel of light is requiring that I relive every moment of my life. I don't care. It's fine with me. I feel safe now. I'm comfortable, and it's kind of fascinating to relive my life in this manner. Besides I don't have anything else to do.

Two years have passed and I'm now nine years old. We live in a different and somewhat newer and larger house, but we're still in Fairfield, California. I have more friends than I've ever had and I'm having plenty of fun. I've discovered that I'm big for my age and a natural athlete; and so far I'm good at every sport—and I play them all. I love sports.

Jim and I have recently joined a Little League baseball team. Jim, who is above-average in sports too, is our catcher. And he's really good at that position. After trying out last week, I've just been moved from center field to the pitcher position. I have a high batting average and so does Jim. My coach, who has nicknamed me "Willy," is going to allow me to pitch in my very first game today. I'm so excited that I didn't sleep even one minute last night, and I can't wait for the game to begin.

I thought the game would never begin, but *finally* it's time to take the field. I run out to the mound and start my warmup. Everyone is looking at me as I take a few pitches, and I like the attention. The umpire yells, "Play ball" and I throw my final warmup pitch. Jim throws it down to second base and then the infielders throw it around the infield. Third baseman Tommy Huong walks over to me and hands me the ball and grins at me and tells me, "Let's get 'em out Willy."

I'm standing on the mound eyeing the first batter closely. I'm nervous and still have the butterflies in my stomach that I've had all day long in anticipation of this game. In practice I've demonstrated that I have a wicked fastball. My blazing speed is beyond my years. There is one problem however: I don't have good control. This may be because I'm naturally left-handed but pitch right-handed. I don't know how that happened, but perhaps it's because my first baseball glove was a hand-me-down from my brother, who is right-handed. Actually I can use either hand for most things. I prefer to write left-handed and shoot my friend Johnny's BB gun left-handed, but I like to bat right-handed and throw a ball right-handed. I fight from a left-handed stance, but I deliver my strongest blows from my right hand because that's my strongest arm. I'm all mixed up in this department.

The very first pitch of my career streaks by about four feet over the batter's head and nearly goes over the backstop. It hits a metal post, ricochet's wildly, and rolls about 40 feet to the dugout. It wasn't lacking velocity, that's for sure. If the ball had hit the batter's helmet, it probably would have knocked his head off.

My brother runs over to retrieve the ball and returns to the plate to throw it back to me. He points at his glove a couple of times to let me know that his glove is the target, not the top of the backstop. Hmm . . . Thanks for that Jim. I thought it was the top of the backstop. Jeez!

The batter now has genuine fear in his wide eyes. It had to scare the ever-loving shit out of him to see that scorching fastball hit that metal post. He doesn't want to be hit by my fastball. He's stepped back from the plate significantly. I reach down and pick up the rosin bag and rub it on my pitching fingers and toss it to the ground. Now I put one foot on the pitcher's rubber and lean forward and eye him for a moment, which seems to intensify his fear of me. I concentrate on the center of Jim's catcher's mitt. I smoothly wind up, and with a perfectly executed follow-through throw a blistering fastball into the center of the glove.

Pow! It sounds like the crack of a .22 caliber rifle as it hits the mitt.

The umpire yells, "*Steeee-rike!*"

Jim points his glove approvingly at me, and throws the ball back. I hear my coach yell, "Attaboy Willy!" I follow with two more perfectly thrown strikes and Jim throws the baseball around the infield to celebrate my very first strikeout. Jim lifts his mask and smiles approvingly at me and gives me the thumbs-up. I hear the crowd clapping.

I hit 13 batters with my blazing fastball that day and I struck out about the same amount. I would strike one out and then my fastball would hit one in the back or conk him on his batting helmet or slam into his thigh. Their batters would stand as far from the plate as possible, but it didn't help much. When a pitch would get away from me there was no telling where it might go. I even threw several pitches completely behind the batters' backs. When the frightened batter would return to the plate, his eyes would be wild with fear. I threw so hard and with such velocity that it was nearly impossible to dodge an errant throw.

Our team handily won the game. Jim hit a home run with two men on base and had several other good hits. I had a great day at the plate too. I actually reached base with solid hits every time at bat and thereby improved my already high batting average.

After pitching and winning my first game my coach congratulated me, my teammates congratulated me, and my teammates' parents congratulated me. Everyone was patting me on the back and saying, "Way to go Willy!" I was so excited and happy that I could hardly contain myself. I'd won my very first game as a pitcher and the coach told me that I'd earned the starting pitcher position. Imagine *me* being the starting pitcher.

My dad and mom went to that game and after it was over I ran to the car as fast as I could in order to hear them tell me what a great job I'd done too. Instead when I pushed inside the car Dad laughed at how wild I was until tears streamed down his face. He recounted the moment that I nearly threw that first pitch over the backstop and was laughing hysterically and kept saying that I was wild as a "March hare." He had to remove his glasses and wipe away the tears from his face because he was laughing so hard.

His laughter soon got Mom and Jim going too. Dad told and retold the story of how batter after terrified batter would come to the plate and I'd either throw it behind their backs or over the backstop. The batters would stand as far from the plate as they could, but it didn't matter. I'd still nail them in the back or conk them on the head. When anyone came to the plate, their frightened eyes were as big as saucers. Dad thought it was hilariously funny and would start laughing hysterically, which would in turn start all of them laughing and laughing. Just when I thought it was over, he'd start again saying, "He hit *13* of them, they were scared to death," and broke out laughing again.

When he finally finishes with me, the subject turns to the game that Jim had played. Dad's tone immediately changes to one of great pride. He can't say enough about the home run and how far it had cleared the fence and how solidly Jim had connected, and in the third inning how he made a great throw to second base and threw out the guy who was trying to steal, and blah, blah, blah . . .

I listen silently and look out the window.

CHAPTER THIRTEEN

My best friend Johnny Lawson and I are outside on the playground with about 20 other kids. Our class is enjoying recess and playing in the warm California sun. My family has been living in Fairfield going on two years now, and it's the longest that we've ever lived anywhere. And I'm enjoying it.

Johnny and I are standing off to the side by ourselves and are pretending to be immersed in deep conversation with each other. Another kid, Jacob Goldstein, has just come over to join us. Jacob isn't very popular at school, but earnestly seems to try to fit in; and he almost always follows Johnny and me around. Jacob is hearing impaired and wears extra-large brown glasses with hearing aids built into the frames.

Jacob's owl-like eyes are frantically peering through his thick eyeglasses at us. His eyes appear larger than they really are because of the thick lenses. They're nervously darting back and forth, first at Johnny and then at me, and he has an expression of sheer panic on his face.

Earlier I had come up with the perfect plan: Johnny and I would move our lips and pretend that we were talking quietly to each other. I told Johnny that when Jacob realized he couldn't hear what we were saying, he'd turn up his hearing aids. I'd seen him do that on two prior occasions. When he turned them up as loud as they would go, we'd let him have it by screaming as loud as we could. I told Johnny that it would be funny as hell to watch Jacob's reaction. Johnny didn't hesitate—he was in.

When Jacob walks up to us we barely look up and pretend not to notice him. We appear to be deeply engaged in our conversation and are nodding to each other and moving our lips; but we aren't saying anything. We are pretending to be jabbering away and for all appearances seem to be completely oblivious to anything going on around us, and to Jacob in particular.

Jacob's face now has a worried look and he's desperately trying to hear what we're saying. He's even trying to read our lips. He reaches up again and again and adjusts the volume of his hearing aids.

Finally he takes his glasses off and turns up the volume as loud as it will go. He puts them back on and adjusts them on his head slightly and once again peers at us through his thick lenses, straining forward to hear better.

I give the prearranged signal to Johnny and suddenly we both simultaneously scream at the top of our lungs,

"AIIIEEEEEEEEEE!"

It's a bone-piercing scream, literally as loud as we can muster. My dark side guffaws with laughter as we watch poor little Jacob jerk back in pain and cover his ears in anguish. It's hilariously funny and we fall to the ground and roll around on the grass laughing. We pulled it off like a couple of Hollywood actors. We're both laughing so hard that we have tears streaming down our cheeks. We hoot to each other and imitate little Jacob's reaction to our trick on him, and then laugh some more.

Now, Jacob is a sickly little weakling of a boy. He's pale white and skinny and his health is poor. He can barely see, even when he's wearing his thick glasses, and he's nearly stone deaf. He immediately runs over to the fence and stands alone, crying. Our homeroom teacher, Mrs. Brown, sees him crying and goes over to see what's wrong.

She bends down to talk to him and puts her arm around him, trying to console him. He's tearfully sobbing and we can see him softly telling her what happened. She appears to ask him something and he looks up and momentarily scans the playground, and when he sees Johnny and me he points directly at us. Mrs. Brown looks in our direction with a frown on her face.

We're no longer laughing.

She's now heading our way at a fast clip. Everyone in our class knows that Jacob is Mrs. Brown's beloved little pet. She feels sorry for him and is protective of him, as if he were her very own son.

Not good.

Even though I haven't been in this school long, I've already been in trouble, and so has my accomplice Johnny. I've been in several fights. In fact just yesterday Mrs. Brown had to break up a fight I was in with one of my classmates. Johnny has been caught throwing spitballs at a girl in Mrs. Brown's classroom. In spite of these infractions, Mrs. Brown has not classified us as problem kids yet, but all of that is about to change. This time we've gone too far. We committed the senseless act of picking on a little defenseless, half-blind, deaf kid. She's not amused.

Mrs. Brown comes over and tersely instructs us to follow her. All our classmates watch as we head to the principal's office. Everyone in the school is afraid of Mr. Baxter, the principal. He's an imposing, intimidating figure and his six-foot four frame looks menacing to a couple of nine-year-olds who are about four-feet-nothing. Johnny and I are told to sit on the wooden bench in the hall outside his office. Mrs. Brown knocks on the door and goes inside and shuts it. Johnny and I can hear her heatedly telling him what we've done.

Johnny looks scared. I whisper to him that I hate this waiting and would rather get it over with. He doesn't reply and gives me an annoyed look, as if he wants me to shut up and not get us into any more trouble. We don't talk anymore.

Mr. Baxter calls our moms and tells them to come to school to pick us up. Mr.

Baxter wants to personally meet with them before he suspends us for the rest of the day. We sit out there for what seems like an hour and finally I see my mom. She's embarrassed, and she's boiling mad that she had to take off work to deal with my misbehavior in school. Johnny's mother doesn't work but is none too happy either.

They both arrive at the same time and start walking together down the hall. I can hear Mom's high heels *click, click, clicking* on the polished tile. She's not very tall and makes up for it by taking fast, short steps. And when she's angry, her steps are even sharper and more hurried—they give off a very distinctive sound.

Both have dark looks on their faces. Johnny and I don't have to ask if we're in big trouble. Mom's jaw is tightly clenched and she pauses just long enough to shoot me a baleful glare before she opens the door and goes into Mr. Baxter's office.

In about five minutes the door opens again. This time it's Mr. Baxter standing there. He looks even taller and more intimidating than ever as he looms over us. He has a deep, gruff voice and he tells us to go into his office. He tersely nods for us to take a seat in the chairs directly across from his desk. He's not smiling and it's obvious that he's very angry.

"Whose idea was this?"

I'm not expecting his loud, deep voice, and I nearly jump out of my chair when he shouts the question. I look at Johnny and he looks at me. Johnny is in tears. Having already learned the hard lesson that it's wiser to confess a misdeed and take whatever is coming, I quickly raise my hand and admit that it was my idea.

Immediately it's as though no other thing on earth exists, just me. I'm the source of his annoyance and anger, and he's now concentrating exclusively on me. He unswervingly stares a hole directly into the centers of my eyes with his penetrating blue eyes. He's staring at me like he's a possessed zombie, and it's spooking me out. Even though my mom, Johnny's mom, Mrs. Brown, and Johnny are all there too, he never wavers. He looks only at me and stares into my pupils like he hates me. He's talking in a weird, low, chantlike monotone, as if he were telling a ghost story or something. He slowly recounts in exacting detail how I had senselessly tortured poor little Jacob.

At first this all makes me very uncomfortable, but for some reason I don't waver. I just stare right back at him. My dark side is now encouraging me to try to look spooky too. I stare harder at him, now trying my best to look spookier than he does. I don't take my eyes off his eyes for even a second and I try not to blink. I'm trying to stare into his pupils too. *Damn,* I had to blink.

Mr. Baxter is fuming and each word that he slowly utters is advancing a burning fuse toward a stick of dynamite. He tells me that he doesn't like bullies. His face is turning deep red and veins are sticking out in his neck, and he's raising his voice really loud again. Finally he explodes!

"Bullies are really just cowards!"

He's screaming now.

"You're a bully and you're a coward!"

He asks, "Why don't you pick on me Mr. Bully?"

He shouts, "Because you're a coward. It is a heinous thing that you have done!"

I don't know what that word heinous means, but I know it has to be bad.

Mom is sitting there with her face flushed-red, looking embarrassed and madder than a hornet. I'm her child and this is a reflection on her, and she didn't raise me to be like this. Now she's chiming in, "You do this to a defenseless little half-blind, deaf child. You should be ashamed!"

Mr. Baxter looks at me in total disgust, as though I'm a diseased wharf rat and says,

"What is wrong with you?"

Chapter Fourteen

I don't have to watch any of this elementary-school drama from my cocoon to know what's coming next for me in my grade-school years. My attitude has turned to shit. So what happens from here on out? Trouble, trouble, and more trouble. And although I know what's going to occur, the story begins to unfold and I'm compelled to watch anyway.

Mrs. Brown steps into Mr. Baxter's office and shuts the door. I sit on the now familiar hard wooden bench and await my turn to go in. It's been only a few weeks and here I am again, sitting outside the principal's office. This time Johnny is not with me. I'm not scared and I have a look of defiance on my face. Mrs. Brown has had it in for me ever since I played that trick on her little deaf pet, Jacob. She's brought me here three more times in as many weeks.

This time she caught me talking to a friend during study period. Any of the other students would simply have been told to go back to studying, but because it's me, I have to go to the principal's office. I don't care. I'm not afraid of Mr. Baxter and I'm definitely not afraid of Mrs. Brown. They just talk and yell and threaten and he stares at me like I'm some nutcase. I don't like them and they don't like me.

Likewise, I'm not afraid of my mom or even my dad anymore. I refuse to cry when he whips me—no matter how hard he swings his belt. I refuse to let anyone see me cry. I'm not afraid of anyone. I can take whatever they want to dish out.

I don't like school. I think it's boring and my teachers are losers. None is worse than Mrs. Brown. I rarely listen while she teaches, and I cut up constantly in class and try to make her life as miserable as she makes mine. When it comes time to take her tests, I can ace them like a breeze without ever so much as cracking a book. Her tests are simple, and she's stupid. She wants me to fail, but I make good grades without ever studying. She hates me and I hate her. I hate her guts!

Today, the principal calls me into his office and once again gives me the "stupid stare" and lectures me in his dumb-ass, zombie, creepy, low ghost-story monotone for a while. Then he gives me a note to take home and tells me that my parents have to read and sign it before I bring it back to school. Big deal! He's a moron too. If I could write a little better, I'd sign the damn thing myself.

After my parents see the note, I receive my customary whipping from Dad and they put me on restriction. They take away my meager 25 cents weekly allowance again. I just got it back and now I've lost it again.

They also confine me to my room unless I'm doing chores. If that's not enough, now I have to do all the chores, including Jim's and not just my own. This is the absolute worst part of it. My brother, their darling little "golden boy," is sure to laugh at me and torment me as I do his chores, and I'm sure to tell him he can go to hell and then I'll probably just be in more trouble for cussing. I know it'll perpetuate the cycle.

Although I'm still on restriction and supposed to be going directly home after school, I stop off on my way home to play some tetherball.

I'm standing underneath the tetherball pole grimacing from the intense pain being applied to my foot. An older kid has just stomped on it and is now standing on it, using his full weight to try and grind my toes into the pavement. He's mad because I just told his little brother that there's no such thing as Santa Claus and it's all just a big lie. He's determined to make me pay for spoiling his little brother's dream about Santa Claus.

My tormentor easily outweighs me by 40 pounds, and looks to be 12 or 13 years old. I may be much younger and smaller than him, but I've had years of daily practice fighting with my brother and others. Something inside my mind just seems to snap when I get mad, especially when someone hits me that first time or hurts me somehow. Rather than shrinking from it, it enrages me and awakens my dark side. It's hard to describe, but it's like a white-hot bomb instantly exploding in my mind. I just snap. I become a wild animal acting on primal instinct. I don't think, my mouth turns dry, and I instinctively react with ferocity. My dark side takes over and launches some innate, primitive desire to hurt, maim, and kill.

I hit the older kid as hard as I can in the stomach and he immediately doubles up and releases my foot. I've knocked the wind out of him and he's standing there bent over gasping for air. I lose control. I hit him in the mouth with my fist as hard as I can and blood spatters all over his face. He immediately falls to the ground.

I start kicking him in the head as hard and as fast as I can kick. He quickly covers his head with his arms, so I savagely stomp him hard in his stomach. He rolls over to protect his stomach. I start stomping on the back of his legs. I then drop my knees and the full weight of my body on the unprotected small part of his back. I manage to roll him over and crunch his head between my legs so he's positioned faceup; and I pin his arms with my knees. I start pounding and pummeling his face as hard and as fast as I can. Blood is pouring out of his mouth and I've opened a cut on the corner of his eye. I concentrate on opening that cut wider by swinging hard with just one fist and aiming each blow directly at it.

His little brother is screaming and crying and some other kids hear him and come running over and grab me from behind and pull me off. I break free of their grip and run back over to where the older kid is lying. Just as he tries to rise to his feet, I savagely kick him again as hard as I can right in the face. I can feel his nose break with my vicious kick, and I see blood gushing from it.

I whirl around and face the other kids with both fists tightly balled up. There are three of them and I recognize them from my class. I scream, "Who wants to be next?"

"YOU?" I point to one of them.

He shakes his head no and backs up.

I'm wild-eyed and have the older boy's blood splattered all over me. I'm breathing heavily—my chest is heaving up and down. All of them back up, shaking their heads to indicate that they want no part of me. I take a step toward them and scream at them again, "Come on! I'll take you all on! *Come on!*"

They back away. Their eyes are wide with fear and there are no takers.

I sneer at them, "You're all a bunch of yellow-bellied cowards!" I grab my books off the ground and walk home. I'm so mad that I'm still shaking uncontrollably.

I didn't know the older kid or his brother, and apparently they didn't report the beating to any teachers or to the police. It happened after school and no one witnessed it but the three boys from my class. They were too afraid to snitch to anyone, but Johnny told me that they did tell all my classmates and it quickly spread all over school. From that day forward no one wanted any part of fighting me.

I enjoy their fear of me.

Chapter Fifteen

Mom and Dad are now heavily involved in church. Growing up on the farm, Dad's parents raised him to go to church, but after he left home he drifted away from it. Mom had never been to church much as a child, and initially didn't want anything to do with it. Something changed, however, and the next thing I knew she'd become a believer and was playing the piano at church services; and Dad was managing the Sunday school.

I didn't like this one little bit. The entire family was now going to church every Sunday. It meant that we could no longer sleep in on Sunday mornings and instead had to get all dressed up and go listen to some guy scream and holler at us for an hour and a half. To make matters worse, we also had to go back Sunday nights for an evening service, where we repeated the process.

Dad talked to Jim and me quite a bit about God and Jesus and encouraged us to go down the aisle and become believers like my mom and him. Sure enough, a few weeks later Jim stepped out into the aisle and went down to the front of the church and told the preacher that he wanted to be saved and baptized just as Dad had told him to do.

This made Dad and Mom very happy, and they cried and beamed and congratulated him for an hour. Not to be outdone, the very next Sunday when the alter call began I stepped out into the aisle and went down and told the preacher that I too wanted to be saved and baptized. Dad and Mom were once again happy and cried and beamed for an hour over me too.

A couple of weeks later we were both baptized on the same day. I waded out into the warm water of the baptistery and the preacher said a few things that I didn't really hear. (I was more focused on the fact that my head was about to be shoved underwater.) I held my breath and nose as the preacher submerged my head. When I emerged the preacher said that I was now "saved" and baptized, and that when I died I would go to heaven.

Someone in the crowd shouted, "Hallelujah!" and the congregation clapped. No doubt they were all thrilled to tears that I would now go to heaven instead of hell.

I was glad to hear that piece of news too, even though as a 10-year-old boy I didn't comprehend in the slightest the concept of death, heaven, or hell.

Not long after Jim and I were saved, Dad decided that he didn't like the big church that we attended. He much preferred small Baptist churches like the one he'd grown up in and soon he and some friends decided to start their own church.

About eight families, including ours, met in an old, rented building located in a seedy section of town. The building was a dilapidated meeting hall and had creaky wooden floors. There was a rickety old wooden podium up front where the preacher always stands, and an out-of-tune piano sat adjacent to it. In front of the podium were some hard, brown, metal folding chairs. That's where we sat. I always positioned myself toward the back where I could sleep without being seen.

They're endeavoring to hire a full-time preacher and are trying out a different one every week. The ones that they've tried all scream and yell and pound their fists on the rickety wooden stand. The little church must not be able to offer to pay them much, because Dad said that so far every preacher they've tried is terrible.

One day the trial preacher who came to church was unshaven and dressed in rumpled clothes. Dad said that he smelled alcohol on him before the service and asked him to leave.

Since we didn't have a preacher that day, Dad preached. So boring . . . it reminds me of one of Mr. Baxter's lectures. I tried to sleep on one of the uncomfortable, hard chairs, but it was impossible. After he finished his sermon, all of the other families went up front to congratulate him and he was beaming and shaking hands. I was hungry and sleepy and just wanted to get the hell out of there.

After months of trying out various preachers, they finally hired a pastor. His name was Ted Runnel. He was a short, stocky man with greasy, black, slicked-down hair and black-rimmed glasses with high corners on them. Soon after, he came he volunteered to take Jim and me fishing at Lake Berryessa, which is a beautiful lake about 40 miles from our home.

Mom's delighted. To me, this new preacher seems to be more than a little attracted to her, and I don't like to see him hanging around our house talking to her. He seems sneaky and has a fake smile, and I don't like him.

Jim catches a big bass and swings him onto the bank, and the fish is flopping all around. Pastor Ted says, "Nice bass Jim. How many does that make for you today?"

Jim says, "I dunno, maybe 10."

Jim's an excellent little fisherman and he loves it. I prefer hunting with my BB gun or pellet rifle, but when the bass are biting, as they are today, I like fishing too. I haven't caught nearly as many as Jim, but I did manage to catch a few good-size fish as well.

Pastor Ted is sitting cross-legged like an Indian and is leaning forward a little holding a fishing pole in his hands. My brother is on one side of him and I'm on the other. Our hooks are baited with live minnows and we're watching our corks and waiting for a hungry bass to take them under.

Suddenly Pastor Ted rolls up on one side, lifts his still-crossed legs, points his butt toward me, and breaks wind. It's a doozy! Loud and long.

Ordinarily I might have thought it was funny, but this man is a preacher, and I say, "You're a preacher and shouldn't be doing that."

He says, "Why? Because I farted?"

I snap back, "That's a bad word and preachers shouldn't say bad words."

He asks, "Well what do you want me to call it?"

I'm stumped because I don't know what preachers are supposed to call a fart. I suggest that he call it a "let one."

He laughs and then in a few minutes rolls up on his side again as if he wants to aim it at me this time. He rips another one that's even louder and longer than the previous one. "Hey Bob," he says, "I just 'let one.' Why not come over here and help me smell it up?" And then he laughs hysterically.

I don't think he's funny and move as far away from him as I can. As we continue to fish, I find Pastor Ted to be foul-mouthed and nasty. He belches and farts with regularity, and each time he laughs like a hyena. I hear him say "damn" several times when he misses a fish. One time he says "shit," when he sticks a hook in his finger.

When I get home I tell my mother what he's said and done and she just laughs. Had that been me and the preacher had told her that I'd cussed, farted, and belched, she would've washed my mouth out with soap and then manipulated Dad into a rage so he'd give me a hard whipping.

It's not right that this lousy *preacher* gets away with farting, belching, and saying bad words—and she thinks it's funny. But if I ever did that, I'd get severely punished. It's just a bunch of phony crap to me!

As I watch from my hospital cocoon, I think that maybe this incident marked the birth of my intense, lifelong hatred of religion, church, and especially preachers. I've wondered about that. It had to start somewhere; I wasn't born hating religion and religious types. To be sure, as I grew older other stuff happened to turn me off to religion and solidify my hatred, but after watching this I think that this just may be where it all began.

Whatever the case, one thing is certain: All that crap about going down the aisle and being saved and baptized and going to heaven turned out to be hogwash anyway, 'cause I'm dead and I'm sure as hell not in heaven. Come to think of it, I'm not in hell either. Am I?

Mom, Dad, and Jim will be surprised to learn that when they die they'll end up here floating around in some damned cocoon on a serene black sea watching their lives unfold, instead of on some cloud playing a heavenly harp.

CHAPTER SIXTEEN

"Guam? – We're moving to Guam?" – *Where the hell is Guam?* – Just when I began to enjoy life and find some stability and happiness in Fairfield, Dad tells us that he is being transferred again.

This time to Guam. Of all the places we could go, he is being sent to some little island nearly 6,000 miles away in the middle of the Pacific Ocean—for *two years.* And we have to go with him.

It's devastating news to me because my life's been going great for the first time ever. I've finally developed some good friends. I have a new teacher, and I like her and she likes me—and I'm making straight A's. I've been an all-star on every team I've played on, and I'm playing every sport. I seldom fight or get into trouble anymore. And now, just when things are going good, we have to move again. I'm heartbroken.

I don't want to move and I beg to stay, but Dad doesn't consider that an option. He simply says, "You'll be fine."

End of discussion.

The entire time we lived on Guam was nothing more than a string of unhappy events. In two years I didn't make one friend. We moved several times on base, then off base, and back on base again as Dad found better quarters. Each time we moved I had to attend a new school (three in all), where there were new teachers, new classmates, new bullies, and new trouble. I fought constantly, screwed up at every opportunity, and took more whippings than ever before. I hated my life so much that I ran away from home.

I don't know where I thought I might have escaped to, but I was picked up by the Air Police less than a mile from home. When I returned home my dad gave me a hard whipping and put me on restriction for a month. How dumb was it to run away from home on *Guam*, a shitty little island in the middle of the Pacific Ocean?

That was my life on Guam.

I was overjoyed when I heard the news that Dad was being transferred right back to my favorite place, Fairfield, California. I let out a *yippee!* and ran all over the house like an excited monkey running through the trees.

When our plane landed in California, I immediately went to my knees and kissed the hot pavement with my lips. It was an awesome feeling for me to be home again. I couldn't wait to reunite with my best friend, Johnny, and see my other friends and pick up where I'd left off two years earlier.

The next news crushed my celebratory mood and joyful frame of mind like a hiker pounding a snake's head into the dirt with his walking stick. We weren't moving back to our old neighborhood. I wouldn't be reuniting with Johnny or any of my old friends, or even going to the same school. Dad said that he couldn't find an available house in Fairfield and we were moving to Suisun City, several miles away from Fairfield.

My first day at the new school was the usual story—I didn't have any friends or know anyone; I didn't know where to go for any of my classes; I didn't know any of my teachers. And, as usual, bullies wanted to pick on the new kid, so I had to go through the process of fiercely defending myself and beating the shit out of a couple of them in order to establish that I was not about to allow anyone to pick on me, the new kid at school.

We left Guam during the middle of the school year, and not only did I lose class time during the relocation process, but I wasn't studying the same curriculum in California that I'd been studying on Guam. I was behind my other classmates and needed to catch up. As for sports, teams were already established and I would just have to wait.

I hated every aspect of it with all my fiber; and not much time elapsed before I was trekking to the principal's office every day for causing trouble with my teachers and classmates. When I went home, it was usually just more trouble with Mom, Dad, and Jim.

I didn't have time to adjust to my new school because after only a couple of months Dad found a house in Fairfield and we moved again. Unfortunately, even though it was Fairfield, we moved to a different neighborhood than the one we'd lived in before. So Jim and I would yet again attend a new school, which meant I wouldn't know anyone or where to go, and the new kid/new school process would repeat itself.

I came home from school one day and my dad was home unusually early and he was crying. He'd received the news that his father had died. Mom didn't have enough vacation built up to take off work, so she could not attend the funeral, and she stayed behind while my dad, Jim, and I made the long trip alone. Early the next morning, the three of us took off in Dad's car and drove from California to Mississippi to attend the funeral—my first.

Jim and I had a great time traveling cross-country with Dad. At home Dad would always arrive home late and then he'd read the paper. At dinner he would talk mainly to Mom and then he would go to the living room and watch the TV news and several comedy shows that he enjoyed. That was his life.

He never went outside to play catch, or talked to me, or paid much attention to me at all at home, but driving across all those states we talked for hour after hour, day after day. He told me about his childhood and life on the farm. They had a horse and cows, and he worked the cotton fields. He used to plow with a mule, and went barefoot. Their farm had lots of woods where he could hunt. I was particularly interested in his hunting experiences. He told us how he used to hunt squirrels and gave us all kinds of tips on squirrel hunting, and he promised that when we were in Mississippi he'd let us go hunting with a real shotgun. It was the first semblance of bonding that I'd experienced with Dad.

Although Dad had never told me that he loved me, for the first time in my life I was beginning to think that he might actually care about me. I'd never gotten along so well with my brother either; and now it was as though we were actually friends.

I wasn't prepared to see my first dead person. Papa was lying in a casket, and as is the custom in the deep rural South, he was being viewed in the parlor room of Dad's old home place. Several people were sitting around the living room watching as each person filed by and took a look at Papa. They would stand there staring at his dead body, cry, and then move on. The family had stationed flowers around the casket and one took the shape of a heart and had "Papa" written in red flowers surrounded by white flowers.

To me, dead people look like they're made of whitish wax. Even their hair looks as though it was carved out of wax. In the parlor everyone was talking in hushed tones and lots of people were crying, me included.

The pastor of a small country church conducted a funeral service for Papa the day after we arrived. They played one particularly sad song, "Shall We Gather at the River," and I don't know what got into me but suddenly I started crying uncontrollably. I was nearly berserk with grief. I didn't even know him, but something about this scene made me as emotional as I've ever been in my life. They had to take me out of the church because I was disturbing everyone with my loud sobbing and hysterical crying. Papa was buried at Topisaw cemetery that same day—the saddest day of my young life.

We stayed on at the old home place for a few days so Dad could visit with his family and friends. My dad was true to his word and allowed Jim and me to go hunting with shotguns, which were supplied by our uncles and cousins. We each carried a single shot shotgun, and Dad's brother—who still lived on the farm—told us where there was one "secret spot" we could go to that was just loaded with squirrels. He didn't know of two places, but assured us that we would easily bag our limit at the big oak tree that he called the "den tree."

Of course Jim and I both wanted to go there and Dad had to intervene. He said Jim could hunt there the first day and I could hunt there the next (and final) day. That afternoon Jim went to the den tree and, as our uncle had predicted, bagged several fat gray squirrels. I went to another location and didn't even see one. I was disappointed, but after seeing Jim's success was anxious for tomorrow to arrive so I could go to the "secret spot."

The next afternoon it was my turn to go to the den tree. I was way too excited to sleep the night before and was excited about shooting my limit of fat squirrels.

Later that day, in the cool of the afternoon when the squirrels began to get active, Jim and I departed for our hunt. As we walked across the field to get there, Jim said, "I'm going back to my same place that I went yesterday—to the den tree—and you can go somewhere else."

I angrily responded, "Oh no you're not, it's my turn. Dad said so!"

He shouted, "I'm going there. It's my spot!"

He then turned around and pushed me down to the ground as hard as he could.

The dark fury takes over my soul. My dark side is deafening, screaming. I get up and cock my sixteen-gauge shotgun. It makes an unusually loud sound as the hammer reaches the cocked position and my brother hears it *click.* The color drains from his face and he tries to back away. I won't let him. I step forward and move the barrel of the cocked shotgun within an inch of his face, aiming the long barrel right between his scared eyes. I'm so enraged that I can hardly breathe. And I'm shaking.

My dark side is on fire, telling me over and over and over again to blow his damned head off. I utter through clenched teeth,

"You son of a bitch. I'll kill you!"

Chapter Seventeen

The old shotgun is cocked and hovers mere inches from Jim's face. My eyes are blazing and my dark side is now in control.

Without saying a word Jim gives me a wounded, almost quizzical look. He lowers his gaze and sadly shakes his head as though trying to comprehend what just happened. He seems almost bewildered by it all and then he just turns and walks off toward the other hunting place, yielding the den tree to me.

He never once looks back.

I slowly lower the gun and little by little my breathing returns to normal. As my anger subsides and I return to a state of sanity, it hits me hard that *I very nearly killed Jim over a stupid hunting place!*

My finger had been firmly positioned on the trigger of the cocked shotgun and I was shaking from the rage. If he'd provoked me even a tiny smidgen more, he'd be dead right now. And even if I hadn't deliberately pulled the trigger, the old gun could have accidentally gone off. At that close range the blast would have taken his head off.

As I sit under the den tree watching several gray squirrels running back and forth, I begin to quietly sob. Then I completely break down crying, uncontrollably, as I did at Papa's funeral. I'm not crying because of the trouble I'll be in when Dad finds out; I'm crying because I love Jim and I almost killed him.

Although I'm jealous of the favoritism my parents show Jim, and I get agitated when his spoiled-rotten demeanor is aimed toward me, I still love him and I know he loves me. With all the instability and moving around, we've never had an opportunity to develop any lasting friendships with other kids; but we've always had the single constant of each other. We've had plenty of good times together, hunting, fishing, riding our bikes, and playing sports.

As for fighting with each other, we've always had a weird relationship: We would fiercely fight each other with bloody fists over the slightest provocation, but we were just as fierce in defending one another against anyone else. Everyone at school knew that if you messed with one of us, you'd soon be facing the other or—worse—*both* of us at the same time.

I never did understand why Jim didn't snitch me out to Dad that day, but uncharacteristically he never once mentioned this incident to anyone (including me), and neither did I. I've often wondered what he thought about when he turned his back on me that day and went off to the woods. As he turned and walked away, did he expect to be shot in the back at any moment? Or did he somehow know that I would slowly lower the gun and let it go.

As he quietly sat by himself in the silence of the forest waiting on squirrels to appear, what ran through his mind? Maybe he realized how close he'd come to death and was frightened by it. Maybe he was ashamed for having pushed me so far. Maybe he was angry, or maybe he was just surprised, like someone who teases and torments a chained dog that one day unexpectedly turns and tears his tormentor's throat out.

Did he come to the realization that there are *limits* to how far I can be pushed without releasing the beast that resides within me?

Although he hasn't said so, I'm sure he doesn't want to face the rage again. As for me, I'm ashamed—and I'm scared shitless of my dark side. I now know that I can't be trusted to control the fury of my irrepressible temper. I have an ominous feeling that it's only a matter of time before sudden disaster occurs, and I hope and pray that it's not aimed toward Jim.

The next day we begin our trip back home to California and in every way it's as much fun as the trip out. I really feel that Dad and I will be great friends from now on. He tells us story after story of how as a young boy he used to ride his horse, hunt, go fishing in the creeks, work on the farm, kill water moccasins, and catch birds and small animals in homemade traps and snares.

He tells us one story about a time his brothers made moonshine whiskey. He was just a small child and his brothers were much older. An old hound dog was with them and his brothers decided to pour some of the moonshine down the old dog's throat. The hound got drunk and started running around the woods with his nose burrowing up leaves and howling and staggering around and acting as though it'd lost its mind. We all laugh to tears as he tells it.

Unfortunately, when we finally return home, it soon becomes evident that nothing has changed. Dad goes back to his old routine of coming home and reading the paper, talking to Mom during dinner, and then watching TV until bedtime. He never plays catch or goes to any of my games, and there is no more talk about hunting or fishing or sports or what it was like to live on the farm, and no more funny stories about hound dogs getting drunk; it is as though I don't exist anymore.

When I try to talk to him, he lowers his newspaper and with an irritated look on his face tells me that he is reading the paper and to quit bothering him and go outside to play. More often than not it is at these times that I turn to Jim and we play some catch or ride our bikes to a playground and shoot a basketball.

Even though the days turn into weeks and the weeks turn into months, the incident with Jim and the shotgun haunts me most nights. I lie in my bed but sleep won't come. Holding that gun in Jim's face and the insidious fury of the moment runs over and over again in my mind.

I think that my angel of light wouldn't give me peace over this as his way of insisting that I find a way to control my dark side before it was too late.

Jim's my only friend. We're brothers and I love him, and I almost killed him. For the first time I finally realize that something is dreadfully wrong with me, and like everyone else I'm now beginning to shake my head and wonder,

What is wrong with me?

Chapter Eighteen

I'm as naked as the day I was born, and I'm hiding in a play area that my brother and I refer to as our fort. The midday California sun is sizzling today and there isn't a cloud in the sky. It's sweltering hot in the fort, which is located in the rafters of our garage. Sweat is literally pouring off my naked body.

A couple of weekends ago Jim and I, with a little help from Dad, built our fort. The plywood floor is carpeted and it's dimly lit with only a single pull-chain lightbulb fixture. We don't have much headroom and have to crawl on our hands and knees everywhere we go within the fort. We enter by climbing a ladder built from two-by-fours to reach the door opening and then crawl into a small room. A hall leads from there to a larger room to the left.

That's where I'm positioned.

I've reunited with my old friend Johnny Lawson. He and I are both 12 years old. His parents and mine have revived their friendship from two years ago and, although we don't live near each other or attend the same school anymore, we get to see each other often because school is out for the summer. Today he's ridden his bike all the way over to my house to visit, and we're home alone.

Johnny has a much older brother named Tommy, who's wild and gets into trouble all the time. He smokes cigarettes, drinks beer, and has had sex with a number of girls. He's been educating Johnny and me about sex. He gave us some nudie magazines with pictures of naked girls and also told us how to have sex.

At the moment, Johnny is trying to coax a girl that we both know from my neighborhood to enter our fort to have sex. She doesn't know I'm already in the fort hiding. Sharon is her name and she's three years older than us. Some kids in the neighborhood told us that she has a crush on Johnny, and he called her earlier and convinced her to come over.

Sharon's not pretty and she's definitely not too smart; in fact she's been held back two grades because she can't pass tests and is probably mildly retarded. Several of the neighborhood kids had recently seen Sharon and a little boy named Curt, who is two years younger than us, having sex under a bridge in our neighborhood. We figure that if she was willing to have sex with Curt, she ought to be willing to have sex with us too.

The magazines that Johnny's brother gave us are now open to nudie photos and are carefully spread out all over the floor for Sharon to see as soon as she enters the room where I'm hiding. Our plan is simple: Johnny will convince Sharon to enter the fort and proceed down the hall to the big room where I'm hiding, at which point I'll jump out naked. She'll see me and the revealing nudie photos, and then we'll all have sex.

At the moment, Sharon's at the top of the ladder peering in and Johnny is standing behind her on the ladder encouraging her to enter the fort. She senses that something is wrong and is resisting his attempt to convince her to go inside. She likes Johnny a lot and wants to believe him, but won't advance. I can hear Johnny coaxing her to go on in and see the fort—that it's cool.

Meanwhile I'm sweltering in the searing attic heat. I've been hiding up here for over an hour, and even though I'm completely naked, I'm roasting and literally pouring sweat from every sweat gland in my body. It must be 110º in that fort. I long for a cool glass of water. In fact I'd give up my allowance forever in exchange for a cool drink of any kind.

After what seems like an eternity, Johnny finally convinces Sharon to enter the fort. She's tentative at first and momentarily stays in the first room by the ladder and refuses to move. Johnny keeps smoothly encouraging her to go on down the hall to the big room, and I'm relieved to hear her finally agree.

When she turns the corner, I jump up and face her and she sees me buck naked, fully aroused in all my glory.

She says, "You're not doing that to me."

I say, "Oh yes we are." Johnny quickly says, "Sharon you let Curt do it under the bridge. Why won't you let us? I thought you liked me."

She looks surprised that he knows about Curt, and smilingly says, "Who told you that?"

Johnny says, "All the kids in the neighborhood know about it. Several people saw you."

She smiles wider but insists that we aren't going to do that to her.

Johnny looks at me and I look at him and we're now at a loss as to what to do next. We were sure she'd be ready and willing, but this was not part of our plan.

Johnny tries again. "Sharon, we just want to do what you and Curt did. It'll be fun." And then he asks, "Don't you love me?"

Love? I look at him like he's lost his mind, but keep my mouth shut.

I'm astonished when she says, "Yes."

"Well if you do, you'll let us have sex with you."

To my utter amazement she says okay and immediately starts unbuttoning her blouse and taking her clothes off. A huge smile forms on Johnny's face and he immediately starts stripping too.

The plan was that I would go first and then Johnny. I awkwardly assume my position on top of her just as Johnny's older brother had instructed and after a few clumsy attempts, soon I am successfully banging away.

I'm looking into Sharon's face and she's wearing odd-looking blue-frame glasses that turn up on the corners like a housecat's eyes. The entire time I'm on top of her she's staring into my eyes with a peculiar, eccentric-looking smile on her face that makes her appear insane. Her weird smile reveals dirty green teeth and it sickens me to look at them. Her hair is nasty, greasy, and unkempt, and it makes her all the more unappealing.

I continue pounding for a while and now we're both sweaty and it feels slippery, like we're covered with fish slime. It's beginning to stink like hell in here and I'm beginning to feel light-headed. My stomach is queasy from the combination of the stench, heat, and repulsiveness of looking at her creepy smiling face. In fact I'm very close to vomiting in her face. Suddenly I gag and almost puke. I can actually taste the vomit backing up in the bottom of my throat, but I catch it; it burns but I force it back down.

That's it. I'm done. I can't reach a successful conclusion.

I want out of here!

Without a word I climb off and yield to Johnny, who still has that huge smile planted on his face as he awaits his turn. I gather my clothes together and put them on in record time. Without a glance back I race down the hall crawling on my hands and knees as fast as I can toward the ladder and fresh air.

I need fresh air!

Bonk!

Shit!

I'd raced down the hall on my hands and knees looking down and had held my head up a little too high and run full speed into a rafter and nearly knocked myself out.

I now have tears in my eyes and I'm rolling back and forth on my back vigorously rubbing my forehead, I can feel a goose-egg-size knot forming.

Shit. Shit. Shit!

I rub my head and moan, cautiously get back to my hands and knees, and resume crawling—only much slower now. I hold my head down low near the floor as I crawl into the smaller room and then on down the ladder.

I'm nauseous when I reach the garage floor, and I run inside the house to the kitchen and drink a big glass of water. My face still feels flushed, my stomach is rolling, my hair is soaked, and a nasty knot and cut decorate my forehead. I pour another glass of water and swig it down and then walk to the back door and peer inside the garage.

In a few minutes Johnny and Sharon appear at the top of the ladder and start to come down. They're flushed too and their faces are as red as a bad sunburn; and both are drenched in sweat. Johnny's curly, black hair is plastered to his head and he looks like he's been swimming; and Sharon's hair looks like a dirty, matted rug.

I'm now paranoid that someone will find out what we did, and I tell Sharon that she needs to leave before someone sees her at my house. (I damn sure don't want anyone in the neighborhood to see her with us, and neither does Johnny.)

I exit through the backyard and then to the street. I anxiously look in both directions, and it looks all clear. I raise the garage door to let her ride her bike on out of here. Johnny tells her that if she loves him she has to promise that she'll never tell anyone about any of this and she nods her head. She waves at Johnny as she rides away and like an idiot he smiles and waves goodbye to her.

As far as I know she didn't ever tell anyone what happened in the fort that day. Johnny and I wanted no more sex with Sharon and we both avoided her like she had bubonic plague. Needless to say, we never told a soul about our encounter either—not even Johnny's brother.

Johnny told me that after I left he couldn't reach a successful conclusion either; but it was of little matter. We had both performed sex and were now real men.

Our very first conquest. Cool . . .

Chapter Nineteen

After we sit down at the supper table, Dad makes an all-too-familiar announcement. We're moving again, and this time we're going to Mississippi. He's decided to retire from the Air Force and move to his home state permanently. He dislikes California and wants to move back to Mississippi and get back to his roots.

I know it's useless to try to talk him out of it. There won't be any family discussion of the pros and cons of such a move. It doesn't matter if we have to pick up and leave school in the middle of a semester—kids always adjust. It doesn't matter if we love our friends, sports teams, living in Fairfield, or our girlfriends—kids always adjust.

We won't even be asked our opinion of this life-changing decision. We'll move to Mississippi like good soldiers. He looks at us and matter-of-factly states, "We'll be leaving California by the end of the month."

End of story.

I feel weak, and then I feel like I'm going to be sick, and then I feel like I'm going to cry. I drop my fork on my plate and without a word stand up from the table and go to my room. I lie on the bed and feel sorry for myself.

I don't want to move again and leave all my teammates, coaches, and friends—especially not my girlfriend. Mom comes into my room and sits on the edge of my bed and rubs my back and tells me that everything's going to be fine and that I can play sports and hunt and fish in Mississippi. She says I'll make new friends.

I don't answer and she quietly leaves. She doesn't say as much, but I don't think she wants to leave California either. Jim stays at the table and continues eating his supper and seems to just take it in stride. I'm not sure if he cares one way or the other. If he does, he's keeping it to himself.

A few days after the announcement, Johnny Lawson rode his bike over to my house to spend Saturday with me. Johnny wants to see me before I leave, and has brought something with him to cheer me up. He stole some cigarettes from his older brother and four cans of beer out of his dad's garage—for my going-away party!

We ride our bikes out to an old, abandoned farmhouse beyond the outskirts of town, and light up our cigarettes. The smoke tastes terrible and makes us cough and leaves us light-headed, but for some strange reason we still want to smoke these cigarettes.

I've learned how to blow perfectly round smoke rings, but Johnny can't seem to get the hang of sailing the perfect ones yet. Johnny and I are taking our very first crack at drinking beer, lamenting my imminent departure to Mississippi.

Like the cigarettes, the beer smells and tastes dreadful, but I drink it anyway and so does Johnny. After the first can I already feel a little tipsy. I discover that I like this feeling very much. Johnny seems to be in similar shape.

Suddenly I emit a long belch, like a donkey braying. I pound my chest like a gorilla as the noise comes from down in my gut. Not to be outdone, Johnny easily tops my belch with a much deeper one, which sounds like what a gorilla belch might sound like. He pounds his chest too. We both laugh and for some reason known only to Johnny, he takes off running in a circle around and around as fast as he can go.

Johnny looks hilariously silly running around, and now he's screeching like an agitated monkey. He gets dizzy from the beer and keeps running in circles. He runs right into an old wooden gate, bounces off, and falls flat on his butt. I laugh and happen to belch again during my laugh, which ends up causing me to emit more belches in between laughs. *Ha, burp, ha, burp, ha, ha, burp, ha, ha, ha.* I can't stop belching or laughing.

Johnny comes back over to where I'm sitting with a sheepish-looking, stupid grin on his face and flops down on the grass. We light up another cigarette and pop open our second beers and soon our conversation turns to that time we had sex with Sharon in my fort. We laugh about how I nearly knocked myself out by running into the rafter in that stifling hot garage, and then we talk about our latest conquests and compare notes.

Since that first sexual encounter with Sharon, Johnny and I have both been successful in convincing our girlfriends to have sex with us. I don't use the fort anymore; instead I use my own bed. My girlfriend and I are going steady now and we've had sex several times. She's a beautiful little Italian girl by the name of Julie DiVito. She has black hair and black eyes and an olive complexion, and we're in love. I'm getting the hang of sex now, and I like it. Julie was a virgin and said it hurt that first time, and she bled some. (Afterward, I had a hell of a time—using plenty of bleach and detergent—cleaning my sheets so my mother wouldn't discover the blood stains.) Since that first time though, Julie seems to like sex as much as I do—which means we do it as often as we can.

Johnny's had good success too. His mother doesn't work and is home every day, but he's been able to score over at his girlfriend's house. Both of her parents work during the day, like mine do. According to Johnny she absolutely loves sex and they have it so many times a day that he gets light-headed afterward when he's walking back home from her house.

Johnny and I hang out together for another hour or so before heading home. After the two beers we're a little wobbly, but we can still ride our bikes. I arrive home long before anyone else from my family. I brush my teeth and use foul-tasting

Listerine mouthwash to cover the scent of the cigarettes and beer; and when my family comes home, no one seems to notice anything unusual or suspect that I'm slightly drunk. I suppose that's one advantage of being ignored.

Smoking cigarettes and drinking beer are really not the norm for me. When Johnny and I are together, my dark side rears his ugly head and we do crazy things together, but I don't have any other friends like Johnny. We go to different schools and it's hard for Johnny and me to get together except on an occasional weekend.

At school I'm making good grades and not getting into any serious trouble or many fights. I'm into sports more than at any other time in my life. Indeed, they seem to dominate my time. I'm big for my age, standing nearly five-feet-eleven, and I stand out in every sport. I have a room full of trophies and ribbons, and my coaches have taken notice and are spending time with me and are very encouraging to me. I take gymnastics and tumbling, and I'm also on the track team. I'm really into high-jumping and have even tried pole-vaulting. In addition, I still play all the normal sports—football, baseball, and basketball. I'm working out with weights and my body is responding well.

My brother is excellent in sports too, and we ended up on the same baseball team this year. As always I was the pitcher and he was the catcher, and we both excelled. Jim and I don't fight much anymore. He has his older friends to hang out with, and I have mine. We're rarely around each other long enough to antagonize one other.

I spend a lot of time talking to my coaches, and actually at times feel closer to them than I do to my own family. They seem to genuinely like me and praise my athletic abilities. I love the attention they give me. With all that I have going on, plus the time I spend with my girlfriend, there really hasn't been much time to get into trouble. I'm really enjoying life for the first time.

It's a shame I have to leave.

Four weeks pass quickly, however, and without much fanfare we pick up and leave Fairfield and head for Columbus, Mississippi. When we arrive, I find it to be nothing like California; instead it's hot, humid, and backward. The entire community looks old and poor, and it's predominantly black.

Lee High School is the first high school I attend. It's very large and is located in downtown Columbus. We have to start school right in the middle of the semester. We were initially told by the school that we might have to be put back a grade because California schools were so far behind Mississippi schools. Nothing could have been further from the truth. I was at least a year ahead of them in everything. My brother and I could have easily skipped a grade without falling behind, and school was all the more boring because of that.

I can no longer walk to school and now have to ride a school bus. On my second day a kid on the bus tried his luck at picking on me, and without hesitation I beat him half senseless. I was banging his head on the school-bus floor when the bus driver stopped at the side of the road and pulled me off him. One thing far different about Mississippi schools: The teachers aren't afraid to use a wooden paddle to exact corporal punishment on those who get in trouble. There are no speeches and stupid stares like Mr. Baxter's, just swift and sure smacks with a well-sanded paddle that's about an inch thick. I got my first paddling after that fight and on a regular basis thereafter. I was made to bend over in my tight blue jeans and when the board hit my butt, it sounded like a rifle going off. *Pow! Pow! Pow!* I had bruises the next day.

For some reason, the students that I've met in Columbus don't seem to like California or anyone who's from California, which of course includes me. To my knowledge, none have ever actually been to California, but they dislike it just the same. This is not restricted to students. It seems that everyone, including teachers and the people I've met in the neighborhood, seems to think that simply because they're from Mississippi, they're better than everyone else. My dad is like this too.

I've never encountered this attitude anywhere else that I've lived, and think it's weird because Mississippi just doesn't seem to be all that great to me. In fact, on first impression, it appears that the opposite is actually the case. Most of the people seem to slowly drawl their words and use poor vocabulary, and take forever to say anything. I had the initial impression that they were ignorant and not all that quick-thinking or smart.

Eventually I did find plenty of smart people in Mississippi, and I learned that the Southern drawl and slow speech were just related to accent for the most part. But I also found that those who seemed to be the most prejudiced and loud-mouthed were among the most ignorant and dumbest people I'd ever encountered.

The sports program in Columbus was an absolute joke. The brand-new gymnasium, multifaceted sports offerings, weight and conditioning programs, and excellent coaches in California were a thing of the distant past. Lee High had very basic sports programs, no tumbling, gymnastics, major track events, or any of that stuff. What little equipment they had was old and worn, and the facilities at the school were unorganized and pitiful in comparison. Football was the main sport in Columbus; and because the season had already started when we got there, it was too late to try out for the team. My sports activity was reduced to an occasional visit to a park near my home to shoot basketball with a few local kids.

I did take up whitetail-deer hunting, thanks to a kid I met in the neighborhood whose father was a deer hunter. I really enjoyed it and killed my first big buck—an eight pointer—not long after taking up the sport. I found that I loved the challenge, peace, and solitude of deer hunting.

Starting at a very young age, I had to have a job. My parents (Mom in particular) insisted. I suspect this attitude came from the fact that both of them were brought up in tough, poverty-stricken backgrounds where every member of the family had to work just to make ends meet. Hard work had its beginning in their early childhood and continued into adulthood. Having a strong work ethic remained a core value in Mom and Dad's lives, and they wanted to instill it in Jim and me as well.

Very few of my friends or classmates had jobs, and sometimes I was jealous of them because they could spend their time doing fun things while I'd be working. But I learned to accept it.

I started selling newspapers on the street in downtown Fairfield when I was just eight years old. I sold copies for 10 cents each, and didn't really know how to make change; but I did very well as the cute little, blond-haired kid with the buzz cut hawking newspapers to everyone who passed me on the street. I'd say, "Paper suh?" or "Paper ma'am?"

For an eight year old, I made big money. When we moved to Guam I started mowing lawns in the neighborhood and built up a solid business of regular customers. And when we returned to Fairfield two years later, the same newspaper company that had me selling individual papers awarded me a regular paper route. In the summertime I also mowed lawns in the neighborhood and made even more money.

One advantage I gained on my friends by always having a job was that I also always had plenty of money—far more than most of my friends—and I liked being able to buy what I wanted.

When we settled in Mississippi, Dad took over managing a federal credit union. One of his customers owned a drive-in restaurant, and true to form, Dad immediately managed to secure a job for me as a carhop. I worked after school from about 3 p.m. until about 11p.m., and on Saturday nights until 1 a.m. With tips, I made good money.

I drove to work on my motorcycle (if you want to call it that). Actually it was a moped, a dorky-looking machine that was like a bicycle with a small engine on it. It was all I could initially afford and it was an embarrassment.

I was glad after I finally managed to save up enough money to get rid of it and buy a real motorcycle—a Triumph. It was used, but to me that Triumph was a thing of beauty. It sat low and had a big teardrop-shaped gas tank with high handle bars. It was British racing green with lots of chrome and loud pipes. And it was fast. A totally sweet ride.

In California I'd been an athlete and, with the exception of Johnny, hung out mainly with other athletes and the coaches; but I'm not an athlete anymore. My attitude has deteriorated and I have no interest in sports. Aside from hunting, my interests now lie mainly in smoking cigarettes, drinking beer, and having sex.

Owning the Triumph seems to elevate my status at school, but unfortunately it's with the wrong crowd. Aside from the few kids with whom I hunt and fish, my new friends are fast becoming those on the wild side, whose interests are darker.

I have a new friend, Jason, who works at the same drive-in restaurant, and he and I steal beer there almost every night. Throughout the night we hide them in one of the garbage cans, and when we take the trash around to the dumpster at closing time, we slip the beers into my backpack. I give him a ride home every night and on the way to his house we stop at a cemetery and drink the beer.

We got drunk the other night, and when I tried to take off on the motorcycle, it reared up and went all the way over backward and landed on us. We were too drunk to be scared and just guffawed, laughing as hard as we could as we pulled the motorcycle off us.

My dark side is mostly in full control these days, and I'm not sure if I even have an angel of light. I'm smoking, drinking, cursing, and fighting, have abandoned sports, and seek sex with every girl I meet. Black clouds are gathering on the horizon and a wicked-looking storm is heading my way.

Worst of all, I don't give a shit.

Chapter Twenty

My mood in my cocoon is as dark as the blackness that surrounds me. I long to be engulfed in the warm blackness of silence and exist no more. I desire to be somewhere that I can simply enjoy some peace and quiet, but this theater of my life will not end. It's becoming quite maddening. I have no interest in reliving all these events; but I have no choice. I know all too well what lies ahead, and none of it is good.

My dark mood seems incongruous. I'm spending time partying down and getting drunk with my friends day after day and getting laid by many of the prettiest girls in school, so it would seem that I'd enjoy reliving this portion of my life. Then why is my mood dark? Aren't these my "glory" days?

No, because I know that this time of my life was the precursor to my fall. Right over the horizon is the evil slavery of drugs, alcohol, crazy violence, and complete domination by my dark side. That serpent will soon become my master and I'm helpless to stop him; and I don't want to even think about this part of my life, much less be forced to relive it from this damned cocoon.

The question in my mind is *why* is this happening to me? Why must I be forced to relive the carnage of my wasted life? I'm obviously powerless to change one second of it. Why can't I simply rest in peace?

I suspect my angel of light wants to say, "I told you so." He's no doubt gloating over this review of my miserable life in order to underline the fact that I could have gone with him but instead chose my dark side. I'd like to tell him to get off my back and let me enter blackness forever, but even if I could speak, no one seems to be around but me.

In the next replay of my life, my mother is sitting at the head of the dining-room table and I'm sitting at the opposite end. My father and brother are sitting across from each other on the sides. All of them are staring at me and all have grim looks on their faces. A family meeting has been called by my mother to try to determine *what is wrong with me.*

Yesterday I skipped school and got drunker than I'd ever been. My friend Charles tried to slip me into the house unnoticed before my parents came home from work. Somehow he got me undressed and into bed, but my mother went into my room later that night to see if I wanted something to eat, and she smelled the liquor. She tried to wake me up, but it was hopeless. I was too drunk to talk or even hold up my spinning head. It would be morning before I'd be coherent, and by then my head would be splitting with a devastating headache.

It's summertime and I'm 16 and a junior in high school and Jim is a senior. In my father's quest to return to his roots, he decided that he wanted to live out in the country. That meant that we would move one more time from our modest little home in downtown Columbus to a little home located in the rural backwoods of Mississippi 16 miles out in the country. The place he found had several acres of land that went with it, and there he could have a garden and would not be crowded by neighbors. He was happy.

I'm well on my way to becoming a full-fledged alcoholic and get drunk every weekend. I smoke a pack of cigarettes a day, routinely have sex with most any girl that I date, and fight at the drop of a hat. I've started skipping school regularly, either to go hunting or fishing, or to drink some beers and have sex if I can convince some girl to skip and go with me.

Jim and I had been given the choice: continue to attend school in Columbus at Lee High School, or attend New Hope High School, which is located near our new home in the boondocks. New Hope is a tiny country school that's not all that appealing, but I didn't like Lee High and have lost nothing there. So I chose New Hope. My brother on the other hand has made several friends at Lee High School and is playing on its sports teams now, so he's decided to remain enrolled there.

New Hope introduced me to rednecks. They are hardy rural souls who like to have fun. They hunt, fish, get drunk, fight, smoke cigarettes, wear blue jeans and white T-shirts with the sleeves cut out, listen to country music, and like to work on cars and race them. The redneck apparel, the racing cars, and the country music are all new to me, but the rest is as comfortable as a well-worn pair of shoes.

Early on I decided that I liked rednecks and in short order I became one. After we moved out to the country I sold my motorcycle and bought a 1956 Chevy and spent nearly all my money souping it up. It's blazing fast in the quarter mile, and I've won several drag races in it. Most of the races take place on some dark and deserted rural highway at night with half the high school in attendance.

One of my new friends (Danny Jones) and I skipped school yesterday and decided to steal some hard liquor. Danny had been in the car with his uncle when he went to a local bootlegger to buy whiskey. After his uncle gave him the money, Danny saw the bootlegger go into a barn behind his house and return with a bottle a few minutes later.

Our plan was to rip off the bootlegger and steal some of his whiskey. We hid in the woods behind the bootlegger's barn where we could see his house and watched and waited for our opportunity. We lingered about an hour keeping watch on the house. We saw several people come and go and saw him enter the barn on three separate occasions, returning each time with a brown paper bag in his hand—no doubt it contained a bottle of whiskey. We finally saw him drive off, and as soon as his car was out of sight, we ran from the woods into his barn. We found an entire case of liquor hidden under some hay bales. We grabbed a couple of bottles and hurried out of there.

It was about 10 o'clock in the morning in the little community of Steens, Mississippi, and we went down to a store that served as the local hangout for neighborhood teenagers. We bought some Coca-Colas to serve as our chasers, and went back out to the car. We drank the liquor straight from the bottle. We would take a swig, make a terrible face and grit our teeth, and then quickly chase it down with Coke. It didn't take long to take effect. Up until this point, I'd tried only beer. I wasn't used to or prepared for hard liquor, and it hit me like a landslide. With no warning I suddenly became *very* drunk.

Danny and I took off in my car and as we headed down the road, we decided to start running over mailboxes. We were laughing as we knocked down mailbox after mailbox for about three miles. We ended up at the community dump, where we drank the rest of the liquor. We then decided to play a game where we would be bullfighters. One of us would be the matador and the car would be the bull. I decided that I'd go first as the matador and would stand in front of the car and Danny would be the bull and drive the car and try to run me down.

I took up my position, standing about 20 yards in front of the car. In my drunken stupor I picked up a dead dog from the landfill and began swinging it by its rear leg around and around over my head yelling taunts to the bull at the top of my lungs. Danny was in the car revving the engine over and over—he was trying to emulate a bull pawing the ground, I suppose. Suddenly he let the clutch out and came right at me, spinning the tires and throwing up dust. The car bore down on me but at the very last moment I jumped out of the way and yelled, "Toro!" Simultaneously I threw my matador's cape (the dead dog) at the car. It hit the windshield and burst open, spreading foul-smelling entrails all over the windshield. We both laughed hysterically as Danny ran my car into a big pine tree.

Fortunately he did not reach a high-enough speed to sustain too much damage to himself or to my car, aside from a twisted bumper. We quickly tired of the game and somehow were able to drive the short distance back to the store. Soon enough I became violently sick and hung my head out of the car door and began puking and continued until nothing was left to puke, at which point I crawled into the backseat and passed out.

Danny lived about a mile down the road and attempted to walk home. I found out later that he ended up crawling along a ditch and passed out with his head stuck in a culvert that ran underneath his neighbor's driveway. The neighbor found him and pulled him out, and then took him home.

I remained passed out for the rest of the day. My best friend Charles got out of school and discovered me at the store. After unsuccessfully trying to wake me, he washed the puke off me and my car with a water hose and then drove me home.

With the help of another friend, they dragged me up the stairs to my room. Charles undressed me and took my puke-laced wet clothes and hid them in the trunk of my car, and put me in bed. He shut the door to my bedroom to try to help me elude detection when my parents came home. Then he beat it out of there.

It was all to no avail, because my mother discovered my sorry state. And even if she had missed smelling the liquor on me, she'd have known something was up because the next day several of the people who had their mailboxes demolished called our home. Word had traveled fast and they found out right away that Danny and I were the ones responsible for destroying their mailboxes. They were calling and threatening to have us put in jail unless we replaced them, and it ended up costing me over $100 of my hard-earned money to pay for all the repairs. Plus it cost another $50 or so to fix my car's damaged bumper and the broken headlights from running into mailboxes. That was big money to me.

I was in serious trouble again and my mother was determined to get to the bottom of it once and for all.

Serving as chairwoman for the family meeting in the dining room, Mom starts off by going around the table to ask each family member what he thinks is wrong with me. The questioning begins with me.

Tension is in the air and the mood is serious. Mom looks at me with her piercing eyes and says, "Bob I have no idea why you're always getting into trouble. Every day it's something different. You're getting into fights and smoking cigarettes, you quit playing sports, and now you're skipping school and getting drunk.

"*What is wrong with you?*"

My head is still splitting and my stomach is rolling. I've had diarrhea all day and I feel very bad. My thoughts are still jumbled from my hangover and my head feels like a slowly spinning top going round and round. I look her directly in the eyes and truthfully tell her, "Mom, I don't have any idea."

She shakes her head in disgust; that's not the answer she's looking for. Now she turns to Dad and asks, "Do you know what's wrong with him?"

He looks uncomfortable, as though he wishes he were somewhere else, and does not answer. Instead he simply looks at me and then down at the table, helpless to identify my sickness. He sadly shakes his head no.

Finally in exasperation, she looks at my brother and asks him, "Jim, do you know what's wrong with your brother?"

Jim turns his head toward me and slowly gives me a close look-over. The room is dead silent. He looks me up and then down, carefully examining me and considering all the options, and he looks back at Mom, shrugs his shoulders, and nonchalantly responds, "I dunno. Bad seed maybe."

Bad seed! We all erupt into laughter. Even I thought that was incredibly clever and funny. From that moment on I was known as the "bad seed" in our family, and Jim's answer was no doubt the all-time best response to date for explaining what was wrong with me. Mr. Baxter would have liked that one.

As for any real punishment, what could they do? I'd long since quit receiving whippings. I was already six feet tall and I towered over my five-foot-eight father and my five-foot-two mother. I'd been coming and going as I pleased for a good long while, and putting me on restriction would have been laughable. I wouldn't have abided by it.

Aside from delivering a stern lecture, my parents were helpless in thwarting my bad behavior. Other than my brother's witty analysis and bad-seed comment, I didn't receive anything from this meeting.

I felt bad about three things: 1. Getting caught. 2. Having to spend my hard-earned money to fix mailboxes and my car. 3. Having to endure the vicious hangover that was racking my body.

I'd be drinking again that night and would drunkenly leer, "I'm gonna bite that dog back" in reference to getting drunk again so I could eliminate the ill effects of the hangover that was making me feel so bad.

My poor parents could foresee me driving drunk and speeding toward another car some dark rainy night. Unfortunately they didn't have a clue of how exactly they could prevent the head-on collision that inevitably took my life.

Chapter Twenty-One

I turned 17 during my senior year in high school. I had worked full time as an electrician's helper through the summer, but when school started back up, I obtained a part-time job working at a local service station, changing flat tires and pumping gas. My jobs are always a tradeoff. I have to work while my friends play, but I always have plenty of money—and I like that feeling.

At this point in my life I'm going to a different beer joint most every night. I'm underage but no one cares, and checking IDs would be laughable. If you're old enough to walk into a beer joint in Columbus, they'll serve you. It's as simple as that. There are plenty of beer joints in Columbus to choose from and they're *rough!*

The strict blue laws of the Deep South prevent the sale of beer, wine, or hard liquor practically anywhere. Columbus is an exception. Columbus is located in Lowndes County, which happens to be the only "wet" county within 150 miles in any direction. In Columbus beer can legally be sold at bars and stores, and hard liquor can be illegally bought through bootleggers as easily as buying a pack of gum in a store.

Columbus is not far from the Alabama state line. All of Alabama is dry, and alcohol cannot legally be sold anywhere in the state. The beer joints start right across the state line on Highway 82 in Lowndes County, and beer joint after beer joint after beer joint can be seen on both sides of the road as one enters Mississippi; and they dot the road all the way into Columbus. Every Alabama redneck that has a paycheck comes to Columbus every weekend to get drunk.

There's also an Air Force base located just outside of town. Beer joints and titty bars line the road beginning just outside the air base and continue all the way into the outskirts of town. Every night the airmen from the base stream south on Highway 45 into Columbus to get drunk, blow their paychecks, and have a good time.

Mississippi State University is located in the neighboring city of Starkville, just 30 miles away, and college kids pour into Columbus from the west to drink at the numerous beer joints that line the road entering Columbus from that direction.

The knife-wielding, redneck pulp-wooders, farmers, and other varied country bumpkins also stream in from their house trailers and tenant farms, and from beneath every rock and out of every black gum swamp surrounding Columbus to spend their money (including welfare checks) at the bars.

Mississippi State College for Women, MSCW, is located right in downtown Columbus. The female students there don't have far to go to enter the beer joints on the weekends. MSCW, or "the *W*" as we call it is like a welcome oasis in the desert for all those horny guys who are coming from all directions looking to satisfy their lusts with the abundance of beautiful girls from that college.

As for us, the local guys, we don't like *anyone* coming into Columbus, period. We especially don't like anyone from Alabama. We consider Alabama to be a backward state and consider the population to be inbred, ignorant lowlifes. We don't like the airmen that travel in from Columbus Air Force Base either, and we refer to them as "propheads." We don't like the college kids that invade Columbus from Mississippi State University every weekend. MSU has an active agriculture program and we refer to it as "Moo U" and the students as cowbell-carrying hillbillies. We New Hope guys don't like those guys from Lee High School either. We view everyone as direct competition for our women and we dislike having anyone on our turf. Hell, if all of that isn't bad enough, we fight each other if we can't find anyone else to fight.

I'm well suited to being a redneck.

To be sure, all these groups don't like us any more than we like them, and every weekend is like preparing to go to war. There's no question concerning whether or not I'll end up in a fight. As I leave for town to go out for the evening, I *know* that I will be in a fight before the night is done. The question is, will I win? Will I end up in jail? Or will I be visiting the hospital so they can sew me up or help my busted-up hands start working again?

Intensifying this strife enormously is a game called bumper pool. This is a very popular game in Columbus. Gambling on bumper-pool games is a big pastime. The game is played on a rather small pool table with bumpers sticking up in the middle, and there are more bumpers and a hole at each end of the table. The players try to put all five of their balls in the opposite hole and whoever sinks them first wins the game.

It's a game of angles and it takes tremendous hand-eye coordination. The mental challenge is similar to the brain work of playing chess, in that complex strategy and thinking ahead must be employed in order to win. Not only are the sides of the table used, but the bumpers are often used to bank balls too. One must have an uncanny sense of angles and be able to think several shots in advance in order to excel at it.

I'm good at bumper pool and have been since the very first time that I shot. I'm not just a little good, I'm *very* good. In fact I'm *amazing* at this game! I'm so good, in fact, that I even astonish myself. I'm unbeatable. I can make all five balls every time and run the table with ease.

I don't know how or why, but I can make shots that no other player can make—incredible shots that might employ the ball banking off four or five rails and bumpers before going into the hole. It's just natural ability. I didn't practice to get this way. I could just always shoot bumper pool. I can shoot one-handed, one-handed behind my back, left-handed, or right-handed. I can even line up my shot and then turn my head and not look when I shoot; and I can still run the table nine out of 10 times whether I'm playing one-handed or two-handed.

Nearly every beer joint in Columbus has a bumper-pool table and I work most of them. I make several hundred dollars a night shooting bumper pool, but it's dangerous work. No one likes to lose money betting, especially when he's drinking and getting drunker with each losing game. I make things worse because I'm constantly hustling players. I have the ability to look like I just barely win by deliberately missing some shots and then "luck" some impossible shot in at the very last moment to come back and win the game and the money.

Actually, unbeknownst to them, I can make that seemingly impossible shot 10 out of 10 times. I only make it look like I barely win to keep them betting. I run my mouth constantly and am exceedingly obnoxious and taunt my opponents. I'm especially hard on them when I make it look like I just "lucked" some shot in and won the game by accident. They turn angry and are determined to knock me off—and it keeps the suckers going until they completely run out of money.

Sometimes when I'm drunk and I see that they have only enough money for one more game, for some perverse reason I drop the hustle and really pour it on. I run the table in the final game just to let them know how good I am and to make sure they know I've been hustling them out of their money all along. It's like rubbing their noses in dog crap and adds to their anger over losing. And it often leads to a fight: I seem to relish beating them in bumper pool and then with my fists.

I also have a nasty habit of cheating. Everyone who has ever watched me shoot naturally bets on me because I'm pretty much unbeatable. When the pot starts hitting the right amount, a secret partner sometimes bets heavily against me and most everyone in the room takes him up on it. Then I deliberately throw the game by barely missing my shot. At the end of the night we split the cash.

This is dangerous work. I'm so good I can make it look seamless, but if I'm too drunk, I sometimes get sloppy and don't disguise my blown shot as an honest near-miss. Those who lose their money by betting on me quite naturally get mad as hell at me for losing. If they think I'm deliberately "putting them in the middle," as the bumper pool players say, it could be exceedingly treacherous and risky to my health.

Even when I'm playing straight up, the people I've beaten have been listening to me brag and taunt them for hours while they lose their paychecks, and they invariably want to start a fight. If they can't win at pool, they try their luck with their fists. The guys betting among themselves want to fight too. Everyone is primed and ready. Bumper pool is where the forest fire of fights is kindled most every night.

Tonight I'm shooting pool at the Southernaire Club. This is the granddaddy of all nightspots in Columbus. Several hundred people are here every night and on weekends, but tonight probably close to a thousand populate the place. It's Saturday night and they have the best band in the South, Big Ben and the Moonlighters, and the huge dance floor is packed. Next to it is a room devoted just to bumper pool. I'm in that room shooting pool, and perhaps 50 people are jammed in there watching the game and betting on either me or my opponent.

My brother is with me and I've won nearly $1,000, easily winning every game from a guy who just doesn't seem to know how to quit. He's not very good, and beating him is as easy as belching after drinking a frothy Coca-Cola. Jim's been placing side bets on me and winning money all night, and he seems mesmerized by the amount of money that he's winning. He's had a big smile on his face all night.

He is in fact trying to expedite the process at the end of each game by putting quarters into the table coin slot, quickly getting the balls out, and placing them on the table so the next game can start without delay. The last ball no more than goes into the hole than Jim's putting quarters in. He seems intent on frantically hurrying along each game as though the meter is running and every second wasted is just so much lost revenue to him.

The guy I'm shooting against is a loudmouth and he's beginning to run out of money. He's been popping off and running his mouth to Jim all night long, calling him Slick. He angrily shouts at Jim at the end of each game, "Rack the balls, Slick!" or "Rack 'em up, Slick!" In fact, he's been talking to Jim in such a derogatory manner that it's beginning to embarrass *me.*

Jim, who is very tough and nobody's bitch, has been uncharacteristically silent, and like some spineless pansy has ignored the insults all night long. I'm becoming disgusted with him. He just stands there taking this jerk's verbal abuse with that stupid wide grin plastered on his face and his eyes transfixed on the table.

I make my final ball and win another game. No sooner has the ball hit the hole than Jim is there putting more quarters in and the balls are dropping down and he's putting them back on the table. But this time the guy looks at me and says, "That's it, I'm done," and he throws his cue stick on the table. He looks at Jim, who is still putting the balls on the table, and says, "What're you doing, Slick? Can't you understand English? *I said the game is over!*"

Jim realizes that there's no more money to be made off this guy. He slowly stands up with a ball still in his hand and looks at the guy and calmly says, "Don't call me Slick, ***SLICK!"*** and then he takes the ball and savagely hits him as hard as he can in the mouth.

He knocked teeth out with that lick, I tell you.

The place immediately explodes into a full-fledged brawl. Bodies are flying, as if someone has just lit a stick of dynamite and tossed it into the middle of the room. All the guys betting on me are instantly fighting all the guys betting on the other guy. The tension was high, and it seems as though we've all been waiting for this spark to set off the explosion.

One of the guys who'd been running his mouth at me earlier gets a cue stick in the nose so hard that I break it. Someone blindsides me, hitting me in the side of the head. I fall backward, out into the dance-floor area. As I'm falling I see Jim hit the guy who hit me. The fight quickly spills out onto the dance floor. Tables are overturned and drinks are spilled onto those sitting at tables surrounding the dance area. A couple of girls are knocked to the floor during the melee.

Now those who had been sitting at the tables are also involved in the fight. It's complete bedlam and chaos. It looks like a hundred people are now fighting, and the brawl is spreading like a fire. More tables are being overturned and more fights are erupting everywhere. I see a girl jump on a guy's back and start trying to gouge his eyes out and claw his face. I see another guy hit someone over the head with a fifth of whiskey. The bottle does not break but the guy falls to the ground like a goose in a hailstorm.

BAM! . . . BAM! I hear two shots ring out and I hit the floor. Two guys have begun shooting at each other with pistols. People are screaming, the lights come on, and everyone is ducking for cover. I'm crawling under tables on my hands and knees as fast as I can, keeping my head low as I make a break for the door. It was reminiscent of my trying to get out of the fort in the attic after having sex that first time.

I finally reach the door and run right into the legs of one of the deputy sheriffs entering the bar to break up the fight. Fortunately he doesn't even give me a second glance as he enters the craziness.

When I'm outside I remember my brother, who's still inside, and I decide to go back in to see if he's all right. As I reenter the bar I see one of the guys I was fighting coming out the door. I immediately hit him as hard as I can in the mouth and he falls to the ground. I jump on him and start pounding his face; and the next thing I know a sheriff's deputy is pulling me off him and handcuffing me. He takes me to a police car, throws me in the backseat, and slams the door.

Chapter Twenty-Two

I open my eyes and see a gray concrete wall. Momentarily I wonder where I am, and then quickly realize that I'm in jail. Suddenly I remember last night. I swing my legs over the side of my hard metal bunk and stiffly sit up and take a look around my cell. It's dimly lit and there's a filthy metal toilet with no seat on it in the corner. A small metal sink sits beside it but nothing else occupies the cell. I stand to go take a leak and then push the button to flush. It's deafening. Does my headache absolutely no good.

My bunk doesn't have a mattress and is nothing more than a steel plate extending out from the wall. No wonder I'm stiff. Filthy words, many of which are misspelled, are scrawled on the painted gray walls.

I'm alone. This is my first time in jail and it's kind of a panicky feeling being cooped up in this tiny cell. I want out of here. I'm wondering what I should do when I hear a metal door creak open and then slam shut, creating an eerie echo. I can hear someone walking down the hall. It's the county sheriff.

His name is Righty Jones and I know him well. He frequents the Southernaire Club and most of my other haunts on a regular basis. He's watched me shoot pool numerous times, and we're fairly good acquaintances. I see Righty come walking down the hall adjacent to the jail cells and when he arrives in front of my cell he stops and greets me with a wide smile.

Righty doesn't look like he fits the part of being the Lowndes County sheriff. He looks more like someone's kindly grandfather instead of the top law enforcement officer in one of the wildest and toughest counties in Mississippi. He's about five-foot-eight and partially bald with silver-white hair on the sides, and a big potbelly hangs over his wide black belt. He always wears cowboy boots and a brown "county-mountie" hat. He also has a continual smile on his face.

He says in a cheerful voice, "Bob! What in hell are you doing in here?" He has a myriad of keys on a giant key ring in his hand but somehow instantly finds the right key to unlock my cell door. He swings it open and starts walking back toward the booking desk, saying over his shoulder, "C'mon out of there. You want a cup of coffee?"

I walk out of the cell and start following him down the hall and respond, "No sir, I don't drink coffee," and then I sheepishly add, "I got in a fight at the Southernaire last night."

He smiles and says, "Yeah, I heard something about that. It was a near riot. What started it?"

"Some guy got mad because he lost some money shooting pool and started swinging. Pretty soon half the place was fighting."

He said with a wry smile on his face, "That's not exactly the same story that I heard, but I suppose it's close enough." Righty has eyes and ears everywhere and certainly did not need to ask me what happened last night. He knew exactly what happened before he ever asked, including knowing that my brother Jim started the near riot by hitting that guy in the mouth with a ball.

"Where's your car? Still at the Southernaire?"

"Yes sir. At least I hope it is."

"C'mon, I'll give you a ride over there."

We stop at the booking desk, and without being told the stern-faced deputy sitting behind the desk unceremoniously dumps out the contents of a large manila envelope. It contains my belt, wallet, car keys, and some loose change. I check my wallet and immediately notice that I'm missing several hundred dollars. I look at Righty with a quizzical look on my face, and he smiles and simply says, "administrative fee."

I say, "Oh yeah, right." I need no further explanation. Righty Jones makes a lot of money in Columbus. In fact, being elected sheriff in Lowndes County, Mississippi, assures a new sheriff a tremendous income. His predecessor made a fortune as did that guy's predecessor before him. I'd heard that all the dice games, card games, bookies, hard-liquor bootleggers, and pimps in and around Columbus were paying Righty Jones tribute and that he was rolling in cash.

Several hundred dollars is a hell of a lot of money to me, but to make my charges completely disappear and be able to walk out of there into the morning sunshine a free man? Heck, I consider that a bargain.

Righty pulls up beside my car at the Southernaire and drops me off. He smiles a golden smile and tells me to "be good." Without looking back, he lifts his hand and leaves it held high as he ever so slowly exits the gravel parking lot, little rocks crunching under his tires. I wave back, get in my car, and crank it up. When it starts, my souped-up Chevy's modified mufflers and custom cam emit a deafening roar in the empty parking lot—it's like I'm firing up a dragster.

I nervously glance toward Righty to see if he hears the loud pipes, but thankfully he's already exited. I say out loud to no one, "Whew, all I need now is more 'administrative fees' for the illegal pipes on my car."

This was to be the first of many visits to Righty's jail, always for the same thing—fighting. Righty remained a loyal friend throughout all my visits to his "home away from home," and he never once lectured me. He even let me slide on his "administrative fees" on those rare occasions when I was short on cash.

Righty later became the object of an FBI investigation, and it cost him dearly because of the bad publicity: He lost his bid for reelection as sheriff. I heard too that after he lost the election his wife divorced him when she found out about his beautiful young girlfriend. Unfortunately, when Righty lost the "money-train," his young girlfriend left him too. Ultimately he ended up all alone and broke, and he committed suicide. It was a real bummer for me to hear that sad news.

My brother escaped going to jail that night, and in spite of being the instigator of the massive brawl was able to talk his way out of it, as usual. There were just too many participants for the police to sort it all out and most everyone escaped any charges or going to jail, aside from me. After the fight, Jim simply drove home and went to bed.

I was mad as hell that he simply went home without even checking on what happened to me or attempting to get me out of jail. Had I not gone back to the bar to check on his well-being, I would have eluded jail entirely. It was especially galling to me in light of the fact that he had made several hundred dollars solely because of my bumper-pool prowess. It was a rotten thing to do.

When I got home I confronted him in the hall and asked him why the hell he didn't get me out of jail. He simply shrugged and said, "I didn't know where you went. I assumed you could take care of yourself. I'm not your babysitter, and besides you're here now aren't you? Get out of my face." He brushed me aside as he headed down the hall.

I yelled at him, "Thanks a hell of a lot for the concern, Jim, you frigging ingrate. I'll remember it the next time you need some help." He gave me the finger without even looking back.

In the weeks that followed, I learned how strongly Dad felt that we should earn college degrees so we could get ahead in life. And he was willing to pay for that education. My parents were both ultraconservative and very tight with their money—I suppose that trait came as a result of their difficult childhoods. But our going to college was a big deal to them and it was a big sacrifice to put up their hard-earned money. They did so willingly.

Jim graduated from high school one year ahead of me and decided to take Dad up on his offer and go to Mississippi State University. He continued to live at home and made excellent grades, as he had done in high school. He was majoring in chemistry but intended to switch to pre-med and become a doctor.

My effort my senior year in high school had been less than minimal and as a result my grades were just a little above average. In the rare event that I found a teacher or class that I liked, I easily made A's, but more likely than not I disliked most all of it. I skipped school so often that the principal told me a full three months before school was out that if I missed another day for any reason—even being in the hospital—I couldn't graduate.

When I graduated from high school I decided to follow Jim to Mississippi State. I began my freshman year at MSU at the age of 17. I decided to live on campus in a dormitory so I'd get out of the house and not have to listen to my parents always raising hell about my getting stoned and zonkered out of my gourd every night.

I didn't like high school and I didn't like college any better. I particularly didn't like attending Moo U and ringing a cowbell while I watched our awful football team lose another game. I liked drinking, having sex, shooting bumper pool, hunting, fishing, and not sitting in a classroom listening to some professor with a Napoleonic complex. I resented all authority and had problems with most all my professors.

As I did in high school, I cut my classes in college regularly. At MSU, the situation quickly deteriorated and I mostly had a straight F average; the lone exception was the one class that I signed up for that I liked (Philosophy) in which I made an A. I mainly just pissed away my father's hard-earned money by skipping classes and making bad grades. Instead of studying, I much preferred to stay up until two or three o'clock in the morning getting drunk and chasing MSCW women, and then sleeping in and not attending class or studying.

This of course had not gone unnoticed by my parents, especially when they saw my midterm grades. In fact my poor grades were cause for many a family meeting, and I was lectured just like I'd been on countless other occasions.

We were at one such meeting and my mother was looking at my grades. I had made F's in every subject. She angrily asked in total exasperation, "Isn't there *anything* you're good at? Can you name even *one* thing that you're good at?"

I replied, "Actually Mom there is. No one can beat me in bumper pool. I'm the *best* there is at shooting bumper pool!"

She wasn't impressed. Plenty of guys around Columbus would have given anything to shoot bumper pool like I could, but my mom and dad were totally disgusted. They both just looked at me with an expression of utter revulsion and Dad would say, "You're totally worthless and you'll never amount to anything."

Those words were very true, but nonetheless they still hurt and stuck with me, especially after hearing my parents lavish praise on my brother for his exemplary performance.

Since I rarely attended any of my classes or studied, I had to cram for my final exams in order to have any hope of passing anything. One night several of us were up late cramming and studying away and someone passed around some Dexedrine diet pills to help keep us awake so we could study all night. After studying for a while we decided to go to the local bar to have a few beers to reward our difficult work and hard study. After drinking a couple of beers on top of that Dexedrine—it's an amphetamine—my mind was racing and I was flying high. This was my first exposure to drugs and I was instantly hooked on that wonderful feeling of alcohol mixed with speed. It's one of the finest highs that can be had, short of shooting up.

I didn't want to stop taking speed and drinking after that night. In addition to buying diet pills at MSU, I started buying them at the Southernaire, at various beer joints, and even from the long-distance truck drivers at some of the truck stops around Columbus. In addition to dex I began buying black mollies, cross tops, "white lightning," and other forms of speed.

Before long I was taking handfuls of speed and drinking large amounts of beer and whiskey every night. I financed it with my bumper-pool shooting and gambling.

At this point I find that I'm no longer content just to get drunk. I want speed and I want it every time I go out drinking, which is every night. My dark side is smiling. He has me right where he wants me now.

I'm hooked on that feeling.

Chapter Twenty-Three

My head hurts. I slowly open my eyes and see a large pool of dried blood on a filthy-dirty concrete floor. I'm lying facedown in it. Instantly I know I'm in jail. I try to stand up, but my head hurts so badly that I can't. I feel like retching. I try to rise again and this time I'm able to get up on my hands and knees.

I rest momentarily as I stare down at the nasty floor. It's grimy where the side of my face and mouth have been resting all night. It looks like a breeding ground for the world's most vile bacteria, and just thinking about it makes me spit bloody saliva on the floor in an effort to cleanse my mouth of it. My head is spinning.

I see a scummy-looking, unshaven bum in dirty clothes curiously looking at me. I move over to the opposite side of the cell from him and lean back against the filthy wall, resting the back of my spinning head on it. I'm in a drunk tank and there are no bunks, just a stainless-steel toilet with no toilet seat, stainless-steel sink, and revoltingly dirty floor. The cell reeks of urine and vomit.

My head is reeling and I'm feeling more and more nauseous. It must be 100 muggy degrees in here, and I need a drink of water. I look down at my sweater and it's caked with dried blood and it's been stretched big enough to fit someone four times my size. I gingerly touch my throbbing head, the worst of my many sources of pain, and I feel a deep gash in it. I look at my fingers and see bright-red blood on them. Fresh blood is oozing out of the deep cut at my hairline above my right eye.

I'm now in my second year of college and have transferred to the University of Southern Mississippi, located in Hattiesburg. In spite of cutting classes daily and having a near straight F average, miraculously I'd aced every exam and ended up with C's in just about all my classes. I owed it all to nonstop cramming for days and nights on end—and to speed.

I convinced my parents that most of my problems stemmed from the fact that I didn't like Moo U, and I asked them to allow me to transfer for my second year, to the University of Southern Mississippi where I hoped to improve. They agreed, hoping that the transfer might change me for the better.

It didn't.

I wanted to go to USM because I'd heard that it was a party school (and I was always looking for a party). It was located near Biloxi and the Gulf Coast and was just an hour and a half from New Orleans, the king of party destinations. That sounded even better to me.

I don't have any memory of what happened to get me into the drunk tank. I've had blackouts before after drinking heavily, but it seems odd that I can't remember much of anything at all about the night before. The only thing I can faintly remember is leaving Hattiesburg after classes on Friday and riding down to New Orleans with a few of my friends to party for the weekend. I remember drinking a few beers on the way down and that's it.

My memory may be nonexistent, but it's not too difficult to know that I've been in a fight. I'm thinking that I must have lost badly. I don't know anyone in New Orleans, but I assume my buddies are working on getting me bailed out. I hope they get me out quickly.

I ask the guy sitting across from me, "Do you know what I did? I don't remember anything."

He answers, "No, but you pissed someone off, 'cause when they brought you in here four cops came in and beat the living hell out of you. They were hitting you with billy clubs and kicking you. It went on for a long time. Be glad you don't remember it."

That explains why I'm so sore. My head is splitting and throbbing, I think my nose is broken, my lip is cut, and my ribs are sore as hell. Crap, I'm sore all over. My badly stretched-out, bloody sweater looks like I was pulled from every different direction. I look down at my hands and notice that my palms are swollen and sore and wonder what caused that.

I sit here for quite some time and finally a jail trustee comes walking down the hall and I yell out to him, "Hey man, can you find out what I'm charged with?"

He looks at me and says, "Yeah give me a minute and I'll see what I can do. What's your name?"

"Williamson. Bob Williamson."

He nods and then leaves. In about an hour he returns and says, "You might as well make yourself comfortable, 'cause you're going to be here for a *while.*"

"Oh shit! What'd I do?"

He pulls out a little yellow sheet of paper and gives it to me. I am charged with some 21 offenses. There are several counts of assault, resisting arrest, obscene language, and battery; the list goes on and on.

The trustee says he talked to the desk cop who was on duty when they brought me in and got the story of what happened during and after my arrest. Later my college buddies would fill me in on the events that led up to it.

It had all started after class late Friday afternoon. Several of my friends and I left school in Hattiesburg and headed to New Orleans to party down for the weekend. Four of us drank two cases of beer on the way down. When we reached the outskirts of New Orleans, we stopped at a Discount Liquor Store and I bought a quart of Smirnoff vodka, which I started drinking straight from the bottle with a 7Up chaser.

We went down to the French Quarter and ended up in a bar named La Casas.

The bar was divided into two sections—one side was Latino and the other American, and each played different music. On the Latin side they had a large conga drum that could be played along with the Latin music. I settled in behind it and wildly beat on the drum, playing along with the Latino music in a vodka-induced frenzy. The music never stopped and this went on for several hours. That explained the swollen palms of my hands the next day.

I would stop playing the drum only long enough to take an occasional swig of vodka and then quickly wash it down with my 7Up chaser. My buddies told me that a long-haired guy in the bar kept coming over to me because he wanted to play the conga drum, and said that he was really making a pest of himself. Vodka makes me meaner than anyone can imagine. This guy annoying me every five minutes and my inebriated state did not make a good combination. Finally I warned him in a loud voice that if he came back over again, I was going to beat the shit out of him; and then I resumed banging on the drum in earnest.

The long hair completely ignored my warning and in a few minutes came back over and once again asked if he could play the conga. My mind instantly snapped and in a flash I was in a vodka-induced, white-hot rage. Without saying a word, I grabbed his head under my arm and began pounding his face with my fist as hard and as fast as I could, spraying blood from his nose with each punch. I began half-dragging, half-walking him toward the back door. We exited through the door into a narrow little alley, and I put my foot beneath the back of his legs and tripped him and pushed him down hard on the ground. I climbed on top of him and grabbed him by his long hair and started ferociously banging his head on the concrete.

Just then someone grabbed me from behind and spun me around. When he did I instinctively hit him. That was a major mistake, because the guy that I hit happened to be the six-foot-six bouncer. He had a slap-jack in his hand (a spring-loaded club that is filled with lead and covered with leather), and he brutally hammered me on the head with it, knocking me out cold. I discovered later that he'd given me a concussion.

When I regained consciousness, the New Orleans police had already arrived and had called for a patrol wagon to take me to jail. My hands were handcuffed behind me and I was lying flat on my back with blood streaming down my face. Several cops were standing around waiting for the patrol wagon to arrive.

One of the cops—he appeared to be grossly overweight—edged over toward me to take a better look, and when he got close I viciously kicked at him. It startled him and he backed up and instinctively moved his hand toward his gun.

When he did I snarled at him at the top of my lungs,

"Shoot me you fat son of a bitch!

"Why don't you shoot me?

"You fat asshole coward! SHOOT ME!"

He just looked at me like I was some kind of crazed animal. The patrol wagon arrived and when they tried to put me on my feet, I fought like a rabid dog. The vodka had snapped my mind and I was in an insane rage. It took all five of them to get me into the patrol wagon. All the while they were beating me with billy clubs and fists, and kicking me. My hands were still handcuffed behind my back and all I could do was kick and curse and try to head butt them as they threw me in the patrol wagon.

They took me to New Orleans Charity Hospital to sew up the large gash on my head. For some strange reason, when we arrived at the hospital they uncuffed me. The doctor put something on my head that burned, and then I hit him right in the mouth.

The doctor was really pissed off and refused to sew me up. He told the cops to get me the hell out of there and not bring me back!

That was it. New Orleans cops see it all and are among the most vicious of all cops, and they don't take this kind of crap from anyone. They took me to the drunk tank and brutally beat me unconscious and left me in a bleeding heap on the floor.

The drunk in the cell told me that after the beating ended, they were leaving and one of them kind of hesitated for a moment as though thinking about it and then came back over and gave me one last fierce kick to the ribs. The old drunk said it scared the shit out of him to see this cop's rage. I had a large bruise and a broken rib where the toe of his shoe met my rib cage. At the time he delivered the kick I was completely unconscious and didn't feel a thing, but I remembered it for months afterward.

Unbeknownst to me, when my college buddies learned about all the charges against me, they realized that they didn't have anywhere near enough money to bail me out; consequently they simply drove back to school figuring I would call my parents to get me out.

They figured wrong. When I am transferred out of the drunk tank and moved upstairs into general lockup, the cop tells me I am entitled to make one phone call. Thinking that my buddies would have me out of here in no time, I tell him I don't want to make one.

Several days later I'm still in jail and haven't heard a word from anyone. I'm beginning to get frantic. I've been moved to a permanent situation in the jail, and using the phone is no longer an option. In the meantime, the large gash on my head has become inflamed and badly infected. It's hot to the touch and throbs constantly. My right eye is completely swollen shut and the swollen area is almost the size of a small cantaloupe and extends all the way to the gash on my forehead. My bottom lip has a deep open gash on it, and the right corner of my lip constantly leaks blood into my throat. My nose is badly broken, is full of dried blood, and is likewise swollen. I have two black eyes and I look as though I've been stung by a horde of angry hornets.

Whenever anyone of authority walks by the cell, I point to my head and tell them it's infected and plead with them to take me to a doctor. Finally one of the trustees convinces a guard to take a look at me. After one look at my swollen head he agrees to take me to a doctor. While I'm waiting for a patrol wagon to transport me to the hospital, I convince the cop who's going to escort me to the hospital to allow me a phone call. He reluctantly tells me okay and hands me a nickel for the pay phone. He tells me to hurry.

With my eye swollen shut I can barely see to dial but manage to call Mom collect. I'm thankful she answers the phone. I'm able to talk to her only for a few seconds and relay that I've been in a fight in New Orleans and I'm in jail and need help.

Almost the second we're connected the cop yells, "Do you want to go to the hospital or not? If so, get your ass off that damn phone and get going. The patrol wagon's here. Let's go asshole!"

My mother overhears all of that and screams into the phone, "Hospital? What happened Bob? Are you hurt?"

I reply, "I'm fine, Mom. Just please find a way to get me out of here," and then I hang up.

I didn't know it, but I had a first cousin, Edward Brodie, who was living in New Orleans at the time. Edward was the administrator of the very large Baptist Hospital there and was a respected business leader in the New Orleans community. My dad called Edward, who happened to know a prominent judge and that judge had me released into Edward's care. It was embarrassing to no end to go to his beautiful big home in my condition and meet his five little children and wife for the very first time.

I soaked the jail grime and remaining dried blood away in a steaming hot bath—it felt wonderful. My body was covered with deep black, blue, yellow, and green bruises, plus assorted cuts and abrasions from the vicious beating that I'd received from New Orleans' finest.

Edward provided me with some clean clothes and it felt good to bathe and clean up. For three days I'd been wearing the same clothes that I wore the night of my fight, and they were covered in dried blood and smelled awful. I threw them in the trash, my treasured $40 camel hair sweater included.

I gingerly ate my first meal since my incarceration, and although I didn't eat much, what I did eat was delicious. I thanked Edward's wife for the great meal and I thanked Edward for getting me out of jail, for the clothes, and for the ticket on a Greyhound bus to take me back up to Hattiesburg. I apologized for all the trouble to him and his family. He just smiled a warm smile and told me not to worry about it.

My head was badly infected and I went into the hospital as soon as I arrived back on campus. I had red streaks running down my head and by now the gash had greenish pus oozing out of it. I was in the hospital for two weeks and my court date came up while I was still hospitalized. Edward was able to convince the judge that I'd suffered enough, and pulled some strings. The judge dropped the charges on the condition that I would never come back to New Orleans. That suited me just fine (for the moment anyway).

During my stay in the hospital I was introduced to wonderful and lovely painkillers. At first I got shots of morphine and Demerol that would make me drift away into bliss and freedom, if only for a few hours. Later, when they would no longer give me shots, they would bring pills every four hours. Those were very nice too. I wondered how they would be if combined with alcohol. I would discover that, similar to what happened with speed, alcohol enhanced their charm on me. I would be adding them to my arsenal as soon as I was discharged.

Chapter Twenty-Four

I was released from the hospital in due time and ultimately ended up with little more than a nasty scar on my head and a few bad memories.

The University of Southern Mississippi had indeed turned out to be a party school. There are far better-looking girls here than at Moo U, and I'm trying my utmost to have sex with every one of them. I'm drinking heavily and combining the alcohol with speed and downers and partying throughout the night. I sleep during the day and am cutting more classes than I'm attending.

As for grades, my second year of college turns out to be a near rerun of my first year. As exam time approaches I pull up my poor grades by taking diet pills and staying up for two or three days straight cramming for final exams. I end up the year once again with mainly C's in the classes that I hadn't dropped.

When summer break arrives, I decide to go down to Biloxi, Mississippi, located on the white-sand beaches of the Gulf Coast. I want to bum around for the summer. This is the first summer since I was 8 years old that I haven't worked and held down a steady job—or two. It's odd that I've chosen to do this, because currently I don't even have a car or any money in my bank account. My parents pay for my tuition, but I have to pay for everything else and I need to work.

My car slung a rod a couple of months ago and I'm reduced to hitchhiking or finding a ride with a friend. In times past I would have been working two or even three jobs, seven days a week, so I could have my car fixed or buy another, and I wouldn't rest until I had put a sizable supply of cash in the bank. But for some strange reason I just don't seem to care this time around.

A good friend of mine, Jim Tucker, has been given a rent-free apartment to use for the summer and it's located between two motels right on the beach. Four of us are living in it. Our two roommates are in the military and we rarely see them except on the weekends, and sometimes not even then.

Jim and I are beach bums and just hang out and sponge off anyone we can. Our daily ritual consists of sleeping in until around nine, and then eating a bowl of cereal for breakfast. We clean up our apartment, which is decorated in a beach theme with an old fishnet suspended from the ceiling. The apartment has cheap rattan-style beach furniture throughout, and wine bottles with melted candles are conveniently situated on tables.

By 10 a.m. we go to the beach and perform our setup ritual. We bring towels, beach chairs, books, games to play (such as paddleball), and a football to throw. We always set up in the same perfect location, which is directly in between the two motels. Jim and I both wear dark sunglasses and have developed exceedingly good tans. My hair has been bleached blond by the sun. Jim has bleached his dark hair with peroxide and it's now an orange-blond color.

Soon beautiful girls start streaming out of the two motels and begin walking up and down the beach, conveniently passing right in front of where we're set up. We fondly refer to it as the "parade of the lovelies."

We review them for a while, and then with wide smiles strike up a conversation with the two best-looking girls we can find. There's something about girls who are away from home and on vacation at the beach that makes them wild and in a party mood. They want to hook up with us just as much as we want to hook up with them. Soon they'll have joined us and we will pair off. After we settle in, Jim or I will smile broadly and casually say, "Today's my birthday." Every day Jim and I switch off—one day it's his birthday and the next it's mine.

The girls always squeal with delight and ask how old we are, and then they'll suggest that we should all go out tonight and celebrate. We tell them that would be great, but unfortunately, at the moment, we don't happen to have any money.

"No problem, we have enough money. It's *your* birthday, and tonight will be on us!"

We flash broad smiles with our white teeth contrasting nicely with our tanned faces and say, "Cool! Let's do it!"

Almost with 100 percent dead certainty, later that day they'll sneak off for a little while and come back and "surprise" us with a birthday cake that they picked up somewhere. (I was sick of birthday cake by the time I left that summer.)

That night we'll convince them to buy us a fifth of Jack Daniels bourbon or Chivas Regal scotch for a birthday present, and then we'll all share it and head down to the local nightclub for a long night of dancing. Afterward it's back to our "cool" apartment for sex.

It turns into a long, hot summer.

We go to the same nightclub every night, and before long Jim and I are in with the "in-crowd" at the Whiskey a Go Go, the hottest bar on the strip. I've become enamored with a local girl, Lindsey Rutledge, who hangs out there. We've become good friends and I'm drawn to her intelligence and quick wit—not to mention the fact that she's movie-star gorgeous and has a ravishing smile complementing thick blonde hair cascading over her shoulders.

Soon we're doing everything together, including going to the beach, partying, dancing, and going to restaurants and the movies. When we're not together, we're on the phone with each other. Lindsey's parents are seriously wealthy and money is not even the slightest issue with her. She pays for everything and does so in a manner that doesn't make me feel like the gigolo bum that I've become. Although she's two years younger than me and has recently graduated from an exclusive private high school, she's as mature and sophisticated as anyone that I've ever met.

It doesn't take long and I find myself deeply in love with Lindsey. I think about her constantly and want to be with her every minute of the day. She tells me that she feels the same way about me.

What a wonderful feeling it is to love and be loved. So far she's rejected having sex with me and sternly told me that she's not the type of girl who just jumps into bed with someone. Oddly this makes me respect her all the more. I'm absolutely crazy about her.

It doesn't take me long to decide to ditch the beach-bum routine. Lindsey is too important to me to waste time on childish college games like hooking up with vacation girls for sex and a piece of too-sweet birthday cake every day. I want to devote myself to Lindsey and our relationship. I'm determined to straighten out my life and it will begin with a job. Much to my roommate Jim's surprise, I start looking for one in earnest.

Then Lindsey drops a bombshell on me. Her parents are going on a European vacation and Lindsey is going with them. She'll be gone for virtually the rest of the summer—nearly six weeks. We're both devastated.

The night before she's scheduled to depart, we go out to eat and then for a night of dancing at the Whiskey a Go Go. I walk her to the door and she begins bawling like a baby. My eyes are moist too and we passionately kiss each other and I can taste the salty tears streaming down her face. We stand there hugging each other for a long time and then she tells me that she has to go inside before her parents come out. She starts crying again and then runs inside her house.

With Lindsey gone, I decide that I'll go back to Columbus to get a job for the remainder of the summer and live at home, where I can save some money. It'll be easier to find work in Columbus, and I desperately need to buy another car and save some money for college. Time will pass quickly and soon Lindsey and I will reunite. I hitchhike home and almost immediately find a job as a carpenter's helper for the remainder of the summer.

A few weeks later, the phone rings and Mom tells me that it's for me. When I answer I immediately hear crying coming from the other end. It's my old high-school girlfriend Pat, and she's hysterically sobbing.

I ask, "What's wrong?"

"I'm pregnant!" she sobs. "It's yours."

I nearly drop the receiver. How could this be? When I returned to Columbus I ran into her one night at the Chuck Wagon, our local hangout. I'd been drinking heavily and asked her out, knowing full well that I shouldn't be cheating on Lindsey. Nonetheless we started going out on some dates while I was home for the summer, and we routinely had sex, as we'd done all through my senior year in high school.

I say, "Are you sure?"

"Positive! My parents know about it too and they're going to call your parents and go over there any minute now."

"Damn!" My mind is racing and my heart is pounding. What am I going to do? What about Lindsey? What about school?

I say, "We need to talk about this and decide what to do. Can you meet me at the Chuck Wagon in 15 minutes?"

"Okay."

Damn, damn, triple damn, hell! Cheating on Lindsey is the least of my problems. A pregnancy of an unwed mother is no laughing matter in 1965. It's a societal taboo and a cause for disgrace and shame. Abortion is illegal. And besides, it's immoral—not an option. Pat is a good girl from a good family and should never have been dating someone like me in the first place. Her parents and mine are very religious and this is going to be ugly. The only options are to marry each other, or have Pat go to an unwed mother's home and have the baby there.

I pick up Pat and we drive off to park and discuss the situation. (Ironically, we park on the same deserted road that we have parked so many times when we engaged in sex.)

There's no doubt that Pat deeply loves me. She loved me all through high school and she remained in love with me even after I broke up with her when I went off to college. She told me so. I like Pat but I don't love her and I've told her that on many occasions.

I tell her again, "I'm sorry but I just don't love you. If we marry each other, sooner or later it will just end up in divorce." I suggest that she go to an unwed mother's home and have the baby there. I vow to her that I will never desert her or the baby and will give our child my surname and financial support, but I emphasize again and again to her that I just don't love her.

After a great deal of tears she agrees that since I don't love her and don't want to get married, the unwed mother's home option makes the most sense. We then go over to my house, where my parents and hers have been conducting a meeting about the situation. When we walk in it's with no small irony that I notice that they're all seated around the familiar dining-room table where I had sat on so many other occasions trying to resolve any myriad of other messes that I happened to be in.

Before we could say anything, our parents announce that Pat and I are *going* to get married and that *they* have decided upon a wedding date—end of discussion.

My parents and Pat's parents are mad as hell. Her father is glaring at me with overt hatred on his face and is staring at me as if he wants to kill me for spoiling his beloved daughter.

Neither Pat nor I say anything. Too much tension's in the air. We silently listen to them tell us how much we have humiliated them and hurt them and how stupid and of course immoral we are.

Mercifully Pat's parents finally depart and Pat leaves with them. After they leave, I recount my conversation with Pat and plead with my parents to reconsider. I carefully explain that I don't love her and in fact am deeply in love with Lindsey and that I want to finish school and marry her. I tell them that Pat is good with the unwed-mothers-home route.

Their terse, sarcastic reply is that I should have thought about my deep love for Lindsey and finishing school before I decided to cause Pat's pregnancy. This is my child and I have to step up and take responsibility for once in my life. The marriage is set and that's it.

The pressure from Pat, my family, and hers and the guilt are too much for me and I have no choice but to agree. The marriage ceremony is small and takes place in a local church. It seems more like a funeral from the looks on the faces of our parents and onlookers, who no doubt are snickering about it among themselves behind closed doors. Pat, with beautiful green eyes, looks pretty in her wedding dress. I look like a moron in my tuxedo. We state our vows, exchange rings, kiss, and are married.

Thus, at the age of 19, I quit school, take a job as an office manager at a small company in downtown Columbus, and move into a tiny rented house.

And now?

Well, now every night I come home at six, eat supper, and watch stupid television shows.

Chapter Twenty-Five

When I initially told Lindsey what happened, she was devastated. It really broke my heart to hear her cry. Most of all she was hurt that I'd cheated on her. She sighed deeply and then angrily told me that she didn't want to ever talk to me again. Then she hung up.

I lost Lindsey, and over time I lost all contact with my college buddies, who'd continued on with their educations. It was just as well because I didn't want to hear about all the fun they were having or about their promising careers and job opportunities after they graduated from college.

Initially I tried to make the best of my marriage to Pat. She was a decent and good person, far better than me, but the simple fact of the matter was that I didn't love her, and a marriage devoid of love on either spouse's part won't work. We never should've married each other.

I worked hard throughout the week and according to my boss did well in my job. But to me it was just so much mindless drivel and I hated it. I saw myself wasting my life away working at that office-supply store, growing old and dying as a small-town Columbus hick. It was driving me crazy.

I tried hard but couldn't help but resent my parents, Pat's parents, and Pat. I felt that my life had been stolen from me by way of a shotgun wedding. I became increasingly irritable and argumentative, and one night after an argument that I provoked, I got mad at Pat and used it as an excuse to move to the spare bedroom. I wanted to be alone in my misery.

The bright spot for me came with the birth of my son. I named him Jim after my brother (who had just about earned his college degree by now). I nicknamed my son "Little Jim." I loved that little fellow and couldn't help but wonder at him. I cherished holding him and watching him staring at nothing, gurgling and smiling. I treasured seeing him smile. For his sake I was glad that I'd married Pat and given him my name. He was my son, my flesh and blood, and that was now firmly established forever.

On Friday and Saturday nights, I would usually go to the Southernaire and shoot bumper pool until the wee hours of the morning. Winning cash by shooting pool was a nice supplement to my meager salary, but more important it provided me with a much-needed mental diversion and time away from Pat and my dark thoughts.

When Friday night rolled around, I'd leave work and go directly to the Southernaire, telling myself that I needed to warm up and get used to the bumper-pool table before my night of gambling began. In reality I didn't need any practice to beat those clowns—I just wanted to avoid Pat and hearing her raise hell about my going out instead of staying home with her and doing nothing.

Not many people were at the club yet on this particular Friday night, and I was just doodling around on the table. I quickly noticed a beautiful girl, Anna, sitting on a bar stool in the bumper-pool room where I was practicing. She was smiling at me and closely watching my every move. She came over and grabbed me by the arm and asked me if I'd give her some personal lessons on how to shoot pool before everyone else arrived.

Anna was strikingly beautiful and I'd noticed her around the Southernaire on many occasions. She often came back to the bumper-pool room and watched the games, but I'd never had anything to do with her. To my knowledge, this was the first time that she ever showed even the slightest interest in me.

I said, "Sure," and we started to shoot a game. As we began to shoot, I noticed that the top two buttons of her blouse were unbuttoned and that when she leaned over the table she revealed most of her perfectly shaped breasts.

She smiled broadly and laughed outright when she quickly looked up at me and caught me admiring them. For some reason I wasn't embarrassed in the least and I actually smiled back at her, pleased that she didn't seem to mind my indiscretion.

Anna appeared to be Italian. She had long, thick, black hair; dark, mysterious eyes; and red, pouty lips, along with a seductive, flashing smile and perfectly straight, very white teeth—they contrasted nicely with her smooth, tanned complexion. She could have been on the cover of any fashion magazine.

Even though my marriage was less than stellar and the same could be said for my character and morals, for some unidentified reason I hadn't run around on Pat and was determined not to do so. Perhaps it was my allegiance to her and my new son, or perhaps I'd learned my lesson when I cheated on Lindsey and lost her, or maybe it was my angel of light. Whatever the reason, I was determined not to cheat on Pat.

As the situation started building steam and it became clear that Anna was overtly flirting with me, I held up my hand and told her to slow down some. I showed her my wedding ring and told her that I was married. I also said that she was stunningly beautiful and that I was unquestionably flattered that she had selected me out of all those guys at the Southernaire to mess around with. But I told her that it unfortunately could go nowhere, because I was already taken.

That brave little speech rolled off her beautifully sculptured and tanned body as easily as rainfall streams off one of those yellow rubber rain suits that kids wear. In fact, after I said it she seemed more determined than ever to flirt with me, as though I had directly challenged her seductive powers. Now at every opportunity she was rubbing her soft breasts against me and hugging me. It was sheer torture because she was gorgeous and my dark side was turning cartwheels.

Soon the gamblers start coming in and I go to work. Throughout the night she acts as my personal cheerleader and brings me a steady string of drinks while I play game after game. Throughout the night we laugh and talk to each other and enjoy each other's company as if we've known each other all our lives. Anyone watching us has to be thinking that we're married.

As the night wears on and I'm getting high on the mixed drinks she keeps bringing me, my mind is zooming from the couple of tabs of speed that I took earlier. For whatever reason, my technique tonight is—in a word—elegant. Sometimes it seems that I enter into a groove where my mind is zooming and I can't miss. When I play like this, even the most ambitious and seemingly impossible shot becomes a sure thing. Tonight is such a night. What a feeling it is to do the things I can do on that bumper-pool table. I can't miss. People are oohing and aahing and I'm soaring high and my pockets are bulging with my winnings. I feel like a cool breeze on a hot muggy day.

Long before I want my night to end, the lights come on and it's closing time. By now Anna is burning hot after me and wants me to go home with her and bed her down. For the hundredth time I tell her that I'm married and have to go home to my wife and child. She pouts and sticks out her bottom lip like a spoiled little baby.

God she's beautiful.

Finally she says, "You don't know what you're missing." And with that she turns and walks away. I stare in awe as I watch her perfectly shaped rear end, which is tightly encased in a short skirt, swaying back and forth. I sigh. She quickly turns around and laughs out loud, because once again she caught me in the very act of gawking at her with my mouth hanging open. Before I can say anything she playfully blows me a kiss, and laughs, and says, "You know how to reach me if you change your mind."

I whisper to myself, "Whew, she's right. I can only imagine what I'm missing. Damn, she's a goddess." My dark side whispers, *And you're a damned moron!*

I hop in my car and drunkenly grin to myself as I review the night with Anna. I agree with my dark side that I am indeed the "village idiot" of the city of Columbus, Mississippi. I drive home with one hand over one eye in order to cut down on my double vision, and arrive there without incurring a DUI or smashing into somebody.

The next morning I'm sound asleep in my bed when all of a sudden I'm rudely awakened by a screeching, startling scream. I'm scared out of my wits as I jump up, prepared to fight whatever intruder has broken in. Suddenly my eyes focus and I see Pat, my mother, and Pat's mother all running around my bed yelling at me at the top of their lungs.

"What the hell?"

Pat has in her hand the white shirt that I wore last night. They're all accusing me of running around on Pat, and Pat is shoving the white shirt in my face and yelling at me. Anna's lipstick is smeared all over it.

I think, *Oh great, thanks for that Anna.* I knew that she'd done that little sabotage number and left her mark on me deliberately. No doubt she was smiling that pouty little smile all the while she was doing it.

Now my dark side erupts. I jump up in my underwear and scream at the top of my lungs as though insane. "Get out of here!"

They scatter like quail as I order them to get the hell out of my house. I see genuine fear in their eyes when, like a madman, I turn over the breakfast table and dishes crash to the floor. They all beat it out of there and I hear them drive away. I assume they're scared out of their wits.

I come back inside and scream as loudly as I can, "Damn, I shoulda got a frigging medal for what I did. This is insane!"

I angrily gather my clothes and put them in a worn-out suitcase. Then I storm out of the house and hop into my Willys Jeep wagon and head to downtown Columbus. I stop off at the office-supply company where I work and leave a note telling them I quit. I leave my keys on the desk.

Anna had given me her phone number and insisted that I put it in my wallet. I angrily retrieve her number and call her from the office.

The phone rings for several minutes and finally I hear a sleepy voice on the other end say, "Hello."

"Anna?"

"Yes."

"This is Bob."

"Oh. Hey . . ."

"Is the offer still open?"

"Sure," she purrs in her sexy voice.

Chapter Twenty-Six

Late that afternoon I head for New Orleans, my radio blaring. I'd decided that since I was going to get blamed for screwing Anna, I might as well screw her. And I did—not once, not twice, but three times.

She was *spectacular*.

I was through letting my parents or Pat's parents or anyone tell me how to live my life. I was heading to the vast oil fields in the Gulf of Mexico off the Louisiana coast. Some of my friends had worked there, and I'd heard that good money could be made out on the rigs. I arrive in Houma, Louisiana, on Monday and within an hour I've secured a job with McDermott working on a derrick barge in the Gulf of Mexico.

I start out as a rigger. I go out for 10 days and I'm in for four. I work 12-hour days, 10 days straight. With overtime I can make a couple of thousand dollars on each trip.

Offshore oil rigs are built onshore. Then tugboats push and pull them out to the oil fields in the Gulf. The derrick barge sits beside the floating rig and then permanently secures it to the ocean floor. There are four leg openings on the floating oil rig. Huge pipes, four feet in diameter, are lifted by a crane and lowered through the leg openings, and then, huge air hammers drive them into the ocean floor and secure them to the bottom.

My job as a rigger is to hook up the cables to the large pipes, which are then lifted up by the giant crane and lowered into position. Once that operation is complete, another large pipe is picked up and put into position over the top of the previous pipe. Then welders spend approximately six hours welding the pipes together. Once welded, another six hours' work by a giant air hammer drives them down far enough for another pipe to be welded. And then the process repeats. The pipes are driven hundreds of feet into the ocean floor to secure the large rigs, and it takes months to finish the job.

During a shift, I might have to hook up three or four pipes at most. The rest of the time I crawl into one of the large pipes and relax. It's an easy job that pays well, but it's a dangerous job. Slipping pipes have crushed riggers, and losing a hand or finger is not uncommon.

The work is also boring, and it's not much better when we finish our shifts. There's really nothing to do but sleep, gamble, or fish. I am an insomniac and can't sleep much, so I choose to fish most of the night after every shift. The rigs and huge lights shining down into the water attract fish, and we can see them swimming around. It's fun catching them, and a couple of other guys and I catch plenty enough fresh fish for the chef.

Some of the men prefer to spend their idle time gambling, either playing cards or tossing dice, but that's a loser proposition to me. My idea of gambling is to win every time, like I do in bumper pool. I'm not about to throw away my hard-earned money based on luck.

I'd rather drink it up, and drink it up I do! With its nonstop partying, New Orleans is my kind of town. I unload from the crew boat, cash my check, and with a couple of thousand dollars in my pocket hit the bars in the French Quarter. College-age girls abound in the many bars, and the drinks are on me.

When I return to the crew boat at the end of four days, I'm flat broke, have a major hangover, and remember little or nothing of what has transpired. I'm beginning to black out more and more frequently from my heavy drinking, and my temper and fighting are becoming problematic again.

I left home about two months ago, and lately I've been feeling guilty about leaving. I suppose my angel of light is responsible for that. I think of Little Jim and Pat often during those long lonely nights out in the Gulf, so the next time the crew boat returns to shore I call Pat to check in and see how things are going. She's happy that I called and seems eager to see me, and tells me that she still loves me and wants me to come home.

I decide to drive the 12 hours up to Columbus to pay them a visit. She welcomes me back with open, loving arms and after a weekend together wants me to move back in.

It's tempting, especially as I look at my young son in his crib, but I just can't do it. I tell her that I need more time and that I'm making far more money in my new job and need to go back to it. Actually I know that I'll never come back, but I just can't bring myself to tell her.

I don't love her—it's that simple. Pat is a decent person and I care about her, but I have known true love with Lindsey and what I feel for Pat is not even remotely the same. Lindsey and I had that "crazy about you" kind of love and she was literally all I could think about day and night, like some lovesick little kid. I want that kind of love in my life and it just isn't there with Pat. I love my son, but I'm not going to stay married just to be near him.

I went back to Louisiana as soon as the weekend was over.

A couple of more months passed and I quit my job. Warnings came in that a huge storm—a norther—was heading straight toward us and that we needed to leave. Our barge captain ignored those warnings because we were behind schedule. We stayed and continued working right up until the day the storm hit.

The storm was much worse than he anticipated, and huge waves and strong winds pounded the barge and the rig. Our bosses ordered us to go up on the rig and bring down 50-pound boxes of welding rods so we could put them on the barge and salvage them from the huge storm. We traveled from the barge up to the rig by walking up a narrow walkway about 30 feet long. The storm was so violent that the walkway was moving up and down 20 or more feet with each passing wave.

A fierce wind was howling and waves were constantly sweeping under the walkway. If someone had fallen from the walkway into the sea, the raging storm would have swept him away and he'd be lost in the blackness of the night. I was walking down the slippery-wet walkway with a 50-pound box of welding rods on each shoulder when suddenly a huge wave violently lifted the walkway and then dropped it back down. I slid down the wet walkway all the way to the deck.

The foreman immediately ordered me back up on the rig, and I told him to go to hell. If he wanted any more welding rods brought down, he could go up there and carry them himself. That was it. I quit right then and there and went inside the warm cabin. Several other guys quit too, and we sat around playing cards while the others worked in the raging storm.

When we returned to port, I went to New Orleans. I hadn't contacted Pat since my last trip up there two months earlier. I was sitting in a bar down in the French Quarter and was in a melancholy and lonely mood and spontaneously decided to go see her and Little Jim. This time I didn't call in advance, because I wanted to surprise her. I drove most of the night, drinking beer and popping some uppers as I went. I arrived a little after midnight and knocked on the door. Instead of big smiles Pat greeted me coldly and asked what I wanted.

Her demeanor caught me completely by surprise because it was diametrically opposite of the "welcome home with open arms" greeting that I'd received last time.

I told her I wanted to see Little Jim. She immediately told me that it was after midnight and he was asleep, and besides I wasn't welcome there anymore, so I should just leave.

I said that I'd been driving all night and just wanted to see my son for a little while. I told her that I hadn't seen him in two months, and that I would leave as soon as I saw him. I assured her that I'd be quiet and wouldn't wake him up or bother her.

She told me that I wasn't going to see him tonight and then tried to shut the door.

After having just driven for 12 long hours to see her and Little Jim, I'm in no mood to hear this crap. Suddenly my face becomes twisted in rage and I snarl, "Screw you! I'm seeing my son."

I barge through the door, pushing it open with my shoulder, brush her aside, and nearly knock her down in the process.

She starts screaming at me to leave and begins hitting me on the arm and back. The baby is loudly crying, no doubt scared out of his wits by her ranting and yelling. In an instant my dark side takes over and I wheel around and look at her with an evil darkness in my eyes, which no doubt scares the hell out of her. I raise my fist to where she can see it, and I growl in a menacing tone through clenched teeth, "If you don't shut your damn mouth and quit scaring the baby, I'll shut it for you."

Pat has known me since high school and knows all too well not to push me any further. She knows I've been drinking and she knows what that does to my brain. She runs out of the house crying.

At this point Little Jim is screaming for all he's worth and I pick him up from his crib and sit in the rocking chair in his tiny room. I slowly begin to rock him back to sleep. He looks up at me with his little blue eyes still wet with tiny tears, and he has his bottom lip stuck out and it's still slightly quivering. I gently sing to him and softly talk stupid baby talk and he finally simmers down. I put him back in his crib. He's dressed in light-blue, one-piece pajamas with his little feet enclosed. I tenderly cover him up with his baby blanket. Soon he's fast asleep again.

I stand there looking at his beautiful, angelic face marveling over his innocence for a few minutes and then I remember Pat and her strange behavior.

Time for me to leave.

I decide to go to my parent's house to spend the night so I can head back to New Orleans tomorrow. I whisper to myself, "This was a bad idea. You should have known better."

Pat had run outside and gone to her next-door neighbor's house, or so I assume. I walk out the door, get into my car, and start to drive off. But when I pull out of the driveway, I notice that a car immediately falls in behind me and starts following. We go about a mile down the gravel road and then he turns on a blue light. As luck would have it, the next-door neighbor is a damned highway patrolman. Pat lied to him and told him that I hit her, and he's pretty fired up. I tell him that what Pat said is nothing but a damned lie and that I didn't hit anyone. He arrests me and takes me to jail and charges me with DUI.

My dad made my bail and hired a lawyer for me. In about a week I had a hearing before a Justice of the Peace, and my lawyer easily got me off on a technicality. The highway patrolman had no legal authority to arrest me on a county gravel road. His authority was limited to highways and in order to arrest me on a gravel road, he needed to declare to me at the time of the arrest that he was making a citizen's arrest and then file the proper paperwork for such an arrest. He had not done so and therefore the charges had to be dropped. I was free to go.

Neither the highway patrolman nor the Justice of the Peace that heard the case is happy about this turn of events, but the law is the law. When I hear that I have been exonerated, a big smirk immediately crosses my face. The judge sees this and has anger in his eyes as he lectures me and duly warns me that he'd better not see me in his courtroom again. I just smirk all the bigger and my dad and my attorney grab me by the arms and usher me out of there before I say or do something that I'll regret.

Later on I learned why Pat had acted so strangely. The bottom line was that she'd grown tired of waiting for me and had started seeing someone else. A couple of my buddies told me that she'd been practically living with some guy.

It all made sense to me now.

After this incident, she immediately filed for divorce and I signed off on it. We were officially divorced. We were married at 19 and divorced at 20; our shotgun marriage had ended just 11 months after it began. My child support was set at $50 per month. That was a lot of money at the time, considering that I didn't even have a job.

I returned to New Orleans and my old habits, only now I was smoking marijuana every day in addition to drinking heavily and taking uppers and downers. I was drunk and stoned most of the time and was living in an apartment with several girls that I'd met at a bar in the French Quarter who allowed me to stay there rent-free. We partied continuously.

I rarely checked in with my parents, but after quite a while I decided to call Mom to see how things were going. She told me that she'd been trying to find a way to get in touch with me. She had some bad news for me. Apparently Pat had turned vindictive and had notified the draft board of my divorce.

At the time, the nonsensical Vietnam War was raging and everyone my age was being drafted to go fight in it. In college I'd been protected from the draft by a 2A classification and had an even safer 3A classification when I was married and we had a child. The day after our divorce became final, Pat had notified the lady at the draft board and my draft status was changed to 1A the very next day.

Less than a week later I was drafted into the Army. If that wasn't bad enough, Dad told me that Pat had already remarried and was in the process of legally changing Jim's name from Williamson to her new husband's name. She was currently running a notice in the newspaper about it. She was also raising hell about my lagging child-support payments, and was trying to get me locked up for that.

I called her.

"Pat?"

"Yes."

"This is Bob."

Silence.

I said, "You should know that if you change Jim's name I'm going to kill you. He's a Williamson and he will remain a Williamson. If you think I'm kidding, *then try me.*

"Everyone thinks I'm crazy anyway, including me. Make no mistake about it. I'll put you in the ground. I might be sitting in a pine tree one morning and I'll pick your ass off with my high-powered deer rifle while you go to work. Or maybe I'll just knock on your door one night and when you come to the door shoot you in the face. Or maybe I'll poison your stinking ass or stab you in the ear with an ice pick. But make no mistake, I'll kill you.

"You'll never be safe as long as I can draw a breath. You can move, you can hide, you can run, but I'll track your ass down like an animal and kill you if it's the only thing I ever accomplish in my life. It might come today, six weeks from now, or years from now, but make no mistake about it, I'm going to kill you, Pat.

"Maybe I'll get away with it or maybe I'll get caught. It will be irrelevant to you because you'll be dead and six feet under the ground in a cold grave. Personally I think I'm smart enough to get away with it. Either way I don't give a shit—my life is horrible anyway."

She said in a trembling voice, "I didn't think you cared about Jim having your name."

I screamed loud enough to be heard two blocks away. ***"Of course I care, you dumb bitch!"***

She said in a scared, consoling tone, "Okay, okay, I'll drop it and leave his name the way it is."

I said, "You'd *better* see that you do. I ought to kill you anyway for turning me in to the draft board."

"I didn't do that."

"You lying bitch. Don't you *even* lie to me. Mom talked to the lady that's in charge of it."

Silence.

I said, "You low-down bitch. I've decided to let you slide on that, but you'd better hear me and hear me good about Jim's name."

She said, "I hear you, I hear you. I promise I won't change it. Ever!"

"See that you don't! You've been warned!" I slammed the phone down in her ear.

She dropped the name-changing effort that day. Dad and Mom paid my back due child support for me, and Dad told me that he would continue to pay it for me until I entered the service and started receiving paychecks and could afford to pay it myself. I told them I greatly appreciated it and that I would repay them as soon as I got my hands on some money.

I immediately head for the recruiter's office. Dad told me that by enlisting in the Air Force I can escape being drafted into the U.S. Army and receiving a one-way ticket to Vietnam. I'm determined that I will not be going to Vietnam under any circumstance, and I think my chances of avoiding it are better if I enter the Air Force instead of one of the other services.

I've lost several friends from high school in that stupid war, and I'm not about to go halfway around the world to fight a political war for Lyndon Johnson and his cronies. As far as I can tell this war makes absolutely zero sense. Hell, I don't even really know where Vietnam is and don't give a rat's ass about those people.

If they were in Mexico or Canada and a threat to our country, it would be different, but a bunch of Asians in a 100-year-old civil war on the other side of the world means nothing to me. As for their dispute over who owns a bunch of snake-infested rice paddies, who gives a shit? I walk into the U.S. Air Force recruiter's office in New Orleans ready to sign up.

"*Where do I sign?*"

Chapter Twenty-Seven

I depart on a Continental Trailways bus for Lackland Air Force Base near San Antonio, Texas, to undergo basic training. I arrive and get a uniform and free haircut courtesy of the USAF. I would describe my new haircut as a "buzzed burr." My long blond hair is now about a sixteenth of an inch long all over my head. I look like an idiot.

The drill sergeants try their best to act like maniacal badasses. They move close to our faces screaming for no reason other than to try to scare us. Some of the guys are scared shitless, but as for me, I don't give a damn. When I was just 16 years old, I saw a lot meaner and badder guys than these clowns. I'd like to see these drill sergeants go to one of those Mississippi state-line beer joints on a Saturday night and run their mouths like they do here.

Both drill sergeants are about five-foot-five and seem to have Napoleonic, short-man complexes—and little intelligence. No matter what we do, whether it's making up our beds, shining our shoes, marching, arranging our lockers, or cleaning up the bunk area, it's wrong. Nothing is good enough for them and they run around with their mountie hats on ranting and raving and getting up in everyone's face and screaming and cursing and tearing our bunks apart and then telling us to make them up again.

I conclude that all of this is just part of their act and is nothing more than a military plan to dehumanize us and make us lose our individuality for the greater good.

Our family moved constantly and I traveled the world a lot while I was growing up, but somehow I was tagged as being from Mississippi. I suppose it's because I graduated from high school and went to college there. This was important because we had a black man as the lead drill sergeant, and he made a black guy our squad leader. And black people don't like Mississippi white people. This was my first exposure to racism, only it was black against white instead of white against black.

Racial tensions are at an all-time high in the country and have been since the early '60s. Blacks are demonstrating, burning down cities, marching, and raising hell at every opportunity. I've been raised in a totally segregated environment and have never gone to school with a black person and really have never been around one or even known a black person until now. Prior to this I didn't have an opinion about them, but based on what I'm seeing I don't like them any more than they like me.

From the beginning, our newly appointed black squad leader ran his mouth about the fact that I'm from Mississippi. One day he called me a "white trash crackah." I hit him hard enough to knock him completely over a bunk, where he landed on the other side, upside down on his back with his legs sticking up in the air. That was all there was to the fight because the drill sergeants heard the commotion and came charging in to break it up.

I gave my side of what happened and told the drill sergeant that I didn't care if he was black or white, no one was going to call me a white trash cracker.

The drill sergeant got about an inch from my face and screamed, "Shut up your big damn mouth you *white trash crackah* Mississippi redneck piece of shit. You're going to do exactly as I tell you! You cocksucker! There will not be any fighting in this squad. You got that *crackah?*"

I glared at him and defiantly responded, "Oh yes suh massa suh. I gets it!"

That was not the right answer. As punishment, I had to do hundreds of pushups, run for miles, and then pick up cigarette butts to put in red "butt" cans throughout the entire week. I was seething mad and particularly enraged about the cigarette butts.

I wanted revenge on that squad leader's ass for getting me in trouble and soon enough I had my chance.

The squad leader enjoyed preferred treatment from the sergeants and quickly became a rat fink and would report our every move. One morning he reported a card game that we'd held the previous night after lights-outs. As a result the sergeants took away the entire squad's smoke-break privileges for three days.

Feelings were running high about this incident. I suggested to a few of the guys that we hold a little "blanket party" for the squad leader to teach him a lesson. Later that night we threw a blanket over his head when he came out of the showers and beat him half senseless with our fists. He couldn't see who was hitting him because his head and arms were tightly covered with the blanket.

After we gave him a good beating, we whispered to disguise our voices and hissed to him that if he ever ratted us out again, including for this blanket party, he might not live through it next time. He learned his lesson and we had no more problems after that.

As we neared completion of basic training, we were told that all recruits had to pull KP for a week in order to graduate. KP—kitchen police—is the nasty process of working in a hot kitchen and washing dishes for the entire mess hall. Some refer to it as hell week. I was assigned to pots and pans, which is the most deplorable and worst job in KP. I was determined to get out of it.

By this stage of our basic training, we had been granted a few limited privileges, including access to the library. Later that evening I went to the library and read up on the symptoms of a bleeding ulcer. I then went to the infirmary and gave them verbatim the symptoms for a bleeding ulcer that I'd just read about. I even told them that I threw up some dark-colored blood this morning that looked like coffee grounds. The doctors immediately admitted me to the hospital and slated me for tests.

I missed the entire week of KP while they ran the tests, and I couldn't help but smile every time I thought about it. I thought my plan was absolutely brilliant. All was not bliss however, because I had to endure an "explosive" enema and then drink barium, which tasted like what I would imagine bird crap tastes like. Then they x-rayed my upper and lower digestive tracts as the barium slowly made its way through my system, all the while tilting me up and down on an electric-powered bed and looking for the ulcer. It was not pleasant.

Predictably they did not find a bleeding ulcer and finally released me. They diagnosed me as probably having a nervous stomach due to stress. My buddies were irate that I did not have to serve KP. I hysterically laughed at them as they described hell week and KP.

Remarkably, I did make it through the six weeks of basic training—it had been quite an experience. Upon graduation I couldn't believe my incredible good fortune: I was being assigned to none other than Keesler Air Force Base in Biloxi for six months of training. I had scored very high on some tests and was accepted to Keesler's technical school, where I would be trained as an intercept operator.

Imagine my good fortune. I'm going back to my old haunts in Biloxi, home of Lindsey, and I'll be just 90 miles from New Orleans and all my drinking and drugging girlfriends and buddies who live there.

Things are definitely looking up!

Chapter Twenty-Eight

I had two weeks' leave before my training at Keesler started, and I decided to return to Columbus to see my family. After Pat screwed me over and had me thrown in jail, I'd vowed that I'd never see or speak to her again.

My parents loved Pat like a daughter and blamed me 100 percent for the divorce. They had a good relationship with her and had been seeing Little Jim often. They made all the arrangements with Pat for me to see Little Jim and brought him to their house for our visit. He was growing up fast and it was fascinating to see how much he'd changed in just the couple of months since I'd last seen him. I was amazed that anything so sweet and innocent could come out of me.

It was a Friday night, and after my family visit I decided to head over to the Southernaire. Almost immediately I ran into an old friend, Lisa Brooks. She'd been married to a very close friend of mine, Nick, who I heard had been shot to death in a bizarre shooting by Lisa's stepfather.

At the time of the shooting, Nick and Lisa were living with Lisa's parents. Her stepfather's side of the story was that Nick started a fight with him. He said that when Nick started wailing on him, he pulled out a pistol and shot Nick in the stomach in self-defense.

Lisa said that wasn't true. She said they got into an argument with each other, but it was entirely verbal. Nick went to the refrigerator to get a glass of milk and when he turned back around, he saw her stepfather with a pistol in his hand aimed at him.

Nick nonchalantly said, "What? Are you gonna shoot me?"

And without a word he did just that. The only witnesses were Lisa's mother and Lisa.

Lisa told me that the cops didn't believe her but believed her stepfather's side of the story, backed up by her mother (his wife). She said that her stepfather literally got away with murder and didn't even have to stand trial. Lisa said the police hardly listened to a word she said, perhaps because she was in shock and hysterical.

Nick was a life-insurance salesman and recently had taken out a very large life-insurance policy with Lisa as the sole beneficiary. When Nick died, Lisa inherited a huge sum of money, and many people around Columbus, including Nick's brother, thought that it was just too much of a coincidence. I had to wonder what really happened. Did the stepfather shoot him for the money? Or had Nick been wailing on him? Nick had a fearsome temper and had been in his fair share of fights. He was one tough guy and didn't take any shit from anybody. I didn't know what to believe about it.

Lisa told me that Nick's death and the resulting controversy about the insurance policy, especially from Nick's family, really devastated her, and after the funeral she moved to Memphis and went into seclusion for about a year. Like me, she was visiting family in Columbus for a couple of weeks and would soon return to Memphis.

I told her that she looked good and I was happy to see her out and about again. She said that she was glad to see me. She hadn't seen anyone else that she knew since she'd been there, and she'd been getting ready to leave when we met.

I smiled and said, "Don't do that."

She hooked her arm in mine and happily said, "Not a chance. C'mon, let's get a table and talk about old times."

"Sounds good to me," I said.

Lisa was very pretty, with dark eyes and medium-length black hair. She was hilariously funny and as witty as anyone that I'd ever known. We ended up spending the entire evening together laughing and talking about Nick and some of the crazy things that we'd all done together. We drank several beers and the next thing I knew she was smiling wickedly at me and saying, "Have you ever taken any speed?"

I said, "Are you kidding? I love speed. I wish I had some."

She reached in her purse and pulled out a prescription bottle, full to the brim with Dexedrine, and then she rattled them around tantalizingly in front of my face and said, "You mean like these?"

"I mean exactly like those!" I grinned.

We both popped a couple of dex and swigged them down with jet cold Budweisers right out of the bottle.

Soon we were zooming and flying high. Speed stimulates talk, and talk we did. I told her my sad story and she told me hers, several times. Often we both were talking as fast we could manage at the exact same time. We didn't care because we weren't listening to each other that much anyway. When zooming on speed, talking—not listening—is what's fun.

We drank some more and we took some more speed, we drank some more, we talked some more, we kissed, we talked about sad times, we drank, we talked about happy times, we kissed, we danced, we drank, we kissed.

I ended up spending the night with her.

We made love and afterward we were lying in bed together, sweaty and exhausted, when suddenly we heard the wind start howling *whoooooooooh* right against the bedroom window above our heads. It was distinctively loud and sounded like the spooky noise a ghost would utter.

As soon as we heard it, at the exact same moment Lisa and I both loudly exclaimed, "Nick?"

I asked again, "Is that you Nick?"

As if on command, just as suddenly as it had begun, the howling was gone and the room was dead silent again. An eerie still descended on us, and we both began laughing, nervously at first, but then heartily, and finally hysterically. It would be just like Nick to come back and haunt us and scare the crap out of us for having sex with one another. We could just see him demonically laughing at having scared us silly.

After that first night Lisa and I were inseparable for the remainder of my two-week stay. We went everywhere together and partied down—drinking, popping pills, smoking weed, and making love every night. This went on right up until the day we departed, when I drove down to Biloxi to begin technical school and she flew back up to Memphis.

I really enjoyed being around Lisa and could feel myself once again falling hard, as I'd done with Lindsey. And from what I could tell, Lisa seemed to feel exactly the same about me. We talked on the phone every night, and she wrote to me nearly every day.

Back on base it was a different story. I hated military life with a passion. It was all I could do to take orders, especially from the "90-day wonders." These were the unbearable nerds who had taken ROTC in college. They bypassed working their way up through the ranks like real officers and got commissioned as second lieutenants with just 90 days of service. Invariably they were skinny, little, dorky jerks who wore thick glasses and swaggered around like supreme emperors in their heavily starched, short-sleeved uniforms, which were too big for them and made their arms look like white strings hanging out.

The military treats officers like gods and enlisted men as lowly scum of the earth, and it burned my ass to have some nerd with just two more years of college than me strutting around like some bantam rooster, chewing me out because my shiny shoes were not shiny enough, or ordering me around like I was a dog and telling me to pick up cigarette butts or some similar demeaning task.

The second lieutenant in charge of our squadron was a real asshole and he didn't like me and I didn't like him. It took all my willpower to refrain from smashing his face. I would have gladly given a month's pay to get him alone for about an hour so I could beat him to a bloody pulp.

Intercept operators eavesdropped and recorded the communications of our country's Cold War enemies around the world, specifically the Soviet Union. After my graduation from technical school at Keesler as an intercept operator, they told me I could expect a transfer to some big listening post in Turkey. I was all right with that. At least it wasn't Vietnam and I'd heard that they had some excellent hashish in Turkey.

Technical school was as boring as boring can be. Usually during the hottest part of the day, we mindlessly marched around the parade field for hours at a time in the torturous Mississippi sun and humidity. The rest of the time we sat in a classroom learning how to take Morse code. I could not fathom how all that marching would help me in my assignment as an intercept operator, in which I'd be confined to a chair, wear earphones, and use a keyboard to record Morse code signals all day long.

It was, however, an easy job. I quickly learned Morse code and honed my typing skills to a fine edge. Soon I was at the top of my class and my instructor was constantly praising my accomplishments. I could have cared less if I were a top-notch intercept operator or not. It really didn't seem to me like much of a challenge nor an accomplishment, but at least the instructor was not on my back as he was with some of my classmates.

I lived for the weekends and as soon as my day ended on Friday, I was driving my little Volkswagen Beetle to the New Orleans airport to pick up Lisa, who by now was flying in weekly to see me.

My brother was close to graduating from college as a chemistry major and had moved to New Orleans to work for the summer. That first weekend Lisa and I stayed in a downtown hotel, but Jim said he had an extra bedroom in his rented house that we could use if we so desired.

So on each of Lisa's subsequent visits we would stay at Jim's house. We'd hook up with him and his roommates and several of my other friends, and have one continuous party throughout the weekend right up until the moment I had to return to base. I'd take Lisa back to the airport so she could return to Memphis, and then I'd drive the 90 miles back to Keesler, usually still drunk and wired up on speed. The next weekend we would meet again and repeat the entire process.

Money was usually no object for us. Lisa was rich from Nick's insurance money and I had my airman's pay and little else to spend it on, but after one weekend of particularly hard partying, neither of us had any cash left. We were walking around the French Quarter, drunk as sailors on leave, laughing and having a good time. We passed a tattoo shop and I decided that, since I was in the military now, I needed a tattoo. Lisa laughed and told me to go for it. We went in and I told the guy that I wanted a cherry tattooed on my ass and asked how much. He looked at me with disgust and said that if I were to get a tattoo on my ass, he would have to close the shop during the process and therefore it would cost $15.

All we had between us was five dollars. I asked Lisa what kind of flower she liked and she replied that she liked daisies. I drunkenly asked the tattoo guy if he could put a tattoo of a daisy on the top of my foot for five dollars.

"Huh?" He said. "How about I put it on your arm, man?"

"Foot," I stubbornly said with a stupid smile on my face.

I guess he needed the five bucks because he agreed. I pulled off my shoe and sock. He started putting the tattoo on the middle of the top of my left foot just above my toes. To merely say it hurt would be a gross distortion of fact. It was *agonizing* to have all those needles on that guy's tattoo gun going in and out of this tender, sensitive area of my body. I didn't want Lisa or the tattoo guy to think I was a candy ass or anything, but tears were filling my eyes and I felt like screaming in pain. I gritted my teeth instead, and then tried my utmost to keep from screaming in agony. Finally he finished and I had a nice little daisy, complete with yellow and white flower petals, on the top of my foot.

He told me that it would scab up in a day or two and not to tear the scab off because some of the color would go with it. He said to just let it fall off naturally when it was ready, and he put a bandage on it.

In my drunken stupor I hadn't considered that having a tattoo on the top of my foot and marching for hours in the hot sun in military combat boots might not be a good combination. I didn't anticipate the amount of swelling that my foot would endure or that I would nearly have to cut my boot off my swollen foot every night. Nor did I foresee the excruciating pain from this seemingly minor little tattoo on the top of my foot.

In an effort to gain sympathy, I told Lisa about my problems. Nothing but maniacal laughter came through the other end of the pay phone. I sighed and told her I'd see her Friday and then hung up the phone, her laughter continuing right up to the point that the phone hit the receiver.

As usual I met Lisa at the airport on Friday and we hit New Orleans with gusto. We had a particularly enjoyable time this weekend. Several of my Columbus friends came down to join us in the revelry, and it was nice seeing everyone. Lisa and I were particularly close this weekend, and she jokingly mentioned in passing that if this kept up we might have to get married. I light-heartedly agreed, but I was wild about her and the possibility of marriage had crossed my mind too.

Lisa was spending some serious money flying back and forth, and when we discussed it over the phone, we decided that maybe it would make more sense for her to just stay over for the week in New Orleans. She wanted to do some shopping in New Orleans anyway. My brother said he didn't mind if she stayed the week at his house, so that was what we decided to do.

Late Sunday afternoon I dropped her off at Jim's house and headed back to Keesler. I returned the following Friday night and Lisa greeted me with a big smile and kiss, and hugged me close and whispered that she'd missed me.

All weekend we scoured the New Orleans nightclub scene from the French Quarter to Fat City, listening to bands, dancing, drinking, and of course drugging. And we made love all weekend too. It was another fabulous time together.

After having been gone for two weeks, Lisa needed to get back home to Memphis, so Sunday afternoon I dropped her off at the airport. We kissed long and hard as we said farewell and for some reason I clumsily blurted out, "I love you."

She looked at me rather oddly and then quickly said with a smile on her face,

"I love you too, Bob." Then she looked at her watch and said, "Damn I need to go or I'm going to miss my flight. Bye."

I watched as she hurried inside the terminal, stopping once to look back and wave. Then she went inside. I waved back and steered my car back onto the highway. Lisa had caught an earlier flight than normal and I had plenty of time on my hands, so I decided to go back down to the French Quarter to one of my favorite bars so I could have a few drinks before I returned to the boredom of Keesler.

My old roommate from USM, Johnnie Bodock, was in the bar drinking his favorite drink, scotch and water.

I greeted him with a big smile and said, "Yo J.B. How goes it man?"

J.B. had been partying with us over the weekend and in fact had been down for the entire previous week. Apparently he had the same idea as me about catching a few drinks before heading back.

He asked me where Lisa was. I told him that I had just dropped her off at the airport. I ordered a Cuba Libre, and when it arrived, resqueezed the wedge of lime and dropped it into my drink. I stirred it a couple of swishes and gulped down a big slug, "Ahhh, that's absolutely perfect!"

J.B. had a really serious look on his face.

"What's up J.B.?" I asked. "You look like you've lost your best friend."

He said, "I don't know how to say this other than to just say it, but while you were gone Lisa pulled a 'train.' She screwed five guys over at your brother's house, including your brother Jim. She was the only girl there with five guys that first night, and they were all smoking pot, drinking, taking pills, and partying hard. And before the night was over she got stoned out of her mind and ended up taking them all on, one right after the other. Then she started hanging out with that long-haired guy, I think his name is Ronnie, and she was with him for the entire week, right up until the time you got here. She screwed Ronnie every night, man. I saw you with her this weekend and she and everyone, including your brother Jim, just acted as though nothing had happened. It isn't right everyone knowing but you. I can tell you really dig her and I really hate it happened to you. I'm sorry to have to be the one to tell you, but that bitch is some kind of a crazy nympho and you need to know it."

I didn't say a word but nodded my appreciation. My mind was numb. My stomach twisted into a knot and I felt sick. A million thoughts were racing through my mind. My dark side was urging me to get even. *Kill every damn one of them. Save Jim and Lisa for last and make their deaths slow and painful!*

After he broke the news to me, Johnny finished his drink, patted me on the back, and left the bar to head back to USM. I stayed behind drinking one Cuba Libre after another until I could barely walk. I felt blinding rage and I felt betrayed and then I just felt very sad. I kept drinking until 2 a.m.

I had to drive back to the base and be in class by 7 a.m. I managed to go about 30 miles out of New Orleans but couldn't drive any more. I just had to catch some

Z's. I decided to pull over and sleep for a few minutes. I pulled my Volkswagen Beetle over to the side of the road and promptly passed out.

I awoke in a hot sweat with the blazing sun beaming down on me. I looked at my watch and it was 8 a.m.

I'd been AWOL for one hour.

Chapter Twenty-Nine

After starting my car and turning on the air conditioner to combat the stifling heat, I sat there for a moment reviewing things in my mind. I had a horrible hangover and was already AWOL. Plus I was still an hour or so away from the base. By now that little 90-day wonder second lieutenant bastard who hated me so would be licking his lips like a hungry fat man anticipating a big meal of fried chicken. He would like nothing more than to see the brass kick me out of technical school and send me to the stockade.

I'd been humiliated and betrayed by my girlfriend, my own brother, and my supposed friends. My parents had forced me to quit college and marry Pat, even after I told them flat out that I didn't love her and the marriage would end in disaster. I had to leave Little Jim. I'd lost the love, trust, and respect of Lindsey, the only truly good person who had ever been in my life. Then I'd gone through an ugly divorce and Pat's subsequent betrayal. She turned me in to the draft board! And that forced me into the same military that I'd hated my entire life and for which I was obviously not suited.

In spite of a good intellect, superb athletic ability, and above-average looks, my entire life had been nothing more and nothing less than a disaster, consisting of abject failure, drinking, drugging, sex, senseless violence, loneliness, frustration, despair, and unhappiness. I was just so much human waste spinning in a giant toilet bowl of misspent and squandered opportunity. I was swirling out of control and heading downward to the stinking cesspool below.

"To hell with it!"

I threw my little car into gear and headed for Memphis. I drove all day and into the evening. I went directly to Lisa's apartment and knocked on the door. She opened the door and I could see Ronnie sitting on her couch. She stood there with a glass of white wine in her hand and her mouth hanging open. She was barefoot and had on very tight hot-pink shorts. Her white blouse was partially unbuttoned, and she was looking at me in total disbelief and shock. I was the last person she expected to see.

Ronnie was basically a long-haired freeloader who didn't have enough money to buy a 50-cent bottle of Thunderbird wine. I knew instantly that Lisa had bought Ronnie a ticket on the same flight that she'd taken from New Orleans. He couldn't have driven to Memphis, because he didn't have a car, and he really had no other way of getting there that fast. He must have met her at the airport shortly after I dropped her off.

I had driven to Memphis because I needed confirmation of Lisa's betrayal—so I could get beyond it. I needed to hear it directly from Lisa. But seeing Ronnie sitting there was all the verification I needed. J.B. had told the story straight.

I felt strangely calm, and my lust for revenge was completely gone. Earlier I was in a rage and felt like beating them all senseless, but after driving 10 or 12 hours and thinking it through, I just didn't care. They weren't worth the bother. I simply felt cold and empty.

At that *precise* moment I vowed to myself that I would never again allow anyone to get close to me: not Lisa, not my brother, not my parents, not my ex-wife, not another girl, not any other person on earth! No one would ever put down roots inside my head and hurt me again. Instead, from this point on I would be the one wreaking havoc with people's lives.

I was in a rather peculiar situation standing at her door because I felt nothing but contempt for Lisa and had nothing to say to her. To me she was just a perverted slut, and she and this loser deserved and could have each other. I'd wanted to tell her that I knew what she'd done, but I even lost any desire to do that. So I just turned around and left without saying a word.

Lisa came running after me and was following me downstairs. She was talking 90 miles a minute, no doubt wired to the gills on speed, and was trying to feed me a line of lame lies to explain Ronnie's presence in her apartment less than 24 hours after we had kissed each other goodbye and she'd told me that she loved me.

I hopped into my car and left. I spent the night in a cheap motel and in the morning sold my VW Beetle at a used-car lot. Luckily for me, I'd just paid my car off and had the title with me in the glove compartment.

I bought an airline ticket to Los Angeles. My next stop would be a well-known hippie community—Venice Beach, California. I'd heard that Venice Beach had bustling streets with hippies everywhere, and I felt I could drop out and disappear there with little notice. Much of the hippie movement was centered on antiwar protests, and I deduced that an AWOL soldier wouldn't have a hard time finding a sympathetic ear in such an environment.

I was wrong. If there was a hippie community in Venice Beach, I couldn't find it. Neat rows of houses and entire subdivisions surrounded the beach area, but save for an occasional sighting of an isolated hippie-looking person here and there, none of the throngs of street people that I had envisioned were to be seen. I spoke to a couple of hip-looking dudes about it and they said that if I wanted hippies and throngs, then I should go to the Haight-Ashbury district of San Francisco.

That afternoon I flew up to San Francisco and took a taxicab to the Haight-Ashbury district.

I found the hippies! There were tens of thousands of them milling around.

CHAPTER THIRTY

The United States was in a mess and not just in Southeast Asia. Race riots were erupting coast-to-coast, the civil-rights movement was gaining momentum, and violent organizations like the Black Panthers and the KKK were emerging and doing battle.

To add to the disillusionment, our country was reeling from the assassinations of John F. Kennedy, his brother Robert Kennedy, and Martin Luther King Jr. The Cold War was at its peak and the threat of worldwide nuclear annihilation was an everyday fear.

Antiwar protests raged in the streets. Young people were burning their draft cards and refusing to go fight in a stupid Vietnamese civil war that made absolutely no sense to anyone, including the Vietnamese who were fighting each other. They'd been feuding for 30 years and would probably be fighting 100 years from now. U.S. youth were fed up with politicians who seemed eager to send thousands of 18-year-old kids to be slaughtered in this God-forsaken, snake-infested, worthless jungle.

It was not lost on my generation that the corrupt politicians who were sending these teenage troops into battle were safely sitting on their fat asses in their overstuffed chairs, comfortably smoking big cigars and sipping whiskey. And that they were doing it in the comfort and safety of the back rooms of Washington D.C., far removed from any danger, bloody gore, or misery of the jungle in which these teenagers were so courageously fighting and sacrificing their lives. The politicians pontificated on destroying the evil "Hanoi communist devils" as though they were in a simple pissing contest that they were determined to win no matter how many died.

What a waste!

Simultaneously, drugs swept through the country like intense wildfires raging out of control, scorching the earth, and burning and consuming every young person within their sinister, demonic path. Rock and roll was adding fuel to this roaring fire with tantalizing, suggestive lyrics that romanticized the effects of drugs, the psychedelic-drug culture, and the antiwar movement. "Make love not war" was the battle cry of millions of young people, especially college students and those of us who were of draft age. A sexual revolution of mammoth proportions was in full swing, and psychedelic music was spurring it on. Nowhere was this attitude more prevalent than in "the Haight."

The turbulent unrest resulted in hundreds of thousands of young people simply dropping out of mainstream society, becoming hippies, "freaks," "heads," and "diggers," and "turning on" to drugs in a futile attempt to elude and escape the insanity and fury enveloping our country. Counterculture guru Timothy Leary, the Harvard professor they removed from teaching (word on the street was that he was fired for expressing his views on LSD), called on our generation to "Turn on, tune in, and drop out." And for many, that is exactly what happened.

Much press was being given to this phenomenon and also to the protests on college campuses—particularly at the University of California at Berkeley—and in major cities throughout the country. The state of California was clearly the undisputed champion for the disaffected, and TV showed you that on the news every night. Thus it was an easy decision for me to go to California to join their ranks. After all, I was the epitome of the disaffected.

I was totally disillusioned with *all* of life, and not merely with the turmoil sweeping the country, whether it was emanating from the Vietnam War, various nuclear "pissing" contests with the Soviet Union, race riots, or assassinations.

I literally didn't care about anything—anybody—anymore!

Including me!

As far as I was concerned, I had no God, family, or friends. I held no hope for some promising career or bright future. I was seething with anger toward life and stubbornly determined to viciously fight the world that I hated so much. I was determined that I would never again allow any person or anything to ever beat me down. I would never trust anyone again, or even allow somebody close enough to hurt me, especially a woman.

I was totally alone but not lonely.

I feared nothing. Never once did fear cross my tortured, twisted mind. I just felt blind rage and hatred, and I wanted to strike back. I was not concerned in the least about being on the run or even the likelihood that I might be caught. If they caught me, I would just face whatever time they offered up in whatever stockade they sentenced me to. I'd serve my time; I would fight my way through it as I had done all of my miserable life. But make no mistake about it, I was very determined to elude capture. The authorities were going to have to catch me first, and I arrogantly felt that I was far too smart to be captured, and doubted they could do so unless I just was unlucky.

I knew that people in the hippie community would be sympathetic to the fact that I was AWOL. My plan was to join them and blend in—lose myself in the multitudes. However, being fresh out of boot camp, my problem was that I was clean shaven, had a short military-style haircut, and was in excellent physical condition.

I wore a clean and freshly pressed, blue oxford shirt with button-down collar; I had on navy blue pants, dark-blue socks, and shiny maroon penny loafers with matching leather belt. Over my shoulder I carried a stylish tan travel bag containing a couple of changes of clothes and a toiletries kit that I had taken to New Orleans for my weekend stay with Lisa. I looked like some rich college kid heading to Europe for a cosmopolitan summer vacation instead of a hippie or an AWOL soldier on the run.

This combination in the Haight made me stand out like an ugly wart on the petite nose of a beautiful fashion model. Nearly all the hippies were skinny and unhealthy looking; had shoulder-length greasy hair, beards and mustaches; and wore dirty blue jeans and grubby psychedelic T-shirts with peace signs prominently displayed on them. Sandals seemed to be the preferred footwear and most of these kids wore headbands, colored sunglasses, and big floppy Jimi Hendrix–style hats.

Initially I was very self-conscious and paranoid. I felt as if eyes were watching me everywhere. But soon enough I discovered that my dress and looks were irrelevant to this community. Everyone was far too stoned on drugs to even notice me.

The Haight-Ashbury district was for all practical purposes nothing more than a huge open market for any drug that you might desire, and everyone was stoned out of their gourds. Thousands of people crowded the streets and all of them were totally obsessed with taking, buying, selling, trading, or giving away some type of drug.

The day I came to the Haight, there were no cops to be seen. At first I felt that was odd; but as I looked around, I realized that it would be a logistical nightmare for the police to arrest anyone in that horde without a riot breaking out.

I made my way through the crowd trying to get acclimated. The smell of marijuana was very strong, and before I had walked 50 feet I noticed a guy standing in the middle of the street calmly smoking a joint by himself—he had hair even shorter than mine. I walked over to him and pointed to his head and smilingly asked, "What happened to your hair?"

He laughed and said, "I just got out of general lockup. They cut it while I was in jail. What happened to yours?"

I nodded and lied, "Me too."

He offered me a toke off his joint and nodded toward my travel bag and asked, "You just get into town?"

I inhaled deeply and, while still holding the smoke deep within my lungs, managed to strain out an answer, "Yeah, how 'bout you?"

"I've been here about a week."

I exhaled and stuck out my hand and introduced myself with my new alias, "Bob Johnson."

We shook hands. "Rick Swift. Nice to meet you man."

Rick and I instantly bonded and he began showing me around the six- to eight-block area of the Haight. As we slowly worked our way through the crowd, we happened upon three absolutely beautiful girls. They were very friendly and Rick offered a joint to them. We stood there smoking weed together and one of them asked us if we wanted to "do" some crystal.

Rick and I didn't hesitate and at the exact same moment we both answered, "Yes."

The most beautiful of the three, Debbie, said she knew where she could score some "dynamite crystal," but they were $15 short. As quickly as she got those words out of her mouth I was handing her $15. Excitedly she said she would score the speed and rendezvous with us back at their pad in 15 minutes. Rick and I went with them the couple of blocks to their apartment.

Inside, we huffed another joint as we waited for Debbie to return. One of the girls asked if we had ever shot up meth before. We both looked at her with disdain as though annoyed that she would even ask such a stupid question, and assured her that *of course* we had shot up speed before, *many* times. *Jeez!*

I lied. I had never used a needle or even known anyone who had, but I was not about to tell those beautiful girls or Rick that I was some pansy newbie.

In a few minutes Debbie showed up with a huge smile on her face. She had a little plastic bag of white crystal meth and was waving it tantalizingly in front of all our faces. As she removed an "outfit" (syringe and spoon) from the drawer in the coffee table, excitement was buzzing through the room like a million volts singing through a high-voltage electric power line. I smiled broadly, but inside was jittery and nervous that soon they'd discover that I'd lied and didn't know the first thing about shooting up.

With precision, Debbie finely chopped the crystal meth with a single-edge razor blade on a mirror and carefully placed a small amount inside a spoon. She squirted water into the spoon with the syringe, and mixed it with a matchstick. The liquid was then briefly heated with a lighter to thoroughly dissolve it. She placed a small piece of cotton in the spoon as a makeshift filter, and drew the liquid from the spoon into the syringe through the cotton. Next, she placed a belt on her arm just above the injection site and tightened it to expose the veins. When she injected the needle and it registered, she released the belt and emptied the syringe directly into her bloodstream.

The girls hit up first. They were obviously experts, and it didn't take long for all three of them to "geez up," as they called it. Rick was next, and he too deftly shot up with no fumbling around. Finally my turn came. They all expectantly looked at me, waiting for me to hit myself up. Instead I looked directly into Debbie's sparkling-blue, dilated eyes, smiled at her, and softly said, "I want *you* to hit me up."

She gave me a wide, gorgeous smile and was obviously delighted that I had chosen her to do the honors. She said in a sexy, flirty, obviously aroused voice that she'd be happy to "do me up."

Unbeknownst to me at the time, many needle freaks think that it's a sexually stimulating experience having someone of the opposite sex hit you up. This pertains not only to the person who is being hit up but also to the one who is performing the hitting up. So asking a very beautiful girl to hit me up was a cool and somewhat kinky thing to do, and everyone in the room understood this request in that manner (except me of course). It was simply dumb luck on my part, because I'd only asked her so I would avoid looking like a neophyte.

She told me that if I wanted a really *special* rush I should kneel down and hold my left arm up in the air. She said that if she shot up the meth directly into my "ditch" vein (the largest vein in my arm, located in the inside elbow area) while I was holding my left arm directly above my head, it would go straight to my heart (also located on the left side of my body) and then directly to my brain. It would give me the rush of a lifetime.

I smiled and told her that sounded good to me. I got down on my knees in front of the couch and held my arm straight up in the air. Rick tied me off with a belt, and Debbie adroitly inserted the needle into the large vein. Next she efficiently and quickly registered, and dark-red blood swirled into the syringe. She nodded to Rick, who released the pressure of the belt that was tying me off, and Debbie pushed the plunger in, cascading crystal meth into my bloodstream, surging directly into my heart.

BOOM, son! She wasn't kidding.

It took me several moments before I could breathe or speak. It's a wonder that the meth didn't explode my heart and kill me, as this was a stupid, dangerous, foolish, idiotic thing to do. But the feeling (appropriately called a "rush") blasting through my brain was like none other. It was like an orgasm to the billionth power rushing up and down my spine and neck and flashing across my brain over and over again. I tingled all over. I stammered for a moment or two and then I started talking at 120 miles a second. I was talking so fast it was just unintelligible gibberish and I breathlessly burst into raucous laughter; and so did they.

This first experience with methamphetamine injected intravenously, dangerously, crazily, with my arm elevated high above my head, solidly hooked me on meth forever.

Crystal meth was my Genesis. Soon enough I would experience the Revelation.

CHAPTER THIRTY-ONE

Rick and I stayed with Debbie and her two friends, Donna and Becky, for the next two days. The entire time we were doing meth, drinking wine, and smoking weed off and on. We'd been speed-talking nonstop while rock and roll blasted in the background. Our minds were zooming at the speed of light and we'd all attained a drug-induced, energized state of Nirvana.

The famous San Francisco skyline, the Golden Gate Bridge, Fisherman's Wharf, and the overall unique, charming, and quaint atmosphere of this often-foggy city was unappreciated by any of us. We had to replenish our supply of crystal meth twice more, and aside from those quick dealer runs made solo by Debbie, none of us left the apartment—or even looked out a window. I'd begun to develop a neat little trail of needle marks running down the ditch vein in my arm, and I was rather proud of my "tracks" and new status as a certified "head."

I hadn't eaten anything but candy bars or slept for two full days, not to mention the ordeal I'd endured the past weekend, beginning in New Orleans. I was near total collapse. I was shaky-nervous, my stomach was rolling, and I badly wanted some rest. Debbie felt the same way. We told the others that we were going to crash.

Rick was wired up. His eyes were wild looking and dilated, and his jaws were clenching and unclenching. He said that he was just getting started and would "keep on keepin' on." Donna and Becky were not ready to hang it up either, and decided to keep the run going for a while longer with Rick. I looked at Rick and then at the girls with a smile, and told them, "Party on."

Rick broadly smiled back at me and gave me the thumbs-up. He loudly said, "Right on!"

Debbie and I headed to her bedroom. I looked at her and started to clench and unclench my jaws and then gave her my most wild-eyed look. I pointed both thumbs up and stridently said, "Right on!"

We both burst into hearty laughter as we fell back onto the bed. I really liked Rick. He was hilariously entertaining and his rowdy enthusiasm and determination to keep the "run" going was contagious. If I wasn't so exhausted, I'd have stayed with him.

Debbie had some Seconal, a barbiturate known as reds on the street. We washed down two of the powerful downers with a swallow of white wine in order to knock us out and allow for some much-needed rest. We stripped off our clothes, crawled under the covers, and soon were fast asleep, utterly exhausted. Sex did not even cross my mind.

I slept for 14 solid hours. When I awoke at noon, Debbie had one arm and one leg wrapped around me and was snuggled up as close as she could manage. Her long blonde hair was naturally thick and wavy and somewhat disheveled. It flowed over her shoulders and cascaded across her face. Damn, she looked good.

I gently touched her shoulder, and her skin felt as soft as velvet. I hugged her and she finally opened her eyes and smiled. We made love and then showered together. It felt wonderful to take a shower, brush my teeth, and put on some clean clothes.

Debbie fixed us bowls of raisin bran and poured two glasses of orange juice. It was difficult to choke even that light breakfast down, and I had to force-feed myself in the interest of eating something. Rick was nowhere to be found, and Donna and Becky looked like death warmed over and were fading fast. They said Rick had gone out for a pack of cigarettes several hours ago and had never returned. Both said that they were tired of waiting for him and were ready to crash. They headed off to bed.

It was just about 1 p.m. when we bid them good night. As they headed for their bedrooms, they reminded me of two pale zombies descending to their lairs in the catacombs.

We'd just finished eating our cereal when Rick walked into the apartment with a wide grin fixed on his face. His eyes were so dilated that they looked like big black pools of oil; there were no retinas, just black pupils. He'd scored some LSD and was "tripping" and talking weird.

He began excitedly telling us that he'd met a dog that talked to him in Spanish, and even though he didn't know Spanish, he was somehow able to completely understand every word the dog said.

Rick was dead serious, but I couldn't contain myself. I spontaneously broke out into loud laughter—and so did Debbie. I finally quit laughing enough to manage to ask, "Was it a Chihuahua?"

Debbie and I burst into hearty laughter again.

He ignored my question and furrowed his brow as though preoccupied with analyzing and thinking through some profound matter of extreme import. As he continued to think, without so much as saying a word or even looking us in the eye, he extended his arm toward us. He was holding a little bag of white capsules and was shaking his hand impatiently toward us as though he wanted us to take the bag. He was offering Debbie and me LSD as though it was a buttered bagel to go along with our breakfast.

He seemed to be thinking on two levels. It was quite bizarre. On one level he was he trying to convince us to "drop" some acid with him. But it was obvious that he was also deeply immersed in thought, trying to solve some complex puzzle swirling through his mind on a completely different level.

Debbie and I looked at each other and then back at Rick, who was still standing there with his hand extended. He was impatiently waiting for us to take some LSD, but he wasn't looking at us and was obviously engrossed in deep thought.

Still not making eye contact with either of us and appearing to be resolving the most complicated and complex problem currently facing the world, Rick finally spoke. He tolerantly recited in a slow monotone as though he was dealing with vastly inferior intellects, "If you want to know what the dog told me, you must partake, *amigos.*"

Debbie punched me in the side, and when I looked at her she was grinning and rolling her eyes. She shook her head no.

Rick was obviously talking out of his mind; but judging from the grin that had become a permanent fixture on his face, he appeared to be having the time of his life. I had never taken LSD before and actually knew precious little about it. I had heard that it was mind-expanding and opened up levels of consciousness that were not obtainable in any other way. That sounded good to me. My mind could use some expansion.

Rick said, "I feel wonderful," and then like a schizophrenic nearly cried as he emotionally begged us to join him, whining that he didn't want to have this experience alone.

I didn't need a lot of convincing. I said, "What the hell, Rick. Maybe we'll meet a Chinese-speaking dog this time and convince him to guide us to the local opium den in Chinatown so we can get turned on to some of that high-grade opium they smoke down there."

Rick did not respond. I saluted him and said, "Captain Rick, I'm officially ready to blast off. Gimme a tab of that acid."

This time Debbie rolled her eyes at me and laughed, "Oh all right! Give me one too."

I smiled approvingly. I was delighted that she was going on the trip with us, and we took two of the pills out of Rick's little plastic bag and returned it to his still-outstretched hand.

The LSD was in the form of a white capsule, and its street name was white lightning. Debbie had taken LSD several times before and said it was rare to find it in capsule form. Most acid came in the form of a little blue or orange microdot blot on a piece of paper or a sugar cube. She'd heard on the street that white lightning was awesome.

I said, "Well my dear, we shall soon find out. Bombs away!" And with that, I popped one into my mouth and took a swig of orange juice to wash it down. Debbie followed my lead and we were ready for takeoff.

Suddenly Rick looked around and asked, "Where are Donna and Becky? They need to be turned on too."

Debbie quickly answered, "They crashed, Rick."

He started walking toward their room, worriedly stating, "We mustn't leave them behind," as though we were all getting ready to depart for Jupiter or some other galactic destination and our entire commune must prepare to go together.

Debbie was not about to go for any of that. She sternly warned him off, saying, "NO RICK! Let them sleep. They're burned out."

He looked like a puppy that'd just been firmly admonished by his master. He meekly nodded okay, still with that wide grin plastered on his face. Then he weakly stammered his final argument: "If they only knew what I know they would wake up and go with us."

Debbie was resolute, "I'm sure they would Rick, but we aren't going down that road!"

Rick never heard her response because for some strange reason known only to him he suddenly changed gears in his mind and was now totally engrossed and engaged in dancing by himself to the Jefferson Airplane music loudly blaring on the stereo.

Debbie and I began laughing at how silly he looked whirling around and around, holding one hand on his stomach and the other high above his head, snapping his fingers. He was stomping his feet, whirling, and rapidly snapping. A short drum solo was hammering in the background and he was wildly gyrating his hips in a vain attempt to keep time with the rapid drumbeat. He nearly fell down.

Rick reminded me of a cross between an Arabian belly dancer in a trance, a psychotic Hawaiian hula dancer, and a Broadway ballerina star wired up on speed. I wondered too if perhaps the Spanish-speaking dog had instructed him to attempt a flamenco dance as if he were a Mexican señorita. His "dance routine" contained elements of all the foregoing.

It didn't take long for Debbie and me to begin to feel the effects of the powerful acid, and soon we began catching up to Rick. At first I felt kind of nervous and jumpy, and then after about 30 minutes, wonderful waves of rushes started swirling through my mind. I started feeling terrific.

Debbie had told me that after about an hour and a half we would begin to "peak" and reach the zenith of the effects. I already felt wonderful and wondered how peaking could possibly be any better than this.

I soon found out.

About an hour into the trip, it was as though someone suddenly flipped a light switch on in my brain and—*PING*—everything I saw was exceedingly brilliant. It was as though I'd been in a darkened, dimly lit room and now dazzling bright lights had suddenly come on. Colors looked like beautiful, glowing, neon lights.

All color was absolutely breathtaking. Even the wooden coffee table was no longer an ordinary wood color. Now its color was beautiful, intense, and vivid, like it was "live" neon. All my sensations were expanded beyond normal. I looked around the room, and the curtains, chairs, walls, and especially the Oriental rug were all dazzling and radiantly glowing. The walls were especially gorgeous and appeared to be breathing in and out in time to the music.

Abruptly I could now actually *feel* the powerful deep colors throughout the room. I not only saw these intense colors but could actually *feel* them permeating and pulsating throughout my body in time to the music. There were colors of every description, some of which were not even in the spectrum and for which there were no names.

Suddenly I could now *smell* the colors. Their sweet-smelling, aromatic fragrance was like a sniff of expensive perfume. It was amazing. Of all things, I was actually becoming sexually stimulated by *smelling* color.

It was astonishing, astounding, remarkable, incredible, mind-blowing, staggering, wonderful, marvelous, mind-boggling; hell did I leave anything out? It was fantastic.

I could see, feel, smell, touch and now even *hear* beautiful colors of every description. The color was making a crackling noise, like kindling burning in a fire. Best of all, it turned me on like I'd never been turned on before.

As I looked around at my surroundings in amazement, I realized that I was grinning wider than Rick! I looked at Debbie and a wide smile was now fixated on her face too. We were all tripping! Somehow, even as he was totally preoccupied and engaged in his frantic dance routine, Rick was perceptive enough to notice that we were now "with him" and incredulously managed a grin even wider than before. He danced over to us, first using a big sliding side step and then tiny little step-over-step-over-steps to where we stood. He stopped right beside us with one arm still suspended above his head and the other on his stomach. Still grinning, he said in a mysterious, weird-sounding voice using a fake British accent, "Welcome to my world."

We decided to go outside, and when we walked out the door it was even more fabulous. The street was a most beautiful bluish-gray color, intense beyond imagination, gorgeously illuminated and glowing with radiant color. It looked like a fresh lava flow of intense color streaming down the side of a volcano. The street was so beautiful that I actually hated to walk on it. The apartments, shops, and sidewalks along both sides of the streets were all lit up. The posters that were on nearly every street corner signpost shone intensely, like beautiful colored beacons—little psychedelic lighthouses glowing brightly.

We saw some hippies dressed in appropriately eclectic garb—flowered headbands, brightly colored robes, and beads—standing in front of a head shop, nodding approvingly at the smiles on our faces. As we passed by, grinning from ear to ear, they knowingly smiled back at us and flashed us the peace sign. As they looked on, they were obviously envious of our enlightened state and had no doubt visited this psychedelic world many times themselves. They seemed to know exactly what was happening in our brains.

"Far out!" we exclaimed over and over again as we pointed out various sights and sounds to each other. *"OH WOW!"*

Rick wanted to go to the Straight Theater, located at the intersection of Haight and Cole. He told us that it was a "trip center": a place for those who have launched their minds on psychedelic drugs and can enhance their trip within a multimedia center of light and music. Lots of big-name bands had played there, including the Grateful Dead, Jefferson Airplane, Big Brother, Country Joe, and others, but today it was limited to music on the stereo. We didn't care if a live band or a record player was blasting, and would never have known the difference anyway.

Inside, someone had strewn some floor mats about on the large dance floor. Three large projection screens filled the walls. Each screen was designed for the enjoyment of different types of drugs—the kind of trip you were taking determined which screen you'd watch.

The screen on the right wall had bands of colors—a horizontal rainbow—ever so slowly streaming across the wall in an endless rivulet of peaceful, harmonious colors. In addition to the rainbow effect, sometimes you'd see a purplish mountain range and at other times what looked like a host of random but very complementary colors of every value creatively woven together and gently streaming a soft, gorgeous hue ever so slowly across the giant screen. The slow, billowy colors suited themselves nicely to mescaline, psilocybin, peyote, and similar mellow psychedelics—drugs that offered more sedate trips for participants who preferred to just lie back and groove.

The center screen was the largest and they had it synced up to the rock-and-roll music that was blasting out of the giant speakers surrounding the theater. The wilder LSD, PCP, and STP trips suited it better, with a myriad of colors dancing in time to the rock and roll. They bubbled up, splashed, appeared, and then faded away; and they danced their way all over the screen. Intricate, psychedelic patterns, shaped like magnified, colorful snowflakes, would appear, enlarge, and then disappear to the music's beat. Or at other times you'd see spinning wheels of color or intricate designs of bright colors blanketing the screen in rectangular or square shapes.

The left-wall screen was solid white. Something resembling a huge drop of water would appear in the center of the screen. Then a solitary, tiny drop of a powerful transparent red dye would land in the center of the crystal-clear water and ever so slowly begin billowing and swirling its way throughout. It really looked cool, and the brilliant hues of color were breathtaking. After the color billowed and permeated its way throughout the giant water drop, the process would repeat—only this time another color would drop into it. The scene repeated itself over and over again. It appealed to just about every drug user in the place, and I found myself intensely staring at it as much as any of the screens.

I preferred to just lie back on the floor mats and grin up at the colors on the screens so I could dig the music that was reverberating within and without. I was on LSD, but all the screens looked good to me. Rick and Debbie were more in a dancing mood and were doing so in fever pitch. They were not dancing together, mind you—no one was dancing with someone else. In fact no one in their right mind would even refer to what they were doing as dancing. Instead it appeared that those who were "dancing" were stark raving mad as they independently jumped around in the air, gyrating and whirling their arms about in what I would describe as a frenzied, maniacal state with no relation to the music's beat or melody.

Rick had sweat pouring off his face and was so engrossed in his dance that he appeared to be caught up in some mystical stupor. Finally, after several hours of this, Rick danced over to where I was lying and plopped down next to me on the mat. He was wearing pointed-toe, Italian-looking boots that came up just above his ankles. He had hidden his stash of LSD there. He told me that he was going to drop another tab of acid and asked if I wanted one too. I said, "Sure," and he unzipped his boot and pulled out his plastic bag of LSD capsules.

There was a big problem. The heat buildup from all of Rick's frenzied dancing for hour upon hour had melted the capsules together. We could no longer regulate the dosage by taking a single capsule, because the capsules were now one big thick glob. Rick resolved the problem by simply tearing off a big chunk and eating it. I did likewise. Debbie came over and we tore off a chunk for her too. I only briefly wondered if someone could overdose on LSD and then quickly became engrossed in the light show again and forgot about it.

We finally decided to leave the Straight Theater and ended up in a little coffee shop located at the lower end of the Haight. Music was playing loudly on a jukebox and suddenly beautiful multicolored music notes began streaming out of it into the air. They floated up in a glittering, gentle whirlwind, arcing toward the ceiling in a kaleidoscopic array, pulsating in time to the music. I excitedly pointed at the jukebox and yelled, "Far out! Check it out."

Rick quizzically looked at me as I pointed and said, "Look! Colored music notes are drifting out of the jukebox."

Rick turned around and looked. Then he looked back at me and dispassionately said, "Yeah man I see 'em. Cool, man."

He turned around again and was furiously puffing on a cigarette without even inhaling. He puffed in and out, in and out, in and out, emitting billows of smoke like an old-time locomotive's smokestack as it strained to climb up a hill. His foot was rapidly dancing up and down and he was staring at nothing.

Rick's apathetic demeanor made me think he wasn't sincere about seeing the music notes, so I quickly looked at Debbie to see if she saw them. But she hadn't heard a word I'd said. She was sitting there with a studious look on her face, muttering something about visiting the pyramids of Egypt and talking to a mysterious visionary. She said he was a little buck-toothed Negro kid with gray hair who told her that he could make known to her ancient laws that would unlock the door to everlasting life, but he should not do so, because it would kill us all.

Huh?

The music notes caught my attention again as they drifted throughout the room and began covering the white ceiling like thousands of shimmering, multicolored, luminous butterflies. It looked as though they were softly alighting on a field of dazzling white roses. I could easily smell the flowers' pungent fragrance. The ceiling—white roses covered with colorful music notes—softly undulated in time with the music as if a gentle breeze was flowing through it.

Suddenly the butterfly notes all took off and began fluttering down like living confetti all over the room. Hundreds of thousands of them floated up and down, whirling around each other like little partners dancing in time to the music. Everywhere tiny music notes, resplendent in vibrant glory, glistened with flashing, burning color—sparkling diamonds with bright iridescent colors vividly reflecting in the brilliant, rich white light. It was intense and penetrated my mind and traversed my spine from one end to the other and back. I felt like crying.

Just then the song on the jukebox ended. *WHOOSH!* From all over the room the colored music notes began surging back into the jukebox, creating an iridescent stream of gushing color that was shaped like a comet. The comet had a long, multihued tail curling and whipping back and forth behind as it streaked through the room at mind-boggling speed. I could hear the colors crackling loudly, just like bacon sizzling, as they hurriedly streamed along and attempted to get back inside the jukebox. It was an absolutely stunning sight.

I yelled, "Far-r-r-r out!"

No one even looked up at me.

It was just breaking dawn and we decided to walk into Golden Gate Park, which was adjacent to the Haight. We entered the park through a concrete tunnel, and as I entered the tunnel I began to have a religious experience. I just knew I was entering into heaven and I couldn't wait to reach the other side of the tunnel to see what it would be like.

As I emerged from the tunnel into the park, I knew that I had arrived in heaven. The green, lush grass and giant sequoias and redwood trees majestically glistened in the morning sun—it was indeed heavenly.

Just then I saw a beautiful young virgin in a long, flowing, white wedding gown, gracefully dancing and skipping along through the green grass to meet me, her bridegroom to be. Don't ask me how I knew she was a virgin or my new bride. I just *knew*. Her magnificent long blonde hair was streaming back behind her shoulders and she was radiantly smiling at me. With arms outstretched, she skipped her way toward me, all the while looking at me with the most intense, beautiful, penetrating deep-blue eyes I'd ever seen.

I left the others behind and took off, joyfully skipping my way toward her through the glowing, green grass, still wet with the morning dew. As I approached her, I spread my arms open to hug her and I was grinning from ear to ear. I longed to hold her and just as I reached for her . . .

She wasn't there.

"Far-r-r-r out!" I smiled widely as I looked around in wonderment at where she might have gone. "Far out!"

I lost track of time as we wandered around, enjoying the beauty and vibrant colors of the gorgeous park. I'm sure our foray into Golden Gate Park lasted several hours, but time had little meaning to us.

Afterward we went back to Debbie's pad. The peak had long since passed and now it felt more like I was coming down from a long speed trip. This was a jittery, nervous, crappy feeling. It was like I wanted something but didn't know what it was. I needed to be fulfilled, but didn't know how to do it. Debbie had some downers and we each took a couple of them, but they had little effect. I was jittery-nervous for hours. I took several more pills and smoked several more joints of weed before sleep finally came, and then only fitfully as my dreams grew dark.

CHAPTER THIRTY-TWO

After only a couple of hours sleep, I woke up jumpy-nervy. I'd enjoyed my LSD trip very much, but I didn't want to go on another one anytime soon. Tripping was very intense and took a lot out of me. My nerves were shot. I looked at Debbie and she was still fast asleep. Rick had crashed on the couch and was loudly snoring and the other girls were nowhere to be seen.

I needed to find a fake ID so I decided to hit the streets. I walked down to the middle of the Haight to ask around, and soon was directed to a guy who worked at a head shop a couple of blocks over. He had long, thin, straight hair that hung down far below his shoulders, and he was dressed in a tie-dyed shirt and blue jeans.

He didn't ask why I needed an ID but told me that he charged $25 for a California driver's license complete with photograph and whatever name and address that I wanted on it. He'd throw in a Social Security card to match, he said.

I was using the alias Bob Johnson and told him to make the card for Robert Leroy Johnson. I chose this name in honor of Mississippi delta blues legend Robert Johnson, who died at the age of 27. He had no equal on blues guitar and some said that he made a deal with the devil—his soul in exchange for tremendous guitar-playing ability.

Long Hair took my photograph and I gave him my date of birth and Debbie's address. He wanted me to pay him the $25 in advance and I sarcastically said, "Yeah right!" I offered a deposit of $10 instead. He put up a brief argument, but when I started putting the $10 back in my wallet, he quickly yielded.

He told me I could pick up my new ID the next morning and then he angrily said, "You'd *better* have the rest of the money tomorrow."

I angrily responded, "Oh yeah, and what'll happen if I don't? You gonna beat me up tough guy? *How 'bout we get started right now?*" I started to climb over the counter, ready to beat the shit out of him.

He looked stunned at my aggressive response and quickly held up his hand and with a weak smile said, "Hold on a minute man. Calm down, calm down. I'm sorry. It's just that I got no use for someone else's ID. You know what I'm talkin' about. You can understand that, can't you man? I mean once it's made, it's made. People down here come and go man. I usually get all the money up front's all. I'm not trying to make waves here. I trust you for it man. Peace, man. Peace."

I gave him a dark look and tersely said, "I'll be back tomorrow for my ID and you'd *better* have it ready."

He looked like he was going to shit himself and I smiled and said, "Just kiddin'. Peace, man. Peace," and I flashed him the peace sign.

He looked relieved and we smiled at each other.

I walked back onto the street. That skinny faggot-looking creep will be lucky if I don't knock his teeth right out of his smart-ass mouth tomorrow. He's definitely messing with the wrong person; I'm in no mood for anyone's shit.

Before returning to Debbie's place I bought some clothes that were more in keeping with the clothes worn by the people in the Haight. I couldn't bring myself to go with the psychedelic tie-dyed look, but I did buy a couple of pairs of jeans, casual shirts, some Hush Puppy style shoes, and a brown hat similar in design to the ones that rock stars like Hendrix were wearing. My hair was ridiculously short, but my beard, although it itched like hell, was coming along nicely.

When I arrived back at the apartment, Debbie was awake and was frantically crying. When she saw me, she quickly came running and threw her arms around me and sobbed, "I thought you left me and weren't coming back."

Baffled, I responded, "You were asleep and I didn't want to wake you. I just went to the store to pick up some things. What are you talking about?"

She cried, "I woke up and you were gone, and I panicked."

I looked at Rick, who was awake and smoking a cigarette. He was sitting there smiling at me, obviously amused by the spectacle that was unfolding.

Warning signs popped up all over my brain about this situation. I wasn't about to become involved with another woman anytime soon and let her screw me over. I was now a free spirit and had every intention of remaining that way. Then I thought, *Yeah, but I don't want to blow her off just yet, either*. Debbie did have a nice apartment and plenty of money, courtesy of her father back in Rhode Island. Not only that, but she was beautiful, good in bed, and fun to get high with; plus, she knew her way around the Haight.

I smiled at her and smoothly lied, "I'd never leave you Debbie. We're a team now. Didn't you see that my clothes were still in *our* room?"

Without answering she hugged me even tighter and buried her face in my chest. She softly whimpered that she loved me as I gently rubbed her back and soft hair. I winked at Rick, who was rolling his eyes at me and trying to keep from laughing at my cornball act.

I said, "How about fixing us some cereal? Do we have any left?"

"No, I need to go to the store. I'll be right back." She grabbed her purse and headed for the door and then stopped and looked back at me with apprehension. "Don't you go anywhere without me."

"I'm not going anywhere, Debbie. Don't be silly."

Obviously relieved and happy now, she smiled widely and left. No sooner had the door shut behind her than Rick burst into laughter and mimicked me: "I'm not going anywhere without you Debbie. We're a team now." More laughter.

"Ha-ha," I said. "Very funny! You can say what you like, my man, but we have a roof over our heads and breakfast will be served momentarily. What was up with that anyway?"

He smiled and said, "It was amazing. She woke me up out of a dead sleep in a panic asking where you were and has been hysterical for an hour. I don't know what kind of spell you cast on her, old son, but she's gut-hooked crazy about you."

"Yeah, the problem with that is I don't want her or any woman tying me down. Man, I'm the original free spirit and want to remain so for the rest of my life."

"I heard that!" Rick smiled. "You and me both, bro."

The next day I managed to free myself from the others long enough to pick up my new ID. Long Hair, whose name was actually Steve, had lost the smart-ass attitude and was now all smiles. He gave me a couple of joints of Jamaican weed, "on the house," and told me it was dynamite stuff. We smoked a joint of it together and I had to agree that it was definitely some good weed. He showed me the new ID and compared it to his own driver's license, which was authentic. It looked identical. The Social Security card looked identical too. I congratulated him on the good job, and he beamed.

I paid him the rest of the money and apologized for getting riled. He told me that he shouldn't have said what he said and that he was glad everything was cool now. We shook hands and said goodbye. As I walked out the door, I smiled and flashed the peace sign at him and said, "Peace, man. Peace."

He laughed and flashed it back at me and said, "Peace, man. Peace."

I'd decided not to tell anyone about being AWOL or obtaining the fake ID. My new friends knew me as Bob Johnson, and now if required I could confirm it with my driver's license and Social Security card.

I knew that the most likely way I'd be caught was if someone were to rat me out; so if people didn't know my secret, my odds of being caught would go down. I didn't trust anyone, including Rick and Debbie. Since I'd gone AWOL, I hadn't called a single person at home, including my brother and parents, and I had no intention of doing so. No one knew my true identity or my whereabouts—and I wanted to keep it that way.

For the next several weeks Debbie, Rick, and I were inseparable. Rick couldn't seem to hit it off with Debbie's roommates, and one day I found out why. Debbie matter-of-factly told me that they were lesbians. It didn't matter to Rick, because all he cared about was drugs. Had he wanted sex, he could have easily obtained it from hundreds of girls on the street. "Free love" was the norm in the Haight. Having sex was referred to as "balling" and everyone was balling as nonchalantly as smoking a joint together.

Actually, drugs were better than sex and we spent the major portion of every day scoring drugs and getting high. We tried every drug that one could imagine. We took all the psychedelics—peyote, psilocybin, mescaline, LSD, and even STP, which I didn't like because it was just too powerful and left me drained. We tried the "nod" drugs, like heroin, opium, Dilaudid, Nembutal, and Seconal. I didn't particularly like downers, except to assist with coming down from acid or speed.

What I really liked was flying high on speed—especially crystal meth—and we would literally stay up for days at a time shooting up and then cruising through the Haight. Everyone smoked pot and hashish daily, and wine was our drink of choice. Like everyone else in the Haight, we stayed stoned every waking moment and our day was totally devoted to finding and taking drugs nonstop.

One day Rick came in and excitedly told me that he could get a super deal on our favorite form of LSD, white lightning. We had to buy $1,000 worth, but he said he could buy it for $1 per cap instead of its street price of $4. I had about $400 left and he had $200. Debbie said she could come up with the rest. Rick said that he heard that it was going for $10 to $12 a tab in Seattle, and suggested that we make a run up there in his dilapidated old car and make a pile of easy money.

We all agreed and within 10 minutes of coming up with the idea, Rick had scored the LSD and we were on the road. When we rolled into Portland, Oregon, Rick's piece of crap car was emitting huge plumes of white, misty smoke from the tailpipe. We pulled over on a side street in downtown Portland as steam was pouring out from under the hood. The car had been running hot for several miles, and Rick didn't bother to stop because he wanted to make it into Portland. When he finally did stop, it died! The engine had become so hot that it had seized up and wouldn't even turn over.

I thought to myself, *Now what?* We had enough LSD on us to turn on half the state of Oregon, but we had only about $50 cash left between us, and that was probably not enough for us all to take a bus to Seattle. It wouldn't be practical for the three of us to hitchhike together, either. It was hard enough for one person to catch a ride much less three, and besides, the police often searched hitchhikers. That much LSD would be a major felony and would carry a distribution charge.

I feared that if we were picked up, they'd soon discover that I was AWOL. The penalty for that alone would put me in the stockade for years. Tag the distribution charge on there and I wouldn't see daylight again until I was an old man. I was mulling over our dilemma and trying to decide what to do when I happened to notice that Rick's eyes were completely dilated.

"Damn!"

Obviously Rick had dropped some of our acid on the sly and was now tripping. This burned me up and I was becoming totally paranoid. Here we were, carrying nearly a thousand tabs of acid, stuck downtown with a zonked-out car, with Rick tripping on LSD and acting like some loony.

I whispered to Debbie that we needed to dump Rick and go it alone. Being in the Haight with 100,000 other stoned-out freaks is one thing, but Portland was from all appearances a "straight" city and we stood out like apples in an orange bin. She nodded her agreement.

I told Rick that I thought it was best for us to split up. Deb and I would take the acid and go on to Seattle and would meet up with him there. By now he was completely oblivious to what was going on and he just smiled at me and said, "Cool, man."

We grabbed our bags from his car and left him standing there on the street corner. As we walked away from him, he was looking up at the sky with a big grin on his face, saying over and over again, "Cool, man," and everyone who passed him was looking at him as if he were insane.

Debbie and I began making our way toward the bus station. We stopped at a sandwich shop to grab a bite to eat and plan our strategy. I suggested to Debbie that she take the bus back to San Francisco so I could take one on to Seattle alone and sell the acid. I would then fly back to the Haight with the money and we'd get high for the next year.

She was not keen on the idea, but she'd been worried sick that she really shouldn't have come with us in the first place. Her apartment was in her dad's name, and she needed to be there to take care of it and keep her roommates from turning it into a den of lesbos or perhaps stealing her stuff. Further, she was supposed to be enrolling at Berkeley, which was her purported reason for even being out there in the first place. She'd been putting off enrolling and her dad was threatening to come out and check up on her—and if he saw where she lived in the Haight, that would be the end of it.

I told her not to worry. If necessary I would even sell the drugs at a discount in order to quickly be back home in a matter of just a few days. She reluctantly agreed and we went to the bus station.

We bought two bus tickets—hers to San Francisco and mine to Seattle. Debbie teared up as we kissed each other goodbye. I brushed aside her tear and told her, "Now don't be going bonkers on me. We'll be back together again before you know it." When she boarded her bus, I waved goodbye and blew her a kiss. She was bawling like a baby as she waved back at me.

As for me, I couldn't believe my incredible good fortune. I had over 10 grand in drugs and with Rick and now Debbie out of the way I wouldn't have to share it with anyone.

Chapter Thirty-Three

I arrived in Seattle in the middle of a pouring-down rainstorm. Bus stations seem to attract street people, and sure enough I saw a hippie-looking guy standing outside, so I walked over to him and said, "How's things?"

He nodded to me and said, "Everything's cool. What's up with you?"

"I just got into town." I stuck out my hand, "Bob."

Disinterestedly, he limply shook my hand, "Mike."

"I'm trying to score some acid. You know where I can get some?"

His eyes lit up. "Yeah, actually I do. I'm heading that way now if you want to come along."

I asked, "What's a tab goin' for?"

"About $4."

I thought about Rick excitedly telling us that it goes for $12 a tab. *That stupid idiot!* That's what it's going for in the Haight. I'd be lucky to sell my stash in quantity for two bucks a tab.

Mike and I entered a crummy little apartment in a rundown building in a seedy section of town, where several long-haired people were sitting around smoking a joint. They all knew Mike and they passed the joint to us. There were no formal introductions because no one gave a crap. Street people just come and go. Mike asked if anyone knew where we could score some acid and one of them said, "I heard Sandy has some."

I quizzically looked at Mike and he said, "Sandy works the street right around the corner. I'll intro you if you'll turn me on to a tab too."

I responded, "You got it. I don't want to trip alone anyway."

Mike and I left and soon found Sandy standing outside a tenement building under a door stoop just barely out of the relentless rain. Sandy was a huge black man.

Mike said, "Sandy, Bob. Bob, Sandy." We curtly nodded to each other and Mike said, "Bob wants to score some acid."

Sandy was at least six-foot-three, muscular, and intimidating. His huge arms were covered with jailhouse tattoos that were barely distinguishable on his jet-black arms. His appearance and prison-hardened look left little doubt that he was menacing-mean. He carefully looked me up and down with penetrating eyes and then nonchalantly said, "Four bucks."

I decided to just cut to the chase. I said, "Actually, Sandy, I want to sell you some acid in quantity. I have a thousand tabs of white lightning, and I'll sell it to you right now for two bucks a tab if you'll take it all."

Mike, who'd been chewing and popping his gum like a speed freak, coughed and nearly choked on it. He wasn't expecting that.

Sandy looked at me with those mean black eyes and said, "I may have some interest in that." He briefly glanced at Mike and told him in a deep, menacing voice, "Get lost!"

I pushed a cap of acid into Mike's hand and said, "Thanks, Mike."

He nodded appreciatively and headed down the street.

Sandy gruffly said, "Follow me."

I followed him for several blocks and we stepped into a deserted building that had been boarded up, but several of the boards had been torn back enough to allow entry. Inside it was dimly lit and rain was leaking through the roof in places. Empty wine bottles and debris were scattered everywhere, and I could smell human waste.

Sandy turned around and was pointing a .45 caliber automatic right between my eyes.

"Whoa!" I said. "What's up with this?"

Sandy said, "Let's see that stash, *boy*."

"Easy man, no problem." I pulled out a plastic bag full of white capsules and handed it over to him.

I was standing there looking down the barrel of his gun and Sandy said, "You want to live or die?"

"I want to live."

"Then get the fuck out of here and don't never come back no more. The next time I see your white honky ass, I'll bust a cap on you."

Oddly I wasn't experiencing fear for my life, rather sheer *rage*. I wanted to kill that black son of a bitch for ripping me off, but I was the one looking down the barrel of a gun. It would've been suicide to rush him. He had my drugs and he had the gun. And from all appearances, I believed that he'd use it. All I could do was back down like a little whipped puppy.

I slowly backed toward the makeshift door opening with both my hands held high in the air. I was watching for any opportunity to make a grab for the gun, but he carefully followed me step for step, always maintaining a distance of about six feet between us, not wavering and keeping the gun aimed right between my eyes the entire time.

Finally I backed all the way out of the building and into the street.

From the shadows inside he snarled, "Now get the hell out of here and don't you ever come back or I'll kill your honky ass."

I walked back toward the bus station in the pelting rain. How could I have been so *stupid*? Aside from nearly getting killed, I'd lost my entire stash. My lame attempt at drug dealing had been the height of incompetence. I should've had my own gun and I should've set up an exchange through that guy Mike or someone else. And I should've never brought my stash with me until I saw some money. Now I had five bucks to my name and was on unfamiliar turf.

Shit!

I was seething with anger for allowing this ignorant, uneducated, criminal street dealer to outsmart me.

Damn it!

I headed back to the bus station because it was really the only place I knew to go. I saw a guy standing outside who was wearing nice clothes, as if he might be working on Wall Street. He had on a black trench coat and, of all things, wingtip shoes. In contrast to his attire, his thick, curly black hair was unkempt, and he was unshaven. He looked oddly out of place hanging out at a bus station with street people. For one thing he was overweight, with an overhanging belly and fat, rosy cheeks—something you rarely see on the street.

He greeted me like I was his long-lost friend from days gone by, and with outstretched hand said in a friendly tone, "Hi, I'm John."

I was in no mood for small talk but instinctively reached out and shook hands with him. "Bob," I wearily replied.

Some people I can just look at and instantly like. John was such a person. Even though I'd just been robbed of my entire net worth at gunpoint and was in a foul mood, I was disarmed by this very likable guy and drawn to him like an inquisitive kid to a clown.

He pulled out a bottle of wine from under his trench coat and asked if I wanted some.

I responded, "Yeah. *Hell, yeah!* Why not?"

I took a big drink and returned it to him and he took a big swig.

He asked me where I was from and I dolefully replied, "Nowhere in particular. How about you?"

"I'm from Oklahoma City."

We continued to pass the bottle back and forth several more times as he told me a hilariously funny story about how and why he came to be standing on the streets of Seattle, Washington, outside a bus station drinking bottle after bottle of cheap wine.

It turns out that John's father owned the largest newspaper in Oklahoma City and he worked there in a senior position. He told me that he had dropped out of sight and left over a week ago because he owed a small amount of taxes to the IRS. He thought the taxes were unfair and in protest he refused to pay them. He could have easily afforded to pay the tax bill, or had one of his father's fancy lawyers fight it, but instead he just decided to take off and drop out of society. He said, "Screw the IRS, I ain't paying."

I looked at him and said, "You're kidding me, right? Let me get this straight. Your daddy is rich and you owe a few hundred dollars in taxes, but you refuse to pay, not because of the money, but because of the *principle* of the thing, and now you're on the run?"

He took a big swig of wine, pursed his lips as he swallowed, and through squinted eyes looked at me and said, "Bob, my newfound friend, that just about sums it up."

I cracked up laughing. "Far out! A tax protestor."

He laughed too and grinned at me with his charming boyish grin, and we instantly bonded. He asked, "Well, what's your story?"

My mood instantly changed and I said, "My story's a lot darker than yours, John. I don't want to talk about it. We won't be going there!"

John looked at me as though he might make light of it or pursue it, but one look at my eyes and I suppose he thought better of it. He let it drop, and then asked if I was hungry. I said yeah, but I was about broke.

"No problem, Bob. Let me show you how this is done."

We walked into a nearby restaurant, and John immediately embarrassed the hell out of me as he made a big production out of putting one hand on his stomach and making a flowery, sweeping gesture with the other. He bowed exceedingly low to a middle-aged waitress and said in a most dignified and eloquent manner, "Ma'am I wonder if you might help my friend and me. You see, at the moment we happen to be down on our luck and temporarily out of a job for the first time in our lives, so we find ourselves in the embarrassing situation of not having any funds.

"We would like to inquire as to whether or not we might be able to wash dishes today in exchange for one of your delicious meals. If you afford us this opportunity, I can assure you that we are both excellent and trustworthy workers and you will no doubt find that we will work exceedingly hard to repay your generosity and make you proud of the job that we have done."

The waitress melted like one of her grilled-cheese sandwiches. She said, "Come over here," and led us to a booth. She gave us each a menu and told us to order anything that we wanted, and that this meal was on her and we wouldn't be washing any dishes—they already had someone to do that.

John reached for her hand and kissed it and gushed his thankfulness like a fawning little ass-kisser. This entire episode embarrassed the crap out of me, but what the heck—it worked. We each ate a salad, the biggest steak on the menu, and fries. Then we topped it off with a large piece of lemon meringue pie for dessert, which she insisted we have.

John feigned an attempt at wanting to wash dishes or help sweep up, or perhaps mop or do *something*, but the waitress would have no part of it. She even gave us $10 from her tip jar and told us that she hoped things turned around for us. John again did his pretentious bowing routine and effusively groveled his most sincere appreciation, kissing her hand again. She smiled and hugged him like he might have been her only son going off to war, and then she hugged me.

When we left, John told me that he'd never had to wash the first dish. He looked at me and said, "I say we take this $10 and find another bottle of wine or two. What say you?"

"I say that's an excellent idea."

It finally let up raining and we shared another bottle of wine sitting in front of someone's house on their front porch steps. I asked John if he had a plan, and he did not. I told him that I'd been thinking of going into Vancouver, British Columbia, a busy port city, so I could land a job with the Merchant Marines. When I worked on the oil rigs, I'd heard that huge sums of money could be made because the ships would leave for months at a time and go to some distant land and finally back to home port and a big payday.

The work was easy, I'd heard, and consisted mostly of chipping away old paint and then repainting. While under way there was little or nothing to spend your money on, and when you returned to port there were heaps of cash awaiting you.

John did not look to be the type for manual labor or rugged adventure, but he smiled and said it sounded good to him. I didn't share with John that I also wanted to get out of the United States and on into Canada as a precaution. Canada was against the Vietnam War; and according to word in the hippie community, it was fast becoming a haven for draft dodgers. I assumed that included those who were AWOL as well. Soon I would be classified as a deserter, and if I was caught, it would no doubt be some serious shit to deal with. Better to leave the country while I'm in the area and near the border.

In the words of someone who no doubt was in a similar dire situation, "I needed to get out while the getting was good."

I figured that I could make Canada my home base and ship in and out of there in the Merchant Marines, see the world, and make lots of money. Besides, I liked the ocean.

There was one small problem, however. How were we going to get from Seattle to Vancouver? I suggested hitchhiking, but John said that Washington State was one of the few states that didn't allow hitchhiking and they strictly enforced the ban. He suggested that we hop a freight.

"Hop a freight? Are you kidding me?"

John said, "Yes, hop a freight. It's easy. How do you think I got here?"

I looked at him to see if he was trying to blow smoke, but he was serious. He'd already proven that he knew what he was talking about regarding hustling a free meal, and I had no reason to doubt him now.

"What the hell," I said. "Let's go hop a freight."

We picked up two more large bottles of wine and made our way down to the freight yard. We saw a railroad worker and John walked right up to him and asked him when the next train to Vancouver was leaving. To my utter amazement he told us there would be one leaving at 6 p.m. and pointed the way to the tracks from which it would be departing. John merely beamed an "I told you so" smile at me, and we headed in that direction.

John informed me that the only concern in hopping freights was rail-yard "bulls." They are the private cops, employed by the railroad companies, that patrol the yards. We would need to stay on the outskirts of the railroad's property and catch the trains after they left the property, or they would bust us sure as heck. Regular railroad workers could care less, but the bulls were not to be messed with, because they would take you to jail and sometimes beat the crap out of you with billy clubs in the process.

John explained that hopping the freights would be easy because the trains take off very slowly and many of the cars are empty. The trains only very gradually built up speed, and there'd be plenty of time to run alongside them and jump in. The same held true when the train came into a rail yard. After it slowed down on the outskirts, we'd simply jump off and then walk around the yard and catch it departing on the other side.

John suggested drinking some wine while we waited. I hadn't realized that there was such a thing as hobos, but we saw little groups of them all over the place. John told me that they are struck with wanderlust. They picked apples in Washington part of the year and then rode the rails south and picked vegetables and fruit in California; or they went out to Texas or even as far as Florida to pick oranges. Some just rode the rails, continuously chasing the wind all over the United States, drinking wine and constantly staying on the move.

John and I got drunker than any two people ever should. We were loudly singing and banging on tin cans and we'd been joined by several hobos who were as drunk as we were. We had one hell of a rowdy band going there for a while. Finally we saw activity with our train.

As it slowly began pulling out of the yard, we went sprinting along beside it. I hopped into the open door of an empty car. John was scampering and hopping along beside it, half dragging and half skipping as he tenaciously tried to hold on to the door handle. He was having a heck of a time climbing in. He was drunk to be sure, but also seemed to be as uncoordinated as anyone I'd ever encountered. Finally I was able to grab him by the back of his trench coat and help pull him in by utilizing every ounce of my strength. This was no easy feat, because he was a large guy and, unlike me, he had a big gut on him.

Inside, we saw a wino lying asleep, rolled up in a corner in the same car. I said that we needed to get rid of him. He might try to roll us when we tried to sleep. I asked John to give me a hand, and we picked him up and threw him off the train. The train was still moving fairly slowly and he rolled down a grass embankment.

I slid the door shut, curled up in a corner, and passed out.

Chapter Thirty-Four

It was about midnight when someone shone a very bright flashlight in my eyes and woke me up. The train had stopped and a rail-yard bull was standing over me and roughly shaking me trying to wake me up; another was standing over John.

They took us inside an office and questioned us. We told them that we were American citizens and had boarded the train in Seattle heading toward Vancouver, where we hoped to find a job in the Merchant Marines.

They told us we were several hundred miles north of Vancouver in White Horse, *Yukon*. We'd both passed out from all the wine, and in our drunken state had slept right through our stop in Vancouver.

Apparently two U.S. citizens stowed away on a freight train into White Horse, Yukon, was not an everyday occurrence, and these guys didn't have the slightest idea as to what to do with us. They told us that their supervisor would sort it all out in the morning. In the meantime we would spend the night in the cabin that was adjacent to their office.

The small cabin served as their temporary jail, but it was unlike any jail I'd ever been in. The building was brand new and was constructed with beautiful tongue-and-groove fir. A set of bunk beds occupied one corner, and they were made up with clean sheets, pillows, and blankets. In another corner was a small bathroom, complete with shower and fresh towels, and in the cabin's center stood a coal-burning, pot-bellied stove, which kept the cabin toasty warm in the chilly Yukon night.

It was clean and much more comfortable than the nasty freight car in which we'd been riding, and I immediately took advantage by taking a long, hot, steamy shower. I brushed my teeth and rinsed out the soured wine taste in my mouth, and then I jumped into bed on the lower bunk.

John on the other hand had turned a chair around and positioned it against the door, and he was sitting there staring at the door's dead bolt.

I asked, "What're you doing?"

He matter-of-factly told me, "I'm going to bust us out of here. I can pick these locks."

The cabin was definitely built to serve as a jail because there were no windows, and we'd been locked inside using not one but *three* extra-heavy-duty dead bolts securing a very sturdy-looking, solid-wood door.

I exclaimed, "Are you serious?"

John ignored my question and was deeply concentrating and vigorously moving a small piece of wire back and forth in an effort to pick one of the locks. He looked like a complete moron sitting there.

I said, "Are you crazy? We couldn't blow our way out of here with 10 sticks of dynamite. Look at those locks. One of them is five inches in diameter. You can't pick those locks!"

Unruffled, he calmly said again, "I'm gonna bust us out of here."

"Fine," I said, "I'm gonna go to sleep."

I crawled under the nice clean sheets and covers and took another look at him. He was deeply concentrating and hard at work maneuvering his little wire in a circular motion inside one of the locks. I shook my head in amusement and soon was fast asleep.

Early the next morning I awoke and John was still sitting in the chair leaning forward. His forehead was resting on the back of the chair and he had fallen fast asleep (apparently while still trying to pick the lock).

He'd spent the entire night in that chair. When I woke him up, he appeared to be as stiff as a 15-year-old dog with arthritis, and could barely move his neck. He had a big red mark on his forehead where it had been resting on top of the chair. He still had his trench coat on and it was now very warm in the room, so his face was flushed and his cheeks were deep red, matching the red indentation on his head.

I cracked up laughing at him. "I thought you were going to 'bust us out.'"

He didn't respond.

Soon someone unlocked the door and told us they'd decided to send us back to the United States by passenger train. We were each given a one-way ticket to Seattle and told that the train had one stop in Bellingham, Washington, before going on to Seattle. We were instructed in no uncertain terms not to get off the train until it arrived in Seattle. I asked if anyone was going with us, like maybe a guard. They said no. I asked if anyone would meet us in Seattle. They said no.

In about an hour, the rail-yard bulls escorted us to a shiny new, aluminum-covered passenger train, and we boarded. The other passengers all were wearing nice clothes and appeared to be mainly families going on holiday or professional business people who were commuting. We on the other hand looked like hobos, with our disheveled, wrinkled-up clothing and unkempt appearance.

John of course was unfazed by his appearance and called even more attention to us by greeting and conversing with most every passenger on both sides of the aisle, shaking hands with some of them as we moved along looking for our seats. Anyone would have thought that John owned the railroad the way he was acting, and didn't have a clue that he was a vagrant bum being kicked out of the country for illegally sneaking in by hopping a freight.

We marveled at our good fortune. Here we were, riding on this sleek, fast-moving passenger train all the way to Bellingham. We were served orange juice and Danishes, and from all appearances we looked just like ordinary commuters. When we arrived in Bellingham, we promptly ignored their instructions and simply got off the train. It was much closer to Vancouver than Seattle, and we were undeterred in our quest to go there.

John and I walked to the local bus station and bought two tickets from Bellingham to Vancouver using all the money we had left between us. We made the short bus ride to the border, but when the bus stopped at the checkpoint on the Canadian side, they wouldn't let us enter the country because they said we didn't have any money and were "vagrants."

In a most humiliating fashion, we were told to leave the bus. We had no alternative but to start walking back toward the small border town on the U.S. side, carrying our meager belongings with us as we went.

This new setback just further increased my resolve to find a way into Canada. I openly wondered if we might be able to walk into Canada later that night. We stopped at a store not far from the border and looked at a road map. We located a road just across the Canadian border that ran parallel to the road on the United States side. It didn't look like there was much distance between the two roads, so I suggested that we wait until nightfall and simply head north the half mile or so through the woods until we hit that Canadian road. I thought that once we were in Canada, we could hitchhike on in to Vancouver and thus bypass the border crossing.

Our plan was not without a few small problems. First, John was inordinately afraid. He was decidedly a city boy and was scared witless of the wild bears and various bogeymen that we might encounter as we walked through the dark forest after nightfall.

Second, he complained bitterly about how far we would have to walk. His feet had already begun to hurt badly, which no doubt stemmed from his fancy wingtip shoes and black silk stockings.

Finally, he was obsessed with putting his hands on a bottle of wine. It got to the point where he was beginning to question whether or not we should just remain in the United States and give up on trying to enter Canada. (I began to suspect that maybe his fondness for wine might be the real reason that he dropped out of society, not the IRS problems.)

I convinced him that we were almost there and that we should just forge ahead because we would soon be in the Merchant Marines steaming into some distant port on a lush tropical island in the Pacific loaded with beautiful Polynesian women.

He reluctantly agreed, and we walked about four miles down the road and arrived at a point that, according to the map, was the closest place to cross over into Canada. It looked like we just could walk right through a pasture and then through a small strip of forest before running directly into the Canadian road just a half mile north of us.

We decided to wait until nightfall to avoid detection. As we sat there waiting for nightfall, the temperature began to plummet and I began shivering. It was freezing, but the serene pasture full of cows lazily grazing on the green grass and the orange sun slowly sinking made quite the beautiful scene.

John was terrified of the cows in the field and kept insisting that they looked dangerous. I tried to reassure him, saying, "Quit worrying about the damned cows already. I've been around cows all my life and they're harmless."

I didn't know what breed of cow these were, but they didn't appear to be your everyday, run-of-the-mill, average-size cows like the ones I'd seen on my grandfather's farm. These beasts were huge. They were black and white and appeared to be some strain of giant Holstein. And although I was not about to admit it to John, they did look a little intimidating to me as well.

As dusk settled, John insisted we go ahead and not wait for pitch-black darkness. I agreed and crawled under the electric fence. John followed. I walked about 25 yards out into the field and John frantically whispered to me, "Bob! That cow over there is looking at us."

I angrily said, "For crying out loud John, just shut up already about the cows. They're more scared of us than we are of them. Just keep walking. *Jeez!*"

Just then that cow lifted its head high in the air, rolled its eyes, and loudly snorted. Suddenly it took off after us at a dead run and so did the rest of the herd. Instantly I turned around and bolted back toward the fence, with John right behind. I glanced back and saw that the cows were gaining on us and I decided to just dive over the fence. Like an Olympic high jumper I easily cleared it with two feet to spare.

John, on the other hand, was too fat to leap over the fence and instead tried to get down on all fours and crawl under it. Unfortunately in his haste, he left his large butt sticking up too high in the air. The electric fence jolted him with a solid hit. He screamed in pain, bawling like a terrified calf separated from its mother. As he struggled to escape the cows, the fence shocked him again and then again. Each time he loudly shrieked in pain. Delivering shock after shock to his huge butt, it kept jolting him as he tried to scoot through on his hands and knees instead of belly crawling underneath it. Finally he slid all the way through.

When he reached the other side, he was wild eyed and furious. He said, "Oh yeah? 'I've been around cows all my life,' you said. 'There's nothing to be concerned about. Just follow me. They're more afraid of us than we are of them.'

"Bullshit! This is bullshit!"

I laughed so hard at the spectacle when he was getting shocked that I had to sit down.

When I recovered enough to be coherent, I told him to calm down. I'd never seen cows behave like these, and it was obvious from their nasty demeanor that we would now have to detour around them. We ended up having to walk all the way around that field and the cows walked with us every step, continually eyeing us as though they were daring us to reenter their pasture.

Finally we reached the end of the pasture and began walking north through the darkness. As night descended, John was scared shitless and was so close to me that he kept stepping on my heels and bumping into me whenever I'd slightly pause. Each time I'd turn around and yell at him, "Get off me," only to have him bump into me again in the next few steps.

Finally we emerged from the forest and reached a small paved road and started walking down it. After about a mile, we saw a farm sign that said British Columbia on it and we started dancing around in the road in our excitement.

"We made it!"

We were elated, but didn't celebrate long because a light, misty rain began to fall and the temperature continued to drop. We were now shaking from the cold. I could see my breath every time I exhaled. I had on a navy peacoat and had turned up the collar to ward off the cold; but I was still shivering. John fared a little better than I did in that regard, because he was wearing a turtleneck sweater and his faithful trench coat to shed the light rain. (Plus he had a thick layer of fat to insulate him.)

We walked on down the road and finally came to a house with lights on, and we noticed that it had a barn out back. John wanted to go to the house to see if they would let us sleep in the barn. He was convinced that he could generate some sympathy for our plight and maybe even talk the owners into providing us with a nice hot meal.

We went to the door and knocked. A light came on and a woman came to the door, cracked it open about an inch, but didn't unlock the safety chain. John politely began his routine and told her that we were heading into Vancouver trying to find work and had been stranded in the rain. Plus, John said, he wondered if she would be so kind as to allow us to sleep in her barn for the night and get out of the rain and cold until morning.

She didn't say a word and immediately shut the door and turned off the light. We looked at each other in bewilderment. I gestured to John with my palms upward and asked, "What was that all about?"

We shook our heads and chuckled at her bizarre behavior and started to leave.

Just then we saw a floodlight come on in the back of the house, partially illuminating the barn. Thinking that the light was for us and that she was coming around to show us the way to the barn, we started walking in that direction to meet her. But without so much as uttering one syllable, she suddenly let a German shepherd out the back door.

We took off running as fast as we could with the dog streaking toward us. Fortunately it stopped at the edge of the yard, where it stood furiously barking at us. John and I ran as fast as we could until we were a safe distance from the house. We looked at each other and I asked the obvious. "Can anything else go wrong?"

John didn't answer. He was visibly shaken. Only a gentle city boy, he'd never been exposed to any of this. "Let's get the hell out of here," he said. "We can just walk into Vancouver tonight." Then he nervously looked around and said, "What are we gonna do if we get attacked by a bear or something?"

"Jeez, John, there aren't any bears around here."

"Oh yeah, there aren't any bears around here, just like those *cows* wouldn't attack us. Do you remember those 'harmless' cows that you said wouldn't attack us?"

"John, I make one little mistake and you want to nail me to the wall like a wanted poster."

"*One little mistake! One little mistake!* We were supposed to go to Vancouver, British Columbia, not to White Horse, *Yukon*. I've been rousted by rail-yard bulls and incarcerated in an extremely hot jail—my neck is still aching. I was kicked out of Canada not once, but *twice!* I was attacked by gigantic cows, repeatedly shocked by an electric fence, and now I've been attacked by a vicious dog that was let out by some insane woman. I'm cold, I'm hungry, I'm soaking wet and getting wetter by the minute. My feet hurt from walking mile after mile through the black forest, and I want some wine. This is not 'one little mistake.' This was *your* plan and it has been *riddled* with all kinds of mistakes!"

"Stop whimpering," I said. "I got us here, didn't I?"

We walked another mile or two until we came across another barn and this time we didn't ask anyone. We just went into the barn and ducked out of the rain. We were both chilled to the bone, hungry, and miserable. We slept on the hard, dirty, wooden floor of the barn and within minutes John was loudly snoring, no doubt thoroughly exhausted from the trauma that he'd endured in the past 48 hours. I tried sleeping, but couldn't. I just restlessly listened to John snore all wretched night as I tried to stay warm.

At daybreak the next morning it was bitterly cold, but at least it had stopped raining. We started walking down the road and tried to stay warm by rubbing our hands together. We were both hungrier than hell. We caught a ride to the edge of town from a farmer who, even though he had room in the cab, made us ride in the back of the freezing-cold pickup truck.

From outside town we walked for miles to reach the waterfront district. We stopped at a restaurant on the way and mooched a meal in much the same fashion as we had before. John poured on the charm and moments later we were served a delicious meal, and once again we didn't even have to wash dishes.

When we inquired around, we quickly discovered that the union to which the Merchant Marine workers belonged was on strike and had been for several weeks.

We couldn't believe that our bad luck was continuing to spiral down. We'd struggled so hard to walk into Canada, only to have this happen. The only good news was that the strike was limited to the West Coast and that they weren't on strike on the East Coast. If we could reach the East Coast, we could ship out from there. John and I looked at each other and shrugged and decided that we would just go to the East Coast.

Like a couple of bumbling idiots, we really didn't think that idea all the way through—or we would have stayed in Vancouver. Primarily, we didn't consider that from where we were standing it was approximately *2,500 miles* to the East Coast. We were penniless and would need to travel across some of the most rugged terrain in North America to get there. Traffic in Canada was sparse and consisted mainly of blue-haired old people on vacation—people who thought that anyone who looked destitute or like a hippie (especially) was a card-carrying communist. They wouldn't have given us a ride if our lives were dependent upon it.

Nonetheless, we decided to hitchhike our way across Canada. We made our way to the outskirts of town and stuck our thumbs out. We stood in the sun for hours and all the while John vehemently protested that his feet hurt and he needed some sleep and he wanted some wine. No one appeared willing to pick us up and give us a ride. He wanted to hop another freight, and I wanted to keep hitchhiking. We were bickering like two old women.

Finally we decided that we might have better luck splitting up. One person hitchhiking can catch a ride far easier than two, and I didn't want to walk all the way back into town to find a freight yard—or more likely a wine bottle.

We decided that we would reunite in Toronto and made plans to meet in the hippie district there in a couple of weeks. I told John I would walk on down another mile from where we were and hitchhike from there. I looked back and smiled as I saw him sitting on a guardrail not even bothering to hold his thumb out to the passing cars. He had removed his shoes and was vigorously rubbing his black-stockinged feet.

I didn't know it at the time, but that was the last I'd ever see of John. He was the funniest person that I'd ever met, and I've often wondered what happened to him.

I caught a ride soon after splitting up, and it turned out that the man who picked me up was a legislator in the Canadian Parliament.

Cool . . .

Chapter Thirty-Five

The man who gave me a ride was nicely dressed and seemed kindly and dignified. He told me that he'd devoted his entire life to public service, and seemed genuinely interested in the sob story I made up. I let it flow like one of the majestic mountain rivers we were following along the highway.

I told him I was in Vancouver to join the Merchant Marines. But, I said, they were on strike on the West Coast and now I had to go to the East Coast in order to ship out. On my way to the bus station, I was robbed of all my money at gunpoint, and now was reduced to finding my way there any way I could. I told him my plan was to work my way across the country, taking odd jobs and hitching rides.

He told me that there were places throughout Canada called hostels, which were government-run refuges for the homeless. He explained that I could stay there for free, and in fact many of them served meals.

He was very pleasant and gave me a ride for several hundred miles before he had to turn off. As I departed the car, he told me that I seemed like a nice young man and that I reminded him of his own son. He opened his wallet and gave me $20 and wished me well. I thanked him profusely and he drove away. I congratulated myself on my sob-story-telling ability. I ruefully smiled as I thought about John's flowery performances hustling meals. He would have been exceedingly proud to know that I was not without skills.

I was on a highway somewhere in the mountains of British Columbia, and had been standing across from a store hitchhiking for hours when a trucker finally picked me up. The trucker had on blue jeans, cowboy boots, a faded-blue Western shirt with white pearl snaps, and a very large white cowboy hat. Country-and-Western music was loudly blaring on the radio.

He was a big, rugged-looking man with a ruddy complexion and steely-blue eyes, and he appeared to be about 35 years old. His name was Ted and he was chewing tobacco and spitting a sickening blackish-brown slobber into a cup every five minutes or so. (At least that appeared to be the goal; it seemed as if much of it never made it to the cup and instead drooled down his chin like stringy brown glue. He'd occasionally swipe off that mess with the back of his shirtsleeve.)

He told me he lived in Calgary and that was where he was heading. We made some small talk for about a hundred or so miles and when I felt he was adequately primed and warmed up to me, I tried my sob story on him. This time it backfired.

Of all things. He offered me a job at his small trucking company.

I didn't want a job! I wanted a free handout so I could be on my way. Rattled, I stammered that I really needed to reach the other side of the country so I could join the Merchant Marines.

"Man, you can't go right now," he said. "We have the Calgary Stampede coming up in two weeks."

I said, "Really? That's great!"

I paused for a moment and asked, "What's the Calgary Stampede?"

He looked at me as if I was from another planet or something, and with a disdainful tone in his voice asked, "You've never heard of the Calgary Stampede? Where you been all your life, numb nuts?"

"No, I've never heard of the Calgary Stampede. What is it? Some local hootenanny, I presume?"

"Dumbass, it's only the largest and most famous rodeo in the entire world. It lasts two weeks and educated people come from all over the world just to be a part of it. There's nonstop bull riding and steer wrestling, covered-wagon races, barrel racing, and calf roping. You name it. It's great!"

"What's so great about a bunch of grown men playing cowboys and Indians?" I asked.

He looked at me as though he wanted to whip my ass, and I broke out laughing. "I'm just hacking on you man. Seriously it sounds like a lot of fun. I like rodeos."

He grinned and simmered back down and continued. "I haven't told you about the best part yet. You wouldn't believe the women that flock into that place. There are dances every night, getting drunk, and partying until dawn. Hot damn son, it's nothing less than a two-week orgy.

"Why don't you stay for it? I'll give you a job loading trucks for my company, and you can stay in my spare guest room—at least until it's over. You can make some traveling money and then be on your way."

"Now you're talking a language that I can understand. Orgies, good-looking women, partying, and getting drunk till all hours—say no more, you can count me in." He greeted my newfound enthusiasm with a wide grin and proceeded to fill me in on every detail of the Calgary Stampede as we drove all the way to Calgary.

He hadn't exaggerated. The Calgary Stampede lived up to all my expectations and more. It was a blast. Ted and all his cowboy buddies, including some gorgeous cowgirls, were hard-drinking, hard-partying animals. And they were as red as any rednecks that I'd ever encountered, even the ones I'd met in those state-line beer joints in rural Mississippi, in the deepest corner of the Deep South.

Ted had a long, pink Cadillac convertible, with high fins on the back and white leather seats. Some furry-looking, light-blue material, which definitely looked out of place, covered the steering wheel. We went everywhere in Ted's Caddy, as he lovingly referred to it, with the top down and pretty girls (including some my age) filling the seats. We partied hard and, just as Ted had predicted, I ended up in bed with a different cowgirl beauty every night. It was one heck of a lot of fun, and I was really enjoying it. But I wished that there was some way to get in touch with John. He'd have loved this scene.

One night we went to a large Country-and-Western beer joint and they were doing a dance called the butterfly. It was similar to square dancing and Ted and his gang insisted that I try it. I laughed and jumped around, trying to follow their lead as they promenaded 'round and 'round and joined hands in a circle going in and out. I always seemed to be going in when they were all going out or out when they were going in, but it was great fun anyway.

Finally I opted out of a dance and was standing on the edge of the dance floor, swigging an ice-cold beer and still smiling at the thought of the spectacle I made with my poor dancing. I noticed a very attractive woman, who appeared to be a little older than me. She'd been staring at me with a wicked-looking smile on her pretty little face, and when her eyes met mine, I detected what I perceived to be sheer lust for me.

I smiled back with my own wicked leer, and it looked to me as if her eyes lit up and acknowledged it.

She had on a short Western-style dress with multiple ruffled petticoats, and was twirling around as she danced. To my delight, when she spun around, her dress and petticoats would lift up and reveal her gorgeous legs and bright-red underwear. I stood there watching her for quite some time, enjoying the show immensely.

BAM! Someone sucker punched me on the right side of my head in the middle of my right ear. I was knocked hard to the floor. A pointed-toed cowboy boot struck me hard in the ribs—and then one more time for good measure. Each vicious kick lifted me off the floor.

I was swimming around on the floor trying to protect myself, but I couldn't tell which direction was up or down. The blow to my head disoriented me, and I couldn't catch my breath after all the vicious kicks. Just then a bouncer came running over and pushed away the guy who'd hit me. He complained loudly to the bouncer that I'd been standing there staring at his wife, trying to make a pass at her.

I was in no condition to defend myself. My ear was ringing and it felt as if my eardrum had burst. I was able to rise up on my hands and knees, and I was trying to catch my breath. Reeling from the blow and sick to my stomach from the pain, I threw up. The bouncer lifted me to my feet and roughly pushed me toward the door. He slapped me hard on the back of the head with his open palm, and I staggered outside, where he shoved me down on the pavement and told me to leave.

Ted and his buddies quickly came to my defense and helped me to my feet. A couple of witnesses told the bouncer that I was just standing there minding my own business when they saw the guy sucker punch me for no reason.

The bouncer would hear none of it, telling them that he had seen me standing there staring at the woman and undressing her with my eyes and if that had been his wife he would have done the same thing to me, only worse.

I staggered to my feet and yelled that I didn't know that the bitch was married. I said that she was flirting with me long before I returned the favor, and "she's a good 10 years older than me anyway." Ted and his buddies continued pulling me away from the bouncer toward the parking lot, trying to get me to shut up. The bouncer told Ted that he'd better get me the hell out of there or someone would be carrying me out.

I said, "What'd you say? Why you talking to Ted? Why not talk to me? You think I'm scared of you? Well, I'm not, you fat asshole son of a bitch! You talk big like that son of a bitch coward that hit me from behind. You want some of me? Why not try it to my face like a man, instead of sucker punching me from behind like that fat pig?"

Ted and his friends surrounded me, separating me from the bouncer and the guy who hit me. Ted pushed me hard and sternly told me to calm down and leave before big trouble broke out. He whispered that he didn't want them to call the cops or they'd put me "under" the jail. He handed me the keys to his pink Cadillac, and firmly told me to take the car and go home. He said he'd catch a ride home later with his friends.

I was furious and my ear and side hurt like hell, but I shook my head okay to Ted. I gingerly walked toward his Caddy, and when I glanced back, everyone who'd come out to witness the spectacle had already gone back inside. I unlocked the trunk of Ted's car, removed the tire iron, and shut the lid. I threw his car keys in the front seat and walked over to the edge of the parking lot, into the shadows.

I wasn't going anywhere.

The guy who had blindsided me was big. He stood at least six-foot-four and easily outweighed me by 60 or 70 pounds. I patiently waited in the dark shadows of the parking lot, smoking one cigarette after another and reviewing events over and over again in my mind. Slowly but surely I was building myself into a seething, blinding, white-hot craze.

After waiting for at least an hour, I finally saw him come out of the bar with his wife. I'd laid the tire iron on the ground while I waited. I didn't want anyone to see me standing out there brandishing a tire iron. I reached down and quietly retrieved it. It was one of those long, heavy tire irons with a lug wrench on one end, and I held it loosely by the side of my leg as I silently walked toward him.

I didn't let him see me as I slowly followed him to his pickup truck. His wife went to the passenger side, and as he walked around to the driver's side to get in, I quickly closed the gap. Neither of them saw or heard me as I snuck up behind him. I tapped him on the shoulder, and when he turned around, I said, "Remember me?"

Before he could answer, I swung the tire iron with all my might. I used both hands, as though wielding a baseball bat, and I aimed directly for that big mouth.

CRACK!

Blood splattered a foot or more out of his mouth, and I heard his teeth loudly crack from the direct hit to his upper lip. It must have instantly knocked him out, because he did not utter so much as a groan as he collapsed to the ground like a felled tree. He was motionless.

Knocking him out cold like that was a great feeling, and I had a rush of adrenaline coursing through me like a hit of speed. I stood over that son of a bitch and I wanted to hurt him bad. He was lying on his back and his mouth was bubbling and gurgling blood like a spring. It appeared dark in the dim lights of the parking lot, but I could easily see a steady, bloody stream flowing down his neck, where it formed a black pool on the pavement.

He was motionless, but I didn't care. This was far from over, because I was going to make that son of a bitch pay! I raised the tire iron high above my head with both hands, as though I were chopping firewood with an ax. I brought it down hard, hitting him squarely in the middle of his right kneecap. The sickening crunch was music to my ears. He didn't move or make a sound as I swung again and again, alternating legs, with as much force as I could manage. Each blow made a cracking, crunching sound. I wanted to shatter his kneecaps into a million pieces. The only thing I hated was that he was not conscious to see or feel me doing it.

I screamed to his unconscious ass, "You want to kick me while I'm down?

"Do you?

"Why not try it now?"

Whap! I hit him again.

"You aren't so bad now, are you?"

Remembering the vicious kicks to my side, I hit him in the ribs. *Whap! Whap! Whap!*

"You big ape, you aren't so tough now, are you?"

His wife had come around the truck and saw her husband lying in his own pool of blood, which was now about two feet in diameter. She immediately began hysterically screaming and crying.

When she screamed I took off running as fast as I could. I threw the tire iron into a creek as I ran by at full speed. As soon as I was out of sight I slowed down to a brisk walk to avoid calling attention to myself. I didn't know where I was or where I was going, but I wanted to put some distance between me and that beer joint before the cops came on the scene.

I was in a bad spot. I was afraid that if I went to Ted's place, the police would find me there. I didn't know how badly that guy was hurt, but I suspected that he was in pretty bad shape. I decided that I better get the hell out of town—the quicker the better.

All my clothes and my bag were still at Ted's, and I only had about $20 on me.

I couldn't risk going back to his place to get my stuff, though. I'd just have to leave my things and the money Ted owed me for working, and haul ass out of town.

So now I was on the run from the Canadian police as well as the United States military. I had no clothes other than what I was wearing, and my only shirt had blood splatters on it.

Everything was going against me, but I was unrepentant and defiant. Actually my dark side was happy and gleefully reminding me of the sickening, crunching sound of that cowboy's teeth being knocked out. And we were laughing at the thought of that poor slob being on crutches.

He hissed in my throbbing ear, *It serves that bastard right for blindsiding you. If only we could've smashed that asshole bouncer too, it would have been perfect.* Smashing that loudmouth bouncer would break him of slapping anyone else on the back of the head and pushing them down in a parking lot.

Just then I heard a siren coming. *Shit! Here come the cops!* There were some bushes on the side of the road and I jumped behind them and watched from my hiding place. My heart was pounding and my mouth was dry. It was only an ambulance speeding toward the beer joint with its lights flashing.

I moved back onto the street and started walking fast. I was in near-panic mode.

CHAPTER THIRTY-SIX

It was as black as my soul on the street that night, and I figured the chances that I'd catch a ride were tiny. But when I saw a car coming, I stuck out my thumb anyway. To my surprise someone stopped to pick me up, and when I looked inside the VW van I was pleased to see a guy with long hair and a beard.

He said his name was Tim and I told him mine was Bob. I asked if he lived in Calgary. He answered yes and straightaway he asked if I was from the states. I cautiously said, "Yes, how'd you know?"

"Accent. Where you coming from?"

"I just came in from Haight-Ashbury in San Francisco." I told him I was heading to Toronto to meet a friend and then would be heading on to Montreal to join the Merchant Marines.

Now that I'd been vetted, he reached into his shirt pocket and pulled out a joint and lit it up. He took a deep toke and handed it to me. I inhaled deeply and handed it back.

"You a draft dodger?"

I was extremely cautious now and fully on guard. Even if I was in Canada, I didn't want anyone to know that I was AWOL. I decided draft dodger was close enough for now and answered, "Yeah, I think Vietnam is a stupid, meaningless war, and I want no part of it. How'd you know?"

"We see a lot of Americans up here these days. I agree with you on Vietnam. You know of course that there's an underground antiwar organization that'll help you get established in Canada don't you? They help all sorts of American protesters, draft dodgers, and military people who are against the war."

"Really?"

"Toronto is the place you need to go for that though. There are lots of Americans living there. If you'd like to come over to my place, I'll hook you up with a contact person in Toronto who works for the underground. In the meantime you're welcome to stay if you need a place to crash for a few days."

I remembered the tire-iron incident and knew that by now the police would be looking for me. I said, "I appreciate it man. I really need to hit the road in the morning, but it would be nice to crash in a warm place for the night; it's freezing cold out there. I got mugged by three guys, and they stole all my money, my backpack, and the few clothes I had. The bastards even took my coat."

"Bummer! I'll take you by the Sally Ann in the morning. They'll fix you up."

"Sally Ann?"

"The Salvation Army. They have clothes that they give away just for the asking. Most look brand-new and best of all they don't charge a penny."

We went to his small apartment and he gave me information on the antiwar movement and the name of a contact person in Toronto. We drank some wine, smoked some pot, and had a bowl of hot vegetable soup and saltine crackers. He asked about the blood on my shirt and I shrugged and told him that the muggers had roughed me up and bloodied my nose some. He wanted to know all about the Haight and was envious that I'd been there.

The next morning I looked in the bathroom mirror and saw that my ear had turned almost completely black where I'd been sucker punched. My broken ribs were so sore that I could hardly put my shirt on. I thought about the guy that I had viciously beaten with the tire iron and smiled, as I thought about how much worse he must be feeling this morning.

Tim took me downtown to the Sally Ann and after hearing my sob story, the lady in charge found me a warm coat, two nearly new shirts, and two worn, but definitely functional, pairs of Levi's. She also gave me some new underwear, toiletries, an old sleeping bag, and a used canvas satchel to carry my clothes in. She let me change into the new clothes right there in the store dressing room.

She was a tiny woman and was wearing a heavily starched, sparkling white blouse and navy blue skirt, and her silver hair was perfectly in place. Her face was wrinkled from the years, but her cheeks were rosy and she had the most loving, kind eyes that I'd ever seen. She was damn-near angelic and as nice as anyone had ever been to me. She told me that God loved me and so did she. I appreciated everything she'd done and told her as much. She stood up on her tiptoes to hug me and softly patted me on the back like I was her only son departing for a long voyage.

When we returned to Tim's car, he said he didn't have any spare change, but he did give me a couple of joints for the road. I grinned and thanked him and said I'd rather have the joints anyway. He asked where I wanted to be dropped off. The last place I wanted to be was on the road hitchhiking because the cops would find me. So I told him that I was going to hop a freight and needed a ride to the freight yard heading out of town. A big knowing smile instantly crossed his face.

It turns out that he had hopped freights and hitchhiked all over Canada himself. I learned something new from him about hopping freights: He told me that at least five engines are nearly always hooked together pulling the freight cars, but the employees ride in only the first engine and the caboose. He said it's far more comfortable to ride in one of the vacant engine's seats than in a cold and dirty freight car. He said no one would bother me as long as I didn't mess with any of the controls.

Tim dropped me off at the freight yard and I thanked him. I asked some hobos where to catch the next train to Saskatchewan, and they quickly pointed me in the right direction.

When the train started pulling out, I ran alongside the third engine and pulled myself aboard, wincing in pain from my broken ribs. Just as Tim had said, it was empty, the seat was large and comfortable, and I had a nice window to look out. Awesome!

I was riding for a couple of hours when a railroad employee came walking through the engine doorway. I thought, *oh, crap*, and prepared to defend myself, but he merely glanced at the gauges and without even looking at me went through the door to the next engine. In a little while, he passed back through and returned to the first engine. He never so much as said a word or even paid me any attention.

The only problem I encountered was after I smoked one of the joints and got pretty stoned. As I looked out the window, I noticed a big moose standing knee deep in water in a pond in the middle of a golden meadow. I couldn't resist pulling the cord and loudly blowing the air horn at him. The same railroad guy who had come through earlier immediately came back and sternly told me that if I touched another control, they would stop the train and remove me. And they wouldn't care if they left me in the middle of the bush, he said. I promised I wouldn't do it again—and I didn't.

The train began slowing down as it approached Regina, Saskatchewan. I jumped off and began walking along the outskirts of the freight yard.

Just then I saw three guys about my age heading toward me. They looked rough and I had a bad feeling that they were up to no good. *Three against one, not good odds. Not good odds at all,* I thought.

I prepared for a fight and planned to hit the biggest of the lot with all I had. If I could hit him hard enough to knock him out or down, I hoped it would scare the others off—or at least the biggest would be out of the way while I tended to the others.

The apparent leader of the trio came up to me and good naturedly asked where I was coming in from. I warily responded, "From Calgary." I was ready to kick him in the nuts or otherwise defend myself at any moment. He told me that they had just been released from a 60-day stint in jail for burglary.

He said, "You hungry?"

"I'm starving."

"C'mon with us—we're going to the hostel to eat a hot breakfast."

I was relieved that they weren't going to try to roust me. I slung my satchel and sleeping bag over my shoulders in backpack fashion and started walking along with them. We crossed the railroad tracks in a seedy section of town, heading toward the hostel when all of a sudden someone yelled, "COPS! RUN!"

Instinctively we all took off running. A cop car had been slowly cruising about a block away from us and when they saw us take off running, they turned their car around and came after us. We all split up and I turned up a side street and was running as fast as I could. In fact I was running so fast that I ran right out of one of my shoes, but I didn't stop. I heard one of the cops yell, "Stop! Stop or I'll shoot!"

BANG! He shot.

I don't know if he shot up in the air or shot at me, but when I heard that shot, it scared the shit out of me and I sped up even faster. I immediately turned into the first street I encountered, to get out of the line of fire. I ran right into an industrial area completely surrounded by a high fence. I was trapped with no way out other than the way that I'd come in.

I saw some large hedges next to an office building, leaped into them, and fell down behind them next to the building. Through the branches and leaves of my hiding spot I could see the cop's legs walking through the parking lot as he looked for me.

He bent down and looked me right in the eye and screamed in my face, "Get your hands up and come out of there."

I noticed he was aiming a revolver at me and badly shaking and trembling. He had "scared eyes" that were wider than his badge.

I tried to reassure him so that he wouldn't shoot me and calmly told him, "I'm unarmed. Take it easy, I'm coming out."

"Shut up, asshole!" His voice was trembling.

I came out of the hedges with my hands in the air and he immediately told me to go down on my knees and put my hands behind my head. He then removed my satchel and sleeping bag from my shoulders and handcuffed me. I asked him if I could retrieve my shoe.

"Shut up, asshole!" He was no longer trembling but was confidently assertive now that I was handcuffed. He roughly threw me into the backseat of the police car.

Surprisingly the cops rounded up all four of us in spite of the fact that we had all run in opposite directions. They called for a police wagon and took us to jail, where they put us in a holding cell and brought us out one at a time to question.

The first question the cop asked me was, "Why'd you run?"

I truthfully answered that I didn't really know. Someone yelled, "Cops, run!" and we all just instinctively took off. I told him that we were merely going to a hostel to get something to eat and that we had done nothing wrong. He didn't believe me and grilled me over and again, asking the same questions for the better part of an hour.

He told me that all the guys I was arrested with had just been released from jail, but I didn't show up on their records. I told him that was because I had just met them five minutes earlier. I told him that I was an American and showed him my fake ID.

Then I made a big mistake. Thinking that the prevailing sentiment all over Canada was antiwar, I proudly told him that I was a draft dodger and was against the Vietnam War and had come to Canada to resettle. It proved to be exactly the wrong thing to say. These cops were not antiwar; in fact they were far from it. They were warmongers and admired the United States for what it was doing in Vietnam, and they wished their own government was doing something besides coddling a bunch of cowardly hippie bastards from the U.S.A.

This cop and the others glared at me and told me that I was a cowardly son of a bitch and an unwanted vagrant, and they didn't want me in their country.

They drove me to the outskirts of the city on a highway that they said led back to the United States, and told me to go back to where I came from and never come back—because if they ever saw me again, not only would they put me in jail, they would bury me underneath it as well.

I was standing there with one shoe on and watched them turn around and drive away. I softly said through clinched teeth, "So long, you Canuck bastards!"

As soon as they were out of sight, I crossed the road and stuck out my thumb to hitchhike back into town.

An elderly farmer picked me up in an old pickup truck and I told him my now familiar "being robbed" story and added the twist that the muggers had even taken one of my shoes so I couldn't chase after them. I asked him if he could direct me to the nearest Salvation Army so I could get a pair of shoes before I continued on my way to Quebec to join the Merchant Marines.

He told me that he was deeply moved by of all my misfortunes, and he reached into his overall pockets and pulled out some bills. He said he was going to give me all the money that he had: $50. I was astounded at his generosity as he handed me the wrinkled bills.

He then took me to the Salvation Army and dropped me off right in front of the door. As I started to depart the truck, my angel of light put the full-court press on my conscience. He wanted me to give this poor old man his money back. I really felt bad about this and didn't want to take any of his money, much less all of it. I tried my best to give it back and even tried to stuff it back in his shirt, but he insisted.

"At least take some of it back," I pleaded.

He just waved me off with tears beginning to fill his eyes. "You need it worse than me, son. You go ahead and take it now, I'll be fine. You'll hurt my feelings if you keep acting this way. Please don't hurt me."

The last thing I wanted to do was hurt his feelings. I wanted to give him the money back. I knew I could find a dozen more suckers, but he needed this money. I looked at him and he again insisted on my keeping it. Finally I reluctantly agreed and sincerely thanked him and waved as he drove his old pickup truck down the street. It really made me feel like shit to take this pitiable old man's money, but he'd insisted. What was I going to do?

I went inside the Sally Ann and they gave me a pair of shoes without even asking me why I needed them. Such kindness from the old man and the Sally Ann folks was overwhelming. I vowed that I would never forget what these kind people had done for me, and swore that if I was ever in a position to repay them, I would.

It took nearly two weeks to make it the rest of the way to Toronto, but finally I arrived. I immediately called the person whose name Tim had given me—the contact person for the underground antiwar movement—and when he answered the phone, I told him my name and that I was AWOL from the United States Air Force.

He screamed at me, "NOT OVER THE PHONE!"

It scared me so bad that I almost hung up. He asked me where I was and what I was wearing, and then he told me to meet him in 15 minutes near the entrance to a downtown hotel that was just a few blocks away.

I agreed and made my way to the hotel. I nervously stood on the street and finally a short, chubby middle-aged guy with grayish, moderately long curly hair and John Lennon–style eyeglasses walked up and said, "Williamson?"

"Yes."

He nervously looked all around and then put one finger over his lips to shush me. "Don't say anything. Come with me."

I followed him down the street. We got into his small gray sedan, and we drove to a nondescript little home on the outskirts of town. He motioned me inside.

He told me that his name was Bill and that he ran an underground antiwar movement to assist those who opposed the war, including draft resisters and military that had gone AWOL or deserted. He matter-of-factly told me that we had to be very careful because the CIA was grabbing people off the street and taking them back across the border, and in fact some people had disappeared altogether.

I'd heard that rumor but didn't believe it. I said, "You're shittin' me."

"No, I'm not 'shitting you.' I'm *dead* serious—and so are they."

"Damn!"

I became really paranoid when I heard that. I'd been AWOL for nearly three months and after 30 days I was officially classified as a deserter. The term "deserter" had a dirty ring to it, and I didn't like to think of myself in those terms. I told Bill that I had a secret clearance and the job that I had at Keesler as an intercept operator was highly classified.

I didn't like the look on his face when I told him that. He told me that I was just the kind of person that was disappearing.

This was far too weird and clandestine for me. I couldn't believe that the United States would be engaged in activities like that. Bill told me that his own life was in danger every day for his role in helping people like me, but that someone had to do it.

I exclaimed to him in a loud voice that I had just started classes in technical school when I went AWOL, and that I had no knowledge of any secrets about anything. I didn't know any state secrets, or information of any kind, and couldn't divulge it even if I'd wanted to. And I definitely didn't want to!

My thought was that anyone listening in on a bug would know that I wasn't giving up any information to anybody. I was nervously looking around as though someone might jump out of a doorway somewhere and tie me up and haul me back to the United States, or dump me in some river with a bullet in my head.

He told me that he could find me a room in a home with several other young Americans who were similarly opposed to the war, and afterward he would assist me in immigrating to Canada and even help me obtain a job. I mentioned the Merchant Marines, but he said I needed an official work permit from the Canadians first, and then I would be free to come and go and pursue whatever career I wished.

It was not what I had envisioned, but what the heck. I looked forward to meeting some other Americans. He made some calls and then took me to an older neighborhood with tall, skinny white homes situated very close to each other. Three American couples were living there in a communal-type environment.

I went in and it reminded me of landing in the Haight. I was welcomed with a joint, a bottle of wine, and all smiles.

Far out!

Chapter Thirty-Seven

The three couples were longtime friends from the same hometown in Pennsylvania and had been married for several years. The guys were all draft dodgers and seemed elated to hear that I was a real-life deserter. They welcomed me into their home as if I was some kind of frigging hero or something.

My enthusiasm for my roommates was short lived and it pissed me off to no end to hear them constantly berate my country. They were far more anti-American than I was, and at night I'd have to listen to them rail for hours about how bad the United States sucked.

I readily agreed that the Vietnam War and draft were idiotic, but aside from those points, I saw nothing wrong with the United States. In fact, I thought the U.S.A. was far superior to Canada in every comparable way.

I nearly lost my temper more than once, but I held it back in the interest of not getting kicked out. Plus, I didn't want to lose Bill's help. I especially disliked Dan, the self-proclaimed leader of the group. He was a know-it-all loudmouth who needed his ass whipped.

So far, Bill had been able to obtain jobs for all the men and two of the women. That left Pam (Dan's wife) and me as the only commune members without jobs. We were home alone together every day with nothing to do, and I suppose it was only a matter of time before we were in bed together, banging away.

Pam was Irish and somewhat attractive, although certainly not beautiful. She had green eyes, naturally red lips, strawberry blond hair, and skin that was a little too white for my liking. It was scattered with freckles. She did have very large breasts, though, and an insatiable appetite for sex.

Considering that I knew firsthand how badly it felt for someone I loved to cheat behind my back, it was odd to me that I had no guilty conscience whatsoever in seducing Pam. In fact, initially it was a challenge in which I was keen to engage, and I relished my success when I easily won her over.

Further, it did not make me feel guilty in the least to be around Pam's loudmouth husband Dan at night, nor did it seem to bother Pam. In the evenings we both acted nonchalant, as though nothing was going on, and as soon as everyone left to go to work in the morning, we'd jump into bed and make passionate love. Sometimes we went for hour upon sweaty hour, and sometimes we made love at different times throughout the day.

During my deeper philosophical moments, especially when stoned out of my gourd, I'd wonder why I went after Dan's wife. Was it because I wanted to punish him for being a loudmouth? Some innate animal-like primal desire for sex? A shallow ego-fulfillment issue where screwing someone else's wife made me feel more significant? Or just another manifestation of black evil pouring out of my soul?

I never did figure it out, but suspected the latter.

Bill told me that I needed to find someone who would send me my birth certificate. He said flat out that I would not be able to immigrate into Canada without it.

I hadn't made contact with Jim or my parents the entire time I'd been gone. The only hope I had of obtaining a copy of my birth certificate would be through them, and I didn't want to exercise that option. I argued to Bill that I didn't have any way of obtaining my birth certificate, and asked if there was another way. He told me that I *had* to find a way to get it. There was no other way around the legalities and without it I wasn't going to be able to immigrate.

Maybe immigration was out. I didn't really want to become a Canadian anyway. It would be taking a chance, but maybe I could slip back into the United States and go to New York City and join the Merchant Marines there. Bill threw cold water in my lap on that idea and told me that the Merchant Marines would fingerprint me and run a background check and at that point would no doubt discover that I was a deserter from the Air Force. I'd end up in the stockade.

That meant that my dream of shipping out with the Merchant Marines was out and the best I had to look forward to was some low-end, meaningless, boring-ass, low-paying office job like Dan and his idiot friends all had, and that would definitely suck. I thought about simply crossing the border back into the United States and bumming around. But if I were to return, I'd end up looking over my shoulder for the rest of my life, and that would suck too.

It looked like I was screwed every way I turned.

One morning after a particularly vigorous romp with Pam, I went for a walk in the neighborhood and ran into one of my hippie neighbors. I could tell he was tripping because his eyes were dilated and he had a big grin fixated on his face. We talked for a few minutes and I patiently listened to his nonsensical diatribe. I laughed again and again as the fantasy world in his mind unfolded in a rash of crazy dialogue full of chaotic bursts of unfinished, illogical sentences—brought on no doubt by the severe electrical storm raging through his brain.

Suddenly he stared directly into my eyes. His dilated eyes were unfocused and reminded me of the blank stare of a blind person. Then unexpectedly he handed me a tab of acid and simply said, "Enjoy!" and with that he turned and walked away muttering something about Edgar Cayce trying to call him.

I dropped the acid—it was called Purple Haze on the street—and my trip was mild compared with most of my other trips. But when I began to peak, I started on a deep—thinking trip that lasted for several hours. I actually thought that I had most of the complex problems of the world resolved and it felt good to know everything about everything.

After the peak, I settled into a mellow groove that was like being up a little on speed rather than tripping in fantasyland. For some strange reason I had a very strong urge to call home as though I *needed* to do it right now. This was weird because the entire time that I'd been gone I hadn't talked to anyone from home or even had a desire to do so.

I went down the street to a pay phone and called my brother collect. He answered the phone and accepted the charges. He told me that Mom and Dad were worried sick about me and that the FBI had been to his house and theirs several times looking for me. He told me to call Mom and Dad.

I had no desire to talk to my parents, and yet I had this strange, irresistible feeling that I *needed* to call home. I dialed the number. My mother answered the phone and excitedly told the operator that she would accept the charges.

She immediately burst into tears and told me that at the exact moment that I'd called, she'd been on her knees earnestly praying and begging God to have me call home *tonight*.

She said, "It's a miracle, a direct answer to my prayer. Praise God!"

"Far out!" I exclaimed.

She asked, "Where are you?"

"Toronto."

I told her that I was fine, but I needed a copy of my birth certificate in order to get a job up there.

She said, "You need to talk to your dad, Bob. We've been worried sick about you."

She told me she loved me with all her heart and then handed the phone over to Dad. Dad and I talked briefly about why I went AWOL. I omitted telling him that Lisa had pulled a train and screwed Jim and his friends; I didn't tell him that after I found out about it I got drunk and passed out on the way back to the base, and that when I woke up I was already AWOL; I didn't tell him that then I just decided *to hell with it* and took off. Instead I told him that I hated the Air Force and their rules and regulations and especially my idiot 90-day-wonder second lieutenant.

I told him, "Dad, I'm done with the Air Force. I need you to send my birth certificate so I can immigrate into Canada and become a Canadian citizen. Without it I can't get a job."

He said, "Bob I'll help you do a lot of things, but I won't be a part of helping you turn your back on your country. You don't need to immigrate to Canada—you need to turn yourself in, son."

Ironically that was the one option that I hadn't considered.

I asked, "What do you think they'll do to me?"

"You'll have to serve some time, but you can probably get some leniency if you turn yourself in. I'll try to help you as much as I can."

"How much time would I have to serve?"

"I'd guess two or three years maybe, but afterward you can go back to school and have a life for yourself and not be on the run for the rest of your life."

Without hesitation I simply said, "I think I'll do it. Bye, Dad," and I hung up.

My conversation was rather short and abrupt, but in fairness I was on LSD at the time. I walked around for a while enjoying the mellow groove of the Purple Haze and the summer evening, and I didn't give another thought to my predicament.

I smoked a joint when I got back to the house and was finally able to crash sometime around three a.m. The next day I awoke around noon, and before getting out of bed I gave my situation another deep think.

As I lay back on my pillow I started reviewing my life. Let's see now, I'd been getting into trouble since I nailed my pet rabbit Bugs to the shed when I was five years old. I was in and out of trouble almost the entire time when I was growing up and attended 19 different schools. I was wild in college and had to quit school because of a shotgun wedding, and lost the girl that I really loved because of it. Just 11 months later I was divorced and said goodbye to a son that I would probably never see again. To avoid the draft and the Vietnam War, I had to join the Air force, which I hated.

My own brother and all his buddies screwed my girlfriend when I was out of town, and then she dumped me for the worst of them, a scumbag freeloader loser. Now I was a deserter. I was on the run from the military police and the FBI; and according to Bill, the CIA would snatch me off the streets if they found me. I was also on the run from the Calgary police because of the tire-iron incident.

I was homeless and penniless and was hitchhiking, hopping freights, sleeping on the side of the road, and breaking into restaurants to steal food. I had even stooped to begging for meals and money.

I'd been robbed at gunpoint, shot at by the police, badly beaten, and jailed. I was in Canada illegally and had no way of getting a legitimate job because I had no birth certificate. I'd started using intravenous drugs, LSD, and any other drug I could get my hands on, not to mention that I was drinking mind-numbing quantities of practically every type of alcohol sold.

Currently I was living with a bunch of anti-American assholes, screwing one's wife, and not thinking a thing about it. I didn't have anyone I could call a friend or that I even liked.

My conclusion was that I disliked everything about life and couldn't find one single redeeming factor in it. From what I'd seen, life was nothing but a screwed-up mess. The world through my eyes was largely comprised of bullies, jerks, and moronic authoritarian figures who thought everyone but them was a stupid sheep that needed to be dominated and told what to do.

I was determined not to be dominated by anyone. No one was going to break my spirit. They could beat me, stab me, shoot me, or lock me up; but short of killing me outright, they'd never break me.

Screw them and screw the world!

Maybe turning myself in was the best answer. After serving my time I'd be free to come and go as I pleased. I figured the longer I stayed on the run, the longer I would be looking over my shoulder and the longer my sentence would be when they eventually did catch me. If I turned myself in now and got two years, as Dad had said, I could probably be out in one, especially if I had time shaved off my sentence for good behavior. Then I ruefully smiled and acknowledged to myself that I was so full of crap. I'd never get time off for good behavior. I'd probably get time added on for bad behavior.

I laughed to myself. *It doesn't seem like I have many options,* I thought. *What the hell, I'll turn myself in and just face whatever is coming and fight my way through it.*

Later that afternoon I walked into the United States embassy in downtown Toronto and told the receptionist that I was an American soldier and was AWOL. I told her that I wanted to turn myself in and return to the United States. (I still couldn't bear to call myself a deserter.)

The lady at the reception desk acted stunned and definitely did not have a clue as to what to do. She stammered around and finally told me to have a seat and she called her supervisor. She talked with him by phone for a moment and then graciously smiled at me and sweetly said, "I'll be right back."

One would have thought we were discussing the weather and she suddenly remembered that she needed to go check on her batch of cookies in the oven or something, instead of my being a wanted criminal desiring to turn myself in. She left the room for what seemed like an interminable amount of time. Finally she returned and told me that Mr. Abbott would be with me in a moment. She asked, "Would you like something to drink?"

She was totally flustered and I looked at her with amusement and said, "No thanks."

In a little while a distinguished-looking gentleman came out and politely shook hands with me. He was slightly built and had neatly combed, thinning, graying hair, and was dressed in a dark-navy suit, white shirt, and red tie. He asked me to please step into his office. He had a large, polished, dark walnut desk with an American flag situated behind it. He looked important.

I on the other hand looked scruffy and was quite the contrast. I had on faded blue jeans, sneakers, and a wrinkled red-and-black-checkered long-sleeved logger shirt, with a beard and hair extending over my ears. I looked quite unimportant.

He was very polite and cordial and told me, "I understand that you are AWOL and desire to turn yourself in to the authorities. Has anyone coerced you into doing this?"

"No."

I assumed that he was covering himself, because of the many accusations by the Canadians and others concerning people being snatched off the street and disappearing. He took my full name, rank, and serial number, name of the base where I was stationed, and other pertinent information, and then he asked me to sign a statement that I voluntarily wanted to return to the United States and turn myself in, and had not been coerced into doing so.

The man told me that I would fly to Buffalo, New York, on a commercial flight in the morning, and that an "apprehension team" would meet me as soon as my plane landed. They would transport me to a nearby Air Force base, where I would be held until Keesler Air Force base could arrange to send a transport team to take me back. There, I'd be held in the stockade until I could undergo a court-martial.

He asked, "Do you understand all of this?"

I nodded yes.

He said, "And you're good with it, right?"

"Yes. I just want to get it over with. What do I need to do?"

He told me to come to his office the next morning at nine a.m. and he would have an airline ticket for me and he'd give me a ride to the airport. There would be no escort on the commercial plane, but I would be met by the Air Police apprehension team as soon as I deplaned.

Back at the house later that day, I didn't share any of this with Pam, nor did I share it with any of the others, especially Bill. The next morning I woke up early, packed my stuff, and left without saying a word to anyone. I laughed to myself that they would probably think I was snatched off the street by the CIA. That would give them some new anti-American fodder to rail about for the next month or so.

I took the subway downtown and met the embassy guy, and he personally drove me to the airport, where I boarded the plane for the short trip to Buffalo.

I thought about it on the plane and actually felt relieved. I was ready for closure on this part of my life. I would serve my time and put it behind me. I missed the United States. Maybe after all of this was over I could go back to school or even join the Merchant Marines.

I wondered what Lindsey was doing . . .

Finally we landed and I departed the plane, expecting to be arrested by the apprehension team. The problem was that no apprehension team came to meet me.

What the . . . ?

Chapter Thirty-Eight

I nervously looked around but didn't see anyone wearing a military uniform. I waited for perhaps 10 minutes and finally everyone in the gate area was gone but me.

Now what?

I decided to walk through the terminal toward baggage claim. I had an urge to just keep right on walking out of the airport, but decided against it. About halfway to baggage claim, I saw two uniformed soldiers hurrying down the terminal walkway. They had to be my illustrious "apprehension team" because they were wearing Air Police armbands and sidearms in black holsters, and black nightsticks were swinging back and forth by their sides.

As they walked past me I said, "Excuse me, but I think you guys may be looking for me."

They rudely brushed past, hurriedly walking toward the gate at a brisk pace.

I was amazed at these numskulls. I turned around and said in a loud voice, "You guys are late!"

They stopped and turned around.

"The plane from Toronto landed 10 minutes ago. I waited at the gate, but no one came, so I started walking toward baggage claim."

They came back over to me. "Williamson?"

I smiled and said, "Yes."

One of them immediately pulled out his handcuffs and started handcuffing my hands behind my back.

My smile turned to a look of puzzlement. "Why are you handcuffing me? If I wanted to escape I'd have just walked out of here. You don't need handcuffs. For crying out loud, I just turned myself in."

The Air Policeman told me through clenched teeth, "Shut up, you deserter son of a bitch, and get your cowardly ass moving or I'll break this stick over your head right here and right now."

If he thought he was going to scare me with that kind of crap, he was badly mistaken. I glared right back at him and bellowed, "Well why don't you just get to swinging then, tough guy? You think you're some kind of badass or something? You think you're scaring me with that nightstick? Well you're not!"

The other AP said, "C'mon Mike. We need to return to base."

The one called Mike told me, "We'll see how bad you are when we get you back on base," and then he shoved me forward, causing me to stumble.

I yelled, "Quit pushing me, you cocksucker! You think you're real tough pushing someone around who can't defend himself, don't you? Get these cuffs off me and we'll see how bad you are!"

People were beginning to stop and watch the scene that was unfolding, and I suppose the APs thought that it might not look too good to start wailing on a handcuffed prisoner in front of hundreds of witnesses.

The other AP took me by the arm and in a subdued tone quietly said, "C'mon Williamson. Just keep moving and quit causing a scene. It's standard protocol to cuff prisoners anytime we transport them."

I curtly nodded to him and started walking toward the exit. At least now they knew I wasn't going to take any of their shit. This incident reminded me of my youth when I'd start my first day at a new school and the school bully would immediately accost me. The bullies learned fast that I wasn't going to allow anyone to pick on me (even if it killed me).

I was taken directly to the stockade at an Air Force base located near Buffalo. Only two other inmates occupied the entire cell block and both were incarcerated for going AWOL. Apparently when the dumbasses took off, they had gone directly home to be with their families (the very first place that the cops were sure to look for them). They'd been captured after just a week.

Too bad for them that they were caught, but at least they hadn't been gone long enough to be classified as deserters, so their punishment would be much less severe than mine.

The stockade itself was like most jails with its austere, bare-bones conditions, but the food was good. On the other hand, the guards hated us and went out of their way to torment us at every opportunity.

It reminded me of boot camp. They would scream and curse and try to insult us and order us around as if we were animals. Like most cops, our guards were bullies and thought they were real badasses. I didn't fear them in the least—and that's what bullies hate the most. In fact, at every opportunity I went out of my way to match their threats and insults with threats and insults of my own.

It always produced results.

This was particularly true of Mike, the guy who'd cuffed me and shoved me around at the airport. He was about my age but was already a sergeant. He was gung-ho military and hated anyone who was against the war. He was always spouting off about it.

He'd sneer at me, "I wish they'd have stationed me on the Canadian border. I'd have liked to have been up there shooting you cowardly deserter sons of bitches just as fast as you tried to cross."

I sneered right back at him, "I wish you'd have been up there too, *Mikey*. It would've been great fun *putting your chicken-shit ass in the morgue when you tried*."

When I said that he pointed his nightstick at me and told me that I'd better watch my big mouth or else he'd come in there and "beat that stupid smile right off my face."

I lost all sanity when he pointed that stick at me. I stuck my face close to the bars and leered and sarcastically taunted him, "O-o-o-ooh aren't you the badass, Mikey? C'mon in here and let's see how bad you are with that nightstick. I don't think you have the balls to fight me, even with that big stick in your hand."

When I said that, you would have thought he'd just caught me in bed with his mother. He tried to hit my fingers with his nightstick but it loudly banged on the metal bars. I nimbly moved them and then tried to grab the stick from his hands. A couple of the other guards grabbed each of his arms and began dragging him kicking and screaming out of the cell block.

I moved up to the bars and screamed, "Where you goin', Mikey? Are you afraid? You're not wetting your pants yet, are you little Mikey?"

They were saying, "C'mon Mike, that son of a bitch isn't worth it. You go in there and you'll lose every one of your stripes and end up in there with him. This punk-ass deserter isn't worth it."

"All talk, little Mikey. All talk!"

He had completely lost all control and was loudly screaming obscenities at me and flailing his arms around and kicking his legs in the air trying to break free from the other two APs because he wanted to come after me. His face was flushed red and looked like a red-hot branding iron—all the way up to the top of his flattop hairdo.

I folded my arms and began flapping them around and squawking like a big chicken, clucking in my best chicken imitation. Then I yelled, "You want some of me, Mikey? I'll be right here waiting for you. You're just a big-mouthed punk. You got no balls, Mikey! You got no heart!"

The other guard said, "Shut up, you son of a bitch!"

"Why don't you come in here and make me shut up you son of a bitch, you? I'm not afraid of you, either!"

The other guard said, "Shut up or we'll all three come in there."

"Why don't you just do that, asshole? Come on in here and we'll see how bad all three of you are! I'm right here. You want a piece of me? Come get it!"

I'd lost any semblance of control and was screaming and shrieking at the top of my lungs. I was banging on the bars of my cell and jumping up and down screaming at them. I was a wild-eyed lunatic running back and forth inside my cell like a caged tiger at a zoo. My dark side had taken full control and I could no longer think rationally. I was completely insane with rage. I wanted to fight!

The cell block was in complete bedlam.

They dragged Mike out the heavy steel door. He was still screaming obscenities at me and I could hear him ranting and raving even after the door slammed shut behind them.

The other guys in the cell looked at me and one of them quietly stated the obvious. "Man, you're one crazy son of a bitch. Those guys are gonna kill you. You ain't gonna make it through the night."

"Maybe so, but I guarantee you one thing, when they come after me, they'll know I've been there."

I was breathing heavily and as I slowly regained sanity I thought, *I have absolutely no idea why I did that. No idea.* My dark side growled his response, *When they come back for you, keep fighting those bastards all the way into the center of hell.*

Amazingly, nothing more came of that incident. Perhaps it was because early the next morning I was interviewed by two serious-looking men from the OSI (the Air Force's Office of Special Investigation, which I understood to be their internal version of the CIA).

I waived my right to an attorney being present when I was questioned. I didn't really see any need for an attorney, because I was turning myself in and was planning on pleading guilty. I knew I was going to serve time and was mentally prepared and ready to move past it.

The OSI was interested in determining just two things: Did I give up classified information, and who helped me elude the authorities while I was AWOL?

I had a secret clearance and was enrolled in technical school to become an intercept operator. This program was highly classified and the OSI's primary goal was to ensure that I hadn't divulged any secret information. This entire interrogation seemed completely asinine and reeked of borderline stupidity to me. At the time I first went AWOL, I'd barely started school. They could have easily verified with one quick phone call that all I'd learned to do was listen to Morse code and type on a keyboard as I listened to groups of dot-and-dash signals coming over headsets. That much of the program was common knowledge and I didn't know any classified information yet.

They seemed to be living in some Cold War, cloak-and-dagger, espionage fantasy world. They just couldn't get it through their heads that I didn't know any secret information. And even if I had known something of a classified nature, I told them I hadn't discussed what I did in the Air Force with anyone the entire time I was gone.

It was serious business to them though. They questioned me for *three full days* and taped all the sessions. It began with my giving them a narrative of all the places I'd gone and what I'd done beginning with the day I took off and ending with the day the APs met me at the airport. After that first full day of narrative and their review of it, the next two days were spent asking follow-up questions to try to catch me in lies.

They now started questioning me in earnest. Over and again they wanted to know if anyone had asked me to reveal secret information. I consistently told them, "No, I didn't know any secret information. Even if I had that knowledge and someone had asked me for it (and no one did), I wouldn't have given it to them."

It was useless because they would just ask me the same question again in 20 minutes or so.

Then they wanted to know who'd given me money and who'd helped me. I told them that no one helped me and aside from selling my car and picking up a few dollars here and there from complete strangers while hitchhiking, I didn't receive money from anyone.

They wanted to know where I went and with whom I'd stayed in each state or province I visited, and then in an hour they would try to trip me up by asking about it again, only in a slightly different manner. A sixth grader could have easily seen what they were attempting to do.

It was hopeless. They didn't believe a word I said.

After the three-day interview I was transported back to Keesler Air Force Base in Biloxi, Mississippi. The stockade at Keesler was not as bad as the one in New York, because the guards didn't take any personal interest in any of the cell mates. They just quietly and professionally did their jobs and, unless we were fighting or participating in some similar offense, they ignored us altogether.

I was assigned a defense attorney named, of all things, Captain *Fink*. He had a little sign on his desk that read "Finks stink" and was quite the likable guy. He had dark hair and was about five-foot-ten and appeared fit. He was young, energetic, and very friendly toward me. What I liked about him was that he was not condescending about what I'd done, and was clearly committed to helping me.

He was very disturbed that I'd waved my right to an attorney and had talked to the OSI without representation. He'd read the transcript and said there was much incriminating evidence of additional crimes that I could be charged with, such as illegally entering Canada.

He told me that the transcript was a fascinating read and would make a good movie script. I told him that during my narrative and subsequent questioning I'd omitted telling them about the fights that I'd engaged in and the more serious crimes that I'd committed, such as taking and selling drugs. I maintained to him that the basic facts about where I'd gone were all true. He found it incredible that I'd traveled so far and in such a short period of time with no outside help or money.

Captain Fink was able to secure my release from the stockade while I awaited court-martial. He pled that I had voluntarily turned myself in and was not a flight risk, and he won. My skinny little 90-day-wonder commander had the mindset of Little Mikey and didn't like it one bit, but what could he do?

After being released from the stockade, I joined my former squadron, at least in a limited fashion. I slept in the barracks and ate in the same mess hall with them, but didn't attend classes or do much of anything else aside from meet with my attorney every few days or so.

No one was assigned to watch over me during this time, and I pretty much just came and went as I pleased. I was supposed to be confined to the base, but most nights I would walk to a bar just outside the gate and drink beer until I was dead drunk. If I'd been caught I would've been sent back to the stockade and it no doubt would have hurt my case, but I couldn't stand the boredom of sitting around those barracks every day and night.

I was the only person on the base with long hair; everyone else had short, buzzed heads. I refused to cut it, stating that I didn't have any money. Captain Fink wanted the Air Force to restore my pay now that I was back, but so far had been unsuccessful in his efforts.

It infuriated my commander that my hair was so long. He felt it made him and his squadron look bad when one of his men was walking around looking like a hippie, which was anathema to any true military person.

One day he ordered me into his office and told me that he wanted me to have my hair cut and then said, "Before you say it, I'll give you the damn money for it out of my own pocket."

I told him in my most sincere/insincere voice that I was uncomfortable with borrowing money or taking a gift from anyone, especially an officer, and that I would just await my paycheck.

Refusing to cut my hair and then feigning a reluctance to borrow money from an officer as my excuse—well, it didn't go over in a good way with him. In fact it pissed him off so much that I thought he might finally lose it and take a swing at me. But he managed to contain his anger and told me through gritted teeth to get the hell out of his office.

When I told Captain Fink about it, he admonished me for antagonizing the commander. He reminded me that as the officer in charge, the commander would have an important say in the ultimate disposition of my case. I didn't care; it was worth it to see the look on the guy's face.

One day Captain Fink summoned me to his office and told me that he'd arranged for me to undergo a psychiatric evaluation. The next day I reported to the base hospital and was shown to a small white room by an orderly. Perhaps half a dozen doctors in white coats were sitting inside in a semicircle. All the chairs were facing a singular empty chair in the middle.

That was mine.

I took my seat and the doctors sat there staring at me with owl eyes. All the men peering at me looked pretty much the same. They were to a person partially bald and graying, and in their late 50s. They all wore glasses, seemed to be studious types, had clipboards and pens, and had their legs crossed in similar fashion. Every one of them was leaning forward slightly as though highly anticipating sliding me under their microscope.

They questioned me extensively for approximately three hours. They politely asked me how I felt about just about everything. They asked about my childhood, my relationship with my parents, brother, teachers, how I liked school, the service, my sex life, and what I thought about my son. I didn't have any friends, so that part of the interview went quickly. They wanted to know about my fights and how it felt to fight, get hurt, and hurt people. They asked me why I went AWOL. I told them about Lisa, but added that I hated the military and would have probably taken off sooner or later anyway.

Finally they told me I could leave.

Captain Fink informed me that the OSI did not believe my story and wanted me to take a lie detector test. He asked me how I felt about that and I responded that I didn't care. I told him again that I'd told the truth except for withholding the parts about the crimes that I'd committed and the fight in Calgary.

He told me that he didn't think that would be a problem because it wasn't relevant to my specific charges, and he was going to review their questions in advance and would limit them in that regard. He told me (as I suspected) that they were convinced someone had helped me, possibly in order to obtain classified information from me. I just laughed and told him that if that was all they were concerned about, then I didn't mind taking the test at all.

I took their lie detector test over a period of a couple of hours and to their surprise readily passed it.

A few days later I was summoned back to the hospital for a follow-up visit in the psychiatric unit. This time I met with just one of them, the senior doctor, a full bird colonel. He asked me into his cluttered office and when I had a seat he told me that I'd been diagnosed as a sociopath.

I asked what that meant. He said that it was a behavior disorder in which the laws and mores of society meant little to those who suffered from it. He pulled out a book and read the definition to me. "Sociopaths have a complete disregard for the rights of others and are incapable of love and don't have any normal feelings of remorse, shame, or guilt. Genuine religious, moral, or other values play no part in their lives. They are often cruel to both people and animals and have no empathy for others and are capable of deadly violence. They are callous and have a reckless disregard even for their own safety. Most are pathological liars and are quick to rationalize the pain that they inflict on others in such a manner as to imply that the other party 'deserved' what they got."

I will never forget his face looking up at me. He had a strange look, and said, "Sociopaths don't have a conscience, Bob. Several serial killers are diagnosed sociopaths."

I asked, "What can be done about it?"

He told me, "All we know is that it begins early in childhood and if it's caught at that stage it can be treated, primarily by altering the social conditions in which the child finds himself. Once adulthood is reached, I'm sorry to say that currently there is no known treatment for it and there are no prescribed medications."

Then he officially told me the good news. "Notwithstanding, it is the determination of this panel that you are not suitable for continuing to serve in the United States Air Force, and we are recommending to your commander that an administrative discharge be given to you."

I was elated to hear their recommendation. Concerning their diagnosis, it really didn't mean much to me. I'd known something was bad wrong with me for a long time. I thought that he'd done a fairly accurate job of describing me (at least my dark side anyway). I realized that I really didn't have much of a conscience and at times had been cruel and violent. I wasn't religious and pretty much had the morals of an alley cat. I really didn't care what happened to me or to those around me, and laws hadn't been much of a deterrent to me if they interfered with what I wanted to do.

I thought the serial-killer crap was a little over the top, but had to admit that I'd often thought about the possibility of killing someone in a fight or whatever, and to be honest it wouldn't have bothered me in the least if I'd killed someone who was trying to harm me. Better them than me.

Another problem with their diagnosis was that I had definitely loved Lindsey and in fact still did, even though he'd said sociopaths were devoid of love.

To tell the truth, I wasn't concerned about being a sociopath. I was more concerned about getting out of the service. Maybe my indifference was another part of my disorder, but I really didn't give a shit about any of this.

Captain Fink wrote to my father on August 26:

Dear Mr. Williamson,

Last week your son took a lie detector test at the OSI Office here at Keesler. Both counsel and interviewee survived the three hour examination. I talked to the OSI on Friday and they informed me that they felt your son had been truthful with them.

Earlier in the week the psychiatrist diagnosed your son as having a character and behavior disorder. This will enable us to seek administrative separation rather than face a court-martial. A character and behavior disorder is not a psychic disorder, but only a personality variance from what the general Air Force norm is.

I just talked to your son and he informs me that he is to take a physical for separation purposes tomorrow morning. Without checking further this leads me to believe that his commander will recommend administrative separation.

Once again I find myself playing the waiting game, but the outlook is favorable toward an administrative separation with, at the worst, a general discharge.

Sincerely yours,
Captain B. Fink USAF
Defense counsel

I was appreciative that Captain Fink had downplayed the extent of my "disorder." There was no sense in getting my dad and mom all worked up about my being a sociopath. My father had honorably served in the Air Force and had worked his way up through every rank from buck private to major. The last job he had prior to retiring was as an administrative aide to a general.

It seemed that the only question that remained was under what conditions I would be discharged. I would either get discharged under "less than honorable" or under "honorable" conditions. An Administrative Discharge under honorable conditions was not bad at all as far as my record went and ultimately would not prevent me from getting hired somewhere when I got out. Getting out on "less than honorable" conditions would haunt me all my life.

Dad was hopeful that the commander would see fit to grant some leniency toward me and that he would allow me to be discharged under honorable conditions. After receiving Captain Fink's letter, he decided to write to the commanding general of our squadron so he could plead my case. His letter follows:

3 October 1968

Dear General McGehee,

I am writing on behalf of my son Airman Robert L. Williamson, Keesler AFB Mississippi, who has applied for administrative discharge from the United States Air Force.

Robert has had some unfortunate experiences which have resulted in abnormal reactions to them. While attending the University of Southern Mississippi he got involved in a courtship which resulted in a pregnancy and an unfortunate marriage; which was later dissolved by divorce. This experience has greatly affected his actions. He seems unable to cope with the problems that have arisen from this broken marriage and having a son that he rarely sees.

As a child Robert felt that his older brother was more favored than he, which caused rebellion. Of course, as parents, my wife and I feel that there was no favoritism. Nevertheless this was a problem for him. Robert is a fine young man, but is just unstable. He seems unable to meet the average problems without abnormal reactions.

I would like for him to go back to college and also obtain assistance from a psychiatrist. I will assist him if this is possible.

Sir my career in the United States Air Force was terminated when I retired in May 1960 after some 21 years of service. Certainly I know some of the problems that servicemen face and some of the decisions that have to be made. I do request that you give favorable consideration to Robert's application and I do hope that my small amount of information will be of assistance to you in your consideration of this matter.

Sincerely,
B. L. Williamson Jr.
Major USAF (Ret)

This letter had to be incredibly difficult and humiliating for Dad to write. He loved the Air Force and to have his son end up serving dishonorably had to be hard for him to take. I'm sure that he took no pleasure in sharing with the general that I had been a problem child beset with serious behavioral disorders. My hat was off to him for "baring it all" in an effort to secure leniency for me.

The general must have been sympathetic, because he responded six days later:

Dear Major Williamson

I have studied the circumstances under which your son Robert requested discharge. In consideration of his being absent without leave from 12 May 1968 to 9 July 1968, the pending court-martial, a medical evaluation, the advice of my staff and the contents of your letter, I directed he be issued a General Discharge Certificate not later than 11 October 1968.

Sincerely,
James C. McGehee, Major General, USAF

On October 11, 1968, I was discharged under *honorable conditions* with an administrative discharge. I was amazed. There would be no time in the stockade and no court-martial, and I was done with the Air Force.

Chapter Thirty-Nine

As I watched from my cocoon, I couldn't help but notice the correlation between my short unsuccessful college career, my short unsuccessful marriage, my short unsuccessful stint in the military, and my short unsuccessful life. My angel of light had made his point, but it didn't seem to be enough. The profound failures of my life merely continued unfolding and all I could do was lie there and watch.

I was *overjoyed* to be out of the Air Force. I didn't just hate being in the military with every *cell* in my body; it was to the *molecular* level. I'd been totally miserable from the day I went in until the day I got out.

I'd narrowly avoided spending serious time in the stockade and being tagged for life with a dishonorable discharge. I was thankful to Dad for the letter, and to Captain Fink, who was my hero.

After my discharge, I went into the hospital with a severe case of hepatitis A, a viral disease that attacks the liver. I'd contracted it from eating raw oysters at the bar outside the gate. The doctor told me in no uncertain terms that I shouldn't drink alcohol for at least six weeks or take anything that might further damage my liver.

When I left the hospital, I took a Greyhound bus to Columbus and reunited with my parents. I stayed at their home for weeks recovering. Although my dad hadn't said anything, I was pretty sure that he was feigning happiness at seeing me again. He seemed uncomfortable and withdrawn, and I had no doubt that he was deeply ashamed of me. It was understandable: He'd spent a lifetime in the Air Force, and loved it with the same passion that I hated it.

Mom on the other hand was genuinely happy that I was home. She felt that God had personally delivered me to her in response to the hundreds and hundreds of hours she spent praying for my deliverance. She was especially thankful for that miracle night—when I called from Toronto at the exact same moment she was kneeling and earnestly praying for me to call home.

Jim was still living at home and commuting to Mississippi State for his final year of college. Aside from discussing where I'd been and what I'd done during my absence, we didn't have much interaction. He was mad that I'd put Mom and Dad through yet another ordeal, but he didn't belabor it.

One day Mom picked up Little Jim from my ex-wife. I was amazed at how much he'd grown. As I looked at him, I sincerely hoped that he wouldn't turn out like me. I wondered what he would ultimately do in life. I hoped he would stay the hell away from alcohol and drugs, continue through school to earn a college degree, and maybe even become a famous doctor or lawyer or something worthwhile.

I wistfully wondered what would become of me now. Ever since I was a youngster, I'd always felt that I would not live to see my 30th birthday. Hell, I now wondered if I'd even make it to number 22—and that was just next month!

After all that had happened to me, I doubted if it was even possible for me to go straight now. I wasn't sure I even wanted to be straight. Straight people seemed wearisome, uninteresting, dull, and monotonous. I especially had no interest in hanging around Columbus. Too much bad Karma permeated the place, and the people seemed to be small-town boring and unaware of the world at large.

Returning to school didn't appeal to me either. I didn't like school, primarily because I disliked attending classes, which I found boring, and I hated to study. It was too much like the military, with too many Napoleon complexes and professors obsessed with their own self-import and holding someone "under their thumb."

It seemed like forever since I'd been 17 and graduated from high school. I'd already lived through an entire lifetime of mind-boggling experiences, including the craziness and mind-expanding excitement of the Haight. Nothing would ever be the same for me. I knew that even if I wanted to, I could never go back.

Much of my problems stemmed from drinking and drugging. The doctor's stern advice and my difficult recovery had convinced me that this bout with hepatitis was serious, and if I continued with my drinking and drugging that it would kill me. I'd stopped for now and I hoped that I could stop permanently, but I knew in my heart that I'd probably start back.

I wanted to give working in the oil fields another try. Out there in the middle of the blue ocean of the Gulf of Mexico, I'd be free from any temptation to drink or drug and—depending upon what kind of a deal I could work—maybe I could manage to stay completely isolated offshore for a month or more and really get clean.

After several weeks at home, I made my decision to give it a try. So I headed out to the road to hitchhike my way to Houma, the oil-rig capital of Louisiana.

My route took me directly through New Orleans, and when I arrived I immediately was drawn to the French Quarter like a sewer rat to a rotten piece of discarded bologna.

Within minutes I happened upon an old friend, someone I'd met prior to going in the service. His name was Bob too. He was a connoisseur of marijuana and always had "primo" stuff. Bob loved smoking pot more than any human being that I'd ever met.

Sure enough, when I saw him, he was on his way to his apartment to smoke a joint. He told me that he'd just scored some dynamite stuff and asked if I wanted to go with him and "burn one."

And just that fast my dark side was out of retirement. It was time to go back to work.

I told Bob, "Sure."

After that first joint, the oil rigs and going straight were quickly forgotten. It was back to business as usual, only worse. Over the next several months I fell right back into the lifestyle I'd left in the Haight. I became deeply entrenched in the hippie community of New Orleans; and I was soon shooting meth and staying up for days on end and then slamming heroin in order to come down and crash.

In between I was smoking weed, taking LSD, popping pills of every description, and taking any other drugs I could put my hands on, not to mention indulging in a steady diet of wine, whiskey, and beer.

In order to pay for my habit, I'd begun rolling queers. New Orleans was full of homosexuals, and instead of hanging out exclusively in their own bars, some of them would stray into the straight bars and brazenly try to pick up anyone they could. Homos always seemed to have huge amounts of cash. They would buy drinks for everyone in the bars, and when they tried to pick someone up, they would often offer money—sometimes big money—for sex.

I rolled a few of them by beating the hell out of them straight up, but it took too long and caused a great deal of commotion. I needed a quick way to mug them and be gone in less than a minute. I came up with the idea of using brass "knuckles" to sucker punch them. I'd seen a guy get hit with brass knucks and was impressed at what a difference the knucks made. It was akin to slamming someone in the head with a brick instead of a fist.

I bought a pair from a guy on the street for $15 and I wore a large black leather glove over them. The glove was an improvisation. The first time I used the knucks without the glove, I nearly broke my wrist because my hand twisted so badly when I hit the guy. When I tried out my idea for the glove, it held the knucks tightly in place and solved the problem.

I engaged a partner in my little business. Josh was a street friend of mine who happened to have a baby face, so every queer within three blocks would invariably try to pick him up. We would work the bars by going in separately, and Josh would stand at the bar alone. Soon enough a queer would come over and offer him a drink. After agreeing to leave with him, Josh would secretly give me the prearranged signal and I'd quietly leave the bar ahead of them.

Josh would suggest to the fag that they go to Josh's place, and he would lead them by a dark alley in a remote, quiet part of the Quarter. I'd be standing there in the shadows wearing a ski mask and the black glove with brass knucks snuggly held in place. When the queer walked by, I'd hit him in the jaw as hard as I could swing, usually cleanly knocking him out with just one efficient blow. On the couple of times I didn't cleanly knock one out with the first blow, the second or the third handily did the job. It was fast and clean and not a one of them ever saw my face or even knew what hit them.

We'd quickly drag him into the dark shadows of the alley, empty his wallet and pockets, remove his jewelry, and leave him there. It was easy money and there seemed to be an endless supply of it.

My split with Josh was 70/30 my way because it was my idea and I did the difficult, dangerous work. Josh only complained about the split once, and when I threatened to use the knucks on him, he shut up his whining. I did agree to split the jewelry money 50/50 with him because I let him take it to the fence, which seemed like too much risk for my comfort.

It didn't bother me in the least to mug those bastards. I felt that they were depraved maggots and deserved what they got and worse. In fact I laughed at knowing that I just smashed some pervert's jaw into pieces. After his mouth was wired shut, it would probably save some little boy from experiencing a nightmare.

As time went on, life continued to rapidly spiral down for me, and I was getting worse and worse as each day passed. One day I was coming down from a two-day meth run and was in especially bad shape. I felt like shit and was drinking some orange juice, and I was deeply depressed as I reflected back on my failed attempt at going straight several months back.

I'd been becoming more and more violent and had recently bought a .45 automatic. I'd quit my operation with Josh and using the brass knucks, and was now committing armed robberies. It was easier and there was no splitting of the money.

I'd pull my ski mask over my face and step out of the alleyway and tell people to give me all their money or I'd blow their damned heads off. I didn't just rob queers, but also targeted drunk tourists or anyone who looked like he had money.

I'd held up a couple of drugstores for both pharmaceutical drugs and money, but I preferred robbing people on the street. I barely escaped capture on the last drugstore heist when they set off a silent alarm. I just eluded capture by running out the back door when I happened to see the cops drive up. I ran through an adjacent neighborhood and ended up hiding in someone's garage for hours while the cops combed the neighborhood looking for me.

I was miserable most of the time and the hard drugs and violence of the street life were wearing me down. What had started as great fun and mind-expanding adventure with drugs was now tedious. I couldn't get high like I used to, but I had to have something. It was very expensive to maintain my need for drugs. It seemed that I had to take more and more just to obtain even a slight buzz, and then it didn't last very long. Those awesome rushes and fantasyland trips like I first experienced in the Haight were a thing of the distant past.

I was always jittery-paranoid and looking over my shoulder. I was in constant fear that the cops would bust me, or that I'd get my hands on some bad dope, or be intentionally slipped a hot shot by someone with a grudge, or have one of those mugging victims take revenge by shooting me in the face.

One day I watched the paramedics haul the limp, dead body of an acquaintance of mine down the stairs of his one-room slum apartment and put him into an ambulance to be transported to the morgue. I call him an acquaintance because there really was no such thing as a friend in my world.

I only knew him by his street name, Domino. He was about my age and we'd shot dope together on several occasions and had some laughs. He'd committed suicide the night before by eating two bottles of pills. He did it because his rich girlfriend dumped him for some rich guy that she intended to marry.

The very first time I saw Domino together with her, I knew their relationship would never last. She was just a bored, spoiled-brat, trust-fund baby, weekend warrior, hippie wannabe looking for some laughs, and Domino was her temporary court jester.

The poor bastard got all caught up in her jet-set world, unlimited supply of money, and riding around in her XKE Jaguar. He actually thought he had a chance with that bitch. In the end she tired of him and dumped him as if she were throwing out a rotten head of lettuce.

I always liked Domino and it was creepy to see his dead body like that. I'll never forget the scene. They had to carry him down the tenement's narrow wooden stairs by hand. One of them had to back down the stairs a step at a time, and Domino's limp body was flopping up and down with each cautious step. When they placed him on the stretcher at the base of the stairs, his very fine, long, straight black hair nearly touched the street. His eyes were wide open and his face looked contorted. Mercifully, they stuffed his hair up under his head and pulled a sheet over his dead face. It was Domino's final curtain call.

The ambulance crew nonchalantly slid the stretcher into the ambulance, slammed the door shut, and drove away. Domino was now history.

I could see the same thing happening to me one day soon, and it creeped me out. For weeks afterward I couldn't get that look on his face out of my mind.

The day after Domino's suicide, I witnessed another troubling event. It was nearing daylight and I was the lone patron in an otherwise deserted local bar called the Seven Seas when a dozen bikers from the Outlaws motorcycle gang came barging in. They were wearing their colors and were out of Daytona, Florida. It was somewhat unusual for bikers to come to the Quarter, but at certain times, like the Mardi Gras season, or sometimes just out of the blue they would appear like invading marauders.

I'd had enough exposure to the Hell's Angels motorcycle gang members, who were all over the Haight, to know better than to mess with bikers. They are the most ruthless, hardened criminals on the street and the lowest of the low. If you were lucky, they'd merely beat you senseless. But make no mistake, they would just as soon kill you as look at you, and if you ever messed with one of them, you would have to deal with *all* of them. Unless you had a death wish or were a masochist, the best thing to do was avoid them.

Ordinarily I would have immediately left the bar—and that is what I wanted to do. However, the bikers were milling around the only exit door and were drunkenly cursing and loudly raising hell about something. Instinctively I could see big-time trouble brewing. But I didn't want to call attention to myself by trying to leave and risk having them jump on me, so I just sat there wishing I were somewhere, anywhere, but trapped in that bar.

The bar was dimly lit and I was sitting in a particularly darkened area in the very back, at the top of some bleacher-type steps. I hoped they wouldn't notice me. The bikers were yelling at a woman who appeared to be with them, although she was not wearing colors. Suddenly they began slapping her face hard, and then one of them pulled out a knife and sliced a big jagged gash down the side of her face at least eight inches long. Bright-red blood gushed out of the sickening-looking wound.

The bartender, Little Jack, was a second-generation resident of the French Quarter. He'd grown up hard and his mother had borne him out of wedlock and raised him in the Quarter. Rumor had it that she still worked on Bourbon Street as a tired stripper who hooked on the side, and that Little Jack had hustled tricks for her when he was just a kid. He grew up to be streetwise and understood the meanness and craziness of the French Quarter's bohemian lifestyle. To be sure, Little Jack was well seasoned and had seen plenty in his 30-some odd years.

He'd been a bartender at the Seven Seas for as long as anyone could remember, and was an iconic fixture there. He was well known and much respected in the French Quarter, and even the bikers, who normally didn't give a shit about anyone who wasn't wearing their colors, gave him a certain amount of respect.

Little Jack was short and of medium build, and had long, thick black hair that was always clean and carefully brushed—like a woman's. It hung well below his shoulders and he wore a little black leather mariner-style hat cocked sideways on his head. He had on a matching black leather vest and Levi's, and had a leather poke hanging off his belt. Stylish, black, Italian-looking pointed-toed boots covered his feet, and to top the look off he had a Frenchy-style mustache with twisted, pointed ends.

When they cut the girl with the knife, Little Jack yelled at them to stop. They ignored him. He always carried a little pearl-handled .25 caliber automatic pistol in his back pocket, and when he came running around the bar in an effort to stop them from cutting her further, he pulled it out and shot a round into the ceiling.

Immediately after he shot, the bikers jumped on him like a pack of wild wolves on a deer in deep snow. As the bikers converged on him, jamming him against the wall, he backed up screaming, "I didn't shoot him, I didn't shoot him." Luckily for Little Jack, he convinced them that he had merely shot in the air and hadn't shot one of their fellow gang members. They let him go.

It was absolutely amazing to me that the bikers showed no fear and no hesitation when they heard that gunshot. Those crazy bastards were going after Little Jack ready to tear him apart, gun or no gun. To me, it was just further testimony to their viciousness and crazy nature.

Suddenly a big black guy walked in the door and they instantly forgot about Little Jack. Like swarming, angry hornets they were all over him. They beat that guy to a pulp in short order. It was 12 against one. I don't think he ever got a punch in. They beat him to the floor and then took turns getting up onto the bar and jumping off and landing on his head and his back with their big black motorcycle boots. These guys were huge and appeared to me to weigh in excess of 250 pounds each.

They beat him and beat him and beat him. I could barely make out the color of his black skin it was so covered in blood. Finally, mercifully, they took him and slung him onto the street.

Then they turned their attention back to the girl whose face they'd cut, and they started slapping her so hard that it sounded like Little Jack's .25 caliber handgun going off, one shot after another after another. Blood from the cut on her face was spattering four feet every time they'd slap her.

I was able to discern from their shouting that the girl was the old lady (girlfriend) of one of the bikers, and she'd taken up with the black guy. One thing you didn't want to do was mess with a gang member's old lady, and one thing an old lady didn't want to do was mess around on a gang member and especially not with a black person.

They were screaming obscenities at her and calling her a whore and a "nigger lover" and suddenly the unthinkable happened. The black guy came staggering and stumbling back into the bar. He was soaked in blood and seemed dazed.

I was stunned! I didn't know if he was brave and valiantly trying to rescue the girl, or if he was just insane, or stupid, or all of the above. I held my breath as I watched and thought, *Does that fool know that he's just signed his own death sentence?*

The first beating had been mellow compared with what they did to him the second time. I looked at Little Jack, who was standing there with his arms folded, leaning backward against the wall where the gang members had shoved him. With a sick look on his face, he was grimly watching the scene that was unfolding and wasn't saying a word. He knew better than to interfere again. There were far too many of them and they would have just killed him too.

As for me, I was trying to turn myself *invisible*. I was not about to say or do anything to call attention to myself either. I wished I had my own gun to defend myself if they turned on me, but a few days ago I'd traded it to a dealer in exchange for some crystal in order to keep a meth run going.

The finale came after they'd beaten him senseless. Two of them picked his unconscious body up off the floor and dragged him to the door, which had glass on the top half. They slammed his head into the glass. His head went completely through and the broken glass shredded his face and cut deeply into his neck. They did it again, and then one more time, knocking out the rest of the glass shards that remained. Finally one of them kicked the door open with a boot and they threw him outside into the gutter of the street.

Instantly, as though an invisible general had telepathically uttered a command to leave, all the bikers left the bar, taking the girl with the cut face with them. In less than five seconds there wasn't a sign of them.

As soon as they were gone, I was out the door and right behind them. I didn't speak to Little Jack and I didn't slow down to look at the carnage of the black man lying in the gutter soaked in blood. I ran the nearly two blocks to my apartment and locked myself inside.

The biker scene, Domino's suicide, armed robberies, and my dismal drug-infested life as a criminal were too much for me. I wanted out of New Orleans and I wanted a new life. I'd reached rock bottom and I wanted out NOW!

Chapter Forty

The problem was, I had nowhere to go and was addicted to drugs. A month came and went and I was still in the Quarter, more strung out than ever. A Fu Manchu mustache now adorned my face. I was gaunt looking, with sunken eyes and greasy, long hair; and tracks covered both my arms.

One Saturday my brother called me at a bar that I frequented. He'd recently graduated from college and moved to New Orleans. He'd obtained a high-paying job as a sales representative working for a huge company out of Chicago, Abbott Laboratories. He called on local doctors and hospitals as a "detail man," pushing Abbott's product line.

I lived in the heart of the French Quarter and Jim lived across the Mississippi River in Gretna. It was odd that he called me, because I practically never heard from him or saw him. I was the black sheep and he was the golden boy, and my life as an addict and a criminal embarrassed him.

Jim told me that his girlfriend's well-to-do father had taken some prescription Demerol intravenously, and that they were afraid that he had taken too much. They wanted to know what they should do about it.

I told him not to worry. I explained that Demerol is very similar to heroin and gives a tremendous rush when you first hit it up, followed by an enjoyable drift called a nod. A user can appear to be sleeping when in the nod, but actually he is experiencing the wonderful pleasures that are coursing up and down his spine.

Jim told me he knew all that. He said her father had taken it many times before, but this time was acting very strange and had mentioned that he was dizzy. He was cold and clammy to the touch and his breathing seemed shallow. He was mumbling incoherently and then drifted off into a deep sleep. Jim said the man had been shooting up all weekend and was afraid that he might have OD'd.

I told him, "Call an ambulance NOW!"

Jim said they were afraid to do that because her father would get mad. His nickname was Bull, which was entirely appropriate because he was very large and aggressive, and if anyone crossed him he could turn mean—*very* mean. With his massive physique and famous temper, he was physically intimidating, and most everyone was scared to death of him.

Bull was very wealthy and had obtained the Demerol from his private doctor, who had a dubious reputation for writing prescriptions for anyone who could afford them. If they unnecessarily called an ambulance and messed up his connection with the doctor, he'd make them pay dearly when he sobered up.

I told Jim that they needed to move quickly and stand him up and start walking him around. I told Jim, "His breathing is the main thing. You need to force him to walk in order to keep him breathing."

Jim asked if I could come over to help, that all of the family members were too afraid to go in there. Bull liked Jim and he wasn't afraid of him, but Bull was so massive that Jim couldn't manage to get him up and walk him around by himself.

I didn't want any involvement in this. I told him that I didn't have a car. Besides, I said, they were all the way across the river and I had no way to get there. Jim said he'd send someone to pick me up.

I reiterated my concern—that Bull was in bad shape and that they should call an ambulance. Jim said the family wouldn't do that and he insisted that I come help him. Finally I agreed and told him to send somebody over. I told him I'd meet the driver at the bar where I was bartending, Bonaparte's Retreat.

In a little while, one of Bull's four daughters picked me up and took me across the river to their house. They lived in a big mansion and, with the exception of Lindsey's home, it was the nicest home I'd ever been in. When I arrived, Jim took me upstairs and told me that Bull was lying on the bed in the master bedroom. He took me to the bedroom door and gestured for me to go in.

I went into the room and saw a dead man staring at me.

His unfocused eyes were looking blankly into space and big blotches of purple were at the base of his neck where the blood had settled. It looked similar to those purplish-looking birthmarks that people sometimes have on their faces. I saw a vial of Demerol and a syringe sitting on his nightstand. I touched his hand and recoiled at its coldness. I was so paranoid I wanted to scream. Here I was with tracks covering both arms and I could just see me telling the police that I had nothing to do with this scene. There was no doubt in my mind that the cops would just assume I was the source of the drugs and thus responsible for Bull's death.

I was freaking out!

I went to the door and frantically motioned for my brother to come inside. I whispered, "He's dead! Man, oh, man, what are we gonna do now, Jim? I can't be here. I have to get out of here right now, Jim. *Right now!*"

Jim went over and looked at Bull and his eyes got wide when he saw those dead-man eyes staring at nothin'.

I was freaking out. "I have to go Jim. *RIGHT NOW!*"

"Calm down Bob! Just calm down a damn minute! Let me think!"

I was frantic. "Calm down my ass, Jim. I have tracks all over me. I have to get out of here right now. They'll bust me sure as hell."

"Okay, okay. But someone has to tell Little Joe" (Bull's 16-year-old son).

Jim continued, "Take my car and take Little Joe with you, and when you get him away from here, just tell him his dad is dead."

I screamed a whisper, "What? Are you crazy? Screw that! You just tell him his dad is dead. I'm not going to do it."

Jim whispered, "Damn it, Bob, I have to deal with the rest of them. Bull's four daughters and wife are standing on the other side of that door and I'm gonna have to tell them and then deal with the cops when they get here. Give me a break will you?"

"All right! All right!" I whispered. "But I have to get the hell out of here right now and you tell them to *forget* that I was ever here."

I was so paranoid that I'd begun hyperventilating and thought my heart was going to explode.

Jim handed me the keys to his car and said, "When you get out of here, tell Little Joe what happened and just deal with it the best you know how. Don't let him come back here and see his dad like this. I'll forewarn you that he won't take it well." He somberly added, "He worshipped his dad."

Little Joe was a misnomer, because he was huge for his age. And like his dad, he had a volatile temper. I told him to go for a ride with me and we left. Little Joe was pumping me for information about his dad. He knew something was up.

I didn't know how to break the news. I couldn't think clearly because I was paranoid to the breaking point. After we'd gone a couple of miles, I simply turned to him and said, "Little Joe, Bull didn't make it."

Berserk! That is what Little Joe did, he went *berserk!* He was screaming and crying and pounding on the dash and yelling that he was going to kill that son of a bitch doctor that gave his dad that shit.

I was freaking out even more. Little Joe was jumping around so much he was actually rocking the car back and forth. He was pounding on the dash and insisting that we go back to his house. *Right now!*

I told him, "Look, Little Joe. I have tracks all over me. I can't go anywhere near that house. There'll be cops everywhere and they'll bust me and throw me in jail and forget about me. You don't need to see your dad like that anyway. Give me a break here, I'm just trying to help out. Let's just go down to the Quarter until they take care of your dad, and then you can go home and be with your family."

When I said that he only got worse. He was stark raving mad, jumping around screaming, cursing, and rocking the car back and forth like a wild man. He insisted on going back. Finally I couldn't stand any more of it. I was one paranoid speed freak and near to having a heart attack. I agreed to take him back, and told him that I'd drop him off a couple of blocks away. But, I said, he'd have to swear to me that he wouldn't tell anyone that I'd been there. He nodded affirmatively, and when I stopped the car, he jumped out and went running down the street toward his house.

I hauled ass back to the Quarter as fast as I could. I knew a guy named "Pokey" who was in the Merchant Marines, and he'd been trying to get me to go to New York

City with him to join up and ship out. When we first talked about it, I was excited to at long last join up and travel the world. Being out to sea for a month would clear my head and solve my financial problems; however I'd been so strung out lately that I didn't want to have to go through withdrawal from the drugs, and even though I badly wanted to join the Merchant Marines, I'd been giving Pokey the runaround whenever he hassled me about joining up.

That was then and this was now! I wanted to get the hell out of town today. I left Jim's car keys with a bartender friend of mine and told him where the car was parked and gave him Jim's number. I told him to call Jim and tell him that I had to leave town. (I didn't mention where I was going.)

I found Pokey and convinced him to leave right away. He was broke and was up for it, and didn't need any further convincing. We hitchhiked out of town that day, heading to New York City.

We arrived about a week later and I went inside the Merchant Marine headquarters to sign up. I hadn't counted on one small hitch. To become a seaman I would have to go through some sort of mini boot camp and get a short-buzz crew cut like in the Air Force. I was told that all new recruits had to go through this program and there would be no exceptions.

I was not about to let them buzz my shoulder-length hair and I was never going to take orders from anyone or go through another boot camp again. This gig seemed far too much like the military, and I told them that they could just "shove it." My dream of becoming a Merchant Marine was officially over. Pokey tried to talk me into signing up, but I was adamant. He went ahead and shipped out without me and I decided to stay behind in New York City to see what this city was all about. I made my way down to Greenwich Village, which I'd been told was the city's hippie section.

It was the meanest place that I'd ever been.

When I got there it was already dark. I quickly learned that it was dangerous just to walk down the streets of the Village. First I saw a deranged man standing in the street yelling at his image in a mirror inside a store. He was screaming and cursing and gesturing with his arms in unintelligible gibberish.

I walked on down the street and saw four guys standing there drinking. For no reason, one of them threw an empty whiskey bottle at me and it shattered in the street at my feet, sending glass shards all over me.

There were too many of them to even think about making a stand, so I just ignored them and proceeded down the street. There I saw two black men in a fight, or rather one beating another senseless, apparently because he'd called him a "nigger." The beaten man was lying on his back in the street and was a bloody mess. The other guy was standing over him with his fists balled up, screaming, "Don't you never call me that name again you son of a bitch. I'll kill your black ass if you ever call me nigger again."

All this in just a couple of blocks! Incredibly, when I continued, I saw two guys mugging a respectable-looking man who didn't look as though he belonged down there. I assumed he was a queer, or maybe he was lost, or maybe just plain crazy, but he had no business being down in that section of town by himself at night, especially all dressed up in that fancy suit and tie.

One guy was holding a gun to his head while the other went through his pockets. I immediately turned onto a side street and got the hell out of there. Next I heard the unmistakable sound of two quick gunshots and that was enough for me—I was running. I took a subway to Grand Central Station. I'd just experienced all of New York City and Greenwich Village that I wanted. This was definitely not the Haight. There was no common bond, no free love, and no flower power in Greenwich Village—just miserable, mean, lonely people looking for trouble and finding it.

Even at the bus terminal I saw crime. A tall, thin, black guy came slowly walking in and it was readily obvious that he was high on heroin. He carried a boom box on his shoulder next to his ear, and he was singing a slow blues song along with the music coming from it. He had a beautiful voice.

He sat down a couple of seats over from me and I noticed that his pupils were contracted to pinpoints, a sure sign that I was right about his being high on "H." In a little while he nodded on out. He was sitting there drifting through his dreams and three big, rough-looking black men came up and one of them put his finger to his lips, warning me not to say anything. Then, while it was still playing, they ripped off that guy's boom box and walked away.

Shit!

What kind of place is this? Now if I leave, this guy is going to think that I did it, or if I stay he'll be mad because I didn't wake him up and warn him.

What should I do now?

I stood up, went to the ticket counter, and told them I needed to go to New Orleans, and I gave them the cash I had remaining. I told them to send me as far as they could for that amount of money. It turned out that I had just enough to buy a bus ticket to Birmingham, Alabama, and that is where I went on the next bus out of there. I'd been in New York City for just one day, but it seemed like a month.

When I arrived in Birmingham, I hitchhiked the rest of the way into the Big Easy.

I wouldn't be staying there long, though . . .

Chapter Forty-One

When I arrived back in New Orleans, the people at Bonaparte's Retreat gave me my old job back as bartender. It really was a seedy bar, and was located in the French Quarter right around the corner from the Seven Seas.

I began to hit the needle again and this time I went at it unusually hard and stayed stoned virtually all the time. It didn't take long until my habit had escalated to the point where I *had* to have drugs. If I didn't take them I'd start feeling physically ill and experience serious psychological withdrawal symptoms.

My insatiable desire for more drugs was expensive, and the small amount of money that I made from bartending was nowhere near enough to support my large habit. I was trying my best to avoid armed robberies, because of the danger involved and the potential for going to prison for a very long time. Instead I began dealing drugs to supplement my income.

I would deal only in large quantities, although this was not without risk. If someone ripped me off or robbed me, I'd be ruined financially. If I was caught by the cops, I would find myself in prison.

The positive side to dealing in volume was that I didn't have to make multiple sales on the street to people that I didn't know, and I made enough money to satisfy my needs by making just one or two large sales each week. As long as a street dealer didn't get busted and snitch me out, I was fairly safe. But I was paranoid—always.

The paranoia was derived only in part from my drug dealing. I was also shooting up huge amounts of meth, which made my delusional paranoid tendencies even more intense. I was so paranoid in fact that I bought a .357 Magnum handgun from a junkie, who'd stolen it somewhere, and I carried it nearly everywhere I went to protect myself from my enemies, both real and imagined.

I became known on the street as the "meth-crazed dealer with a gun." I could fly into a rage at the slightest provocation, but particularly if anyone started pumping me for information about my connections or otherwise acting suspicious. (Of course everything seemed suspicious to me. I was, after all, a speed freak.)

More than once I was all stoked up on meth and shoved that big chrome revolver in someone's face and screamed, "Why you asking me all these questions? You a cop? You a rat fink? I'll shoot you right between the eyes, you asshole you! You ever snitch me out and I'll hunt you down and kill your ass if it takes me the rest of my life."

Most of the street people and dealers were too afraid of me to rat me out.

I'd rented a rundown apartment on Royal Street and would gain access to it by passing through a locked gate and a tunnel-like entry into a courtyard surrounded by two stories of crummy apartments. One night I was walking through the dark tunnel to go to work, and I had a strange, powerful feeling come over me. It was as though I was suddenly compelled to stop and look down. I did so and, although it was very dark, I noticed a book lying on top of a box in the tunnel.

I picked it up, and when I moved into better lighting I discovered that it was a book on witchcraft. Although I needed to go to work, I felt compelled or almost *required* to take it upstairs right then. I did so and quickly examined it. The book was hardbound and appeared to be quite old. It was black, with half an inch or so of red trim around the edges and gold lettering on the front, and seemed about the same size and thickness as a Bible.

I quickly leafed through the pages and noticed all sorts of black-magic spells. Each spell would have incantations that the user needed to recite, along with special instructions concerning how to implement it.

It looked interesting but I was already late for work; so I put the book down and left. That very night a guy was sitting at the bar and out of nowhere told me that he was a warlock. I didn't really know what a warlock was, but I didn't want him to know that so I didn't ask. He solved the problem for me by expanding on it. He told me that he was a male witch and that he could invoke the unseen forces of the dark underworld to do his bidding.

I didn't believe in that shit, but thought I would have some fun with him. I looked directly and intently into his eyes, trying to look mysterious and dangerous, and said in a low, menacing voice that I too was into black magic. I told him, "In fact I own one of only 12 original copies of the ancient *Black Magic Bible*."

He asked me about it, and he seemed visibly shaken and very frightened when I described it to him in detail and told him how I was led to it one night by a powerful force that I could not see but somehow understood.

He seemed really upset and immediately said, "I'm sorry man, I didn't mean nothing by it," and then he left in a hurry.

I laughed and thought, *What an idiot.*

Over the next two weeks I felt compelled to read the book, and I decided to try my hand at casting a spell. My first attempt had startling results. Several love spells spiced up the book, and I decided to cast one of the easier ones. All I had to do was light a black candle and chant an incantation and supposedly it would work.

I was standing on the street with a guy who smoked weed with me on occasion, and we met a girl who told us she'd just hitchhiked into town all the way from Big Sur, California. We asked her if she wanted to smoke a joint with us and she agreed. We went over to my apartment, and although she didn't look all that sharp to me, I decided to cast a love spell on her.

We smoked a joint and talked for a while. I had a black candle on my mantle and without telling her or him what I was doing, I went over and lit it and softly chanted the incantation. I left the candle burning and walked into the kitchen to get a Coke. When I came back into the room, my friend was having sex with the girl on the couch.

Whoa! I was genuinely amazed. I laughed out loud and said to myself *These damn things work fast.*

I went back into the kitchen and smoked a cigarette and waited. In a few minutes the guy came into the kitchen with a big grin on his face. I whispered, "What the hell?"

He replied, "Well, when you walked out of the room I asked her if she wanted to ball, and she said yes. So we got it on."

"Far out!" I said. "I cast a love spell on her right before I walked out of the room. That's what I was doing when I lit the candle and began chanting."

He stuck out his hand and said, "Thanks man!"

I shook hands with him as I laughed my ass off. "Holy cow, I guess this stuff really does work after all."

I was amazed at the number of people involved with witchcraft who began hanging around me. Prior to finding the book, I hadn't known even one person involved with black magic. But after I found that book, it was as though everyone that I met was into it. It seemed the dark forces had let the news out all over the Quarter that a new kid was in town. I wasn't seeking them out; they were seeking me out. It was most weird.

To be sure, the French Quarter had its share of shops that sold witchcraft and voodoo paraphernalia, but I always thought they were really just for tourists. I'd never been inside one and didn't know anyone else who had. I started going though, and was amazed at the number of people seriously involved in it.

I started telling people that I was a warlock, and I tried casting several more spells. To my surprise they all seemed to work. It was either one hell of a lot of coincidences, or there really was something to this black magic. Even though I had seen some things happen that seemed to indicate it was working, I still wasn't 100 percent convinced that there was anything to it. But whatever the case, it was kind of cool to see everyone's reaction and to see their fear of it.

One day Terry, a buddy of mine, and I decided to go to the horse races. I saw a fortune-teller set up on Jackson Square and paid her $5 to read my palm. During the course of the session she told me that my lucky number was three.

I didn't think much about it, but when I began to handicap the third race I noticed something that appeared too good to be true. It was the *third* race, *third* horse, *three* to one odds—and between us, all the money that we had amounted to a *$30* bet. I remembered the fortune-teller telling me that my lucky number was *three.*

I pointed all this out to Terry and said, "Hell, we can't lose!"

We put all our money on it and my horse won by three lengths. *Damn son!*

Word quickly spread around the French Quarter that I was a powerful warlock. My buddy had told everyone that he knew about what happened with my love spell and the girl from Big Sur, and Terry was spreading the word about the horse race.

Soon I was totally enamored by the tremendous feeling of power over others and seeing their fear of me as a warlock. People around the Quarter were spooked when in my presence, and I'd further their fear by staring at them like some insane, crazed madman. It became great sport to me and I was really digging it.

Then came the ultimate spell, which convinced even me that black magic was not only real, but also an undeniably powerful and dangerous force. One couple, Greg and Sandy, had been hanging around Bonaparte's every night for about a week. I'd smoked pot with them a couple of times, and we'd done some meth together on two occasions.

I thought Sandy was gorgeous with her long blonde hair, blue eyes, and beautiful smile. Neither of them had been on the street long enough to be hard core, but they were slowly getting there. Sandy in particular seemed to really like the needle. She especially liked heroin, which I was trying to steer her away from.

I decided to cast a love spell on Sandy, and this time I chose the most elaborate love spell in the book. I would need to create a drawing on paper and then say a bunch of incantations. Next, the book required that I give the paper to her and that she had to keep it in her possession.

Following my witchcraft bible, I carefully created two circles—an inner and an outer ring—leaving about half an inch in between. I drew the inner circle to be about four inches. I made my drawing on a letter-size piece of cardboard I found that kind of resembled parchment. Next, in between the inner and outer circles, I used black ink to meticulously draw in various symbols. I had no idea what they stood for, but re-created them to look exactly like the ones in the book. The symbols filled the entire ringed area between the two circles. When finished, my spell looked identical to the one in the witchcraft bible. Then I lit a black candle and chanted the incantation word for word, reading it right out of the book.

That night I brought the piece of cardboard with the spell drawn on it into the bar with me. When I saw Sandy and her boyfriend Greg, I gave it to her and told them that it was a good-luck spell and to keep it close at all times.

Greg said, "Awesome, we could use some good luck."

Sandy smiled that beautiful smile and softly said, "That's so incredibly nice of you to do that for us."

I just smiled and nodded.

That very night their apartment building burned to the ground. They'd hung the spell on the wall and, as I had instructed, lit a black candle before it. Apparently after they went to sleep, the candle caught the cardboard on fire; the spell fell to the floor and ignited the long curtains on the wall. Within minutes the entire apartment was ablaze, and they barely escaped with their lives.

Poor Greg was now terrified of me and was convinced that I'd put a curse on him. He was so afraid of me, in fact, that he left town the next morning heading for Texas. He implored Sandy to go, but she refused.

Instead, that very day she moved in with me.

Call it a coincidence or whatever you like, but this event utterly convinced me that black magic was no hoax and that powerful forces could be summoned up to do my bidding. I could actually feel their presence. I loved my newfound power.

A few weeks later, Sandy and I were approached by a weird-looking guy with frizzy black hair and little beady brownish-black eyes. He told us he was "into witchcraft" and had heard from some friends that I was a warlock. He had some drugs and wanted us to come over and party. When we got there, he put on the Rolling Stones' *Beggars Banquet* album and turned up the volume. We all smoked a joint and listened as he kept playing "Sympathy for the Devil" over and over again.

I went to the restroom and when I came back Sandy looked distraught. She whispered to me that we needed to get the hell out of there. She said that while I was gone, this guy had told her he'd give us drugs in exchange for allowing him to watch us perform sex.

Hearing that was akin to setting off a blasting cap wired to the end of a stick of dynamite. I instantly turned around and hit him as hard as I could right between those beady little eyes. He fell backward into an entire wall of beer cans that had been meticulously stacked to the ceiling along the wall of his apartment. All of them came crashing down on top of him. I then savagely kicked him in the mouth. Next I pulled out the .357 Magnum from inside my waistband behind my back.

Sandy was begging me not to shoot him, but I very badly wanted to blow his damned head off. The music was blaring and I could hear Mick Jagger chanting, "Pleased to meet you. Hope you guessed my name . . . oh yeah." accompanied by the Stones' singing the demonic chants of the chorus, "Who hoo, who hoo."

It was surreal and seemed as though I was possessed—my dark side was screaming at me, demanding to be bathed in bright-red blood.

The guy was shaking and trembling and begging me not to kill him. I told him to give me his drugs and his money. He handed over a small quantity of meth, a lid of pot, a dozen or so Quaaludes, and $400.

I put the gun barrel in his mouth and shoved it hard against his teeth until he opened his mouth. When the barrel went inside his mouth, I forcefully pushed it until it rammed into the back of his throat and he started gagging. I told him I was going to allow him to live because Sandy had asked me to, but if he ever came around me or Sandy again I'd kill him. I asked him if he understood and he nodded yes. Tears were streaming down his cheeks.

His mouth was bleeding and his blood coated my chrome-plated gun barrel.

I wiped it off on his shirt and then savagely hit him on top of the head with the gun butt. It made a sickening thud—once, twice, and then again (just for the hell of it the last time, because he was no longer feeling anything).

Sandy and I went home and downed some of Frizzy Head's Quaaludes with wine, and then had fabulous sex.

CHAPTER FORTY-TWO

A couple of days went by and I was approached by a black junkie who wanted to deal on the street for me. A friend had told me that he knew the guy and he'd been a street dealer to the blacks forever, and that he'd be a good contact for selling dope to the blacks. I had a good connection for blue morphine tablets, and I was told by the black guy that he could move them for me. Like all junkies, he insisted upon trying a free sample first.

I didn't like being around junkies even for one minute, but Sandy loved morphine and heroin and had been bugging me all afternoon about getting high. I decided that all three of us could geez up—I could get her off my back and accomplish some business while I was at it. If I could move even 50 tabs a week to the blacks in addition to my already thriving business with the whites, it would amount to some good money for me. So I agreed.

I was obtaining my morphine tabs directly from a drugstore, so it was pharmaceutical grade, which meant it was pure and it was powerful. A junkie's standard procedure was to split a tab four ways with a razor blade, and dependent upon their habits, two or even three could get fixed on a mere quarter tab. There were only three of us and Sandy and the guy wanted to split an *entire* tab just three ways—a third of the tab for him, a third for Sandy, and a third for me.

I was concerned that it would be too much and someone would OD, but Sandy insisted that she and I had built up a good tolerance to it. We'd been hitting it pretty hard (thanks to her strong desire for it), and I felt pretty good about it not being too much for us. But I didn't know about the junkie.

He told me that he had a significant habit and it would be no problem for him, either.

I said to him, "This shit hasn't been cut."

"No problem man. Damn! What da hell you talkin' 'bout? I'm doing $100 a day. Shit, man, I can do half a tab by myself."

I said, "Oh yeah, and you'd be one dead junkie in about three minutes too. This shit is pure, I'm telling you."

"I'll be all right, son. You let *me* worry about *me*. I was shooting up when you was crawling roun' shittin' yellow."

"I'm not your son and don't talk to me like that or I'll bust a cap on your sorry black ass—*boy*."

He was immediately apologetic. He wanted no part of the .357 Magnum that I was known to carry. He said, "I'm sorry man, I din't mean nothin' by it."

We went to an abandoned tenement building just down the street from the bar where I worked. We divided the tab into three hits with a razor blade. I crushed one in a spoon, added some water, and heated it with my lighter. Sandy shot up first, and then I fixed myself in like manner. The junkie did his thing last.

Sandy and I were sitting on the floor, leaning against a wall enjoying our rush; but as soon as the black guy did himself up, he stood and kind of made a gagging, gurgling sound and started staggering around like he was drunk. There was a nonfunctioning toilet in the tenement and the next thing I knew he'd staggered over to it and pulled down his pants, sat down, and excreted a foul-smelling load of diarrhea into it. Suddenly he keeled over and fell to the floor and was jerking around like he was having convulsions or something.

Sandy and I beat it the hell out of there.

I never saw him or heard from him again, and I don't know if he OD'd or not. We ran in different circles, so it might be that he just didn't come around anymore, especially after bragging so much about his big $100 habit and then shitting himself and keeling over like it was amateur hour. I kept my ear to the wind but didn't hear a word on the street of anyone OD'ing. I assumed he'd made it.

A couple of nights later, a clean-cut, straight-looking guy dressed in a white shirt and nice slacks came into the bar and ordered a beer. I served him and then went down to the other end of the bar, where a friend pointed to the guy and mentioned that he'd heard that he was some kind of powerful warlock.

I went back down to him and said, "They tell me you're into witchcraft. Is that true?"

He gave me a hard, mean look and, without answering, immediately left.

I thought, *Well, screw you too, buddy.*

The next afternoon the same guy came in and sat in the exact same chair and ordered a beer. I turned my back to get it for him and when I turned back around he was gone. But he'd left a small bouquet of white carnations wrapped in waxed paper on the counter.

I was pissed off that he ordered a beer and left without paying for it. I jerked the flowers off the bar and angrily threw them into the garbage can and drank the beer myself.

Later that afternoon a guy came in who owned a tattoo parlor in the Quarter. He began telling me he knew some junkies that had knocked off a drugstore and scored a big bottle of liquid meth. He'd heard that I was a speed freak and also that I had a blue morphine connection, and he thought I might be interested in him setting up a trade.

I was suspicious of this guy. Not long ago he had started coming in out of nowhere and talking to me like I was his old, long-lost friend. He'd been in the bar several nights that week bragging about geezing up, but when I asked him where his tracks were, he tried to give me some lame shit about covering them with tattoos so no one would know that he was hitting up. He had tattoos all over both arms, but I looked at them real close and I couldn't see any needle marks anywhere. Something wasn't right about this guy.

He was always trying to score from me, but I didn't trust him. So I told him I didn't care what he heard on the street, that I didn't sell drugs. Now he wanted to bring me a deal where I personally would have to deal with junkies and use him as the go-between. I was turned off by the entire thing. I didn't trust him and I didn't trust junkies; I knew from experience that junkies would do anything when they needed a hit. I had to admit the liquid meth was a big temptation, but I told the tattoo guy that I wasn't interested.

He asked me to at least come to his shop and meet them and maybe sample the meth and let them sample the blues. He said, "We're talking pure meth, man. An entire bottle. A *big* bottle."

The vision of a big bottle of pure pharmaceutical liquid meth proved to be too much for me. Finally I agreed. The next morning Sandy and I walked the several blocks to his shop to meet up with them at our prearranged time of 10 a.m. When we arrived there, the junkies were obviously in bad need of a fix. They were locked onto me as the one who could quell the beast inside them that was demanding to be fed. They were nervously insisting that I come through for them on the sample.

One was very tall, maybe six-foot-four, and went by the name Frog. The other guy was about medium height and his name was Bobby. Both were gaunt looking and strung out. I could tell that they were both ex-cons from their hard eyes and prison tats. Frog looked to be about 40 and Bobby was in his early 30s.

Frog said, "Just give us a taste man. If it's good stuff we'll deal you the meth. We got no use for it."

I had my doubts about the tattoo guy, but I knew Frog and Bobby were for real. You can't fake being a junkie. I got those morphine tabs dirt cheap and the meth would be a good deal for me. I had a morphine tab stashed in an alley by the bar where I worked that I could turn them on without a lot of trouble, and I decided to do it. If nothing else I could get them off my back and maybe have someone else do the deal with them and take the risk in exchange for a hit or two of the blues or the meth.

"Okay, what the hell. I'm warning you, though. You have to be careful with this shit. This is pharmaceutical-grade morphine and there are four super-hard hits to the tab. You could OD on this stuff real easy. I've seen it happen."

They said, "C'mon, we'll take a ride over and do our business."

The tattoo guy told us to go ahead without him—that he needed to stay at his shop. Sandy and I got into their beat-up 1960 Chevy Impala and headed the few blocks to the bar. As we drove over, I saw an unusual number of cops driving through the Quarter, and it started making me nervous.

We parked on the street and when we walked around the corner, I saw an unmarked car with a guy sitting in it pretending to be reading a newspaper. It was parked right beside the alley where my stash was hidden.

I told them, "It's the heat; we have to get the hell out of here."

The junkies needed a fix and didn't want to leave. Frog said, "Calm down. Are you sure that's a cop? He doesn't look like a cop to me."

I hissed, "It's unmistakable. I'm getting the hell out of here."

Frog was insistent and he grabbed me by the arm, "*WAIT!* Let's just all stay calm and go in the bar, have a beer, and wait until he leaves."

Just then a marked police car came slowly cruising down the street and the cop was looking right at me.

I jerked my arm out of Frog's grip and said, *"Screw you! I'm getting the hell out of here right now."*

In typical junkie fashion, they were relentless. Frog said, "We're staying with you man. We need to fix . . . *bad.*" He reached over and grabbed my arm and looked me in the eye and squeezed my arm and said again, "*Bad!* Let's all just stay calm and go back to the tattoo shop and wait it out. We're staying with you. You're just going paranoid, man. It's the meth. We all need to just chill!"

I could see in their eyes that they were badly in need of a fix and weren't going to let me out of their sight. There would be no way out unless I fought my way out right there on the street with cops everywhere. I was tempted to do it, but seeing those cops and thinking that Sandy might get hurt cooled me down. Better to just go with the junkies and ditch them later.

I said, "Let's go then. Anywhere but here. Something is going down. I live down here, man, and the heat is everywhere. Something bad is going to happen SOON! This is not good. This is not good."

Sandy and I got in the backseat of the car and Frog and Bobby sat in the front, and we slowly wound our way through the Quarter heading back to the tattoo shop. A cop car had pulled in behind us and was following us through the Quarter.

I was petrified. I said, "Is anyone holding anything?"

I looked at all of them. Bobby, Frog, and Sandy all shook their heads no.

"*Are you sure?* We're going down. IS ANYBODY HOLDING ANYTHING? Outfits, dope, anything?"

Again they all said no and were nervously looking around, sensing the danger. Just then a cop pulled in front of us. One cop was now in front of us and one was behind. We were sandwiched in between.

Shit!

When we drove up in front of the tattoo shop, all hell broke loose. Cops came from all directions, sliding their cars in with tires screeching. They all jumped out brandishing guns and ordered us to put our hands where they could see them. "Get out of the damn car," they shouted.

We all piled out onto the street and they searched us. They handcuffed us behind our backs and sat us on the curb while they literally tore the car apart. They even took the seats out, but found nothing. I'd been afraid those junkies had overlooked something in their car, but it looked like they hadn't. I was very glad that I had decided to leave my .357 Magnum at home. I had a premonition about this. I should have listened to it.

I thought, *At least we're all clean. It looks like we're in the clear.*

There must have been 20 different cops milling around on the street as though they didn't know what to do now.

I saw one of them whispering to the tattoo guy.

I whispered to the others, "Look at that asshole. Right over there is your snitch. *I knew that guy wasn't right.* Look at that son of a bitch talking to those pigs. They're asking him why it didn't go down like he said it would."

When he saw me looking at him, he looked scared and quickly turned away and went back into his shop.

I softly said, "You'd better run you son of a bitch, 'cause me and my .357 are gonna be coming to see you real soon."

Frog said, "If you need any help, just let me know."

After about 45 minutes of sitting there with our hands cuffed behind our backs and growing numb, I heard a lone siren coming. First it sounded as though it was far away and then it began to get closer and closer. Finally an unmarked car slid to a stop behind the marked cop cars.

A cocky-looking, skinny little asshole, plainclothes cop wearing aviator sunglasses, a white shirt, a thin tie, and a cheap suit jumped out of the car. He didn't look old enough to shave and reminded me of that 90-day-wonder second lieutenant I hated so much. He walked directly over to some bushes and reached down as though he was picking something up and said, "Here it is. I found it. We got 'em. Arrest those sons of bitches."

He had a syringe in his hand and it didn't come from any of us. That asshole brought it with him. We looked at each other and knew that we were being set up.

They took us all to jail and booked us for possession of heroin. During the booking process, Sandy and I talked to different cops at adjacent desks. I could plainly hear what she was saying and that dumb bitch was going on and on about how much she liked heroin. I couldn't believe she was that stupid.

The cop interviewing me kept asking me about heroin and I told him I didn't like heroin and I didn't use heroin. He didn't believe me and kept asking me over and over again.

Finally I had had enough of his shit. I rolled up my sleeve and showed him my tracks and said, "Look. I'm not trying to act like I'm some friggin' priest or something. I'm a speed freak. I admit it! I like meth and not heroin. I've tried heroin and I don't like it. You can keep asking me the same damn question until hell freezes over, but it's not gonna change one damn thing. I'm a speed freak, not a heroin addict."

Finally I'd gotten through to him. I could see it in his eyes. He looked at me and sadly said, "Son, don't you know that meth will fry your brain?"

I somberly replied, "It will *all* fry your brain. I'm just waiting to die anyway. To tell the truth, I don't care if I die. In fact I'd welcome it. I already feel dead anyway."

I was sincere and had finally verbalized what had been on my mind for quite a while.

The cop looked stunned. I shall never forget the look on his face when he fully understood that I knew meth was frying my brain and killing me and that I just didn't care.

How could anyone not care about whether they lived or died? That was insanity.

At least to him it was insanity; it made perfect sense to me. I wanted out of this screwed-up, perverted world. I just hadn't had the balls to take myself out, as Domino had done. Yet.

I asked, "What's going to happen to us?"

He told me the syringe would be tested for heroin residue and if it came back dirty, we'd go to trial or plead out. If it was clean we'd go free. He told me if we ran water through it after hitting up (which is standard procedure), it would likely come back clean.

I looked at him and told him, "You know and I know that syringe was not ours. Say what you want, but that guy brought it with him."

He just laughed and said, "That's what they all say."

We were arraigned the next day and we all pled "not guilty." The judge, who was an old man with a foul disposition, looked down at us with sheer disgust on his face and said, "Let's get these damn junkies off the street. Bail is set at $5,000 each."

I thought my public-defender attorney was going to swallow the gum he'd been furiously popping. He told me no one with a chicken-shit beef like we had ever has bail set that high. He said, "They must have wanted you guys off the street really bad. Why do they want you off the street so bad?"

"I don't know."

I used my one phone call to call my brother. I told him I'd been arrested for possession of heroin and my bond was $5,000. A bail bondsman would require 15 percent of the bond as his fee for making my bail. Jim said he'd see what he could do, but that he'd just gotten married and didn't have money like that. I didn't even know that he'd gotten married. I congratulated him.

Sandy called her parents in Florida and they were on the next plane to New Orleans. She ended up making bail and returned to her parents' house in Florida, where she was under their custody while awaiting trial.

Frog, Bobby, and I went directly to Parrish Prison in downtown New Orleans to await trial. As we were being transported from the jail to prison, Frog looked at me and somberly said, "Bob, when we get inside, you just stick close to me. I been in there before and it ain't no picnic."

I wasn't thinking about prison. I was thinking about that warlock and his damned bouquet of flowers. I was sure that son of a bitch had cast a spell on me and landed me in this mess.

Frog continued, "We're going to be housed in a big tier. There are 40 guys in one open cell. It was built for 20. There are guys in there for murder, armed robbery, rape—you name it. We'll probably be sleeping on mats on the floor until someone gets moved out. All three of us need to stick together. You got anyone on the outside that can get some money to you?"

"Nope, no one."

"Are you sure? Money goes a long way in there. It could really help out."

"I got no one."

He could see I was telling the truth and he said, "That's all right, we'll be fine; just stay close. Bobby and me, we'll help watch out for you."

"Thanks, Frog."

Chapter Forty-Three

The prison guards issued us uniforms, sheets, a thin wool blanket, soap, toothbrush, toothpaste, and two visitor's passes. We entered the tier, which was a giant cell filled with over-and-under steel bunks and a 20x20 open area. Approximately 40 men were milling around, for the most part dressed in boxer shorts and T-shirts or no shirts.

We were immediately met by a black man wearing white boxers and a sleeveless white tee that looked even whiter in contrast to his black skin. He had a wicked-looking, jagged scar that ran diagonally from his temple to the base of his jaw. Two burly, heavily tattooed men stood on either side of him, and I assumed they were his enforcers.

He was the boss and was in for murder. He stopped me and, without a word, disinterestedly rifled through my stuff as he had no doubt done to other inmates hundreds of times before. He took my two guest passes and then dismissively motioned me on into the tier.

Frog knew several people inside, and they were yelling out to him and he was waving back. It was like a reunion for him. I was surprised that a junkie seemed to have so much stature.

Parrish Prison definitely had its pecking order. It not only held inmates awaiting trial, as we were, but housed criminals already convicted and serving their sentences. Everyone's rank was determined primarily by the crimes they were in for—the most prestigious, of course, was murder, followed by manslaughter, armed robbery, and felonious assault. Drug-related crimes fell somewhere in the middle, as did burglary and so forth. Our status was neither revered nor reviled.

The only exceptions to the priority ranking fell to those vicious muscle-bound inmates of huge physical stature who could literally beat the shit out of someone and kill him with bare hands. Qualities like that were admired in Parrish Prison and generally moved these men up in stature. The guys who had money or could obtain money also had a special ranking; and although the pit kingpin still controlled the tier, money talked and the money guys pretty much had it made.

The most reviled were pedophiles, rapists, homosexual sex-crime perverts, and wife beaters. They were in constant danger of being beaten, stabbed, raped, and killed. They were the ones who were gang-raped late at night (which happened most every night I was there, and sometimes even in broad daylight).

Everyone had a story to tell of how he ended up in prison. One guy that I met was in for bank robbery. From his appearance, he seemed to be the least likely person to be in Parrish Prison, much less incarcerated for bank robbery. He was about my age—maybe 22—and was a nice-looking, clean-cut college kid.

He told me he had been walking downtown, thinking about needing some money, and on a whim decided to rob a bank. With no prior planning he just went into the bank, wrote a note, and handed it to the teller. It said, "Give me all your money or I will kill you."

He told me that the bank teller was terrified and quickly gave him all the money in her drawer. He then calmly walked outside.

His brilliant plan of escape—his absolute stroke of genius concerning his getaway after robbing a bank in downtown New Orleans with cops on every street corner—was to walk outside and hail a cab.

Not one cab stopped, and the cops caught him standing directly in front of the bank still holding one hand up to every cab that passed and clutching a bag of the bank's money in the other.

It irked me to no end that this moron had a higher status in prison than I had, because he was in for bank robbery and I was in for my lowly possession-of-heroin charge.

As predicted by Frog, no beds were available and we all had to sleep on mats on the floor. It didn't matter. We were all sick as hell due to withdrawal. My physical withdrawal symptoms were minor compared with Bobby's and Frog's. They were in exceedingly bad shape from their big heroin habits. Both of them had the dry heaves and were shaking; they also were experiencing cramps and shooting pains running up and down their bodies.

I hadn't realized just how strung out I was. As a speed freak I didn't have physical withdrawal symptoms that were as bad as the ones they had, but the mental torment was every bit as awful. The craving was far beyond anything I'd experienced to date. It was somewhat akin to crawling through the sand of the blazing-hot, 140-degree Mojave Desert for 100 miles and then being denied water. I was damned thirsty for a fix of any type.

Drugs were readily available in prison, but you had to have money to obtain them. I was sure that's why Frog had asked me if I knew anyone on the outside who could get money to me. I was subsequently grilled by Scar Face about it too, but I told him that when I was on the outside, I put all my money into my arm. It took a while, but I finally convinced him that I had no money, no family, no friends, no nothing.

I saw Frog shoot up with his buddies several times, but he got only tiny little hits that were barely enough to take the edge off his severe withdrawal pains. I saw him smoke some weed too. I was never asked to join in, but true to his word, Frog did watch out for me. He told the right people that I was "good people" and no one ever bothered me.

Prison life is like being diagnosed with terminal cancer. At first you are desperate to escape the sentence and you're expecting a miracle. It's all you can think about every second of every day. You just want to take off running with reckless abandon, but there is nowhere to run. Most inmates are afraid when they first walk through those gates. Later they just become angry. With the realization that you ain't getting out comes dark depression.

Finally, you comprehend that you'll be staying there and aren't going to be the recipient of some frigging miracle. When all hope is gone, only then can you accept it; and that is when the routine kicks in. Prison life is routine. There can be no peace until you submit your spirit to the routine.

You eat, you shoot the shit with other inmates, you sleep, and you *always* try to stay out of the path of dangerous psychopaths; you eat, you shoot the shit with other inmates, you sleep, and you *always* try to stay out of the path of dangerous psychopaths.

Routine.

Every day is just the same as the last and will be no different than the next. You do not think about getting out. It's not going to happen to you; maybe someone else, but good stuff never happens to you.

I never had one visitor or one piece of mail, nor did I expect any.

They fed us sandwiches for the most part—two pieces of dry bread and bologna with no condiments—and they gave us boxes of lukewarm milk and half-rotten apples. If we received a cookie or something good, Scar Face or one of his men would take it. I didn't give a shit—I wasn't ever hungry anyway. I never had a penchant for eating and ate only to survive, even on the outside.

I kind of lost track of time while I was inside. Most of our days were spent talking about how we were busted, or what we were going to do when they finally let us out. We mostly wanted to get stoned, get laid, and make some money by committing more crimes. I must have had 10 different guys who wanted to partner with me in my drug dealing.

After about two or three weeks, a guard called out my name and told me to gather my stuff together, that someone had made my bail. It was totally unexpected and I was ecstatic. Frog and Bobby came over and seemed genuinely happy for me and slapped me on the back and congratulated me. Scar Face smiled and saluted with two fingers, similar to the Cub Scout salute. I smiled and saluted back in like fashion. Frog and Bobby both told me that if there was any way I could get some money to them, it would be appreciated.

I nodded. "I'll see what I can do. Thanks for keeping me under your umbrella, Frog."

"No problem man."

My brother Jim was waiting for me when the steel door slid open. The first thing he said was that he had to hock his wife's wedding ring to get me out. He was none too happy about it. I told him I was sorry, but that I was very appreciative for what they'd done and that I'd pay him back somehow.

I'd lost my apartment, which I rented by the week. My brother had gone by my place and gathered everything I owned into a cardboard box. Inside was my witchcraft book, toiletry items, a couple pairs of underwear, two shirts, two pairs of worn-out Levi's, and my .357 Magnum. He lectured me for an hour about the pistol and I promised him that I would sell it as soon as I could find a buyer.

He told me that I could stay at his house until I found a place of my own and secured a job. I thought of what my attorney had told me: that it would be a couple of months before we went to trial and I should stay out of trouble. So Jim's house sounded just about right.

Prior to his marriage, Jim had two girlfriends at the same time. Their names were Brenda and Julie and he loved them both with all his heart. And they felt likewise about him. I was never clear on how he decided upon which one to marry. When he was dating them he was constantly sneaking back and forth from one to the other, and eventually they found out about each other. Somehow Brenda won the tug-of-war and ended up being his bride, but I don't think Jim ever quit loving Julie.

The marriage didn't end the tension, and Julie was a constant source of trouble between them. Brenda was insanely jealous, and every time Jim left the house, she thought he was going to see Julie (probably for good reason).

I'd been staying at Jim's for about a week and had been able to secure my old job bartending at Bonaparte's. I was laying low and trying my utmost to stay off drugs. One day Jim and I both had the day off and we were sitting around smoking a cigarette and just talking, and he asked me if I'd like to go to a movie and just spend some time together.

We hadn't done that in years. Come to think of it, I don't remember ever doing that with Jim. I said, "Sure, that'd be fun."

Brenda was in the kitchen and Jim yelled out to her that we were going to a movie, and we walked out and sat in the car. Here came Brenda. She was irrational and screaming, cursing, crying, and clawing at Jim. She thought we were going out partying—probably with Julie and friends—and she was having no part of it.

Jim patiently tried to reason with her, as did I. This went on for a good 10 minutes, with Jim telling her over and over again that we were just going to see a movie. But she could not be consoled. She was convinced that we were going somewhere to meet some girls. Finally Jim started the car. She reached in and grabbed the keys out of the ignition and threw them as far as she could into the bushes against the house.

I exclaimed, "You stupid bitch, why'd you go and do that?"

Jim angrily turned toward me and said, "Don't you call her a stupid bitch, you junkie. She just hocked her wedding ring to bail you out. You get the hell out of my car and while you're at it get the hell out of my house."

"Fine!" I said, and I got out and slammed the car door and started walking. I didn't even bother to take my stuff.

As usual, I was broke with nowhere to stay. I made my way down to the French Quarter and the Seven Seas, and I hung out for a while trying to find some speed in order to stay awake until I could find a place to crash.

A guy I knew said he didn't have any speed but he had a tab of acid and he didn't want to trip alone and would be glad to split it with me. I'd taken acid hundreds of times, but it no longer had much of an effect on me. Half a tab would never even get me off, but I guessed that it might be similar to dropping some speed. I thought maybe I could substitute it and stay awake long enough to find a place to crash for a few days. I said, "Yeah, half a tab of acid would be nice right about now."

He broke the orange tablet in half and then we each dropped a piece. We went over to his girlfriend's apartment and after about 30 minutes I began feeling rather tingly and kind of clammy all over. I felt like I was going to have diarrhea, so I ran toward the bathroom. All of a sudden both my arms went flying off my body, torn off by some horrific force. Then the force tore off my legs in similar fashion, and they went flying through the air. It seemed as though they were connected by some sort of invisible springs, because they came flying back on, only to fly off again. I was terrified.

I looked in the mirror and my face was covered in blood and big boils. It looked horrific. Suddenly the loudest noise I'd ever heard in my life blared in my ears like a highly amplified air-raid siren going off in my head.

WAHHHHHHHHHHHHHHHH!

I was so afraid that I literally thought I would shake to pieces.

I saw a flash of burning white light and then I went blind. Total darkness. The siren suddenly began blaring in my ear again, and it scared me so badly that I took off blindly running. I couldn't see and ran into the door frame, cutting my forehead. I fell to the floor and my vision came back. I saw thousands of poisonous snakes crawling all over me and the room.

Then the room started filling up with blood, and the snakes were swimming in it. I was horror-struck, but the noise in my head was so loud I couldn't move. I was drowning in blood. The snakes smelled like a sewer, but I just sat there letting them crawl all over me, holding my ears with both hands, rocking back and forth as the blood rose over me like floodwater in a basement. I was trying to keep my head above it, but kept sputtering and spitting blood out of my mouth as it continued to rise. The blaring siren was relentless and kept emitting wave after wave, beating me down. I was weeping and crying, scared shitless.

Abruptly the siren stopped and the snakes were gone. And so was the blood. I slowly returned to my feet, dazed and shaken. I was still trembling uncontrollably and sobbing. It was as though I was now looking down from a balcony into a seedy-looking, very dimly lit small theater with maybe 30 rows of red seats, 30 seats across, descending at an angle like an amphitheater down toward a well-worn wooden stage. The stage was elevated about four feet above the first row of seats. Bunched red drapes hung to the floor on each side. A solid-black backdrop stood behind the stage.

No one was in the theater but me, and it was deathly quiet. All of a sudden a menacing, portentous figure began shuffling across the stage. It was difficult to see him clearly because the lighting was very poor, and it almost seemed as though a barely visible, hazy smoke was covering the room.

The figure looked to be a big man, with large shoulders almost like a hunchback, and he was dressed in a full-length black overcoat that hung nearly to the floor. He wore an oversized black fedora pulled low over his face. I could not see a face, but the figure was ominous and revolting—the personification of evil ever so slowly shuffling across the stage. When he finally reached center stage, the figure suddenly whirled around to face me.

WAHHHHHHHHHHHHHHHHH!

The blaring siren knocked me down to the floor again. I was scared beyond comprehension. I was petrified and was screaming over and over again with fright. I could not see his face, but the black and foreboding figure stood there facing me.

Suddenly the siren stopped and the figure started ever so slowly shuffling away. Then it whirled around and faced me again and the siren wailed.

WAHHHHHHHHHHHHHHHHH!

This happened over and over and over. Each time I would cover my ears and scream in fear. I'd never been afraid of much of anything in my entire life, but I was struck with the horror of it all.

The guy with whom I'd dropped the acid was not experiencing a bad trip. Several other people were now at the apartment and heard my excruciating screams, and saw me hysterically crying. They knew I was having a bad trip, so they herded me into a back bedroom. They were all trying to figure out what to do with me. I was totally berserk and stayed that way with no letup for perhaps 10 or 12 hours.

Finally the hallucinations lifted for perhaps a minute. I was terrified as I looked around the room, trembling like a scared child. Suddenly it resumed—this time for nearly five solid hours. It lifted again for maybe a couple of minutes and then came back—wave after wave after wave. During the times it would pause, I was shaky but coherent. I was begging them to give me a gun so I could kill myself. They were all stoned and the guy who was tripping finally agreed to bring me a gun.

WAHHHHHHHHHHHHHHHHH!

Chapter Forty-Four

The LSD-induced fright would continue furiously ravaging me for hours on end and then mercifully it would suddenly stop. It was akin to being pounded by a devastating hurricane, because just when it seemed that all was lost, the fury would suddenly pass and I could take refuge in the peaceful eye of the storm for a few moments. Then, without warning, its horrendous wrath would return with unbearable intensity, unleashing unimaginable hallucinations of horror. The process repeated itself over and over again.

Mercifully, the periods of relief in between the horror sessions were growing longer as time went on. At first there were periods of perhaps 15 or 20 minutes of precious relief, and later they increased to 45 minutes or even more.

During those times I would experience a sense of nervous normalcy. But then the horror would return and I'd sit on the floor, rocking back and forth, trying to cover my ears. I would scream in terror and cry uncontrollably, and I was shaking like an aspen leaf. I'd lose any semblance of sanity for hours on end.

When it would finally lift again, I'd cower on the floor in the fetal position, nervously anticipating the next horrendous blast. I was shaking with fear, crying, sobbing, and begging the others to "please, please" find me a gun so I could kill myself before it started again.

As time moved on, I slowly began to understand that I was undergoing a bad trip on LSD. Just knowing what was happening to me seemed to help calm me down little by little. It was during one of the brief periods that the terror had momentarily lifted that I began to wonder if this bad trip was what being in hell was like.

I reasoned that if indeed there was a hell, surely I would go there. My black-magic experiences had undeniably and demonstrably proved to me that dark forces definitely exist. Logic began to dictate to me that if Satan, demons, evil, and hell exist, then God, angels, goodness, and heaven must exist too.

My dark side and my angel of light suddenly showed up in my mind.

I thought that maybe the wonderful trips on LSD that I'd enjoyed and this nightmarish bad trip might be small samples of heaven and hell. Then I had a horrible thought that sent cold chills coursing up and down my spine.

What if I were to die and go to hell and stay like this *forever*?

What if hell was even worse?

I was mortified by the very thought of it.

In the meantime my buddy had scoured the Quarter looking for a gun. But nobody was going to loan a gun to someone whose friend was freaking out on LSD and wanted to use it to kill himself.

It was just as well he couldn't come up with a gun for me. If hell could end up being a permanent bad trip, I didn't want to take the risk.

My buddy's girlfriend was finally able to reach my brother on the phone. She frantically told him that I was freaking out on acid and wanted to kill myself and that he needed to come and get me and take me to a hospital. Jim told them he'd come right over. And he did.

It had been two days since Jim had kicked me out and I'd dropped the acid. He took me back to his house and stayed with me. Jim was scared. He knew firsthand what it was like to freak out on acid. I could see the fear in his eyes. The one and only time that he'd ever dropped acid, he'd freaked out. He'd hallucinated that a giant book was chasing him down the street, slamming shut with a sound as loud as thunder. He had feared that at any minute he would be squashed like a bug. Later on in the day he was tripping and I had to physically stop him from jumping out of a window when he hallucinated that he could fly. It sounds comical but it was deadly serious—and very real to him.

By now the freak-out sessions were lasting only about two hours at a time and then would lift for about an hour or so. It was still every bit as horrific as before, because that damnable siren would start blaring again, announcing a new wave of hallucinations. But tucked away somewhere in my mind was the knowledge that soon the insanity would lift, and that small amount of reassurance made it bearable. Eventually the calm was lasting longer than the pain, and I knew the acid was wearing off and my worst nightmare was coming to an end.

In between waves, Jim and I would talk. He'd initially wanted to take me to the psych ward so they could give me a shot or something, but I told him that it wouldn't do any good. When I was in the Haight I'd heard stories of people freaking out on LSD and taking the powerful antipsychotic tranquilizer Thorazine. It would knock their bodies out, but their minds would just keep going. Nothing could stop someone's *mind* when it was in this state. As badly as I wanted relief, nothing was going to relieve my misery—not Thorazine, not even death. I would just have to tough it out.

During the breaks, Jim told me that when the horror came upon me, I went completely out of my mind crying and screaming. I'd howl something about going down into the catacombs and talking with the dead and evil spirits, who screeched and cursed at me and wanted to taste my blood.

I told him that those visions were as real to me as talking to him was. I was glad he didn't see me when the trip was at its worst. Jim was just getting in on the tail end and seeing only a small sample of the horror that I'd been experiencing for two full days.

By the third day, the drug had completely worn off and my nightmare was over. I slept fitfully for nearly 12 hours; and considering that I normally slept three or four hours a night at most, that was quite an accomplishment.

Over the objections of his wife, Jim let me stay at his house for another week. It took me that long to save enough money from my bartending job to come up with the $20 in advance weekly rent money for a dumpy room located upstairs from Bonaparte's.

One thing was certain: I would never take LSD or any other hallucinogen again. I couldn't understand why I freaked—I'd taken LSD hundreds of times without the slightest problem. I wondered if I had the bad trip because I was in such a terrible frame of mind at the time I dropped the acid. After all, my brother had just kicked me out of his house and I didn't have any money or anywhere to go. I'd just been released from Parrish Prison and was out on bond awaiting trial for possession of heroin. I'd failed at everything in life and had been contemplating suicide for a month.

Had the LSD merely pulled the trigger and exploded the extreme pressure built up in my mind?

As I was mulling it over, all of a sudden it hit me right between the eyes like an ax. *Wait a minute. I know what caused it, and it wasn't any damned nervous breakdown, either. That asshole warlock put a curse on me the day he left those flowers! I got busted the very next day after that, and right after I got out of prison I had a bad trip on acid even though I'd had literally hundreds and hundreds of good trips.*

It was entirely too much coincidence for me. I knew he'd put a curse on me.

The more I thought about it, the more it made sense. The madder I became, the more I wanted to get even with that son of a bitch. I wanted *revenge!*

I decided to fight fire with hellish fire. I'd been in a voodoo shop recently, and a woman there told me that if I went to St. Louis Cemetery and drew three Xs on Marie Laveau's tomb, her spirit would grant me a wish. I figured that doing this would be a good place to start. I wanted that son of a bitch warlock to *die* for what he'd done to me.

Marie Laveau was a potent voodoo priestess in the 1800s who had legendary power and was still widely acclaimed in the Quarter. It was reputed that even today her spirit roamed the streets of New Orleans. I was told that Laveau was laid to rest in St. Louis Cemetery in an above-ground family crypt belonging to the Glapions, a New Orleans family. The lady at the voodoo shop gave me directions as to where to find it, and I went right there.

There were numerous other marks already scrawled on the tomb, and little scraps of paper and even some strands of hair in a rubber band were carefully placed in various little niches around the gravesite. It was kind of spooky. No telling what spells and curses those people were casting. I made my Xs on the tomb and wished a curse of death on that jerk. Then I beat it the hell out of there.

That wasn't enough for me, though, and I wasn't through with him yet. That afternoon I scoured my witchcraft book for curses. I found the worst curse that I could find and decided that I would cast it later that night.

Much spiritual power was said to exist around rivers and mountains, and if spells were cast around them it would greatly facilitate a curse. There weren't any mountains around, but the mighty Mississippi River was just a couple of blocks away.

At midnight I went down to the Mississippi River ferry and caught a ride. I'd brought a black candle with me and had situated myself in an isolated portion of the ferry, where I could cast the spell. It was pitch black and the swirling water smelled like the sea. The entire scene seemed ominous and foreboding.

As the ferry was churning across the river, I tried to conjure up a demon. I'd never done it before because frankly I'd been a little afraid of it. I'd heard stories of people's attempts to conjure up demons: When they succeeded, they'd become possessed by the demons and in some cases were even torn apart.

I brushed those risks aside. Regardless of what might happen, I'd decided that I was going "all in" with this curse and was going to get even.

I began chanting furiously and almost instantly felt something dreadful begin to occur. A sinister, powerful sense of boding evil was overtaking me as though rising out of the murky black water. I could hear the wind pick up like it was sweeping across a barren desert. Suddenly I heard the most vicious, vile, and hideous voice that I'd ever heard screech, **YOU SON OF A BITCH, I'M GOING TO GET YOUR ASS!**

I was so petrified I couldn't move. I thought I might have a heart attack. I didn't see anyone, but I knew that I'd just heard the horrid, abysmal voice of Satan himself, audibly speaking to me. It was ghastly. The deep voice was gravelly, and it coursed through me like it was being broadcast through a synthesizer, just like the ones the rock band Black Sabbath used to say, "I am Iron Man!"

I threw my black candle into the river and ran to the front of the ferry, where a few people were standing around. I hoped there might be safety among them. I was so frightened that when the ferry reached the Algiers side of the river, I ran off it as fast as I could and continued running down the street and kept running until my lungs felt like they might burst and I could run no more.

Even though I could have crossed the river in minutes by riding the ferry back across to the New Orleans side, I ended up going through some of the worst Algiers' ghettos and neighborhoods imaginable, taking a series of buses and finally crossing back over the Mississippi River bridge to work my way back to the Quarter.

It took me several hours to return to my apartment, and my hands were still shaking when I arrived there. As soon as I was back, I gathered up everything that had to do with black magic, including my book, black candles, various spells I was currently casting on people, scraps of paper, and notes, and I put it all in a plastic garbage bag.

I took the bag downstairs and put it in the garbage can, and went back upstairs. But I began thinking of Sandy's apartment burning down from my love spell, and I worried that it was still too close for comfort. I ran back downstairs and dug the bag out of the trash can and took it all the way across the Quarter and threw it in a big garbage bin there.

I was through with witchcraft and my dark side, but unfortunately my dark side was not through with me. In fact he was just getting warmed up . . .

Chapter Forty-Five

I continued working at Bonaparte's for several months, and finally my court-appointed attorney notified me that I was to attend a hearing concerning my drug charges. The attorney told me that the syringe that we supposedly had in our possession had come back clean, and the charges were going to be dropped and the hearing would be a mere formality.

When I saw my attorney at the hearing, I said, "I guess the cops forgot to put any 'H' in the syringe they brought with them."

He looked at me with a dipshit smirk on his dumb-looking face and winked at me. "Yeah, right."

What a moron. It really made me mad when even my own attorney didn't believe my true story of how that dirty asshole cop had planted the syringe on us. What the hell, I didn't give a shit now. I was just glad that it was finally over. This charge looming over me had been on my mind constantly—I felt like someone on death row awaiting word on his final appeal.

The ever-present feeling of dread that had been hanging over my head for months lifted, and I felt pretty damn good about it. I saw Sandy at the hearing and she looked tanned, healthy, and very pretty in a bright yellow sundress with bare shoulders. I met her dad and he seemed to be a cool guy. He was not condemning in the least, and in fact told me not to feel bad about getting busted. He said that when he was young, he once was busted for possession of opium. He was similarly healthy, tanned, and fit, and I remember thinking that he didn't look the part of someone who had smoked opium in his youth.

He invited me to come to their home in Florida and said he would help me find a job. Sandy was hanging all over me and wanted the same thing. I told them that I had some things that I needed to take care of first, and that I would see them in two weeks. They gave me their phone number and address, and Sandy's father told me that if I needed any financial help getting there, I should just give him a call.

I thanked him again, shook hands, and kissed Sandy goodbye; they left for the airport. Actually I had no intention of ever seeing her again. As soon as they were out of sight, I threw away the phone number and address. She was the jealous type and had been smothering me before we were busted. Sandy's lust for heroin was also going to be a forever problem and I was moving on without her. I didn't want a relationship with anyone ever again, especially some junkie.

About two weeks after we all were cut loose, I ran into Frog on Bourbon Street.

He was standing in front of a titty bar handing out discount coupons and cajoling customers to come inside and "see it all."

I was genuinely happy to run into him and stopped to talk for a few minutes.

He asked, "Hey, you hear about Bobby?"

I said, "No."

"He OD'd."

"You're shitting me." I felt like I'd been punched in the stomach.

"It happened the very *first* day that he got out, man. He did up a hot shot of H in some flophouse. I heard that no one found him for three days and the city buried him in one of those pauper graves."

I felt sick. I'd seen Bobby at our hearing just two weeks ago. After being in the joint for several months with no drugs, he didn't even look like the same person. He'd lost that gaunt, hollow-eyed, walking-dead junkie look. He had gained some weight and looked real good. It was mind-blowing upsetting to learn that he was dead, buried, and gone.

"Damn! I hate to hear that. I *really* hate to hear that, man."

"Yeah, same here. Hey, you still got that connection for the blues?"

Apparently Bobby's death did nothing to quell Frog's need for the same thing that just killed his pal.

"No, I've been laying low and running scared since we were busted."

"Yeah?"

I knew he didn't believe me.

"You know I could move some real fast for you, bro."

I smiled. "If I come out of retirement, you'll be my first customer. Hey, I gotta get to work. I'll see you around, Frog. Good seeing you again."

"Yo, we'll be seeing you around, Bobby boy. Be careful."

As I walked on down the street, he called out after me, "Hey Bobby boy, if you get those blues going again, don't you forget me now, you hear?"

I just smiled back at him and held up my fingers in the peace sign as I made my way through the crowded street of drunken tourists.

I didn't like his calling me "Bobby boy." It was all just a little too ghastly for me. I could still picture Bobby's smiling face at the hearing. The thought that he'd been dead three days at that flophouse made me sick. Damn! He had to be rotting and smelling bad by then. I'd bet the smell is how they found him. It creeped me out.

After I beat the heroin rap, I started slamming meth like there was no tomorrow. I'm not sure why. They fired me from my job for not showing up for days at a time, and soon after I began running with a guy named Ryan, who was the only person I ever met who could shoot more meth than me. The guy had a death wish.

Ryan was third-generation New Orleans, born and bred. He had that distinctive "coon-ass" Cajun brogue, and was about six-foot-two and good looking. He didn't look like a hippie or street person at all , and combed his short black curly hair straight back, slicked out with some kind of gunk that made it look greasy. He wore New Orleans–hip clothes and pointy fake-alligator shoes, and he had the appearance of a street hustler shyster.

I met him through a mutual speed-freak acquaintance, and we instantly became pals. Ryan was off-the-charts intelligent, and if drugs had not enslaved him, there was no doubt in my mind that he could have been anything he wanted to be. The problem was that, like so many people on the street, he just wanted to shoot speed until it killed him—nothing more and nothing less.

Our drug use had reached a point where we didn't ever go to the Quarter or bars anymore. We were quintessential drug addicts and all our time was consumed by the arduous task of acquiring and shooting up speed. We almost never left our rented house unless it was to mug someone or rob a store and then score our drugs.

Ryan taught me to write prescriptions as well as any doctor in New Orleans could. Medical people invariably left prescription pads lying around in examination rooms in hospitals and private offices, and the pads were easy to steal. Most of the time we would ask various hangers-on (girls mainly) to steal the prescription pads. We'd write the prescriptions, primarily for Desoxyn, which is pharmaceutical meth and is as pure as it comes. We'd then find someone to take the prescription into a drugstore and have it filled.

If the cops were going to bust you, chances are it would be at the time the illegal prescription was filled. Ryan and I were far too smart to take that kind of risk ourselves. We were both charismatic leaders, and we attracted a following. Invariably someone in our entourage would be either too stupid to know the risks, too knocked out to care, or so eager to belong that he'd do practically anything we asked of him regardless of the risk. He just wanted to become a part of our troupe.

We called it "busting scrips," and we would send the sacrificial lambs into the drugstores with our forged prescriptions. Dieters and fat people used Desoxyn, so we had a bit of a problem: Speed freaks are skinny, and even the dumbest druggist could spot one a mile away. We loved it when some fat chick would start hanging around and become our scrip buster.

The other danger in writing prescriptions is being the one who actually writes them. Invariably I convinced Ryan to write them, because I knew it was a felony rap to forge a medical document. I played to his ego, telling him that he could write them better than me. Usually that's all that it would take.

We'd been lucky so far, and none of our crew had been busted. I was kind of worried about Ryan, though, because I knew he'd been arrested on a big-time bust two years earlier. Somehow he'd gotten out of it, but he told me that it was still pending. He said his dad had hired a good lawyer, but I had my doubts. Usually when someone is still on the street after a bust like that, it means he's now ratting people out as part of a deal to stay out of jail. I was delusional paranoid, but it was no delusion that people around Ryan were getting busted right and left.

I'll give you an example: Just prior to the Mardi Gras parades, Ryan went down to the Quarter and brought about 15 scummy bikers back home with him to party. This was completely out of character for Ryan. I always disliked being around bikers, but after witnessing that incident at the Seven Seas with the girl getting her faced sliced and the black guy being beaten to a pulp, I hated to even *see* one, much less have them partying down where I lived. I raised holy hell with Ryan for bringing them home, but he acted really weird about it and insisted that they were all right. His dad was paying our rent and I had no leverage.

They wanted to buy some drugs and Ryan set them up with a dealer. Then somehow they all were busted the very next day. The bust was all over the news and the city bragged about cracking down on "undesirables" and taking them off the street prior to the Mardi Gras parades.

I noticed too that someone had repeatedly stuck a knife blade into the drywall and cut slits in the walls of our apartment. I went outside our apartment and peered through them and was amazed at how clearly I could see inside. So I covered them up with duct tape from the inside. After only a day or so, there were more slits providing a peep show into our apartment. I knew someone was watching us and it made me nervous all the time.

Ryan was totally unpredictable, with huge mood swings. When he was methed up, a violent rage might overcome him at the slightest provocation; and when that happened, no one, including me, wanted to be around him or mess with him.

He was in a particularly mean mood one day and started in on me. I'd already moved my .357 Magnum to my lap under the table and just sat there listening to him as he worked himself into a meth-inspired rage.

After listening to him rant for a full 10 minutes, I finally had enough. I told him, "Maybe you scare everybody else, Ryan, but you don't scare me. I'm not gonna take any of your shit! Why don't you just shut up your big mouth?"

He started yelling, "Oh yeah? You think you're some kind of badass?"

He was standing there with his fists balled up, screaming at me. He took one threatening half step toward me and raised one of his fists as though he was going to hit me. But before he could so much as blink, I raised my revolver, cocking it as I brought it, and pointed it right at his face. I stood.

I said through gritted teeth, "Yeah, as a matter of fact I do think I'm pretty damn bad, and you take one more step in my direction and I'll kill you."

He stopped cold in his tracks. I could see the fear in his eyes as he looked down the barrel of that big revolver.

I didn't waver, nor was there any sign of fear in my eyes. It was explicitly clear that I wasn't bluffing. I had made up my mind the moment he started screaming at me. My .357 Magnum was cocked and I was aiming it right between his blue eyes. My finger was on the trigger and I had every intention of shooting him if he so much as blinked at me. I was in as much of a meth-inspired rage as he was, and he'd picked the wrong person to bully this time.

He looked in my eyes as though he was thinking about pushing it, but I could see that he knew better.

Abruptly he broke into a big smile and said, "C'mon, BOBBY, I'm just playing with you man." He laughed. "Put that cannon down man; we're brothers forever."

I didn't say a word as I slowly lowered it to the table. It was still cocked and my finger was still on the trigger and my eyes were still filled with rage. I knew he was acting like he was just kidding around to save face and I didn't press the point, but I knew better and so did he. I could see it in his eyes and he could see it in mine. I wasn't smiling.

He did well to back off that day, because I would have sure as hell shot him in the face. It must have made an impression on him, though, because after this incident, no matter what the situation, he didn't ever push me again. Not even a little bit.

One weekend some time later, his girlfriend dumped him and he got doped up out of his mind. All weekend he was mixing downers and uppers and shooting huge amounts of speed and drinking whiskey straight up. He became so stoned and was slurring his words so badly that I couldn't understand him. Then he started crying like a little kid and talking out of his head, saying that his life was nothing but shit. I'd never seen anyone cry like he was crying, hysterically boo-hoo'ing and wailing. I attributed it to the cocktail of drugs that he'd been slamming for days on end.

I was going to hit up some speed. So I started looking for him to see if he wanted to join me. But I couldn't find him. I went to the bathroom door and could hear moaning noises coming from inside. I called out to him, but all he did was moan louder. I tried to open the door but it was locked. I tried to ram my shoulder against it like they do in the movies, and I nearly broke my shoulder, bouncing off the solid-wood door as if I were a rubber ball. Next I tried to kick it open and badly jammed my knee in the process.

I was screaming at Ryan to open the damn door, but all he did was moan. Another guy and his girlfriend had been hanging out with us for several days, and they helped smash a hole in the door with a fire extinguisher.

Ryan was lying on the floor in a huge pool of blood, which appeared to be half an inch deep and five feet in diameter. I looked at his wrists and he had slashed each of them at least a hundred times with a single-edged razor blade. Large shreds of flesh were hanging off them and bright-red blood was ebbing and flowing. I could see all the way to the white bone inside his wrists.

I screamed, "Holy mother of God! Ryan, what have you done?" I wrapped his wrists with some towels and applied pressure.

He kept moaning and holding his stomach and I looked on the sink and there was a box of rat poison. That crazy son of a bitch not only had sliced both his wrists to shreds but had eaten half a box of rat poison as well.

It was two o'clock in the morning. All of us had tracks galore, and dope and drug paraphernalia littered our house. There was no way we could call an ambulance without getting busted. I was as paranoid as I'd ever been and was panicking badly.

The guy with me had an old beat-up car and I told him to help me put Ryan into the car so we could take him to Charity Hospital, which was just a few miles down Canal Street from where we lived. Ryan had passed out and it took all three of us to half carry, half drag him to the car.

We drove to the hospital's emergency entrance, and I tied rags very tightly around both his wrists as we sped along. I told the guy driving to stay in the car and leave it running. His girlfriend and I leaped out, pulled Ryan out of the car, dragged him over to the emergency-room door, and rang the bell. Then we hauled ass back to the car and jumped in as I screamed, "GO! GO! GO! GET THE HELL OUT OF HERE!"

He gave it gas and we spun away, squealing tires as we left.

I thought my heart was going to burst. I told him to go to the Quarter; I wasn't about to go back to our house. I couldn't get out of the car and be seen in public, because I was covered in blood.

Finally I couldn't stand it any longer and I told him to drive back by the hospital. We made our way back down Canal Street and slowly drove by where we could easily see the hospital emergency entrance. Ryan was gone and all looked quiet. I hoped he would make it, but I really had my doubts.

CHAPTER FORTY-SIX

The next day we called the hospital and found out that Ryan was indeed alive and well. They'd transferred him to the psych ward. (Anyone attempting suicide has to spend 30 days in psych; it's Louisiana state law.)

We visited him a few days later and he seemed completely normal. He'd undergone several transfusions after they sewed him up, and he seemed to have survived the entire ordeal just fine. He'd cut a tendon or two in his wrists and caused some permanent nerve damage, but at least he was alive.

Apparently the rat poison had prevented his blood from coagulating and he'd nearly bled out. He was passed out when we left him, and with no one to tell the doctors that he'd eaten rat poison, they probably would have missed it. He likely would have died had I not had the presence of mind to take the half-empty box of poison and leave it on his chest.

A guy named Brad and his girlfriend Beth were visiting Ryan in the hospital when I arrived. Brad and Beth had known Ryan since high school. Brad seemed like an arrogant punk to me, but I kind of had the hots for Beth, who was a sexy-looking redhead with nice red lips. Her eyes were emerald green and very distinctive because they were shaped like a cat's.

When we left the hospital, they accepted an invitation over to our house to do some drugs. We hit up some speed and I told them about a drugstore that I had cased out and wanted to burglarize. I asked if they were interested. They were up for it and about two a.m. that morning, we hit it.

Our plan was simple. I would drive the car and drop the two of them off. They would go around to the back door and use a gigantic pry bar that I'd purchased for just such an occasion. I learned this tactic as well as where to buy the commercial-grade pry bar while I was in Parrish Prison. That giant piece of steel could easily pop open practically any door in seconds—and with minimal effort.

I told them I was sure there was no alarm system in the small drugstore, but just in case I'd be parked right down the street. If I saw any cops, I'd honk the horn before driving off. If they heard the horn honk, they were to haul ass out the back door, go through the backyard of an adjacent house, and meet me on the street one block over from the rear of the store.

I gave them two small flashlights and a long list of all kinds of drugs to look for, with Desoxyn topping the list. I told them that I seriously doubted that small store had a safe, and told them not to rush around when they got inside—just to look for the drugs on the list. "No one's going to see you. You have plenty of time and I'll warn you if anyone comes. Just take your time and make sure that we make it worth our while."

They both nodded in agreement and headed for the back of the drugstore.

No cops came, and after about 30 minutes they came running out to the street laughing like two school kids out for recess. They were carrying a shopping bag full of every kind of drug imaginable. Even though it appeared to be a mom-and-pop drugstore, we scored big. We had two huge bottles of Desoxyn, plus uppers and downers of every description. It was like Christmas morning.

After the drugstore heist, we began doing drugs in dangerous amounts. One morning I noticed that Beth had a black eye and split lip. I also noticed that Brad treated her like she was a dog, and I was none too pleased to think that he was slapping her around. I'd just hit up some speed and was zooming into outer space when I saw Brad stand up and slap Beth's face hard.

I jumped up and hit him and knocked him at least five or six feet across the living room, upsetting a lamp and small table in the process. I grabbed him by his hair and started slamming his head repeatedly into the wall.

Beth began screaming at me, "Stop! Stop! You're hurting him."

I dropped him on the floor and turned around and quizzically looked at her. "Here I am defending you and you're taking up for this piece of crap? He just slapped you in the mouth."

She softly said, "Bob, we're into S&M."

"Huh?"

"Sadomasochism—S&M. I *like* being hit."

Brad was crawling up off the floor, wiping blood from his mouth. I looked at her and she showed me the cut on her mouth with delight in her eyes. She was smiling and licking the blood off with her tongue.

I couldn't believe it. "You like getting hit?"

"Yes."

I slapped her in the mouth and knocked her to the floor and she came up smiling the sexiest smile one could imagine.

"Well I'll be damned." I'd never encountered a masochist. "*Far out!*"

For a supposed tough-guy sadist, Brad didn't impress me. He was scared shitless of me. He looked at me kind of sheepishly and then slowly backed out of the room and left without a word. Maybe the .357 that I had holstered in my back pants waistband creeped him out, but he didn't waste any time hightailing it out of there.

He'd no more than driven out of his parking spot before Beth stood up and went into the bedroom. When I went in she was lying on the bed with her cute little round ass sticking up in tight blue jeans, smiling broadly at me over her shoulder. I walked over to her and slapped her hard on the butt with my open palm. "Mmmm," she purred, and then she seductively gyrated her hips back and forth in a stripper's bump and grind.

I pulled off my belt and popped her hard on the ass a few more times, and I thought she was going to have an orgasm right then and there. We both stripped off our clothes and had sex. The sex was rough and I pulled her hair and bit her on the shoulder and she went nearly insane.

I'd never been into anything like this and I suppose the novelty of it was sexually appealing to me at first. I'd practically given up having sex and was devoting most of my time to my first love—doing drugs—but I did enjoy this brief interlude.

Beth moved in with me, and over the next several weeks we were two fiends doing the drugs stolen in the drugstore heist. After that first experience I found that I was not really into S&M. I didn't mess around with it again, except for an occasional "warm-up" spanking the few times I wanted sex. I found that I definitely was not a sadist and took no pleasure in knocking a woman around, whether she liked it and wanted it or not.

Ryan came home and joined in on the final days of our drugfest. He thought it was exceedingly funny when I told him about Beth being a masochist and the incident with Brad.

One day I was stoned beyond stoned and I showed Ryan a hammer and told him that I was going to see how Beth liked it. Ryan nearly freaked out and grabbed the hammer out of my hand and asked me if I'd lost my mind.

Next I found a rope and made a hangman's noose and told Ryan that I was going to hang her. He again freaked out and gave me a look that I'd never seen before. He thought I'd gone over the cliff.

Actually I'd just been kidding around and had no intention of hammering or hanging Beth, but he didn't see it for what it was—simple, warped humor. I was just clowning around, but he thought I was serious. He kept acting nervous and kept telling me to calm down.

We'd gone through all the good stuff from the drugstore stash and went back to writing scrips for Desoxyn. The day after the hangman's noose incident, Ryan insisted that I personally write the prescription for the Desoxyn. I tried to convince him to write it, but he'd have no part of it; further, he wanted this half-wit guy who'd been hanging around our house (who I didn't know or trust) to drive us to the drugstore.

Ryan was insistent. He demanded that I write the prescription and that we go to the Canal Street drugstore that he specified. Beth had to bust the scrip, he said, and the half-wit would be the one to drive us there.

He could demand this because indeed he'd written hundreds of scrips. It was not lost on me that I was living rent-free in Ryan's house either. He was insisting that it was only fair that we share some risk, and I saw no way to avoid it.

I was paranoid about the way Ryan was acting though, and so was Beth. As soon as we sat in the car, I decided to change the plans. I told the half-wit to go down to a drugstore on Esplanade instead of the one on Canal. Before we got there, the half-wit said he had to make a call and drove to a Laundromat with a pay phone.

I viewed this with extreme suspicion. Beth and I found a torn piece of paper on his dash with "Po Lise" written on it along with a phone number. We looked at each other and she said, "Does that mean police?" Now we were freaking out. We laughed nervously and I said, "Surely not; we're probably just paranoid."

At that moment the half-wit came back and got in the car. We were only a couple of blocks away from the drugstore and I thought that even if he did call the cops they wouldn't have time to drive there that quick, so I didn't say anything about the call. We pulled up outside the store and dropped Beth off. She went inside.

I told him, "Drive!"

As we went down the street, I saw one unmarked car and then another speeding down the street in the direction of the drugstore. I told the half-wit to keep driving. In about five minutes I told him to turn around and head back toward the drugstore. Esplanade was a divided street with trees planted in the median strip, and we were driving down the side opposite the drugstore. I saw Beth standing outside with a look of terror on her face, as if she'd been crying and was ready to cry again. She was holding a white paper bag—I figured she'd busted the scrip—and was waiting on us; but she was obviously scared shitless. When she looked up and saw our car, I saw her shake her head no ever so slightly.

A well-built middle-aged guy with thin black hair and dark sunglasses was pretending to wash off the sidewalk beside her with a hose. But he was wearing a brown suede jacket in the heat of the summer day. Duh! Do you suppose that coat was covering up a gun?

I screamed at the half-wit, "If you stop this car, I'll kill you." I jammed my .357 hard in his ribs. "You drive, you son of a bitch!"

I didn't want to go down on a felony rap and there was the complication of having an unregistered .357 magnum. My heart was pounding and I was in a rage. We went down the street and I shouted at him to make several turns zigzagging our way toward the Quarter. I kept looking back, but no one was following us. Finally after several miles of this, I screamed at him to stop and let me out.

I put the gun to his head and told him that he was nothing but a scummy snitch and if they caught me I was coming after him; and if it took me the rest of my life I'd find him and cut his tongue out and then slash his throat. I then yelled, "Now get the hell out of here!" and he drove off.

I made my way back down to the French Quarter and ran into a speed-freak buddy of mine and told him what had happened. He told me I could crash at his place for a few days and lay low. I didn't call Ryan or go back for my meager belongings.

Later that night I went out for a pack of cigarettes. I was walking down the street and a very drunk tourist stopped me and said, "Hey man, are you from around here?"

I said, "Yeah."

He asked, "Do you know where I can find a hooker?"

I told him, "Sure do, just follow me. I'll take you to the best little whorehouse in New Orleans. It's right down the street."

He slurred his words, "Thanks man."

He was dead drunk and staggering. I had to actually help him walk for a block or two. I led him to the darkest, quietest place I could find and then turned around, pulled my gun on him, and told him to give me his wallet.

I thought he was going to faint when he saw that big silver gun in his face. He handed over his wallet. I looked inside and he had about $200. I removed the money and returned his wallet along with his credit cards and driver's license and told him to enjoy the rest of his stay in New Orleans. I melted back into the dark shadows.

Now I had some operating capital.

My pal Ronnie was also one of those third-generation New Orleans coon asses and had known Brad, Beth, and Ryan all his life. At my urging, Ronnie went to see Beth after she was out on bond. He learned exactly what happened at the drugstore and reported the story back to me.

Beth was being a good soldier and was refusing to finger me as the one who forged the prescription. She had an excellent attorney who was defending her pro bono, apparently because he was into S&M too.

Her attorney had big-time underworld connections with the Carlos Marcello crime family, and he was able to determine through their connections that Ryan was indeed a snitch. In fact, he'd been one since his drug bust two years earlier. It was Ryan that had set us up; the half-wit was in on it too as a paid informant.

What I didn't realize at the time was that the incident with the hammer and noose had been monitored by the police. It was a very big deal to them and probably precipitated my bust. Apparently they were worried that I'd gone off the deep end. This was crazy. Beth and I had actually laughed about the hammer-and-noose incident when Ryan freaked out about it. She knew I was just clowning around, but apparently the cops and Ryan didn't get the message.

The cops felt that they already had a good enough case against me, and the time had come to take me off the street. It all made sense to me now: The slits in the walls were for the undercover cops to watch the activity, the place was probably bugged, and Ryan was indeed on their hook. Come to think of it, that might have explained, at least in part, why he tried to kill himself. He was tired of turning his friends in and being a rat.

Maybe Ryan needed a little help with his failed suicide attempt. Maybe instead of a razor blade and rat poison, Ryan just needed a bullet in his brain. Quick. Plain. Simple.

I was angry—very angry—at Ryan.

Chapter Forty-Seven

I used the $200 that I stole from the drunk to buy a large quantity of meth. Ryan and the half-wit would just have to wait. I started shooting up huge amounts every couple of hours as though I had a death wish.

Usually other speed freaks would shoot up with me, but I wanted to be by myself. I kept hitting up again and again. I occupied my time by sitting by myself in a very dark room with my foot nervously dancing up and down tapping time to a Jimi Hendrix album that I played over and over again.

For one of my hits, I shot up a syringe that was so full of meth that not even one more drop would fit in it. I thought my heart would explode when I pushed the plunger forward.

A few minutes after I did that monster hit of speed, I looked into the mirror in the bathroom and suddenly it dawned on me that it was a two-way mirror and cops were on the other side watching me.

I casually turned around and went inside the bedroom closet and shut the door behind me. Once inside I hid my .357 magnum by wrapping it in a T-shirt and putting it on the floor with some dirty clothes. I opened the closet door and nonchalantly walked back out. I hoped that it appeared to the cops as though I had been searching for something in the tiny closet.

I grabbed my coat and left the apartment. I knew I was being followed, so I headed down toward Canal Street—away from my gun and the Quarter. I boarded a trolley car at Canal Street and started riding down St. Charles Avenue. I could *feel* someone looking at me, and when I looked around, sure enough I spotted two FBI agents. They were closely watching me and I heard one whisper to the other that at the next stop they should take me.

I casually stood up, walked to the door, and jumped off the moving trolley car. I rolled onto the hard concrete street and narrowly missed hitting a light pole. But I landed squarely on my knee, cutting it badly and nearly breaking my leg in the process. I started limping and running down the street as best I could manage in an effort to elude them.

I noticed several unmarked cars cruising the street, and they were looking at me and talking into microphones in their cars. Suddenly I thought about my jacket. It had obviously been bugged and I knew the cops were using it to track me. I took my jacket off and stuffed it down a United States Postal Service mailbox.

I ran through the dark streets for several hours, but every time I turned a corner, undercover cops would be right there with me. They were following me with different teams and using different vehicles to pursue me all over the city. I ran from one section of the city to another and then back again. I was totally exhausted from the chase. I wished I hadn't left my .357 behind because maybe I could just shoot it out with them and go down fighting and with guns blazing.

Finally I had had enough. I just sat down on the side of the street and started crying. I was physically spent and couldn't run anymore. I had nowhere to go anyway. I was ready to face my tormenters, even if it meant my death.

They left me sitting there for hours just watching my every move. Finally about midnight a marked cop car pulled up beside me and stopped. I thought, *Well this is it. They'll either kill me or arrest me, but either way it's finally over.*

A big burly cop got out and asked me what was wrong with me and why I was crying. He knew damn well what was wrong with me and this was just an act. I didn't say anything.

The cop asked, "What's your name?"

I started talking gibberish to baffle and confound him. I answered, "Yes, I'm aware that it rained last night; however it was hot and dry in the Mojave Desert. I know because a crow told me."

"What the hell?"

He took me to the station and sat me down and tried to question me to determine what was wrong with me. Had I been mugged? Was I drunk? Was I on LSD? Was I just plain crazy?

I was determined not to divulge any information, and in response to his questions I either did not answer or made up some gibberish.

Finally he said that he'd have to book me and lock my ass up unless I told him who I was. I decided to play along. I told him my name was Bob and then I gave him my brother's name and phone number. He called Jim and told him that I was undergoing "extreme anxiety" and some kind of emotional breakdown and to come down to the station.

When Jim got there, instantly I knew he was in on it too. I could tell by his demeanor and I saw him whispering to the cops when they thought I wasn't looking. I couldn't believe that my own brother was in on the conspiracy. The cops told him to take me to Mandeville, which was the Louisiana insane asylum. Jim told them that he wanted to take me home to my parents' house in Mississippi, and they released me into his custody.

I knew of course that this was all part of the master plot and that he was working with the FBI and they wanted certain information from me concerning various crimes that I'd committed. I was determined not to divulge any information.

Jim drove me to Mississippi and I was fully aware that our conversation was being recorded from a device hidden in the ashtray. I also knew that a camera had been concealed in his car, so I talked in a circuitous manner and was careful not to incriminate myself. He of course denied that he was in with the cops and asked me if I was crazy.

I knew better.

When we got to my parents' house I couldn't believe it. *They were in on it too!* There was another two-way mirror in their living room and the place was bugged.

Shit!

I told them that I knew they were working with the FBI and that I didn't have any information aside from what I'd already given Jim and to please leave me alone. I started crying again.

My mother looked at me with a worried, frantic expression. My father, mother, and brother left the room and went into the kitchen. I heard my mother crying and asking my brother in a shaken voice, "What is the matter with him?"

At that moment I realized that everything I had been experiencing had been in my head. I was having paranoid delusions. No one was chasing me, no one was recording me, and there were no two-way mirrors. I hallucinated the entire two-day ordeal. It had seemed so real but it was all in my mind.

I gradually adjusted to a semblance of normalcy and the extreme paranoia began to leave; but I was still clearly on edge. My mother asked if I was hungry and I said yes. I hadn't eaten anything in a couple of days. She fixed me a bowl of vegetable soup and a bologna sandwich. In about an hour I threw it all back up. The odd thing about it was that none of the food that I threw up looked digested. It had obviously been chewed, but not digested in the slightest.

In a few hours I ate again with the same result. There didn't appear to be anything wrong with my appetite, but I couldn't digest anything. My mother took me to a doctor and I was quickly admitted to the hospital. They found out that I had taken an overdose of meth. When I told the doctor how much meth I'd recently shot up, he laughed and called me a liar. He told me that much meth would kill an elephant.

"Believe what you like doc. I have no reason to lie about anything. That is how much I took."

He looked at me and saw in my eyes that I was telling the truth and slowly, incredulously, shook his head. He muttered, "I don't know how you're still alive, son."

Apparently my liver and gallbladder were not secreting bile because of what he described as "meth crystals clogging them up." He gave me an IV and some medication, and in a few days I was back to digesting my food and keeping it down.

After I left the hospital I told my parents I was immediately hitchhiking back down south to work on the oil rigs. Actually I wanted to get back to my drugs. *I needed them.* I also had my .357 hidden in the closet and I didn't want anyone to find and steal it in my absence.

I asked my mother to drop me off on the outskirts of Columbus and told her that I'd hitchhike the rest of the way. She reached into her purse and pulled out a small bank envelope and handed it to me. Inside were five $20 bills. "Here, this is for you. I stopped by the bank and withdrew it for you this morning. DON'T use it to buy drugs. Use it for food."

She looked at me anxiously and then she tenderly told me that she loved me and would continue to pray for me.

I weakly hugged her and said, "Thanks Mom, I appreciate it. I'll see you later."

I stepped out of the car and waved goodbye as she drove back toward town. I didn't give a rat's ass about her God or her prayers, but I looked at the money she had given me and figured that I could get high for at least a week on this score.

I knew my parents were worried about me and loved me, but I'm sure they were relieved that I was leaving. They didn't even know what meth was, much less have a clue how to deal with a full-blown drug addict hell-bent upon destroying himself. They were helpless and so was I. They didn't want to give up on me but just didn't know how to help. The only one who was amused was my dark side, who was gleefully laughing his ass off.

I arrived back in New Orleans and picked right back up where I left off, shooting up a big hit of speed as soon as I got there. I just wanted drugs in my arm and in my brain.

I used the $100 to shoot up drugs and more drugs over the next couple of weeks. I wrote several prescriptions and got them busted using her money. I had just enough money for one more scrip. I got another speed freak and his girlfriend to bust it for me, and I split it with them. I was penniless but I had a brand-new bottle of Desoxyn watered down and ready to go.

At the time I didn't know that I'd just written my final prescription and soon would be dead.

Chapter Forty-Eight

The review from my cocoon is nearing the conclusion of my life. I calmly watch as I shoot up a big hit of speed and then walk out the door of a crap-hole apartment. A few minutes later I'm jamming my .357 Magnum right between the eyes of a would-be mugger and maniacally screaming at him at the top of my lungs. At the last possible second, I veer the big gun slightly and pull the trigger, discharging it into the door jamb right next to his ear instead of blowing his brains all over the street. I slam his head repeatedly into the door jamb and leave him in a heap.

The next day I watch as I elude the police in New Orleans and I hitchhike out of town, heading for Atlanta. There I observe myself in a bloody fight in which I break a beer bottle over some guy's head and repeatedly stab him in the face with the remains.

Finally I view my last night on Earth, beginning with my unsuccessful attempt to pick up a pretty blonde at an Atlanta nightclub and then drinking myself into a drunken stupor. Lastly I watch the deadly head-on collision that I caused, the wild ambulance ride to the hospital, and then dying in the emergency room. Last, I view my shitty funeral "celebrating" my shitty life.

Okay. So I'm dead and have watched my life play out in its entirety. What's next?

Suddenly something radically changes and I see a dazzling, beautiful warm light in the distance. I think it might be God, my angel of light, and heaven. I badly want to reach that warm brilliant light, but the serene black sea in which I've been calmly and peacefully drifting is no longer serene nor is it calm or peaceful. I'm rapidly being swept away from the light and I can no longer feel the angel of light's presence. I'm being swept away in a raging current like a raft on a rain-swollen river.

At first I'm irritated at this new event, but I'm helpless to change anything. I hear a roaring sound like a waterfall and the strong current is whisking me toward it at a frightening pace. Now I'm scared. What the hell is going on?

What was once a calm black sea is now an enraged and unruly river, and it's acting possessed. It's plunging me toward the deep at mind-boggling speed.

Unmitigated terror is what I feel as I'm violently swept over the edge. The thunderous, churning waterfall is deafening. I plummet into space and free-fall, tumbling over and over again into a swirling, furious, black hole cascading for miles beneath the surface of the earth. I scream in fear as the black vortex spins me wildly into the abyss.

I'm thrust far into the deep. Suddenly I find myself floating in a filthy cesspool alongside a dark shoreline. My cocoon no longer encases my body and I'm washing back and forth, banging against the rocks in black, nasty tidewater and a pile of assorted debris and human waste.

I sense the boding, evil presence of my dark side. He's been missing all this time. No one has spoken to me, but somehow I know that my angel of light has now released me to him.

It's dark and I can see an evil, menacing creature walking back and forth in the shadows. It's looking for me, scavenging through the debris that is floating in the nasty, dirty pool at the edge of the shoreline. It's emitting coarse, guttural sounds, as though muttering to itself in some strange, frightening language. It's using a long, pointed stick to poke about in the water's edge.

I'm mortified with fear of this huge, vile creature.

I can distinctly hear aboriginal tribal drums and mysterious twanging didgeridoos in the distance. Suddenly the creature spears me in the chest with his pointed stick, picks me up, and slings me. I go flying through the air for several hundred yards and land in the center of a mammoth cavern. The top of the cavern flickers with reddish-orange light from a smoky fire, which reveals hundreds of tombs carved in its sides. Each tomb has a steel door locked shut with giant steel padlocks and chains.

The creature is now running from cave to cave unlocking the doors and removing the chains. He's stirring up his pack and calling them to action, casting them from their tombs in the eerie flickering shadows.

Black and red streaks paint his wicked, despicable face, which is covered with shiny, reptilian scales. His glowing, malevolent, yellow serpent eyes and horns shine brightly in the eerie firelight. His depraved, evil smile revolts me.

I know that I'm in hell in the center of the earth. All kinds of dreadful creatures are frenetically and wildly dancing around a fire, as if to celebrate my death. They are led by the satanic creature I saw earlier on the shoreline.

I hear chanting and drums beating, strange weird music, and spooky animal howling and growling, and sounds like gnashing teeth. I hear people moaning, screaming, cursing, crying, and wailing, chains clinking, and huge metal doors clanging shut. I'm horrified and scared beyond scared from the deafening sounds.

On the fire is a stinking cauldron and I look inside and immediately jump back. I'm aghast because I see *myself* floating in the steamy, bubbling kettle. Maggots and long worms are churning the water as they eat the flesh off my bones. The worms go in my eye sockets and exit from my ears and mouth like slimy snakes. Maggots are everywhere. They cover my face, chest, arms, and legs, and strip my flesh to whitened bones. The worms are writhing in and out of my body cavities. The stench is overpowering and reeks of sulfur and sickly, rotten flesh. The water is putrid green.

The pain is excruciating and unbearable. I feel myself literally being eaten alive. The sharp bites of the maggots feel like thousands of painful stings from yellow jackets. I cannot breathe and it feels as if I'm drowning. My throat is completely filled with wriggling black worms, suffocating me and stifling my screams of agony. I feel the worms biting their way through the inside of my head, piercing the backs of my eyes until they literally pop my eyeballs out of their sockets.

The boiling cauldron sears all the flesh off my bones. I feel my body sizzling. My scorched throat is on fire and I thirst an unquenchable thirst. My tongue is swollen to twice its normal size and is covered with biting maggots.

My white, fleshless skull appears to be sardonically grinning back at me. Clumps of my hair are floating in the bubbling, putrid, sickly cauldron. The evil creature has thrown his head back and is hysterically laughing like a madman and roaring like a lion. It's deafening! I tremble in fear and am so scared I begin to wet my pants.

I've never seen my dark side before, but I see him clearly now. He's a beast of mammoth proportions, standing a full eight feet tall. His demonic horde craves my flesh, but he lusts for and is now demanding my soul.

I'm dead but alive and experiencing incomparable pain. Somehow I realize that I'm immortal. *I cannot die. I'm eternally doomed to unimaginable horror and pain.*

My angel of light has now relinquished me to him. I am *forever damned!*

I shut my eyes and mercifully it becomes exceedingly dark and quiet again. I cautiously flutter them open again and see bright white lights. I try to focus and I see my mother's image peering at me from just inches away.

I cry out, "Mom? Mom is that you?"

I see tears streaming down her face as she sees me open my eyes and hears my hoarse whisper. Her voice breaks as she attempts to explain where I am and what happened. "Bob! Can you hear me? You've been in a car accident and you're in intensive care."

"I'm alive?"

"Yes, you've been unconscious for nearly two days."

I whisper to her, "I just had a vision that I died and was in hell!"

Mom's eyes widen and she looks terrified. I see my dad standing behind her, and his jaw is tightly clenched. He says nothing.

Mom sobs, "We've been on our knees praying for you Bob."

Chapter Forty-Nine

I close my eyes and it's very dark. My head feels as if it's being tightened in a giant vise while someone is simultaneously pounding . . . pounding . . . pounding a nail through my forehead with a hammer. The pain is incessant.

Am I alive? Did I just see my mother? Where am I?

Oh God, the pain coming from my leg is excruciating!

I force open my eyes and see monitors and lights blinking, and I hear something beeping. Tubes are coming from various areas of my body, IVs penetrate both arms, oxygen tubes snake out of my nose. Heavy bandages garnish my face, arms, chest, shoulders, and hands. My right leg is suspended above the bed in traction. I make out what appears to be a large blood stain on my sheets.

I see Mom. I try to focus, but just can't quite achieve it; she's blurry.

"I'm gonna die, Mom. I just know I'm gonna die."

Mom comes into focus. Something does not look right. Her hair looks disheveled instead of perfectly groomed and her normally pristine, freshly starched clothes are wrinkled.

What the hell?

She looks tired, and is frantically looking at me with a worried, anxious look on her face. Her eyes are red and there are dark, almost black circles underneath them. She's been crying. I see my dad and his eyes look moist.

Why are they crying? I wonder if there's something they're not telling me. Am I dead? Am I in my cocoon again watching this? Is this all a bad dream? What the hell is going on? Where am I?

The room begins to spin. The entire ceiling looks like some giant ceiling fan spinning around. I feel dizzy and sick to my stomach. I want to puke but can only dry heave. When I move slightly I'm racked with nearly unbearable pain that comes from deep within my right thigh. *Damn!* I feel intense, agonizing pain unlike anything I've ever experienced.

I hear Mom say, "Are you okay, honey?"

"Pain!" I grimace as I look at my tormentor, my right leg, suspended above my bed.

"I know, honey."

I look around as though looking for something, so Mom asks me what I need.

"Water," I hoarsely whisper.

She holds a cup of water with a straw in it to my dry lips and I take a sip and gag. Water streams down both corners of my mouth.

"You're in intensive care. The doctor said your right leg is badly broken and you'll need a major operation as soon as you're strong enough. You've lost an enormous amount of blood and already had two transfusions."

She goes on telling me other stuff that barely registers, but it's clear that for some time my life has been erratically spinning like a quarter on a diner countertop, with a 50-50 chance of landing heads up or down. Only in the past hour or so was I upgraded from "very critical" to "critical but stable." The sound of her voice comes in and out like waves at the ocean.

I'm overwhelmed and the severe pain is agonizing. I just experienced the most traumatic, horrible experience of my life, and I'm afraid of dying. If I die I'll go to hell, and I'm still shaking from seeing the horror of it.

I blurt out, "An angel showed me my whole life. I saw all the bad things I've ever done and when it was finished I was damned and went to hell. It was *horrifying.* Demons were celebrating my death and I saw Satan hysterically laughing. He looked *hideous.* I was being boiled in a huge pot with evil creatures dancing around it, and maggots and worms were eating me alive. I was being *burned alive* and the pain was unbearable . . ."

I'm shivering badly and shaking as though I were outside in the freezing snow.

Mom softly says again, "We're praying for you, Bob." She's trying to look confident, but I see fear in her eyes.

"My leg is killing me. I need something for the pain."

Mom pushes the call button clipped to my bed and the nurse appears and smiles to see me finally awake, and says she'll be right back with some pain medication.

Mom lovingly puts her soft palm on my cheek. "I know it hurts, honey. It won't be long." She turns her head slightly and gazes at me with a tenderness that only a mother can show a hopeless son. I can see the pain in her eyes as tears stream down her cheeks.

I've become a monster. She does not deserve a son like me.

"How long have I been here?"

"Two days. We came as soon as they called. They told us that if we wanted to see you alive again, we needed to hurry." Her voice breaks and trails off.

She regains her composure and softly says, "Let's look at the bright side. You survived and what is important now is for you to get well."

I don't say anything, but think, *Get well? Now just how in the hell does an addict "Get well"?*

I drift in and out of consciousness. They talk with the doctor while I doze, and he tells them I'm going to make it. I open my eyes and see Mom. She smiles that wonderful smile and tells me that I'm going to be all right.

She looks down at her watch as if she has to be somewhere and then says, "Now that you're stable and past the worst of it, we're going to have to go home. We both need to get back to work, and it's a nine-and-a-half-hour drive home."

I don't want them to go. I don't know anyone in Atlanta and I'll be left all alone. I'm like a five-year-old kid. I want my mommy and daddy.

Mom sees the disappointment and pleading in my eyes and quickly adds, "We'll come back to pick you up after the operation. You can live with us. I'll take care of you. It's going to be a long recovery. The doctor says you'll be on crutches for two years."

"TWO YEARS?"

"Yes, and then you'll need another operation to remove the metal rod that they're going to put in your leg. Bob, it's going to take a very long time for your body to heal. You've been to the very brink."

"I'm glad you both came."

She starts gently crying and says for the third time now, "Bob, we love you more than you'll ever know, and we'll continue to pray for you every day."

Dad does not say anything but is choking back tears too. How it must hurt him to see me like this. As I look at Mom and Dad, I think that I have made them cry too many times.

I'm uncomfortable and want to change my position. I put my hands down, shift my weight, and move ever so slightly. Abruptly blinding, intense, white-hot pain surges into my brain. I bawl like a wounded animal and ferociously scream at the hurt that is attacking me. My piercing scream is so loud, in fact, that the nurse hears it in the hall and comes running. The unset bones in my leg do not like to be moved and are announcing their extreme displeasure.

I need relief and I need it now. Sitting atop the little tray in the nurse's hand is what appears to be a syringe full of amber liquid.

Hmmm . . . Wait a minute, I know that liquid. I know that liquid well. Demerol! It's in the same family as heroin and morphine. Good choice!

She swiftly and expertly sticks the needle into the muscles of my thigh and slowly pushes the plunger down, down and I instantly feel the healing balm as it enters my body. She efficiently removes the needle and deftly puts a cover on it. She's a pro.

Immediately the warmth begins to swirl its way up toward my neck. I can feel it slowly creeping its way, as if my body is a tube being filled with liquid forbidden fruit: wonderful, soothing, delightful, delicious, sensual, calming, breathtaking, magnificent, fantastic, brilliant, amazing juice . . . up my spine first and then continuing up my neck and into my brain.

It is called a rush on the street. Addicts live for it. It takes your breath away. Wave after wave gently rolls back and forth across my brain until the drug completely blankets it with a sensation that I know and love all too well. I like it! No, I LOVE it!

I'm addicted to that feeling. I'm smiling. The rush from an injection in the muscle is not nearly equivalent to an injection directly into a vein, but this large dose of pure, pharmaceutical-grade Demerol is a close second. Sweet! Sweet! Sweet!

Pain? What pain? I'm loopy now and I smile at the nurse. She smiles back at me with a knowing look in her dark eyes. No doubt she has delivered these soothing afternoon, morning, and nighttime "delights" to many patients on many occasions. The reason that she's a nurse is that she has a kind heart and wants to take care of people, and she likes to alleviate suffering and pain. Mother Teresa. Kind one. She has a need to help those of us who are tortured.

Her mission has been accomplished. She looks good in her cute little hat and starched white uniform that so nicely exhibits her firm breasts and shapely buttocks. Thank you my sweet one, maybe after this is over . . .

My eyelids are heavy and I begin the nod.

As I prepare for the drift, Mom gets up and bends over my bed and kisses me on the cheek and Dad gently shakes one of my bandaged hands with his big paw.

Mom says, "We love you, son."

"Thanks, Mom."

Dad nods and I smile and nod back. He's never verbalized those words to me, but maybe that's just his way. At this moment I feel sure that he loves me too.

I watch them walk out and lift my bandaged hand to wave goodbye. Mom is gently crying again, fighting back the tears, and Dad has a sheepish, helpless, almost embarrassed look on his face as he follows her out of the double white doors. I'm glad they came to see me even if I did make them sad again.

I've been alone so long and am so tired of the fight.

My melancholy mood is short-lived, though, as I'm cheered on by the pain medication that is now coursing through my body.

I drunkenly say aloud, "Comrade Demerol, I salute you!" and then raise my bandaged hand and manage a snappy salute.

I begin to gently slide down the hill and into the Nirvana pools. The spa has been heated to perfection and the warm waters covered with rose petals are lazily swirling. The heated, soothing fluids begin the massage, undulating their way back and forth across my brain, numbing it to perfection.

Nice.

Very nice.

Chapter Fifty

I dream of playing catch with my brother Jim. We're little kids again and it's a nice sunny day in Fairfield, with bluebird skies. I'm the pitcher and he's the catcher. I'm smiling as I throw strike after strike, and with each toss he nods his approval and pounds his mitt and yells, "Attaboy, Bobby. Way to hum! Way to hum, Bobby boy!"

Someone is persistently shaking me, but I don't want to leave my dream. Finally I open my eyes and I see my nurse and someone in a white coat peering at me.

"Hi, Robert, I'm Dr. Jacobs. When you came in I worked on you all through the night and on into the next morning. You gave us quite a scare."

I've been here nearly a week and this is the first time I've seen my doctor. He doesn't look much older than me. "Hi, doc." I shake his limp hand and cannot help but notice that he has the smallest and softest hands for a man that I've ever encountered.

"Am I gonna live?"

"Yes, you're stable now and you seem to be steadily improving. In fact, I just authorized moving you from intensive care to a ward first thing in the morning. You still have a ways to go though. Your right femur is badly broken and it's going to require major surgery.

He immediately launches into his spiel, talking as fast as a greyhound runs at the dog track. "During the car crash, it appears that the front end of your car was crushed forward with such tremendous force that it hit your right shin about halfway up your lower leg."

He points to a spot midway on the front of his shin.

"Oddly, it did not break your shinbone, but it snapped your femur like a pencil. We'll need to make an incision about 12 inches long on your right thigh in the area where the bone is broken."

He points to his thigh area and draws an imaginary line on it where the incision will be made.

"We'll go in and clean up any bone shards and splinters, and we'll then align the two bones together. After that, we'll make a four-inch incision in your hip area."

He points to the top of the right cheek of his ass and draws another, smaller imaginary line.

"We'll drill a hole in the end of your femur into the center of the bone where the marrow is located. Then we'll insert a beryllium rod called a Kirshler rod—similar to this one."

He shows me a sample of a metal rod that appears to be perhaps three-eighths of an inch in diameter and perhaps 24 inches long. It's triangular and hollow, and it's tapered on one end.

"Once the broken pieces of your femur are properly aligned, we'll drive the rod through those holes in the center of both bones. The rod will reside inside the broken bones all the way from your hip to a point just above your knee, and your bone should then heal nicely around the break.

"With the assistance of crutches, the metal rod will support your weight until the bone grows back and is strong enough to support you on its own. That process usually takes about two years, at which point most people elect to have the rod taken out."

"Two years?"

"The femur is the largest and strongest bone in your body, Robert. Sometimes patients die just from the shock of breaking it. That bone supports your entire weight. You have the advantage of being young and should heal quicker than most, but it will take significant time for the bone to grow back. The alternative to this procedure is not good. Without this operation you would be in a full body cast for possibly nine months.

"As with any surgery, I must warn you that there are significant risks. Your body may try to reject the rod, especially since it's so large. If so, we may have to go back in later and remove it and put you in a body cast whether we want to or not.

"It's a long, complicated surgery and will probably take a team of surgeons 12 hours or more. During that time you'll be under anesthesia and anytime you're under for that amount of time, it's not without some risk.

"You're in good hands. Even though Grady is a charity hospital, we have some of the finest surgeons in the world that work out of here on a volunteer basis. The outstanding team of orthopedic surgeons that will operate on you is out of Emory University Hospital. They'll be demonstrating the innovative techniques of this new surgery to several Emory medical students during your operation."

"So I'm a guinea pig."

He smiles, "No, you are the very lucky patient who will receive a revolutionary procedure from a team of the finest orthopedic surgeons in the world."

I'm grim. "When?"

"You lost a lot of blood and we gave you several transfusions. I want you to get stronger. We must allow some time for your body to recover before we can operate. We won't be performing the surgery for at least two weeks.

"Any more questions?"

"How bad are the others hurt? The people who were in the ambulance with me."

"There were two young women in the other car. One had a badly fractured ankle, and the other had minor injuries—a few cuts and bruises mainly. You were hurt far worse than anyone and are quite lucky to still be alive."

Ordinarily I would have sneered and remarked, *Lucky to be alive, my ass. I wish I could've just died and finished the job once and for all.* But after the vision of hell that I just saw, I don't make any smart-ass remarks about wishing I'd died.

"Whose fault was it?"

"I don't know the answer to that."

"Thanks, doc."

"No problem; see you soon."

Since Mom and Dad left I've been living a junkie's dream. Like clockwork, every four hours a smiling nurse hits me up with a big dose of what I affectionately refer to as "pharm-fresh" Demerol, and then I lay back and groove and drift until it's time for my next shot.

I don't have to write any scrips, rob anyone, rip anybody off, or otherwise try to scrape any money together to buy my drugs. Everything is free of charge. When I'm hungry for my treat, I just push my call button and someone magically appears with it. Far out!

Unfortunately, all is not bliss, and one huge problem plagues my situation. They cannot give me too much Demerol or I'll OD. I can have a shot only every four hours and the previous shot wears off in *three*. This leaves me suffering in agony for nearly an hour before I get relief.

Similar to when I was in prison, my time here in the hospital has already become a routine. I drift. I suffer. I drift. I suffer. I drift.

When the pain monster pushes me, I in turn start pushing my call button. The nurse comes and patiently explains that it's too early and I'll just have to wait. I keep calling and begging and calling and begging and finally, right when I think I can't stand the pain for another second, she appears with her little tray in hand. Sitting atop it in all its glorious splendor lies a syringe fully loaded with that beautiful amber liquid that I so dearly love.

It is time . . .

The next morning, as promised, I'm moved out of intensive care and into a ward. (I suppose there aren't any private rooms in a charity hospital.) I'm in a large room with six or seven other patients. One is a black kid about my age with a gunshot wound to the thigh. All the rest appear to be very old and in some sort of near-vegetative state. One old man looks like a holocaust survivor. He is nasty looking, with jaundiced skin, long gray hair, and a gray beard, and is so skinny that I can actually see his skeleton showing through his flesh like a Halloween costume.

The nurses on this floor don't seem to like their jobs and don't provide the high-quality attention that I received in intensive care. After only a couple of days elapse, I figure out that one in particular does not like me at all. She is as black as midnight on the Mississippi River and grossly overweight, and she talks like an ignorant farmhand. Her dislike for me probably stems from my relentless requests for another pain shot. When the pain starts, I press my call button over and over again, begging for my shot and some relief.

It's terrible for me to move even a little. It's especially agonizing when they change my sheets or when I have to use a bedpan. In intensive care they would not attempt to move me until they'd administered a shot of Demerol. These clowns seem too stupid to realize that the bones in my leg are not set and if I move, it sends shock waves of intense pain tearing through my brain at the speed of light.

I need a shot and summon for help with my call button. I see the nurse who doesn't like me coming in. She looks at her watch and unsympathetically sneers that it's too soon and I'll just have to wait. Then she tells me she needs to change my sheets. I tell her that I don't want to go through that until I get my pain shot, but she impatiently insists that it will only take a minute and that if she doesn't change them, I'll develop bedsores.

As predicted, she jostles my leg as she pulls the sheet out from underneath me, and horrible pain hits me with a vengeance.

"You damned idiot! I told you to wait to do that until I got my shot! I HURT! Get me a pain shot NOW!"

With eyes blazing, she defiantly stands with hands on her hips and says, "Fo yo infomation, slavery done went oudt 200 yeahs ago!"

I angrily respond, "Yeah, well it's a good thing or I'd have your black ass whipped! *Get me a pain shot now!*"

She stands looking at me with hands still firmly placed on her hips and with hot anger snapping in her eyes, says, "You know not evrbody gits out of heah 'live."

That does it. I go ballistic. I scream loudly enough to be heard two floors down.

"Let me tell you something you WHORE. You don't scare me in the least. Are you threatening me? You think I'm scared of you? You'd better be scared of ME! When I get out of here I'm gonna track your ass down and kill you and every member of your family. I personally guarantee that you'll die a slow, painful death. I'll cut your heart out and while it's still beating cook it up for dinner."

She says, "Calm down, calm down." She's now nervously looking around to see who might be observing the commotion.

"Let me talk to the doctor right now," I demand. "We'll see about this shit!"

"Calm down Mr. Williamson." She looks scared.

"Calm down, hell. You're telling me that I won't make it out of here alive? *You bitch! I'll kill YOU! You want to threaten ME? You have no idea who you're messing with. You're dead! YOU'RE DEAD!*"

Chapter Fifty-One

The nurse is afraid; I can see it in her eyes. She promises that if I'll quit screaming, she'll go ahead and give me my medicine *right now*. I give her a tortured look and sullenly nod my approval. She leaves and is back in less than a minute with my pain shot.

As she administers it, she softly says, "I'ze sorry I hurt yo leg. You right, I shoulda wait till you hadt yo shot befo' tryin' to change dem sheets."

By this time my body and mind are blanketed in silky velvet and my rage is gone.

"No problem. What's your name?"

"Lydia."

As if she didn't already know it, I drunkenly say, "Mine's Bob." I don't hear her response as I drift away.

The next morning when Lydia arrives, she comes straight to my bedside with a big smile on her face and hands me an orange. I'm meth-paranoid and I vividly remember her telling me that some people never get out of here alive. The first thought that crosses my wary, twisted mind is that the orange might be poisoned; however, she's radiantly smiling and acting very friendly. She seems as though nothing ever happened.

I cautiously accept the orange and mumble, "Thanks."

From that day on Lydia faithfully brings me an orange every day, and whenever she gets a chance, stops by to talk. It becomes apparent that she really does regret hurting me, and soon we become friends of sorts. Although she appears to be no more than 30, she's trying to raise five kids. She had her first when she was just 15. Having all those kids did not flatter her figure—she's short and overweight, and her butt is enormous.

Lydia never had a husband, just various boyfriends who did little more than get her pregnant, mooch off her for a while, and then move on to their next "old lady." Her mother lives with her and watches the kids when she's at work, but Lydia says her mom drinks way too much wine and is tipsy most all the time. I have the impression she's just one more problematic mouth to feed.

I can't imagine how Lydia managed to go to school and then on to become a nurse. It must've been very difficult. Not surprisingly, she seems lonely, depressed, and highly stressed. And I'm sure her job doesn't help her attitude. To my way of thinking, caring for the type of people who end up in a charity hospital must be a miserable way to earn a living.

I don't like being here with dregs of humanity like me. I wish I could be in a private room instead of in a ward with beds crammed together. Most of these people look like they haven't bathed in a month and probably have the crabs. I can only imagine what it must be like for her to constantly be changing bedpans and sheets and listening to all these scummy patients and visitors bitching and moaning.

Initially I thought my death threats were what brought Lydia around. But now I'm convinced that what really terrified her was the possibility that I might rat her out to the doctor and she might lose her vitally important job. I can tell that she is struggling mightily trying to make ends meet on her single mom's salary. She's almost overwhelmed with maintaining her difficult full-time job while caring for all those kids at the same time.

Lydia and I often joke with each other and routinely swap demeaning insults, which (as odd as it may seem) tends to add some cheer to our otherwise dismal lives.

One day she is bitching about her bleak financial situation and I sarcastically ask, "You're a registered nurse right?"

"Yeah."

"It seems to me that after getting knocked up a time or two—much less five—a registered nurse would figure out what caused her pregnancies. I've come to the conclusion that you just like to screw."

"You funny. You real funny! You be cryin' fo' you gets yo nextd pain shotd, you white-ass crackah."

I smile at her. I've grown to enjoy our daily jousts and insulting banter. It gives me something to look forward to and oddly makes me feel half normal again. I haven't smiled in a long time. It feels good.

I change the subject and mention to her that I'm bored shitless, and ask if she'd mind going to a library somewhere and checking out some books for me. She readily agrees, telling me there's one on her bus route home, and then asks what kind of books I want.

"I don't really care. Just ask the librarian for the latest best sellers and ask her to pick out a couple that look interesting."

The next day Lydia brings me two murder mystery books that are on the best-seller list. By the time she finishes her shift, I've finished them both and I ask her to bring me some more. She looks at me and asks, "Damn, you a speedt readah or sumpin'?"

I laugh and tell her that I've always had the ability to read fast, and when I was a kid I used to read several books a night.

The next morning Lydia comes in with that big, beautiful smile I've come to know. It reveals her gleaming white teeth, which contrast nicely with her ebony skin. She has perhaps a quarter-inch gap between her front teeth, and that gives her a whimsical look.

She brings a couple more books and this time hands me a printed list of current best sellers. She says the librarian sent it to me so that next time I could pick out the ones I want.

I choose a few off the list, and Lydia returns the ones I've already read; the process repeats itself for a few days. Then late one afternoon Lydia is preparing to leave and I'm once again perusing the best-seller list. I happen to notice that the Bible is listed as the best-selling book in the world.

I say to myself, *I've never read the Bible; maybe I'll just read it.*

"Hey, Lydia, how about just bringing me a Bible to read for tomorrow."

"'*Scuse me*? Did I heah you say you wants to readt a *BIBLE?*

"You kiddin', right?"

Lydia and I have discussed my personal situation at length, and she knows exactly what kind of person I am, so she's wondering why I would possibly want to read a Bible.

"No! I'm not kidding," I scowl, feigning anger that she dare question me for wanting to read the Bible. "I've never read it and just want to readit's all. Jeez . . ."

Lydia smiles broadly and says, "Nevah dreamt that you go gittin' religion on me white boy, but de Lawd, He works in misteerus ways. It 'mazes me sometimes. I be delightedt to brings you a Bible, crackah."

Then she just can't resist another stab at sarcasm and adds, "'Specially since you ax me so nice an' all."

"Whatever."

Lydia is delighted because she figures that I'm gettin' religion. What I don't tell her is that I want to expose it as a fairy tale. The Bible is what all those weak-minded religious nuts are always touting, and since I have some time I want to actually read it word for word just so I can use their own manifesto to prove how ridiculous their beliefs are.

The next day I see Lydia making a beeline for me. She proudly hands me her own personal Bible and, of course, my daily orange. She lovingly looks at the Bible; obviously it's one of her most prized possessions. She refers to it as the "Goodt Book." It is well worn and she's underlined sentences and written little notes throughout.

"Have you read this?"

"Not all de way, but I studies it when I has de time."

I smile at her old-time Negro dialect. She's a good-hearted person and being a nurse was a good choice for her. Her accent and vocabulary are deceiving; she is intelligent and keeps me laughing with her quick wit and keen sense of humor. I like being around her and listening to her down-to-earth, commonsense analysis of most any subject we discuss.

"Well, I'm going to read it all today, word for word, and will tell you what it says tomorrow."

She rolls her eyes. "Bullshit! I gwon believe that when I sees it. That Goodt Book is long and pawts of it is hardt to readt and unerstan. You might get though wif it in a yeah."

She starts walking away toward the hall, and then as an afterthought, she abruptly turns and puts her hands on her big hips and says in an exaggerated and highly irritable tone, "And befo' you asks, I'll be in with yo pain shot soonze I can. Don't be bug'n me 'bout them damn shots or nothin' else today! I ain't in no mood fo yo shit. I'ze up all night long with two sick young'uns."

I'm already engrossed in reading the Bible and without looking up, flip her the bird. She patiently waits until I finally look up. She's standing there giving me the finger right back, twirling her middle finger around and around. I laugh and go back to reading.

I give her some time to walk to the nurse's station and then press my buzzer. She comes back in, and even though I just had one, I ask for my pain shot. Without a word she turns and stalks back out of the room in a huff, cussing me with every nasty adjective she knows. I laugh heartily.

I start in Genesis. At first it's interesting, but soon I'm bored to tears. This guy begat this guy, who begat this guy, and that guy, and this guy, and that.

"Damn! Who gives a shit? What's up with this crap?"

I can't stand it. I'm ready to toss this project, but as I thumb through it I notice that Lydia has marked more of the New Testament than the Old Testament with her underlining and scribbled notes, so I decide to start reading the New Testament.

The book of Matthew starts with more of the genealogy diatribe, but soon the story picks up and turns interesting. I find the New Testament fascinating. I read on and on throughout the day. The drugs are not affecting me like they did when I first started taking them. The shots merely deaden the pain for a while, and I have built up such a tolerance by now that unfortunately I'm not getting stoned like before. When the Demerol begins to wear off, I have to stop reading because of the intense pain, but almost immediately after my pain shot settles in I'm right back on it.

After I read the first four books (Matthew, Mark, Luke, and John), I pause to reflect on what I've read. The Bible is actually nothing like I envisioned it to be. As Lydia had warned, some of it is hard to understand, but as I read about Jesus, I actually liked Him. This is surprising to me, because up until now I hated religion and so-called religious people.

I honestly don't know why I developed such a hatred of religion. I'm not devoid of religious training. As a kid my parents made me go to church. But I disliked it intensely, and I suppose those early experiences with it may have contributed to some of the hatred of it later in life.

I detested the crummy, ignorant preachers who would scream and yell in the small churches that my parents attended. I loathed the hypocritical people in the congregations as well. I remember my dad being politically involved in those tiny churches. The people were always fighting with each other over anything and everything, and invariably a bunch of them would get mad and take sides and then the church would split up. Sometimes they'd hire some sorry preacher, only to discover that he either had a drinking problem or was chasing every woman in church like a mangy dog in heat, or both.

Eventually I despised going to church, and as I got older refused to go. I carried that hatred with me after I left home, and as time went on it intensified. One day I was down in Jackson Square in the heart of the French Quarter in New Orleans, and a street preacher was standing on a little box and was preaching to no one in particular.

He was all fired up, yelling and pounding on his Bible, and as I walked by he pointed at me and said that if I didn't find Jesus I was going to hell. I turned around and without a word hit him hard in the mouth, knocking him off the little box. I stood over him with both fists clenched and snarled that if he didn't shut his damn mouth, I'd kill him.

According to what I've just read in Lydia's Bible, that preacher was right, and without Jesus I'll end up in hell. (And I'd already seen enough of that place not to want to go there.) I've never had much of a conscience but oddly find myself wishing I hadn't hit that preacher now.

I used to consider myself an atheist, but rest assured I believe in the unseen spirit world with absolute certainty now. I saw it firsthand when I practiced witchcraft. I saw things happen with my own eyes, and I know of no other explanation: Spiritual forces of evil definitely exist in the world. They are real, and they are frightening, and they are active.

I think back to that black night I was practicing witchcraft on the ferry crossing the Mississippi River. I was chanting an incantation, trying to summon an evil spirit to appear, when suddenly Satan began screaming at me in that horrible, gravelly voice, "I'M GOING TO GET YOUR ASS!"

I shiver. He *almost* did.

Chapter Fifty-Two

Over the next several days I finish reading the entire New Testament. Much of it was downright mesmerizing, some of it was boring, and some of it (like the book of Revelation) was utterly impossible to understand.

I largely just skimmed through the boring parts and also those that I didn't understand, but felt strangely drawn to other verses, many of which had been underlined by Lydia. I would read those verses over and over again, often stopping for an hour or more to ponder their meaning. I even asked Lydia to give me a little notebook so I could record them in order to refer back to them later.

One of the most perplexing verses that I encountered seemed simple enough at first glance, but after I thought about it, I couldn't stop thinking about it. It was Philippians 4:13, which simply stated, "*I can do all things through Christ who strengthens me.*"

I read it and then reread it. And then I felt compelled to read it again. I just couldn't seem to get past that one statement and it bugged me to no end. I fell asleep thinking about it and the next morning woke up thinking about it. *Why* was this little statement bothering me so much?

Suddenly I blurted out in a rather loud voice, "Well, if you really could do anything that you wanted, what would it be?"

Embarrassed that I'd spoken aloud to myself, I quickly looked around to see if anyone had heard me. Luckily no one on the ward seemed to have heard, or if they did, they didn't seem to care.

If I could rub Aladdin's magic lamp and make a wish and be able to do *anything* that I wanted to do, what would it be?

I didn't hesitate.

I'd change my life!

I wanted off the streets. I wanted to be far away from the never-ending violence of guns, knives, and vicious fights. I wanted to *permanently* kick drugs. I was weary of spending my every waking moment thinking about how I was going to find my next fix, whether or not a "hot shot" might kill me, or if bad dope might send me freaking out to an insane asylum. I was worn down from being a criminal, I was sick of the paranoia and looking over my shoulder for cops, and I was damn sure sick of being around other dangerous psychopathic criminals and drug dealers. I wanted to make my family proud of me instead of ashamed. I wanted to find a good job that was interesting and paid decent money. I wanted a girlfriend who was wholesome and not a two-timing slut whore. I wanted some intelligent happy friends who weren't losers, and most of all I just wanted to be happy for once in my life.

Can Jesus give me all that?

I exploded with rage. *This is all just a frigging Cinderella story!* I'm a hard-core drug addict, alcoholic, exceedingly violent criminal, twisted freak of nature with a death wish. I'm a lonely loser, and there is no hope for someone like me. People like me don't ever change. According to this verse, Jesus Christ can change me. Just like that.

BULLSHIT!

I know better. Time after time I've tried to change my life and failed, and I've watched scores of others do the same. There is one way out for addicts like me and that's to be lowered six feet under into a pauper's grave in a $100 pine box just like the one they put Bobby in.

I angrily ring my buzzer. When Lydia comes in I heatedly demand an answer. "Your 'Goodt Book' says right here" (I tap my finger on the page) "that I can do *ANYTHING* through Christ who strengthens me.

"Jesus or no Jesus, there ain't no damn way, Lydia! Once you stick a needle in your arm, it's 'til death do you part,' baby. It's a damn death sentence. You know it and I know it; and I'll tell you something Lydia, if there was a God, He'd know it too.

"There ain't no cure for an addict. This 'Goodt' Book' is full of damned lies!" I defiantly look at her with glaring eyes and in a loud voice, irately demand, "What you got to say about that Lydia? Huh?"

Unfazed by my outburst, she snorts contemptuously and calmly says, "Jesus pefom miracle after miracle dat was lots hardah dan changin' yo sorry ass. Jesus raise Lazrus fom the dead and you ain't even dead, crackah. What you talkin' 'bout, white boy? *Jesus is God.* He do anything he want. Quit botherin' me with yo crazy shit, I gots work to do, fool."

Lydia stalks out of the room and I lie back on my pillow and close my eyes. Maybe she's right. I'm now all but certain that the angel of light in my life was actually Jesus all along, and my dark side was undoubtedly Satan. I thought that whole scene was a crock: a Sunday school fairy tale of a devil on one shoulder and an angel on the other, a fable that was made up in an effort to control impressionable little kids. Now I'm not so sure. Was Jesus trying to help me all those years? Was Satan like a roaring lion trying to tear me apart and devour me?

It seems logical to me that indeed Jesus must be God, just as Lydia had said. The Bible said that He performed miracle after miracle and possessed supernatural powers. He cured lepers, walked on water, stilled storms, healed the sick by merely touching them, and fed thousands of people with just a few loaves of bread and a couple of fish. And as Lydia lectured me, He brought Lazarus back to life from the grave. Jesus predicted that He would die on a cross and then rise from the grave in three days, and that is exactly what He did.

Only God could do such things.

As to the validity of it, there were plenty of witnesses to all of it. And although plenty of people have tried to discredit Him through the ages, I cannot ignore the fact that I'm lying here reading about it 2,000 years later in the number one best-selling book in the world. If it were a lie, it wouldn't have made it this far.

If it's true, and Jesus is God, then changing my life is not beyond His power and ability.

Okay, I suppose He *could* do it, but why would He bother? Why would He help someone like me? I'm rotten throughout.

I remembered the Bible describing Jesus's Crucifixion. He'd been horribly beaten, whipped, and tortured, and was nailed to a cross where he was suspended with His arms completely dislocated and out of joint. A crown of thorns had been pounded onto His head with a stick, and He was soaked in blood. He hung there in the hot sun in terrible pain and agony, left to die a slow, horrible death while the throng of angry people who had just crucified Him looked on with their twisted, hate-filled faces. They were jeering and cursing Jesus, and spitting on Him and taunting Him to come down and save Himself if He was God.

Jesus looked down on them with compassion and said, "Father, please forgive them for they know not what they do."

I've done some terrible, rotten, black things in my life, but my rottenness hardly compares with the rottenness of those people who cruelly tortured and murdered Jesus Christ. Yet He was willing to forgive them all.

If He forgave them, why not me?

As to *why* Jesus asked God to forgive the very people who were putting Him to death and spitting in His face, I don't have a clue. If I'd been Jesus, I would've shouted, "Father kill them all, but before you do, kill their damn families, including their infant children. But make sure that before you do it you gouge the kids' eyes out, and be sure Father and make the parents watch. Kill 'em all, Father! Make every damn one of them die in a slow, painful manner. Oh, and by the way, the sooner the better. Could you start right now?"

How can I understand the love or thinking of Jesus Christ/God?

I can't, but after reading the New Testament, there is one thing that has become clear to me, I must either choose to go with Jesus or continue on with my dark side. I can't have it both ways. I'm now convinced that Jesus and Satan not only affect this brief life, but more important, extend far out beyond it, as well. They cross over death's doorstep with us, as it's a mere threshold separating us from an entirely different dimension of eternal life, where our souls will reside either in heaven or in hell.

So far in my life I've chosen the darkness over the light. The results have not been good. In fact, I've hit absolute rock bottom. I'm all alone, addicted to drugs and alcohol, miserable, filled with hate, paranoid, reviled by society, and dead tired of it all. I hate everything about myself and all of life. Suicide is no longer an option because now I know it's not the ultimate escape. We don't just die and become so much carbon matter or fossil fuel. We have a spirit and soul, and they live on.

I think about my vision of dying and then floating on the serene black sea in my cocoon, watching the review of my life. At the end I was thrust into hell and I wonder if the vision was all that far off from what I've just read about in the New Testament.

I'm not afraid of fists, guns, knives, dark streets, or dangerous shooting galleries in tenement buildings, but that visionary experience taught me to fear God and what could happen to me after I die.

Before I can think any more about it, Dr. Jacobs walks in. As usual he's smiling. "How we doing today?"

"*We* be doing fine doc, except for the pain. My pain medicine isn't working. Can you increase the dosage?"

"No, but I can switch you from Demerol to morphine and that should help. It's normal to develop a tolerance after this amount of time, but we can't just keep increasing the dosage or it'll kill you."

"We're going to perform surgery on you at the crack of dawn tomorrow. You up for it?"

"If it'll reduce the pain, you can cut the damn thing off right here and now. It's excruciating when I have to use a bedpan or when they change my sheets."

"Robert, I'm going to be honest with you. I'm afraid it's not going to be any easier for a while to come. We'll control the pain as best we can with medication, but fair warning: This surgery is *major*, recovery will be *major*, and you will experience some *major* pain for several weeks to come."

"Thanks for cheering me up, doc."

He smiled even wider. "No problem, Robert. I have some consent forms that I need you to sign. Basically all this fine print says is that you agree to the surgery and that you've been told that anytime you undergo major surgery there is the possibility that you could die and/or suffer serious complications. You will be under anesthesia for approximately 12 hours. Patients have been known to not wake up after undergoing anesthesia and/or suffer serious reactions to it, especially after that length of time.

"Also, I've already told you that the femur is the largest bone in your body and that yours is very badly broken. Your treatment will require insertion of a large metal rod to support the broken bones. Your body might violently try to reject the rod, and there's no guarantee that this surgery will even work for you. But with all that said, it's my best recommendation to get you back on your feet again as quickly as possible.

"There are risks, but rest assured you have an excellent team of surgeons. Even though this procedure is relatively new, they have performed it many times. You're in good hands and I don't anticipate any problems.

"Do you have any questions?"

"Where do I sign?"

"Right here."

I sign his consent papers and he leaves with that smile still firmly fixed on his face.

I'm completely alone and for a change it's unusually quiet on our ward.

I rest my head back on my pillow and shut my eyes. *What if I don't make it out alive?*

Abruptly I open my eyes wide and reach over and retrieve my little notebook and start flipping pages back and forth. Soon I find the note that I'm looking for. I frantically thumb through Lydia's Bible, flipping pages back and forth trying to locate John 3:36.

Finally I find it.

"He who believes in the Son has everlasting life; and he who does not believe the Son shall not see life, but the wrath of God abides on him."

Almost without thinking, I whisper, "I believe, I believe in you Jesus." And suddenly I feel this gentle, soothing, calming presence softly blanket me. I say it again, a little louder this time, and the presence grows.

My little notebook is still open, and I see another verse that I've written down, Romans 8:38-39.

Incredibly I open the Bible to the *very* passage for which I'm looking without needing to turn a single page. Lydia had underlined the verse in red ink.

"For I am persuaded that neither death nor life, nor angels nor principalities, nor powers, nor things present nor things to come, nor height, nor depth, nor any other created thing shall be able to separate us from the love of God which is in Christ Jesus our Lord."

The hair on my neck is standing on end and tears are streaming down my cheeks.

I buzz.

CHAPTER FIFTY-THREE

I was excited and wanted to talk to Lydia about my extraordinary experience. Unfortunately, while I'd been talking to the doctor, her shift ended and she left for the day. The other nurse, Mrs. Wilson, answered my call.

I was disappointed beyond words. I wanted so much to share what I felt with someone, but I hardly knew this nurse. With Lydia gone, there was no one else. Mrs. Wilson had, however, anticipated that I'd want a pain shot, and a fully loaded syringe sat atop her tray. That in itself was delightful, but even better news was that the syringe contained morphine instead of Demerol. I smiled, "Good ol' Dr. Jacobs came through after all." The morphine was much better than the Demerol and I actually got loopy from it and quickly drifted off to sleep.

Before daylight an orderly came into my room and moved me to pre-op to prep me for surgery. He shaved my leg and a nurse brought me some mild (but good) drugs to "calm and relax" me. I hoped to see Lydia before going under the knife, but she didn't show.

With little fanfare, I was wheeled into the operating room. The last thing I remember was an exceedingly bright light shining in my eyes and someone in a green gown and white mask staring down at me with ultra-blue eyes. He injected something into a tube with a syringe and then waved and curtly said, "Bye-bye." And I was out.

I awoke to the absolute worst pain that I'd ever encountered. I didn't know that pain like that could exist. Before my surgery I'd felt the occasional excruciating jolts when they moved me to put a bedpan underneath me or change my sheets, but that was just a temporary blinding jolt. This was *constant* agony in the form of deep, throbbing, relentless, gut-wrenching pain coming from deep within my leg.

My throat was raw and my head was spinning from the anesthesia. I was moaning and a nurse instantly appeared. She efficiently injected pain medication into my thigh, and I was out again. When I awoke the pain was so devastating that I became nauseous. The nurse quickly gave me a shot and I went under again. The process repeated itself several more times.

Lydia finally came to see me and for once didn't joke around or trade insults with me. She took one look at me and she *knew*, so she quietly sat on the side of my bed. I'd been excited to tell her about my personal redemption, but I hurt so badly that I couldn't even think straight, much less converse with anyone about such a complex subject.

I was wet with perspiration and all I could do was lie there and moan and endure the agony. I began to feel sick and retched into a plastic pan. Lydia took the pan and then carefully wiped the vomit from my mouth and chin with a damp washrag. The throbbing, blinding pain tore at me, emanating pulse wave after pulse wave from deep within: *leg to brain, leg to brain, leg to brain.* I was crying from the pain and groaning, mumbling that I just knew I was going to die.

At one point Lydia lost her composure. Trained nurse or not, seeing me suffer like that seemed to overcome her, and several big, shiny tears slowly streamed down her black face; her eyes glistened. She kissed her finger and touched my forehead with it and whispered, "You hang in deah, crackah, you heah me?"

I was so anguished by the intense pain that I could barely manage a weak nod, but when our eyes met, she felt the unspoken message: *I appreciate your friendship.* She bit down on her trembling lip and left the room wiping at her eyes.

I had about 10 inches of wire stitches down the side of my thigh where an incision had opened my flesh. The doctors had gone in through that opening to manipulate the broken halves of my femur and piece them back together. It was through this incision that they also trimmed the broken bone shards so that the two bones could fit precisely back together. I had six inches of additional stitches on my hip area, where the metal rod had been inserted and driven through the center of the two broken bones.

I didn't know if it was night or day, but I remember that it was very dark in my room. As I lay there in torment, I'd never felt so alone. I thought of my mom and wished that she were there with me to hug me and tell me she loved me and say that everything would be all right. But aside from that brief initial visit after my accident, my parents hadn't been back—and I hadn't had any other visitors.

Families of criminals and drug addicts get worn down by the years of nuttiness and being used and abused, and they eventually learn that avoidance makes life easier; friends are nonexistent for the same reason.

I'd snarled my embittered battle cry and waged war against them all without prejudice. *Screw 'em all! I don't need anybody! I can make it on my own!* Unfortunately, the war that I'd waged against the world had only resulted in humiliating defeat. I'd lost that war and was now forlorn, crippled, and hurting.

It was when my loneliness and pain were most intense and I had nowhere else to turn that I first cried out to God for help. I simply pleaded, *Oh my God help me. Please help me.*

At that moment a blanket of gentle, peaceful calm descended upon me. It seemed as though that blanket had been suspended above my bed anxiously awaiting me to summon it. It slowly covered me from head to toe. The frenetic chaos of the raging storm obediently subsided, yielding to the mysterious peace of God. Could it be that God Himself just answered me?

As if God wanted to personally confirm that indeed He was right there at my side, the following words came to my mind: *Be anxious for nothing, and the peace of God, which surpasses all understanding, will guard your heart and mind through Christ Jesus.*

Where did those words come from? I'd taken copious notes while reading the Bible and had recorded verse after verse in my little notebook, but I didn't remember seeing that particular verse. *Could it be that Jesus Christ Himself was here in my room talking to me?* Is this how God communicates? Not with a thunderous, booming voice, but with soothing inspiration, gently swirling through my mind and soul like a miraculous healing balm?

I could actually *feel* God's reassuring presence in the room. He seemed to be standing right beside me, smiling down at me—a loving Father showering His prodigal son with His radiant, gentle love and softly speaking to me through my thoughts. The hair on my neck was literally standing on end, tingling in excitement. Tears of relief filled my eyes.

I finally came to understand that night that I would have to surrender to God before peace could ever come into my life. Surrender had not been in my vocabulary before this moment. Up until now I'd have preferred death over surrender. And I'd ferociously fought all authority, including my parents', and that of school teachers, college professors, police, military leaders, supervisors at work, and yes, even God's.

God made me understand that night that I was fighting an unwinnable war. *My* way hadn't worked and wasn't ever going to work, and unconditional surrender was the only option left to me. The message I received that night was, "Yes, you can do all things (including changing your life), but it has to be through Jesus Christ and not on your own."

I was emotional as I blurted out my simple prayer to God. *I don't understand You God, but apparently You understand me. I'm worn out and exhausted and a complete failure at everything. I know I can't make it on my own, and I know that I need Your help. Your Bible says I can change my life through Christ, and I don't have the slightest idea of how to do that. But I'm willing to listen and learn.*

My prayer may have been clumsy and ineloquent, but it was sincere. And it did not come easy. Imagine me, a hardened criminal who'd sunk so low that I wouldn't have flinched at putting a bullet in someone's brain, sobbing like a child as I surrendered to God and asked Him to give me His peace.

It seemed bizarre, but yet strangely natural. I, the original son of disobedience, had just meekly acknowledged for the first time ever that I needed something other than my fists or my gun. I needed God.

I wish I could say that after that prayer and God's response the agonizing pain instantly stopped and my leg was miraculously healed—like when Jesus touched the leper and his lesions were instantly gone and perfect flesh had been restored—but that was not the case. The excruciating pain was still very much with me and my shattered leg had not miraculously healed.

What had changed was that I now had *hope* where heretofore there'd been only hopelessness. I'd tried to kick drugs and go straight, but I'd failed miserably on numerous occasions. This time was different, though. I'd only known Satan before and now I knew God. I had hope!

In a few days I was back on the ward and feeling much better. The pain—still severe—was slowly but surely subsiding. I was beginning to heal and feel better, and was confident that I could make it now.

When Lydia and I had a chance to talk, I told her about my life-changing experience and how I'd asked Christ to forgive my sins and save me. I told her that I was going to take Him up on His promise that I can do all things through Christ who strengthens me, and I smiled at her and said, "Surely if He could raise Lazarus from the dead, He can change my sorry ass."

Lydia seemed deeply moved by this and said in a shaken voice, "I believes dat God have big plans fo you, crackah. All you been thugh, and you ain't deadt? He save you for sumpin' special. Dat much I know."

I nervously laughed at the idea that I might accomplish "sumpin' special." I'd settle for just being a normal person for a while.

I actually felt good enough to insult her and said, "You don't 'know' crap, Lydia. Have I told you that you look like Aunt Jemima today, with that stupid-looking bandanna on your frizzy head and that big wide butt? I think all you might 'know' is how to make pancakes. Or more likely how to *eat* pancakes; lots and lots of pancakes to get a butt that big and wide."

She said, "I like you bettah when you *cryin'* all de time 'stead of makin' dem smart-ass comment. I suppose you gettin' bettah, crackah, and dat's goodt 'cause you be out of heah, an befo I know it I won't have to mess with yo sorry ass no mo'."

Someone paged her over the intercom, but she stuck her tongue out at me as she headed toward the nurses' desk. Abruptly she turned around and put her hands on her hips in what had become her classic lecture pose. She said, "An' let me tell you 'nother thing. You call me Aunt Jemima again and I'm gonna whup yo little white ass."

"Whoooo . . . I'm scared Lydia." I sailed an empty plastic bedpan at her and it barely missed hitting her head as it clattered to the floor.

She didn't even flinch or try to dodge and contemptuously snorted, "Dat was a pitiful shot, crackah. And I tells you one mo' thing, I wouldn't be talkin' 'bout nobody's big wide butt. Just remembah I was de one dat put yo catheter in and *I ain't impressedt.*"

I responded, "That was just a low-down thing to say Lydia, but it ain't gonna wash, 'cause I know you're lying. If you were lucky enough to get a peek at the 'babe' much less handle that bad boy, you'd be hanging around me 24/7—night and day, day and night—every day of your life, even more than you do now."

She laughed and said, "Dream on, crackah, dream on! Dat li'l fella ain't gwon do nobody no goodt. *Da 'babe,'* now dat's funny." And with that she wheeled around and left the room without picking up my bedpan.

CHAPTER FIFTY-FOUR

After Lydia left, more somber thoughts dominated my mind. I thought about the number one problem in my life, drug addiction. No one really ever kicks drugs. Do they?

I quickly told myself that I could and I *would*. God was with me now.

My thoughts were interrupted when I saw Dr. Jacobs walking into my room. As usual he was smiling. "Mr. Williamson, you're greatly improved. We're going to get you up and let you take a few steps on crutches today, and in a few more weeks, when the bone around the break heals just a tiny bit more, we're gonna get you out of here."

"Great news, doc. I'm ready to go home."

He smiled, "One more thing, Robert, I'm going to have to switch you from pain shots to pain pills today."

"BULLSHIT YOU ARE!" I was in full panic mode and started talking faster than a bullet exiting the barrel of a gun. "It's too soon! You don't understand doc, I'm still in pain—terrible pain every hour of every day. I can't make it without my pain shots. I can't doc. There's no damn way . . . *I have to have it!*"

The ever-present smile on Dr. Jacobs face dimmed slightly but quickly returned. It reminded me of a lightbulb that went through a power fluctuation. He skillfully ignored my sudden outburst and cheerfully said, "Sorry, Robert, we wouldn't want to make a drug addict out of you, now would we? You'll be fine." And before I could muster an answer, he turned on his heel and briskly walked away, still smiling.

"You'll be fine." Yeah right, easy for him to say. That smiling son of a bitch isn't the one who's addicted to drugs.

Instantly I thought about the bold statement that I'd just made to Lydia about God being with me now, and that I was going to change my life forever. Where was all that bravado now? "I can do all things through Christ who strengthens me." *Bullshit!*

I immediately caught myself and felt ashamed of what I'd said. At the very first hint of taking away my drugs, I'd crumbled like a stale cookie. Already I was having serious doubts that I could win the drug war.

Where was my faith in God? In an effort to shore up my shaky belief, I reminded myself that I'd felt God's unmistakable presence beside my bed in the recovery room as I suffered in agony. He'd helped me through that ordeal and He'd help me through this one too.

It wasn't long before the weaning process began and I was put to the test. I'd just returned to my bed after taking my first difficult steps. I'd had problems using the crutches and had stumbled and nearly fallen. My leg was hurting like hell. But when I frantically buzzed for my pain shot, Lydia brought me a little minicup with a white pill in it instead of a syringe.

When I looked at her in desperation, she said, "Sorry, crackah, I gots no choice."

As I'd feared, the pain pill took its sweet time taking effect. It dulled the pain some, but just barely. It was eons away from being a hit of morphine or Demerol. The longer I thought about it, the more I wanted a pain shot. I soon began to work myself into a lather and wanted a shot so badly my insides were heaving.

I nearly lost control. I told myself, *I can't take this shit anymore, I need to score. If I could only get on the street for five minutes.* I wondered briefly if I could talk Lydia into slipping me a shot or scoring something for me on the street. I knew she'd never do that. Then I thought that maybe I could just start screaming as loudly as I could, pretending I was in intense pain, until they brought me a shot.

Even if screaming worked, it would never work more than one time and then I'd be right back where I started. I tried to remind myself that the reason that I'd hit rock bottom in the first place was drugs, and the only way I'd ever change my life would be to kick them once and for all. I needed to bear down and tough it out. I prayed to God to help take away the craving. It didn't work.

In order to kick, I knew that I'd have to go through withdrawal. Drug withdrawal is a twofold process, because you're addicted both physically and mentally. I'd gone through physical withdrawal time and again: when I'd gone to prison, the time I freaked out on LSD, when I'd overdosed on meth, and after my escaping the New Orleans police and heading to Atlanta.

The physical craving, whereby your body actually needs drugs, lasts only two or three days, and although it makes you acutely sick, it's manageable. The real challenge is controlling the insatiable mental craving for drugs, and that's not a two- or three-day process. Everyone I ever talked to has said mental withdrawal lasts *forever*. Only a tiny percentage of addicts ever resist the call of drugs for any significant length of time, and many experts agree that five years of total abstinence are needed before someone is considered free from their lure. Groups like Narcotics Anonymous say you're never safe.

Most addicts, including me, have tried kicking drugs multiple times. The fight begins by slugging your way through the physical withdrawal process and then advances to the mental-addiction phase. The mental craving anguishes your soul and weakens you, just as kryptonite weakens Superman.

When trying to kick, the addict will vow, "This time will be different! I'll never give in!"

But then a girlfriend or boyfriend will dump them, or maybe a job opportunity will fall through, or perhaps they'll just become bored shitless with their mundane lives. It's then that drugs become the refuge, the haven the addict goes to so he can escape the disappointment, pain, discouragement, depression, and sheer boredom that everyone else on this planet seems to endure every day.

Drugs are the addict's out. When you hit up, the drugs make the misery of this world less miserable for a few moments. It's called a fix, but it never fixes anything. In the end, drugs just make matters worse and, like a malignant cancer metastasizing, begin to destroy life.

I knew that my drug dosage was being carefully monitored at Grady, so physical withdrawal wouldn't be a factor this time. But the mental addiction was already gnawing at me. Just knowing they would be ending my pain shots had panicked me. Now that the shots were gone, I wanted to take off running—but there was nowhere to run. Hell, my legs couldn't support me anyway.

I thought of Jesus again. He helped me through my surgical recovery; maybe he'd help me beat this.

I prayed, *God, please help me get through it this time and stay off drugs forever.* But although I listened hard, this time there was no response to my earnest prayer.

I questioned why God didn't just take away the cravings altogether. After all, I was one of His followers now. I was a Christian. I'd said that I believed in Jesus and I even did something that I thought I'd never do: I surrendered. I asked God to forgive me my sins, and according to what I read in the Bible, I'd now been "born again" and was a new person.

Then why did I still want drugs? Nothing had changed.

What the heck did "born again" mean anyway? My dark side was still licking his lips, wanting me to take a hit. My angel of light wanted me to kick. I'd been fighting this battle all my life—and losing. How was I any better off than before?

What did being a Christian mean anyway? Shouldn't fireworks have gone off in the sky, a lightning bolt popped me in the head, and my chains fallen off, suddenly meaning I was free? How was I any different now than before?

I still wanted drugs!

This was all very perplexing to me, and I didn't come to any solid conclusions.

I thought about the term "born again" and I remembered near verbatim the verse in the Bible where Jesus was talking to a man named Nicodemus.He said, "Most assuredly I say to you, unless one is *born again* he cannot see the kingdom of God."

What does God mean by those words?

Nicodemus asked the same question and Jesus gave him an explanation, but I didn't understand His answer and I don't think Nicodemus did either.He said something about being born of water and spirit, and these were spiritual and heavenly things to which He referred, and not earthly things.

What the hell does that mean? It sounds like mumbo jumbo to me.

Maybe He wants me to just think about it and figure it out on my own.

For something this monumentally important, I theorize that Jesus must have chosen those words very carefully. After all, God had suffered unparalleled pain and agony on the cross for this purpose. Doesn't common sense dictate that He would not have taken these words lightly, especially in light of the fact that He had said that gaining admittance to heaven was reliant upon being *born again?*

I concluded that He would not just leave selecting these words to mere happenstance, and indeed He'd chosen those particular words for a specific reason. There simply had to be some deeper significance to that terminology that I could understand.

What is He trying to tell me with these two little words?

I thought about my current situation. After 22 years of walking this Earth I would describe myself as being a totally evil person. I was so far gone that evil was dripping out of my fingertips. I didn't want to be that way, but it was what it was. Now that I wanted to change my life and follow Jesus instead of Satan, I would in effect need to be reborn.

Okay, I get it: "reborn" = "born again."

What does that entail, I wondered? I thought about what it meant to be born. When someone is born they are a baby. Logically I deduced that when I became "born again" I became a *baby Christian.*

Okay, if I'm a baby Christian, what does that mean? I thought about newborn babies. All they seem to know how to do is *scream and shit.* I laughed out loud.

That pretty much describes me all right. Babies mess in their diapers and then scream at the top of their lungs until their parents come and change them. I chuckled, thinking, *My entire life has been one continuous case of major diarrhea and now I'm screaming for God to come and change me. He'd have to love me to do that!*

My train of thought continued, *If a baby cannot care for itself, wouldn't it be totally reliant on its parents to take care of it? Especially in the infant stage? Until a baby learns enough to fend for itself, it's pretty much totally helpless, isn't it?*

I'd hit on something with this thought. That perfectly described how I felt about kicking drug addiction: *totally helpless.* Like a newborn, I'm totally helpless against drug addiction without God.

I liked God's terminology, "born again." I liked the analogy. I was being compared to a helpless little newborn baby who doesn't know what to do or how to act until he begins to mature. That's exactly how I felt. I didn't know how to go about changing my life. I'd need God's help and it was going to take some time to figure out how to do what He wanted me to do.

I happened to notice Lydia's Bible sitting on my nightstand, and I figured that reading the Bible would be a good start. I'd already read the New Testament and much of the Old. I use the term "read" loosely, because although I physically looked at every single page, I skipped all those long genealogy sections and other boring sections and concentrated on the sections that I could understand and in which I could take an interest. I felt that the Bible was God's communiqué to the world, and I wanted to read it firsthand for myself. I can read and I can comprehend, and I want to take my instructions directly from the source—I don't want anyone telling me what to believe.

Each day I read volumes of the Bible. Most of the Old Testament was boring, but I took notes whenever I came across anything particularly meaningful to me. I did like parts of it, like Psalms and Proverbs; however, when I started rereading the New Testament, it was like taking a cool drink of pure water after being scorched all day in the hot desert sun.

I loved reading about Jesus and His love for all humanity. He ate dinner and conversed with criminals and sinners, and had compassion for them instead of condemning them. It didn't matter how far someone had sunk; He was there for them. I drank it down and was refreshed.

Each day I made steady progress with the crutches, until one day Lydia came in and told me that I was being released in the morning and that the hospital had notified my parents and they were coming to pick me up.

She looked down at me and softly said, "I gonna miss you, crackah."

I retorted with a grin, "Yeah, well I ain't gonna miss you, Aunt Jemima. I'm sick of eating oranges."

"You gonna miss me all right, 'cause ain't nobody else gonna deal wif yo *shit*."

I laughed heartily. "No doubt Lydia, no doubt. Seriously, I'm gonna miss you too, and I want you to know that I appreciate your letting me read your *Goodt* Book. And I appreciate the oranges, and especially your hanging out with me through the worst of it. You really helped me out."

She smiled widely and then that mischievous look that I'd grown to know and love appeared on her face, and she quickly said, "Dat's my job, crackah. I ain't done it 'cause I likes you or nothin'. You too full of meanness to like."

I shot right back, "Yeah, right. I know you don't *like* me. That's because you're in *love* with me, Aunt Jemima, and I don't blame you one little bit, especially if you really did put my catheter in and got a peek at the *babe*."

She snorted, "Love? I loves to get you out of heah. You a pain in the ass's all you are. An I done tole you dat I damn sho ain't got no intrist in no 'babe'. I tells you dat reel quick." She shook her head, "Da *babe*. You one sick puppy, crackah."

She looked at me with disgust on her face and then we both burst into laughter. I was going to really miss her and she was really going to miss me.

Early the next morning Dr. Jacobs came to visit. Drug addicts are masters at convincing otherwise sane people to enable them, and I was the master of the masters. Although quite the challenge, even Dr. Jacobs was a sucker. I told him that I was going to have to ride in the backseat of a car for nine hours, making the long trip to my parents' house in Mississippi on terrible roads. I pleaded with him that the pain would be excruciating for a trip that long, and that I needed one last pain shot prior to leaving.

He looked at me and his brow was wrinkled, and lo and behold for the first time ever, he actually frowned. I assumed he was getting ready to lecture me about drug addiction again, but to my surprise he nodded and agreed to allow me to have the shot. He instructed Lydia to give it to me immediately prior to my discharge.

"Thanks, doc!" I was elated and licked my lips in anticipation.

"No problem." The smile was back.

It was great to see Mom and Dad. She was smiling broadly and so was Dad. After our hellos and some small talk, they went to fill out some paperwork and check me out and bring the car around. Lydia came in to give me my shot and wheeled me in a wheelchair downstairs where I could be picked up at the front entrance. By now I was grooving from the pain shot and I drunkenly saluted her and said, "Well, Lydia my dear, alas I must depart. Bon voyage."

She leaned down and kissed me on the cheek and affectionately whispered, "Goodt-bye, crackah."

When she bent down to kiss my cheek, I suddenly reached up and grabbed one of her big boobs and give it a firm squeeze. Then I quickly grabbed the other one and did likewise. She recoiled and said, "*What da hell?*"

I laughed like a schoolyard kid and giddily told her that before getting out of there I just had to know whether or not those bad boys were real. I said, "They're real all right. Hot damn those are two big bad bumpers you got there Lydia. You be black, and you be *proud*, big mama."

She said, "You's a damn *pervert,* dat's what you is. Da Lawd got His work cut out fo you. It take some kind of powful miracle to evah gits de devil out of you and straightens out yo craziness."

I looked up with a silly drug-induced grin on my face, trying my best to emulate a devilish leer at her.

Just then my parents drove up. Lydia looked down at me and now had a serious look on her face. She smiled a nervous smile and I looked up from my wheelchair with a serious look on my face and smiled back at her. Our eyes briefly met and we both saw that the other's were moist with tears slowly beginning to work their way down our faces. We both quickly dabbed at them, embarrassed by the show of affection.

"Bye, Lydia."

"Bye, crackah. You take care of yoself. You unerstan'?"

"I *unerstan,*" I smiled.

Lydia and Dad helped me into the backseat and put my crutches in the trunk, and off we went. I waved at her as we pulled out. She waved back and stood there and watched. And we continued to wave until we were completely out of sight. Lydia was one of the most kindhearted people that I'd ever met. I was going to miss her.

Chapter Fifty-Five

The drive to my parents' house was gruesome. It went fine for about three hours, and then the shot wore off. The instructions on my pill bottle said not to exceed taking one pill every four hours. I assumed that it really meant "take four every hour." *My logic was if one is good, two should be twice as good.* Dr. Jacobs would have been aghast, but it did enable me to sleep for much of the trip.

During the next several weeks, I recuperated at home. Mom cooked for me and I slowly began to regain a little weight. When the hospital discharged me, I looked like a skeleton and weighed in at a scant 110 pounds instead of my normal 185. The meth, the hard lifestyle, and the car accident had all taken their toll and ravaged my body.

Talking with my parents was difficult. They were normal people, far removed from the sewer in which I'd been living. We mainly made small talk about the things that normal people talk about—the weather, the news, what the people that I had known in school in Columbus were doing now, and mundane topics like that.

I was 22 years old going on 100. I'd experienced psychedelic drugs in the Haight, perversion, sex, depravity, fear, and crazy violence. I'd seen and done things that no person should ever see or do. I'd watched people die right before my eyes. How could I relate to normal people and carry on a normal conversation when I was anything but normal?

It was 1970 and the war in Vietnam was still raging; and it dominated the news. Tens of thousands of brave young men had been slaughtered; and it pissed me off to see guys my age dying and then Lyndon Johnson's ugly face on television telling us their deaths were for a noble cause and entirely necessary for the greater "good."

Dad would stay glued to the news and passionately and loudly defend our country's leaders for making the insane decision to be in Vietnam. It was no use arguing with him—he was convinced he was right and there was no reasoning with him. I'd hobble outside on my crutches to escape the insanity of the illogical.

I shared with Mom and Dad that I'd read the Bible while in the hospital and had accepted Christ as my Savior. And, I told them, I was determined to change my life. My mother was thrilled and the next day bought me a Bible of my own.

Dad was delighted that I was claiming God, but didn't think too much about my conversion. He still clung to the belief that I was saved when I was a little kid. He adamantly stated that Jim and I went down the aisle and accepted Christ as our

Savior and were Baptized and it was "real." He knew it was real.

He fervently told me, "Once saved, always saved. *I raised you right!*"

To my way of thinking, the real issue with Dad was not whether I'd actually accepted Christ as my Savior as a child or in Grady Hospital after reading Lydia's Bible. The real issue was that he was humiliated and deeply embarrassed by me, and didn't want to claim any responsibility for my turning out like crap. He'd raised me "right" and brought me up in church. I turned out like crap in spite of my stellar upbringing, so none of it was his fault.

As for why I turned out to be a piece of crap, I didn't blame Dad or Mom. "Bad seed" still sounded reasonable to me; however, he had no right to tell me when or how I found God. I went down the aisle as an impressionable little child because my brother went down a week or two before. And I went down that aisle because it made Dad proud of me and he showed me some attention for once. I was no more saved that day than a stray cat, but what would be the use of telling him all that? Let him believe whatever he wanted.

I saw Little Jim a couple of times while I was home. He was about four years old now and was much different from the last time I'd seen him. He didn't know me, but seemed to absolutely adore my parents, which made me a little jealous. I felt guilty and depressed about not being around him much during the past four years, but I also knew that an innocent little kid didn't need to be around a crazy speed freak either.

I finally talked to my brother by phone, and he reamed me out for wrecking his car. He reminded me—as Dad had already reminded me several times—that the Malibu had been Jim's college graduation present. I promised that I'd buy him a new car as soon as I got back on my feet (literally). Jim said, "I won't hold my breath," and then went on to remind me that he'd hocked his wife's wedding ring to bail me out of Parrish Prison. He ended by telling me that I was driving Mom and Dad and him crazy, and that I should just stay out of everyone's lives.

Finally I'd had enough. I told him to go screw himself and angrily hung up. I didn't blame Jim for being mad about his car, his wife's wedding ring, the times he had to intervene when I was freaking out on LSD and meth, and all the other craziness; but he could've saved the speech. I didn't need any lectures from Jim. I already knew that I'd screwed up, *again*, and that I was worthless, low-down scum. In fact, my opinion of myself was much worse than his was. My depression and low self-esteem were already as bad as they could be, and his piling on added nothing.

After about a month my leg had healed enough for me to walk on crutches with ease, and the horrible pain had all but subsided. On Sundays I attended church with my parents, and it felt good to be there. I could literally feel God's presence in the reverent atmosphere, and I felt His comforting peace when I attended.

The sermons, however, meant little to me. Their preacher had been a Christian since he was a little kid and had never so much as drank a beer, smoked a cigarette, or had illicit sex, and the dark side of life to him was hearing someone say "damn" or "shit." He would stand up there and rail against the slightest infractions of God's law, and I'd be sitting in my pew marveling at his sermon and wondering why he didn't address the unhappiness, loneliness, suffering, grief, sadness, despair, sorrow, misery, and *real* problems that people were enduring all over the world at that very moment. How could he relate to someone like me, who would've bashed his head in for 20 bucks in order to buy some meth?

I desperately hung on to God, especially when I was depressed, which was most of the time. Reading and studying the Bible, which I did most every night while everyone else was soundly sleeping, inspired me much more than listening to sermons on Sundays. I came to the conclusion that God was more interested in compassion than condemnation. In His own words, Jesus said He came to save the world and not to condemn it.

As the time neared for me to return to Atlanta, I prayed to God to help me with my anxiety, depression, low self-esteem, and hopeless outlook. I also renewed my prayer for help avoiding drugs. I knew that it would be only a matter of time until I was put to the test. And I feared failure. Briefly I thought about praying for help in eliminating the crazy violence from my life too, but one look at my broken body convinced me that my car wreck had already taken care of that issue for a while. I'd be on crutches for the next two years, and I couldn't envision being in a violent fight anytime soon.

Finally it was time for my return to Atlanta. My job at Martin Sprocket and Gear was still available, and the plant manager had made special arrangements for someone to drive me to and from work until I could resume driving again. Considering that I'd only worked there for a short time prior to my accident, I was flabbergasted at their generosity.

Before the car wreck, I'd considered my job at Martin to be a shit job, working with a bunch of losers. In reality the people were good and caring folk. In fact, a number of them had gone down to Grady and donated blood for me after my accident. I was ashamed of my thoughts about my job and fellow employees, and viewed my shame as a sign of positive change occurring in my life.

My parents and I drove the long, arduous trip back to Atlanta. They had secured a tiny, furnished efficiency apartment near my workplace for me. Mom stocked up the refrigerator, bought dishes, groceries, linens for my bed, towels, washcloths, and everything I needed. She put everything away and left the place absolutely spotless and in immaculate order.

They also purchased an older model Chevrolet Impala for me. It was somewhat dilapidated, but the engine was in relatively good shape and it ran well. The best news was that when the doctor released me to drive again, I would have my very own car. I hadn't owned a car in years.

Finally it came time for them to head home. Mom couldn't help but sob as she said goodbye and we hugged. As usual, Dad stood to the side, silent, with moist eyes. He nodded his customary nod to me and shook my hand with his big gnarly paw.

I don't know what I'd have done without their support—slept at a mission, I guess. I wouldn't have blamed them for giving up on me. I'd screwed them over too many times to remember. It was a tremendous expense for them, and I knew in the back of their minds that they were wondering how long I would make it; I wondered the same thing.

I didn't make any promises this time; I didn't think they would be legitimate. I'd gotten clean and made promises before that I'd never kept. I knew that they wanted me to succeed, but fully expected me to fail; it was understandable. We all felt it, but left it unspoken.

As she was walking out the door, Mom stuffed $200 in twenties into my hand and said, "This will help get you going until your first paycheck, honey." She kissed me on the cheek, said "We love you, Bob," and was gone.

I stared down at the money and remembered the last time she stuffed money into my hand. All I could think of back then was that I couldn't wait to use that money to buy meth. Strangely this time, I was thinking that it would come in handy to upgrade my skimpy wardrobe and go for a haircut so I wouldn't look like a hippie when I returned to work on Monday.

Maybe there was hope after all. For once my cynical, pessimistic attitude was overshadowed by a glimmer of optimism, albeit a tiny glimmer. I felt that this time it really might be different. I felt it in my *soul*. I whispered a promise to myself, "I'm staying clean this time," and then quickly added, "with Christ's help of course."

My pain-pill prescription had long since expired and I was clean and determined to stay that way, but there had been plenty of times recently when my entire being craved getting high. My life at home, crippled up and living with my parents, going to church, and studying the Bible had been a fairly easy environment in which to stay clean, but five minutes ago Mom and Dad walked out of my apartment and my support group went with them.

I was all alone again.

My doctor hadn't released me to drive yet, but he told me that in a couple of weeks I'd likely be strong enough to push down the brake pedal, so I'd be ready to go. Very soon now I would be back on the street with a car and a pocket full of money.

The test of a lifetime was right around the corner . . .

CHAPTER FIFTY-SIX

I returned to work and was greeted like some long-lost friend back from the dead. The office girls lined up to hug me, the guys shook my hand, and even the top dog himself—the senior VP and general manager—strolled out of his plush office, smiled widely, vigorously shook my hand, and said, "Welcome back!"

The show of affection for someone who'd only worked in a low-level job for a couple of weeks seemed odd, but genuine. I was embarrassed by all the attention and happy when the hubbub quelled. I hobbled back to the production office, where I clumsily stowed my crutches and plopped down at my desk.

Martin Sprocket and Gear was a small company. Approximately 60 manufacturing employees worked in the plant; three of us were located in the production office, and a handful of sales and administrative people worked in the front office.

The plant manager, who insisted that I call him Hank, was in his early 30s and took a liking to me right away. He was intelligent and energetic, treated employees in a fair manner, and had a thorough knowledge of his craft. I admired his style: He was confident and sure of himself, but unpretentious.

My job was to produce the blueprints that were utilized to manufacture the sprockets and gears that our company sold. The manufacturing process would begin with giant plates of steel, which would be burned out in circular blanks and then transformed into the sprockets and gears. Some were huge and some were tiny; all had to be machined to exacting dimensions. I had to know how to calculate the dimensions, but I also had to understand the manufacturing process, including which machines would be used, so that each drawing would direct the various stages of production.

We manufactured and kept an inventory of standard sprockets and gears, and we also produced custom, made-to-order items. Drawings already existed for the standard stuff and I merely copied them and annotated how many to make. The custom items had to be engineered in their entirety, including calculating dimensions and making shop drawings—and that was far more challenging and fun.

Initially, fighting through the learning curve and creating the few custom designs that came along made my job interesting and thought provoking, but soon even that became routine and boring.

At Martin, the chances of tackling something new were zero, because it was such a small company. Everyone, save me, had worked there for many years and they were all proficient at their jobs and seemed content to come in every day and do the exact same thing they had done the day before. All the good jobs were already taken, and the people holding them weren't going anywhere.

I was just the opposite of my coworkers. Once I mastered something, it immediately became boring. I was on fire. I wanted to learn another job and then another and another, and work my way up the ladder to the very top. I felt condemned to a life of daily tedium and mired up to my neck in a mud hole of monotony at Martin; and I wasn't making squat—only $300 a month. The job was wearing on me and I yearned for something better.

It was almost completely out of character for me, but I'd grown to actually like and respect most of my coworkers. It would seem bizarre to an outside observer who was familiar with my life, but I felt brazenly confident that I could handle any job in that company, including the plant manager's job, or even the general manager's position. This newfound confidence in my abilities was not something that I was consciously trying to develop; rather it just seemed to descend upon me quite naturally. I *knew* I could do those jobs if given an opportunity.

It would be an understatement to say my life was a drag. My doctor hadn't released me to drive yet, so after work I couldn't go anywhere in my new old car. I didn't have a television, radio, stereo, or even a telephone. That last one didn't really matter, because I didn't know anyone to call anyway; I didn't have any friends, including a girlfriend. I wasn't taking drugs or drinking. It was an incredibly boring time for me and I was turning antsy. At night, when I was bored out of my mind and depression began to overwhelm me, I would think of drugs and begin to crave getting high.

One night I finally succumbed to the urge. I thought *screw it*, and I decided to drive down to 14th Street and score some weed. I told myself that after a few tokes on some "huff" my "gray day would go sunny." It would be just what Dr. Bob ordered for the doldrums-depression mud hole.

I hobbled outside to my car, threw my crutches in the backseat, got behind the wheel and turned the ignition key to start it. *Click, click, click. Click, click, click* was all I heard. My car hadn't been started in over a month and the battery had run down.

I banged the steering wheel with my fist and then immediately thought of Jesus. I smiled and in a subdued tone muttered, "This ain't no coincidence, is it Jesus? I know you're standing there laughing at me. Not funny! Not funny at all!"

I angrily grabbed my crutches and limped back inside and went to bed. The compelling urge had subsided and my angel of light had defeated my dark side. I could almost hear him growling his displeasure from his lair deep within my mind.

That was a close call.

My routine was such that after work I'd come home, prepare some soup and a sandwich, and then voraciously read. I had plenty of reading material because my

Mom, who also loved to read, had given me boxes of books and, of course, my new Bible. Most nights I would read on through the wee hours of the night; generally I slept only three or four hours until it was time to go to work.

I was on a Bible-reading kick for a while and read it most every night. I soon discovered that the Bible was no ordinary book. I could whiz through a regular book or sometimes two a night, but as I got more involved with reading the Bible, I began to read it ever so slowly—just a chapter or maybe even a solitary verse at a sitting.

Normally I wouldn't think of rereading an excerpt from a regular book, but I would routinely reread the same verse in the Bible numerous times on end. Quite often I found myself putting the Bible down altogether as I stopped to think about something I'd just read and reflect upon its meaning. I might spend an hour or more turning it over in my mind, struggling with it, and trying to determine what God was saying to me and whether or not it might be instrumental in changing my life.

One night I read Hebrews 4:12 and, as often happened, I stopped to think about it. It stated, "The word of God is living and powerful, and sharper than any two-edged sword, piercing even to the division of soul and spirit."

I contemplated that statement at length, asking myself, *What does that mean? How can a book be "living"*?

I thought about those times I'd been racing along, reading the Bible at my normal reading pace when suddenly I would stop at a particular verse and be unable to move on until I carefully reflected on it.

Sometimes I'd be stuck on some concept for days on end. The verse "I can do all things through Christ who strengthens me" was a prime example. When I happened upon that verse, I couldn't get it off my mind for a week. Had God somehow wanted, or maybe even *directed*, me to stop on this particular verse so that it would come alive in my mind? Did He want me to realize that I'm no loser; that I'm a child of God created in His own image and that with His help I can conquer my demons and achieve great things?

I asked myself, *Is this what it means when it says the Bible is "living"?*

This was incredibly deep, but I wondered if the Bible was not some kind of a mysterious "Gateway to God." Is this how God actually communicates with us? We read and then we listen to God Almighty communicate with us as the words come alive.

I remembered reading that God is not physical like a person, but is a spirit and is everywhere at once. When I happened across this, I thought about it for quite some time too. I couldn't understand it. Was God some kind of a ghost? How could He be everywhere at once?

I resolved that issue to my satisfaction late one night when I thought of God as being similar to a television signal. Although it can't be seen, touched, heard, smelled, or felt, it is there just the same and it's everywhere at once. It emanates throughout space from a power base transmitter located somewhere. That is how I envisioned God, as some potent, evocative power base located on His throne in heaven, pulsating His spirit throughout all creation and blanketing the Universe with it.

It was a cool thought.

I'd felt His presence at times, just as I'd felt dark forces. I concluded that God undoubtedly influences me directly through my thought processes—as does Satan.

I assumed if that was the case, then it must have been God who stopped me when I read that verse "You must be born again." As with other verses, I couldn't find peace with this little verse until I'd thought about it for hours on end. It was only after I thought of the analogy between a newborn baby and a baby Christian that I could actually find any peace with the verse and move on.

Was it possible that reading the Bible was God actually teaching me what "born again" meant? At that *exact moment*, I looked down at the open Bible before me and a verse leaped out of the page and into my eyes.

> 1 Peter 2:2
> *As newborn babes,*
> *desire the pure milk of the word,*
> *that you may grow thereby.*

I physically recoiled and the hair on my neck stood on end. Goose bumps were tingling all over the back of my head and neck. *I'd just opened my Bible exactly to the very subject that I was thinking about just five seconds ago!*

After recovering from my initial shock, I read the verse again and then reread it one more time. My hand was shaking and I felt scared for some reason. This was creeping me out.

I went to find a pencil and some paper, and I wrote down the following:

- Newborn babies need milk to physically grow
- Newborn Christians need the "milk of the word" (Bible) to spiritually grow
- Newborn babies demand milk with every ounce of their fiber
- Newborn Christians should desire the word of God with equal fervor

Slowly it began to sink in. *God had just given me the next step to changing my life without saying the first word (aloud).* I would need to study His word and He would enlighten my mind as to its meaning. That was the key I'd been looking for so I could learn how to bring about the change in my life that I so desperately wanted.

If the first time wasn't enough to scare the crap out of me, I tried flipping through the Bible again. This time when I stopped, the following verse leaped into my eyes. Matthew 4:4: "It is written, Man shall not live by bread alone, but by every word that proceeds from the mouth of God."

"Help me, Jesus!" I slammed my Bible shut and anxiously looked around the room, scared out of my wits. I was so spooked now that I was near wetting the bed. Christ, it was as though God was carrying on a direct conversation with me and reinforcing what I'd just thought! "Man, this is *Jesus* talking directly to me! Could this just be a coincidence? Is this what the Bible means when it says it is *living and powerful?*" I looked down at my arm; it was covered in goose bumps.

Sleep was impossible that night and for several nights thereafter.

I hobbled around on crutches for another six weeks and then went to the doctor for my checkup. At long last he released me to drive. He suggested that I press the brake pedal down with my left foot instead of my right until I gained more strength in my right leg. Aside from that, he said, I should be good to go.

The problem was that after my horrendous accident, I was terrified of driving and none too anxious to sit behind the wheel again. I was glad that no one had to shuttle me to work anymore, but was very careful whenever I drove the few miles myself. For the first few days of that week I didn't go anywhere at night. Frankly I was just too fearful of having another wreck and going through that pain again. Then Friday night came around and with it came the urge to get out on the town and see what was hopping. Maybe I'd drink an icy beer or two to help me to overcome my fear of driving.

My new apartment was located completely on the other side of Atlanta from where I'd lived prior to my accident, and the few bars I was familiar with were much farther than I wanted to drive. I'd heard that they'd opened a brand-new disco called the Candy Store right down the street, and I thought I would go there to have a few cold ones and check it out.

I arrived there early and managed to secure a prime place to sit adjacent to the dance floor. I put my crutches under the bar and sat on a bar stool. I wouldn't be dancing, but from this excellent vantage point I could watch all the young lovelies twirling around and gyrating to the beat. Excellent!

Pretty soon both upstairs and downstairs were packed to capacity. I estimated that over a thousand people were crammed into the place. The small dance floor was jammed full of people hypnotically dancing to the rhythm and pounding of the loud disco beat.

Every so often I would have to stand up to stretch my leg. I still had stitches in one of the incisions, and it itched like crazy. And if I sat too long my leg would begin to ache. I stood there for several minutes nursing my beer, stretching my leg, and watching the dance floor.

When I turned around to sit back down, some girl with long blonde hair was sitting on my bar stool. I thought, *This ain't gonna get it*, and tapped her on the shoulder and yelled over the blaring music, "*Excuse me, you have my seat.*" I pointed to my crutches up under the stool. "Those are my crutches," I shouted.

She looked up at me and began laughing.

I was a little taken aback that she would laugh at someone on crutches and with a quizzical look on my face said, "What the hell? You think it's funny that someone's on crutches?"

"Don't you remember me?"

I looked at her with a blank look.

"The Store? I gave you my phone number."

I looked more closely at her. Just then one of her friends walked up, grinning from ear to ear too. I immediately recognized the friend as her watchdog the night of my accident. *This was the pretty little blonde that I'd met at the bar in downtown Atlanta the night of my car accident; the one that would not let me go to the party with her. And the other girl was the one guarding her like some prison warden that night!*

"Why didn't you call me?" she sulked.

I said, "Thanks to *you*, I had a head-on collision that night. I very nearly died, that's why."

"Thanks to *me*?"

"Yeah, thanks to *you*. If you would've let me go to that party with you like I asked, I wouldn't have had the accident." And then as an afterthought I asked, "Did you break up with that guy that night?"

"Yes, we broke up and he left for Germany and I haven't heard from him since."

"So," I said, "are you dating anyone in particular now that he's gone?"

A flirtatious smile lit up her face. "Not at the moment."

Hmmm. I asked, "What did you do to your hair? I remember it being shorter and now it's below your shoulders. I think maybe that's why I didn't recognize you."

She laughed and said, "I was wearing a shag wig that night. This is my natural hair."

"Far out!"

"I was hoping you'd call, but you never did." Her lip had an enticing little pout on it signifying her displeasure, and it was obvious she was not used to being ignored.

I had not even so much as thought about her again, and of course had lost the phone number in the melee surrounding the car crash.

I retorted, "Well *excu-u-u-use* me! Somehow between numerous blood transfusions, a badly mangled body, broken bones, operations, and fighting for my damned *life*, I somehow managed to lose your phone number." Then, in a nicer tone, I asked, "How about giving it to me again?"

She smiled. "Are you just going to lose it again?"

I shot back loudly, "Are you going to let me go to your party this time?"

"Maybe," she teased as she fumbled in her purse looking for something to write with.

I told her, "I'm sorry but I don't remember your name. How 'bout you write it down too, will you?"

"No problem, I don't remember yours either, ***BOB!***"

"Hey, thanks to *you*, I had a brain concussion! Cut me some slack, will you?"

She smiled and said, "My name is Teresa."

CHAPTER FIFTY-SEVEN

After our amazing reunion, Teresa and I became inseparable; it was love at first sight. I liked everything about her, and she made me feel good about myself. From all accounts, the feeling was mutual. She told me that I was the most interesting and fun person she'd ever met or been around.

Imagine that.

Teresa was the diametric opposite of me. She still lived at home at age 23, and loved to spend time with her family, which included her parents, her grandmother Mam-Maw, and her sister, Bobbie, who was also her very best friend. She was not into the drug scene and didn't even know anyone who was.

She was a good person from a good home and was what I would describe as a Goody-Two-Shoes: someone who strictly follows the rules no matter what. Although she was not a religious zealot, she had professed her faith in Jesus Christ, was baptized in her early teens, and attended a local church. She wanted to do the right thing, *always*, and there was not a rebellious bone in her body.

Her parents, Shelby and Jenny, were down to earth, hardworking, blue-collar types. They didn't have much in the way of formal education, but were blessed with good hearts and an enormous amount of common sense. Shelby was a brick mason who was good at what he did and always seemed to have work. Jenny was a smart woman, and despite her limited education and her West Virginia mountain accent, had been promoted to a top job as one of the purchasing agents for a large Atlanta hospital.

Shelby was raised in the isolated backwoods and mountains of North Carolina, and during his youth was reputed to have been somewhat of a wild child himself. He was said to have made and run moonshine along with his older brothers during Prohibition. He was about six-foot-four, lean, and quite the colorful character, with a shy, congenial demeanor that often conflicted with his hair-trigger temper.

When we initially met, he didn't seem to like me much. When I arrived to pick Teresa up for our first date, he was sitting on the front porch. I smiled my most endearing smile as I stepped out of the car and began the arduous task of using my crutches to walk over to where he was sitting. I wanted to shake hands and introduce myself. Without saying so much as one word, or even nodding to me, he stood up and walked inside the house.

I was just thinking *what a rude son of a bitch* when Jenny appeared and warmly greeted me. Where Shelby was a man of few words—introverted, shy, and hard to know—Jenny was extroverted, warm, and friendly, and she treated complete strangers as if she'd known them all her life.

I loved Jenny almost from the first day I met her. She was a charming and gracious Southern lady, and a genuine "people person," with a heart as pure as the deepest mountain spring. Jenny could have inherited those traits from her mother, Mam-Maw, who was as close to being a saint as anyone I'd ever met. She did most of the cooking, and the meals she prepared were awesome.

Teresa's parents had moved to Atlanta from North Carolina when Teresa was just a baby, and she'd lived in the same modest house all her life. And she had friends galore. Her parents had instilled their strong work ethic in her, and right after graduating from business college, she began working at a local insurance agency as an executive administrative assistant.

They were the type of family that did everything together. They'd visit a local park, go on picnics, gather for huge meals during the holidays, decorate the Christmas tree, and spend weekends camping, water-skiing, and fishing. Everything was done *together!*

I was very secretive about my dark past and didn't share any of it with Teresa. Whenever she'd mention it in passing, I'd quickly change the subject. She just wouldn't let it lie and finally, exasperated, I told her that my family had moved around constantly during my childhood because of my dad's job and I attended too many schools to remember. As a result of my Gypsy lifestyle, I didn't develop any close lifelong friends like the ones she had.

After high school, I recounted, I'd attended college for a couple of years and worked in the Louisiana oil fields in the summers. At 19 I got a girl pregnant and then married her. I didn't love her, I said, and just 11 months later was divorced. I lied and told her that I avoided the draft through a medical deferment. I told her that college had become too much of a financial burden and I wanted full-time employment and dropped out to come to Atlanta to find work.

That was it: short, sweet, and simple; no mystery, no intrigue here.

I looked clean-cut. My hair was short and I was well dressed, thanks to the money that Mom had given me to buy a new wardrobe. I wasn't using drugs and was trying my utmost to avoid anyone who did. I sometimes drank to excess, but most guys my age did the same. She really had no way of knowing that I'd been a violent drug addict/alcoholic/criminal, and I wanted to keep it that way—not just with her, but with everyone.

The first time she came over to my tiny apartment she was shocked—this in spite of the fact that I'd warned her about it. I had told her that I just couldn't manage to clean it very well on crutches and I'd "allowed it to slide a little." I had pretended that I didn't want her to come over and see it in its current condition, but really was hoping that she would come clean it up for me.

As anticipated, she insisted on coming over to help me get it whipped back into shape, and one Saturday Bobbie followed her over to my apartment to help out. When they walked in, I could see the look of shock on their faces. Aside from being a dump located in a seedy section of town, my apartment was in foul shape and in bad need of cleaning.

Mom had left it spotless, sanitized, and sterile, but since then a couple of months had elapsed. It was grubby now and nowhere was it worse than in my kitchen. Beginning early in childhood I'd developed an aversion to washing dishes. The thought of any slimy crap stuck on dirty dishes getting on my hands just gave me the willies. Consequently I refused to wash them until there was no other option and I was completely out of clean dishes. In fact, if I could have afforded it, I would have just thrown away the nasty dishes and bought new ones.

Teresa very nearly threw up when she walked in and saw the carnage. Dirty dishes were piled high and little gnats were buzzing around like miniature airplanes circling a busy airport trying to land and refuel on the dried food lodged on them.

I acted embarrassed that they were seeing my place in such a deplorable condition, and donned my most pitiful look as I hurriedly hobbled over to the sink, acting as if I was going to clean it. Just as I reached the sink, I clumsily on purpose dropped one of my crutches to the floor. I awkwardly bent down to retrieve it and when I tried to kneel I feigned losing my balance and started hopping around on my good leg, trying to keep from falling. Teresa came running over and nimbly grabbed my crutch off the floor and handed it to me.

I told her thanks and shot her a "tortured" look of appreciation and a grim smile. I then turned to face the sink with a crutch under each arm and with great difficulty managed to turn the water on as though I was determined to wash those dishes in spite of my pitiful infirmities.

With a mother's tenderness, she sweetly told me to just get out of the way and go sit down—she'd clean up.

I meekly said, "Are you sure?"

She smiled, nodding affirmatively, and gently pushed me away. "Go sit on the couch; we'll be through in no time." After I sat down, she brought me a beer and even popped it open for me.

I beamed and thought about my performance and persuasive skills. *Legendary* came to mind.

She and her sister spent nearly an hour washing, drying, and putting away my dishes and taking out trash. From there they moved to mopping floors, vacuuming, and dusting. Then they headed for my bathroom. In a word, "sick" would have described the bathroom. In two words, "very sick." Undaunted, they broke out the rubber gloves and Lysol and gave it a thorough scrubbing too.

All the while I was lounging on the couch, drinking beer and thumbing through a hunting magazine. Every now and then I would stand up with my crutches and limp over to where they were working and ask if there was anything I could do to help. I already knew that Teresa would smile and refuse, but Bobbie was on to me and would sullenly glare. It was obvious that but for Teresa she wouldn't be there. I smiled my nicest smile right back at her, all the while thinking, *I know you don't like me bitch. Not to worry, I don't like you either.*

Finally they were finished and Teresa's sister curtly said she needed to go. I smiled broadly and thanked her for helping out. She quickly gave me another glare of disdain and then produced an equally disingenuous smile of her own right back at me and left.

Teresa didn't even notice the animosity in the air. She stayed and gathered up my dirty clothes, which had been tossed into a large stinking pile at the base of my closet. She took them to the Laundromat and returned in an hour or so and ironed them for me and neatly hung them in my closet. She then folded the towels and put them away.

If all that wasn't enough, she went to the grocery store, bought groceries (with her own money), and came back and prepared me a delicious meal, complete with a bottle of wine. It was the first bona fide meal I'd eaten in my apartment since Mom had cooked one for me. I'd been living off soup, sandwiches, candy bars, Cokes, pizza, and cookies since my parents dropped me off. The meal she cooked was terrific, the wine was excellent, and the company was superb. After dinner she quickly cleared the table and washed dishes again. She left everything spotless and gleaming.

By now I'd swigged down more than a couple of beers and of course had helped myself to the majority of the wine. I was feeling pretty darn good. To my way of thinking, the only thing missing from this splendid day was an evening of glorious sex. I asked her to come over and sit on the couch and rest for a few moments and relax. I put my arm around her and kissed her. She was a good kisser and was hugging me tightly. I smoothly encircled her breast with my hand and gave it a good squeeze. To my complete surprise she grabbed my hand and sternly pushed it away and told me that she wasn't "that kind of girl." She warned, "Cool it with the hands!"

In my slightly inebriated state I was not easily dissuaded. I drunkenly thought that she was merely toying with me and when she'd said, "No," she really meant, "Try a little harder; I'm not going down that easy, 'cause you might not respect me." I continued to try to fondle her breasts as though I hadn't heard a word.

Whap! She slapped me hard on the face and said she'd leave if I didn't stop.

I was caught completely off guard. Rejection just didn't happen to me. The bitches I'd known would have been out of their pants before I had mine unzipped. Ordinarily anyone who slapped me would have gotten slapped back, only harder.

For some strange reason, her rejection of my advances actually greatly enhanced my respect and admiration for her. I sheepishly told her I was sorry and that I didn't know what had gotten into me. I immediately stopped trying to seduce her. She smiled and snuggled back close to me, relieved that I wasn't harassing her anymore.

Teresa was the marrying type—a class act—and I was beginning to fall deeply in love with her. I didn't want to ruin our relationship by treating her like she was some New Orleans slut ripe for the picking.

Since returning to Atlanta, on occasion I'd go to the pay phone down the street and touch base with my parents and even my brother. I was doing great in my job and had stayed off drugs for longer than any time before. I was reading my Bible quite often and trying hard to make it. Slowly they'd begun to dare to hope and were cautiously optimistic that this time around I might actually change my life and make something good of myself. They were especially excited to hear that I was dating a good girl from a good home. It was on just such a phone call that my brother invited Teresa and me up for a visit to his home in Tennessee.

We drove to Jim's house in Teresa's new car and had a great weekend of fun in the Tennessee mountains with Jim, his wife, and his young son. I was shocked to learn that he'd named his only child after me, and everyone referred to him as "Little Bob." He was a beautiful little boy with sparkling, deep-blue eyes and long, curly blond hair. I'd never cared to be around kids much before, but this little guy was smart as a whip and I quickly grew to love him as if he were my very own son.

Jim nor his wife ever mentioned a word about my sordid past to Teresa.As far as anyone might tell, we were just one big, well-adjusted, normal family gathering together for a grand old weekend and having a great time.

On the drive home, Teresa and I were riding along talking, and out of the blue I asked her if she loved me.

She looked puzzled, hesitated, and then softly said, "Yes."

I told her, "I love you too. You wanna get married?"

Her mouth dropped open and she quickly glanced at me to see if I was serious. When she saw that I was, she simply replied, "Yes."

There was no expensive ring that I dug out of my pocket to give to her, no flowers, no fireworks, no candlelight dinner, and no rehearsed speech. And I didn't hire a plane to fly over with a sign saying, "Teresa I love you. Will you marry me?"

It was all spur of the moment. I asked her if she wanted to get married, she accepted, and a month later we did the deed.

We were married in a beautiful Christian church that had stained-glass windows valued at over a million dollars. Ironically, it was located directly adjacent to the intersection of West Peachtree and Peachtree streets, where I'd been in my head-on collision months earlier.

It was a beautiful ceremony. Teresa's family and friends filled the church to overflowing. My parents and my brother were the only ones who attended from my side. My brother was my best man, and he handed me the $35 wedding band for Teresa and her niece handed her the $35 matching wedding band for me, and the ceremony went off perfectly.

We spent our honeymoon not far from my little apartment, staying at the Stone Mountain Inn just outside of downtown Atlanta. We could only afford to rent the motel for a one-night stay, but that was all right with us. We were madly in love.

I consider that reuniting with Teresa that night was nothing less than a miracle of God; and next to my relationship with Christ, Teresa proved to be the best thing that ever happened to me.

There is absolutely no doubt in my mind that God directed Teresa to come sit down in my chair in that crowded, dimly lit place that night.Consider: It was the very first night that I'd gone out after my accident and I'd never been to that disco. Teresa had never been there either until that night, and had decided to go there at the last moment because one of her friends had heard it was a fun place. Located on the opposite side of town, the disco was miles away from where we'd originally met downtown some six months earlier. The place was packed, with over a thousand people milling around the multilevel disco, and finding me there was like finding the proverbial needle in a haystack.

I believe that when I stood up to stretch my leg, God sat her down in my chair for a purpose. He knew that I would never make it on my own. I needed a help mate, a soul mate, an anchor who would love me and keep me from drifting back into the abyss. I needed someone in my life who was the opposite of me. Someone stable, caring, loyal; someone who was normal. I needed Teresa.

I never would have imagined in my wildest dreams that a scumbag like me could ever even meet, much less marry, a nice person like her—and still be married to her nearly 40 years later.

It just goes to show that miracles do happen and we can indeed do all things through Christ who strengthens us.

One would think that after all the lessons learned, having discovered God and finally getting married to a decent person that I loved, I might now happily ride off into the sunset with "Happy Trails to You" serenely playing in the background. There was one thing that I didn't consider.

Satan wanted me back!

CHAPTER FIFTY-EIGHT

Soon after we were married, I took a job at Glidden Paint Company, in a sprawling, 17-acre paint manufacturing plant and distribution center. Over 400 employees filled a wide variety of positions there. I had liked my job and the people at Martin, but I hadn't made a lot of money and had virtually no opportunity for advancement.

My new position was perhaps the worst job in the plant, but I wasn't discouraged in the least and actually looked at it in a positive light. As bad as it seemed, I was still making $50 a month more than I was making at Martin. I optimistically figured that starting at the very bottom in such a large operation meant that my opportunity for advancement was unlimited. My position was merely a starting point and not the final resting place.

With my limited education, criminal record, military background, and pitiful résumé, I knew up front that I would be at a decided disadvantage going up for a promotion against practically any worker in the plant. I accepted full responsibility for my past mistakes and figured that I ought to have to start at the bottom with a past like mine.

Logic dictated that, with all that bad stuff going against me, I'd need to work longer, harder, and smarter than my cohorts if I was going to get ahead. I committed myself to doing just that and from day one I was the first one to arrive at work and the last to leave.

I didn't mind hard work. It kept my mind off drugs and it made me money. My parents had instilled a strong work ethic in me, and when I lived at home from the time I was eight years old I'd always had a job. Invariably I had money when I was a kid, and I hadn't forgotten how nice it was to have some as opposed to having none.

In fact, money was without question the primary motivating factor in my quest to succeed. I wanted a house, a car, a ski boat, and other nice things, and it took money to buy them. I knew that I wasn't going to win any lottery or inherit some fortune, so if I ever wanted anything, I'd have to work long and hard to obtain it. Teresa and I were already beginning to see the rewards from our joint efforts: She was making $400 a month; and with my $350 a month, we were now able to move out of my rat-hole apartment and rent our very own two-bedroom house in Decatur.

My job at Glidden was to take care of the paint labels that would be put on every can of paint that was manufactured. The label room was located in the bowels of the plant, and was a filthy dirty, dimly lit, nasty little room with labels strewn everywhere.

I befriended a maintenance man and convinced him (with the help of a six-pack of beer) to install some fluorescent lights in my label room, along with some shelving. Then, even more important, I had him put up a chain-link fence to stop the plant workers from just wandering in whenever they pleased and helping themselves to entire bundles of labels when they needed only a fraction of that amount.

I asked for and received permission from my boss to come in on a Saturday (off the clock) to paint the floor, ceiling, chain-link enclosure, and shelves a brilliant white. When I was through, the label room was dazzling white-on-white-in-white and brightly illuminated. It was much less depressing to work in after I'd painted it, and I beamed at my handiwork.

I separated the labels, and neatly bundled and stored them in bins that had been logically numbered and identified. I took a physical inventory and determined a valuation. I established a policy whereby production workers were required to come to the window and hand me their production ticket before I would pull the required labels, which I meticulously counted out one at a time (allowing just 10 percent extra for spoilage). I created a manual inventory-control system so I'd know how many of each label I had on hand, and I developed a method whereby I could quickly reorder.

I didn't have formal training for any of this. My education consisted of common sense and a determination to figure out a better way of doing things. Soon my little operation transformed the label department. It was neat, organized, efficient, and so clean you could have eaten off the floor.

Immediately I became very unpopular with everyone but my supervisor. The plant workers were for the most part surly, hard-core union guys, and were not enamored at all with the idea of saving the company money. They were used to coming and going in the label room as they pleased, and any excess labels that were left over after a run they would just throw away.

My being anal about a few lousy labels did not go down too well. They would glare at me, but I was undaunted and would glare right back at them. I wasn't trying to win a popularity contest, and could care less if they liked me or hated me. I was solely interested in obtaining an increase in salary and a promotion.

It wasn't long in coming either. My label program was wildly successful and I saved some serious money on wasted labels. I also saved the company more money by virtually eliminating label outages, which heretofore had halted production on a regular basis. My newly implemented reordering procedures kept adequate inventory on hand at all times.

And of course I developed a report that chronicled everything I'd done since I'd arrived: from initially making the improvements to the label room, to chronicling the annual label savings with a before-and-after financial snapshot, to reducing production stoppages that took place because of label shortages. My boss immediately reported my progress to his boss, and the next thing I knew I was promoted to the inventory-control department.

I took on that challenge in the same gung-ho manner. As far as I was concerned, the inventory-control department was a joke. Four of us shared the responsibility of placing paint orders for Glidden's stores located throughout the Southeast. We would utilize computer printouts that detailed how much paint a store had on hand and the store's sales usage by month. We each controlled inventories of a small number of stores, and we would place orders for them weekly.

I was trained in about an hour and considered it a simpleton job that a trained monkey could probably have done. I placed an order for my very first store using their criteria, and then my boss carefully checked it for errors. There were none. He beamed and said he was impressed with the superb job I'd done. As I settled in to the routine of ordering for all my stores over the next several weeks, a problem soon developed. I could order so fast that I would complete my entire week's workload in just one day.

Finally one Tuesday morning I went to my boss and told him that I was already through with my entire week's workload, was bored silly, and needed something else to do.

At first he appeared skeptical, as though he thought I'd just rushed through it and done a crappy job. He took my orders and went into his office to review the accuracy of my work. In a little while he came back out of his office with a big smile on his face. He told me that I could order even better than he could. Then he gave me a special project to work on that he'd been trying to finish for months.

Shortly after my meeting with the boss, he called the other inventory-control workers into his office and chewed them out. He pointed out my sterling accomplishments versus their sluggard performances. He ended the meeting by angrily telling them that they'd better pick up their pace, or else. This did not go down well with my coworkers, and when they got back to their desks they were all livid. One of them whispered to me, "You need to slow down, pal. You're making us look bad."

It was as though he'd pulled the pin on a hand grenade and tossed it to my dark side. I exploded in near full-fury mode and angrily snarled, "Let me tell you something, **PAL.** I'm the one who has to pay my bills and support my family. If you guys want to sit around on your asses and do nothing all day, I could care less, but you either mind your own business or meet me in the parking lot after work. Or we can get it on right here and right now and I'll *beat the shit out* of you, one at a time or all at once."

The spokesman recoiled as though he'd just been stuck in the eye with a red-hot fireplace poker. He quickly looked down at his desk and didn't utter another word, nor did any of the others. They were all dumbfounded and shocked at my violent diplomacy.

Not one of them ever mentioned it again—at least to me. In fact, from that point on I was completely ostracized. None of them went to lunch with me or even talked to me. It didn't matter to me. I was used to being alone and I didn't like those lazy sons of bitches any more than they liked me.

I was promoted eight more times in the ensuing two years, and during that period my salary nearly doubled. Teresa's career was taking off as well, and she'd taken a job as the executive assistant to the regional vice president at Union Pacific Railroad. She had an unbelievably good job and still made more money than me, and although happy that we were doing so well as a family, I was personally disappointed. I was motivated to work even harder to surpass her.

I was now in the management program, and as far as I could tell I was the only one without a college degree that had ever made it this far. I'd worked as a supervisor in nearly every department in the plant, including manufacturing, the paint filling department, warehouse, shipping, and plant scheduling. During this time I learned a tremendous amount about paint manufacturing and distribution, and developed a reputation among upper management for doing an excellent job wherever I went.

Soon they created a new position for me. With such a variety of experience under my belt, someone came up with the idea that I should become a "roving foreman." I would cover for any supervisor in any department throughout the facility who went on vacation or was out for any length of time. This meant that at different times I had to work on all three shifts, sometimes for a week or two at a time. I liked it because it gave me an even greater opportunity to learn various operations throughout the organization. I calculated that the more jobs I knew, the more valuable I became, which in turn meant more money. And money was always on my mind. They also gave me extra pay for shift work, so I eagerly accepted the new position.

One night I was working second shift and I came out of my office to check on my men. One of them was missing. I asked the others where he was, but all I got were sullen looks and "I dunno."

I searched for him and finally went to the locker room. As I turned the corner, I heard music playing and saw my man leaned back in a chair with his locker door open. His radio was hanging on the open door and he had his hands folded back behind his head. He was listening to it as though he didn't have a care in the world.

This infuriated me. My dark side ignited my brain like a stick of dynamite and I went over and kicked the chair out from under him. He went sprawling on the floor.

He blurted out, "What the hell?" I answered with a hard kick to his mouth. When he got up blood was trickling down his face. I hit him with my fist and he fell back to the floor like a 50-pound sack of flour. I jumped on top of him and, with his head between my knees, I began to pound his face with my fists.

Suddenly I stopped. Why, I don't know. I suspect Christ grabbed my fist midair and said ***STOP!***

I was breathing hard and blood was all over the floor, my worker, my white shirt, and my fists. I climbed off him and went for some paper towels and water, and got him to his feet. I helped him clean up his face with the towels. He appeared dazed and frightened.

I gruffly told him to gather his stuff out of his locker and leave, that he was fired. He quickly gathered his belongings, glad to be getting out of there, and I escorted him to the parking lot.

As soon as I watched him drive away and leave the premises, I began to panic. I'd just beaten the hell out of a *union* employee and fired him. That just doesn't happen to union employees. Glidden supervisors don't do that. In the short time that I'd been in the management program, I'd already accumulated more grievances against me from the union than any other supervisor. I'd documented each incident to the hilt and had won them all, but this was major.

I couldn't sleep that night and I called my supervisor just as he arrived at work the next morning. I told him what had happened, except I lied and told him that when I confronted the employee and ordered him back to work, without warning he had attacked me and hit me in the eye and nearly knocked me out. I'd defended myself, I said; and after I subdued him, I'd made him clean out his locker and escorted him from the building.

To make my story more believable, when I went home I stood in front of my bathroom mirror and hit myself as hard as I could in the eye several times. It hurt like the dickens and the eye began to swell a little, but now I had the physical evidence and swollen face to support my story.

The employee had far worse than a slightly swollen eye. At the hearing he still looked as if he'd been in a train wreck. His nose was obviously broken, his lip was cut, his face was swollen, and he had several assorted bruises and abrasions where I'd pummeled him. It was my word against his and the only witnesses were a couple of guys that could only verify that the guy had gone missing. And that prior to looking for him, I'd asked if anyone had seen him.

The arbitrator ruled in my favor, saying the guy shouldn't have left his post and shouldn't have attacked me when confronted, but oddly he then allowed him to keep his job. I breathed a sigh of relief that I'd won another one. I looked at the employee and I'll never forget the look in his eyes. It simply said, "You're a lying son of a bitch."

In spite of winning the arbitration hearing, I couldn't convince my boss to buy the story. Word had gotten back to him more than once that my temper was foul and that I'd challenged several people to fights in the short time I'd been there. He called me into his office and reamed me out about it. He told me that Glidden was not the Wild West and that if I wanted to remain a supervisor or even an employee, I'd *better* get a grip.

I acted hurt that he didn't believe me and made a half-hearted argument, asking him, "What else could I have done? I was just trying to defend myself." I quickly shut up when he informed me that he wasn't an idiot and neither was the arbitrator. I barely got away with it this time and it could have ended up costing the company a ton of money, *literally!*

Things cooled down in a few days, and not long after that incident Teresa and I bought our very first house in Kennesaw, Georgia. We were ecstatic, and one night not long after we moved in, one of my neighbors came over and told me that he wanted to nominate me to the Jaycees. The Junior Chamber of Commerce was an organization for fine, upstanding young men to develop and assume leadership roles in the community.

I was flattered that I could become involved in such a prestigious organization and accepted. Teresa and I went to the Jaycee annual dance and all of us fine, upstanding young men and women were mingling.

Teresa had never given me any reason to be jealous, but I was, and it was about the only bone of contention in our marriage. I was always fearful that she might be running around on me, and I was jealous of her boss, male coworkers, and virtually every other guy with whom she came in contact. I assume that my jealousy stemmed from the deep psychological scars that had formed when my "fiancé" pulled a train and screwed my own brother and all his buddies that time in New Orleans.

The dance had an open bar and I'd been heavily drinking hard liquor and mixed drinks, and I was feeling mean. Some guy kept coming over and talking to us like he'd known us all his life. He seemed to be taking an inordinate amount of interest in Teresa and in my mind was flirting with her. When I came back from getting another drink, that same guy was standing there again and they were laughing and talking.

Snap, Crackle, Pop! I exploded. I walked over to him and hit him, and he hit the ground. The fight was broken up before it really even started. We were surrounded by all those fine, upstanding young men holding our arms behind our backs. I grinned widely and said that it was all just a slight misunderstanding, and as soon as they loosened their grip on me, I head butted the guy. Blood spurted from the corner of his eye where my forehead had solidly landed.

As far as I could tell, I was the only member of the Jaycees' organization for fine, upstanding young men to ever be kicked out. It was not very subtle. My neighbor friend, who happened to be the president of the organization, called the next day and told me that perhaps the Jaycees was not such a good fit for me after all.

"No problem, man."

I told Teresa that I didn't want to be around all those phony people anyway. I then started in on her about flirting with that guy. She denied it. I responded by giving her the silent treatment. I sullenly sat by myself and drank a case of beer and passed out on the couch.

I just couldn't get the sight of Teresa and that guy laughing together out of my mind. Three days later I was still steamed. I was standing next to her giving her hell about it as she was preparing our dinner. She angrily told me that the guy was just making conversation and inviting us to go water-skiing with him and his wife. She said that I'd made a fool out of myself and embarrassed her.

I loudly screamed, "I don't give a damn if you were embarrassed! You lying whore, he was trying to screw you and you wanted it just as badly as he did!"

She was standing at the kitchen sink peeling vegetables. She screamed back at me, with tears now streaming down her face, "You're crazy! I'd never do such a thing!"

She sobbed, "I love you! Can't you understand that?"

"You're a lying whore!"

At that she violently threw the knife that she'd been using into the kitchen sink. It bounced out of the sink and flew by the side of my head, narrowly missing my eye.

Instinctively I hit her hard in the stomach with such force that I knocked her all the way across the room. She landed sprawled on her back by the refrigerator. She was lying there writhing around on the floor making a gagging sound like she couldn't catch her breath and her face began to turn purple. When I saw what I'd done, crazy fear swept through me.

Frantically I ran to her side and asked if she was all right. She couldn't catch her breath or talk. She was sobbing and crying and gagging for breath. I was frantic and had no idea what to do to help her. I feared for her life and choked back tears as I blurted out, "I'm sorry! *I'm sorry!* I didn't mean to hit you, Teresa."

She was finally able to catch her breath and, still trembling, recovered enough to whisper, "That's it. I'm leaving you! I can't take it anymore."

Chapter Fifty-Nine

Teresa meant more to me than any other person in the world. I helped her to her feet and she could barely walk. She was bent over, clutching her stomach and sobbing. I begged her to forgive me and solemnly promised that I would never lay my hand on her again.

She shook her head and said, "It's too late. I can't deal with your crazy jealousy anymore. I won't live with someone who beats me. I'm going home."

Without thinking, I angrily screamed, "*You **are** home!*"

She flinched and cringed at my raised voice, and held up her hand as though she were a small child trying to ward off another smack in the mouth from an abusive father. She backed away from me with terror in her eyes and then turned and ran down the hall to our bedroom, where she quickly began packing her clothes. Tears were streaming down her face.

I was devastated to see her afraid of me and sickened at what I'd done. I was scared beyond imagination that she was going to leave me. I meekly followed her down the hall and into the bedroom; I softly told her that I was sorry. I pleaded with her to just please, *please* give it another try.

She was trembling all over as she turned and looked at me with tears flooding her eyes, and I could see the hurt. Seeing her hurt made *me* hurt—*badly!*

She said, "You're *insane*. I've never run around on you. I've never even wanted to. I'm not like that. I love you! Can't you understand? It's hopeless. You'll never believe me and I can't live like this. Please just leave me alone. I'm going back home to Mom and Dad."

I truly loved her and couldn't bear the thought of losing her. She gazed at me with a tortured look on her face and then resumed packing. I didn't hear a word she was saying because I thought that I saw something in her eyes. I gently turned her around to face me again and looked closer.

I could see in her eyes that deep down she really didn't want to leave, but I could also see the fear. She was afraid of me and my violent temper.

I sorrowfully begged, reassured, and pleaded. I promised that I would never hit her. Never again!

I blurted out, "I just couldn't stand the sight of you standing there laughing and talking to that guy. I can't get it out of my mind. I was frantic that I would lose you! When that knife bounced past my eye, I just reacted out of instinct. I didn't even think. I don't even know how it happened. I don't remember hitting you, I swear to God. You just have to believe me. I'm sorry. God knows that I didn't mean to hit you, Teresa."

She turned and faced me and simply buried her face in my chest and began crying uncontrollably. By now tears were streaming their way down my face too. We remained standing there crying like that for several minutes. She began to cry more and more and finally hysterically. She was shuddering like a scared child who'd just awakened from a horrible nightmare. I didn't say anything and just hugged her and gently rubbed her back and let her get it all out. Finally she began to calm down and became subdued.

She softly whimpered that she loved me and I told her that I loved her. We kissed and I looked her squarely in the eyes and solemnly promised that I would never, ever lay a hand on her again.

I could tell that she wanted to believe me, but months later, anytime we had even the slightest disagreement about something, I could see the tentative look of fear that remained in her eyes. I felt the apprehension too, and wondered when my temper would snap again. I feared that it was probably only a matter of time.

I didn't lose my temper anymore but things were still uneasy. I wasn't home on the weekends much because I'd picked up on my childhood hobby of whitetail-deer hunting and would spend each weekend in the woods in pursuit of whitetail bucks.

It was the height of deer season and it was a beautiful day. As I sat on my deer stand enjoying the fall weather, the woods bustled with activity. The big buck that I'd been hunting had remained elusive since opening day. I knew he was frequenting the area, but so far I hadn't seen so much as a glimpse of him.

It was such a beautiful day that I really didn't care whether I saw the buck or not. I was enjoying the warm morning sun and observing other wildlife in close proximity to my stand. I was greatly amused by a squirrel that was perched on a limb in the same tree in which I was sitting. He was eating a white-oak acorn and a blue jay was loudly berating and scolding him from a perch a mere inch or two above his head. The squirrel seemed oblivious to the blue jay's screaming and calmly munched away, his jaw moving 90 miles an hour as he enjoyed his meal.

I wondered at the squirrel's unmindful disregard of this nuisance bird and his incredible patience in totally ignoring it. I smiled as I began thinking that if I were that squirrel, I'd reach up and grab that chattering, raucous asshole by its throat and before he ever knew what hit him, I'd rip him to pieces. I'd begin by wringing his neck and twisting his head off. No, even better, I'd bite it off and then spit it out with blood running down both corners of my mouth. I'd then calmly go back to enjoying my breakfast, only now I'd enjoy some peace and quiet. He wouldn't be bugging anyone else who was sitting there minding his own business trying to enjoy a nice leisurely acorn breakfast, I tell you.

The instant this thought crossed my mind, it was as though God slapped me hard in the face. *Why would you even think such a twisted thing? This is the very kind of thinking that has been destroying your life. This is coming from Satan.*

This revelation was nearly identical to the one I had with drugs. After seeing the extreme devastation that drugs had on my life, I realized that if I didn't stop taking drugs, *I would come to no good end.*

Now it was obvious that another terrible, demonic plague was devastating my life. I was facing the same dilemma that I'd faced with drugs, only this time it was the disturbing violence. If I couldn't stop the violence, *I would come to no good end.*

As I sat there in this beautiful setting in the quiet forest, I wondered why I was so angry all the time. I asked myself, *Why do I hurt people?* I'd worked hard for two years and had finally been promoted, but nearly lost my job because I lost my temper and pounded some guy. I became friends with my neighbor and he got me in the Jaycees, but then I pounded some guy and got kicked out and lost my friendship with my neighbor. Now I'd hit my own wife when my temper exploded, and I'd nearly lost my marriage.

My marriage, my job, my friends all at risk of being lost, because I can't control the violence that rages within me. Is this what I want? *Why am I so violent?*

My behavior certainly wasn't coming from God, which meant it could only be coming from my dark side. I remembered back to when I was recovering from my accident and I was first contemplating changing my life: I'd cited drugs as my biggest problem, and violence as the next. I'd looked down at my leg and figured violence wouldn't be a problem because my body was broken. That was then and this was now. I was no longer on crutches and the violence was back. I needed to address it now.

"I can do all things through Christ who strengthens me" had been my creed back then, but God was now missing from my life. After I met Teresa and things had started going well, I'd forgotten about the Bible and drifted away from daily Bible study. I was spending time with her or on hunting expeditions on weekends, or I was consumed with building my career and getting ahead. I hadn't left any time for God or picked up my Bible in months. Or was it a year? Hell, I didn't even know where my Bible was. As I thought about it, I couldn't remember the last time I even thought about *God*, much less the Bible.

Sitting right there in the forest I bowed my head and prayed to God to help me. When I got home I finally found my Bible stuffed in a box on the top shelf of my closet. I dug it out and went into the kitchen. There at our little breakfast table, while Teresa slept in the other room, I opened it at random to the following passage, which I'd underlined in red ink:

Proverbs 3:5
Trust in the Lord with all your heart.
And lean not on your
own understanding.
In all your ways acknowledge Him,
And He shall direct your Paths.

I smiled as I felt God's warm, uplifting, reassuring presence in the room with me. I bowed my head, shut my eyes, and whispered, "Thank you, God. I'm no longer leaning on my own understanding because I have failed miserably and am helpless in solving this problem in my life by myself. I acknowledge that I need You in my life and I trust in You. Please help me to control my violent temper."

I said, "Amen," and then randomly began flipping ahead a few pages and abruptly stopped and immediately read the following passage:

Proverbs 19:19
A man of great wrath will
suffer punishment . . .

The hair stood on end on my neck and my heart was pounding so hard I could see it moving through my T-shirt. When I got over the initial shock of having God direct me to a passage that was precisely the answer to the question that I had just asked, I took a pen and underlined that passage and sat there and continued to stare at it for several minutes, tingling all over. God had said that if I acknowledged Him, He would direct my path; and right after reading that I'd turned to this passage dealing with wrath.

Then I glanced across the page,

Proverbs 19:11
The discretion of a man makes
him slow to anger
And his glory is to overlook a
transgression.

I leaned back in my chair and put my hands on the back of my head and thought about it. I'd learned in the hospital to read and then just stop, sit back, relax, and wait on God to communicate with me and enlighten me as to what He was telling me, as thoughts slowly swirled through my mind.

I whispered, "This method of communicating with God is just too far out for anyone to ever believe; I have trouble even believing it myself and yet it's happening to me right now." I sat there and intensely thought and *listened* for God to advise me. I didn't have to think too long about the verse that I read pertaining to a man of great wrath suffering punishment. I was that man of great wrath and I'd suffered punishment because of it. If I didn't get a grip, I'd suffer even greater punishment and possibly lose the best thing that ever happened to me—my wife. I'd also lose my job, friends, family, and everything.

The next verse that I examined was more thought-provoking and I even looked up the word "discretion" in the dictionary. It means good judgment. I substituted good judgment and the verse simply stated, "The good judgment of a man makes him slow to anger."

I thought about that for a moment and reasoned that in order to use good judgment, I needed to first stop and think and consider all alternatives prior to reacting with my fists. That doesn't sound like an easy thing to do for a man with a hair-trigger temper. I needed to get a grip on my temper.

And then came the real kicker. In order to receive God's *glory*, I must overlook a transgression against me. As I mulled this one over and over in my mind, I thought, *Forget about transgressions. If someone so much as even looked at me wrong, I'd drive a fist right through his face. Here God is telling me that if I want His glory, I must overlook an actual transgression against me. Hell, I don't have a chance. Damn, how can I ever do that?*

I thought about the little squirrel calmly sitting there eating his acorn, completely oblivious to and ignoring the blue jay that was screaming away at him at the top of his lungs mere inches above his head. The squirrel was unruffled and unfazed by the jay's antics, and simply disregarded the commotion. The squirrel continued to sit there enjoying its meal and the beautiful morning.

The blue jay, who'd tried its utmost to torment the squirrel, couldn't stand being ignored, and when it couldn't stir up the trouble that it desired, soon grew tired and flew away to try to find someone else to bother.

I thought about those in life who love to torment me, and I considered that if I were to ignore them, they too would soon fly away and leave me to my peace and quiet. If I confront them, there will be chaos and big problems and I will enjoy no peace. By ignoring its tormentor, the little squirrel enjoyed peace. God's GLORY is peace!

I understand, and I want it.

I laughed at my personal conclusion: God wants us to enjoy this life and live in harmonious peace, but in order to achieve it we must ignore raucous, obnoxious assholes.

I don't think God would have put it quite that way, but it was my street version and I understood it.

Could I do that? The answer was clear: "I can do all things through Christ who strengthens me!"

In the 39 years of marriage since I mulled this over, I never once raised my hand against my wife again, or even had the desire to do so. And in those nearly four decades, although I've had thousands of disagreements with a variety of people and admittedly caught myself sometimes at the last moment, I have restrained myself from violence. Only twice did I get into scuffles, and both were in self-defense and unavoidable, and are not even worthy of further discussion.

I'm particularly proud of winning this battle against the unrestrained, mindless violence that had plagued me for—literally—as long as I could remember. Yet again I attribute my success to being a *miracle* of God. I can find no other plausible explanation. I compare it to the Bible lesson in which Jesus stills a raging storm by simply admonishing it. I assume in similar fashion that He stilled the raging storm inside me by admonishing me that day when I wanted to strangle and bite the head off that stupid blue jay.

How did He do it? He spoke to me through my mind and I obeyed. I consider it a *miracle*, just like I consider it a miracle when the storm on the Sea of Galilee instantly obeyed and became calm when Jesus told it to be still.

How could anyone expect to explain a miracle? By its very definition a miracle defies human logic and understanding because it is an act of God that defies the laws of nature. Mystery surrounds the power of God, and it is far beyond our intellect. The Bible tells us that we were created lower than God and that His ways are higher than ours. It says we can see things only dimly now, as though looking into a dirty mirror, but that one day we will see clearly and understand what has been hidden from us in this life.

I look forward to that day. Maybe then I will understand. For now, all I can truthfully say is that after I prayed to God and asked for His help, from that day forward I have been able to control my temper and stop the violence that had plagued me since childhood. That is enough for me. As far as I'm concerned, "Seeing is believing."

The raging and ferocious battles against drugs and violence were hard-fought victories, but the fierce war for my soul was far from being over and would only intensify. Satan wanted me back even more than before and went after me with everything he had in his formidable war chest. I would soon be faced with evil so heinous that it would shake my newfound belief system to its very foundation like the worst earthquake in recorded history.

Tragedy of a magnitude of 10.0 on the Richter scale was right around the corner . . .

Chapter Sixty

Teresa and I had been married for almost four years and were both nearing our 28th birthdays. We decided that it was time to have some kids, and within a month she was pregnant. We were elated. Nine months rocketed by and our first son, Michael Ryan Williamson, arrived without the slightest complication.

As you might expect, Teresa was the quintessential loving mother, and I loved him just as much or even more than she did. I simply couldn't wait to come home from work to see him every day.

This was the happiest time of my life. I immensely enjoyed every segment of his development, from the time he changed from a gurgling baby staring into space (I referred to this as "the vegetable stage"), to an active, crawling, jabbering personality. Every phase of development was a blast to experience.

Unfortunately I hadn't had the chance to experience that with Little Jim. I was able to see him only every month or two, whenever I would make the arduous nine-and-a-half-hour drive to Mississippi to see my parents. Sometimes I could take him for the entire weekend and sometimes for only an hour or two. I missed practically all his early childhood years and that makes me sad.

I tried to make up for being an absentee father to Jim by being there for Michael. I couldn't bring myself to change diapers—it was too revolting— but I would often feed him from his bottle and later from a spoon as he sat in his high chair. We even took our baths together every night, and to his absolute delight I would sing his favorite song at the top of my lungs.

I took my responsibility as a father *seriously.* I didn't know that I was even capable of loving my son that much. I was especially determined to raise my kids in such a manner that they would never turn out like me.

It was during this time that my brother and I began to develop a bond stronger than we'd ever had before. It started with a few tentative phone calls and then some visits. I think when he finally realized that I'd indeed actually changed, he lowered his "drug-addict alert" and we began hanging out together.

As with me, one of the best things that ever happened to Jim was to move out of New Orleans and escape its evil influence on his life. Once he left that satanic stronghold, he seemed to find his groove. His marriage was blossoming, his son was doing great, and he owned a beautiful house in the suburbs of quiet Kingsport, Tennessee. They had all the trappings of "the good life"—a big color television set, brand-new company car, shiny new van for his wife, sparkling new bass boat, dirt bikes, camera equipment—and he even had a long-haired sheep dog the size of a Shetland pony, which completed the yuppie scene.

Jim was very successful in his job with Abbott Laboratories and he made big money. He was their number one salesman and received an engraved plaque, gold lapel pin, and an all-expenses paid vacation (the only thing that he really cared about).

Practically every weekend either they would come see us or we would go see them. Jim's wife and Teresa quickly became friends, and while our wives talked and did their thing with the kids, Jim and I would either go fishing or, more likely than not, dirt biking.

He'd gone "all in" to racing dirt bikes, and had two highly tuned, jazzed-up bikes that would virtually scream rpm's. We would fearlessly race at top speed, tearing over steep and perilous Tennessee mountain trails, leaving caution at sanity's doorstep, laughing and yelling like two wild teenagers at an amusement park. When we returned, we would be unrecognizable. Our helmet visors would be so completely covered in muck that we couldn't see out, and nasty Tennessee mud covered us from the top of our heads to the toes of our boots.

Jim and I became more than just blood brothers or even best friends—we became soul mates. My former life was a filthy, black secret and I was ashamed of it. I refrained from ever discussing it with anyone, preferring to keep it locked away deep within the catacombs of my mind. I wanted it to remain forever hidden.

Jim and I lived through some dark times together, and although we rarely talked about them, they were always there. I think our situation might have been similar to the camaraderie felt among soldiers who have experienced the horrors of war together. Although the horrors remain unspoken, there is comfort in just being around others who have lived it and know what it was like.

Jim's son, Little Bob, was something to behold. He had beautiful, long blond hair that was naturally thick and wavy. It was curly on the ends and he had perhaps the deepest blue and most piercing eyes that I'd ever seen. He was full of energy, laughed constantly, and was just happy. Jim and his wife idolized Little Bob and had never left him with a babysitter (not even once in his entire life). If Little Bob couldn't go, then they couldn't go. It was as simple as that.

Although he was only five years old, Little Bob was a prodigy with an astounding vocabulary, and he could speak intelligently about a variety of subjects. He constantly amazed us. I would spend an enormous amount of time with him, and soon we developed a very deep love for each other, almost as though he were my own son. If Jim and I were on the phone and Little Bob found out I was on the line, he would pitch a fit and insist on talking to me. When he got started, he would talk so fast that I was amazed he could even breathe. He would have talked on for an hour or more if we would've let him.

He followed me around like a little pup, asking a million questions about every subject imaginable. Sometimes just the two of us would sit downstairs in my den and have deep conversations about a host of subjects.

One day Little Bob looked up at the trophy whitetail-deer mount that adorned my den wall and asked me why I had killed that deer. I told him that hunting whitetails was a challenge of the highest magnitude. I went on to describe in minute detail the tremendous skill that is required to match wits with the elusive whitetail buck, which has a keen sense of smell, vision, and hearing. I told him it was the ultimate challenge to go up against these wild, intelligent creatures in their home territory. Success depended on putting in significant hours in the woods, learning their haunts and habits, and also being patient, I told him. And, I said, a hunter needed to learn certain skills—how to figure out where a deer was likely to frequent, how to position a stand in order to get a shot, how to use camouflage, where to shoot the deer to make an efficient kill, and more.

I told him that being smart like me was also a big advantage.

He grinned widely and vigorously shook his head no when I said that.

I pointed to my buck and said, "I spent months scrutinizing that wily old buck's routine. I found his well-used trails and all the skinned-up trees where he rubbed the velvet off his antlers. I saw where he conducted mock battles against other bucks in preparation for the breeding season, which is called the rut. I researched all the buck's favorite areas, and after months of study I set up an ambush where I could waylay him as he moved between bedding and feeding areas looking for receptive does.

"When hunting season opened," I continued, "I parked my jeep perhaps a mile away. And then long before daylight, I silently sneaked toward my stand—I had to be careful not to step on a twig or make a sound. I approached downwind of where I expected the buck to approach, and when I got there I climbed 30 feet up into my tree stand. Donning full camouflage, I perched myself near the top of the tree. I remained motionless for hours, trying not to move or make any noise. My back ached. It was freezing cold and I could barely feel my fingers and toes. I waited motionless for the big buck to appear."

As I spun my hunting story, Little Bob seemed fascinated and his blue eyes were twinkling with excitement. They reminded me of the sun dancing off the Pacific Ocean, glittering like two little sparkling blue diamonds in the bright sun.

I continued, "Just then I caught a glimpse of movement out of the corner of my eye.

"*There he was!*

"I was so excited that my heart started pounding. He was indeed the trophy buck that I'd been pursuing all these months. He was huge and even bigger than I'd imagined, with an enormous rack and a neck swollen from being in rut.

"He was silently gliding down the trail like a ghost. His head was down and he was heading straight for me! My mouth was so dry that I started choking. I would have given anything for even a tiny sip of water. I wondered if I might asphyxiate.

"I slowly began moving my rifle into place, but suddenly the big buck stopped and shot his head straight up in the air. He sensed that something was not quite right, and he was staring right at me. I trembled as I held my scoped rifle midair, trying not to move or even breathe. The gun weighed 200 pounds, it seemed, but I dared not move, even an eighth of an inch, or the big buck would see me and bound away."

Little Bob was spellbound as he nervously sat on the edge of his seat waiting to hear what happened next.

"Finally, mercifully, the ancient buck twitched the 'all clear' sign with his tail, dropped his head back down, and resumed walking. I breathed a sigh of relief as I gratefully exhaled, and I thanked God that the buck hadn't seen me. I slowly lowered my gun into position and took aim. I pushed the safety forward to the fire position.

"I winced as I heard it make a loud *click*. It sounded as loud as a firecracker to me and I nearly panicked when I heard it; but the buck didn't even look up and kept slowly walking toward me.

"I picked out an opening between the trees, and when he stepped into it, I put the crosshairs right behind his shoulders in the heart-and-lung area, took aim, and ever so gently *squeezed* the trigger.

"BANG!"

When I loudly screamed, "**Bang**", Little Bob flinched and jumped six inches off the couch as though he'd been shot through the heart himself.

I smiled and beamed down at him. "And there you have it, Bobby boy. *That*, my young friend, is what it's all about; going to the arena, competing with a worthy opponent, and of course, *winning*." I winked at him and slapped him on the shoulder.

I casually draped one arm around Bob and with the other I proudly pointed to the whitetail mount that was blankly staring down at us with glass eyes. I said, "I conclusively demonstrated on that fine sunny November day that I, your Uncle Bob, possessed the superior hunting skills required to take the elusive and much sought after trophy whitetail buck. Indeed one would do well to rightly conclude that I'm undeniably a Great White Hunter.

"I'll tell you what, though, my Little Bobby boy. For short you can just call me 'Uncle Bob the Great!'

"How about that?" I patted him on his precocious little head and paternally smiled down at him.

As I looked at Little Bob, he was smiling widely and seemed totally enchanted with my narrative. From all appearances, he seemed to be swept away by it all. He was gazing at me with those penetrating blue eyes, and was speechless for maybe two full minutes as he mulled it over in his bright little mind.

I thought, *This little rascal is truly enamored by my skills. He's even smarter than I thought. When he comes of age, to be sure I'm going to donate some of my time and train him up and mold him into a great hunter too.*

Just then he looked up at me with a slightly amused look and said, "Uncle Bob . . . uh, excuse me . . . I meant to say, Uncle Bob *the Great.*"

I smiled and nodded approvingly.

"Couldn't you have accomplished the same goal by just taking a photograph? That way you could still prove that you are the Great White Hunter, but you wouldn't have had to kill him and he would still be out there running around in the forest for others to enjoy."

I stammered, "What the . . . uh?"

I was stunned. It was as though he had deliberately kicked me in the groin. I glared at him and gruffly said, "Okay urchin, it's time for your nap."

His question sounded like it was voiced by some midget-in-disguise Harvard University philosophy professor instead of a five-year-old kid.

He followed me upstairs still jabbering away about it. I grabbed a Coke out of the refrigerator and glowered at him. I wanted no more of his stupid questions, but he was undeterred and kept following me all over the house. I only occasionally grunted "yeah" or "no" to the onslaught of his persistent follow-up questions. I finally told him to "get off it," that I didn't want to hear any more about it.

Fun times like these were far away from the precarious world that I had come from. I was living a wonderful dream and felt true joy and peace in my life, and I liked it. The dangerous life on the streets, with its violence, drug addiction, loneliness, despair, and hopelessness, seemed a million miles away. But as I was about to start learning, God is a Teacher who teaches through vigorous testing. You get comfortable, you get smug, and when you least expect it, He hands you a very difficult test that is no doubt designed to ensure that you're really understanding it.

About three weeks later, I developed a relentless cough. I just couldn't shake it, and one morning while I was shaving, I had a coughing fit and up came a smattering of bright-red blood. I looked at it on the white porcelain sink, not believing what I was seeing. I went to the doctor the very next day and he took some chest x-rays, which revealed a suspicious-looking dark spot on my lungs.

I asked him what it was, and he said in an almost bored, rehearsed monotone that he didn't know.

Aggravated with his nonchalant demeanor, I persisted, "Well, what do you *think* it might be?"

He impatiently asked, "Do you smoke?"

"Yes."

"How long have you been smoking?"

"Let's see, I started when I was about 11 or 12, so I guess it's been about 16 years now."

"How much do you smoke?"

"I'm up to three packs a day."

"If I was a betting man, I'd wager that you probably have lung cancer."

"Lung cancer! I'm just 28 years old!"

"Well son, 16 years of sucking up tar and nicotine is plenty enough time to develop lung cancer. I'm not saying that it *is* lung cancer mind you; we'll need to run additional tests to determine that. But in the meantime, I'd highly recommend that you quit smoking cigarettes—today."

I was completely taken aback. I couldn't believe it. This guy acts like he is reciting from a dictionary or something. Where is the emotion?

Lung cancer! *That shit'll kill you!*

I'm too young to have lung cancer. *Aren't I?*

When I stepped out of his office, I nervously lit up a cigarette and took a deep drag. My heart was pounding. There was a time when I would have welcomed death, but now that I finally had something to live for, it looked like God was poised to snatch it away from me. What kind of perverse joke was this?

As I drove home, I thought about the doc telling me I should quit smoking "today." He sounded urgent. How should I go about quitting? Should I taper off or just hit it cold turkey?

I thought, *Hell, if I can quit the needle, I can quit smoking cigarettes. Cigarettes are nothing compared with hard drugs.* Cold turkey it would be. I reached into my shirt pocket and grabbed my just-opened pack of Winstons, lowered the window, and tossed them out.

In less than an hour, all that bravado about kicking the needle had evaporated and I desperately wanted a cigarette. My nicotine withdrawal was making my skin crawl. I wanted a cigarette so badly I could have smoked one a foot and a half long. I longed for my pack of Winstons. I envisioned finding them on the side of the road and fantasized about sitting down right there with cars whizzing by on the busy freeway and smoking one right after the other. Taking a deep drag off a cigarette was all I could think about, night and day.

The pressure from not knowing whether or not I had lung cancer just intensified my need for a cigarette to calm my nerves. It was a true test of sheer willpower and determination.

I asked God to take away the temptation, but it was as though He was stone deaf. Instead of having less temptation, my cravings intensified. I assumed that He didn't want to be bothered, or more likely He was just telling me to "man up" and handle it on my own.

Subsequent tests showed that I didn't have lung cancer. The doctor told me that the spot was probably a sore that had developed on my lungs, and that smoking had aggravated it and made it bleed. He told me in no uncertain terms that I needed to permanently quit, or it could develop into cancer.

I did quit smoking, but I can assure you that I still wanted a cigarette a year later. And there is no question that it was more difficult to quit smoking than to kick drugs. I think this was in no small part because everywhere I went, people—including most of my friends—were smoking cigarettes. I didn't hang out with druggies and thus was never exposed to the temptation from seeing them using. If everywhere I went the fragrant smell of marijuana was drifting through the air, or if I saw people shooting up in restaurants, at work, and virtually everywhere else I went, it might have been a different story.

The entire time that I was sweating out whether or not I had lung cancer, I'd been praying incessantly. Once the all-clear signal sounded and I didn't have cancer, I quickly put the danger out of my mind and didn't give it another thought. This Christian thing seemed to be working out pretty darn well. I called Jim and immediately launched into telling him all about it. I thought he'd be delighted that I didn't have lung cancer and had quit smoking, but he sounded really down and preoccupied. I could tell he was worried about something, so I asked him what was wrong. He told me that one of Little Bob's eyes was "drifting" and they had taken him to the doctor.

"What do you mean 'drifting'?"

"One of his eyes is cocked off to one side and not facing forward as it should be."

"What could cause that?"

"They don't know. They're running some tests, but they're afraid that it might be caused from pressure on his optic nerve."

I repeated myself, "What could cause that?"

"Perhaps a growth, or maybe even a tumor of some kind."

"*Tumor!* Naw, it couldn't be that. Surely there's another explanation."

Jim didn't answer.

I continued to worry about it and even prayed to God that all would turn out well, as was the case with the spot on my lung. The following Friday night we loaded up the car and made the long drive to Tennessee. When we arrived, our absolute worst fears were realized. Little Bob's neurologist had determined beyond a doubt that Jim's precious little five-year-old had a brain tumor!

We were in shock.

Monday they performed brain surgery on Little Bob. I got down on my knees and I fervently prayed with all the energy that I possessed. I'd never prayed so long or so earnestly. I begged God to please spare Little Bob and to *please, please* let the tumor be benign and not malignant.

The family sat in the waiting room for an agonizing nine hours as the operation progressed. Much of the time I was on my knees together with Jim, Teresa, and my parents. We intensely begged God to heal Little Bob. The wait was grueling, as hour after distressing hour ticked off the clock.

Finally the phone rang and Jim went to the front desk to talk to the doctor. I saw his shoulders slump forward and he almost fell to the floor. He had received the horrible news from the surgeon that the tumor was malignant and was growing at an incredible pace. They removed some of it, but it was in an inoperable position on Little Bob's brain. It would kill him if they took any more. The doctor said he was sorry, but this particular cancer was as malevolent and as nasty as they come.

As the news spread among the various family members assembled around the waiting room, the scene became chaotic. Grief surged from person to person like a sickening, pulsating shock wave from a nuclear blast. Through the din of cries and wailing, somehow I determined that Little Bob would be taken to recovery and it would be several hours before anyone could see him. Jim and his wife would stay at the hospital and the rest of us would go to Jim's house.

I stood and hugged Jim and cried with him. It was nearly unbearable to see him so afraid and helpless. He'd always been so tough—hard like a rock—but now he looked like a scared little boy who was lost and didn't know how to get home. I could feel him shuddering and crying in my arms, and I felt helpless in trying to comfort him. Finally he turned to console his by-then hysterical wife. I gathered up my Bible, and Teresa and I headed for the elevator.

We walked onto the elevator accompanied by one Jim's wife's sisters and when the doors shut, she screamed, **"Fuck God!"**

I dejectedly looked at her and didn't say anything. I asked God a simple question.

"Why?"

I listened for my answer.

There wasn't one . . .

Chapter Sixty-One

Little Bob went through chemo and radiation treatments, both of which made him extremely sick and weak. He steadily declined for about three months. All his beautiful blond hair fell out, and he suffered as no little child should ever have to suffer.

The tumor was located at the base of his brain. It started out about the size of a walnut but quickly metastasized to the size of a softball; and then the cancer cells migrated down his spinal cord and seeded up and down his spine. This affected the nerves throughout his entire little body, and he experienced constant, unbearable, excruciating pain *everywhere*, especially in his joints. He screamed in nonstop, heartbreaking agony, and it was so bad that finally he had to leave the home that he loved so dearly and enter the hospital.

They were giving him enough morphine to kill a horse, but within 15 minutes of receiving a shot, he would resume screaming. It was extremely emotional and difficult beyond imagination to see him like that, and no one grieved more than Jim. The doctor explained that an adult would have long since succumbed to the pain and died, but a child could endure more pain than we could imagine.

At one point they tried an experimental hallucinogen to try to alleviate the pain, but Little Bob was so frightened by it that he screamed in terror and waved his arms as if he was frantically trying to ward off his tormentors. Jim made them immediately stop that treatment and threatened to beat the shit out of the doctor for giving it to him.

One bitterly cold dark night I returned from the hospital after seeing Bob like this all day long, and I was emotionally spent. I collapsed on my bed and fervently wept. The anguish was overwhelming and I didn't think I could bear it. Grief stricken, I sobbed and bawled and turned on my side and beat my pillow with my fist.

Finally, exhausted, I rolled over on my back and stared up at the ceiling. I thought of Little Bob smiling at me and gently making a case for photographing that old whitetail buck instead of shooting it, and tears once again filled my eyes, flooding them into blurs.

I moaned and blurted out, "I'm the one with blood on my hands. I've done evil, unspeakable things and sinned dark sins against You God, but this little boy is innocent and gentle and just five years old. His whole life is ahead of him. Why would you take him and spare me? *It's just not fair!*

"What kind of God are you?

"One who cruelly tortures innocent little kids?"

At that moment I felt God's Spirit gently unlocking my mind. I was spellbound as I envisioned Jesus Christ surrounded by an angry mob. I saw the madness, the angry twisted faces that were spewing hatred and cursing Him as He was being crucified. I saw the violent rage in the mob's eyes as they gathered at the base of the cross and howled for more and more blood. They were shaking their fists, cursing, and spitting on Him.

I saw the anguished look of pain in Jesus's eyes as blood oozed out of His wounds. I saw the nails driven through His hands and feet and the crown of thorns that the soldiers had beaten onto his head, I saw whip marks covering his chest and legs. And although it must have hurt Him greatly just to speak, He looked down upon the swarming multitude and gently said,

"Father, please forgive them, for they know not what they do."

At that moment I felt deeply ashamed. There among the crowd I had seen my own angry face. I was standing right there with them cursing and screaming and shaking my fist at the one who died for my sins and saved me, Jesus Christ.

The Jesus that I knew from the Bible was full of love and compassion and as gentle as a newborn lamb. Jesus would have never done something to harm *anyone*, much less a beautiful, innocent child like Little Bob. I knew with certainty that the only reason He came to this Earth was to save lives, not to destroy them.

No, Jesus wasn't the one responsible for this. The culpability was Satan's and his alone; he's the one who cruelly delights in death and suffering. I vividly remembered when God opened a window to hell to let me see this vile creature firsthand. His gloating evil head was tilted back, laughing that horrendous, wicked laugh, while his demons danced in the flickering firelight and delightfully celebrated my death.

I take much personal pleasure in the knowledge that he will burn in hell forever as payment for what he did to Little Bob and for all the other atrocities that he and his horde of demonic followers have committed, beginning with Cain and Abel.

We prayed and prayed and prayed for a miracle, but it was to no avail. Finally one night Jim delicately lifted Little Bob from his hospital bed and tenderly cradled him like a little baby in his arms. It was frightening to see how badly the cancer had ravaged, and emaciated his body in just three short months. Now weighing barely 30 pounds, he looked so tiny and fragile. He was ghostly pale and noticeably exhausted, and was soaking wet with sweat. His little brow was furrowed and clearly he was still being wracked by the now constant pain.

Little Bob weakly looked up into Jim's eyes and softly whimpered, "Daddy, I want to go home."

And at that very moment, Little Bob died in Jim's arms and the glittering blue sparkles in his beautiful eyes flickered slightly and then disappeared.

Bob's tiny casket was snow white with gold-colored handles. I wanted to quietly grieve with Jim from the obscurity of the family pew, but was asked to be one of the pallbearers. I wore dark sunglasses in an effort to hide the steady flow of tears that gushed from my eyes and broken heart. And I prayed fervently to God to hold fast to His promise, that "I can do all things through Christ who strengthens me." I was so grief stricken that I could barely walk as we carried his little casket to the hearse. It was without question the saddest time of my life.

Jim suffered as no human should ever have to suffer. It was as if his heart had been ripped from his chest. He wouldn't talk much about his loss, even years later. He told me that unless you've been through losing a child, it's impossible to relate the grief to someone who hasn't gone through it.

When Jim told me that, I reflected upon how much I loved Little Bob. I was sure that I loved him as much as I loved my own sons; however, when I looked upon my own son Michael playing outside, I was quite sure that Jim was right. *No parents should ever have to outlive their children.* I don't think I could have stood up to it.

In an effort to relieve some of Jim's misery, I gently advised him that he should draw close to God and that God would draw close to him. I reminded him that God lost a son to an agonizing and cruel death too, and that God could comfort him in a way that no one else could.

Jim would have no part of it. He was bitter and fiercely angry at God for not answering his prayers and saving Bob. He heatedly snapped, "He could have saved him. He could have spared him the pain. Bob never even got to go to school. That son of a bitch is mean!"

"I'm no preacher Jim, but the Bible states that God created us to serve His purpose and not our own. I remember someone told me once that it would be hard to imagine heaven being a place of immense joy and peace without children being present. Perhaps all along the purpose that God had in mind for Little Bob was to be realized in heaven and not on Earth. Can't you picture him at this very moment walking along streets of gold in heaven holding hands with Jesus Christ? He's probably chattering away like a magpie asking the Lord a million questions.

Jim began tearing up and I hastily and clumsily tried a different approach.

"Jim, Bob isn't suffering anymore and will never suffer again. The Bible says that '*Eye has not seen, nor ear heard, nor have entered into the heart of man the things which God has prepared for those who love Him.*' There will never be sickness, death, or sadness in heaven, and the Lord shall wipe away every tear from that place. This life is just like a vapor, Jim. Heaven is forever and Little Bob will enjoy total happiness forever. One day we'll all join him and celebrate. Little Bob will never have to deal with the tragedy of this world. He'll never have to experience what you've experienced in raising up a beautiful little boy only to see him cruelly torn apart by

Satan. He will reign as a prince in heaven with the Lord God almighty forever. Just think of it, Jim."

"Go to hell!"

I should have kept my big mouth shut. I wasn't a preacher and in fact was just a baby Christian who didn't know crap. All I did with my stupid preaching was drive the wedge between Jim and God a little deeper. And I hated myself for it.

Jim and his wife were never the same. She insisted that they return to New Orleans, where she could be near her family. Jim asked his boss for a transfer and his request was promptly granted, so off they both went to that evil city that never sleeps and where there's always a party going on. Jim's idyllic life in the suburbs was over. It wasn't long before he and his wife were divorced and embittered to the millionth power.

Jim began drugging, drinking, and fighting. Sometimes he fought with fists in the mean bars of New Orleans. Other times he'd just spew bitterness at anyone and everyone, including the boss who'd encouraged him to throw himself back into his career, and our parents and me, when we tried to encourage him to move on with life.

Mainly he fought with his ex-wife. They fought over money, the house, every stick of furniture in it, and real and imaginary lovers of whom they were both extremely jealous. Before long they hated each other with a strange passion. They raged at each other like two crazed pit bulls trying to tear each other apart, as though somehow lashing out at each other would relieve the miserable sadness that had been burned into their broken hearts with a branding iron of desolation.

It didn't.

About this time Teresa was pregnant with our second child. She called me at work and told me to meet her at the hospital, that she had started having contractions. I took off from the paint plant and drove like a wild man to reach the hospital in time. When I arrived I was told that the baby was in a breech position and that they would have to deliver it by cesarean section. Then they told me that Teresa had developed very serious complications—her blood pressure had risen to extremely dangerous heights. At one point the doctor came out to the waiting room and sat me down and told me that he knew he could save the baby, but wasn't sure about the mother. He said, "If I were you, I'd get down on my knees and pray. I'll do my best, but it's a dangerous time. She's critical."

I did get down on my knees right there in that waiting room, and with tears streaking my face I prayed with all the energy I possessed for God to protect Teresa and not take her away from me. Hour after hour ticked by and I didn't hear a word.

I was frantic and went to the desk so often that whenever they saw me approaching they would simply shake their heads to indicate that there still wasn't any word. It was a lonely, frightening time and I begged God to spare her life.

Finally the doctor appeared and told me that both mother and my new *son* were doing fine. Jonathan Lee Williamson (middle name the same as my brother Jim's), and my beloved Teresa would see me in about 15 minutes, after they were cleaned up. I breathed a sigh of relief and thanked God profusely.

Shortly thereafter I left Glidden. The company had been hit with an affirmative-action lawsuit and announced as part of their settlement that no one but minorities would be promoted for the next two years. They also immediately promoted to department head practically every secretary that worked there.

Management tried their utmost to convince me to stay, but I told them there was no way. I wanted promotion opportunity; heck I wanted the president's job. I wasn't about to work for some unqualified secretary who got the job only because she didn't have a penis, or some minority whose promotion was based upon skin color. I wasn't hanging around to run their department for them and make them look good while they made more money than I did.

I took a job at Sanders Paint Company as a project engineer and began working with a vengeance. I convinced my boss to allow me to develop a computer-software system for warehousing and distribution. Software was just coming on the scene and I'd discovered that I had a natural talent for it. My last major project before resigning at Glidden was to assist with developing computer software to convert Glidden's manual system to a computerized one. With that huge successful project still fresh in my mind, developing a similar system for Sanders would be easy.

After getting the "go for it" from my boss and building it into an enormously successful program, I was puzzled to no end and madder than heck that I didn't receive any recognition or, more important, a raise for putting the system into action. It was saving them an enormous amount of money and I received absolutely nothing for it, not even an "attaboy." I was steamed.

A few months later they unexpectedly fired my boss, and not long after he left I got word that he'd taken credit for my idea. He'd told the president of the company that he was working in his garden and leaned against his rake and "had a brainstorm." His brainstorm for handling warehousing and distribution was in reality *my* brainstorm. After my boss was fired, a paint chemist buddy of mine who was familiar with the situation went to the president and told him the truth about the computer software being my idea and that I was the one who made it reality.

The president promptly called me into his office. He was rather sheepish as he apologized for not being aware that it was my idea. He thanked me profusely for my contribution, but then told me that his budget was rather strained at the moment and he couldn't offer me a monetary reward. He smiled broadly as he mentioned that he did, however, want to give me something to show his appreciation. He went to his closet, where he had all sorts of promotional items that he gave away to customers, and he fished out a Coleman Lantern.

No raise, no promotion, just a Coleman Lantern. He handed it to me with a big grin on his face, as if he'd just signed a check over to me for a hundred grand.

I felt like breaking it over his head.

I was raging mad, but couldn't stand to sit back and coast and not develop new and innovative ideas. I immediately launched another project for improving the utilization of an extra warehouse, and it required transferring an enormous amount of paint from one warehouse to the other. When the project ended, I conservatively estimated that it would save the company about $100,000 a year in labor costs alone. I planned to demand a raise, and he would be hard pressed to refuse. I meticulously documented the savings to show him, and any argument of not having the funds to pay me for my innovativeness would be gone.

The problem was that I couldn't get it done during the week because we were too busy. And my new boss, who was a jerk of the highest order, wouldn't let me pay my men overtime to accomplish it on weekends. I was determined, though, and the following weekend I came in by myself and worked all day Saturday and Sunday to move the paint; I hoped to have the project completed by Monday. I didn't want to work on Sundays because the Bible said it was a sin, but I wanted to complete this project and rationalized that God wouldn't mind.

About two o'clock on Sunday afternoon, as I was nearing completion of my project, I heard the warehouse phone ring. When I answered, Teresa was sobbing that my mother had gone to the doctor with a headache and had collapsed in his office. She was in a coma in a hospital in Tuscaloosa, Alabama, and was not expected to recover. We needed to hurry.

I was stunned. I shouted, "What do you mean, *'Not expected to recover?'* What's wrong with her?"

Teresa sounded frantic. "I don't know, Bob. She's in a coma and your dad said there's no chance that she'll ever recover. He was frantic and kind of out of it, and said we should hurry and go there. She's on a life-support machine."

When Teresa and I arrived, Jim and several members of Dad's family and some of his friends were already there. Dad was crying and said that Mom was brain-dead and on life support. A massive brain tumor had exploded an artery in her brain. Dad said she'd experienced a sickening headache that morning and it became so severe that she told Dad that something was "bad wrong" with her. She asked him to take her to the doctor and when she stepped inside the doctor's office, she suddenly gasped and then collapsed. And just that fast she was gone—brain-dead.

Dad escorted me into Mom's room. I was appalled by what I saw. She was lying there with her eyes blankly staring into space. I'd seen that look before. She was dead. A hose had been placed down her throat to pump oxygen and a machine was busily forcing her chest up and down. A monitor showed her heart beating, solely because of the machines to which she was hooked up.

It was very difficult to see her like this, and I was in shock. Mom was a beautiful woman; and for as long as I can remember, she'd insisted that she didn't want an open-casket funeral so curious onlookers could file by and gawk at her only to remark later as to how "dead" she looked. She definitely didn't want to be on life support either, and in fact had stipulated that in her living will. Mom would never have wanted anyone, including us, to see her in this condition.

Dad was frantic, lost, and incoherent. Carte blanche he was allowing his family members and friends to see her. Jim and I were furious and tried our best to convince him to stop allowing it, but he insisted. Finally Jim asked a nurse to tape Mom's eyelids down so at least people couldn't see her dead eyes staring blankly at nothing; this would allow her some final dignity.

Dad didn't want to let her go, but finally the doctor, Jim, and I convinced him and he agreed to take her off life support. Within minutes of removing her from the machine, the nurse came and got us and told us that time was very short. We went into her room and watched as the heartbeat on the monitor pulsed a couple of times and then went flat. Her arm moved slowly in a reflexive movement, and she was gone. I'd told her that I loved her, but she never got to hear it.

I hadn't talked to Mom by phone in about two weeks and hadn't seen her in over a month. Her death was totally unexpected. She didn't ever display any symptoms prior to the day she died and seemed to be in perfect health. Michael was just two and our most recent addition, Jon, was only six months old. She'd seen Jon only once and that is how I try to remember her, sitting on the swing at her home in Mississippi with a big smile on her face, cooing at Jon and remarking how his eyes looked just like hers.

I couldn't believe it. She was only 52 years old. I was devastated, but Jim was much, much worse. After Little Bob died he went through his messy, bitter divorce and his life began spiraling out of control. He'd come to rely on Mom to help him cope. He called her daily and she comforted him long into the night. Now his beloved mother, who'd babied, spoiled, loved unconditionally, and pampered him all his life was gone, along with his son and wife. Jim was a complete wreck and looked as bad as I'd ever seen him.

I felt tremendous guilt when Mom died. I felt bad for being such a rotten son all my life, for not calling or going to see her lately, and even for working on the Sunday that she died. My only comfort was that I knew Mom loved Jesus Christ and I had no doubt that she was with Jesus and rocking Little Bob in her lap. And I knew that one day I'd see her again. I also knew that she lived long enough to see me turn my life around, and for that I was thankful.

We buried Mom near the family home in Columbus, right next to Little Bob's grave site. I helped pick out her casket and vault, and the ceremony was heart wrenching.

I grieved her loss and it *hurt.*

Chapter Sixty-Two

Losing Little Bob in the horrible manner in which we lost him and then helplessly watching my tortured brother free-fall from sanity into the demonic insanity of New Orleans was destructive and demoralizing. I wanted to turn to my Mom for advice and draw from her strength in dealing with it, but now she was gone too.

I tried to block the tragedies from my mind by throwing myself back into my work, only to receive more bad news. Sanders Paint Company announced that it was being bought out by Porter Paint Company, and they told me that I'd have to transfer to another plant, probably the one in Louisville. That was like a vicious kick in the teeth to me.

I wasn't about to leave Atlanta. I'd been shuffled all over the world as a child and as a result had attended some 19 different schools; I darn sure wasn't going to put my kids through that same kind of destabilizing experience in order to enhance my personal career.

I resigned from Sanders and took a job just a couple of miles across town as plant manager of a small industrial-paint company. By now I hated working for others. I hadn't been compensated for my innovation and hard work, and I'd seen my good ideas used to further others' careers and paychecks. I'd seen lazy and incompetent employees promoted ahead of me simply because they were ass kissers or had more education.

Most of all I had grown to despise working for managers who screwed up everything they touched and then tried to shift the blame to others, including me. In short, I was sick and tired of taking orders from people who I considered to be idiots.

I quickly discovered that this new job was no different from any of the rest. I liked my new responsibilities just fine, but I intensely disliked having to take orders from the guy who was at the top. He was about five-feet-nothing and had a "short man" complex. He didn't have the slightest idea of how to run a paint company, but his daddy owned it. When he finally did show up for work at midmorning, he'd spend most of his time stalking around yelling at people as if he was some kind of tough guy.

He had yet to raise his voice at me—and for good reason. I was the first to arrive on the job and the last to leave. I worked hard and smart, and did an excellent job. The first thing I did was fire nearly every employee in the plant and replace them with employees who'd work. Within six months the programs that I'd implemented turned the little company around and nearly doubled its profit margin. With each success the bosses would give me more responsibility and soon, in addition to the manufacturing plant, I was managing the warehouse and the shipping and purchasing departments. With the exception of the sales and administration department, I was now running the entire company.

One day the little runt, who was appropriately nicknamed Junior, called me into his office and immediately began yelling at me like I was a four-year-old. He hadn't checked his facts and what he perceived to be a problem hadn't even happened.

When he raised his voice at me, it was as though he opened my dark side's cage door and released the dark fury that'd been impatiently waiting for an opportunity to rip someone to pieces. My mind snapped and then exploded. All the pent-up rage and frustration that'd built in me over Little Bob, Mom, Jim, and all the assorted jerks for whom I'd worked through the years bubbled to the surface and spewed out all over him like a Coke that had been dropped on the floor and then popped open in his face.

I angrily screamed at him, "You little sawed-off son of a bitch runt! That's it! I'm sick and tired of your stupidity and your big mouth. I quit! Now you either write my check this very minute or I'm gonna beat the shit out of you right here and right now!"

I was standing over him with both fists clenched and if he even blinked I was prepared to bash his head in. I was breathing like a raging bull and was just as wild eyed. Several office workers were present, but to a person sat with eyes lowered, too afraid to breathe, much less offer assistance. No one moved or looked up, and no one so much as said a word.

With a shaking hand and a scared look on his face, he wrote my final paycheck. As I drove home I was still as mad as a wasp knocked off its nest. I was sick and tired of working for others. Suddenly I banged my fist on the dashboard of the car and shouted, "I'll never work for anyone else again!"

And with that bold statement my entrepreneurial career was born.

As I look back on that decision today I realize that it was reckless, rash, impulsive, irresponsible, and naïve—or, more correctly, just outright stupid. I had no start-up capital, no formal education in business management, and no research on revenue potential or the competitive landscape. And I certainly didn't have a business plan.

Hell, I didn't even know what kind of business I would start!

As I drove home I decided that I would open a taxidermy business. I was naturally attracted to wildlife art through my passionate love of the great outdoors. By now I'd become an avid sportsman and had taught myself taxidermy as a hobby. I found it to be a very enjoyable and rewarding pastime, and a nice outlet for my creative side. Practically all my spare time was being devoted to my hobby and working in my little art studio. Often I'd work throughout the night and on into the early morning hours trying to create some masterpiece.

Others had seen and liked my work, and I'd begun to develop quite a following. I was making a nice supplementary income as a part-time taxidermist. My work backlog consisted of two freezers completely full of birds, fish, deer heads, and other trophies that needed to be mounted. I was brimming with confidence and knew I could easily build upon my current workload; and with my strong work ethic, I'd be wildly successful. As I drove home, I decided to name my new venture Bear Claw Taxidermy Studio.

The more I thought about it, the more fired up I got; and by the time I got home I was excited and ready to conquer the world. Teresa on the other hand was livid. When I told her that I'd just quit my high-paying plant manager's job and was going to start "some lowly, crazy, taxidermy business" (her words), she pitched an absolute foaming-at-the-mouth fit. At first she screamed and yelled at me, then she cried, and finally she settled in on the silent treatment; she didn't speak one syllable to me for at least two weeks.

I liked the silent treatment the best.

Unfortunately, everyone else I knew wasn't silent about my new career path, and I still had to listen to disparaging, discouraging remarks. My dad told me that it was one of the stupidest things that I'd ever done, and wanted me to go back and apologize to my former employer and see if he would give me my old job back. My brother told me that I was a moron. Teresa's dad, my friends and neighbors, and essentially everyone that I knew told me that it was insanity to even think of giving up my high-paying job and start my own business as a lowly taxidermist.

The only exception was Teresa's mother. One Sunday afternoon shortly after I quit my job, the entire family was assembled in Shelby and Jenny's backyard for a cookout. They were all sitting around berating me about quitting, and telling me how many new businesses fail and how I needed to find a regular job.

Jenny listened to them beating me up and then got fighting mad and angrily told them in a stern voice, "Listen, if Bob Williamson says he's going to make it, then he's going to make it, clear and simple! That's all there is to it."

I loved Jenny with all my heart for expressing such confidence in me that day. She was the first person that I can ever remember who showed me any respect or exuded confidence in my ability to succeed. Her unwavering faith in me meant more than anyone could imagine, and it's something that I'll continue to cherish until the day I die. I loved her like I loved my own mother.

Someone could've pulled my fingernails out and I still wouldn't have admitted that I was hurt by people's lack of confidence in me. But deep down I was very hurt. The only positive thing about it was that their lack of faith in me was very motivating. I became steadfastly resolved to wipe those damned smirks off their faces and show them all that they were wrong.

Unfortunately, motivation alone doesn't pay anything, and soon I was facing mounting bills and scrambling to find money to pay them. Teresa and I had made decent money, but like most families, we'd spend right up to the limits of our income and had no savings. My start-up capital consisted of the final paycheck that my ex-boss had written, and it was needed to pay our regular household bills.

I quickly mounted the remains of what I initially thought was a huge backlog of work. In just a couple of weeks, the two freezers full of trophies were ready for customers to pick up. I didn't realize that working around the clock on a full-time basis (my typically disciplined, unrelenting work ethic) would wipe out my backlog in such short order. I also didn't anticipate that those customers who'd been clamoring for me to finish their trophies would be so slow to come pick them up. No doubt this was because they didn't have the extra cash to pay for them.

I'd mistakenly thought that merely hanging my taxidermy sign in my yard meant that soon I'd be inundated with work. After about a week without a single call, I realized that my marketing plan was less than stellar.

Faced with looming disaster and the distinct possibility that I might have to eat the mounted crow staring down at me from my studio wall, I came up with an idea to jump-start my business by selling taxidermy mounts to various businesses around Atlanta. I immediately began to call on decorators, interior designers, collectors, country clubs, doctors' offices, attorneys, bars, and the like, and began selling all kinds of mounts.

I even sold a mounted moose head for $1,000 to a radio station to give away as a promotion for Moosehead Beer. I rented mounts to swank nightclubs in Atlanta like the *Limelight*, and even had an ad in the exclusive *Atlanta* magazine. High-end customers who saw the ad bought all kinds of mounts, such as swans and little birds in glass domes.

I quickly learned that the more exorbitant the price, the more people seemed to like it. I began selling my wildlife art at ridiculously high—even astronomical—prices. I was selling everything from mounted exotic pheasants to 500-pound blue marlin mounts, to zebra-skin rugs, to life-size brown bear mounts.

I sold a mounted longhorn bull's head and several other mounts to highly successful entrepreneur George McKerrow for display in the very first Longhorn Steakhouse restaurant, which he founded in downtown Atlanta in exclusive Buckhead. George was a little tight on money for that first entrepreneurial challenge, and he bartered for the mounts by offering Teresa and me dinners there at no charge as part of my compensation.

George McKerrow was a marketing genius and, from that austere beginning, went on to build Longhorn Steakhouse into a fabulously successful, multimillion-dollar franchise. It was inspiring to me to see what George accomplished, and it made be proud just to know him and to have been a tiny part of it at the very beginning.

Not long afterward I did some mounts for a movie being shot in Atlanta. The pay was excellent, but it was the nastiest job I ever agreed to take on and one that I had nightmares about. I mounted several wharf rats for a movie about Jim Jones, the infamous religious nut of poison Kool-Aid fame in Guyana. I attended a party conducted for the cast one night, and one of the actors was running all over the hotel with one of my mounted rats perched on his arm trying to scare the starlets.

There was also a scene in which Jim Jones's family dog was thrown through his living-room plate-glass window to scare him into leaving the neighborhood. It seems that the KKK didn't like him hanging around with black people. The movie people brought the mounted dog prop with them from California, but each night would bring it to my studio for repair because the plate-glass window would cut off its feet and gash up its body. They must have shot that same scene five or six times, and each time I made several hundred dollars for the repair. They must not have ever perfected the shot, because when I watched the movie, that part was excluded.

I did several jobs for celebrities, including mounting a largemouth bass for Atlanta Braves knuckleball pitcher Phil Niekro. He's one of just three or four knuckleball pitchers who have reached baseball's Hall of Fame. He came over one day and my oldest son Michael sheepishly stood there with a baseball in his hand and Phil graciously signed it for him. A few days later I caught my boys outside playing catch with it and it was covered with red mud. So much for a Hall of Famer trophy baseball.

One job that I contracted reminded me too much of my not-so-distant past. The former record promoter for Elvis Presley was building a huge mansion and wanted to buy thousands of dollars of mounts to decorate it. He lived on the highest point in the subdivision, and he told me that he negotiated with his realtor for that particular spot for months because he wanted to be able to "look down on everyone."

I drove out there in my old pickup truck. My truck was quite a sight for this exclusive gated neighborhood; in fact, the guard wouldn't let me in until he called the mansion and verified that I was an authorized visitor. The hood on the old blue pickup had blown off one day and I'd found another one at a junkyard and replaced it. The problem was that the truck was blue and the replacement hood was white. It had a manual shift and barely had enough power to manage his steep driveway. I had to jump out and quickly put a brick under the tire to prevent it from rolling back down the hill—the truck was so worn out that the gears on the straight shift would pop out and the emergency brake didn't work. I parked right in front of his 20-car garage, which was loaded with Ferraris and other exotics.

I had mounted a sailfish for him, and he commissioned an artist to weave a custom-made rug designed to complement the sailfish's colors. He'd built an Olympic-sized indoor pool and its structure was two stories high, and he wanted me to hang the sailfish squarely in front of the pool and over the middle of the rug, where a spotlight would shine on it.

I didn't like heights, but the money he was paying me to do this was obscene, so I warily climbed a wobbly double extension ladder trying to hold the heavy sailfish mount two stories above the pool area. Just as I prepared to hang the fish, the loudest music that I'd ever heard began blaring in my ears. It was the music that always played just prior to Elvis entering the stage for a performance. The horns blared and the bass pounded and my extension ladder was shaking from the vibration of the huge speakers, which were as big as refrigerators and hung on either side of me. I came down off that ladder like a frightened squirrel scrambling down a tree.

The promoter was standing up on his balcony overlooking the pool, laughing at me as if he'd lost his mind. He was clutching perhaps 20 bottles of pills in his hand and underneath his arm, and carried a bottle of whiskey in his other hand. He was obviously stoned out of his gourd and enjoying himself immensely. I refused to go back up on the ladder until he turned off the music.

He always paid me from a huge roll of $100 bills. It was a weird process. He would pay me thousands of dollars, but would only peel one $100 bill off at a time and give it to me. I would quite naturally look down at the stack of bills accumulating in my hand, but he wouldn't peel off another and give it to me unless or until I would raise my eyes and look him squarely in the eye.

One day his chauffeur brought me a big largemouth bass to mount. The record promoter had actually stabbed the bass with a barbeque skewer as it was lazily swimming underneath the dock where he kept his houseboat moored at Lake Lanier.

Unfortunately, his chauffer, who was a city boy, didn't know that the fish had to be refrigerated or it would spoil, and he'd left it in the hot trunk of the limo for a couple of days prior to bringing it to me. When he opened the trunk, the smell almost knocked me down. I told him that it couldn't be mounted and he was scared out of his wits that he'd be fired. I was able to find a replacement fish of equal size and promised not to tell, and he tipped me $500 of his own money in addition to what I received for mounting the fish.

I didn't have nearly enough time to personally mount everything I was selling, and soon became adept at buying and selling other artists' work. It was from this experience that I learned a valuable lesson that I would remember the rest of my life. I learned how to *buy low and sell high.* My profit margin was enormous and the money began pouring in.

I was having loads of fun and was making loads of money. I was netting over $90,000 a year, which was over three times what I was making as a plant manager and was an enormous amount of money back in the late '70s. I was the exception as far as taxidermists went. Most of the taxidermists in my area made closer to $12,000 a year, but they concentrated primarily on the sportsman market and competed with each other with very low prices and lower-quality work.

I offered high-quality mounts at exceptionally high prices, and in fact charged the highest prices in town. The high prices didn't deter my high-net-worth clientele of wealthy sportsmen. Ironically, whenever I would raise my prices, it seemed to increase the demand for my services. These people paid me promptly and I made more money mounting fewer trophies.

I combined my rapidly increasing vertical market of wealthy sportsmen with my vertical market of aggressive wildlife-art buying and selling, and complemented them with my outstanding marketing and salesmanship skills to excel in both.

Teresa also made good money and was bringing home $30,000 and a full range of union benefits working for Union Pacific Railroad as an executive secretary. We were flush with cash, the kids were doing great in school, and we were flourishing.

In an effort to improve the quality of my work, I'd begun experimenting with various paints to develop an airbrush-paint system that was decent. An important part of every taxidermist's job is using an airbrush to re-create colors of mounted fish and do touch-up work on mammal and game-head mounts.

I'd been disappointed with the results I was seeing from automotive lacquers, which at the time were the only paints available to airbrush artists. Automotive paints were designed specifically to paint cars and not wildlife art, and wildlife artists needed a system that was designed specifically for them.

Having worked in several paint plants, I knew a great deal about paint chemistry and how to develop and manufacture paints. I wanted to design a system that utilized transparent paints with clean, vibrant colors identical to the colors found in nature.

I lowered my swimming pool and covered it, and then added about a foot of fresh water. I put live bass and other live fish in it. I set up a workbench and had all kinds of pigments and resins on it. I would dip a bass out of the pool, examine it closely with magnifying equipment, and then try to replicate the bass's coloration by mixing my various paints and combinations right there on my workbench.

I experimented with every imaginable resin and pigment to achieve perfection in these paints. I even used the same pigments found in women's mascara to match the brilliant shimmering iridescence of fish and other wildlife.

I received an enormous amount of advice and help with various formulations from Jim Stanley, an exceptional paint chemist and good friend of mine, whom I'd met at Sanders. Jim in fact was the same chemist who'd told the owner at Sanders that the computer program that my boss had taken credit for was actually mine. After about a year of experimentation, we developed a superb formulation for an amazing paint system, and I loved it.

During this period I'd become active in my state taxidermist association. I wanted to learn everything I could about my new profession, and I also wanted to share what I'd learned with others. I was elected to their board of directors and then one year later was elected president.

I spent that year building the membership of the organization to unprecedented levels, and even spent my own money to help advertise their annual convention. It turned out to be the largest convention in their history, but instead of receiving thanks for our volunteerism, Teresa and I were criticized for holding the convention at a resort instead of a less-expensive alternative.

A few ignorant people who were jealous of our achievements launched other assorted gripes. These people were jealous of our achievements in the association and my financial success in the taxidermy market. It was enough to dissuade me from ever agreeing to run for any kind of elected office again.

I didn't need politics.

It was at this time that I attended an airbrush-painting seminar by world-renowned wildlife artist Jim Hall, from Idaho Falls, Idaho. Jim's seminar was excellent as far as describing how to paint with an airbrush, but was laced with technical errors as he clumsily tried to explain paint chemistry.

Rather than embarrass and correct him during his seminar, I decided that when I was home I would write him a letter and explain how the combination of paint, color, and light actually worked. I told him that if he was going to go all over the country giving paint seminars, then he needed to give the correct information to his attendees. I drew several diagrams with detailed instructions about how paint reflects and even transmits light, and how the human eye perceives color. I also provided some other technical information that he needed to know.

He was very appreciative. We soon became good friends and often corresponded and called each other. I told him in one such call that I'd developed some airbrush paints and wondered if he might like to try them. He agreed and I shipped him a few samples. A few days later he called and I thought he was going to jump through the phone. He loved my paints so much that he wanted to pour out all his old paints and replace them with mine *right then*. He was nearly too excited to talk.

This started me thinking. I surmised that if one of the best artists in the world liked my paints that much, then maybe I really had something here. Jim was scheduled to conduct a seminar at a convention for wildlife artists in North Carolina, and he told me that he was going to paint a mounted fish using my paints during his seminar.

I invested $1,000 in raw materials and made up as much paint inventory as I could. I drove up to North Carolina in Teresa's little car with all those paints in the trunk and backseat, and was half drunk from smelling the fumes when I arrived there. I rented a booth in the tradeshow and set up my paints on the table with a mimeographed price list. I hadn't even had time to make up a sign for my booth.

Jim gave his seminar and referred to my paints as a "technological *breakthrough*" in airbrush fish painting. The fish he painted for the seminar looked so lifelike that when he was finished with the thing it appeared as though it might actually swim away. Afterward he put it on display in my booth.

"Seeing is believing," as the old adage goes, and after that demonstration my paints became the rage of the show. Anxious customers lined up at my booth all the way through the convention center and out the door, and they formed a line literally a block and a half long trying to get to my booth in order to buy my "*miracle*" paints.

I was selling one-ounce bottles of the stuff for $12.50 each. My cost was a mere 50¢. My $12 profit margin was phenomenal, and the axiom that I'd come to know and love, *Buy low and sell high,* was once again working extremely well.

I came home with the front pockets of my blue jeans bulging with big rolls of money and I carried a brown paper bag full of more bills. I'd sold out my entire stock of paint and had a stack of orders that was 10 inches high.

I would go on from there to incorporate my little company as Master Paint Systems, and I named my new paints Polytranspar ("Poly" for polymer and "transpar" for transparent). I would soon have 28 employees working out of my house, and we would grow so fast that we'd have to move into a new building and then another and another.

I would discover that I had an exceptional knack for marketing and salesmanship, which would lead me to secure seven major distributors for Polytranspar and directly service 268,000 customers worldwide.

I would be an overnight success, netting $30,000 per week before I was 35 years old. I would have come a long way from homelessness and selling pints of blood and chopping mortar off used bricks.

I would wipe those damned smirks off my detractors' faces with mind-boggling overnight success and wheelbarrows of cash.

But for now I was just giddy from the tradeshow. I emptied my pockets of those crumpled bills and poured out the rest of the money onto the bed. And then I lay down in it and rolled back and forth for a few minutes. I'd always wanted to know what it felt like to be rolling in cash.

It felt pretty damn good!

CHAPTER SIXTY-THREE

I was putting in tremendous hours at work every day, and I was there seven days a week. I'd typically start at 7 a.m. and work all day, and then I'd come home and spend two or three hours with my family and eat dinner. After the boys went to bed, I'd head downstairs to work on various projects until 4 a.m. The next day I'd do it all over again. In part, my lifelong curse of insomnia was helping me build my career.

Business was great though, and I was riding high. But it seemed that every day I'd experience a major headache. Like a tropical thunderstorm it would begin building in the morning, continue throughout the day, and be raging by nightfall. These were no ordinary headaches. They were so intense that sometimes they made me vomit, and an almost continuous stream of tears would run down my face from my left eye.

At first I simply attributed the headaches to the pressures of managing a wildly expanding business, but one morning I awoke to discover that two of the fingers on my left hand were completely numb. I also felt numbness on the left side of my face.

I hadn't been to a doctor about the headaches, but this seemed serious. I wondered if maybe I'd had a stroke. I went in for a checkup and was promptly referred to a local neurologist who, after hearing my family history of brain tumors, promptly conducted an MRI.

After the brain scan, the neurologist called me into his office and dispassionately told me that I had a *brain tumor*. He displayed the black-and-white image on a screen in his office, and there at the base of my brain was a massive dark area, easily distinguishable from the light-gray areas that he said were normal. He told me that the tumor was like a cyst and was very similar to the one that took my mom's life.

By then I was in complete shock and stammered, "How long do I have?"

I'll never forget the callousness of that doctor. With his detached, unemotional approach, he was very similar to the lung specialist that I'd seen. He looked almost bored as he nonchalantly said, "Well I had a lady in here not long ago with symptoms exactly like yours, and three days later she was dead."

Wahhhhhh! Suddenly I was freaked worse than I was during my bad trip on LSD.

I went home and awkwardly told Teresa. She bawled like a baby, which started me crying. I tenderly held her, trying to console her, and then my two young boys came running over wide-eyed and scared—and each of them hugged one of my legs and started crying too. They were too young to understand what they were even crying about, but instinctively they knew that something was wrong.

Over the next several days, reality began to set in. Each subsequent test only confirmed the previous ones. And it seemed that the doctors administered every test on a Thursday, so I'd have to anxiously await the outcome until Monday or Tuesday of the following week. All weekend we'd be down on our knees fervently praying, "Please God, let the test be negative. Please God, don't let this happen."

Finally Monday would come and I'd anxiously call, only to be told that it would be Tuesday before the results were in. More anxious waiting, more fervent praying. Tuesday the doctor would call me in and tell me that the prognosis was not good.

This went on for about six weeks, and each test led to the same diagnosis. The final test involved injecting a dye into my spinal fluid, which then moved on into my brain. I lay down on a table, and the technicians tilted that table into every imaginable position so the dye would swirl into various parts of my brain. Then each brain section was mapped by a whirring, clicking MRI machine. When I arrived home, the iodine from the dye caused a violent reaction, and I developed a splitting headache that was so intense that I had to go to the emergency room.

I suffered from the reaction all weekend and then had to wait until Tuesday for the test results. Finally the doctor's office called to tell me the doctor wanted to consult with me in his office and that I should bring my wife. It wasn't a good sign.

Later that afternoon our worst fears were confirmed. The dye-imaging test indicated that the first diagnosis was right and, if anything, the massive tumor was larger and even more dangerous than the doctor had first imagined. It was similar to my mom's and was cystlike in nature, covering a large section of my brain in a web like a spider weaves. It was totally inoperable and I would immediately die if they tried to remove any of it.

It was only a matter of time before I died, he matter-of-factly told me. "Mr. Williamson, to be perfectly honest with you, I don't know how you've lived this long." I was shaken to my core and not at all sure that I wanted the doctor to be "perfectly honest with me."

First Little Bob—POW! And then Mom—POW! And now me. The knockout punch was streaking through my brain to finish me off.

I couldn't bring myself to call my brother and tell him. He was still insane with grief over losing Little Bob and Mom. I was fearful that he would completely disintegrate when he found out that he was going to lose me to a brain tumor too.

Dad was still grief stricken and was nearly as bad off as Jim. Mom had been the dominant figure in our household from day one, and Dad relied on her for so many things. Without her he was like a lost child, and I didn't want to burden him.

Teresa was a complete wreck. She'd leave for work with eyes red from crying, and she'd arrive home in the same shape. She was so emotional we couldn't conduct a conversation, and I tried not to bring it up in front of her. I didn't have any close friends and was reluctant to tell anyone at work because I didn't want to talk about it.

My wife and sons were my life. My boys loved me with all their hearts and I loved them with all of mine. No matter how busy I'd been in managing my company, I'd always made time for my sons. My dad had been too busy for me as a kid, and I was determined to never make that same mistake with my boys.

Whenever I was home, they followed me around like my shadow. We'd go swimming in our pool, fish in the 2½-acre pond in our backyard, play basketball on the court that I built for them, play soccer or football, or play catch in the front yard. At night we wrestled together on the bed and they'd pull my hair and laugh and giggle when I tickled them back.

I had no idea how or what to tell them in order to prepare them. Michael was 10 years old and Jon was just 8. I decided that Jon was too young to understand, but Michael might be old enough.

I was wrong and failed miserably. Michael was indeed too young and didn't understand the concept of my dying and then some day reuniting with him in heaven. He became frightened and began hysterically crying that he didn't want me to die. This was brought on in part by my breaking down and crying a little as I clumsily tried to tell him that I wouldn't be around that much longer.

It broke my heart to see him like that.

I'd never felt as lonely and forlorn as this, even during my blackest days in the darkest sewer. I tried to draw close to God by pulling out my Bible and searching it for answers, but this time I didn't hear or feel God's comforting, gentle reassurance or presence. This time God was strangely silent.

In the past, when my life was teetering on the verge of total collapse, I'd dig out my Bible, dust it off, and start reading it daily and praying with fervor. God always drew near and answered my prayers and graciously helped me recover.

Then almost as soon as the dust would settle and I'd start doing well again, I'd promptly forget about Him and discard Him like a used Kleenex. Now that I needed that Kleenex to wipe away fresh tears, it was nowhere to be found.

I couldn't say that I blamed Him for remaining aloof this go-around.

I admitted to myself that I also lacked any semblance of faith now. I'd prayed that somehow Little Bob's initial diagnosis was wrong; it wasn't. Then I'd prayed that the surgery would reveal the tumor was benign; it hadn't. Then I'd prayed that the chemo and radiation treatments would put his tumor in remission; it didn't. Finally I'd prayed that he would be healed by a miracle; he wasn't.

In spite of all my months of intense prayers and receiving the best treatment known to man, Little Bob had withered away like a beautiful little delicate flower and died a horrible death. Just two years later, Mom died suddenly—and I didn't even have the opportunity to tell her goodbye or that I loved her.

I knew all too well what being diagnosed with brain cancer meant. Jesus wasn't drawing close to me because He was fresh out of miracles and I was doomed. I suppose you could call this a lack of faith, but it was just reality to me.

I became melancholy and slept most of the time. I'd stay in my pajamas all day, not bothering to shower, shave, or even brush my teeth. I had zero appetite and couldn't bring myself to get out of bed. For someone who was a complete insomniac, it became readily apparent that I was clinically depressed.

During this time, my business had begun to flounder without my leadership. But I just couldn't bear to think about that. All my big business plans scarcely seemed important anymore. All I could think of was my little family and how badly I hated to leave them.

I cried more than I'd ever cried in my life. It was sheer torture to look out the window and see my sons happily playing in the yard without a care in the world; because then I'd realize that I'd never live long enough to see them play sports, bag their first whitetail buck, graduate from college, or accomplish any of the other goals that I'd envisioned for them.

Late at night I'd slip into their bedroom and quietly stand by their bedsides, looking at their innocent little faces as they slept. I'd stand there literally biting into my hand to control my sobbing and not wake them.

If I wasn't around to protect them, who'd keep them off drugs and the mean streets? Who'd encourage them to stay in school and root them on when they were down? Who'd teach them to hunt and fish or drive a car? Who would provide for them?

I hurt so bad I felt like screaming.

One morning after the boys went off to school and Teresa left for work, I wandered into their bedroom and dejectedly sat down at their little desk. I just sat there in silence for a few moments and then began looking at some of the stuff that was lying there. I recognized Jon's handwriting, complete with misspelled words, and smiled. It appeared to be some sort of story that he'd written.

The Deer and the Hogg

One day I saw a deer. I shot him. He fell down and I went to see him. He was dead all right. I brought him home and mounted him. I went back and saw a hogg. I didn't won't to shot at him becose two people was shoting at him. They both mist. I shot at him. I went down to look at him. He was dead all right. I brought him home and mounted him. I didn't won't to go any more becose there was not any more.

I laughed out loud as I rifled through more of his papers. I picked up another.

Autobiography

Jon
Who listens, helpful, kind, and nice.
Sibling of Michael and Jim Williamson.
Who loves hunting, fishing, sports, and pizza.
Who feels sad sometimes, happy sometimes, good.
Who needs love, care, and someone to talk to.
Who gives time, cares, and listens.
Who fears bear, hogs, and winoes.
Who would like to see Christy Brinkely, France, and Statue of Liberty.
Resident of Walton.

Jon Williamson

I laughed again, even more heartily this time. I wondered how in the world he'd come up with such an "autobiography." I hadn't realized that he even knew what a wino was, or that he knew he lived in Walton County, or that at eight years old would notice the beautiful model Christie Brinkley or know who she was.

I turned my attention to their latest report cards. I smiled as I looked at Michael's. He'd received all A's and the teacher had written,

"Michael is an excellent student. I have really enjoyed having him in my room. He is a pleasure to teach."

Jon had E's (Excellent) mixed with a few S's (Satisfactory) but he had good comments too.

Jon is a sweet, happy child with a good attitude toward learning. He is a model student for others. He is still young and needs time to grow and mature.

I knew what that last comment was all about. Jon loved to talk and most of all to play. He had a hard time focusing on his studies and would have much preferred to be playing any kind of sport instead.

The boys were polar opposites, and in fact after you'd been around them a little, it was hard to believe that they even came out of the same womb. Jon was as mischievous as Dennis the Menace and was as hyper as an excited puppy. He didn't care too much about anything other than sports. Michael was calm, gentle, and sweet, and although he was good in all sports, he was levelheaded and studious and wanted to achieve straight A's, which he did.

They both had excellent manners. I'd taught them to be courteous, especially to their elders. I insisted that they always answer any adult by saying, "Yes ma'am, No ma'am, Yes sir, No sir." There was none of that "yeah" business. I never let them fight and was particularly proud that neither had ever even been in a fistfight, not with each other or with anyone else.

Jon took after me a little too much and was always getting into some type of mischief. He liked to make up his own rules, and probably would've been better off doing as I had done—wearing an extra pair of pants each morning in preparation for the spankings I gave him on almost a daily basis.

Michael rarely if ever did anything that required his being disciplined. He took after his goody-two-shoes mother, always wanting to be good, do the right thing, and follow the rules. I'd given him maybe one or two spankings in his entire life.

I remembered the time that a rare winter storm hit Georgia. We'd accumulated several inches of snow and all the ponds had frozen over with a layer of ice perhaps an inch thick. I'd begun to worry about Michael because it was getting dark and he still hadn't come home. He'd been playing in the snow with a neighbor's kid, and I walked down the road to our neighbor's house to try to find him.

The parents of the other kid said they'd seen them playing together earlier, but hadn't seen them lately and didn't know where they were. I went into the neighbor's backyard looking for him and saw several large rocks sitting on top of the ice covering their pond. Then I saw a huge hole in the ice where apparently they'd thrown a large rock and broken the ice. As I thought about it, I became petrified that maybe Michael and his friend had gone out onto the ice and fallen through it. I panicked and started screaming for him. But I heard no answer.

I went running back to the road and just as I was getting ready to go back to the pond and perhaps start diving into it looking for them, I saw the two boys coming up the road. I began screaming at him, "Where have you been? I've been worried sick about you."

Michael was devastated that I was angry with him and started crying. They'd found our neighbor's dog and were worried about it, and had walked over a mile in the freezing, blinding snow to take it home. When I saw how devastated he was by my admonishment, I gently brushed away a tear with my mitten and softly told him not to cry—that I was just worried sick about him was all.

Michael always felt bad for scaring me so badly that day. In his own words, this was the worst thing he ever did as a child. Imagine that: He'd rescued a little pooch and took it home in the blinding snow so it wouldn't freeze to death, and that was the worst thing he ever did. As I thought of my past, I just shook my head in amazement.

Being in their room and reflecting about them in this light changed my mood. My boys had turned out very well, and quite unexpectedly I was confident that they would stay that way in spite of anything, including my imminent death.

I returned to my bed and pulled out my Bible. Immediately I felt God's gentle presence descend upon me like a familiar warm comforter. The passage that I began to read described the wondrous glory of heaven. As I reflected about this passage, I began to understand that the next step for me after dying was to spend eternity with Jesus Christ in heaven. My dread of dying dissipated almost immediately.

I could hardly bear to think about saying goodbye to my family, but the more

I read and thought about it, heaven began sounding pretty good. Further, as I compared the eons, millions, billions, trillions, and infinity of years of the next life to the 70-some odd years that most people live in this life, I started developing a different perspective. I understood for the first time what God meant in James 4:14 when he was describing the brevity of this life: "For what is your life? It is even a vapor that appears for a little time and then vanishes away."

I think the Spirit of God opened my mind right then and there and made me realize that as a born-again Christian I shouldn't try to cling to this life. Death is just one of many ugly phases of this "fallen" life that we must all pass through on our way to a new life. For Christians, that coming life is so wonderful that "eye has not seen, nor ear ever heard" of all the marvelous things that God has prepared for His children. Death shouldn't be dreaded or feared. Soon I would be reconciled with Jesus forever, and the years of trials of this mortal life would seem inconsequential. Soon my little family would join me and forevermore we'd bask in God's presence together in paradise.

As I was flipping through the pages in my Bible, I noticed something that I'd written during a sermon and all but forgotten:

Some situations I can't control;
I can however, control my
attitude toward the situation.
I can't run from it.
I must deal with it.
And there is no place for bitterness.

I realized that I couldn't run, hide, or control my own destiny, but I could control my attitude. One thing was certain: Death was inevitable and being bitter would not add one day to my life. I needed to get the most out of whatever time I had left—and lying around in my pajamas every day crying about my situation wasn't going to allow me to make the most out of anything.

After 8 weeks or so of living through fear, anger, and depression, I finally experienced acceptance. I accepted my death sentence—and that day I found my peace.

The dark clouds of my depression lifted. I took a shower, brushed my teeth, put on some fresh clothes, and went back to work. I threw myself into preparing the company for the transition from my leadership to others. Over the next week I started putting all my affairs in order to try to ease the burden on Teresa and the boys. I prayed every day for the strength of Christ to help me through this period, and I asked that He not take me home until after I'd completed what needed to be accomplished.

I planned my funeral and made all the necessary arrangements. When I'd helped make the funeral arrangements for my mother, the shrewd funeral director had "up-sold" me, utilizing the same sales pitch that I'm sure he uses to up-sell others who are totally out of their minds with grief.

He said, "Now this vault is the least expensive, but it's only guaranteed for five years. Now this one over here will last 100 years."

I blurted through tears, "Gimme that one. I don't care how much it costs! I want the best for my mother."

The same was true of the beautiful shiny casket that we selected, and on and on. I was determined that Teresa would not have to go through that, and I picked out a plain pine box for myself and told the guy that I didn't even want a vault.

He was none too happy when I chose not to listen to his insane logic. A dead, decaying shell is all that would be in that grave, but I'd be in paradise walking on streets of gold. I selected the economy model for everything, much preferring that Teresa and the boys spend the saved money on their needs.

I picked out the songs that I wanted sung at my funeral. I chose only two, "Amazing Grace" and "How Great Thou Art". I felt that both of them were appropriate for my life. The following words to Amazing Grace pretty well summed it up for me:

Amazing Grace! How sweet the sound,
That saved a wretch like me!
I once was lost but now am found
Was blind, but now I see.

Through many dangers, toils, and snares,
We have already come;
'Tis Grace hath brought me safe thus far,
And Grace will lead me home.

When we've been here ten thousand years
Bright shining as the sun.
We've no less days to sing God's praise
Than when we've first begun.

Most important, I spent as much time with my family as possible. I'd go to work in the morning, but would arrive home in time to meet the boys when they came home from school. Then I'd meet Teresa when she walked through the door from work.

Finally all the details were taken care of, and I was ready.

My doctor sent all my records and tests to the cancer clinic at Emory University Hospital in Atlanta. He told me that they'd decide how best to treat me from now on.

I was not keen on receiving *any* treatment, and was prepared to simply refuse anything but pain medication. My tumor was incurable and there was no sense in prolonging the inevitable. I was actually hopeful that the tumor would grow rapidly so I'd die quickly and relatively painlessly, as Mom had. Whatever time remained, I wanted some quality to it without the incessant vomiting, extreme pain, and hair loss that Little Bob went through. I didn't want to be merely kept alive at all costs.

I was sitting at my desk at work one morning busily updating our new catalog, when I received a call from the chief radiologist at Emory.

"Mr. Williamson?"

"Yes."

"Are you sitting down?"

"Excuse me?"

"I think you should sit down. I have something I need to tell you. I have reviewed your MRI and all your collective tests. Good news son. You don't have a brain tumor!"

Wahhhhhhh!!!! The siren went off again but this time it was a welcome-home blast.

As the hair stood on end on my neck, the doctor went on to explain, "You have a large pocket of brain fluid located at the base of your skull. It's a very rare condition that is found in less than five percent of the population, and that's what is showing up on the MRI. We all have brain fluid in our skulls, but yours has collected in a rather large pool located near the base of your brain. It's totally harmless, but appears on an MRI to be a cystlike brain tumor. That, combined with your family history of brain tumors, is probably what threw your doctor off with his diagnosis."

YEEEEEEE-HAW!

The rush that doctor gave me was unbelievable and far exceeded any rush I'd ever experienced on drugs. I felt happy, giddy, wonderful, liberated . . . simply unbelievable! I felt like a 1,000-pound weight had been removed from my shoulders.

The doctor was ecstatic too. "In my line of work I don't often get to deliver such good news, and I'm personally delighted to make this call, son."

Just then I remembered the headaches and the numbness of my fingers and face. I cautiously asked the doctor, "If I don't have a brain tumor, then what is wrong with me?" He said he didn't know, but reconfirmed that it definitely wasn't a brain tumor. He was going to order more tests, he said.

Additional tests revealed that my symptoms were being caused by what I originally suspected—stress. When stress hit me, the muscles on the back of my neck involuntarily contracted and put pressure on a nerve located underneath the muscles. This is what caused the numbness, and the headaches were stress related as well. They prescribed a cocktail of a muscle relaxant and the antidepressant Elavil.

When I heard I was going to be treated with an antidepressant, I told the doctor that I wasn't even slightly depressed when I first started experiencing my problems. He told me that what he prescribed had absolutely nothing to do with depression, and that they had discovered quite by accident that the two drugs, when combined, worked in cases similar to mine.

I agreed to give it a try and it worked exceedingly well. In fact, on the very first day, all my symptoms were gone. I continued to take this drug cocktail for quite some time, until my prescription ran out. But I was too busy to have it refilled, so I quit taking the medication. My symptoms didn't return, and from that point on I never took it again.

I shouldn't have doubted my God and I should have maintained my faith in miracles. My whole life was a miracle.

This nightmare was over.

Chapter Sixty-Four

Staring into death's menacing black eyes and surviving one more time created nothing short of a spiritual rejuvenation in me. I was very thankful to God for what I considered to be a mighty miracle, and I was overjoyed at being alive. I was especially thankful that He was allowing me another chance to see my boys grow into men and to take care of Teresa.

I began studying my Bible daily, stopped working seven days a week, and started attending church every Sunday. I drew closer to the Lord than ever before, and I made the conscious decision not only to base my personal life upon His Holy Scripture, but also to make sure my business's foundations were set entirely upon biblical concepts.

After considerable thought and prayer, I produced a mission statement that I felt was appropriate for a faith-based business. I didn't look to sample mission statements produced by Harvard or Wharton Business School; instead I looked to the Bible. I asked myself, "If Jesus Himself were to go into business, what would His mission statement be?"

I turned to a Bible verse where Jesus was asked, "Teacher, which is the greatest commandment in the Law?"

Jesus responded, "Love the Lord your God with all your heart and with all your soul and with all your mind. This is the first and greatest commandment. And the second is like it: Love your neighbor as yourself. All the Law and the Prophets hang on these two commandments."

The two greatest commandments in the Bible seemed like a good place to start. The task seemed simple enough—I needed to put God first in all aspects of my life, and then incorporate this philosophy, "*Do unto others as you would have them do unto you,*" as the centerpiece of my mission statement.

I envisioned myself as a customer and thought about how I'd like to be treated by a company, and then I wrote the following mission statement to reflect how my company needed to treat our valued customers:

1. Provide *outstanding* customer service.
2. Create state-of-the-art products of the highest quality.
3. Offer fair prices.

I believed then and I believe now that if Jesus had His own business, He would abide by a similar mission statement. He and His entire company would be dedicated to providing *outstanding* customer service, and He would no doubt serve every single customer with tremendous respect. Likewise He would never offer a product unless He was genuinely convinced that it was of the highest quality. And no doubt His pricing would always be consummately fair.

I used that mission statement for many years, and it was only after I founded my ninth company, Horizon Software International, that we added a fourth component to it that dictated our character.

4. Work together in a spirit of honesty, integrity, and pride.

I insisted that everyone in my employ take the mission statement seriously—beginning with me—and it was prominently displayed in every cubicle in our offices. As I look back today, nearly 40 years later, I really don't know how to improve upon it and wouldn't change a single word. I credit my mission statement for much of the success that I've enjoyed.

In nearly four decades of being in business for myself, I've never been sued by a vendor or customer, and I've never sued anyone. I believe that this astounding accomplishment was due in no small part to my mission statement. I also believe it was due to a slogan that I read somewhere and adopted into my personal management policies: "Always endeavor to be fair, friendly, and firm."

To me, being "fair" meant, being fair to the customers and employees while simultaneously being fair to my company and me.

I interpreted being "friendly" as dealing with every circumstance in as pleasant and as gracious a manner that I could manage. The Bible teaches in Romans 12:18, "If it is possible, as far as it depends on you, live at peace with everyone," and that is what I have tried to do.

"Firm," I deduced, was an important part of the equation. Without it, customers and employees alike wouldn't remain reasonable.

As to how effective I was in implementing this policy? Sometimes I was successful and, unfortunately, sometimes not so successful.

I feel that I've done a good job being fair and objective throughout my career; however, try as I might, I have often struggled with consistently being "friendly," especially in the heat of battle. No doubt this is due in no small part to the remnants of my dark side, which occasionally surfaces in the form of a torrent of white-hot anger. I fought my way through the business world just as fiercely as I did when I was fighting for my life in a back alley somewhere, and there were times when my dark side ruled my spirit—almost like the dark days. Without question I sometimes overused the part of the slogan dealing with being "firm." Even though I was not physically beating anyone up and bloodying my knuckles, I can assure you that no one in my employ wanted to be summoned to my office for "counseling" when I was in a rage. The same was true for others with whom I dealt in the business world.

I developed a reputation for being a fearsome, tough, take-no-prisoners, aggressive CEO, which makes it even more incredible that I was never sued. Losing my temper has *always* caused tremendous angst, both for me and those on the receiving end. Through the years, I've so intimidated some of my employees that it cost me dearly in a lack of innovative ideas, simply because they were too afraid to speak up; and a few have just given up and resigned so they could move on to calmer waters, taking their intellectual capital with them.

I've always deeply regretted that aspect of my personality and have worked extremely hard to conquer it, and although I've made progress and mellowed some, even today I can't entirely shake it.

Fortunately the Lord is forgiving and, in spite of my faults, has stuck with me through my temper eruptions and myriad of mistakes. He continues to bless me enormously.

As time progressed I developed a very powerful marketing *machine* to sell products. I initially began implementing this strategy for selling my airbrush paints by producing what I called a "clinic-in-print" for airbrush artists. It started out quite simply as a two-color newsletter 16 pages long.

The concept was simple but brilliant. Teach the users how to apply the paint properly and they will achieve better results. When they do, they'll be grateful and attribute their success to my products and company, and then become loyal customers.

With my paint background I knew that airbrush painting was a very complex process and that most users (even the most accomplished artists) knew little about the intricacies of rendering it properly. I knew I could easily remove the mystery of airbrush painting with my little clinic-in-print.

I taught my customers how to select and utilize the right equipment and paints. Then I showed them how to properly apply the paints to produce excellent results. I taught the correct application techniques, such as using base coats to reflect through subsequent transparent topcoats. In that way, the artist would create depth and realistic color combinations. I taught which solvent combinations to use to achieve proper viscosity and what air pressure to use to achieve an even spray. I recommended equipment, such as moisture traps to control humidity and solvents to combat temperature fluctuations. I established a troubleshooting guide and loaded the newsletter with informative tips.

I developed paint schedules that contained detailed instructions for painting various fish and other species rendered by Jim Hall and other famous artists. My customers could use the exact same equipment, techniques, and paints as the pros, and I sold every single item they would need. It was very nearly a paint-by-the-numbers system and yielded superb results.

A few days after I mailed out a newsletter, I would receive thousands of orders for every piece of equipment, paints, and supplies mentioned in the paint schedules and clinic-in-print. It was great fun.

My system became the talk of the industry, and that's how the little clinic-in-print derived its name, *Breakthrough* magazine. It was a revolutionary concept and the industry recognized this system as a breakthrough for airbrush artists.

At first I mailed out my clinic-in-print free of charge to all my customers. They had excellent results, loved it, and clamored for more articles. It was as though they were starved for information. Initially I restricted *Breakthrough* to airbrush painting, but soon expanded it to include instructions and tips for all kinds of wildlife-art mediums; and it became a full-fledged four-color magazine. Simultaneously my little paint company expanded to include wildlife-art supplies for every form of wildlife art.

The magazine helped my customers improve the quality of their work, whether they were mounting a whitetail buck or carving a mallard decoy. The educational tools were enormously popular and highly educational to struggling wannabe artists and pros alike. I took the mystery out of everything, from tanning deer hides to carving a fish out of a block of wood, and made it all seem as easy as 1, 2, 3. Readers could use the exact same supplies, techniques, and step-by-step procedures as the best artists in the world. How could they fail?

Eventually *Breakthrough* became so popular and expensive to produce that I quit mailing it out free and started selling subscriptions. I also founded several more companies in the educational realm, including a company that published how-to books for wildlife artists and a video-production company that produced wildlife-artist how-to videos. I established the World Taxidermy Championships, the World Fish Carving Championships, the World Wildlife Photography Championships, and the World Wildlife Sculpture and Bronze Championships; and one of my companies conducted live how-to seminars, workshops, and competitions all over the country.

I founded another company, Serious Sportsmen, to conduct sportsman shows, and I combined all the foregoing entities under one roof. Tens of thousands of wildlife artists, sportsmen, and various interested parties attended the largest sportsman show ever held, in the World Congress Center, in Atlanta, where we utilized two full convention halls. We offered over 68 seminars and events, which were put on by leading outdoorsmen. One of the events was the Levi Garrett world turkey-calling championships, with nationally recognized turkey hunter Ben Rodgers Lee. We conducted bass-fishing clinics with bass pros, whitetail clinics, duck-calling contests, decoy competitions, taxidermy classes and competitions, decoy carving seminars, and on and on. We even hired country music legend Mel Tillis and his band to entertain everyone one night with his country music and stuttering jokes.

I began making obscene amounts of profit selling books, videos, and magazine subscriptions, and collecting seminar and workshop fees; but truth be told, I would have given all those educational tools away free of charge to get people to order their supplies from my mail-order distribution company. The real money was in the supplies. For example, I would sell a book or video for $24.95, and as soon as he or she read or watched it, the customer would order $500 worth of supplies. It was an awesome concept.

I recruited the most respected wildlife artists in the world to create our how-to books, videos, and magazine articles, and to conduct live seminars and workshops detailing step-by-step how they created their wildlife-art masterpieces using my products. Included were fish carvers, flat artists, sculptors, decoy carvers, tanners, and leading taxidermists with specialties in birds, small mammals, fish, whitetails, reptiles, and big game.

Many of these men and women were far better artists than writers, and I ended up writing (under their direction) the majority of the books and articles myself. The artists didn't mind lending their name to my products, because they were excellent products of the highest quality and I paid them well and made them internationally famous. They began endorsing my company and products at every opportunity, which of course was greatly appreciated (particularly at the cash register).

It was a win/win/win situation because my customers loved it too. And even though they didn't have the artistic ability of some of these legendary artists, they achieved far superior results than they would ever have achieved on their own—simply because they followed the step-by-step guides utilizing my great products.

I adopted the slogan "It's all in the system," and all my marketing was geared toward using the "system." The best thing about it was that it worked, plain and simple. And those who tried the system became fiercely loyal customers, so our company soon was the number one wildlife-artist supply company in the world.

Time flew by and before I even realized it, seven years had elapsed since my brain-tumor scare. I was swept away by my success. I was feverishly working to keep up and was adding 100 new products to my mail-order catalogs every month. Product descriptions had to be written, pricing determined, and a thousand other details taken care of, and I handled it all personally—in addition to all my other writing, editing, and management responsibilities.

I invented numerous products for wildlife artists and founded a manufacturing company to produce urethane injection molding, paints, papier-mâché, tanning supplies, and clay.

For those items that did not make sense for me to manufacture, I became a reseller and sold them through my company Wildlife Artist Supply (WASCO). Soon I was selling 4,000 or 5,000 different items, including every conceivable supply for any type of wildlife artist. I was a one-stop, A-to-Z market for wildlife-artist supplies.

My schedule most weeks was now back to seven days a week, and I worked from 7 a.m. until 4 a.m. By day I was frontline-managing the employees of my seven businesses; by night I would write. During this period of time I published 19 books, produced 68 videos, wrote and edited articles as publisher and editor of *Breakthrough* magazine, and every other month produced new catalogs for my mail-order businesses.

My instincts were extraordinary. For me, business was like knowing where to dig for gold, and every avenue I explored was like a lane to an open vault at Fort Knox where I could help myself to some bullion. I was innovative and visionary, and had a knack for knowing what my customers wanted and how to market it to them. I found myself becoming nauseatingly arrogant and I wallowed in pride.

As I approached age 45, I began going through what I would describe as a midlife crisis. I recognized that I was beginning to get old, and I didn't like it. To compensate, I began intensely working out with weights and performing aerobic exercises. I was disciplined and never once failed to carefully follow my stringent workout routine. It seemed odd that someone who'd led the early life that I led could possess as much self-discipline, but such was the case. Once I made up my mind to go after a goal, I was determined to achieve it or die trying. This was true in every aspect of my life, and no amount of hard work, sacrifice, or pain would stop me.

Soon I was very muscular and in great shape and even started hiding the gray in my hair with Just for Men hair products. I bought several cars, including a sleek black Cadillac. Often I'd wear garish-looking clothes that made me look almost like a pimp. I'd strut around wearing loudly colored, expensive shirts unbuttoned halfway down to expose my expensive gold chain, tight pants that nearly cut off all circulation to my genitals, and Gucci pointed boots. As I reflect back on it now, I must have looked like a strutting peacock to those around me.

I even found a way to make money from my obsession with health and fitness. I founded a health-and-fitness mail-order business, complete with retail-outlet store. I began selling weight-lifting equipment, vitamins, supplements, sports drinks, and a myriad of other health and fitness products. I called it Weight and Shape Company (WASCO), and named it that way so I wouldn't have to install another 1-800 line. My order takers for the other WASCO (Wildlife Artist Supply Company), could answer the phone, "Good morning, this is WASCO, may I help you please?" and take an order for either company.

I utilized many of the same techniques that I used to build the wildlife-artist business, including the clinic-in-print concept, and it too became successful, almost overnight. It seemed as though I had the Midas touch. In just a few years I'd become enormously successful and was managing seven different companies simultaneously.

Things were good; in fact they were *very* good, but my walk with the Lord was suffering. I had what seemed to be an unquenchable thirst to make more and more money, and I'd let nothing get in the way of it. I wanted to create an empire, and I worked like a maniac to achieve my goals.

This burning desire to succeed was due in no small part to my strong desire to continue to prove all my detractors wrong—and actually to rub their noses in my success. I was determined to prove to every single person who'd ever told me that I would fail that they were wrong about me. All my life nearly everyone had looked down on me and asked, "*What's wrong with you?*" and I was determined to show them that I wasn't a loser (especially my dad and brother).

I began spending less and less time with my family and drifted far away from God. My drift started slowly, but as the years ticked away I couldn't seem to find time to read the Bible, or even to pray; I'd stopped going to church entirely and had resumed working on Sundays. Eventually I forgot about God altogether and He rarely, if ever, crossed my mind.

Soon this obsession was taking a toll on our marriage, and Teresa and I were beginning to experience serious problems. She'd quit her job at Union Pacific and was working full time for me. We worked in different areas of the building and hardly ever saw each other. And aside from attending our sons' various baseball, soccer, basketball, or football games, we rarely did anything together.

Spending precious little time with me hurt her, yes, but she was also jealous because I was working alongside a number of younger, attractive women. Two pregnancies had changed Teresa's good figure some and she was beginning to age, so she felt threatened by all the pretty young girls running around our office (who on occasion, I must say, flirted with me).

I was in the best physical shape of my life, I was rich and full of myself, and I didn't shy away from younger women flirting with me. In fact, I often encouraged it with some flirting of my own. It made me feel young and vibrant. It made Teresa livid.

She'd reached a point where she had a very bad attitude toward me, and to further complicate things, she wouldn't follow orders like the other employees. Recently she'd failed to mail a very important letter that I'd instructed her to mail. It seemed to me that, since we were married, she thought she didn't have to follow instructions like everyone else.

I found myself constantly arguing and bickering with her, and I was becoming miserable and looking for a way out. She wanted me to be the good husband and father that I'd once been, and I wanted her to get off my back. I told myself that she was lucky to have me. I'd made her rich beyond her wildest dreams and she had every material possession that a woman could want.

I know today that I was the one who was lucky to be married to her and that the happiest time of my life was right after we had been married: We were broke most of the time, living in a tiny apartment, and struggling to pay our rent and electric bill, but we were madly in love and did everything together. We were close to God and we were exceedingly happy.

Now, in spite of having more money than I knew how to spend and being the most powerful figure in my industry, I was miserable. I blamed Teresa, but it was I who had turned my back on God and galloped full speed ahead to satisfy my lust for the power and money that my dark side had tendered up for the taking. Satan undoubtedly had his despicable serpent head cocked back, laughing that wicked, hideous laugh and reveling in the knowledge that he once again owned me.

The situation was tense and something was bound to happen. One day she walked by my office and suddenly stopped in front of my open door and stood there with her hands on her hips until I looked up at her. Without so much as saying a word, she just stood there glaring at me as though she hated my guts. I had no idea what she was mad about and I didn't care.

My temper exploded. "Get in here!"

She stalked into my office still glaring and with fire jumping out of her eyes.

I didn't even ask what was bothering her this time. I shouted, "Get your things together, you're fired!"

She looked at me and said, "You can't fire me."

"Oh, but I can. You don't work here anymore. Get your stuff together and get the hell out of here."

Chapter Sixty-Five

I was completely unaware of the intense spiritual warfare that was still being waged against me by my dark side. In retrospect, I was foolhardy to think that Satan might've just amicably conceded my soul back over to God and with bowed head gone slinking to his lair to lick his wounds while I enjoyed my newfound Christian life. Satan was hardly through with me and in fact was just getting started.

When I eradicated drug addiction and violence from my life, I'd naively thought that I'd won the spiritual war against my dark side. I wasn't even consciously aware of it when my dark side merely replaced those demons with new ones named *Money, Power,* and *Pride.*

The transition had been subtle and had occurred over time. In the beginning I walked very close to God, but I slowly drifted away. It began one Sunday when I didn't attend church, saying that I needed to work because I had a deadline that I just *had to meet.* Then I skipped another Sunday and another, and soon that behavior morphed into never attending church at all. In similar fashion I quit reading my Bible, and the same was true with my prayer life. It finally reached a point where I'd blotted God completely out of my life and rarely if ever thought about Him anymore.

My new demons came to me innocently enough and were very well hidden in their disguises as the very pinnacles of societal success. Before I even understood what had happened, I was already trapped in their raging fire. The fire was kindled by making too much money too fast, and soon flames of intoxicating power and pride were burning uncontrollably and devouring my body, spirit, and soul.

I'd greatly underestimated Satan. He had the whole world to offer me, and once I'd gotten a taste of it I wanted more and more. In the end these new addictions were no different from my addiction to drugs, and my new demons dominated my every waking moment every bit as much as drugs did.

I owned the mighty WASCO "machine," including the most popular magazine in the world for wildlife artists. If an artist was lucky enough to have one of his renderings hit the cover of my magazine or receive a full-color feature article, he would instantly become famous. Likewise, if I offered someone a book or video deal, selected him as a judge at the World Championships, or featured him in my catalog as a world-class artist, he (or she) would instantly leap to stardom within his chosen field and financial reward would shower him.

People disingenuously fawned over me and showered me with compliments trying to gain my favor. The power was intoxicating and I lapped it up like a puppy drinking water. I was so infatuated with myself, my money, and my power, that I hardly took notice of their insincerity, or even cared about it. For that matter, I didn't care about anyone else. It was *me* that I was interested in. I was full of arrogance, ad nauseam.

Local community leaders further stroked my large ego when they took notice of my success and began to routinely invite me to their luncheons around town, which included all of the who's who: the bankers, attorneys, insurance executives, smart money businesspeople, and politicians, who all referred to themselves as the "movers and shakers." Soon I'd become one of them as they accepted me into their exclusive little club.

I attributed my success to my own brilliance. I blotted from memory the fact that prior to God's entering my life, my lifetime achievements had consisted of a penniless, forlorn life of hopeless drug addiction, alcoholism, insane violence, homelessness, loneliness, and suicidal tendencies.

Indeed, it was only when God entered my life that I was transformed. He miraculously sat Teresa down in my chair in that crowded disco that night and through her provided the love and stability that were missing in my life. That love and stability were, without question, necessary to conquer my addictions and eventually become a loving husband, doting father, and successful businessman.

Those were the realities, but I was blinded by pride and attributed my amazing success to my own intellect, perseverance, and hard work. I didn't give God any credit for anything, nor did I give Teresa any. In fact, I'd begun to want out of my marriage altogether. I wanted to be unfettered and take wings like a free bird so I could go wherever my heart desired. I resented being tied down and lusted for the excitement and allure enjoyed by the rich and the famous.

My visions of grandeur bordered on insanity. I sometimes dreamed of hooking up with a couple of young beauties half my age and hanging one on each arm and becoming one of "the beautiful people." I envisioned hopping on my own private jet and following the sun to a topless beach on the French Riviera and then into Paris for some shopping, perhaps take in some polo at Monaco, engage in who knows what in Amsterdam, ski the Swiss Alps, and then put together a gambling junket and take in some shows in Vegas.

Spiritually and mentally I was sinking deeper and deeper into a darker and darker abyss. It was a perilous time, but in spite of firing Teresa and humiliating her in front of the entire company, somehow it began to appear as though our marriage just might miraculously survive.

This was because of her efforts and not mine. I fully expected her to leave me and I was prepared for it, but either because of her deep love for me, not being willing to subject our kids to divorce, her religious beliefs that divorce was wrong, or perhaps a combination of all the foregoing, she determined to swallow her pride and accept my decision to fire her.

Initially I was resolute that she would never work for me again, but after calming down some, I decided to form another little company to collate and bind the various wildlife-art softbound books that were printed through our publishing company. I set her up as manager of several other ladies, and together they worked out of the basement of our home.

I was adamant, however, that under no circumstance would she be allowed to work out of headquarters again. She accepted and seemed content with the new arrangement. After that we didn't see each other enough to argue much, and it seemed to relieve much of the tension. Although our marriage was still rocky, it had somehow endured a tsunami event and remained standing.

My personal life might have been a failure, but my business life couldn't have been going much better. I'd come up with a plan that I was sure would propel my already multimillion-dollar business into the really big time, where I could knock down some serious money. I'd used the computer skills gained so long ago at Glidden and elsewhere to write my own comprehensive software systems for managing each of my companies. Much of my business was direct mail, and I'd worked very hard in designing mail-order software so that my mailings became an exact science.

The secret to being successful in direct mail is first and foremost to have an excellent mailing list. It's essential to identify within the database exactly who will buy, and then mail to them often. It was a numbers game. Each mail-out would yield a predictable percentage of response (depending on the promotion, of course).

I spent a tremendous amount of time and effort developing my system. I even hired a University of Georgia statistics professor to help predict buying behavior and develop a mail-out strategy. I analyzed everything, from the amount of money that the average customer was willing to spend per order, to how often I should mail, to being able to predict what my percentage of response in dollars received would be by week.

I learned that a typical mail-out, whether it was promoting a new book, video, seminar, or product, would at first slowly begin to produce results and then pick up speed rapidly until it peaked. After peaking, sales would endure a steep and *fast* decline. I of course wanted to develop a system in which a mail-out would peak just prior to the decline of the previous one, so there'd be no down time. Therefore the timing was crucial for each subsequent mail-out after the first. If a mail-out went out too soon after another, it would inundate the customer with too many choices; delaying it would result in dead time with no orders being generated between peaks.

It didn't take me long to perfect the system, and soon I was producing a steady stream of maximum revenue. For taking mail to the post office, I bought an extra-long extended van and took all the seats out of it except for the driver's seat. We filled canvas postal bags with mail-outs and crammed the bags in from ceiling to floor, beginning in the front of the van and going all the way to the back—to a point where we could barely slam the door shut.

Within days, as a mail-out began hitting state after state, our order-processing phones would begin to light up as thousands of customers began responding.

While business was great and I was making money, I was not content. I wanted more; I wanted to hit the big time; I wanted to rock the world; I didn't want millions or even tens of millions, I wanted hundreds of millions.

One day I came up with what I affectionately referred to as the "Big Idea." It was my ticket to the big time. My Big Idea was to use my mailing list, mail-order software programs, and spectacularly successful mailing techniques and strategies in order to sell more than just wildlife-artist supplies to my fanatically loyal customer base.

My customer base consisted of 268,000 wildlife artists, which just also happened to include the world's most intense, hard-core sportsmen. Most of them started in the wildlife-art field because of their fanatical love of hunting, fishing, camping, wildlife, and the great outdoors. They loved these things so much that they chose wildlife art as their vocation. A career in taxidermy or whatever meant they could pursue something that was not merely a job to them but a passion.

I reasoned that, in addition to the wildlife-art supplies they were already buying, I could also sell hunting and fishing gear, camping supplies, clothing, and so forth. My customers trusted me and knew that I wasn't about to sell shoddy products to them. I knew that I could select and offer excellent products that worked, just as I'd done in the wildlife-art business. A business like that could generate $100 million or more in additional revenue every year for me.

I was going to utilize my mailing list and direct mail know-how as a launching pad to become the next Bass Pro Shops, Cabela's, or L.L. Bean. I'd run the numbers on my Big Idea, and had become too excited to eat or sleep or do little else but dream about the potential of all those dollars hitting my bank account.

But just as I began putting my business plan and pro forma together, the bottom fell out. Teresa's mother, Jenny, suddenly developed a blood clot in her leg, and within two weeks died at the young age of 62.

I was completely devastated. Jenny had been my sole supporter when I began my first business. She more than anyone believed in me from day one and had remained my most avid cheerleader.

At her funeral I reflected back to an event that was indicative of her unswerving support for me. It was that exciting day that I looked on my personal financial statement and realized for the first time that I'd achieved my goal of becoming a *millionaire*.

I was so thrilled that I literally couldn't wait to tell someone. I excitedly picked up the phone and called my dad. I'd sacrificed so much in order to achieve this goal. I'd overcome tremendous odds, worked gruesome hours, and endured great risk for years. After wasting 23 years of my life, I'd gone on to become a millionaire by the time I was just barely 37 years old. I was so excited at achieving this milestone I could barely contain it, but Dad acknowledged it almost with a yawn. My brother was even worse and almost immediately got off the phone, saying he had some things to do.

I didn't expect them to stop everything and organize a parade, but I thought that at the very least they'd be happy for me and perhaps even be a little proud of how far I'd come since shoving a needle in my arm at every opportunity. Their responses were underwhelming, and all those bitter memories of my youth suddenly descended upon me in a landslide.

When I told Jenny about my accomplishment, you'd have thought that she'd just hit the lottery herself. She was so excited and happy for me that she probably damaged my eardrum with her excited squealing into the phone. She'd always thoroughly enjoyed hearing of the success of our companies, and couldn't wait to hear all the latest. To be informed that I was now officially a *millionaire* delighted her, and best of all her excitement for me was genuine.

Reminiscing about it just made me all the more depressed and sick with grief at her death. Another good-hearted person, someone I loved so much, had died young. Losing such a close friend, confidante, and loyal supporter was devastating to me, but I was thankful that, unlike when my own mother died, I did have an opportunity to talk to Jenny at length in the hospital before she died.

I told her I loved her and she told me that she loved me. I talked to her for long periods of time about many things, including Jesus Christ and salvation. She'd reached the point where she knew that she was going to die, and she assured me with certainty that she'd accepted Christ as her Savior and would join Him when she died.

At her funeral, my mind drifted and I envisioned Jesus standing with outstretched arms to meet her as she stepped across the threshold of death and entered into her new life. I could see Him gently reassuring her and telling her not to be afraid, and that all bad things had forever passed. He took her by the hand and together they entered into that dazzling paradise of unequalled beauty and peacefulness. She looked beautiful and was clothed in a brilliant white robe and was widely smiling the charming smile that was her trademark. She looked around in wonderment and seemed to actually radiate light and glow as a choir began singing "Victory in Jesus" in perfect harmony to celebrate her entry into her new home.

Sitting in my pew I whispered to her, "I'm happy for you, Jenny. You'll enjoy your time in heaven and I know Jesus will enjoy spending time with you." At that moment I understood that heaven was no doubt created by God for people like Jenny.

My thoughts of God and heaven were short lived, however, and soon I was back at work. It was one more indication of how gut hooked my new demons had me. Losing Jenny was a major traumatic event in my life. One would have thought that I would have *run* back to the Lord with tears streaming down my face, but sadly I was more interested in picking right back up where I'd left off on Earth.

Soon after the funeral I put together a deal in which I sold some copyrights to a competitor so that he could reproduce some of the largemouth-bass sculptures that I owned and use them to manufacture fish manikins. He wanted to sell them to his own customers. It was a good deal for me. He paid me $50,000 cash just for the rights to reproduce them, and he brought the money to my house in a brown paper bag and counted it out for me on the bar in my basement. Back then that was a lot of cash, and seeing it stacked along that bar top in 50 separate bundles of $1,000 each mesmerized me.

During this time Teresa and I had resumed fighting with each other. I spent less and less time at home. We never went out to eat anymore or did anything socially with other couples; we never even sat down and talked to each other in a civil tone. She claimed that all I cared about was my next business deal and I claimed that all she cared about was criticizing me.

She wanted the "old Bob" back and had taken to nagging and berating me, beginning whenever I set foot inside the house and ending only when I left. It was a miserable existence, and one day after a particularly bitter fight I'd had enough.

I walked back into our bedroom and pulled the .44 Magnum pistol that I used for hunting wild hogs from the top shelf of my closet. I sat down on the side of the bed, cocked the trigger, and put it to my temple. I sat there with that cocked revolver tightly jammed against my temple and my finger on the trigger for what seemed like an eternity before I slowly lowered it.

I couldn't do it.

I carefully uncocked the pistol and put it back up and walked back into the living room and told Teresa that I was leaving. I would give her the house and all the furniture and take care of her and the boys financially for as long as I could take a breath, but I wanted to be free.

She begged me not to go and said that she was sorry for the fight. She told me that we could work things out, "if for no other reason than for the kids." But I told her that I just didn't think things could work out and I was sick of all the fighting. I told her that we should try a trial separation for a while and see if it would help.

That was disingenuous of me. I already knew what I wanted and I wouldn't be coming back. I wanted a divorce!

The hardest thing for me was telling my boys. They were just 11 and 9 and were way too young to understand the complexities of marriage, or much of anything. They were both scared because Mommy was crying and Daddy had been yelling a lot. They didn't want me to leave and begged me to stay, but I reassured them by telling them that I wasn't going to the moon, or even leaving town, and would still go to all their games and just like always see them every day.

I found my bachelor pad: an immense house in a neighboring community. It came complete with marble floors, wet bar, an elaborate room-to-room stereo system, hot tub, and grandiose master bedroom. I leased it with an option to buy and prepaid a month's rent out of my $50,000 cash.

I'd decided that just as soon as I was divorced I'd hook up with some beautiful girl somewhere, start chasing the sun, and party on.

I moved in on a Saturday and was standing in my new kitchen smiling as I popped open a jet cold Budweiser and said, "Let the games begin."

Chapter Sixty-Six

I'd moved out early on a Saturday morning, long before anyone else got up. I knew it would be less stressful that way. All I took with me were my clothes and shaving gear. My new place was already elaborately furnished and even included kitchenware. All I needed to do was hang my clothes in the closet, buy some food and household supplies, and stock the bar. That was important. By midmorning I was well on my way to becoming a bachelor again and couldn't wait to get out on the town to see what I'd been missing.

Outside of work I had a few casual business acquaintances, but no real friends, so my first night out on the town was solo. I didn't want to get too involved with any females until I was divorced, but now that I was officially separated, I did want to start meeting some people and paving the way toward establishing my new life of bachelorhood.

I decided to begin my search by checking out the Atlanta bar scene. That first night I got slicked up in my flashiest designer clothes, put a roll of cash in my pocket big enough to finance a Third World country uprising, took my black Caddy to the car wash for the superwash/wax/buff special, removed my wedding ring, and headed out into the night.

I didn't want anyone to know that I'd moved out, including my dad, brother, employees at work, or anyone. It was nobody's business but Teresa's and mine, and so I'd told no one. Without divulging why I wanted to know, I'd surreptitiously nosed around work and asked the hippest people I could find to identify the hottest clubs in Atlanta for me.

When I walked into the first one, I wondered if perhaps I'd inadvertently stumbled into a high-school prom or something. Everyone in there appeared to be half my age, and the earsplitting noise could hardly be called music. Those kids may have been stylish for their day, but to me they appeared dirty, with uncombed, unkempt hair. They were dressed in ragged, sloppy-looking clothes similar to those worn by the winos and hobos on the freights that I used to hop.

No one even noticed me and even if they had, I'm sure they would've just assumed that I was someone's dad looking for his wayward son or daughter. I turned on my heel and walked right back out without even ordering a beer.

After visiting three of the "hottest" clubs on the Atlanta bar scene with identical results, I decided to ditch the recommended hot-clubs list and head to downtown

Atlanta to find something better suited to someone my age. The first nightclub I visited was called the Sans Souci. It was dark and smoky and it was as dead as a cemetery. Tired-looking, worn-out people sparsely filled the place. Most were sitting at the bar with cigarette in hand, nursing a mixed drink and looking straight ahead.

The bored, empty looks on their wrinkled faces creeped me out and it briefly crossed my mind that I didn't want to end up like them. I quickly exited and headed for a hotel bar that was just down the street in the heart of Atlanta.

This bar catered mainly to hotel conventioneers, and most of its patrons were still dressed in their business suits from that day's meetings. It was readily obvious that they were already well on their way to getting drunk and satisfying their quest for female companionship. They were sitting at tables surrounding a small hardwood dance floor, and overhead a cheap sparkle ball flashed twinkling lights in a 20-foot circle.

Two or three couples had already paired up, and one couple was slow dancing. Actually, they were standing still and rocking back and forth in a lewd-looking grind. The guy was firmly gripping each cheek of his partner's butt and pressing her tightly against his groin, no doubt foretelling what would come later (after a hundred bucks was exchanged).

Little red-glass candleholders with faint yellow flames decorated each table and barely illuminated the dimly lit bar. As my eyes began to adjust to the darkness, I could discern a few hookers circling the tables like vultures looking for a dead animal to devour. They're easy to spot: Their caked faces are made up like a circus clown's; their hair is fried, frizzy, and bleached-blonde, or they wear jet-black wigs; and their skirts are so short that they expose their red or black undergarments whenever they take a step.

When I walked into the bar, one immediately started walking toward me with a gleam in her eye. But I quickly held up my hand and shook my head no. I wanted no part of that. She gave me a go-to-hell look and turned back around to search for easier prey.

That scene was not for me, and once again I left without even ordering a beer. I drove my Caddy all over Atlanta trying to find some of my old haunts from years gone by, but they were all long gone. The scene had changed.

I was getting desperate and decided to check out a country-music place that I knew of. Mama's Country Showcase was located on the outskirts of town. The place was hopping and it was filled to capacity with what appeared to be a good mix of young people and people my age. And to be sure there was no shortage of pretty girls. Everyone was wearing faded Levi's, pearl-button Western shirts, big belt buckles, and cowboy boots and hats.

I was the lone exception. I was dressed similar to an Italian mobster in my Gucci shoes, brightly colored silk shirt, and navy blue, tailored trousers. I stood out like a white man at an NAACP convention.

The band was terrible, especially the lead singer, who talked like he maybe had a second-grade education and sang like a whining hick with a hemorrhoid. Even if the band had been decent, I wouldn't have cared—I hated country music anyway.

They were extraordinarily loud and my assumption was that perhaps they'd cranked up their amps to full capacity so that someone would notice them. It didn't work and no one (aside from me) seemed to pay them any attention; everyone else was too drunk to notice. They were too busy line dancing or taking turns trying to stay atop a mechanical bull that immediately sent their drunken, uncoordinated bodies flying through the air onto the mats that surrounded it.

It gave me such a headache that I just decided to call it a night.

I went out every single night that first week and had similar results each time. I couldn't help but notice that of the few people that I did meet, none seemed to be genuinely happy. To be sure I observed a few smiles and some laughter, but it seemed artificial and shallow and lacking to me. Without even probing, I could easily see that something dark was eating away at most of them. I didn't see any joy in anyone. More important, I didn't feel any either.

It was depressing.

One night I went back to my bachelor pad and as I lay there wide awake, I thought about my new life. I'd discovered years ago that all the sex, booze, and drugs in the world didn't bring me joy, no matter how much I indulged myself or how desperate I was to find relief. I'd been there and done that, and yet here I was again. It seemed as though I hadn't learned anything.

I was all alone again. I was in the same place mentally and spiritually as I was when I first came to Atlanta; the only difference seemed to be that instead of being addicted to drugs, I was addicted to cash, cars, clothes, jewelry, and ruling my little empire.

I couldn't sleep, so I just decided to go on in to work. I feverishly worked all night and on through the early morning hours, continuing nonstop into the late afternoon of the next day before returning home. Exhausted I entered my large empty house and my footsteps echoed loudly as I *click, click, clicked* my way across the polished marble floor in the foyer. When I tossed my car keys into the silver tray on the kitchen counter, they clattered noisily for a moment and then I heard nothing but profound silence.

I said aloud, "This place reminds me of a mausoleum." And as if to emphasize my point, my words echoed back through the room with a resounding hollow tone.

I was never one who enjoyed eating out and I didn't cook either, so I threw a three-day-old piece of pizza into the microwave, popped open a can of Coke, and sat on a barstool at the kitchen counter as I waited for it to heat up.

This scene was a stark contrast to my home with Teresa. I didn't watch much television or listen to the radio, but my family was just the opposite. I smiled as I thought of the melee that was probably occurring at that very moment, with the kids playing and scampering through the house yelling at each other while Teresa rattled dishes as she prepared dinner. No doubt the television, radio, and probably stereo were all simultaneously playing and the washer and dryer would be chugging in harmony.

It had to be sheer pandemonium by now. I chuckled as I envisioned the chaos. I thought back to happier times, when I used to come home from work and excitedly share my dreams and relate to Teresa something fascinating that had occurred at work. Sometimes we'd talk for hours while she cooked one of her fabulous meals, and then after dinner I'd wrestle with the boys or play catch with them or help them with their homework.

BEEP, BEEP, BEEP, BEEP

Abruptly the microwave interrupted my pleasant thoughts as it irritatingly informed me that dinner was ready. The pizza was rank and after just one bite I threw it away. Suddenly it all seemed to catch up with me and I felt brutally exhausted. I slowly walked back into my huge bedroom and with a giant sigh flopped down on my gigantic bed and stared at the high ceiling. Tears began trickling down my cheeks.

"What am I doing?"

I thought of God. I knew that He was angry with me and I didn't blame Him. I was mad at myself. After all I'd been through, I still had been stupid enough to allow my dark side to gain the upper hand in my life again.

Abruptly I got up and drove over to our home and softly knocked on the front door. Teresa answered and I couldn't even bring myself to look her in the eyes. I looked down and sheepishly asked if I could come back home. She didn't hesitate even for a moment. She excitedly threw her arms around me and hugged me for all she was worth. I could feel the hot tears running down her cheek as they mixed with mine. When the boys heard my voice, they came running in and like excited little puppies began running around circling me, tugging at my pants legs and clamoring to be hugged too. It was one of the happiest moments of my life.

I determined right then and there that if anyone ever left again, it wouldn't be me. Today I can honestly say that since that day the word "divorce" has never even one time crossed my mind again. Teresa is my wife for life, and as the Bible so eloquently describes, we are "one."

Inasmuch as it's up to me, death is the only thing that will ever make us part. We might choose fists, guns, knives, clubs, arm wrestling, water pistols, or words to settle our disputes, but divorce will never again be an option that I consider. As proof of this commitment, as of the publication of this book we have been married for 39 years and are still going strong.

I told my landlord just to keep the prepaid rent, and I picked up my stuff and moved back home.

Meanwhile I was making tremendous progress on my Big Idea. In order to pull it off, I needed investment capital, and I'd been working two potential investors against each other.

One was from Denver and headed up an investment fund that was keen to take WASCO public right away. The other was a local businessman that had the means to invest solo and provide all the additional cash needed to grow the business. He was highly motivated to invest because he wanted his son to be involved in a good opportunity; there was the added bonus that both father and son loved hunting and fishing. This seemed to be a perfect fit.

After weeks of negotiations with both parties, I opted to go with the local businessman instead of the Denver group. I met with his acquisitions guru and after about three days of tough negotiations, we hammered out an acceptable deal for both sides. Some fine details would still need to be reduced to writing by the lawyers, but it was mere formality from here.

We had forged one of those deals that businesspeople always dream about: one that made everybody happy. Amazingly I'd ended up with majority ownership of the stock—51 percent versus their 49 percent—and I considered it to be the best deal that I ever negotiated.

We shook hands to seal the deal, and I was well on my way to making my Big Idea a reality.

I couldn't wait to go home and tell Teresa and then go to work to tell the employees. Everything was going to change now. Little did I know that in just three days my life and business would be changed all right. It would be ruined and lying in utter devastation.

CHAPTER SIXTY-SEVEN

I looked forward to announcing to our employees that we were on our way to stardom. I called the entire company together at lunchtime so I could finally reveal my top-secret Big Idea to them. Heretofore the project had been shared only with my executives and a couple of secretarial employees who'd helped prepare the presentation for the potential investors.

This would be a Friday everyone would remember!

The entire company began to gather in our large showroom. The room was massive but it looked small as our 65 employees began to fill it up. Some were standing and others were sitting on brown metal folding chairs that had been hastily set up.

As I stood there with Teresa by my side, waiting for the employees to assemble, my mind drifted. As I watched them stream in laughing and talking and cutting up, I mused that there weren't any suits and ties at WASCO. We all dressed casually, including me in my blue jeans and plaid shirt. I considered that to be one of the best benefits of working in a company geared toward wildlife artists and outdoorsmen.

I noticed how small groups of employees seemed to band together. I saw the creative group, headed up by Ken Edwards. Ken was the absolute genius who did the creative design for our catalogs, magazine, and marketing materials. Ken was sitting next to Sallie Dahmes. Sallie was another incredibly talented artist and had won Best in World at the World Taxidermy Championships as a whitetail taxidermist, and she sculpted all our whitetail and duck species manikins. She was one of our hardest-working, most talented, and most loyal workers.

Ken and Sallie were sitting with Greg, our printer. Greg was always smiling, and his white teeth contrasted nicely with his handsome African American face. He was in charge of all of WASCO's printing operations and was a very talented printer. Greg was deeply religious and always had a Bible by his side. I smiled when I saw it in his hand. I'd ordered pizza for the entire company and after the meeting, I'd call on him to say grace before we ate.

Other groups included the warehouse workers, and the accounting and purchasing departments (headed up by Ralph, our controller, who smiled and nodded to me when we made eye contact). The manufacturing people were sitting together as were the order processors and operators. (I'd taken the rare step of not answering the phones during this important meeting.)

It was a great bunch of people and I considered most to be good friends as well as good employees. I was really proud of them. They'd all worked their tails off and the result of their hard work would soon be realized.

When everyone was assembled, I whistled loudly to quell the conversation and bring the meeting to order. I started off by saying that I had some great news. I explained that soon we would greatly expand our operation to include "sportsman-ware" and I'd struck a deal with a major investor to help finance the expansion and make it become a reality. I told them that our goal was to eventually take WASCO public.

I informed them that prior to taking our operation public, I was going to issue stock options to each employee according to their personal contributions toward our success and according to tenure. The next step, I said, was to conduct a three-year audit, sign a few legal documents, and get ready to rock and roll.

I said, "We're going to be rich!"

As soon as those words left my lips, a raucous cheer went up and I saw high fives being exchanged all over the room. Everyone seemed genuinely excited and grateful for such an awesome opportunity. They were in the right place at the right time, and this deal was destined to enhance all our careers.

As the meeting came to a close, I asked for questions, but there were none. The room was buzzing with excitement and people were enthusiastically talking amongst themselves. I whistled again and held up my hand for silence and asked Greg to say grace. When he finished delivering his elegant prayer, I shouted, *"Let's eat!"* and immediately everyone rushed the pizza tables.

I circulated through the room, shaking hands and congratulating employees and in turn being congratulated. Then Teresa and I left for the day. I practically never took a day off, but this was a special day and in fact was so special that I decided, what the heck, I'd take the entire weekend off. I'd earned it!

Teresa, the boys, and I went out to eat that night to celebrate over an all-you-can-eat dinner of snow crabs. My youngest son, Jon, embarrassed us by going back for more at least three or four times. The rest of the weekend was spent lounging around our pool with our closest friends and their families and just enjoying life.

Monday I went in to work completely rested, with a huge smile on my face and ready to conquer the world. I was astonished when Ralph, my controller, immediately came into my office and told me that he was resigning. Ralph had worked for me for *seven years* and was one of my most trusted and key employees. Moreover, he had been like a son to me and even had a key to my house and would house-sit whenever our family was out of town.

I was doubly taken aback by his resignation because he was one of the select few that I'd kept informed of the progress that had been made on the Big Idea. I'd made it vividly clear that when this deal went through I was going to promote him to senior vice president, give him a nice raise and bonus opportunity, and give him substantial stock options. I couldn't understand how, in light of all this good news, he wanted to resign; it was just too weird.

When I questioned him as to why he was leaving, he told me that his father-in-law had offered him a management position and partial ownership in their small South Georgia family business, which was a glass and mirror installation business.

I exclaimed, "You gotta be kidding me!" I was aghast. This was just too bizarre. Here we were, about to become a hundred-million-dollar company; Ralph would become a senior vice president and would be offered enough stock options to make him filthy rich the moment that we took the thing public; and he was going to throw it all away in exchange for a partial ownership in a cheesy little glass and mirror installation company?

I said, "For crying out loud, Ralph, have you lost your mind?"

He soberly looked at me and said that his decision was final and he was resigning *effective today*.

I went two-stage ballistic when he informed me of that. He was in charge of payroll, payables, receivables, general ledger, and taxes, not to mention being solely responsible for all our computer backup tapes. There was no second in command! This was a major blow to our company, and I told him so.

He told me that he couldn't give me any notice because his father-in-law wanted him to start right away. I told him that I didn't give a damn what his father-in-law wanted, he was too vital to our operations to just leave us twisting in the wind like that. No professional person would ever leave that suddenly, especially after seven years.

"For Christ's sake, Ralph, you're like a son to me. What do you mean you aren't giving me any notice?"

By now I was standing face-to-face screaming, and I could see fear in his eyes. He reluctantly agreed to give me one week. When I complained that one week was not enough, he said he'd work long hours, all night if necessary, and he promised to leave us in good shape. But he was adamant that he could stay only for one more week. He said that once he brought everything up to date, he could bring my CPA up to date in an hour or so; and then the CPA could easily handle it from there until I could find, hire, and train another controller.

I realized that it was hopeless and his mind was firmly made up. Sadly I agreed and shook hands with him and wished him all the best with his new opportunity. That night Teresa and I decided to throw a going-away party for him and hold it the very next weekend, which just happened to be the Fourth of July weekend. We would have it at our house and have a caterer bring in barbecue, order a keg of beer, and even hire a band. I would invite the entire company and their families and give him a send-off to be remembered. And while we were at it, we could celebrate the Big Idea deal at the same time.

True to his word, he worked far into the night each night as he prepared to leave. He brought me hundreds of checks to sign for various vendors as he brought payables completely up to date. He did all the month-end reports and informed me that all the files were current and the bank reconcilement was finished; and he said that he would brief my CPA on the taxes. He also said that he'd spend time with me on how to conduct computer backup and he'd explain related details no later than the end of the week.

Wednesday, my local insurance man, Jerry Jackson, came by to see me. He was the ringleader of the movers and shakers in the community and was young and popular, and he was considering running for mayor. He would often come by to update me on the local happenings and gossip around town. When I saw him standing outside my office, I heartily greeted and welcomed him.

I noticed that he was acting uncharacteristically uncomfortable. His eyes nervously darted back and forth, looking behind him as if he was being followed or something. He had a strange look. Then in what amounted to little more than a strained whisper, he asked if he could come into my office.

I boomed back at him, "Sure man, come on in."

As he walked in, he asked if I'd mind if he closed the door.

I answered, "Of course not Jerry, have a seat." By now I was as curious as a cat, wondering why he was acting so peculiar.

He softly closed the door behind him and took a seat directly across from me.

I smiled and asked in jest, "What's up with all the cloak-and-dagger stuff, Jerry? You're acting like the spy who came in from the cold and its 90 degrees outside." I chuckled. "Are you being tailed or something?"

He replied in a very serious tone, "There's something that I think you should know, Bob. Your controller came by my office at lunch and told me that he plans to open a wildlife-artist supply company identical to yours in Grayson." That was a small community about 20 minutes from my headquarters in Monroe. "He wants me to write an insurance policy for it. He's setting up shop to compete with you."

I was stunned. "Are you kidding me?"

His stone-cold serious expression and silence were enough for me to understand that he wasn't kidding.

"That son of a bitch!"

"Bob you should also know that he's been going all over town, including to the bank, telling anyone who will listen that you've been keeping two sets of books and are a crook, and he's quitting because he doesn't want any part of it. I don't know what's going on. I don't think you're dishonest and don't believe a word of it, but felt you should know."

I was in shock and totally speechless. I said, "I can't believe it. Two sets of books? That's nothing but a crazy lie. I'm gonna get him in here right now."

Jerry held up his hand and said, "Wait! Please! I know you wouldn't have two sets of books, Bob, and you're certainly no crook. I'm sure the others around town feel the same. This whole thing is just really wacky. I'd appreciate it, though, if you wouldn't tell him that we had this conversation and wait until I get out of here before confronting him with it. I don't want to be caught in the middle."

I nodded, "Sure, sure, no problem, Jerry. I don't know what's going on, but I intend to find out. I can't believe he'd say or do something like that."

Jerry left and I could feel white-hot anger rising. I immediately stormed into Ralph's office and asked him if it was true. I was nearly floored when he calmly, almost nonchalantly, answered yes. He went on to admit that he was opening his own company in Grayson and there was nothing I could do about it and then he looked at me in a very defiant manner as though he hated my guts.

I balled up my fists by my sides and screamed loud enough to be heard in the neighboring county, "Get the hell out of here!"

His face turned beet red and he hastily headed for the door. I wanted to beat him to a pulp, but somehow I contained my rage and didn't physically attack him. It's a good thing I didn't know then what I would soon find out, or I'd probably have killed him.

The events that followed were nightmarish. Several key employees that worked in operations didn't show up the next day, including my sales manager, purchasing agent, and warehouse manager. Approximately a dozen of my high- and low-level employees quit with no notice and went to work for Ralph's new company, which he immediately began running out of the basement of his home.

When I examined my accounting records, I discovered that my general ledger had been completely erased and that all our backup tapes were missing. Computer records were not the only thing missing: Hard-copy paper files were gone too. All my vendor files were empty and I had no way of knowing how much, or to whom, money might be owed. The same held true for receivables and taxes; even our bank reconcilements were nowhere to be found. All my accounting data had disappeared!

I hastily ordered a physical inventory to be conducted and made the sickening discovery that approximately $300,000—or about 80 percent—of my inventory was missing. In effect, my shelves were bare.

Next we checked with the bank and discovered that my bank account was empty. It got worse: Not only was it empty, I was bouncing checks like crazy. (WASCO had never bounced a check.) When we reached overdrawn status, the bank honored them for a while, but then I got the call that they'd cut off the credit line and were returning checks. An unbelievable $275,000 in bad checks had amassed.

When I heard this piece of news, I remembered my controller working late nights and bringing me hundreds of checks to sign, along with a report showing that I would still have $25,000 available after signing all those hundreds of checks and bringing payables to a completely current stage.

The entire operation was in complete bedlam. In a panic, I called my investor in the hopes that he might help me out. He wouldn't even take my call. I persisted and was so insistent that finally his acquisitions guy got on the line and told me that my former controller had called and told them the same story that he spread around town about the two sets of books and that I was a crook.

I immediately denied it, of course, but he said that the investor had an unbreakable rule of never investing in any company with even a hint of dishonesty. He told me that if I straightened it all out, I should give him a call; otherwise don't bother. In other words, they believed Ralph and not me. So much for all the smiles, handshakes, pats on the back, and glowing remarks about what a brilliant businessperson I was.

I soon discovered that it wasn't just the investor who dropped me like a hot rock; it was everyone with whom I had any financial dealings. At the first sign of trouble, my so-called friends scattered like rats in a dark room when you flick on a light. I quickly found out that I didn't have any friends. My entourage and supporters were gone as soon as the money disappeared. In spite of Jerry's ringing support in my office, members of the movers-and-shakers club were among the first to go, beginning with my banker, who was threatening to sue.

My suppliers were next. The bank had closed my account when the checks started hitting, and as soon as they quit covering those payments, nearly 300 of my vendors received nonsufficient funds checks that couldn't be sent back through the bank again. To a vendor, all my former "good" friends throughout the industry were refusing to provide me with credit or even ship to me until I made those checks good. Many were threatening to sue.

In just three days I discovered that I had no inventory and no money to buy more, that none of my suppliers would extend me credit, and that no one in their right mind was going to loan me money with my financial records in ruin.

With no inventory, I couldn't ship orders and receive money. Further, I couldn't make payroll, pay utilities, pay UPS, or pay anything. The situation was critical and I had no choice but to immediately order a massive layoff. I reduced our workforce from 65 employees to just 19 in three days. I completely closed down our plant in Idaho and all those employees lost their jobs, including my good friend Jim Hall, who declined my offer to leave his Idaho home and work out of Georgia in such tenuous circumstances.

I called all the remaining employees together and briefed them on what I knew so far. I explained the situation in excruciating detail and I was honest in telling them that I wasn't sure if we could even recover from what appeared to be a massive theft of the majority of our current assets. I told them our cash on hand and inventory were gone, and we'd been deliberately sabotaged. Someone had destroyed our financial records and spread lies all over town about me.

I warned that, as we fought our way through this situation, there were no guarantees I could pay them on time. I also said that if they remained on board, paychecks might be sporadic and would depend entirely on cash receipts.

The situation was grim and they needed to know. These were the most loyal of the loyal employees that I had, and as I looked around the room, I could see the concern on their faces. They loved the company but they had bills to pay and mortgage payments to meet. I wouldn't blame them if they resigned too.

It was as though God had allowed me to experience the utmost height of elation—I was so tantalizingly close to consummating the deal for my Big Idea—and when super-success was seemingly within my grasp, I was crushed like a cockroach crawling across the floor. A giant foot had come down hard, twisted back and forth to ensure that my back was broken and my body was thoroughly smashed, and left me as a greasy spot on the concrete.

If God's goal was to humble me, He had succeeded. I didn't feel arrogant anymore, and I definitely didn't feel much like the marketing-genius boy wonder that I'd convinced myself that I was. Helplessly I looked around at what had once been the mighty WASCO machine. I thought of all the hard work, planning, and awesome results. It was all I could do to keep from crying.

In the days that ensued, every adviser with whom I discussed my situation, including my CPA, attorney, and banker, all advised me that it would be impossible to avoid bankruptcy and that I might as well just get it over with.

The party was over!

CHAPTER SIXTY-EIGHT

After piecing together enough information to determine where I stood, the devastation was more widespread than I ever imagined. From a strictly financial perspective, the following was our situation:

1. We owed approximately $980,000 to some 300 different creditors.
2. Our bank balance was in the red to the astounding tune of $278,000.
3. My warehouse was nearly empty. I estimated that 80 percent of my stock was missing.
4. We were three months behind in payments with practically every supplier.
5. The bank had closed my corporate bank account and cancelled my credit line. (I had to go to another bank just to open an account.)
6. Our tax situation was grim. The IRS claimed we owed $50,000 in payroll taxes alone, and we had no financial records to verify the case one way or the other.
7. I now had only 19 employees instead of 65 to run a very complex operation.

How did I land in such a mess? I'd made the stupid mistake of allowing someone else to watch over my finances in their entirety, with virtually no checks and balances in place. I was too ignorant to even do my own bank reconcilements. Had I done that one thing, I would have immediately seen that the actual bank accounts were not matching the falsified reports that I was being given.

As an example, the last financial report that I received just prior to all hell breaking loose indicated that we were in excellent financial standing, with $25,000 in the bank and all payables current. The report was all fabricated.

I was honest and trusted others to be honest too. In other words, I was dumb and gullible.

I was also preoccupied. At the time this occurred I was simultaneously writing/editing three different books on three different subjects. I was editor and publisher of our magazine. I was responsible for adding hundreds of new products to our catalogs monthly, and was CEO of seven subsidiaries with management responsibilities too numerous to mention. I was engrossed with working on the Big Idea and a zillion other projects.

Accounting was not my job and I trusted the man who was doing it. Why he suddenly resigned the day after I announced that we would immediately need to begin conducting a three-year audit made sense to me now. But *now* was too late.

If any singular word described my mood it would be MAD! I was mad at myself for allowing this to happen right under my nose, I was mad at my "friends" for turning on me, but most of all I was mad at Ralph and the disloyal employees who joined him. I was determined to make them pay for what they'd done, but more urgent matters faced me—like trying to prevent the total collapse of my companies.

Jerry Plant, my CPA, called and asked for a meeting and then invited himself to dinner. He suggested that we could talk while we fished and afterward Teresa could fry up our catch and we could continue our discussions over dinner and a beer (or two or three). I welcomed the idea; fishing would be a good diversion from the crushing pressure that I was undergoing.

He came over later that afternoon and we went out onto the dock that overlooked the pond in my backyard. We baited up our hooks with crickets and started fishing for the hungry bluegill and channel catfish that were abundantly milling around the surface, eating the fish food I'd thrown in to attract them. It was a beautiful day with hardly a cloud in the deep-blue sky. We both had a cold beer by our sides and if a casual observer had seen us in that peaceful and serene setting, they would have never guessed the utter ruin, devastation, and chaos I was facing.

Characteristic of someone short and round, Jerry was always jovial and in a good mood. He fit the stereotype of an accountant by appearing to be somewhat of a nerd, with his thick glasses, pudgy appearance, and partially balding head. He was a smart man and had been doing my taxes and advising me for five or six years. I respected his opinion on most matters of finance.

I could tell he was greatly distressed and something was on his mind. It seemed completely out of character for him to have such a dead serious look on his face. Finally he seemed to muster enough courage to get what was bothering him off his chest. He said in his most solemn voice, "Bob, I'm your friend and what I'm going to tell you is from one friend to another. You are an incredibly smart guy and you made a good run at this, but it's time to give it up. I've analyzed it from every angle and WASCO is just too far gone for you to salvage. You can easily find a job making good money and without question will excel at whatever you do. I'm advising you to do just that. You really shouldn't be in business for yourself."

Jerry was no different from any of the rest of them. Everyone was advising me to take bankruptcy and call it a day. I don't know why I kept stubbornly refusing to heed their advice, but I'd taken the position that as long as no one sued me, I was not going to quit. He started to further reinforce his point, but I just held up my hand and said, "Shut up and fish Jerry!"

That was the last time he ever suggested that I quit.

All my life I'd been told that I couldn't/wouldn't succeed, and this situation made me even more determined than ever to prove people wrong. This was a deep hole, however, maybe even a bottomless pit; and short of another miracle in my life, it just might be impossible to pull this one off.

After I finally realized just how bad my situation was, I went to my knees and fervently prayed. I didn't come away with any warm and fuzzy feeling. I was quite sure God was angry at me for acting the way I had, and it was not beyond the realm of possibility that I was being punished by Him for my bad behavior. In fact, I was pretty sure that this was the case. I wasn't anticipating any miracles dropping from heaven like manna to pull me out of this one.

I questioned whether or not I was up to the daunting task of pulling WASCO back from the brink, and that bit about "I can do all things through Christ who strengthens me" rang hollow as the enormity of the task overwhelmed me.

Not that long ago, God had rescued me from far worse, and He'd blessed my life beyond measure. But my faith that God would help me out this time around was now at its weakest point. I knew in my heart that God had transformed me, but then I'd turned my back on Him.

When I enjoyed some success, I screwed up big-time by becoming pompous and arrogant and taking credit for all the accomplishments myself. Now it was time to try to dig out of the hole that I'd dug for myself, and I had the distinct feeling that God had decided to step aside and allow me to fight my way out of it *by myself.*

I smiled as I thought of Jenny's unwavering support for me. I mused that if she were still alive she'd no doubt be encouraging and cheering me on with her reassuring million-dollar smile. I missed her more than ever, but she was gone.

Teresa was just plain scared. Many times in our marriage when our finances looked bleak, I told her, "Don't worry, something will turn up." And something always did. But we'd never faced a situation this dire, and she'd never faced real adversity in her entire fairy-tale life. Like me, she wanted to have faith but was having a tough time with it. We were almost sure to lose our home and everything we owned, and she was frightened.

After mulling over whether it was right or wrong, tough or impossible, I decided to forge ahead. I reasoned that WASCO was still an excellent company with excellent products, and *Breakthrough* magazine was the best of its kind in the world, as were our books and videos. Polytranspar was unequaled and in high demand, and the World Championships that I'd established were the most coveted events in our industry.

I didn't think the majority of our loyal customers would ever desert us. I just needed enough resources to get back on track before our *outstanding* customer service turned into *crappy* customer service. Too many back orders and not enough personnel to ship within 24 hours would have done that. I knew that I had to act quickly. It was only a matter of time before the service would begin to head downhill fast, and I knew that many customers wouldn't like it, not even a little. I hoped most of them would remain loyal and refrain from adopting the philosophy, "What have you done for me lately?"

My first thought was to borrow some money, but after thinking about it I realized that it would be virtually impossible. Lenders make loans based on the three C's.

1. Collateral
2. Credit
3. Character

I didn't have any remaining collateral. My home had already been heavily mortgaged to provide money for earlier expansion of my business. All my other assets had been pledged to the bank as collateral for our credit line, which had been completely exhausted paying overdrawn checks.

As for our credit, I had checks bouncing everywhere and my bills were all overdue. I could only imagine how bad my credit rating was at that moment.

The character issue was the most frustrating of all and caused me the most consternation and angst. Longtime "friends" believed the crook instead of the victim. It was as though they *wanted* to believe the worst. The very person who was dishonest was telling everyone that it was *me* who was dishonest and amazingly they believed *him* and not me.

On a long shot, I called the other investor from Denver who wanted to take us public with his fund. He was delighted when I called because he was hopping mad at me for selecting the private investor instead of him. He'd been waiting for an opportunity to tell me what a lowlife I was for stringing him and his fund along in order to gain leverage in my negotiations with the private investor.

As for my current dilemma, he got a good laugh out of it.

Borrowing money was out. I would just have to make it on my own. I put a positive spin on it by telling myself that it was actually a good thing. I already had too much debt now and borrowing more money would just aggravate the situation.

In our business model, the bulk of our revenue came from shipping orders directly to customers via UPS with collect-on-delivery terms. The balance of our revenue was primarily money that we received from distributor orders for my Polytranspar paints. They paid on 30-day terms.

In order to conduct business, we relied on regular shipments from our suppliers. We marked up and resold some products, and utilized others as raw materials in manufacturing our own products. Without these materials, we couldn't ship goods to our customers and collect cash. The problem was that practically all my suppliers had now put me on a COD-only basis (it had to be a cashier's check) due to the bounced checks.

I needed cash in order to generate cash. We were receiving orders from our loyal customers every day, but the overwhelming majority were COD. Only a small percentage were prepaid, and we had begun back-ordering nearly everything on each order because our inventory was so low. To sum it up, our deposits were low and our bills were high.

To complicate things further, everyone and his brother was threatening to sue. I decided to write to our customers and explain what had happened. I told them that we had a large sum of money embezzled from us and as a result were struggling. I expressed confidence that we would recover and asked them to please be patient with the back-order situation. If it had happened in this day and age, I could easily have sent them all an e-mail, but e-mail had not been invented yet, so I had to actually send letters to 50,000 of my best customers—and that in itself cost a substantial amount of money.

Next I made a list of critical needs and expenses that we had to address in order to survive. It was essential that we keep the lights on and the toll-free order phones ringing; we needed to pay UPS, make payroll, and keep sufficient inventory on hand to service enough orders to keep money rolling in. It became imperative to manage our precious cash with the utmost precision—we didn't have one dollar to spare.

I considered how I'd feel if our situations were reversed. To be sure, if I were one of my creditors, I would be upset about not being paid in a timely fashion. But as long as I was receiving at least some money each month and saw that WASCO was trying its best to do the right thing by me, I wouldn't sue. (That's just good business.)

I wrote every creditor and explained what had happened and told them that I didn't like the situation any more than they did. I explained that I was a victim of a crime and I asked them to put themselves in my position. I reminded them that but for the grace of God, the same thing could happen to them. I emphasized that I was honest and had done business with them for years and they knew that I was honest. I assured them that I was determined to pay them every last penny they were owed; but if they sued me, I warned, I'd be forced to go into bankruptcy and they'd receive pennies on the dollar (if anything).

I was adamant that I would pay principal only, and was very up front in informing them that I absolutely refused to pay any interest, late charges, fees for bounced checks, or similar charges under any circumstances. If their firm insisted on those kinds of charges and they were willing to take me to court to force the issue, then they should go ahead and notify me. I told them I would immediately file bankruptcy because I was not going to pay anything but principal. My bank was the most vehemently opposed to this policy, but I wouldn't budge even a little. They ultimately "blinked" and waived all their many charges.

As for payment terms, I offered no guarantees, aside from my solemn promise that I would pay every last one of them at least something each month (even if it was just $5). I said that it would take a while to repay everyone totally, but as conditions improved I would increase the amount of my payments until they were paid in full.

I promised to send them a letter updating the situation each month along with their payment. I closed the letter by reemphasizing that if any one vendor sued me, I would necessarily be forced to file bankruptcy.

Even though I owed an enormous amount of money in total, I was fortunate that I owed it in relatively small amounts to numerous vendors. Aside from the bank, most of the debt I owed was more like $1,000 here or $1,500 there, and so on. Most vendors would not sue for such a small amount, but they could effectively cripple me if they cut my shipments off. So I had to be careful in dealing with them.

I made a list, ranking the most vital suppliers down to the least. Any money that I received that was in excess of my critical-needs list was divided amongst them, beginning with the most vital. Some of them actually were sent as little as $5 a month in the beginning; others received considerably more. It was all determined on a pro rata basis according to how much I owed, how critical they were to my operation, and how much cash became available to dole out.

The key was not to avoid their calls but to keep them informed. And most important, I had to try my utmost to pay them something every month (come hell or high water).

It was a miserable time for me and I dreaded going to work. Every call I took was from some angry creditor. Though I was determined to take every single call and not avoid anyone, I was resolute that I wasn't going to be anybody's whipping boy. I was a *victim* of a crime and I was quick to remind them of it. I told them that I didn't like the situation any more than they did, and was working hard day and night to resolve the crisis.

I made the mistake one time of smarting off to my banker and angrily telling him, "You can't get blood out of a turnip." He turned beet red and angrily replied, "Yeah, but I can sure as hell get the turnip." After that incident, no matter how tempted I was to pop off, I kept my big mouth shut. Like it or not, I had to allow them to vent, if for nothing more than to make them feel better. I needed them more than they needed me.

I was nauseous throughout most days, as vendor after angry vendor let me know what they thought of me and my company. I would hold the phone away from my ear and when they were finished spewing, I would grit my teeth and softly say in the nicest voice I could muster, "Things will be back to normal soon. Please just bear with us a little longer." Then I'd thank them kindly for their patience.

It wasn't long before customers also started calling to complain. I'd worked so hard to earn the reputation of having the best service in the industry; it was just heartbreaking to hear them angrily denouncing me and our great company.

Here I was, the former king of the industry, and now everyone in the industry was talking to me as though I were some common check-bouncing criminal. My reputation had been severely damaged and I was humiliated daily. It'd taken me seven long, hard years of mind-numbing work to build WASCO into the number one company in the industry. And God had allowed the company and me to be struck down practically overnight. His lesson in humility was not an easy one to endure.

As for cutting costs, everything was on the table. I called my insurance guy and canceled all my insurance policies. Since I didn't have a single financial record in the building to back up what had happened, I had no way of proving that a theft had even occurred, and my word apparently counted for nothing. My cash, inventory, and even office supplies had been stolen, and my business records had been willfully sabotaged. And yet my insurance company didn't pay a single dime.

I reasoned that if they wouldn't pay this catastrophic claim, they wouldn't pay any claim. I mused that I probably was going to end up bankrupt anyway, so what the heck. The insurance refund from my canceled policy came in very handy, and I immediately put it to better use. I was now operating uninsured but didn't give it a second thought.

Things changed drastically at WASCO. In days gone by someone would come into my office and say that they needed a computer or similar item and I would angrily scold them, "Well order it already! Why are you bothering me with crap like that? Can't you see I'm busy?"

Now if someone came in my office and so much as asked for a replacement pencil, I would demand, "Where's your stub? Bring it to me for inspection, and I'll forewarn you now that it had better not be over an inch long."

I coined the term, "Get by or justify!" and no money would be spent unless someone built a strong case for spending it; they also had to submit the request in writing as a purchase requisition and had to bring it to me in person before receiving an approved purchase order. Considering the mood I was in, not many wanted to venture into my office for any purpose, much less to request that we spend money.

Once I had my operation stabilized and had put a good system into place, work became exceedingly boring. I was an entrepreneur who loved to build and expand, but I was in a bare-bones/cut back to the absolute minimum/survival mode, and I could easily have run the greatly reduced operation of WASCO and its subsidiaries in my sleep. For the first time ever we weren't expanding or building anything, and we had nothing spectacular to look forward to. We were strictly a meat-and-potatoes operation now. I hated going to work for the first time ever.

My passion was gone.

All the anger that had been seething and bubbling inside me now began to channel toward one source: Ralph and his little band of followers. One way or the other I was going to make them pay. When I was in my bed at night, I thought for hours about breaking every bone in Ralph's body with a baseball bat, beginning with both of his knees. I wanted to make him suffer for days on end in an agonizing pain, and only then would I finish him off. It wasn't long before I put one of my son's baseball bats in the backseat of my car for just that purpose.

Once I thought I saw him driving down Highway 78. I immediately turned around in the middle of the four-lane highway—with cars coming both ways. I barely avoided turning my car over and/or crashing into somebody. With tires squealing, I gunned it for all it was worth, swerving back and forth in and out of traffic, until I caught up with what I thought was his car.

My pistol was in my hand when I pulled up beside the car, but it wasn't Ralph. It was fortunate for him (and for me) that he wasn't in that car because I do believe that I would have shot him right then and right there.

I was on a dangerous path to a dark place. Now that I had somewhat stabilized my business, I was turning my full attention to Ralph.

My dark side was insanely laughing in anticipation. Violence was back!

CHAPTER SIXTY-NINE

I drove back to my house, walked into my bedroom, and shut the door. I sat on the edge of my bed and dejectedly reflected upon what I'd become. I slowly shook my head in disbelief as the insanity of it sunk in. Yes Ralph had stolen from me and wrecked my company, but I was driving around with a baseball bat and handgun in my car fully intent on beating him senseless and then shooting him right between the eyes as he begged for his life.

This mind-set was pure evil and straight out of hell. My dark side had returned with a vengeance, and I was fearful that Satan was regaining possession of my soul. I was terrified to even think about that possibility. I realized I was right back where I was when I arrived in Atlanta some 18 years ago. I knelt down beside my bed and asked God to forgive all the stupid things I'd done—leaving my family, having foolish pride and arrogance, and lusting for power and money. I especially asked for forgiveness for wanting to maim and kill Ralph. I begged Him to please forgive and help me—one more time.

Afterward I put my son's baseball bat back in his closet and my handgun back on the top shelf of my closet. Those options were completely off the table now. My urge to kill Ralph was gone, but I still wanted to see him go down.

A mature Christian would have obediently allowed God to avenge Ralph according to His promise in Romans 12:19, "Do not take revenge, my friends, but leave room for God's wrath, for it is written: 'It is mine to avenge; I will repay,' says the Lord."

But I was not a mature Christian. I was still just as determined to retaliate and seek vengeance as before, only now I was determined to work within the confines of the law. I now was totally obsessed with putting Ralph behind bars and could think of little else.

I found that it was far more difficult than I anticipated. Shortly after I'd discovered the plot and realized the scope of what had happened, I'd called the police to report the crime. WASCO was located in the tiny rural town of Monroe, Georgia, and the town's investigative and prosecutorial resources were very limited. They sent over a detective and I explained in detail that cash, inventory, and supplies were missing, and that my general ledger had been erased and financial records destroyed. I also told him who did it and where he lived, and I revealed the motive: his stated desire to start a business similar to mine in order to compete with me.

The detective was negative from the beginning, stating that I had little to go on. He said such is often the case with white-collar crimes and a lack of evidence is why they're among the toughest to prosecute. In this case, there were no eyewitnesses to any theft and no one actually observed my financial records being destroyed. Neither could they could garner fingerprints off broken-down doors or smashed windows where someone forced his way into the building. For all practical purposes, there was no sign that anyone had even committed a crime. Without hard evidence, it would be impossible to prove anything in court. It would be my word against Ralph's.

The detective summed it up by saying, "Had these thieves broken into your building during the dead of night and stolen from you and destroyed your records, you would have been far better off from a prosecutorial perspective. (That was the same line my insurance man had given me right before he rejected my claim.)

That is not what I wanted to hear. I wanted that cop to obtain a search warrant and go over to Ralph's house and recover my stolen property; there he would find all the proof he needed. I was livid and told him that half my damn warehouse was in Ralph's basement at this very moment and *I wanted it back!*

He shook his head and said he was sorry, but there just wasn't enough to go on. No judge would issue a search warrant without more evidence. Frustrated, I decided to go over his head and went downtown to see the district attorney and plead my case directly to him. I was promptly shuffled off to the assistant DA, and to say I was disappointed would be an understatement. For one thing, he didn't look like he was old enough to be out of high school, much less be a graduate of law school. He had a high-pitched voice like a little kid and I sardonically wondered if he had even reached puberty yet, much less ever tried a case.

After hearing me out, he repeated nearly verbatim what the detective had told me. He summed it up by saying, "Bring me some hard evidence and we'll talk; otherwise there is little else I can do."

I caustically shot back, "Do I look like a policeman? Why not make your detective *investigate* the crime by obtaining a search warrant, and let *him* bring you some hard evidence?"

That just made him angry. I could see it was useless and left.

Over the next several months I spent hundreds of hours poring over various bits and scraps of evidence that I could scrounge. I found some old reports that depicted my before-and-after inventory balances. These reports clearly showed that massive amounts of product had disappeared off the shelves. I went to the bank and requested electronic copies of my bank records. I reviewed deposits and withdrawals, and they also showed a significant change in activity and lower deposits for the six-month period prior to my discovery of the theft. To me, this indicated that someone was stealing money.

I furnished the assistant DA with mounds of documents, accompanied by my extensive written analysis detailing the significance of the evidence and how it implicated Ralph.

I don't think he even looked at any of it. Every time I brought him a new batch of evidence, he would smile and tell me he would review it, and then I wouldn't hear another word from him.

Frustrated, I started calling his office every day; it finally reached a point where he wouldn't take my calls. When he stopped taking my calls, I started dropping by his office. Soon his pimple-faced secretary wouldn't allow me in to see him. I was furious.

I was Furious, but helpless, and then I finally got a break.

Soon after we'd discovered the embezzlement, I'd identified the name of Ralph's new company by name, both in a letter sent out to all my customers and in an editorial in *Breakthrough* magazine. I'd informed them that Ralph, a trusted employee of ours, had just stolen everything that he could get his hands on and was now starting a company to compete with WASCO. I warned them to beware of him because he was a criminal.

When his catalogs started reaching some of my loyal customers, they recognized him as being the person I'd cautioned them about, and immediately called to notify me. I asked them to send me their copy of Ralph's catalog and they did.

When I saw the first one I immediately noticed the mailing label and, lo and behold, there was the expiration code for *Breakthrough* magazine.

Gotcha!

We printed this code on all our mailing labels to make subscribers aware of their subscription's expiration date. The month and year appeared at the bottom of the mailing label, below the name and address, as in the example shown below.

John Doe
2323 Pine Street
Greenville FL 32331
6/88

The 6/88 meant that this customer's subscription to *Breakthrough* would expire in June 1988. These codes were unique to each subscriber and had absolutely nothing to do with the mailing address, so it would be impossible for Ralph to explain how my magazine's proprietary subscription-expiration data was printed on his catalog's mailing labels unless he had stolen my mailing list. I now had irrefutable hard evidence that he'd ripped me off.

This was no insignificant crime. A customer list is the most valuable and treasured asset of a mail-order company. It is how the company makes its money. Finding out who will buy through the mail and then mailing to them often is the secret to success in this business. WASCO's list represented seven years and millions of dollars of advertising and my grooming and development work, and I had no doubt that it was the most comprehensive list of wildlife artists *who would buy through the mail* to be found anywhere in the world.

Had Ralph been smart, he would have deleted the subscription expiration codes before using the list, and no one would have ever been able to prove that he did not come by the names legitimately. Either he was too lazy, or too confident that he could get away with it, or (more likely) too stupid to realize what he'd done. It was a bonehead move!

This was the break that I'd long been awaiting—finally some hard evidence that would prove once and for all that Ralph was a thief.

I excitedly took the catalogs down to the ADA's office. The pimple-headed secretary tried to stonewall me again, but this time I told her I wasn't leaving until I saw him. If necessary, I said, I'd sit there all day. I excitedly told her to inform him that I now had in hand the hard, conclusive evidence that would break the case.

She frowned at me over her red horn-rimmed glasses and absentmindedly flipped at her heavily bleached, straw-looking hair as she weighed my request. Obviously she was perplexed. She had standing orders to dust me off and not allow me to see him, but she didn't want me hanging around her desk all day either. Finally she went into his office, and in a few minutes he came out to greet me. I followed him into his office and excitedly showed him my "smoking gun"—Ralph's catalogs with my mailing labels on them.

At this time, desktop computers were just beginning to come of age and very few offices even had one yet. It was obvious to me that the ADA was one of those people who didn't have one, and it soon became crystal clear that he knew absolutely nothing about computer technology. He seemed mystified as I tried to explain to him how Ralph had accessed our computer system in the dead of night and downloaded my customer list, and then utilized it to mail his catalogs to all my customers. He acted as though I was talking in a foreign language.

I showed him the expiration codes and explained how they worked, and then nodded approvingly, expecting a positive reaction from him. He just looked at me with a near glaze in his eyes, like someone who had just undergone a lobotomy. It was apparent that he didn't have a clue. I explained it again and again. I don't think he ever understood what I was telling him. If he did, he wasn't impressed in the least. He told me that he would take this new evidence into consideration and get back to me in a few days.

I felt like a deflated balloon. Here was the break that I'd been waiting for, and this guy was just blowing me off again. I waited a week for a response, and then I went back to his office. When I was shown in, I saw several large stacks of file folders cluttering his desk and various papers strewn everywhere. He pointed to the piles and told me that my file was just one of many and that he was too busy working other cases to put any time into my case yet.

When I began to complain, he held up his hand and sarcastically replied that he had more important crimes to work on than a white-collar crime.

That was it. I had had all I could take! I screamed, "You **idiot**, 46 Georgians lost their jobs because of this white-collar crime and I'm facing financial ruin! You asked for hard evidence and I gave it to you. Now I want this criminal prosecuted! If you're too stupid to understand computers, then get someone in here to help."

His face flushed crimson red and he almost choked up as he told me to leave.

When I returned to my office I was so mad that I called the governor's office. Perhaps Governor Joe Frank Harris was interested in prosecuting someone who had caused 46 Georgians to lose their jobs. I wasn't put through to him and some secretary gave me the runaround. I drove to the state capitol in downtown Atlanta and walked into the governor's outer office. I told the secretary that I wanted to see him and briefly explained what was happening. She of course would not allow me to meet with him, but I did meet with three different people on his staff and finally ended up with the name of an investigator at the GBI (Georgia Bureau of Investigation) whom they said would help me.

Unlike the local authorities, the GBI agent was sympathetic, professional, knowledgeable, and very helpful. He told me that there was a new law on the books that dealt with accessing a computer for fraudulent purposes. The best news was that it had some teeth to it. The crime was classified as a major felony punishable by 15 years in prison and a $50,000 fine. The GBI agent told me that computer-technology cases were very new and many prosecutors were not up to speed on them yet. He graciously volunteered to call my local DA's office so he could offer assistance from his office. He also told me he would do what he could from an investigatory standpoint.

"Awesome!" I thanked him profusely.

The GBI agent's call to the DA's office made all the difference and seemed to magically unlock the gate. Within a month my case went before a grand jury.

It was an open-and-shut case and the evidence was irrefutable. I was the only witness to appear before the grand jury. I showed the jurors Ralph's catalogs with my expiration codes on them and explained their purpose and made it vividly clear that they were unique to our company. When I finished my testimony, the ADA asked the jury if they had any additional questions for me and there were none.

I was excused and went back outside and sat on an old-time wooden bench that looked like an antique church pew, and there I waited while they convened in secret. In less than a minute, the ADA came out and said they had indicted him.

"YES!" I was elated.

Ralph was promptly arrested and charged with the major felony of accessing a computer for fraudulent purposes and he spent the night in jail. Subsequently he was released on $25,000 bond. I was as happy as a kid with a new puppy and felt vindicated. Justice just might prevail after all.

Or maybe not. Now the problem was setting a trial date. The ADA kept putting me off and the case languished for months. Finally I got the long-awaited call to see the ADA. I excitedly drove over to his office and assumed that I was going to be interviewed in preparation for the trial.

When I arrived the detective and the assistant DA were sitting there, and both appeared to be blazing mad. The ADA told me that Ralph's attorney had called and revealed that I'd called Ralph and tried to get him to pay me $15,000 in exchange for my "dropping the case against him." Before I could respond, the ADA told me that what I had done was illegal and a *serious* crime, and that he had a good mind to put *me* in jail.

I came completely unglued. ***"You want to put ME in jail?***

"ARE YOU CRAZY?

"I haven't so much as seen that idiot since he left my company, much less talked to him. I didn't try to bribe anyone. I wouldn't drop this case for a million dollars! I want that asshole behind bars!"

Then I went off on him again, at the top of my lungs. ***"You want to believe that pathological liar criminal instead of ME? ARE YOU CRAZY?"***

"Mr. Williamson, either you *shut up* and get the hell out of here or I'm going to have you arrested!" the ADA warned.

I left.

This was the ultimate insult. I decided that I was through with the ADA. I called the DA himself and, as expected, they wouldn't put me through to him. It didn't matter. I left a message for him that was hot enough to fry an egg. I told his secretary to relay to him that I was going to contact every newspaper reporter in Georgia and tell them how badly his office had botched this case and how the DA's office was now taking sides with a low-down criminal and persecuting a victim of a crime.

This criminal had cost 46 Georgians their jobs and instead of prosecuting him, they wanted to go after me. I railed against the ADA, stating that he was incompetent and ignorant and didn't even know how to turn a computer on, much less prosecute a crime involving one. I said that his office was a disgrace to the legal system and I intended to let anyone and everyone who would listen know about it.

I told his secretary to inform him that today I was going to make an appeal directly to the governor's office and the GBI to initiate an investigation of him and his office to determine why they hadn't followed the indictment with a trial and to determine if anyone in his office had accepted a bribe in connection with this case. I then told his secretary to wish him my best in getting reelected next year after this story hit the newsstand.

Early the next morning I received a call from the ADA. He told me that he had a deal for me. He said that if I'd be willing to take a polygraph test concerning the attempted bribe (and pass it, of course), he'd prosecute Ralph.

I was flabbergasted. "Let me get this straight. You want me, the victim of the crime, to take a lie-detector test before you will put the criminal on trial (who, I assume, has not been asked to take a polygraph test to back up his charge against me). Does that just about sum it up?"

"Mr. Williamson, this offer comes directly from the DA and not from me. It makes no difference to me. Take it or leave it."

I defiantly said, *"I'll take it!"*

The test was administered at GBI headquarters on the outskirts of Atlanta. When I arrived, the ADA and the detective were already there. Both had smirks on their faces and I angrily smirked right back at them and silently mouthed the words, "Go to hell" to the ADA.

I went back into the examination room with the GBI agent and he asked me if I was nervous.

I said, "I'm madder than hell about being subjected to this crap. I'm an innocent victim of a crime and here I am taking a polygraph test. Do you see anything wrong with this scenario? . . . Don't bother to answer—that's a rhetorical question."

I quickly apologized to him. "I'm sorry, it's not your fault. I'm going to tell the truth. The only thing I'm remotely concerned about is whether or not that machine is accurate; otherwise I'm fine with it."

He smiled and said, "You can rest easy Mr. Williamson, it's extremely accurate."

I calmly said, "Then let's do it."

Chapter Seventy

I'd undergone a lie-detector test in the military and already knew the drill. Look straight ahead, no moving around or tapping my foot, and simply answer yes or no and add nothing more. The GBI examiner hooked a strap around my chest and some sensors to a couple of my fingers.

I answered about 50 questions, including . . .

"Have you offered Ralph and/or his attorney $15,000 in exchange for dropping the case?
"Did you illegally maintain two sets of books at your company?
"Did you try to illegally take cash out of the company?
"Have you committed any crimes at WASCO of any nature?"

And every now and then he would throw in control questions like . . .

"Have you ever eaten a hamburger?
"Is today Monday?
"Is your name Robert?"

When he'd finished, the GBI examiner came over and began unhooking me from the machine. He was about my height but thinner. The olive tone of his skin and his short curly black hair indicated to me that he was perhaps of Italian descent. His face was pockmarked with acne scars and he didn't smile. I mused that he looked more like someone in the Italian mob than a GBI agent. He even wore a dark suit, white shirt, and thin blue tie.

I asked, "How'd I do?"

His countenance seemed to change in an instant and a warm smile replaced his frown. He replied, "You did just fine, Robert."

We walked together back to the waiting room where the ADA and detective were sitting. The GBI agent curtly told them, "This man is telling the truth."

I thought they were going to fall out of their chairs. I could see by their faces that they were convinced I'd been lying.

The examiner then abruptly turned his back on them and shook hands with me. In a very nice tone he gently said, "Thanks for coming in, Mr. Williamson. I apologize for your inconvenience and having to put you through all this trouble."

I shot him an appreciative glance and told him, "No problem. I'm just glad it's behind me."

Our deal was that if I agreed to take a lie-detector test and passed it, then the DA's office would prosecute Ralph.

They didn't.

What happened next was bizarre, to say the least. Because Ralph was a first-time offender, the DA's office offered him a plea bargain—no jail time, five years' probation, and a $15,000 fine.

Ralph's savvy lawyer promptly refused the deal and demanded a jury trial. He, of course, knew there'd only been three jury trials in the entire county the preceding year. The sparsely populated rural area just didn't have the resources or budget for such things. The lawyer knew that they wouldn't spend money prosecuting a white-collar crime when they had murders, child molestations, drug dealing, and other, more heinous offenses to deal with.

And that is exactly what happened. The case remains open, but it has never been prosecuted, even to this day. The ADA encouraged me to sue Ralph in civil court and even offered to assist, but that would have cost me an additional $16,000 in court and legal fees, not to mention another thousand or more hours of preparation. If I ultimately did win a judgment against Ralph, I felt he'd just file for bankruptcy.

This was the proverbial straw that broke the camel's back. I'd endured all that I could, and my two-year battle with the DA's office and my intense pursuit of Ralph was finally over. I went home, got down on my knees in my bedroom and did what I should have done long before. I surrendered to God and finally yielded to His command to leave vengeance to Him.

Immediately and miraculously, I felt His warm loving forgiveness, and for the first time in a long time, I felt His presence in the room with me. In an instant, I achieved total peace of mind in regard to Ralph and from that moment on I haven't given it another thought.

Today I consider this to be a major tipping point in my spiritual life.

The Bible states in Job 22:21, "Submit to God and be at peace with him; in this way prosperity will come to you." I didn't realize it at the time, but I had been at war with *God* and not Ralph. In order to achieve peace with God, I needed to submit to Him. According to the Bible, submission would yield prosperity, not just with WASCO, but with my family and my peace of mind. I had been too blind with anger and lust for revenge to turn my life over to God.

I was determined to go back to my roots and do what I did to originally achieve success. I determined that I would put God first in my life. I would love my wife and boys and conduct business in a fair, friendly, and firm manner.

I thought back to the day that I initially started my little company. At that time I had no business experience, no customer list, and my start-up capital consisted of just $1,000 that I'd borrowed on my credit card. Yet in just six months my little company had grown to multimillion-dollar status and become wildly successful.

Even though I was still heavily in debt, I had far more going for me than when I started, including a couple of hundred thousand loyal customers, excellent marketing skills and business savvy, a great line of products with superb brand recognition, and a small but solid cadre of loyal, smart, experienced, hardworking, dedicated employees.

I reasoned that if I were to quit spending thousands of hours trying to get even with Ralph and instead return to being a responsible leader for my company and concentrate on rebuilding, WASCO would again be the finest organization of its kind in the world.

Sure enough, as soon as I turned my full attention back to running my business, it immediately began to flourish. The verse from Job about submission to God and His promise of prosperity in return for obedience came alive for me.

In the end, true to His word, God took care of avenging Ralph, and his life became a nightmarish hell. I was told that his wife divorced him. She left Atlanta to return to her south Georgia home to live with her parents. And she took with her their twin sons, whom he loved with all his heart.

In spite of all the stolen assets that he used to launch his business, his fledgling artist-supply company went belly-up in just three months. He lost his home when he couldn't make his mortgage payments. He was sued for fraud by his next-door neighbor, whom he had convinced to obtain a second mortgage on his home in order to invest $50,000 in the fledgling business. And although he was never convicted of any of the crimes committed against WASCO, he did spend one night in jail and had to pay a bail bondsman to get him out. This garnered a police record for a felony arrest, and an open case on file at the courthouse—something no controller wants on his résumé.

I never saw Ralph again and have no idea where he is today.

I'd undergone hellish torment and been through excruciating punishment for my sins for years now. And I felt that God had soundly punished me and would lighten up and welcome me back into the fold now that I'd come to my senses.

I suppose God saw it differently. I think maybe He was tired of cleaning me up only to see me return to the pigsty. It was a pattern that I'd developed. I would get into serious trouble and then in my anguish call on God to rescue me. He'd do so, and as soon as the pain had passed, I'd drift away from Him and soon be right back where I started. I reminded myself of the Israelites, who throughout their history would turn to God in time of need, and then as soon as God intervened and helped them, they'd turn their backs on Him again. He punished them severely for their sins and I expected no less from Him.

I believe that God knew that I needed even harder lessons. And although I'm sure it grieved Him to see me suffer, He didn't withhold the tumultuous sad times that would soon be overwhelming me. The worst thing about it? Just as I thought I was home free, I'd once again feel another lash of the whip.

Chapter Seventy-One

Bobby Joe Crawley stood a lanky six-feet-three inches tall. He was rangy looking and had big ears. On the back of his head, his coarse black hair formed a cowlick that stood up like a tuft of stubborn grass ascending from a crack in a sidewalk. He had hazel brown eyes, a ruddy complexion, and crooked teeth. He was the spitting image of Abraham Lincoln—without a beard.

He'd been raised on a farm and still loved working in his garden on late summer evenings. He didn't look the part of a gifted computer programmer, but he was among the brightest I've ever had the pleasure of working with.

I began developing computer-software applications in-house for WASCO and its subsidiaries beginning sometime around 1982. Back then, computer technology was in its infancy and desktop computers were primitive. The first computer that I bought for our company was an Apple that had a tiny hard drive with a total storage capacity of just 16K. (That's right, 16 kilobytes, not megabytes.) It utilized big, removable, vinyl floppy disks to store both the data and the programs. I still have it today in my basement.

Improvements came quickly, however, and it seemed that with the passing of each month, companies would release computers that had bigger hard drives and faster processors, beginning with the IBM 286, then continuing in rapid succession with the much improved and faster 386, and 486, and then the unbelievably fast 586 with a whopping *gigabyte* of storage capacity on its hard drive and 64K of memory.

With the improvements in hardware came improvements in software, and I was there as a pioneer working my way through each phase. I personally designed all the software applications for WASCO and hired several programmers through the years to write the code for the various applications that we needed for our different companies.

Bobby Joe had worked for the state of Georgia and wrote software for the large IBM mainframe computers that were used by the state. He told me that he responded to my want ad for a computer programmer because he was a country boy at heart and didn't like working in downtown Atlanta. His home in the tiny rural community of Social Circle, Georgia, was not far from our operation in the small town of Monroe. He took a huge cut in pay and benefits to come to work for me, just so he could distance himself from the traffic and big-city atmosphere of Atlanta.

My customer list contained a huge number of names, and quickly sorting and finding customers within such a gigantic database required a robust computer language that would run on desktop computers and handle mega-indexes, such as ours. I researched various languages and selected DataFlex, primarily because of its speed in handling large indexes. Bobby Joe's expertise was writing code in C, which was a far more challenging and complex language than DataFlex, so he had no problem learning it.

Since WASCO was in survival mode and wasn't adding new products or expanding in any way, I had ample time to develop my software applications. I relied heavily on software to do practically everything, and considered it essential to efficiently and cost effectively conduct mailings. We also relied on it to maintain proper levels of inventory. I was constantly trying to improve the software so it better served our company's needs, and Bobby Joe and I worked on it as a team day in and day out, side by side, for about four years. During that time the recovery slowly took place and WASCO healed.

I think at quantum speed and I have never had the patience or necessary skills to slow down and explain things. Most employees who have worked directly for me have had trouble dealing with my poor communication skills, intensity, and lack of patience.

I had no need to slow down for Bobby Joe, and he liked intensity just as much as I did. We got along famously. He had a keenly inquisitive mind, was exceedingly smart, had a thick skin, and loved solving the many problems associated with software development. It was fascinating work for both of us, and we reached a point where we practically knew what the other was thinking at all times. The result of our many thousands of hours of hard work together was the development of an entire host of simply outstanding software applications, most notably our supply-chain system for inventory control, purchasing, warehousing, and shipping.

Throughout my career, I've always tried to avoid getting too close to employees. I've found that when employees begin to think of you more as a friend than as a boss, it creates undesirable and sometimes serious management problems. Through the years, with just a few notable exceptions, I've remained aloof from anyone in my employ. Bobby Joe was one of the notable exceptions. We became best of friends and I loved him like a brother.

Little Jim, the son of my first marriage, was still attending Mississippi State University when he first expressed an interest in joining WASCO. While still in college, he'd told me that after he graduated with his computer-science degree, he'd like to join our team. He was a little shorter than me, standing five-feet-ten. He was a good-looking young man with a fair complexion, blue eyes, sandy blond hair, a great sense of humor, and a ready smile. He had my wide shoulders, which seemed even bigger because he loved to work out and lift weights.

Regretfully I'd missed out on much of Little Jim's early life and had little to do with his upbringing. I'd only seen him on occasional visits to my father's Mississippi home, or when he'd stay with us for a few weeks in the summers. I think we both tried very hard to bond, but sometimes it seemed awkward and strained. I was delighted when he asked about coming to work with me because I felt that this would be our opportunity to make up for lost time together. And since software development was something near and dear to both of us, we could have some fun working together. I offered him a very nice compensation package and he accepted.

But by the time he graduated in 1990, WASCO was in full recovery mode from the Ralph fiasco, and money wasn't available to give him the compensation package that I'd previously offered.

I explained what had transpired and related that our situation had dramatically changed. I told Jim that times were hard now, but I was sure that in time they'd improve. And as they improved, I told him, I would increase his compensation package accordingly. But for now all I could afford to offer him was a much-reduced package.

He ultimately decided to work for WASCO for the lower compensation package. Unbeknownst to me, however, it remained a bitter issue for him and he eventually came to believe that I was taking advantage of him. He became deeply resentful.

When he came to work for me, I decided to personally mentor him. It didn't work out as I'd envisioned, and almost immediately we began to butt heads. Bobby Joe, the other employees, and my other two sons trusted my judgment implicitly and like good soldiers would follow my instructions to the letter. Jim on the other hand had to be convinced that whatever I told him to do had merit and was the correct way to do things. He was stubborn and would heatedly argue with me about the minutest of issues.

At this point in his career, Jim was still at the junior programmer level. Problem was, he didn't know it. By that I mean, like many young people who first start out in their careers, he was overconfident and thought he knew more than he actually did. He was the college graduate who knew everything and thus was reluctant to take advice.

I, on the other hand, was not the kind of boss who took kindly to some still-wet-behind-the-ears young pup arguing with me and challenging my authority.

We had some heated exchanges, and often Jim would not acquiesce until my legendary anger surfaced and he could see in my eyes that he should stop talking. He knew he was risking my fierce wrath, at a magnitude he wanted no part of, including physical punishment.

These arguments had begun to wear on me. I didn't tolerate that kind of conduct from anyone (which was blatantly obvious to all when I fired my own wife for insubordination). Son or no son, I was not about to waste my time day in and day out arguing with a college boy who had zero experience in writing software or in the real world of business.

This problem was compounded even more because Jim, although highly intelligent, was not particularly a fast thinker. At that point in my career, I was almost entirely devoid of patience in any form, and it frustrated me to no end to try to explain projects over and over again or attempt to teach anything to anyone. It was maddening to wait for what seemed like eternity for the information to gradually sink into his brain—it did so at an excruciatingly slow pace, like cold syrup being poured out on a cold day. His brain would seem to leisurely process the information until finally, mercifully, I would see his eyes light up.

During this process I would sometimes complicate matters by repeating, again and again, what I'd initially said. The more exasperated I got, the louder I got. Before it was over I'd be screaming at him and then would start berating him. Sometimes in the heat of the battle, I'd call him a "stupid idiot" or worse.

Rightfully so, he resented these exchanges, and it was becoming painfully clear to both of us that Jim and I could not work together.

Finally I decided to put him under the direct supervision of Bobby Joe. I'd pass the design criteria for the software on to Bobby Joe instead of to Little Jim, and then he and Jim would take it from there. They would write the code and test it under Bobby Joe's brilliant direction and patient, good-natured management style.

When the work-related interaction between us abated, the relationship between Jim and me dramatically improved.

I always thought that Little Jim was very fortunate to have begun his computer-technology career under the excellent tutelage of Bobby Joe. He benefited enormously from learning a practical, common-sense approach to writing solid code, and Bobby Joe was the one who taught Little Jim the DataFlex language.

One day Bobby Joe bent over to pick up a box of printer paper and I happened to notice a large lump on his back that was readily distinguishable through his T-shirt.

I asked, "Bobby Joe, what's that lump on your back?"

He replied, "It's a mole. It's been bothering me a lot and has grown quite a bit lately. Yesterday I noticed that it was bleeding a little."

"Have you seen a doctor about it?"

"I haven't had time."

I was visibly shaken, "For crying out loud, Bobby, don't you know that those are warning signs of cancer?"

Before he could answer, I went into my office and called my dermatologist. I had endured extreme sun damage as a kid and as a result routinely went to the dermatologist so he could remove various precancerous growths. The doc and I had become friends, and the receptionist put me right through to him. After I described Bobby's symptoms, he told me to send him on down to his office *right then.*

Bobby Joe was diagnosed with a melanoma, the most malevolent and aggressive of skin cancers. They scheduled surgery to remove it the very next day. My doctor told me that it was the largest melanoma that he'd ever seen; it was the size of a grapefruit and had grown deep inside Bobby Joe's back.

Despite the surgery, the cancer quickly metastasized, and within just eight short weeks it had spread to his brain, kidneys, liver, and other vital organs. Bobby Joe stayed at home for most of the battle, but deteriorated to a point where they finally had to admit him to the hospital.

When I came into his hospital room for a visit, he managed a weak smile and whispered, "This is hell."

His face was gaunt and jaundice-yellow from the cancer having spread to his liver. He told me that he was embarrassed because he had to wear a large diaper—he could no longer control his bowels.

I've never felt more compassion for anyone in my life. I told him not to be embarrassed about anything. I carefully wiped his brow with a damp cloth to remove the sweat, and then I held his hand in mine. We talked about Jesus at length. He weakly smiled and told me that he looked forward to meeting Him. Bobby Joe wanted to see if there might be some software systems that needed to be developed in heaven. I assured him that no doubt there was plenty going on up there, and no one was better qualified to design software for God than him; I had no doubts that Jesus would put him in charge of the entire project, I said.

Bobby Joe died soon thereafter and it was like ripping a huge hole out of my chest. I broke down crying when I heard the news, and I grieved for many months afterward. He was a true friend—and I never had many true friends.

As with other tragic events, Bobby Joe's death drew me close to God—closer than I'd been in a long time. And even though I was depressed over the death, I felt God's warm presence. I was strangely optimistic that things would soon dramatically improve in my life.

CHAPTER SEVENTY-TWO

Ken Edwards and Sallie Dahmes were close friends of mine too, and it would have been impossible to build WASCO into the most successful wildlife-artist company in the world without them, much less salvage it after the fall. I've never had harder-working or more fiercely loyal people in my employ. They were highly talented, intelligent, and . . . did I mention hard-working and absolutely loyal?

Sallie was attractive and had a warm, friendly smile, a great sense of humor, and a heavy New Orleans Cajun accent. She was tall and thin, and had long, thick, brown hair. She'd won two world championships as a whitetail and waterfowl taxidermist and was truly a gifted artist. Like many artists I'd met, Sallie was not without her quirks. She was an obsessive-compulsive perfectionist who could be smiling one minute and pitching an emotional tantrum of legendary proportions the next.

I originally hired her to sculpt a line of whitetail and waterfowl manikins for WASCO; and later, after a little prodding, I talked her into writing a couple of very popular books and numerous articles for the magazine. She ended up being quite the celebrity in the industry, and to the delight of our customers would perform book signings and offer advice at our trade-show booths.

After the Ralph fiasco, we quit adding new sculptures to our already extensive manikin offerings, and stopped spending our scarce resources writing or publishing new books. Without so much as the first complaint, Sallie switched gears and volunteered to do anything required to keep the company going, including taking and pulling orders, and then boxing and shipping them out. And if needed, she'd even sweep the warehouse floor after she was through. No job was too menial or too dirty for her. She took a particular liking to our paint-manufacturing operation and before long was completely managing it—and doing an excellent job.

She was the type of employee that every business owner desires: smart, loyal, reliable, hardworking, and willing to do whatever it took to help the company—without ever complaining.

Ken had all the great employee attributes of Sallie; plus he was a certifiable genius with an incredibly high IQ. He looked like a nerd, stood about five-feet-nine, had a slight build, and sported a mustache. His brown hair was always neatly groomed—with the exception of a cowlick that stubbornly stuck up in the back. He wore thick glasses that were always down on his nose and made his eyes appear bigger than they really were; and he generally dressed in khaki pants and out-of-style button-down shirts, complete with shirt-pocket protector full of pens and pencils. He always had one of those quizzical smiles on his face that geniuses often muster, and it made him appear amused at the rest of us mere mortals.

Ken was a wonderfully talented artist. He was also a musician who could sing just like Willie Nelson and professionally play most any instrument by ear. He was a commercial graphic designer extraordinaire, computer guru, and excellent photographer. He concentrated primarily on producing the magazine and helped me design and conduct the mailings that stimulated orders and kept the cash flowing. I'd also trained him in the money-management and operational aspects of the business, and he was a reliable second in command. He did the work of four people and the quality of his work was superb. He was very congenial and had a sense of humor second to none.

The business was on the mend, and as the years slowly churned their way along we made dramatic strides toward recovery. I became a master at managing our meager finances and had implemented strict new controls, including stringent checks and balances to prevent a recurrence of what had happened before. I subscribed to the theory that there is nothing wrong with making an *honest mistake* the first time around; however, if you make that same mistake again, it becomes a *stupid mistake*, which is intolerable. I vowed that I would never again allow anyone to steal from me, at least *in the same manner* as Ralph. To my knowledge, I've achieved that goal.

In spite of our steady progress and success, I'd become deeply disillusioned with the wildlife-art industry (mainly because the people I'd thought were my friends turned on me). It was a small enough industry for news to travel fast; and when the rumors started flying about WASCO's disastrous fall, outright lies ran wild about the company and me personally. Tongues began wagging in overtime; and with each successive passing of the vicious gossip, it moved further and further away from the truth—to the point of sheer absurdity.

People jealous of my success or competitors in the industry who wanted to see us fail spread deliberate lies. Many of our competitors were irked to no end when WASCO expanded from selling paint and paint-related items to selling any and everything an artist could want. This resulted in our directly competing with our own paint distributors and selling deer manikins and other items that they sold.

As distributors of my paints, they were in effect financing their strongest competitor. It was a serious loss of revenue for them, especially since we had the competitive advantage of owning the WASCO machine and could utilize *Breakthrough* magazine, the World Championships, books, videos, and more to maximum advantage in marketing our own products. Many in the industry were deeply resentful of that success.

I cannot ignore the facts that I'd become arrogant and flaunted my power and money, and that I had treated some people in the industry shabbily. It was only natural for them to gloat when I got my comeuppance. Well-deserved or not, it added to my angst just the same.

Although I was now rebuilding WASCO to its former glory, my fiery passion for this industry had grown bitterly cold. Too much garbage had piled up. Managing the debt-reduction program and taking angry telephone calls from vendors and customers day in and day out for years had taken its toll on me, and the entire scenario had just soured me on the industry. Then when I endured the severe personal loss of my dear friend Bobby Joe, I became so depressed that I began to yearn in earnest for a fresh start.

I was still an insomniac and all through the night I began to search the Scriptures for answers to what God might want me to do. I spent an enormous amount of time in prayer. I just couldn't find peace while I was running WASCO, and an uneasiness was beginning to gnaw at me. To my mind, this signified that I wasn't on the path God wanted me to take with my life. The trouble was, I didn't know which path He did want me to take; and since God wouldn't come sit on the edge of my bed and say, "Okay, Bob, here's the direction that I want you to go," I was clueless as to what to do.

Prior to his illness, Bobby Joe and I had developed a business-management software package for professional wildlife artists. We made some decent money selling this little system, and I'd enjoyed developing it.

This minor project started me thinking about all the software I'd developed through the years for the WASCO machine. Our software was well designed and—more important—it wasn't riddled with bugs. Unlike much of the software that was out there in those early days, our software performed extremely well in the real world. The mere fact that I managed *my own money* with this software system is the best indicator of how good it was. I would have never used the software to manage our companies if it wasn't good—*real good.*

After thinking about it, I felt sure that other companies would benefit from my software too. Soon I began earnestly exploring the possibility of starting up a software-development company.

I shared my plans with my boys and they were immediately fired up about it. In fact, from that moment on they all began enthusiastically hounding me to get it going. Like me, they loved computer technology, and it seemed to come quite easily to them. It was as though we were all blessed with some sort of God-given computer proficiency that was built into our brains.

I was very close to Michael and Jon, and it'd been a joy to have them working at WASCO with me day in and day out after school and throughout our summers. They had begun doing odd jobs for my various companies as small children, and as they grew older had helped out in every conceivable position. They helped with conducting mail-outs, answering phones, pulling orders, sweeping up the warehouse, processing subscriptions to the magazine, working at our sportsman shows, working in the paint plant, and more. They even wrote an article or two for *Breakthrough*. I wanted to instill a strong work ethic in them because I knew that later on they would have no free rides.

As for Jim, to be sure we had our problems, but things had dramatically improved between us, particularly after he went to work directly for Bobby Joe. He'd gained some experience and maturity during that year and his attitude seemed much improved. I wanted him to be a part of my new company too, and I was confident that in time we could overcome our problems. He seemed as fired up about the new entity as the rest of us. And all looked well.

Ken and Sallie, on the other hand, cherished WASCO and were not at all interested in starting a software-development company. They still loved the wildlife-art industry and they were unhappy about my state of mind. Instead of us being "All for one and one for all," they now saw me as a traitor wanting to abandon them and desert the "WASCO team." I tried to explain my feelings to them by detailing my frustrations with the industry and my strong desire to do something *fresh*, but they couldn't understand and were insistent that we stay the course.

One day I told them that I'd finally made up my mind to sell the WASCO machine and was going into the software business full time. I told them my first preference was to sell the company to them. Ken really wanted to buy it, but couldn't come up with the money. Sallie on the other hand came from a very wealthy Louisiana family and was in a better position to buy it.

Her father, who was an excellent wealth-management consultant, was somewhat receptive to the idea, but wanted her to start off slowly. Wanting to see how well she fared owning her own business before overcommitting, he initially gave her just enough financing to buy our paint-manufacturing company, Master Paint Systems.

That was fine with me. Although we had improved dramatically, we were always strapped for cash and the money generated from that sale was timely and a much needed shot in the arm. I immediately began looking for buyers for the other WASCO components while Sallie began managing Master Paint Systems.

After only a short period of time, it was readily apparent to me that she would succeed. She was very smart and as hard a worker as anyone that I'd ever known. And she surely had *passion* for that little company. She dove in with vigor and did an excellent job, but managing this operation in its entirety meant she would now need to manage people (without screaming at them), file taxes, manage payables, take care of the payroll and receivables, and handle insurance and legal matters. All of that was really too much for her and beyond her capabilities and expertise.

It became evident that Sallie was more of an artist than a businessperson. Unless she had someone helping with that side of things, I feared she would struggle mightily. I warned her that there was no way she could run such an operation on her own, and suggested that she give Ken some stock and let him run it. I knew they could be successful if they worked as a team. Sallie ultimately took that advice and it was a good move for her and also for Ken. He added tremendously to the business success of the operation, and the move allowed Sallie to remain creative (and thereby stay happy).

As Sallie and Ken prospered, she soon wanted to buy the entire WASCO machine. Her father acquiesced (to a degree) to his persuasive daughter's constant nagging, and she managed to acquire WASCO's main supply business and all its manufacturing operations and copyrights, including Polytranspar, WASCO sculpture lines, urethane injection molds, chemical division, and more.

I sold *Breakthrough* magazine, all the copyrights to my publishing company's books, and the World Fish Carving and World Taxidermy Championships to my good friend Larry Blomquist, of Louisiana. It was a solid deal for all concerned. Larry was also best of friends with Sallie and Ken, and that relationship continues to blossom through today.

I sold my how-to video and mail-order correspondence course to a husband-and-wife team that wanted a small business they could run out of their home. And I decided just to close down and liquidate the health-and-fitness company.

It was 1992 when the WASCO machine was officially and finally transferred to its new owners, and I'd finally wrapped everything up. It had taken me seven years to build WASCO and seven brutal years to finally recover from the ordeal with Ralph.

In the end I repaid every dime of the $980,000 that we owed, just as I'd promised those 300 vendors. Miraculously we were never sued by anyone. Teresa had spent three years fighting the IRS. She found a few old records and was able to use them to rebuild all our payroll records for the period that was in dispute, and in the end, instead of owing them $50,000 plus penalties and interest, they ended up owing us a $1,280 refund.

WASCO was once again a force in the industry, and its sales revenues were even higher than before. Only now it had half the overhead and thus was more profitable. We'd made a *miraculous* full and healthy recovery, which astounded all those detractors who'd advised me to take bankruptcy and call it a day.

It had been a brutal experience, but in retrospect, this was the best thing that ever happened to me as far as furthering my business career. I ended up much improved in virtually all areas of business acumen. I didn't ever get an opportunity to go to Harvard or Wharton Business School, but I went to the school of hard knocks and earned my Ph.D. in business management and received an A+ in money management and budgeting.

As for my cash on hand after the deal, I was able to repay all my personal debt with the proceeds from selling my various companies. I paid off everything but the modest first mortgage on my house, and ended up with $350,000 in assets to start my new company. Considering the severity of my situation (at one point being

$278,000 overdrawn, $980,000 in debt and three months behind on mortgage payments), I had achieved quite an accomplishment, one of which I remain very proud.

Even more important, my struggle had resulted in my becoming a much better person than I was prior to my ordeal. My character had dramatically improved. I was very close to God again, going to church regularly, and reading the Bible daily.

All things considered, I was light-years ahead of where I'd been prior to the WASCO experience, and I felt that I was ready for my new beginning. I truly believed that I'd just experienced one of God's most intense training sessions. I had accomplished my mission, and some valuable "lessons learned" were branded and *seared* into my mind. Yes, for seven long years He'd harshly punished me for turning my back on Him, but I knew that I deserved every minute of every year of agony that I'd endured.

I was just glad that it was over. And I was totally optimistic about my upcoming fresh start and feeling good for the first time in a long while.

CHAPTER SEVENTY-THREE

When I left WASCO, Little Jim, Jack Oaf (a programmer), and Lee Johnson (my secretary of 10 years) were the only employees that accompanied me. Teresa was quick to ask if she could work at our software-development company too.

My response was, "You're hired." I was glad to have her back. She was my one true friend and aside from my sons was the only person that I really trusted at this juncture of my life. We now had five full-time employees, including Teresa and me. We were able to utilize Michael and Jon on a limited part-time basis; they both were still in school and available only infrequently after school and during summer breaks.

The first order of business was to select a name for our new company. In passing I'd recently overheard someone say, "There's something good on the horizon." That little saying was so representative of the unbridled optimism and enthusiasm I felt about my new venture that I decided to name my new company in its honor. I called it Horizon Software International.

Unlike the wildlife-art industry, with its limited and finite number of wildlife artists, the entire world and its billions of people were now my potential customers. The computer revolution had created a global marketplace overnight. I hung International on the end of my new company's name because I wanted to take it global. I knew it would probably take years (maybe even decades) to grow it into an international company, but from the onset I had high ambitions of becoming the best in the world with my software technology.

All the software source code I owned was excellent, including software applications for publishing, manufacturing, retail, direct mail, and supply-chain distribution. I was especially confident that our supply-chain software application was the finest ever written. I had over a decade of experience in managing my own inventory control, purchasing, warehousing, and shipping operations. Many software developers will create software for third parties without a real clue as to how it should best work in an actual work environment. That was not the case with me.

My money was on the line when I created this system, and I wrote it to make the very most out of my limited funds. I didn't want too much inventory on hand needlessly tying up my precious few dollars; and I didn't want too little inventory on hand or we'd have too many costly back orders and emergency resupply orders. I needed accurate forecasts of inventory needs, and I didn't want a repeat of the situation where people were stealing my inventory right off my shelves.

I designed a very efficient inventory-control system that was tightly integrated with other modules for order processing, shipping, receiving, asset management, and a verification system for paying bills (nearly foolproof). I'd built all of that and more into my products; and best of all, unlike many software systems on the market during this early period of software development, my system worked extremely well, was bug-free, and had been thoroughly tested under live conditions for years.

Unfortunately, after taking my first, brief look at marketing the system, I encountered a major stumbling block. I discovered that the software business was nothing like I thought it would be. I'd mistakenly thought that I could market this new product as I had marketed Polytranspar paints. I wanted to first sell it through established distributors, and then start selling it directly. I naively calculated that I would quickly garner a few distributors and large retailer chains, and then stand by and watch as their powerful marketing machines propelled my excellent products into the major leagues; and then I'd start selling the software directly and garner more profit.

I envisioned our little company becoming a very large company in short order.

That was just so much wishful thinking. I soon realized that even though I owned a great product, it would take money—*real* money, an *enormous* amount of money—to place software products in retail-store chains or with distributors. The brutal facts were that a software company had to pay to put its product on the shelves of the retailing giants. And they had to pay to place them in the catalogs of the major software distributors. Further, the distributors' terms were deplorable. A software developer had to front their inventory to the distributors and not receive payment for six months after the products had sold; plus the developer had to guarantee that they would take back any unsold product and pay a penalty if that happened. It wasn't a game in which a meagerly funded company like mine could play.

I realized that I would have to abandon my original plans and instead start selling directly to customers within small niche markets. In essence, I'd have to build my business one customer at a time. That would take time, money, a direct sales force—and creating an operation that a mail-order guru like me had zero experience with.

I was undeterred, however, and felt that in time I could build my supply-chain business into a major force. In the meantime, I would just have to find a way to fund and sustain the company while I was building my mainstream business. As I saw it, there were two basic choices for software developers. They could either build their businesses around a great product—that's what I had with my supply-chain system—or develop custom applications for those entities that desired them.

I was not enamored by the latter. I much preferred to write an excellent system that I would ultimately own in its entirety and that I could sell to clients with similar needs *over and over again*.

The one-shot custom route meant writing a one-time package exclusively for a singular customer. And although I could make some money in the process, after a job was completed I would necessarily have to move on (hopefully to find another one). True, I could make a little cash supporting the custom application and occasionally in modifying it, but I could have had a full lobotomy and still figured out that the custom route was a loser compared with the great-product route.

Now I faced the brutal reality of paying expensive programmers for months on end and then pouring hundreds of thousands of marketing dollars into building a great brand. It was readily obvious that I would need to at least temporarily conform my business model to whatever was needed to survive. No job that put green dollars into my company was beneath me, including jobs that entailed the custom route.

I was looking for any reasonable course of action when my programmer, Jack Oaf, came to me with a proposal from his former boss. Jack had worked several years for a very successful law firm owned by John Sanko, a locally famous personal-injury attorney. I'd seen his smiling face in his ambulance-chaser-type ads on television for years, and was familiar with his name. Jack suggested that I meet with him. He told me that John wanted to develop a bankruptcy-petition filing system in DataFlex. Attorneys would be the main users, and we could market it throughout the country; Jack thought that it might prove to be a good opportunity for Horizon.

I met with John and it was easy to see how he'd become so successful. John was charismatic and smooth talking, and he quickly convinced me that we could make a fortune selling these systems. He enthusiastically told me that no one else had a similar system (save a few "cheesy" ones, which he dismissed offhand as being irrelevant).

He had 32 attorneys working in his law firm, and all of them routinely handled bankruptcy cases. He told me that Horizon could move into his building and he and his other attorneys would help me with the design requirements. Once the software was written, he said, his firm could test it under actual conditions until we had it ready to take to market.

He assured me that virtually every attorney in the United States routinely filed bankruptcy petitions, and "incidentally" there were over *800,000* of them scattered around the country! He thought we could sell these systems for at least a couple of thousand bucks each, which was mere chump change to attorneys. He said they'd gladly pay that small amount to computerize this otherwise cumbersome manual process.

I quickly did the math in my head and a smile widened on my face; I could see dollars pouring into my little company by the wheelbarrow load. I calculated that with my marketing skills and mail-order prowess, we would be able to sell these inexpensive systems strictly by mail at very little expense, and the profits would be enormous. It all sounded good to me, and we shook hands on the deal. He invested $50,000 in Horizon and supplied the office space in exchange for his minority interest. We went to work.

Unfortunately when I started work on the project, I soon discovered that it was far more complex than I'd been led to believe. Laws varied in every state, as did the format of the bankruptcy petition and the criteria that had to be filed. John was familiar only with the laws in Georgia; the other states had different regulations and filing requirements. This necessitated the expensive process of researching filing requirements state by state. The states were also constantly changing the laws, which meant that the system would need continual updates (and management thereof) to reflect those changes. We began spending more and more money, and we both had to inject more and more investment capital. Soon my budget was demolished and my meager cash reserves were all but gone.

By the time we finally finished the software and I began to look into marketing the system, all was not as I'd originally been led to believe. It was painfully apparent that I should've conducted due diligence on my own. Contrary to what John had assured me, the market already featured several good software systems for filing bankruptcy petitions, and our competitors had been in the market for years on end. Worst of all, to a competitor, their systems were feature-rich and far exceeded the capabilities of our little system. Competing against them was going to be brutal.

If that wasn't bad enough, as soon as I did begin to sell a few systems, I discovered that attorneys were slow to pay (if at all). Worst of all, they were highly belligerent and threatened to sue over any little problem or bug that they encountered within the software.

Our financial standing was bleak. I'd spent nearly a year writing this system and had almost exhausted my remaining start-up capital; and the few systems that I'd sold didn't provide enough revenue to pay our bills.

I wanted out.

I made a deal with John whereby he would exchange his total equity in Horizon for a lake house that I owned. The home was located on Lake Oconee and I'd obtained it in a trade for one of the WASCO companies I'd sold. It was a valuable piece of property, worth about $200,000. I also gave him all rights to the bankruptcy package as part of the deal, while exclusively retaining all rights to all other software source code that we owned, including my coveted supply-chain system.

Giving him the house troubled me, but giving away the bankruptcy software package code didn't bother me at all. Even though I'd spent most of my start-up capital and thousands of hours developing it, I was so sick of dealing with attorneys by then that I would have gladly *given away* that software system completely free of charge—and included a bottle of John's favorite wine just to be rid of it.

He accepted my offer and both he and the bankruptcy package were out of my life forever.

It was an expensive lesson about the absolute necessity of conducting due diligence and thoroughly researching opportunities prior to pouring resources into them. This project had left me dangling from a precipice and fighting for my financial life; however, I was undaunted. I chalked it up to learning the software business the hard way, which was entirely consistent with my life so far. It seemed that the hard way was the only learning curve I could comprehend.

Aside from the hard lessons about looking before leaping, a bright side emerged from this experience. Working with John on the project benefited me in my new role as a software developer. Through his legal expertise, I learned all the important complexities of software licensing agreements—knowledge that was absolutely essential if I was to proceed in this field.

That alone was worth the angst, but I also learned about programmers, code development, and managing project development during this period of time. Not that I was doing all that great managing people or projects. Back in the WASCO days, when Bobby Joe had become too ill to work, Little Jim had become the lead programmer and we'd hired Jack Oaf as our new programmer.

Almost immediately after Bobby Joe got too sick to work, I had a case of déjà vu as Little Jim and I resumed clashing with each other. Jack Oaf was causing problems too. He had more programming experience than Jim and was a quick thinker; but even though he was smart and a blazing-fast programmer, he was exceedingly sloppy and his code was riddled with bugs.

This was the diametric opposite of Bobby Joe. By the time Bobby Joe gave some extremely well-written code to me, it had been well tested and rarely displayed any bugs. Jack and Jim's code creations were practically unusable, and I would be incensed that they would give it to me in such a deplorable state. It was as though they expected me to test it and debug it for them.

I missed my senior programmer Bobby Joe for more reasons than one. I would've loved if he were managing these guys and patiently dealing with their inexperience and training them instead of me. I would have given practically anything to just sit down and discuss the situation with him, but it was not to be.

After all was said and done, in spite of my financial and personnel problems, I still felt very optimistic and enjoyed designing computer software immensely. I knew it was a growing market with tremendous potential, and I recognized that I could eventually succeed in this business. I just needed to weather the financial storm and I knew we'd be fine. I was resolute that a few little setbacks were not about to deter me from succeeding in this field. After all, when I considered what I'd been through in life, this was *nothing*.

I didn't have a clear direction in which to take my fledgling company next. I had a few independent sales representatives who were occasionally selling my supply-chain system to local companies, but the revenue those sales generated was not nearly enough to sustain us.

I soon happened upon an opportunity for some custom work. A handful of very successful sales guys with State Farm Insurance wanted Horizon to develop a system to monitor and manage their sales processes. We went to work on it and soon developed an elegant system for them. Unfortunately, they ran out of money for the project and abandoned it.

Next we took some contract work for a French company, CATCO. It had formed a partnership with GE to develop a DataFlex-driven monitoring system for a nuclear power plant in China. They wanted software that would employ some prototype handheld devices to remotely monitor various gauges and record important data from control rooms all over the plant. The system would then compare the most recent data with previous readings to determine whether there were any fluctuations in temperature, pressure, and other parameters—vitally important information in a facility of this nature.

We grossed several hundred thousand dollars in the months that we worked on it, and I was thrilled to garner some work (and much needed cash). But I was well aware that these one-shot deals were not the direction that we needed to be going, and I was determined to keep my supply-chain system moving forward at every opportunity.

I'd just about reached the bottom of my working capital during the bankruptcy-software fiasco, and I still hadn't been able to recover. Funds were dangerously low, and even though I was taking in some cash from these custom projects, I was burning through money as fast as it was coming in. I'd had no choice but to hire additional programmers so that Horizon would meet CATCO-related deadlines. And with the burden of paying these additional salaries, I was finding it all but impossible to regain momentum. No bank would offer me a loan with my financial history, and I realized that I didn't have any financial room to make any more mistakes.

I had to make every penny count.

I decided that my best course of action was to ramp up selling my supply-chain system to other distribution companies. I hired Allen Brown, an independent sales representative, to do just that. He already represented another company and was selling Point of Service software to K-12 (kindergarten through 12th grade) school districts for their school-lunch programs; but he had some time to rep for us too. It wasn't long before he began selling a few of my systems.

One day Allen came to me and told me that I needed to modify my supply-chain system to meet the "back office," (supply chain) requirements of school food services. He'd uncovered the need for a system like this when he called on one of his public-school accounts and tried to sell the Point of Service software for his other client. He told me, "There isn't another system out there that handles supply chain. We'd have it to ourselves." He went on to tell me that my supply-chain distribution system would be a perfect fit. He said I'd need to modify it to meet a school's food-service needs, but from what he'd seen it wouldn't need that much modification to make it work.

Yeah, right! Where had I heard that before?

I'd just lost several hundred thousand dollars after listening to a similar sales pitch about a bankruptcy-petition filing system, and that still smarted. I immediately referred to my lessons-learned-in-life file: "The first time you make a mistake it's an *honest mistake*, but the second time it's a *stupid mistake*!"

I told him to buzz off.

I credit Allen with the persistence of a bulldog. He was a stocky little guy with red hair and a red beard; and although he stood just somewhere around five-feet-five, he was fiery. He talked way too loudly, but was intelligent, articulate, and charming enough to keep you interested in whatever he was saying. He'd been more successful than any of my other sales reps, and I liked him.

He just would not quit! His jaw stuck out resolutely, and it fit him perfectly. He was as persistent a person as anyone I'd ever met, and when he wanted something he was incessant in his determination to achieve it. Such was the case with the K-12 back-office push. He literally tortured me for weeks on end to pursue this market, insisting all the while that my system was perfect for their needs and no one else had a similar system, and blah, blah, blah.

Finally one day he had either worn me down or caught me in a weak moment, and I agreed to go on a sales call with him to see for myself. Much to my surprise, the school food-service director that we called on confirmed everything Allen had said. She was kind enough to show me how they manually took physical inventories, kept up with their inventory-on-hand balances, processed orders, and so forth. Her crude manual system was reminiscent of the way people did things 50 years ago with legal pad and pencil. It was laborious and time consuming, and she desperately needed computer automation. My system would without question revolutionize her operation.

Practically everything she needed was already included in my supply-chain system, and I felt that with some slight modification I could quickly develop a usable system for her (probably in a month or so). According to her, school systems throughout the country had a tremendous need for this type of software, and no other vendor had it.

Still wary, I told her I'd contact her in a week or two after I'd spent some time analyzing her needs. I spent the next several weeks researching the industry with a vengeance. I looked at everything from competitive promotional materials to the size of the market (17,000 school districts and 94,000 public schools with lunchrooms). I found out where I should advertise and which trade shows to attend. I researched pricing and how the school systems were funded, length of sales cycles, government regulation, and lots more.

I was convinced.

I took some standard reports from my supply-chain distribution system back out to the school food-service director and showed her how it worked. I emphasized how it would save her vast sums of money compared with her manual system. One thing was certain: When it came to managing inventory, I was an expert and *I knew what I was talking about.*

She was overwhelmed by the power of the system and completely flabbergasted with what I showed her. She wanted to order it immediately. Such a tool would undoubtedly help her and her overworked staff enormously.

I told her my price was $30,000 and she didn't bat an eye. She said she'd gladly pay that much for it and knew plenty of other school districts that would follow her lead if it worked well for her.

She had plenty of money in her budget and, after approval from the school board, issued me a purchase order. The problem was, I had hundreds of hours of modifications to make before I could deliver the product and collect those badly needed funds.

My pitiful resources had dwindled to such a low point that it would be very difficult to pay for modifications to accommodate her specific K-12 needs. I hadn't taken a salary in weeks, and Teresa was beginning to give me that worried look.

I still had confidence that we could accomplish the job, but I knew that it would be tight. By now, in addition to Little Jim and Jack Oaf, I'd hired two other programmers. They were very experienced and we had an elite work force, albeit an expensive one. With luck, I could trim delivery of the K-12 supply-chain system down to three weeks of long hard days and perhaps a weekend or two.

Like a hungry shark, I could instinctively smell blood. I was thoroughly convinced that this was the break I'd been waiting for. I was positive—100 percent, no-risk certain—that this was the market that would pave the way to making Horizon Software International a financial success.

I could feel it in my bones.

Chapter Seventy-Four

One thing I pride myself on is being able to motivate people, and the very next day I gathered my seven employees together and did just that. I gave a rousing motivational speech, stating that this was "our moment." I warned that such an opportunity to achieve greatness often eludes those who fail to recognize or seize it. I stressed that while it was true that we'd have to hunker down and work long hours, in the end our total domination of the K-12 food-service market was *going* to happen.

I assured them that I'd done my homework in researching this industry. I'd dotted my i's and crossed my t's. This mega market was like a gigantic orchard loaded with juicy fruit ripe for the harvest, and we were the only harvesters who were ready to pick. Our tiny company was destined to become a giant company. Fate had dealt each of them a winning hand and to a person every last employee would benefit enormously from being there at the right time and the right place at the very beginning of something grand.

As hoped, the speech fired everyone up, and big smiles, high fives, and unbridled enthusiasm filled the room. We were on our way!

Wrong!

It was as though someone had absentmindedly noticed a little piece of wayward yarn hanging off a hand-knitted baby blanket and had given it a tug, causing the entire blanket to start unraveling. As I looked on in horror, Horizon began unraveling in just such a manner.

Just three days after my stirring speech, Jack came into my office and turned in his resignation. He'd taken a higher-paying job. He referred to it as "his very own opportunity of a lifetime." He was moving to Augusta, Georgia, to start a career with industry giant Oracle Software. He offered no notice (and no apology for not giving one), and in a matter of a minute or so was out the door.

While our impending deadline was crucial and I needed more resources and not less, I considered Jack's departure only a minor setback. It certainly wasn't a death knell. I felt that if everyone would bear down and work just a little harder until I could replace him, we'd be fine. I'd grown to dislike Jack. His work was sloppy and riddled with bugs, and he'd argued almost as much as Jim. I felt that he was a bad influence on Jim, and lately the two of them had often sided together against me over practically every little issue. I was actually relieved that he was leaving and hoped that Jim and I would get along better after he did so.

Just two more days had elapsed when two of my remaining three programmers turned in their resignations on the same afternoon. Unbeknownst to me, a huge DataFlex project was under way in Atlanta, and the company developing the software had fallen far behind schedule on the project. Millions of dollars were at stake, and this company was offering any and all DataFlex programmers in the Atlanta area virtually open contracts to work for them at obscenely high hourly rates.

Our company hosted the local DataFlex User Group meetings at our office, and our monthly meeting was naturally the first place they began their recruitment effort. My two best programmers were stolen right out from under my nose at that meeting.

There was no way I could match the high pay the other company was offering them, and even if I could have, I wouldn't be able to match the same gold-plated health-insurance plan also being offered. Both programmers apologized and told me they hated to leave me in a bind, but said their families had to come first and that financially they'd be stupid to turn down this offer.

They left without so much as an hour's notice. Again apologies were forthcoming, but their new company urgently needed bodies and as a condition of their new employment they had to start immediately.

I called a meeting to bring Teresa, Jim, and Lee up to date. I took a deep breath, put on my bravest face, and told them not to worry—we'd be fine. The situation was brutal, but not insurmountable. We now had one remaining programmer in Jim. Lee was taking the documentation that I was writing for the system and integrating it into a user manual. Teresa was paying bills, answering phones, and assisting me with a variety of tasks, including management of my many sales appointments.

By day I was calling on K-12 food-service directors around the state with my independent rep Allen, trying to sell more systems; and by night I was designing software, testing code, and writing documentation for our software. I was working 18 to 20 hours a day seven days per week, and soon had reached my limit.

I leveled with the remaining staff and told them that our most serious problem would be recruiting additional programmers. DataFlex programmers were scarce because the big DataFlex project in Atlanta was snagging every available DataFlex programmer within 150 miles. I'd already called every programmer I knew, and to a person they'd already been heavily recruited for the project. Most were either taking jobs with that firm, or their current employers were giving them huge raises to entice them to stay.

This was a significant setback, but I reminded the staff that we'd been in tighter spots—namely WASCO, when we dropped from 65 employees to 19 almost overnight. I was positive that we could weather this storm too.

And on the brighter side of things, Allen and I had sold our system to three more school districts and were awaiting purchase orders totaling in excess of

$100,000. That money would be released as soon as their school boards approved the purchasing process. Sales potential was really looking good, and every customer to whom I'd shown our new system was genuinely excited about its potential.

I told our employees, "Just imagine what sales will be like once we have the software in place and start garnering some good references. We just need to 'work and not worry,' bear down, and focus on finishing the system. We'll be fine."

Jim could have been like the other DataFlex programmers and jumped ship like a big wharf rat, but he'd stayed. I fully appreciated his loyalty. I called him aside and confided privately to him that I was proud of him for hanging in there with me, but there was something that he should know.

In addition to our personnel problems, we'd run out of money. We were only a few weeks away from completing and installing the software, but even if we could find someone to hire, we'd need some cash in order to pay that person.

I told him that I was willing to bridge the crisis by borrowing the last $25,000 credit available to me using my home equity as collateral, but I didn't want to take a second mortgage unless I was sure that he was going to hang in there with me.

He told me, "*I'm sticking!* You can count on me."

"Are you sure?"

"*I'm sticking!*"

"Good!"

I went down and borrowed the money that afternoon, and the four of us resumed feverishly working on completion of the modifications.

The next day—more unraveling.

Lee Johnson, my administrative assistant of 10 years, came into my office, shut the door, and handed me her resignation letter. I was really hurt by this. Lee had begun working for me when she was just 17 years old. Over the past 10 years we'd enjoyed the good times together and we'd weathered the bad. She'd always maintained a positive attitude and was a trusted employee and a friend.

I was completely baffled when she told me that she was quitting in order to take what I considered to be a crap job engraving plastic signs for a small trophy-and-sign shop near her rural home. Times were hard for Horizon, but this new job was, in my estimation, a large step downward. Lee was an attractive, smart, and skilled administrative assistant with advanced computer skills. It seemed entirely bizarre that she would quit Horizon to accept such a low-level manual job.

I knew that she was concerned about the stability of Horizon because she'd met with me privately a few days earlier and told me that she was worried about the programmers leaving and Horizon's financial strength. Lord knows she needed a stable job; she'd just gone through a messy divorce and now was the sole breadwinner. In our meeting, I reminded her of the desperate situation in which we'd found ourselves with WASCO and how we'd not only survived that crisis but thrived as well. I assured her that our current dilemma was not nearly as bad and that we'd breeze right through this in good fashion.

She asked what would happen if Jim left too. Trying to reassure her, I told her that Jim was just a coder, and although programming was an important aspect of our business, it played a relatively small role in determining whether or not the business would succeed or fail. I told her that I was the driving force behind Horizon and I would get us through the day, just as I had at WASCO. I told her to trust me and not to worry; orders were beginning to come in and we'd be fine.

I tried my utmost to talk Lee out of quitting, but she refused to discuss it further. When it became obvious that her mind was made up and nothing was going to change it, I wished her the best and regretfully accepted her resignation.

Lee worked one more week and left on a Friday. I hated to see her go. Our little company was now down to just three family members: Jim, Teresa, and me. (My other two sons, Michael and Jon, were still in school and had time to help out only on rare occasions.)

The following Monday the unraveling was complete when Little Jim walked into my office and resigned too. He told me that he was taking a job with the same company that his buddy Jack Oaf just went to work for in Augusta. He told me that Oracle Software was a better opportunity.

I was livid. "What about all that crap about, 'I'm sticking'? What about, 'You can count on me'?"

He said, "I'm sorry but I have to look out for what's best for me."

"What's best for *you!* What about what's best for your family? Teresa? Michael? Jon? Me? What about keeping your word? What about my borrowing my last $25,000 available credit just *one week ago* based upon your 'I'm sticking' assurance?"

He tried to change the subject and promised to work for three more weeks. He said he thought he could finish the modifications within that time frame or at least get us very close. Then, he said, Horizon could collect its much-needed funds and we'd be on our way. He told me that after he left, he'd help train and support his replacement for as long as needed.

At this point I was totally disgusted. "Fine, Jim, if that is your decision and your mind is made up, then so be it." I walked away without even looking at him.

What else could I do or say?

Little Jim began working out his notice. But he'd worked only two weeks when he called me at home one night to tell me that the Augusta firm insisted that he start his new job without further delay. He told me that if he didn't start with them, they were going to give his job to another programmer. He said he was going to have to cut short his notice to Horizon, but he promised that he would work nights, weekends, or whatever it took to help finish the system. He'd also support us by phone, he said.

Before I could verbalize a protest, he dropped another bomb. He told me that there was something else that he'd "been meaning to tell me." He and Lee Johnson had been secretly dating for quite some time and had fallen in love. Not only that, but they had eloped and were married in Gatlinburg, Tennessee, several weeks before.

It would be an understatement to say that I was surprised. I didn't have so much as an inkling that they'd even been seeing each other, much less that they'd secretly gotten married. According to Little Jim, they were married before Lee ever turned in her notice. I couldn't believe that the two of them had been going to work day in and day out, pretending to be mere coworkers, and all the while were actually married. They'd been carrying on their romance for months without anyone so much as noticing that anything was going on between them.

Several months back I'd observed Jim, who was a bachelor, flirting with Lee in the hall. I'd angrily warned him not to mess around with Lee. I told him that she was going through a nasty divorce and he should steer clear of her. I also advised that "having a honey where you make your money" was not a smart thing to do by any account.

Jim said that because of that conversation, he was afraid to share the news of their relationship.

Lee's sudden departure from Horizon made sense now. She'd been working for me for at least two weeks while she was married to my son. It had to be a wee bit uncomfortable for her.

I could also now better understand Little Jim's desire to leave Atlanta. Lee's ex-husband hadn't been content to just ride off into the sunset after his divorce. Even after it was final, he continued calling and harassing Lee both at home and at work. I knew him, and he was not the type of person who would just give up without a fight and then wish Lee well with her new life. Lee had been his high school sweetheart and they'd married right after graduation. He wasn't going to be enamored with the idea of the love of his life getting remarried so soon after their divorce, and he no doubt would continue to cause them trouble. Moving would solve that problem for Jim and Lee.

When I overcame the initial shock, I simply said, "Congratulations, Jim. Lee is as fine a person as you'll ever meet, and I wish the best to both of you."

He sounded relieved and thanked me. I told him that I was in a serious bind and I'd take him up on his offer to help us finish the modifications. He assured me that he would be there for me and said, "You have my word on it."

We said goodbye and that was the end of the conversation.

Teresa and I were the last persons standing at Horizon Software. Remarkably, I wasn't even slightly worried about moving forward with the company. I *knew* I could surmount the serious obstacles facing me. I didn't know how at the moment, but I knew with absolute certainty that I would get it done. I immediately recited my favorite verse, "I can do all things through Christ who strengthens me" and felt a familiar inner calm descend upon me.

I put my arm around Teresa, smiled, and said, "Something will turn up."

She looked up at me with tears in her eyes and squeezed me tight and said, "It always does."

Chapter Seventy-Five

Our situation by any objective analysis could have been best described with one word: *grim!*

I thought back to another time in my life when I would have assessed my situation similarly. It was when I first came to Atlanta and the consequences of my dark, depraved lifestyle were showing their devastating toll upon me. It was then that I had sunk down to the very bottom of the pit.

In complete remorse and submission, I'd literally begged God to forgive and save me. He bestowed mercy upon me, and like the prodigal son, I was forgiven. God not only forgave me but He welcomed me home with open arms—and then proceeded to shower me with His blessings. He removed the slavery of my addictions, honored me with a wonderful wife and happy children, and bestowed a rewarding career with financial success that few people ever enjoy.

Instead of continuing to glorify and obey God for miraculously transforming my life, I slowly but surely drifted away from Him. I became infatuated and obsessed with everything my dark side could conjure up, including money, power, lust, material objects, fame, and a nauseating arrogance and infatuation with myself as being the brilliant boy wonder that my entourage told me that I was.

I turned my back on my God and my family and finally God said, "Enough!"

His retribution was fast, furious, and certain, and my world came crashing down around me in a matter of just three days. Seven long years of punishment and hard lessons ensued—and now this.

As I surveyed my bleak situation, I felt inexplicably calm. And I wasn't worried about where I was going from here, or whether or not Horizon would ultimately succeed. As I'd told Teresa, something *would* turn up, and I knew we would succeed!

I was convinced that everything had happened exactly as God had ordained. He was in control and had me right where He wanted me. Teresa and I were starting with practically nothing. What appeared to be insurmountable obstacles lay dead ahead of us. When I succeeded this time around—*and I would succeed*—there could be no question that it was God working another miracle in my life. And when that day came, I would be the first to tell others that all my success came from Him and not from me.

I'd placed a want ad in the *Atlanta Journal* when Jack Oaf quit, and Monday morning a young man called me in response. He'd recently graduated from prestigious Georgia Tech as a genuine rocket scientist. But by the time he had graduated, NASA was no longer hiring rocket scientists. He'd taken a job teaching computer software programming at a small community college in South Carolina, near his parents' home, but had just moved back to Atlanta to find something more interesting.

He didn't have DataFlex experience, so I was leaning toward eliminating him out of hand, but he was insistent on coming by to see me. He said he'd taught several computer languages at the college level, and although he'd never heard of DataFlex, he was confident he could learn it in short order. I looked around my empty office and told him, "Sure why not? Come on by and we'll talk."

His name was John Sims. Similar to every other programmer I'd ever encountered, he dressed casually, wearing sneakers, blue jeans, and an open-collar shirt. He had a high, squeaky voice, slight build, freshly washed shoulder-length fine brown hair, and a constant smile.

Several things initially jumped out at me concerning John: He was intelligent, he had a tremendous attitude and was highly motivated to work, and he was the type of person who loved a challenge. That was the combination I wanted.

I explained my situation, including our limited resources, but I also was quick to point out the potential for greatness once we overcame these initial hurdles. I told him the supply-chain software system I'd built at WASCO was spectacular, and I was dead certain that we would have no problem selling it once we'd finished modifying it to meet the school food-service business model. He was unfazed by the challenges and anxious to start.

I hired him on the spot and we went to work right then. I spent the rest of the day orienting him to DataFlex and our existing code. John was amazing. According to the DataFlex tech-support people, who were located in Miami, John learned the DataFlex language faster than anyone they'd ever encountered.

Another programmer's software code is difficult to understand at best, but after Bobby Joe left us, Horizon's code had become sloppy. It was devoid of notes and lacked an intelligible data dictionary. John tried his best to decipher the code and understand what Little Jim and crew had done, but some of it looked like gibberish. As he poured through thousands of lines of code, John would call Little Jim numerous times throughout the day, trying to make sense of it.

Initially Little Jim spent some time answering these questions, but then he became harder and harder to reach. After a while, he quit taking John's calls altogether.

In frustration, I called Jim at home one night. A friend of mine had told me that he'd run into Little Jim at a store the previous day. Apparently Jim had lied to me about starting his new job early, and was actually taking a vacation during the week that he had promised to work for us. He hadn't even moved to Augusta yet, and in fact was still living in Atlanta. Had he wanted to help us, he could have easily been up there helping and training John.

I was madder than hell about that piece of information, but I was also desperate to finish the system; therefore I swallowed my pride and in my nicest voice tried to convince him to live up to his promise to support and train John.

I decided to sweeten the pot by offering Jim a tremendous opportunity—a lifetime royalty of 15 percent on the modules (pieces of software applications, such as inventory, order processing, and bid analysis) that he'd worked on in exchange for his help in this final drive to finish the system.

This was an act of sheer desperation on my part and not well thought out at all (actually, "idiotic" describes it best). Had Jim accepted my hastily contrived desperation offer, it would have cost Horizon millions of dollars in due course.

Fortunately for Horizon, the offer didn't matter because Jim just turned up his nose and sneered at it. His biting response is eternally burned into my brain, "I don't know why you need me. After all I'm just a 'coder.' You're the 'driving force' behind Horizon." His demeanor was poisonous and he spat those vengeful words at me with unbridled bitterness.

Instantly I remembered my conversation with Lee in which I'd said those same words. My comments had been made when I was trying to reassure her about her job security; obviously when she later shared them with Little Jim she'd done so out of context. He'd come away mistakenly thinking that I'd slighted him and had failed to appreciate his contribution to the Horizon effort.

It was at that moment I realized he wasn't about to help us—at all. In fact I now surmised that he actually wanted to see Horizon *fail.* His desire was to teach me a lesson and he had no regard for the consequences, including the possibility that if Horizon failed, Teresa, his brothers, and I would face financial ruin and the real possibility of forfeiture of our home.

I responded, "All right, Jim, if that is how it's going to be, then so be it. I won't bother you again."

And with that I hung up.

I resolutely told John not to call Jim again under any circumstance. We were done with begging for his cooperation. Over the next several weeks and months, our calls were directed to the DataFlex technical-support desk. They were aware that we'd suddenly lost all our programmers and were sympathetic to our need—so they were very supportive. We called so much over the next several months that we were on a first-name basis with all of them, including the lead programmer that actually developed the DataFlex language, Ken Ross, and we all became long-distance friends.

To his credit, and under unimaginably difficult circumstances, John finally completed the system and I could deliver it. Obviously God had sent the right person in my time of need. We collected our funds and celebrated with a dinner and then a trip to a local pub, where we played darts throughout the night.

Within the next few weeks and months, we were able to sell several more systems and the business really began to start clicking. I found a smart contract programmer to help John on a part-time basis, and as we expanded I recruited and lured away another experienced programmer to help out full time.

I also hired one of my son Michael's lifelong friends and classmates, Robbie Payne, to support our customers and test software. Although Michael and Jon themselves were still keenly interested in Horizon, their school responsibilities allowed them to work only summers and on occasion after school.

These days were, in a word, *fun*. We were all driven to succeed, and when word would come down that a purchase order was about to be faxed into our office, we'd all run into Teresa's office and gather around the fax machine like a bunch of excited kids. The moment that it began to print, we would hoot and holler and wildly cheer and dance around her office high-fiving each other.

That first year was the absolute best of times. We had a bunker mentality and would work unbelievably long hours to stay on schedule with whatever module we were developing. All five of our employees were fiercely loyal and dedicated. They saw our success unfolding right before their eyes, and to a person were highly motivated. At one point, John actually asked for permission to bring a couple of cots up to work so they could work until they were exhausted and then catnap for a few minutes. After a short rest, they'd arise again so they could continue working—what amounted to 24-hour days.

During this time, if I was not out on the road selling more systems, I was right there with them. Sometimes we'd all be up working and I'd look at my watch and discover that it was already 1 a.m. I'd gather all the employees together and we'd go out for a pizza and a pitcher of beer, only to return for more work afterward.

All the hard work transformed into amazing success for Horizon. Our revenue increased an astounding 480 percent in our second year. I streaked across the country selling Horizon software, beginning first in our own state of Georgia, then expanding throughout the Southeast, and finally going nationwide. Allen had long since abandoned Horizon and I was our sales force. I found myself traveling constantly and staying in a different city every night, but I was selling our software with ease—and loving it.

I felt that God was closer to me than at any other point in my life, and I was amazed at how He was blessing our company. It was like knowing where to mine for diamonds.

Everything was progressing nicely, with one aggravating exception. I had yet to sell my first "mega" account. To date I'd been able to sell our product only to relatively small and midsize school districts. I had also sold it to one large district, in Lexington, Kentucky, which had 50 schools; but they were well aware that they were our first large account and had used that knowledge as leverage in some hard negotiating. I practically gave the software away because I needed a reference from a large school district. I needed someone who would tell potential clients at other large school districts, "You should buy this system. It's great!"

Large school districts were nice, but in the K-12 market, the mega school districts were the real crown jewels. They represented potential windfall profits that were more in keeping with my goals of succeeding *mightily*. Our software pricing model meant selling individual software licenses to each school. A small school district might have anywhere from one to eight schools, and we would sell licenses at a cost of approximately $3,500 per school; but a mega district might have 400 or more schools. Sell one of those babies and we were talking *real* money.

One problem was that these elite districts were akin to exclusive clubs. Breaking the entry barrier seemed harder than an African American trying to attend a southern university in the early '60s. The rules were simple: If no other mega district had purchased your system, then you didn't gain entry into the club.

The first question they'd ask was, "What other mega districts are using your system?"

I'd look at them and sheepishly reply, "Well you'll be the first. BUT if you go with our system, you can believe I'll take care of you like I'd take care of my own *mama*!"

No matter how sincere my message, no one wanted to be first. These folks were first and foremost seasoned bureaucrats. If one of them made a multimillion-dollar decision and it went badly, he or she could end up losing a job; so that decision would not be made. The first rule for bureaucrats was to avoid risk at all cost (even if it was blaringly obvious that our software could save their district millions of dollars). They were not about to put their jobs on the line and become guinea pigs. To be sure, seasoned bureaucrats were definitely risk averse.

I'd worked feverishly for months trying to sell our product to one of these mega districts. I was positive that if we could just install our excellent software system in one, we would no doubt do an excellent job for them and the rest of the mega districts would follow like lemmings walking to the sea.

It was at this time that I met Dennis Barrett, who was with the Dallas Independent School District. Dennis was a bright and shining star in the field of school food service. He was my age and about my height, but he was much more potbellied. He was an amiable man with a quick wit. He was as bald as a cue ball and didn't mind if you kidded him about it. He'd been a food-service director in Anchorage, Alaska, in Las Vegas, and elsewhere, and had done an excellent job everywhere he'd been.

He was hired at Dallas ISD to bring sound business practices to the district and clean up the huge mess that the food-service department was in. He appeared to be the right man for the job. He was intelligent, articulate, and experienced, he understood business concepts, and he was politically savvy in this very political district. He was also a great delegator, and was determined to turn the district, which had more than 200 schools, into a model for the rest of the nation. I liked him a lot.

Over a period of several months I'd been trying to convince him that our company's products were a good fit for Dallas and could be instrumental in accomplishing his goal of streamlining their business processes and making this mega district efficient (and in so doing become the envy of the industry).

Dennis told me that he was disgusted with his existing system and seemed impressed with my overall knowledge of the subject. He admired my tenacious enthusiasm, straightforward, genuine approach, and the quality of our products (an opinion he developed at my initial presentation). My overriding goal had been to project an image of consummate professionalism—both my own and our company's, and so far anyway, my strategy seemed to be working.

I knew it was going to be a tough battle because no other district of their size had installed our system. Plus, he already had a very bad taste in his mouth from his current software vendor, and that bad taste translated to software companies in general. My experience had been that potential customers had a tendency to unfairly throw all software vendors into the same pot when in that frame of mind.

The bottom line was that it was going to be a very difficult sale, and if I was to be successful, I had to make the impression of a lifetime.

After months of calling on him, I finally got him to agree to a major demonstration. But he insisted that I had to show the actual *live software* and not a canned demo. I agreed, and he lined up nearly 50 people to view it. Heretofore the most I'd ever shown the software to in one sitting had been six or seven people.

Wow!

This was the chance I'd been waiting for and I was determined to make the most of it. I'm not sure that I even slept at all the night before in my motel room, but one thing is certain: I was up and dressed and mentally preparing for this presentation long before the sun began to peek over the horizon.

I was dressed fit to kill in a brand-new, navy blue Armani suit; double-starched white shirt; new tie with a fashionable, superbly tied double Windsor knot; and sparkling, freshly shined shoes. My teeth were scrubbed, my breath smelled like mint mouthwash, and every hair on my head was perfectly combed into place.

I was only two minutes from the meeting place, and I saw no reason to leave too early, so about ten minutes prior to the meeting I whispered a quick prayer and out the door I went. As I briskly walked down the sidewalk enjoying the bright sun, blue sky, and crisp air, I walked under a tree and suddenly a bird pooped on my head and partially on my right shoulder.

Apparently it was a big bird. And whatever it'd been eating had not agreed with its stomach, so there was no shortage of poop. It was a direct, splattering hit, and I was covered in it!

Aghast, I ran back to my room, only to discover that I had locked the key inside.

I fruitlessly shook and rattled the door handle and screamed, "Oh, no!"

To obtain another key, I ran down to the lobby with speckled, white, creamy bird poop splattered all over my head and neck, and the shoulder of my navy blue suit.

The clerk took one look at my eyes and my menacing countenance, and knew better than to smile or even so much as ask about the bird poop all over me. He nervously handed me a replacement key, and I ran back to the room. I didn't have time to take a shower or change clothes.

I frantically used a damp washcloth to try to remove the poop from my hair, neck, shirt collar, and suit. I was frantic. By the time I was finished, I was completely flustered. When I looked in the mirror for the final time, all the color in my face was gone.

I looked at my watch. I was going to be late for the meeting of a lifetime.

Minutes later I arrived at their main office. I was sweating profusely, shaken, and nervous. I saw my software engineer and nodded a sick smile in his direction. He was very overweight—obese, actually, at 450-plus pounds—but he was our best programmer. He wasn't much of a conversationalist or appealing to look at, and normally I would have never brought him to meet a customer. But this one had wanted to see a demonstration of the actual live software system, utilizing live data. I didn't feel confident showing live software myself with a deal this important, and had decided that it would be absolutely essential for me to have our best programmer there for additional insurance in case something went wrong.

Envision this for a moment: Approximately 50 people are crowded into a very small room, standing in a semicircle, focused on a single computer terminal with a chair in front of it. (Back in those days LCD projectors had not been invented.) I'm standing there trying to smile, but internally my mind is racing and I'm frantically wondering if I've removed all the bird poop from my hair and clothes.

Suddenly I distinctly think I can smell bird poop.

I quickly try to think of something else.

That was the scene, and at that point my mind went to prayer. I began praying that no one would notice or smell the bird poop; I prayed that the live software would perform well and not lock up, or have some other malfunction as I'd seen happen a hundred times before; finally I prayed for strength.

Just then my 450-pound technician stepped over to the chair to begin the demonstration. But as he tried to sit down, the chair suddenly rolled out from under him and he fell to the floor and landed with a loud thud. I could literally feel the floor shake when he hit the floor. He was rolling back and forth on his back, flailing his arms and legs straight up in the air, and floundering around struggling to get right side up.

So much for projecting an image of professionalism! This was not what I wanted to leave imprinted in their minds about Horizon Software International!

Dennis and I and several of his employees rushed to my programmer's side to help him up and determine if he was injured. After what seemed like an interminable delay, we were successful. Aside from his pride being damaged, nothing else appeared to be wrong with him. His face was beet red and so was mine. I could see his face and could *feel* mine.

Oddly, no one laughed and it was so quiet that you could have heard a spider walking across that room.

I should have been saying to myself, "I can do all things through Christ who strengthens me! I can do all things through Christ who strengthens me! I can do all things through Christ who strengthens me!" Unfortunately what I was saying to myself is not fit to be repeated. I was humiliated, unnerved, and wishing I was anywhere but in that room.

I felt that this deal was now gone, over, kaput!

That was all in my head and I know it was coming from my dark side. No one at the meeting but me knew about the bird-poop incident, and to a person everyone felt compassion for the programmer and knew he was embarrassed to no end. They were extremely impressed with the system that we showed them and were convinced that it would solve the majority of their most troubling problems and revolutionize their business processes.

In spite of our missteps, we had breezed through the demonstration in fine fashion and the software had performed flawlessly. My programmer did a splendid job with it, and we answered all their questions to their satisfaction.

Indeed, in the ensuing months we did win their business and many more mega accounts after that.

I think even God has a sense of humor.

CHAPTER SEVENTY-SIX

Over the next 15 years, Horizon expanded exponentially in virtually every area. By 2007, we'd greatly increased our product-line offerings, vertical markets, customer base, and number of employees; we'd enlarged our office space from 400 to 44,000 square feet, and established numerous satellite offices throughout the country. We'd built a state-of-the-art call center, customer-training facility, quality-assurance lab, modernistic sales and marketing department, and high-tech research and development center. We'd transitioned our technology to best of class, and most important, we earned a well-deserved reputation for providing excellent customer service and product satisfaction. All of this translated into improved revenues and profit.

We weren't perfect by any stretch, but we had assiduously worked to execute every aspect of our mission statement. And it was working. Horizon was nearing $30 million in annual sales revenue (much of it recurring), with excellent double-digit margins. We were experiencing good growth, had no debt, and enjoyed Dun & Bradstreet's highest credit rating. And incredibly, in all those years of doing business, we had never been sued by a customer, nor had we ever sued one. In fact, our customer-satisfaction rating (as determined by an outside agency) was over 98 percent, as was our customer-retention factor. We'd become wildly successful by most any measure.

Much of our success can be directly attributed to our great people. My objective was to hire only the brightest, happiest people—people of good character and a great attitude. If I could find those phenomenal but rare individuals who were also poor, smart, and driven, then all the better. Our 180-plus employees made up one of our most cherished assets; and true to biblical concepts, we tried our utmost to treat them like we would want to be treated. With precious few exceptions, they greatly appreciated Horizon, its leadership, and their opportunity to be a part of this great company.

Early on, we had become the overwhelmingly dominant player nationwide in the K-12 school food-service market, but that success was insufficient to meet my aspirations. I had my eye on bigger and better goals for Horizon. I'd begun researching other food-service markets, and early analysis confirmed my hunch: Food service was food service. Whether it was a K-12 school or a college dining hall, or for that matter a senior-living community, military base, correctional facility, hospital, or corporate dining hall, there really wasn't a whit's difference in business processes.

Basically, all the facilities in these vertical markets had to do the same things that our software readily managed, including inventory control, order processing, menu planning, food preparation, sale of food products, collecting cash, credit-card processing, accounting, video surveillance, biometric identification, keeping up with fixed assets and personnel, and so forth. I sensed that with a few minor tweaks to our K-12 system to address any specific vertical market's needs, we could eventually dominate those segments of the market too.

I knew that we had to become singularly focused on our goal of becoming the number one provider for the entire food-service industry, (a global mega market which in itself was plenty big enough to meet our most ambitious aspirations). We now aspired to be the number one food-service technology company in the world for *all* institutionalized food-service vertical markets—not just K-12. Over the next several years, we developed product lines and private labels for all of them.

To be number one in anything, however, we would have to stay laser-focused. As CEO, I was bulldog determined that Horizon was going to do just that.

As we expanded and improved, so did our technology. We eventually progressed to a position in which Horizon technology was generally acknowledged in the industry as being the most sophisticated, elegant, comprehensive, and sought-after food-service technology to be found anywhere on the planet. Our mission statement called for our products to be "only of the highest quality," and I took that pledge seriously. And our great people worked hard to make it a reality.

Early on we'd moved away from DataFlex and had gone on to become gold-certified Microsoft developers. The first improvement was converting all our applications from DOS to Windows. Several years later I made the monumental decision to rewrite (in their entirety) all our applications on the most sophisticated platform available. We selected Microsoft's .Net and SQL Server database as the desired platform and back end, and began rewriting the system in Microsoft's beta one version.

Subsequently Microsoft honored Horizon by selecting it to participate in their *Whidbey* .Net and *Yukon* SQL programs. These were highly esteemed programs for Bill Gates, and at the time he indicated through press releases that he was betting the future of Microsoft on this state-of-the-art technology. Out of all the software developers that Microsoft had available to them, they selected Horizon as one of just 15 elite companies *worldwide* with whom they would partner to develop a large ERP (Enterprise Resource Planning) system. These partnership programs gave us unfettered access in person or by call-in technical support to Microsoft's development teams and also to their testing lab, which was located at their headquarters in Washington. This was ample testimony to the excellence and high quality of our development team, which was by this time being led by my son Michael.

Few software-company CEO's would have ever made the ambitious decision to rewrite a comprehensive ERP system of this complexity. It had grown to include some 28 different integrated modules with thousands of features, and it was sold under numerous brands and private label offerings for multiple vertical markets. In all, Horizon's food-service offerings contained some 5½ million lines of code and had been written at tremendous expense over a period of 21 years. That includes the decade spent writing the system's original core offering, the WASCO supply-chain and distribution system.

But in the end it was all worthwhile. Horizon had undertaken a bold, unique, creative, and imaginative step, and the net result was that in record time we'd created Horizon's next-generation software system, *Horizon OneSource*™.

Just three years after we'd begun the project, we released the major components, and customers worldwide responded overwhelmingly. Our client base quickly shot up to some 18,000 small, medium, large, mega, and ultra-mega customer installations. We'd garnered business from some 28 food-service management companies, including Aramark (with $10 billion in revenue), Sodexho ($14 billion), and the world's largest food-service management company, Compass food group (a whopping $21 billion). We also became the exclusive service provider for military schools all over the world and achieved preferred vendor status for the Army Air Force Exchange Service (AAFES), which was a $7 billion entity.

We had developed a myriad of innovative products, like the *Horizon Meal Pay*™ system, which enabled parents to go online to see what their children were eating every day and to refresh their lunch-money accounts. We also had the *Horizon Student Nutrition Guide* (a computerized child-obesity prevention system), *Smart Vending*, and other products. We ended up on *Good Morning America*, CNN, *Fox News, ABC News,* and other TV programs, and our innovative products received coverage in over 650 other media outlets, such as the *Boston Globe, Atlanta Journal and Constitution, USA Today, Los Angeles Times, Forbes* magazine, the *Washington Post, Better Homes and Gardens,* and even the *London Times.*

Our technology was repeatedly honored by the Technology Association of Georgia (TAG), and we were a recipient of the prestigious Deloitte Technology Fast 50 Award for four years running. We were recognized as one of the fastest-growing privately held businesses by *Inc.* magazine and made its highly esteemed Inc. 500/5000 list.

I was showered with accolades. The Gwinnett County Chamber of Commerce—the third largest chamber in the country—chose me as its 2006 businessperson of the year from among hundreds of nominees. A year later, I was a finalist for the prestigious Ernst and Young Entrepreneur of the Year award, which had previously been won by the likes of Michael Dell of Dell Computers. I appeared on television and radio shows. I was featured in newspapers and magazines, including *Inc.* and *Reader's Digest.* I was on the Internet on MSN and on Yahoo Daily Business. And I was asked to speak all over the country.

Amazingly, in spite of all our tremendous success, it still was not enough for me. I wanted to go after the big daddy of them all, the United States military. They fed more people on a daily basis than any other entity, and there could be no greater prize than selling Horizon's technology to the U.S. Department of Defense. I had a problem, though: I had absolutely no idea of how to sell to them. I spent months knocking on doors and making phone calls, just trying to make contact with someone—anyone—but I'd gotten absolutely nowhere. The Department of Defense was proving to be the mother of all bureaucracies.

After months of trying, I had dejectedly decided that, short of a miracle from God, I might not ever make my sale of a lifetime.

It was during this time that I boarded a plane in Los Angeles, heading back to Atlanta. It had been a difficult week for me. I'd been working with my West Coast salesperson for five solid days, giving sales presentations to K-12 school districts in five different cities. I was exhausted and happy to be heading home. I plopped down into my seat and let out a sigh, and with a weary look on my face smiled and nodded to the distinguished-looking gentleman sitting next to me. I hoped he wasn't the talkative type, because I just wanted to rest and maybe even sleep a little on the four-hour flight back.

"Hard day?" he asked.

I responded with a weak smile, "Brutal!"

He stuck out his hand. "Bob Shadley."

We shook hands as I replied, "Bob Williamson. Pleased to meet you, Bob."

After we took off, he immediately struck up a conversation and asked what I did for a living. He seemed to take an unusually keen interest when I told him that I owned a food-service technology company.

I asked him what he did and he told me that he was a major general in the army and was stationed at Fort McPherson, an army base in Atlanta. Then he dropped a bombshell. He was the base commander and food service was a major part of his responsibility.

"As a matter of fact," he said, "food service is my first love. Feeding the troops has always been one of my top priorities. Providing good meals is the key to maintaining good morale, especially in combat theaters."

I could feel goose bumps and the hair rising on my neck. I nervously glanced around like a dimwit, as though somehow I expected to see God standing behind me, smiling and asking, "Is this the miracle that you've been whining for?"

How fortuitous it was for me to sit down next to an army general in charge of the food-service department for an entire army base! I'd been trying for months to talk with anyone in the military. Talking with a master sergeant would have made me happy, but here I was sitting on a plane next to an army base *commander* who had a passion for providing excellent food service for his soldiers.

I can tell you that I no longer wanted to doze on the flight back to Atlanta. I excitedly began explaining our excellent technology and told him of our years of experience in food service—we had some 18,000 food-service installations all over the world in various vertical markets. I told him that I'd been trying for months to make headway breaking into the military market, but had met a hardened and reinforced concrete wall when I requested a meeting with someone at the department of defense or any of the military services. I told him I also tried the legislative route, and my meetings with my arrogant, blowhard congressmen and senators in Washington D.C. had gone nowhere.

He laughed heartily and said the army could make it extremely difficult to do business with them sometimes, but he would be happy to help steer me through the maze and make some introductions to some people he felt could help me. He would start by having his colonel, who managed his food-service operation, brief me on how the army's food-service system worked— as early as Monday if I liked.

I liked!

General Shadley spent much of the remainder of our flight explaining how food service worked in the military and detailing many of the problems that he faced with his current system. I told him how our software resolved those problems and did even more. He seemed genuinely impressed and even excited with the way we handled menu-plan forecasting and other problems, and he was especially interested in the cost-cutting measures incorporated into our technology.

The time passed quickly and soon our plane was nearing Atlanta. I remember thinking that I did not want our conversation to end, and it was almost as though God said, "Okay, I can handle that for you." Immediately the pilot came on the intercom and said that thunderstorms over Atlanta were causing them to redirect our flight to Memphis to ride it out.

I smiled broadly in amazement and then quickly resumed my conversation with General Shadley. We stayed in Memphis several more hours and had lunch together before finally hearing the announcement that our flight to Atlanta had been cleared to depart. All in all, we'd spent nine hours together that day, and before we parted he invited my wife and me to dine with him and his wife, Ellie, the following weekend. This was the beginning of an enduring friendship.

General Shadley introduced me to his mentor and friend, General Ross, who was a retired four-star general and a real-life hero. General Ross had orchestrated the mind-boggling logistics for the Gulf War, coordinating all aspects of pre-positioning millions of tons of vehicles, supplies, ammo, tanks, rations, and other supplies to the Gulf region.

Like General Shadley, General Ross can best be described as a perfect gentleman of the highest caliber and integrity. He was a kind-looking, soft-spoken person. He stood about five-feet-eight and had a medium build, and he was a marathon runner in excellent condition, like many of the other army brass that I would eventually meet. He was not an imposing, big bull of a figure like General Schwarzkopf, but he definitely had what is referred to in the military as a command presence. When he walked into a room, you just automatically *knew* he was in charge. Even though I was not a military person, I answered his every question with a respectful "Yes sir" or "No sir." And when he spoke, I listened . . . *attentively.*

An army colonel who'd worked for General Ross for years told me that a certain aggressive general in the Pentagon with an office right down the hall from where General Ross worked had ruined some really good colonels by screaming and cursing at them—to their breaking point. He told me that he'd never heard General Ross even so much as raise his voice or utter a curse word, and yet he achieved phenomenal results. I yearned to be like him, but unfortunately had a long way to go and was wired more like that screamer down the hall from him.

After retiring from the army, General Ross had begun a career with a consulting firm in Washington D.C. that catered to a clientele who wanted to do business with the military but needed help. His firm also employed a retired navy admiral, an air force general, a marine corps general, and numerous colonels and other high-ranking military officers with experience in all areas of procurement. They had all the services covered and they had excellent contacts, from officers in the field, to the Pentagon, to Congress, and even to the White House. It was like a dream come true for me.

Ordinarily General Ross's firm took on only huge clients, such as major defense companies, but because of his personal friendship with General Shadley, he graciously made an exception for me. Not only did he do that, but after seeing the quality of our offering, he personally worked Horizon's account with me. It turns out that he too had a passion for feeding the troops, and after seeing what we offered, he believed that Horizon's system would be an enormous improvement for the army. (And trust me, he loved the U. S. Army.)

In the ensuing months and years, he and others on his staff introduced me to generals, admirals, the undersecretary of defense, and various important bureaucrats. These people were from all over: Washington D.C., Philadelphia, the Pentagon, West Point, the Naval Academy, the Air Force Academy, and military bases all over the country.

It was all helpful, but the wheels at the Pentagon and Department of Defense still turned slowly. Nonetheless, with bulldog determination to succeed, I forged through five long years of hard work, presenting to virtually anyone who would give me an audience. At long last, the DoD released a Request For Proposal, or RFP—they wanted to consider purchasing a common food-service technology system for the army, navy, air force, and marine corps, which was to be installed in every dining facility on every land base, ship, submarine, and remote battlefield for all services.

Each service had been using its own homegrown technology system and none of them worked very well. Plus, the technology they used was inefficient and costly to maintain. At the time of the RFP, Secretary of Defense Donald Rumsfeld was on an efficiency and cost-cutting binge, and the DoD launched this effort to comply with his marching orders to streamline every process in the military or else.

Accenture, Computer Science Corporation (CSC), and IBM, the world's largest integrators of software systems, all responded to the RFP for the mammoth $100 million project. In addition to rolling out the actual food-service technology that operators would use all over the world, one of these companies would also integrate and roll out other systems covering SAP, security, food procurement, communications, and more. I was told that 85 technology vendors originally competed to become the food-service technology vendor for this project and yet incredibly all three—Accenture, CSC, and IBM—chose Horizon Software as their vendor of choice.

This was amazing because invariably when these fiercely competitive integrators bid against each other, they would try to gain an advantage by offering something different. In this case, Horizon's technology, experience, and good references for mega projects were so superior to those of other vendors that all three of the RFP respondents selected us. I still think of this as being incredulous and unheard of. To a company they'd all tried their utmost to obtain exclusives from me, but I was in the enviable position of being on the winning team no matter which integrator won. I diplomatically, but firmly, turned them all down.

IBM ultimately won the bid, and we were in right along with them. DoD purchased the technology directly from Horizon and we partnered with IBM for the integration aspect of the project. It was the largest single sale we ever made, amounting to over $10 million for licensing fees alone, and long-term profits would amount to many, many millions more over the years ahead as each service began fine-tuning to its own exacting specifications.

I was delirious . . .

Chapter Seventy-Seven

How did I hold up to all the flash and the cash through those years? In times past, whenever my dark side would come calling and beckon me with money, fame, and success, I'd answer his call and soon thereafter abandon God. This time was different. My relationship with God had remained intact. In fact, I was closer to Him spiritually at this point than at any other time in my life.

On that fateful day when Teresa and I (the lone remnants of Horizon's meager workforce) stood together hugging in our tiny 400-square-foot office, I'd promised God that I would never again turn from Him no matter what happened, no matter how tough the temptation or situation.

I remained true to my word. My faith in Jesus Christ was absolute.

Throughout the ensuing years, during which I attained fabulous success, accumulated tens of millions of dollars in personal wealth, and received accolades and awards at every turn, I steadfastly attributed my success to its rightful source. These were *blessings from God.*

I believe with all my heart, soul, and spirit that God has directly intervened in my life numerous times, molding and shaping me into what He desired. (Although, I must admit, in typical rebellious fashion I was often kicking, screaming, and fighting Him as He dragged me along.)

My explanation for my success did not sit well with the overwhelming majority of those writers and media people who interviewed me. Maybe it was a sign of the times, but by and large, they all seemed to want to ascribe my success to my hard work, perseverance, and brilliance, or to dumb luck, coincidence, or Karma, or to some combination thereof. Most did not want to even discuss the subject of blessings from God. Much to their dismay, I always insisted upon it because I'm absolutely convinced that "blessings from God" was the case.

After all the hard lessons in life that I endured, beginning with the first ones in Atlanta and culminating with seven years of recovering from the Ralph fiasco, it had all boiled down to one thing. And I was determined to live and die by "I can do all things through Christ who strengthens me."

The key to my understanding this verse was to carefully examine it. The verse begins with **"I."** It does not say that **Christ** will do all things for me. It says **"I"** can do all things. This meant to me that I had to do my part, which entailed hard work, being passionate, and maintaining a positive attitude; I also thought that it meant working smart, being dedicated to success, and persevering through the obstacles that were invariably in my way.

Most important, I discovered that I had to truly commit my work to Christ and **"His"** purpose for my life. I couldn't ever commit myself again to my own selfish ambition or to lusts or to foolish pride. Logic alone dictated that I could not reasonably expect Christ to strengthen me to accomplish *anything* that I might want to do. What if my goal was to establish a pornography empire?

No, whatever the opportunity was that presented itself had to be within God's will for my life, and I needed to spend the necessary time trying to determine if it was being launched for God's purpose or my own before embarking on a certain course.

So what about Horizon? What noble purpose did it serve for God? I believed then as I believe now that Horizon would ultimately serve dual purposes to advance the kingdom of God. One, from a philanthropic standpoint, it would provide me sufficient funds to help those in need and further God's ministry. Second, and perhaps more important, I had made the difficult decision to go public with my past. I wanted to help others find Christ, especially those who were hurting—and my reputation could just be damned. Heretofore it had been a dark family secret. I'd shared my life of drug addiction and criminal behavior with my children so I could warn them about my firsthand experience with the dark side and its devastating consequences in my life. But I hadn't shared my story with anyone else. I agonized over whether or not to reveal my lurid past to others. I knew it would be an embarrassment to my family and personally humiliating to me.

As I mulled this over, I thought of Biblical examples of God's using weakness to exemplify His power. He did it with David and Goliath, when a puny kid with a slingshot overcame incredible odds and slew the most feared warrior of the day. God demonstrated His power through Moses, a weak, frightened shepherd with a speech impediment, who God used in a mighty way to fiercely and boldly defy Pharaoh, the most powerful man in the world, as he insisted that Pharaoh let God's people go.

God's strength worked through these men just as it had worked through me. I was a weak, wicked wretch with no hope, and yet by the wonderful grace of God I've been mightily transformed. I didn't become a revered king of the Jews like David or watch the Red Sea part like Moses, but nonetheless I witnessed a mighty miracle of God in my own life. My life story glorifies God in a smaller but similar fashion, and is a tribute to God's awesome power. It really isn't so much about me. Mine is a miraculous, true story of redemption that needs to be told in order to inspire others, and to offer hope to the hopeless.

I felt that if Horizon was not only successful but *wildly successful,* it would have an even greater impact upon those who heard my testimony. If I could build Horizon into a $50, $60, or even $70 million entity, I believed that people would listen to me even more. I hitchhiked into Atlanta penniless, found God, and through Him had amazing success.

I'd become accustomed to studying the Bible every morning. Generally I would arrive at work around 4 a.m., and the office would be empty-quiet and conducive to deep spiritual reflection. My early morning Bible study had become a wonderful way of starting my day off in a good mood. If I was facing a particularly troublesome problem in my personal or business life, I would research what the Bible had to say about it and thereby receive soothing comfort and wise direction. It was ironic: Despite how far I'd come, I was right back where I'd started, reading and studying the Bible every day just as I had done in Grady Hospital so long ago.

Admittedly, my good moods didn't always stay around for very long. The intensity associated with resolving the perplexing problems of a large company would grind me down. But the way I looked at it, at least I could start off every morning in a good mood.

One day I was thinking about how most of the personal and business problems and pressures I faced were not unique to me but were common to all our employees—and in fact to all humanity. I couldn't help but think how unfortunate it was that many people didn't even own a Bible, much less spend time studying one on a daily basis. I knew from personal experience that facing the problems of this pressure-filled, tough world alone was a losing battle, and that we all need God in our lives in order to succeed.

I think God opens opportunities to everyone who submits to Him. Opportunity is like a taxicab: When the taxi pulls up, either we climb in or we wait for another. We might have a long wait if we don't seize on an opportunity when it presents itself. I believe that too many people miss out on their opportunities in life due to their inaction and because of their lack of faith in God and in themselves.

Against tremendous odds, I'd become incredibly successful, by most any measure. And it occurred to me that if others would do the same things that I had done to achieve success while avoiding those things that I'd done wrong, they too could become successful. I wanted to motivate and inspire others so they might have the same success that I was enjoying, and I came up with an idea of how to do just that.

In early 2000 I decided to start sharing the conclusions I reached from my daily Bible study, and I would do so by relating my real-life experiences to friends and employees. Every morning I'd research the Bible about whatever randomly came to my mind, and then my interpretation and conclusions on what the Bible had to say about that particular subject or problem would be sent out as a daily e-mail message to anyone who wanted to be on my mailing list.

I entitled it *Words for the Day.* The topics were all over the place, and included marriage, raising children, drug abuse, lust, anger, unbridled ambition, pride, helping others, attending church, drinking to excess, the love of money, tithing, trials and tribulations, death of a loved one, abortion, homosexuality, lying, stealing, heaven, hell, obtaining salvation, giving to the needy, and an entire host of other subjects.

One of my programmers, Ken Ross (who ironically was an atheist), volunteered to design a website to house and manage all the daily messages, and he designed a searchable database so viewers could easily find information on subjects that interested them. He also designed a method for me to compose messages and send them out, and also set up an easy way for people to subscribe or unsubscribe online. In effect he created a blog (**www.wordsfortheday.org**) for me years before the word "blog" was ever coined.

I made it vividly clear to all employees that choosing to receive the daily messages was entirely voluntary, and I let them know that I did not monitor the subscriber list. I had decided early on that I didn't want to know who subscribed or unsubscribed in my company, because I didn't want that to influence my relationship with them in any way. If *Words for the Day* was, or was not, their cup of tea, then so be it; it was nobody's business but theirs.

Eleven years have passed since I started my daily messages, and to this day I still don't know who subscribes and who doesn't. I do know, however, that the list of subscribers has grown exponentially outside the original Horizon base, and I now have readers scattered all over the world. People write to me daily to offer comments or seek advice, including some pastors who tell me that they often use my messages as inspiration for their Sunday sermons.

It never ceases to amaze me to see how God has used this resource to comfort His children. Not a week goes by without some reader writing to inform me that a particular message hit home with him or her. Invariably this reader tells me that whatever I'd written that morning was the very thing that he needed to hear that day. It's almost as though that morning God put into my mind the very subject that was tearing someone apart so that my *Words for the Day* could help lighten his burden in a timely fashion. It's eerily uncanny, because sometimes I open my Bible to the very passage that pertains to my chosen subject for the day, and I can feel the hair on my neck sticking straight up as I sense God's presence.

Below is an example of just such a *Words for the Day* entry that I sent out. Also below is the letter that I received from a reader and part of my excerpted response to him:

Isn't it amazing how God works in our lives! On a Saturday night several weeks ago, a certain pastor was working late and decided to call his wife before he left for home. It was about 10 p.m., but his wife didn't answer the phone. The pastor let it ring many times. He thought it was odd that she didn't answer, but decided to wrap up a few things and try again in a few minutes. When he tried again she answered right away. He asked her why she hadn't answered before, and she said that the phone hadn't rung at their house. They brushed it off as a fluke and went on their merry ways.

The following Monday, the pastor received a call at the church office. It was on the same phone that he had used that Saturday night. The man calling the church wanted to know why the pastor had called on Saturday night. He couldn't figure out what the man was talking about. Then the man said, "It rang and rang, but I didn't answer." The pastor remembered the mishap and apologized for disturbing him, explaining that he'd intended to call his wife.

The man said, "That's okay. Let me tell you my story. You see, I was planning to commit suicide on Saturday night, but before I did, I prayed, 'God if you're there and you don't want me to do this, give me a sign now.' At that point my phone started to ring. I looked at the caller ID, and it said, 'Almighty God.' I was afraid to answer!"

The reason it showed on the man's caller ID as coming from "Almighty God" is because the church that the pastor works at is called Almighty God Tabernacle!

Matthew 7:7

Ask and it will be given to you;
seek and you will find; knock and
it will be opened to you.

My reader's response:

Bob, I can really relate to today's WFTD. I have been going through some amazingly bad times lately and have had numerous encounters with God.

I recently got a pistol to commit suicide with, but I was unable to pull the trigger. I put it in the drawer until a few days later, when I tried again. Again, I was unable to pull the trigger and I put the gun back in the drawer. A few days later I decided to let my truck run in the garage. After 10 or 15 minutes I felt euphoric, like I was on laughing gas. I was tingling and numb, and my thoughts were all over the place. I got scared and turned my truck off and went outside until I felt better.

A few days later, while eating dinner, God told me to get rid of the gun. I said "okay" and the next day I took it back to where I got it. That evening, my wife finally admitted to her affair and went into detail about having sex with her boyfriend at a hotel while the kids were at school and I was at work. That night was it. I didn't have the gun, so I had to sit in my truck in the garage again. There was nobody to stop me. I said a prayer apologizing to God. I told him that he was the only one who could stop me tonight. I sat in my truck for 2½ hours that night, and the only thing that happened was that I got really hot. Somehow that night God gave my truck the cleanest emissions ever.

All my problems are still here. The world seems hopeless and unrelenting, but I don't have a choice anymore. God wants me here, so one way or another I will get through it. I pray constantly, and I can tell you that God has taken a lot of my pain and sorrow away. Every waking minute is not filled with agony anymore. The problems are still there, but the pain has subsided.

I just wanted to tell you that I look forward to your e-mails every day. I appreciate what you do.

Thanks.

My partial response to the reader:

I want you to know that when I wrote that WFTD yesterday I was in a hurry and just decided to search the database for an old one instead of writing one from scratch like I usually do. As I got ready to type in the search criteria, the word "suicide" suddenly popped into my mind, and that is what I typed in the search field. I truly believe God made that word pop into my mind yesterday in order to help YOU. He loves you more than you can imagine and this is no coincidence, just like it wasn't a coincidence when the man in yesterday's WFTD got the call from the pastor of Almighty God Tabernacle.

Remember God is there for you 24/7. If you don't have anyone else and need someone to talk to, please feel free to call me personally. God bless you, my brother—I'm praying for you. These things will pass and in time God will take away your pain.

Your friend,

Bob

I didn't know it at the time, but soon enough my own faith would be severely tested under raging fire, and I would be the one who needed comfort and guidance.

CHAPTER SEVENTY-EIGHT

I'd been keeping in touch with my brother Jim, but we weren't getting along at all. Whenever he called, he wanted to pour out his heart about all his problems and current tribulations and how much he missed Little Bob and Mom. Yet when I tried to offer advice or encourage him to get involved with God and go to church to find comfort and peace, he'd turn violently angry and curse me out, call me a "Bible thumper," and hang up.

One night he called me and he was very distraught. He and his wife had been arguing, and she'd told him that she was going to leave. This was Jim's third wife and he just couldn't bear to go through another divorce, especially since it meant that she'd be taking their little son with her (not to mention cleaning out his bank account, which he had suffered through during his previous two divorces, and possibly getting his home).

He'd already lost his two daughters to his first wife's custody. He didn't have any children with his second wife. He told me that shortly after he married her she emptied his bank account, bought a large quantity of cocaine, and ran off to California with a male stripper.

As usual, I tried to advise him to start involving his family in church. He let out a string of oaths that would melt a candle, cursing me and God with all the vile energy that he could muster. It became so bad that I hung up on him. I went back to my bedroom and got down on my knees. With tears flooding my eyes, I asked God to take over. I told Him that I'd tried and had said everything that I knew to say.

I said, "God, I give up. I'm not qualified to help Jim. I'm turning him over to you."

I immediately felt as though a huge burden had been lifted from my shoulders and couldn't help but ask myself why I hadn't done this earlier. Jim was in God's capable hands now.

The very next night Jim called and he was crying uncontrollably. He and his little son James had found his wife near death. She'd attempted suicide by taking a large amount of sleeping pills. He had barely arrived in time to save her life by rendering artificial respiration until an ambulance arrived. His quick action saved her. She was subsequently committed to a psychiatric ward for mandatory evaluation and observation for 30 days. When Jim went to see her, she told him that when she was released from the hospital, she was leaving him for good and taking their young son with her.

Jim was devastated. He sobbed into the phone, "I just don't get it. Look at you. You have a wonderful wife . . . happy, successful kids . . . a great career; you have tons of friends; you're happy . . . you have everything going for you. But me?

"My life's a wreck, my kids are a wreck, my third marriage is in shambles. My company forced me into early retirement. I'm all alone. I don't get it; we came out of the same womb . . . had the same upbringing . . .we even look the same, and I'm just as smart as you."

He agonized, "I was the golden boy when we were growing up. But you're the one sitting on top of the world now and my life's a complete disaster? *Why?*"

I softly replied, "The answer is simple, Jim. I have God in my life and you don't."

I told him, "Go to the airport and I'll have an airplane ticket waiting for you in your name. Come up here for a while and let's work through this together."

To my amazement, he meekly agreed. Jim had finally reached that point known to many alcoholics, drug addicts, and others who have resisted God until they hit absolute bottom. And then he reached out. He finally recognized that he could no longer fight the fight alone.

He flew to Atlanta and I met him at the airport. He looked like hell compared with the last time I'd seen him at my father's house several years earlier on the Fourth of July. He'd lost a lot of weight, needed a shave and a haircut, and was showing far more gray in his black hair than the last time I'd seen him. He was wearing a loud outfit with white pants, a royal-blue-and-white flowered shirt, and dark sunglasses. He looked like a pimp.

When he sat down in the car, he removed his sunglasses and I noticed that his eyes were bloodshot and sunken. He really had a haggard appearance, as if he'd been on a drinking and drugging binge for weeks. His face was marked with deep lines, and it was razor thin. He was chain-smoking, even though doctors had recently performed heart bypass surgery and warned that smoking would kill him. He had a long white scar down the back of his tanned neck where he'd undergone surgery after a car accident; they'd had to fuse his spine, and his neck was permanently stiff—he had to turn his entire body to look behind him.

I fought against crying when I saw him like that, brushing back tears and pushing down the choking, sobbing feeling in my throat. We shook hands and I patted him on the shoulder and told him that everything would be all right.

We headed to the church I attended and met pastor Dr. James Merritt in his study. I had called him ahead of time to ask for his help in counseling Jim. Dr. Merritt explained that in order for Jim to reconcile with God, all he needed to do was ask God to forgive his sins and accept Jesus Christ as his risen Savior. Jim, Dr. Merritt, and I all got down on our knees, and Jim asked God to forgive him his sins and for Jesus to come into his life. Right there in Dr. Merritt's study, Jim fully submitted his life to God and accepted Jesus Christ as his Savior. Tears were streaming down all our faces before it was over.

Dr. Merritt spent considerable time talking to Jim about Jim's inner demons, including the unexpected deaths of Little Bob and my mother, his divorces, his problems with his present wife, and a host of other demons that had been torturing him for years. Dr. Merritt related Bible verse after verse, and not only did it help Jim, but it also helped me better understand some things.

Later Jim and I went by Borders and he bought a Bible. We talked about God, we studied the Bible together, we reminisced about our childhood, we visited my office, we cooked steaks out in the backyard, and we just hung out together for the two weeks that he remained in Atlanta.

By the time he returned to New Orleans, Jim looked like a different person. He was relaxed, clean shaven, and fuller, and he had a smile on his face. He arrived in time to meet his wife as she was leaving the hospital. She noticed the change in him, and amazingly they reconciled that day.

One point of disagreement between them had been their house. Jim's wife wanted to move out of their old, dilapidated neighborhood, but Jim couldn't sell the house and didn't want to reduce the price and end up giving it away. Within a couple of days of returning to their home, amazingly they received a fair offer on the house; and they ended up selling it and moving into the new home of their dreams.

Jim, his wife, and their young son all joined a local church right down the street and were baptized together as a family two weeks after moving into their beautiful new home in the suburbs.

Was all of this just coincidence, luck, or Karma? No, it was a miracle of God.

Jim stopped drinking and drugging and playing guitar in his band in the wild bars of New Orleans. Instead he got into some good clean fun, like hunting, fishing, photography, and wildlife art. He even bought a boat for fishing offshore.

My family visited his and we had one of the best times of our lives. Jim showed me all of his new toys, including his hunting equipment, four-wheeler, maps of his hunting lease, his boat and fishing equipment, photos from his photography hobby, and a fish rendering that he had carved out of wood. (It was an excellent piece of art.) We went offshore in his new boat and caught a boatload of fish out at the oil rigs in the Gulf of Mexico; when we came home we had a huge fish fry.

Before we left, he assured me that all systems were go in his life and he'd never been happier. He and his family were going to church and he was reading his Bible daily—and I was elated for him.

A couple of years passed. I was traveling constantly all over the country, selling Horizon's products, and I was running our large corporation in between road trips. I would call Jim periodically and we'd talk about all kinds of things. After a while I began to grow concerned about him. He rarely called me, and when I called him and inquired if he was still going to church he'd reply, "Naw, I know that I need to but I just haven't gone lately."

I'd say, "Well, are you at least studying your Bible?"

"Naw, I know that I need to but I haven't picked it up lately."

I found out that he'd been playing music again and hanging out in the same bars with the same bums that he'd hung out with before he found Jesus. I warned him about it, but he said he needed the extra money that he made playing because his wife had run up his credit cards gambling in the casinos near his home. He assured me he could handle things.

In frustration I told him, "Jim, you should be careful. God turned your situation completely around when you hit bottom and you begged Him to come into your life. If you turn your back on Him, there's a danger that He'll turn His back on you; and if He does, bad things can happen. I know firsthand because it's happened to me more than once.

"Please, Jim, get back in church."

Jim told me he would, but from that point on he wouldn't answer his phone when I called. His answering machine would pick up and I'd say, "C'mon, Jim, pick up the phone; I know you're there. This is your brother, Bob." But there would be only silence until I heard the recorder beep to tell me it had reached its limit.

One night I was in Chicago and the weather was blustery rainy and cold. Lightning was popping everywhere, and I was hopeful that my flight wouldn't be cancelled. I was with John Sims, my rocket-scientist programmer, and we'd been making a presentation for a large client a few miles south of Chicago. Traffic control had already canceled several flights, and I really didn't want to spend the night in a Chicago hotel.

My cellphone rang and it was Teresa. She was crying uncontrollably. I anxiously asked, "What's the matter, Tree?"

She sobbed, "Oh, Bob, it's Jim. He just shot himself!"

I slumped down in my chair.

She said that Jim had committed suicide. He'd shot himself in the temple with a 9-millimeter handgun and had died instantly. She told me that Jim's wife had finally left him and taken their young son with her. Jim had called her and begged her to come back home, but she angrily refused and told him that she was going to seek a divorce and this time there would be no reconciliation. He put the gun to his head and pulled the trigger.

When I got off the phone with Teresa, I was in shock and oblivious to the tears streaking down my face. John Sims asked me what was wrong. I simply stared straight ahead and hollowly replied that my brother had just committed suicide. John didn't know what to say or do, aside from mumbling that he was very sorry, and then he nervously sat looking straight ahead saying nothing further. What does someone say to a person whose only brother just committed suicide?

I sat in silence, tortured with my thoughts, as I awaited news of whether or not the last plane scheduled to Atlanta would be cancelled like the dozen or so flights before it. I desperately wanted to get home and be with my family. I didn't want to be alone tonight, and I prayed to God that air-traffic control wouldn't cancel my flight.

Around midnight our plane, which was the last uncanceled flight, did indeed get out. The plane lurched and bumped through the turbulence as it ascended into the stormy clouds and into the pitch-black night. The scene seemed entirely appropriate for the moment. I blankly stared out the window, thinking of all the good times that Jim and I had enjoyed together. I was frantic and desperately wanted to somehow reverse what had happened. I wanted it all to be just a bad dream. But the cold, hard reality was that it wasn't going to go away. My brother Jim was gone.

Thoughts were racing through my mind. What could I have done? Why didn't I get on a plane and go see him when he wouldn't take my calls? Why didn't someone tell me he was suicidal? Why would he do such a thing? Why? Why? Why?

Jim and I once had a discussion about understanding the grief he felt over losing his five-year-old son, Little Bob. He told me that unless you've lost a child of your own, you could never understand how much it hurts. I can say the exact same thing about losing someone you deeply love to suicide. I believe that it's the absolute worst thing that can happen to someone, including outliving one or more of your children.

Heartbroken is inadequate. Sad cannot address it. Painful, upset, torn apart, gutted, hurting, anguished, sorrowful, agonized, aching, grief stricken, tortured, tormented, inconsolable, crushed, devastated, overwhelmed, shocked are all far too mild.

No superlative, adjective, or adverb is adequate to describe the crushing, dreadful feeling that slams into you when you hear that someone you deeply love has committed suicide. And if the grief is not enough, there's the guilt. I've never talked to anyone who lost a loved one to suicide that didn't feel that somehow they were responsible for not preventing it. I was no exception.

The haunting question "Why didn't I do something?" tortured me every waking moment. I should have somehow known that he was having these kinds of problems. Had I known, maybe I could have intervened and done something to ease the situation. The reality was that it was impossible for me to predict that Jim was contemplating suicide, and even if I had known, I doubt that I could have stopped it. I felt riddled with guilt just the same.

When I returned home, my entire family was waiting for me. When I saw them I just couldn't control my emotions any longer and broke down completely. I started weeping and sobbing. I lay down on my bed with them huddled around me and wailed, "It hurts so much" over and over again. I cried and cried and cried, until I could cry no more.

The tears dried up but the emptiness remained.

The next several days and weeks were like a horrible nightmare come true. Jim's funeral was the absolute pits and sadder than any I've ever attended before or since. Aside from family members, only two people (one druggie who said he was a friend, and Jim's former boss) came to the viewing; neither came to his funeral service. My sons and some other family members served as pallbearers. Unequivocally, this was the most traumatic thing I've ever endured. I couldn't imagine someone living 53 years and not having a single friend attend his funeral service.

To this day I still have a horror of not having anyone attend my funeral service and my family not being able to muster enough friends to serve as pallbearers. In fact, I've asked my wife to cremate me and spread my ashes in private because of this fear (whether it's founded or unfounded).

I got down on my knees and asked God to take away the pain. It was a useless prayer really, because you don't ever get over the pain of something like this; you just learn to live with it. It takes time—lots and lots of it.

My only comfort came from knowing that Jim was in heaven. Some might ask if suicide is a sin. Sure it's a sin, but Jesus Christ forgave Jim his sins, *all of them*, including committing suicide. On the cross, Jesus willingly took Jim's punishment for his sins. I have absolutely no doubt that today he is in heaven with Jesus, Little Bob, and Mom. Ultimately that knowledge enabled me to move on.

At the time of Jim's death, I'd made dramatic progress on many fronts in my spiritual life and had conquered many of my inner demons. But I still had a major stumbling block in my walk with God. I'd never given up drinking alcohol and although I drank mainly at home, I was drinking far too much and far too often. It became especially bad after Jim died. I began drinking heavily and it was adversely affecting my life.

I didn't like what alcohol did to my personality. It was as though drinking alcohol separated me from God and swung open a door to my dark side. Black thoughts, worldly lusts, and obnoxious behavior abounded in there.

When my inhibitions were lowered by mind-numbing alcohol, my dark side would come calling, beckoning me to venture to the darkness within. Unfortunately, like a dumb sheep going to slaughter, more often than not I did. I rarely drank in public, but recently I'd made a complete fool of myself at a Christmas party for our employees. After way too many drinks, I began dancing around on the dance floor thinking I looked cool; but in reality I was just another drunken idiot in a stupor, making a fool out of myself in front of our employees. It embarrassed me to no end and I was determined to quit alcohol.

Of course I realized that drinking was not good for me and knew I should do something about it. I'd quit taking drugs, I'd stopped smoking cigarettes, and I had found ways to control my urge to solve every problem by beating someone senseless. But after trying repeatedly to quit drinking, I always started back. Usually the temptation would overcome me whenever we'd go out with friends and everyone else would be having a beer or wine with dinner. When it was my turn to order, I'd yield to the temptation and say, "Sure, why not? Give me a glass of wine; in fact, bring a bottle will you?"

My drinking was hurting my Christian witness—how my daily life reflected my belief in Jesus Christ—in more ways than one. The worst incident in this regard was with a friend who had received numerous DUI's. I'd been trying to convince him to seek help at Alcoholics Anonymous. As I stopped to talk to him in the aisle of the local supermarket, I couldn't help but notice his eyes fixated on my shopping cart full of Lambrusco wine and beer for a pool party in progress at my house. He didn't say it, but I knew "hypocrite" was written in bold letters across his mind, and rightfully so.

It was painfully obvious to me that I needed to quit drinking. But simply put, I couldn't do it. I was an alcoholic. I didn't frequent bars or get into fights anymore, but I couldn't wait to get home every night after work and have a glass of wine, which translated into a bottle before the night was over. Over the weekends it amounted to several bottles, and then I started buying wine by the half gallon. I didn't drink because I liked the taste; I wanted that "feeling"; I wanted the mind-numbing buzz. I wanted to get obliterated.

One Sunday morning after a weekend of heavy drinking, I awoke with a particularly bad hangover. My wife and I had gone to our lake house for a weekend of relaxation, and I'd consumed two bottles of wine that Saturday night. I overslept and didn't go to church in the morning. As I lay in bed with my head pounding, a bad taste in my mouth, and a churning stomach, I realized that drinking had reached a critical point in my life. Alcoholism was adversely affecting my Christian life, my Christian witness, and my health.

I sat on the edge of the bed and then knelt down and begged God to help me quit drinking. I was so despondent about it that I literally fell flat on my face and cried out to the Lord for help.

The very next morning (Monday), bright and early I got a call from my doctor. A few days earlier I'd taken a blood test for a "key man" life-insurance policy for Horizon. The company was buying the policy, valued at several million dollars, to insure itself against the possibility that I would unexpectedly die and leave it in a lurch. Horizon needed to obtain the policy so we could secure an equity investment. The theory behind the policy was that, in the financier's opinion, much of the success of Horizon was due to me. If I were to die, the policy would provide them some financial protection and buy some time to bridge any gaps while they trained my replacement.

Due to the large amount of money involved, the physical exam and blood tests were extensive and very thorough. My blood work revealed something of grave concern that had never before been identified in any of my annual physicals and routine tests. I learned that I had hepatitis C, a devastating, deadly virus that infects the liver and is generally fatal. The only treatment for it is radical, debilitating chemotherapy using a drug cocktail of interferon and riboflavin, and that cocktail is effective for just 25 percent of those who use it.

My doctor told me that hepatitis C is transmitted only through the blood and I either got it from sharing dirty needles when I was using intravenous drugs, or through the many blood transfusions that I had at Grady Hospital.

Either way I knew that it was a direct consequence of sin. Even if a sin takes 30 years to exact its price, a sinner ends up paying for it.

My doctor told me that I needed to see a specialist, and advised that I shouldn't drink alcohol or do anything that might further harm my liver.

Wahhhhhh!!!! The shock of the siren was back . . .

My prayer asking God to help me stop drinking had been immediately answered, but I didn't know whether to thank Him or shake my fist at Him for allowing this fatal disease to infect me.

I went to see one of the top hepatitis C specialists in the world, Dr. Eugene Schiff of Miami, Florida. He examined me and conducted a liver biopsy. The biopsy showed minimal viral damage to my liver. He told me that the virus appeared to be inactive at the moment. He said that he'd seen cases where it had remained inactive or near inactive for decades, only to suddenly become active and very rapidly begin destroying the liver. He also warned that because I had hep C, the odds of now developing liver cancer were much greater than the average person's.

He didn't advise me to begin chemotherapy, however, because the virus appeared to be inactive and the chemotherapy was so devastating. In some cases, the treatment was considered to be nearly as bad as the disease. He told me that researchers were developing promising new drugs all the time, and if I could hold off for a year or two I might have an easier time with one of them when it was released.

I'd been living with the virus for over 30 years with no ill effects. He told me not to be deceived or build up false hopes, because the virus would never go away. If I lived long enough, he said, sooner or later I would have to deal with it. He also said that I might live out the rest of my life and possibly even die from something else before it took me. He sternly warned me not to drink alcohol or take anything that might further damage my liver.

As I write this, and to the best of my knowledge, my hepatitis C remains exactly as it was the day that doctors discovered I had the disease. It now has been 40 years since I contracted it. I no longer drink alcohol and so far, at least, God has held it at bay.

CHAPTER SEVENTY-NINE

In spite of everything I'd been through in my life, I finally reached a point where my absolute faith in Christ enabled me to maintain a positive attitude through the hard times and the good times—and even when I stared death in the face. My faith better prepared me to lead and encourage others through the best and worst of their lives.

Of course, nowhere did I drill the hard lessons that I'd learned more than into the heads of my two sons. I loved them more than life itself, and I didn't want them to ever have to experience the horror that I'd gone through. I knew they'd make their own mistakes, and in reality there's no better way to learn than to *suffer* through the consequences of a serious mistake; however, I didn't want them to make the *same* mistakes that I made. They could make new ones, but it would be foolish on my part not to help prevent them from making the same ones that I made.

I taught them everything I'd learned. I concentrated on character issues, such as always making the Lord their number one priority. I insisted they always be honest, and told them that when they gave their word on something, they were to live up to it—even if it cost them dearly. If they made a rash promise and it cost them either money or inner turmoil, they needed to live up to their word. They would not be so quick to do the same thing again after paying for it the first time. I instructed them that they had no other choice than to always honor their word. I taught them to try to live in peace with everyone if they could. I taught them the value of reputation and demonstrating a high level of integrity at all times. To be sure I taught them business acumen too—how to prevent someone from stealing from them; how to negotiate; how to avoid lawsuits; how to treat employees and customers in a fair, friendly, but firm manner; how to hire great employees; sales and marketing secrets that I'd developed over decades; the need for products of the highest quality; how to set prices for products; and much, much more.

I taught them so many things that it would take 10 books just to record it all. I went over it time and time again until finally, if I were to start a sentence, both of them would finish it for me; and then we'd all smile at each other.

I felt that very successful families reached that success over time. They did so, I believed, because way back in the beginning, the patriarchs of the family were willing to take time out of their busy schedules to mentor their children and share what they'd learned. If those lessons resonated with that next generation and they listened to the wisdom of the patriarch, they would avoid making the same mistakes the patriarch made; but in time they would make some mistakes of their own. Then the next generation would avoid the ones that Grandpa had made, plus the ones that Dad made, and then they would be left to make a few of their own. This learning would continually pass on to coming generations.

Provided that each successive generation spent the necessary time to educate their children, the mistakes would soon be minimal, and dynasties and fortunes—like those of the Rothschilds, Kennedys, and Rockefellers—amassed.

I wanted my kids to far exceed anything I'd ever accomplished, and I spared nothing in my efforts to prepare them. The effort was not without its rewards. Nothing in life compared with the immense pleasure that I derived from working with my family every day and watching my boys mature into successful businessmen in their own right.

It's an incredible experience to watch one of your children conduct a high-level meeting with very intelligent men and women in a consummately professional manner, or see them skillfully present complex multimillion-dollar technology solutions to a sophisticated group of clients.

We all worked in different departments and didn't see each other constantly, but we saw each other enough in meetings and of course when we went to lunch together. Our family became very tight knit and we truly enjoyed each other's company. There were no sibling rivalries or other family feuds. We had a common goal of success and worked together as a team to achieve that goal.

Michael and Jon, like many siblings, were diametrically opposite of each other. Michael was gentle, quiet, serious, reserved, and committed to following the rules. He was more like his mother. Jon was loud, fun loving, boisterous, and wild, and rules meant little to him. He was more like me. Their personalities nicely fit their roles in Horizon.

Michael was a child prodigy in computer technology. He had started his career with Horizon as a programmer, beginning part-time after school and during the summer. He joined Horizon full-time immediately after graduating from the University of Georgia with a degree in MIS (Management Information Systems). Before long, his exemplary people skills, technological prowess, and keen intellect propelled him into his role as director of research and development. He later was promoted to chief operating officer and began the difficult job of running Horizon's entire day-to-day operations at a very young age. His management style was much less aggressive than mine and yet he was very effective. He reminded me of General Ross: He had *command presence.*

I treated Michael harder than I treated the average employee because I didn't want it to appear as though I was favoring him. To his credit, he weathered this just fine, and his character was rock solid. He earned the respect and admiration of his fellow employees because of his skill set and accomplishments, and no one resented his success or his position within the company.

Even though Michael was admired and respected, senior executives still wanted to come to me with their difficult problems instead of going to Michael. In effect, he became COO in name only. This was a problem that was so pervasive that I finally decided to take drastic action.

I left. Well, kind of. I had grown tired of Atlanta and wanted to move to Florida, so I relocated to Jacksonville and commuted to work in Atlanta every couple of weeks by plane. It was my plan to force senior executives to go to Michael in my absence. And it worked. Without me there, Michael was the one who made decisions on critical issues, and soon he was running Horizon's daily operations in their entirety. Once they gained confidence in him, no one came to me unless their problem truly deserved the involvement of the CEO. I concentrated on sales and on visionary matters concerning new products and the growth of the company, and Michael handled everything else.

I was always a true entrepreneur—a charismatic, big-picture, visionary type, long on ideas but short on patience for the details of execution (which I found to be quite boring). Michael was a spreadsheet guy who loved numbers. He was very detail- and budget-oriented and was more of an operations guy. And honestly, he was running the daily operations of Horizon better and more efficiently than I'd ever run them. No one could have been happier than I was about that situation.

Jon, with his aggressive, gregarious, outgoing, fun-loving personality and charming smile, was better suited to sales. He graduated from the University of Georgia with a degree in marketing and started out by shadowing me on sales calls for almost a year. He was an excellent student and seriously wanted to succeed. He took copious notes and studied hard.

I was a natural-born salesperson and was selling more software than our entire sales department put together, and I taught Jon everything I knew about sales during his training period.

When I felt he was ready to go out on his own, I didn't want to appear as though I was favoring him, either; therefore I assigned him the worst sales territory in the company. In fact it was so bad that nobody else wanted it, and essentially no one was working it. Georgia was part of the assignment; it was the state where Horizon first started selling and we had literally worked it to death through the years. People generally accepted that every account that could be sold in Georgia had already been sold. Jon's territory also included Alabama, which was controlled by a competitor whose accounting software was directly tied in with the state. (Alabama had a state mandate that all vendors had to interface with that company's accounting system, so they had a monopoly.) His other state was Mississippi, and those customers just didn't have any money.

He took that awful territory, and much to my surprise and everyone else's, somehow sold more software that first year than anyone else in the company. He won our *Sales Person of the Year*. He also won it every year thereafter for as long as he competed. Jon was the type of person who not only could sell firewood in hell, but could also get reorders every week or so.

He was eventually promoted to sales manager and he did a spectacular job, although his management style was perhaps a little too aggressive. Jon and I were not different in that regard. He displayed little patience with people and was not hesitant to let them know when they screwed up. This caused some resentment from time to time. But I worked hard to get him out of that mode and after a few years finally succeeded.

Michael married his beautiful high school sweetheart, Michelle. She's so much like Michael that it's scary. She's very intelligent and she graduated from college *cum laude* with a double major. All the medals and honor banners and braids that she donned at the commencement made her look like a South American general in full dress. Michelle came to work for Horizon right out of college and assumed a role with Teresa in our accounting department, where she excelled and later became manager.

Jon married a beautiful girl he met at Horizon, and her name is also Michelle. That's right, two Michelles. In order to eliminate confusion, I suggested calling Michael's Michelle "Number 1," and Jon's Michelle "Number 2," but that idea didn't flush with them. So instead we nicknamed Jon's Michelle "Shelly" and resolved the problem.

Shelly worked in customer service and did a stellar job. Eventually she rose to supervisor level. If that was not enough family in the company, we also hired Teresa's sister Bobbie to work in purchasing and her husband Nelson to work in marketing. We also hired an entire raft of Michael's and Jon's lifelong friends.

Some might question my methods, but I was effective in building companies and especially in motivating the troops. Take, for example, the time our sales team was presenting our software to the largest school district in the country, New York City Department of Education. The day of the presentation I felt very good and was totally relaxed and ready for battle; this in spite of the pressure associated with a very important deal that represented tremendous national prestige, millions upon millions of dollars in revenue, profit for our company, and plenty of sales commissions to go around.

Unfortunately, my sales team was not feeling as confident as I was. There were about 10 of us and we were preparing to face the school district's committee of 30-some men and women. Another vendor was presenting first, and we were in the waiting room as they finished up their presentation. I looked around the waiting room, and to my chagrin, not one person was smiling. Every one of them had a grim, stressed-out look on his face, and a few seemed to be scared out of their wits. Fearing disaster, I knew I had to do something drastic.

I called everyone together and told them that they all needed to smile and not have grimaces and frowns on their faces when we went in. Then I had an idea; I told them all to take out their cellphones and turn the ringers to vibrate. I then instructed them to put their phones in their right front pockets. Finally I instructed one of them to call the receptionist at our home office and give her the presentation schedule; she was to call each presenter precisely at the start of a presentation and was to keep calling every minute or so until that presenter finished.

I told them that when the receptionist called, the phone would begin vibrating and give them the thrill of a lifetime, which no doubt would put a big smile on their faces. Each successive time she called, I said, their smiles would only broaden.

With a wide grin I beamed at them, "What do you think?"

They all laughed heartily and the mood instantly lightened up. When it was time for us to enter the room, I turned to them and said, "Okay men, vibrators on!" We filed into the room with everyone smiling a big, warm, wonderful smile, which no doubt put our audience at ease.

I'd like to relate another incident, which took place after the terrorist attack on September 11, 2001. The entire country sat glued to their televisions, and no one could think of much of anything but those murderer terrorists that dared to attack our country. The plane that crashed into the Pentagon hit 100 feet from the office of the undersecretary of defense that I'd visited when I was working the DoD project. He was spared because he was at the dentist, but his staff did not survive.

It was a scary time and no one could concentrate on business. The tremendous loss of American lives, the audacity of those who dared attack us, and the fear that more was to come was on everyone's minds, including ours. Our sales were nonexistent for three full months. We had ramped up our development project for *Horizon One Source* and were burning through a million dollars a month in overhead. Something had to give soon, because funds were sinking low and debts were piling high. I called a meeting of our executive council to deal with the problem.

When I walked into that room, those seated around our large conference table all had scared, shaken expressions on their faces. As I pondered what to say, I remembered a movie that I saw. General George Patton, with bombs bursting everywhere, was walking up and down the trenches of a battlefield. He'd occasionally stop to shake hands and ask the scared soldiers crouching in the trenches where they were from; he was completely oblivious to the danger around him and showed no fear whatsoever. He solidly clamped down on his cigar as he encouraged soldier after scared soldier. His troops responded and were greatly encouraged by his bravery in the face of tremendous pressure and danger.

As Patton had done, I wanted to encourage the troops. I also wanted to be sure they would never see the slightest hint of fear in my eyes. As I looked around the table at them, my life flashed in front of my eyes. I'd seen death, I'd slept on the side of the road, hopped freights, been hungry and penniless, fought through addictions, been inside prison, experienced mega embezzlement, fought vicious fights, and faced tragedies innumerable; and yet I'd endured and God had seen me through it all.

I wasn't scared in the least. I was mad! I was mad at those terrorist bastards who had attacked our country, and I was mad because they were succeeding in disrupting our way of life.

I contemptuously snorted, "This is nothing! We'll make it through this crisis and look back one day and smile at how we overcame the hurdles that we now face. I lit into that executive council with all the vigor that I had. I told them that we would not be defeated. Yes, bureaucrats were using the attack as an excuse for not conducting business and they would continue to use it until we convinced them that the time for mourning was over. I said, "We are the UNITED STATES OF AMERICA! We don't let terrorists dictate our way of life.

"We need to get out there and call on our customers and if necessary *camp out* in their offices until they gave us a 'yes' followed by a purchase order. We need to renew our sales effort and I'm personally going to lead the charge."

Immediately every expression at the table changed. They no longer had defeated looks on their faces and all appeared ready for battle. In order to cope with the money crunch, I instructed each department to reduce its workforce 15 percent across the board. Horizon had never initiated a layoff before, and no department would be immune . . . I told them to eliminate all waste. I borrowed from my WASCO days and educated them that they must either *get by or justify*, because we weren't spending any money on anything unless they could justify it to my satisfaction.

I told them I'd worked out a deal to obtain some capital through an equity investor, and that the money would help us bridge the crunch and ease our burden somewhat; but what we needed was sales. Finally I told them just to *work and don't worry* and soon they'd see our problems disappear.

In a matter of days, it was as though I'd opened a spigot because orders began flowing again. In a month, we were well on our way to recovery and the crisis was behind us. Within a couple of months we were in a position to rehire those employees who'd been laid off (at least those we wanted to rehire). Eventually I bought out the equity investor and we were completely back to normal. The best thing about this terrible experience was that Horizon's leaders were now seasoned by fire and better off for it.

In spite of all the success I'd had at Horizon and our great employees, products, and service, I was beginning to get antsy and couldn't find peace. For one thing, I was incredibly bored and had begun searching my soul, wondering if I should cash out and do something else. I spent three months praying and meditating about it, trying to seek God's will for my life.

His answer, as always, was interesting . . .

Chapter Eighty

I estimated that I could sell Horizon for no less than $30 million, and if we could obtain the highest multiples of our earnings and profit ratio, maybe even a little more. I'd given each of my sons a fairly significant amount of stock, so if we sold Horizon, which had no debt, they (along with me) would be well compensated and set up for life.

I felt that $30 million was plenty sufficient for our needs, and I was leaning toward selling and possibly even retiring. But after months of prayer and meditation, I couldn't find peace with that decision and came to the conclusion that God didn't want me to sell at this particular time.

I came away with the distinct impression that God wanted me to build the company much larger in order to further demonstrate His great power in transforming me. More money meant more success, more funds available to finance good causes, and more of an impressive story to share with people in order to inspire them.

I felt sure that the $30 million I could muster at this point was sufficient to serve *my* purposes, but it was insufficient to serve *His* purposes. I yielded to that inner voice and faithfully obeyed God. And that shows how far I'd come toward surrendering my life to Him.

It was at this time that a friend and a client, Glenn Davenport, was retiring from Morrison Management Specialists, a food-service management company. The company serviced health-care facilities, such as hospitals and senior living communities, and Horizon had done business with them for years.

As CEO he'd taken Morrison from about $50 million in sales to approximately $100 million, and then he took it public. Once it was a public company, he grew it even larger, to approximately $280 million. At that point, Compass Food Group acquired Morrison and retained Glenn as CEO. In a few years he took it to nearly a billion dollars in sales.

He was only 52 years old and had made plenty of money, but in spite of his success, he didn't like the big-public-company scene and decided to retire. Glenn owned a vacation home in the Florida Keys. I had moved to the Keys from Jacksonville and was now living in Islamorada full time. We'd gotten together and gone fishing a few times, and had become good friends. I knew that Glenn had tremendous integrity and was an excellent businessman. I also knew that he loved the Lord with all his heart and was a great steward of the fortune that God had entrusted to him. He had in fact given millions upon millions of dollars to his church and various Christian-based causes—something that was near and dear to my heart as well.

Michael was doing an excellent job as COO running the operations of Horizon, and Jon was doing similarly well managing the sales team; but I wanted more for them. I wanted Michael and Jon to benefit from someone else's mentoring, experience, and expertise aside from mine. Glenn was the perfect choice, not just because he could share his business acumen, but also because he was a great example in living for the Lord.

So when Glenn retired, I used my formidable sales skills to convince him to come to work for us as a consultant, which meant I had to overcome his desire to sit around fishing every day. I wanted him to assist in budget matters and devise incentive-based bonus plans for our key employees. I knew from the Morrison days that Glenn was an expert at this, and I felt that Horizon would benefit greatly from his expertise.

Glenn agreed to help out, and after working for a few months he really began to take a liking to Michael and Jon and the Horizon team. One thing led to another, and soon we worked out a deal whereby he joined us full-time. We allowed him to invest in Horizon, and he received a small amount of equity. He was already financially set and didn't really need any more money, but he was always on the lookout for new ways to make more money so he could give it to his many philanthropic endeavors.

I made him president and assigned Michael, who was still the COO, to report directly to Glenn. I wanted Glenn to mentor Michael and take him to the next level, and I wanted Glenn to teach him all those spreadsheet things that I didn't know about or care to know about. I remained as chairman and CEO, and concentrated more on sales and marketing.

Sales was not Glenn's strongest suit, but I asked him to mentor Jon too whenever he could. I instructed the boys to be like big sponges and soak up all the knowledge they could from this once-in-a-lifetime opportunity. I told Glenn that I'd taken the boys as far as I could, and it would be great for them to work with someone with a different management style and perspective, especially someone as learned and successful as him.

I felt that it was very important for Michael to receive a better education in finance; that was something I was weak in. I was one of those "shoot from the hip" entrepreneurs who ran the company strictly with my business instinct rather than by spreadsheet and hard budget. I'd done well as an entrepreneur to take things to this point, but I knew that to take it to the next level we'd need a more polished approach.

Glenn was not an entrepreneur but an operations and finance guy like

Michael. I could take an *idea* and turn it into reality by creating a profitable business from brainstorm to brick, but Glenn and Michael could take an already *established business* and take it to greater heights than I could ever achieve on my own.

Neither Glenn nor I wanted to work forever, and we set an ambitious goal to dramatically increase our revenue. In just three to five years, we wanted to double or even triple the value of the company and then sell it, or take it public. We thought that $100 million in revenue (with a 15 percent net) was a nice round number, and that became our goal.

Heretofore I'd been content to increase the size of Horizon about 20 percent every year, because I was more interested in keeping profits high than in growing the company rapidly. (I'd learned the hard way that bigger is *sometimes* better, but profitable is *always* good.) It'd been a good model and it worked well for us; we didn't outgrow our management team's capacity to deal with the growth, we lived within our means and had no debt, we were rock solid and very profitable, and we were considered a "blue chip" company.

Doubling or tripling the size of the company in such a short period of time was an entirely new strategy for us. We had an excellent staff, but not nearly enough top managers for that much growth. We knew we'd have to invest heavily and decided to forgo much of our profit for the short term and instead use it to enhance our infrastructure and shore up our executive staff in anticipation of the rapid growth storm that was coming.

Michael and Glenn were joined at the hip and concentrated on operations. I spent two years revamping our marketing department, which I considered vital to our growth. In my absence from sales, Jon rose to the occasion and took over as top salesperson, working mega and large deals. We hired some powerful new executives in vitally important areas, and our plan began to gel.

Our strategy was working and our revenue began to increase. We were right on schedule with our three-to-five-year plan of reaching $100 million in revenue and 15 percent profitability.

After just two years and in spite of making excellent progress, I began to start having really bad vibes. Actually I felt it was a premonition coming directly from God. I sensed that an economic *"perfect storm"* was forming and bearing down on our country.

Personal credit-card debt was staggering for the American public and high interest payments were drowning people, who had no hope of ever paying off their cards. Personal bankruptcies were at an all-time high. Fuel prices were astronomical, and I was worried that if Israel hit Iran with a preemptive strike to eliminate their nuclear ambitions, the Strait of Hormuz would be affected—and 40 percent of the world's oil moved through that strait. Everything seemed to be affected by the high oil prices and I knew that it would be devastating to our economy if the Mideast exploded.

I sensed also that there was a huge housing bubble that was ready to pop. I'd known some guys who lost everything in the early '80s in the real-estate crash then, and I knew that it was only a matter of time until the real-estate bubble again popped in the United States, especially in California, Florida, Arizona, and other locales where real-estate values had grown way out of proportion to real value.

In traveling to California, I noticed that even tiny homes were selling for a million bucks. I'd moved to Jacksonville and then to the Florida Keys and seen firsthand that Florida real estate was far overvalued. Ordinary working-class folks could never have afforded these expensive homes without some sort of weird financing. The problem was that sooner rather than later, that money would eventually come due; and when it did, people wouldn't be able to pay. Then financiers would be stuck with those homes. I calculated that, just like in the early '80s, people would soon be jumping out of windows. Lots of people were going down hard and surely they would take a lot of others down with them.

The fire was being fueled by the federal government and its social policies gone awry. Poor people couldn't afford homes, due in part to the astronomical prices being asked for them. The feds decided that was unfair and elected to provide anyone who wanted to buy a home with a government-backed loan through Fannie Mae and Freddie Mac. Loan officers were structuring crazy deals to give practically anyone who could breathe a loan without so much as their making a down payment or undergoing a credit check. The loans came with balloon terms and there was no way some of these folks could ever repay them when the balloons came due.

I personally knew a couple of bankers who were cashing in big-time on writing loans daily for this phenomenon. They'd turn around and sell the crummy loans to a mortgage fund and collect their $5,000 fee with absolutely no risk to their banks. The mortgages might be sold two or three times, and each time a big, fat fee would be collected. It was a racket and people were becoming rich and trying to write as many loans as they could to get even richer.

I was also concerned about big unions and poor management driving companies into mind-boggling losses—GM and the airlines are examples. No company can lose billions each quarter without a day of reckoning. Union workers were making close to $100,000 a year with $50,000 in benefits working menial blue-collar jobs on an assembly line. How could U.S. car manufacturers compete with lower-paid workers in other countries? No wonder they were losing money hand over fist.

Although generally I didn't pay much attention to the stock market, I'd been seeing some signs that things weren't going that great for Lehman Brothers. I wondered what would happen if a large firm like that collapsed. It could trigger a bunch of bad things happening.

The same held true of Congress. They were spending money like there was no tomorrow. I learned early on in business and my personal life that I had to live within my means. *Get by or justify!* Spending money you don't have can result in only one thing—DISASTER! Everywhere I looked the government was spending, spending, spending. The national debt was growing to astronomical numbers.

The worst of the perfect storm that I foresaw was of grave concern. It came in the form of an ultraliberal senator from Illinois named Barack Obama, who was gaining momentum in the polls. I knew that if he was elected, capital-gain taxes and other taxes would go through the roof. His liberal agenda would not be kind to business and I didn't want to work for the next several years investing heavily only to pay astronomically high taxes and give all my hard-earned money—for which I'd risked everything—to some welfare program that would give it to some crackhead bum too lazy to get out of bed and go to work.

It seemed to me that our entire economy was teetering on the verge of collapse.

I called a meeting with the boys and Glenn and explained my concerns and logic to them. When I was finished with my spiel I said, "I think we need to get out and get out NOW!" They unanimously agreed, and within weeks we employed Jefferies, an investment banking group in New York City. And amazingly, in just two months' time, we sold Horizon for $75 million cash to a multibillion-dollar public company, Roper Industries.

Imagine how I felt going from zero to $75 million.

With the stock that I gave them early on, Michael and Jon both became instant multimillionaires and were set for life. Glenn had doubled his investment in just two years. Many of our employees who'd remained loyal through the years made out very well with stock options given to them in the early days.

And me, well I made out like a bandit!

Part of the deal was that we would not leave Roper in the lurch—we agreed that upper management would remain in place. I was adamant that I would not stay. I knew I could never work for anyone else; but Glenn, Michael, and Jon had worked for someone else their entire lives. It was agreed that Michael was the one who would take over the top management role as president, but Glenn would stay on for a year or so, just for some "old-guy" insurance. Jon would remain in sales and other various executives would stay as well.

In August of 2008 the deal closed and with a big smile on my face, I pushed my wheelbarrow of cash right down to the bank and left Horizon for good.

I truly believe that God gave me that premonition and told me that the time had finally arrived for me to get out. Incredibly, just a couple of weeks after we received our money, Lehman Brothers indeed collapsed and the stock market crashed and our economy tanked. The mortgage bubble popped, GM and Chrysler were taken over, and many companies collapsed. We just barely averted a depression.

The recession of 2008 indeed turned out to be a very bad one and things might not improve for many years to come. The most liberal senator in congress, now our president, Barrack Hussein Obama, turned out to be even worse than I could have ever imagined. The antibusiness tax increases, ill thought out stimulus, excessive regulation, health care debacle, entitlement giveaway programs, and antibusiness policies that I feared are currently being put into place by a radical administration and an equally liberal, free-spending Congress.

It makes me sick to watch.

Fortunately for Horizon, much of its business was government-related, so it was spared the worst of the bitter economic downturn that the rest of the country endured. Actually, in spite of the economic meltdown, Horizon turned a profit and outperformed many of Roper's subsidiaries after they bought it. I'm very happy about that. Had we decided not to sell, we undoubtedly would have survived the crash; but had we waited, we wouldn't have sold Horizon for anywhere near its value for many years to come.

Glenn didn't have to stay a year and was able to leave not long after the sale—Michael had demonstrated that he was ready to take over and Glenn assured me that he'd already taught him everything he could.

Michael performed extremely well in his role as president and proved to himself and others that he is an excellent executive in his own right. Jon could not adjust well to the public-company environment and after a year left Horizon and joined Teresa and me in our 10th start-up company, Honey Lake Plantation Resort and Spa. It's a development in north Florida where we're building a resort and spa retreat on my 4,700-acre hunting-and-fishing plantation; and we also have some luxury vacation rental homes in Islamorada.

As for me, I'm now in a position to complete God's purpose for my life. I intend to tell anyone who cares to listen how God completely changed my life. This book, which took more than two years to write—two difficult, gut-wrenching years of reliving my worst nightmares—is my first installment. I expect that I will spend the remainder of my life trying to inspire people to do as I have done and turn their lives over to God Almighty. I will continue in business because, like Glenn, I want more money to fund worthwhile projects. And besides, it's fun to be in business.

If it were not for God entering my life, there is no doubt in my mind that I would be dead, in prison, or perhaps locked up in an insane asylum somewhere. He alone is responsible for my success, and there is no doubt in my mind that if I can do it, so can you. I hope you will make Philippians 4:13 your battle cry and burn in your brain that indeed *"I can do all things through Christ who strengthens me."*

If you are not a believer, then I encourage you to become one. It's easy to call upon the name of the Lord. Start with this verse, John 3:16: *For God so loved the world that he gave his one and only Son, that whoever believes in him shall not perish but have eternal life.* Ask for forgiveness, and ask God for help in turning from your former life—beginning as a baby Christian and following Jesus Christ to your maturity.

I recommend that you do as I did and read the Bible. I've read it many times since I first read it in Grady Memorial Hospital. I like the New International Version, the New King James Version, and the Living Bible.

If you are new to the Bible, I would advise that you first read the book of Romans and then go to Matthew and read the entire New Testament before tackling the Old Testament. I also urge you to find a church that you like and attend regularly. (There will be hypocrites there to be sure, but they need to be there. Sick people need to be in the hospital.)

I hope to see you in heaven . . .

EPILOGUE

Teresa and I

We are very committed to our sons and of course our grandchildren. We remain happily married and are getting ready to celebrate our 40th wedding anniversary. We both still enjoy working long hours and are passionate about the many business opportunities that God has blessed us with. We live full time on the plantation, where we ride horses and view the wildlife most every day. We visit the Keys often to relax, fish, and boat.

Dad

Dad remarried two years after Mom died. His was a remarkable story in itself. My Uncle Jake and Aunt Betty (Mom's sister) were going to retire in Columbus and spend the rest of their lives near Mom and Dad. Unfortunately Uncle Jake was tragically killed in a car accident about six months prior to Mom's death. After Jake died, Betty moved to Columbus to be close to Mom. But then she unexpectedly died of the brain tumor, giving Betty the double whammy.

Dad and Aunt Betty were both devastated, but God was merciful to them in providing comfort to them through each other. Approximately two years after Mom's death, Dad and Aunt Betty got married and the empty holes that had been ripped in their hearts were filled by God. They were married some 30 years and were very much in love and happy together.

Betty recently died and Dad was devastated. He is 89 now and is in very poor health with Parkinson's disease. Although he's quite feeble, he still faithfully teaches his senior men's Sunday school class each and every Sunday—as he has done for the past 40 years. Betty, who was 87 and in poor health, taught the senior ladies' class right up until her death.

My relationship with Dad is excellent and I love him dearly, as I did Aunt Betty. I call him every Sunday afternoon and visit as often as I can.

Michael and Michelle

Michael and Michelle are happily married, and both are Christians. They had twin girls, Hailey and Lauren, who are now four years old. Michelle resigned from her position at Horizon after having the girls in order to pursue being a full-time mom. Michael continued on as president of Horizon for a little over two years after we sold it, and he did a stellar job. He resigned to start up his own software business and is currently writing the specifications for it. I consult with him on the project and hope to help him with his project as it matures.

Jon and Shelly

Jon and Shelly are happily married and are both Christians who love the Lord. They have two boys: Owen is one and a half years old and Ryan is an infant. Shelly resigned from Horizon after she gave birth to Owen and became a full-time mom. Jon stayed at Horizon for one year and then joined me as a partner in my Honey Lake Plantation Resort and Spa endeavor, which is transforming my 4,700-acre plantation into a corporate retreat, destination wedding location, hunting-and-fishing mecca, and high-end bed-and-breakfast.

Little Jim and Lee

Little Jim moved to the suburbs of Portland, Oregon, and still lives in that community. He works out of Portland as a senior Oracle consultant and project leader, and is very successful and respected in his job.

After he and Lee left Horizon, we had little contact with each other. One day the Lord put it on my heart to tell him that I had forgiven him, and I did. I consider it one of the most rewarding things I ever did and I'm exceedingly glad I reached out to him.

Jim and Lee have three children—a girl and two boys—and they are super-nice, well-adjusted kids. Ashley is a cheerleader, and both boys, Nick and Evan, are star athletes and play every sport. All three are excellent students and make terrific grades. The entire family loves the Lord and they attend church together each Sunday.

A couple of times a year all my family, including Jim, Michael, and Jon, their wives, and the grandkids, get together either at my home in the Florida Keys in Islamorada or at my quail-hunting plantation in northern Florida. It's quite a sight to see them all together and interacting. All my boys are Christians, at peace, college educated, well adjusted, and happily married; and by far my greatest achievement has been that they did not take after me in my early days.

Lydia

Unfortunately after I left Grady Memorial Hospital I never saw or spoke to Lydia again. It is one of my deepest regrets that I didn't stay in contact with this wonderful woman. I fully intend to see her again in heaven and pick right back up where we left off.

WASCO Machine

Though broken up and sold in pieces upon my leaving, most of the components of the once-mighty WASCO machine are still alive and well today. Ken Edwards and Sallie Dahmes are at the helm of WASCO, and it's still a viable entity that continues to manufacture and distribute wildlife-art supplies all over the world. Polytranspar is still the best airbrush paint on the market and has the awards to prove it.

Breakthrough magazine, the books I published, the World Taxidermy Championships, and the World Fish Carving Championships are still the best in the industry and are a significant industry force. They remain owned and operated by Larry Blomquist and his wife, Kathy.

A couple of years back I was staying at a hotel way down in Texas close to Old Mexico. I was standing in the lobby and a guy walked by with a WASCO camouflage hat on. It was an unexpected reward to see that a company that I dreamed up was affecting people so far from where it all began.

I've been lucky enough to experience this feeling many times since, particularly with Horizon. As I travel the country, I'm rewarded to see customer site after customer site in city after city. We installed 18,000 sites all over the world that rely on our technology every day.

That was my idea to come up with that technology and now I see it everywhere I go, be it in Los Angeles Unified school district, a submarine or military base, John Hopkins University hospital, or wherever.

Way cool to do this! Way cool.

Miracles, Answers to Prayers, and Strange Things

There are miracles, answered prayers, and strange things that occur in the background of our lives, confirming that an unseen spiritual war is being waged for our souls. Many times they are overlooked, or chalked up to coincidence, Karma, or luck, but I believe that unseen spiritual forces are in play in our lives on a daily basis; and the Bible tells us the same.

There is no question that I've been blessed throughout my life, and God transformed my life through a series of mighty miracles, answered prayers, and strange spiritual occurrences in order to demonstrate His awesome power. I've created a bullet-point list of some of the more important ones for you below.

- Found a nickel on the street, and that was the exact amount of money required to catch a bus out of New Orleans to escape hell
- Saw a newspaper ad for a computer school in Atlanta on the bus as I was trying to escape, and decided to go to that city because of it
- Arrived in Atlanta at the intersection of Fairlie Street and Luckie Street—Fairly Lucky for me, wouldn't you say?
- Survived a head-on collision. If you had seen the car, you would have agreed that it was a miracle that anyone got out of it alive
- Met Teresa on the night of the accident and then reunited with her the first night out after my recovery, when she sat in my chair in the dark, crowded disco

- Called home from Canada at the very moment my mom was on her knees praying for me to do so
- Car wouldn't start the night I had given in to temptation and tried to go out to find drugs
- Kicked intravenous drugs without rehab or therapy
- Kicked violent behavior after observing a blue jay squawking at a squirrel; overcame my inclinations even though a psychiatric team had diagnosed me as being an incurable sociopath
- Kicked cigarettes after spitting up blood and cancer scare
- Kicked 30-some-odd years of alcoholism after hepatitis C diagnosis
- Master Paint Systems built into a multimillion-dollar entity in just six months, with no start-up capital or prior business ownership experience
- Diagnosed with a brain tumor, told I could die at any moment, discovered that it was harmless brain fluid
- Avoided bankruptcy of WASCO despite incredible odds
- Along with Teresa, revived Horizon after every employee had quit and our money had been depleted
- Sat down next to General Shadley on a plane when I was trying to sell Horizon software to the Department of Defense and needed a military contact
- Jim reunited with his wife and immediately sold his house after accepting Christ as his savior
- Premonition from God to sell Horizon—a deal that closed two weeks before the stock market crashed

I encourage you to list the miracles, answered prayers, and strange things that have occurred in your own life. If you look, you'll find them.

Lessons Learned

I'm much grayer, wrinkled up, and wiser now than I was nearly 40 years ago when I first hitchhiked into Atlanta full of hate and spewing bitterness. Mine has been an amazing journey and I've garnered some rich lessons learned, and some hard lessons learned. I thought it might be helpful to summarize some of the ones that I deem to be the most important to me, and it's my hope that they can benefit you as well.

Pyramid of Life

Perhaps the most important thing I've learned is to keep my priorities in order. I developed what I refer to as the *Pyramid of Life.* It graphically represents how I think every aspect of my life should be prioritized.

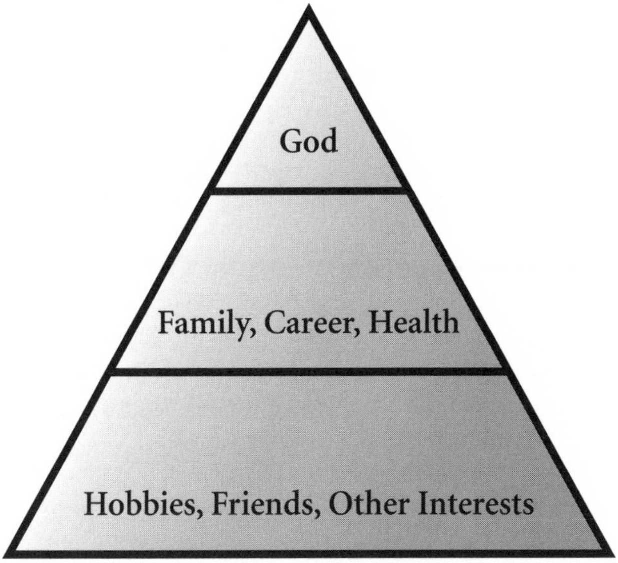

Pyramid of Life

God is at the top and is more important to me than anything else in my life, including my wife, kids, and grandkids. He must always be put first, above all other things. Next I put my family, career, and health all on the same plane. Underneath that are the other things in life. Something from a lower section should never trump something in the section above it, and items on an equal plane should be given equal emphasis.

I've often been heatedly told, "My family comes above my career. What do you mean putting career on an equal plane with wife or family? It should be God, family, and then career."

I simply respond, "Do you love your family?"

"Well of course I do!"

"Then please tell me how you intend to provide for the family that you love without making your career just as high a priority? Your career provides the financial means to buy a home for them, clothe them, send them off to college, vacation with them, and otherwise care for them. Basically if you love your family, you must love your career too.

I cannot tell you how many times I've had to suck it up in order to resolve some difficult problem at work at the cost of not being able to go somewhere with my wife or family as I'd originally planned. As I look back on it now, I don't regret making those tough decisions and neither does my family. My family is financially set for life because of my sacrifice.

Now if I'd ALWAYS made the decision to sacrifice my career in favor of my family, that would've been different. Indeed there have been times when I did exactly that. It's a balancing act, and sometimes there are not any clear-cut answers. I remember one time when I was given an opportunity of a lifetime: Some wealthy landowners offered me tremendous money to move to South Africa and open a mega tannery for them.

I declined the job because I didn't want to move my kids out of their schools and away from their friends. Having moved constantly as a child, I knew firsthand how difficult it was on kids to move them out of their schools and a stable environment. I couldn't in good conscience put their stability and happiness above my own ambition. My kids lived in the same house in the same neighborhood from infancy through college graduation.

Likewise, if you fail to take care of your health and you become too sick to care for your family, what good will you be to them? You must allot the necessary time to exercise and eat right in order to stay healthy and serve your family.

When I refer to keeping things on an equal plane, I mean devoting equal time to all priorities on that level. If you really love your family, you'll partition your time and fully embrace spending time with them as well as fulfilling the responsibilities of your demanding career and doing your part to stay healthy.

When I get the priorities of the pyramid out of order and put something higher than it should be, it generally causes serious problems. For example, if I decide to go fishing instead of going to church on Sunday, then I'm taking something on the very bottom of the pyramid and treating it as a higher priority than what's at the very top. I've found that there are always repercussions when I do that.

This concept works for me and I think it will work for most Christians.

Why Bad Things Happen

I now realize that exhilarating triumphs and agonizing defeats are an integral part of everyday life, and every human being on this planet ultimately will have a taste of both. To be sure, God punishes sin and I've experienced that phenomenon firsthand; but I've also learned that I shouldn't always interpret hard times as being some form of retaliatory punishment exacted upon me by an angry God.

At the time of my brother's suicide, I was as close to God as I'd ever been. I was attending church every Sunday, and I was studying my Bible daily. In fact, I began each day by writing my daily devotional, *Words for the Day.* I was praying throughout the day, and at every opportunity I was encouraging others to become Christians. I had tremendous faith in God and loved Him with all my heart.

So the question loomed, why did the Lord allow this to happen to me?

The answer that I came up with is that "I" am not the center of God's universe and not everything that happens in this world is directly related to me. Sometimes bad things affect many people, including innocent bystanders.

No matter if bad things happen to others or directly to me, God's purpose for allowing bad things to happen is often known only to God. And that is His prerogative as our Almighty Creator.

I believe that Jim's unhappiness was a direct consequence of his drifting away from God and directly toward his dark side and sin. Did God punish Jim for drifting away from Him? Does God sit up in heaven with a big flyswatter just waiting for someone to get out of line so he can swat them one?

I don't think so. It seems to me that consequence is an incontrovertible result of sin. Sin is the cause, and consequence is the effect. Once sin is set in motion, consequence always results. For example, if I throw a rock at a window, it will shatter the glass upon impact. I might regret throwing the rock the instant that it leaves my hand, but once it's set in motion, all the regret in the world won't prevent it from continuing on to shatter the glass.

Similarly, I might regret committing a grievous sin the moment after I commit it; but unfortunately the sin has already been set in motion and along with it the consequence of that sin shattering my life. I've come to the conclusion that it's an irrefutable axiom that consequence cannot and will not be denied. For every action there is an automatic reaction.

Can anyone reasonably deny that there will be life-shattering consequences for murder, stealing, lying, drug and alcohol abuse, adultery, and the like?

The consequence might be strikingly severe—prison, divorce, venereal disease, dark depression leading to suicide, getting fired, bankruptcy, debilitating sickness, dying from AIDS, driving drunk, OD'ing, or being shot by a jealous husband.

Sometimes we escape the life-shattering consequences—for example, all those times I drove home drunk without crashing my car, which amounted to hundreds or possibly even thousands of times. And then sometimes we don't escape them, like the one time that I drove drunk and had the head-on collision that nearly killed me.

One thing is certain: Even if we escape those severe consequences, we will not escape the litany of less debilitating but nonetheless severe and more-subtle consequences, such as unhappiness, hopelessness, guilt, loneliness, misery, despair, and sadness.

Make no mistake about it—there are no free rides when it comes to sin. There are always consequences.

Bible

I've often wondered if God's word, the Holy Bible, was actually some sort of spiritual owner's manual designed to spare us from the consequences of sin. Did God create us and then mandate that the Bible be written so that we could first and foremost find salvation and then it could guide us through this life? I thought of an owner's manual for an automobile, which details what should be done in order to ensure maximum performance and extended life for that vehicle. If I observe the manufacturer's recommendations about changing the oil every 3,000 miles, rotating the tires, changing filters, and more, then that maintenance will enhance performance and extend the life of my car.

Could God our Creator (or if you will, *Manufacturer* of life) have given us the Bible to ensure that we might enjoy maximum performance in our lives? Does His owner's manual tell us not to commit murder, lie, steal, commit adultery, cheat, covet, lust, or commit a multitude of other sins so that we might avoid those harmful things and instead do those things that will enable us to enjoy life to its fullest? Are all the commands in the Bible designed to help us be all we can be in this life and the next?

It seems logical to me that if God loved us enough to send Jesus to die for our sins, then He would also provide us with a set of guidelines to follow so we could find peace and happiness in this life and the next. I believe the Bible contains those guidelines, and I read it daily.

I do not think an all-powerful God would make mistakes in His Holy Bible. Indeed it states of itself that every word is true. Many atheists have tried to disprove it and none have succeeded. Most, like me, after reading it for themselves, became believers convinced that it was the *living* word of God, powerful and sharper than a two-edged sword.

My tip to others reading it is to not read it as a novel. Take your time and reflect often upon what God is telling you as you read. I have no doubt that He will gently speak to you through your mind and open up His scriptures to you in an amazing way. I believe that God directly communicates to us through the Bible.

Forgiveness

I have found that forgiveness is more about us than the person we forgive. It's difficult to forgive others. Some don't even want our forgiveness, or don't think they have done anything wrong in the first place to warrant forgiveness. But if you can't decide whether or not to forgive someone, and it eats away at you, then do it. I think it's one of the most difficult things in life to do, but is no doubt one of the most rewarding.

Raising Kids

I believe in discipline, and that includes corporal punishment on occasion. Kids cannot raise themselves and the Bible states that if you spare the rod you will spoil the child. It also states that if you won't discipline your kids, it means that you hate them. We should follow God's lead. He loves us with unimaginable love, but when it becomes necessary, He disciplines us for our own good—and sometimes that discipline can be severe.

With that said, the most important thing involved with raising kids is to *love* them and spend time with them. Don't get so caught up in the world that you fail to spend time with your kids. If you do so, you will know their friends. I believe more kids go astray because of crummy friends than for any other reason.

Marriage

This December my wife and I will have been married for 40 years. She is my best friend and my soul mate, and I believe with all my heart that God picked her out for me and put her in that chair beside me in that crowded disco so many years ago. She is the best thing that ever happened to me, aside from my securing my salvation. The Bible tells us that our spouse is a blessing from God and we should treat her as such.

As for my thoughts on marriage: First I think that both parties must be devoted to God. Second we need to realize that the only thing in life that is perfect is God. You are not perfect and neither is your spouse. A happy couple overlooks and learns to live with the imperfections of their mate. Divorce should never be an option to working out problems; knives, fists, guns, arm wrestling, water pistols, maybe, but never mention or think about divorce.

Addictions

I've spoken to thousands of recovering addicts and alcoholics from Anchorage to the Florida Keys, and I've never met one who had set a goal of becoming an addict or an alcoholic. It starts out with having a beer or smoking a joint, and before you know it you are hopelessly ensnared. I do not believe that freedom from addiction can be achieved apart from developing a relationship with God.

Compassion

I have a tremendous amount of compassion for others. I try to model my life after Jesus Christ. He was compassionate and not condescending. If I don't care about the unsaved among us—the poor, the suffering, the sick, and those who have lost hope—then how can I be a child of God? We all need to take our eyes off ourselves and our own needs long enough to take a look around and then do something about it.

Death

The Bible tells us that we should think of our own deaths often. Why?

I wonder if it's because after we die, we face eternity with God in heaven, or are forever separated from Him in hell. I think maybe that this is the answer.

The saddest thing in the entire world is to attend the funeral of a non-Christian; Christians, however, should not fear death. In Psalms 23:4 death is referred to as a shadow and we are told that we "should fear no evil as we walk through the valley of the shadow of death."

A shadow is harmless. Imagine the dazzling, intense, wonderful light of Jesus Christ. The Bible states that all of heaven will be illuminated by His radiant light.

Death will be defeated forever and there will be no shadows in heaven.

Witnessing

Few things are as important or rewarding as sharing the word of God with others. The Bible tells us to do it and we need to obey that command for sure. I actually feel very fortunate to have lived the wicked life that I've lived.

Before you freak out, hear me out. The wicked things that I've done have convinced me that I'm deserving of going to hell and I know that I know that I need Jesus.

I witness to so many people who think that they are basically good and decent. They refuse to believe that a loving God would send them to hell to suffer for all eternity.

The Bible tells us that we have ALL sinned and will be eternally separated from God unless the blood of Jesus covers those sins. We cannot be good enough to get into heaven. If we could, why would it have been necessary for Jesus Christ to come to Earth and suffer so horribly and die on the cross?

Now, either the Bible is lying or even the little white lies will send us to hell without Jesus. I believe the latter. We all need Jesus and we need to tell others.

Judging Others

As one might imagine after the sordid life that I've lived, I'm not the judgmental type. I've done so many wrong things I'm not about to condemn others for whatever they might've done. I have, however, been the recipient of such behavior on many occasions right through today, and it's not a good feeling. I overcome the judgment of others by taking comfort in Ephesians 2:1–10

"And you were dead in the trespasses and sins in which you once walked, following the course of this world, following the prince of the power of the air, the spirit that is now at work in the sons of disobedience—among whom we all once lived in the passions of our flesh, carrying out the desires of the body and the mind, and were by nature children of wrath, like the rest of mankind. But God, being rich in mercy, because of the great love with which He loved us, even when we were dead in our trespasses, made us alive together with Christ—by grace you have been saved—and raised us up with Him and seated us with Him in the heavenly places in Christ Jesus, so that in the coming ages He might show the immeasurable riches of His grace in kindness toward us in Christ Jesus. For by grace you have been saved through faith. And this is not your own doing; it is the gift of God, not a result of works, so that no one may boast. For we are his workmanship, created in Christ Jesus for good works, which God prepared beforehand, that we should walk in them."

All I can say is that the Bible insists that no person is free of sin. When the adulteress was brought before Jesus and the raging crowd was accusing her and wanted to stone her to death, Jesus told them that whosoever among them was without sin should throw the first stone, and then He stooped down and began writing in the dirt. I believe that perhaps He was writing the Ten Commandments.

They immediately started dropping their stones and began leaving, beginning with the oldest and continuing until there was no one left.

> *Jesus then said to her, "Woman, where are they? Has no one condemned you?"*
> *"No one, sir," she said.*
> *"Then neither do I condemn you," Jesus declared.*
> *"Go now and leave your life of sin."*

Now if Jesus did this, how much more so should we?

Success

Success to me is being able to achieve peace and happiness in your life. It has nothing to do with bank accounts, material possessions, or job titles. I know some folks who have very little in the way of education, money, power, or fame but are exceedingly successful because they know peace and are very happy. Conversely, I know a good many very wealthy, famous, powerful people who are considered by the world to be successful, but are miserable.

Money does not bring happiness; if anything it's a serious distraction from the Lord, and with it comes a barrel full of temptation. Having a close personal relationship with God has everything to do with success and being successful.

Faith

The Bible teaches that it's impossible to please God without faith. It also states that faith without works is dead. This means that we all need to find some purpose greater than ourselves and do more than just talk about it.

Purpose

We were created to serve God's purpose and not our own. Find your purpose in life and fulfill it to the best of your ability. In order to do this you must take your eyes off yourself and put them squarely on God.

I've spent an enormous amount of time trying to discern God's purpose for my life. And I've determined that sharing my testimony is my primary purpose. That's why I wrote this book. It wasn't easy to write and I didn't want to relive all those dark moments, much less share them with others. I worked thousands of hours on it and that was time that could have been spent fishing, relaxing, hunting, or whatever. I did it for my God and my Savior. Considering what He did for me, it was a small thing.

Temptation

The Bible teaches that with temptation comes an escape route. Know that temptation is coming, and look for the escape route, find it, and take it.

Finale

My early, sinful life left its mark on my body and mind. Remarkably I lived through two head-on collisions; two cars that rolled; thousands of fights in which I was beaten with fists and clubs and was kicked, stomped, and gouged; and I was shot at on at least three occasions. I introduced all kinds of drugs into my body, freaked out on LSD, OD'd on meth, engaged in crime, and on and on. The consequences of those sins are still exacting their price upon my body today.

After I was married, I had numerous flashbacks from LSD. This phenomenon would cause me to actually start tripping again regardless of the fact that I hadn't taken any LSD. Thankfully the trips didn't last long and stopped altogether approximately two years after our wedding.

I wasn't so lucky with my teeth. Years of abuse and using meth ruined my teeth and gums. I endured major reconstructive surgery on four occasions, including having painful bone grafts to replace the deteriorating bone in my jaws; and virtually every tooth in my head has either been pulled or crowned.

As detailed in the book, I have hepatitis C and will have the dangerous virus until it either kills me or I die of something else. As far as I know, it's still inactive and my hope and prayer is that it will remain so.

I now have severe arthritis in the leg that was crushed in the Atlanta accident, and in the mornings—and especially when it rains—I'm like an old dog as I stiffly hobble around. I've repeatedly broken my hands, fists, and fingers, as well as my ribs and collarbone. All that abuse took its toll and ended in painful arthritis too.

My nose was broken seven times and later in life I endured not one, but two operations to repair a severely deviated septum and straighten it.

The surgeon looked inside my badly mangled nose and said, "God what a mess! Your nose isn't just broken, it's tied in knots! *What in the hell happened to you?*"

I looked at him with a smile on my face and shook my head and said, "I had a rough life doc."

That just about sums it up, does it not?

Jim and me in Okinawa

Me in Fairfield

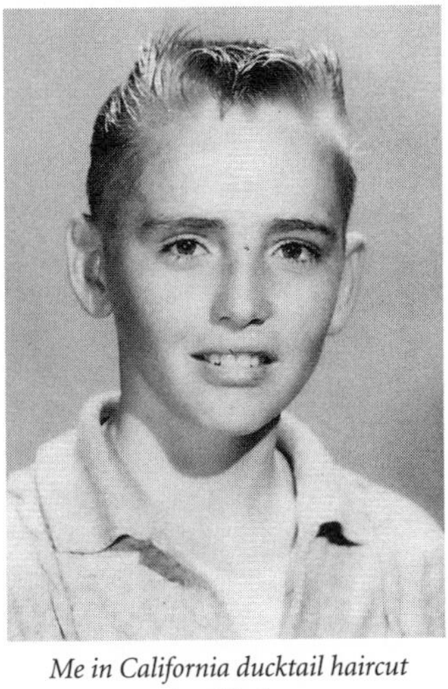

Me in California ducktail haircut and scabbed nose

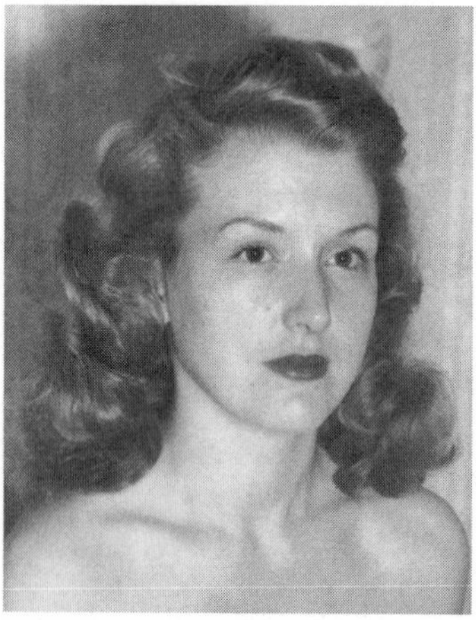
Mom

Betty and Dad

My beloved brother Jim

Mom and Uncle Jake (Betty's husband)

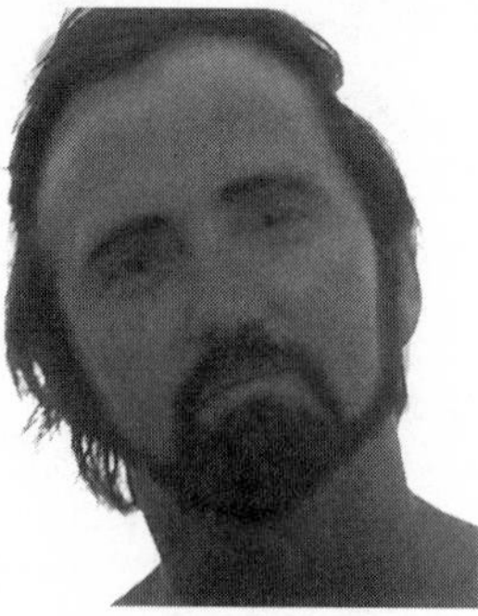
Me when I was still bad to the bone

Old ways die hard

Mom and Little Bob

Teresa and me - engagement weekend

Back: Teresa and Bobbie;
(front) Shelby and Jennie

Bobbie and Teresa

Michael and Jon – Starting young
on a WASCO mail-out

Horizon building

Teresa and me

Dusty and me

Little Jim, Me, Jon, and Michael

Top row: Michelle K, Jon, Nick, Michael, Little Jim, Teresa, me
Bottom row: Evan, Ashlee, Hailey, Lauren, Michelle C., Lee, Owen

Nick, Lauren, Evan, Hailey, Owen, and Ashlee

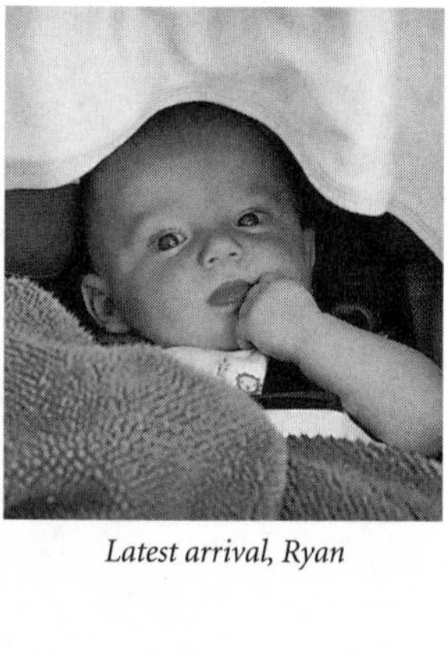

Latest arrival, Ryan

Acknowledgements

I'm delighted to be finished writing this book. Living through the darkest days of my life was bad enough the first time, so reliving the same experiences all over again years later was painful. With that said, I'm glad I struggled through it, because my autobiography clearly demonstrates the power of Jesus Christ to miraculously save even the worst among us. It is Jesus Christ who I wish to acknowledge and thank the most. Without Him I would certainly be locked up in a prison somewhere, or buried in a pauper's grave and long since forgotten. Thank you Lord Jesus!

The people I will acknowledge here are, simply put, the best: My wife Teresa, my three sons Jim, Michael, and Jon, their wives Lee, Michelle C., and Michelle K., and my seven grandchildren. Also my mom and dad, and my stepmom, Betty; all of whom prayed for me throughout my life. I would also like to acknowledge my beloved brother Jim; may he at long last rest in peace.

I appreciate and admire all the great employees whose hard work and commitment to excellence made all the great companies that I founded what they are today. I won't name you all because I would likely omit someone and I couldn't bear to do that to you. You know who you are and how much I appreciate what you contributed.

I would like to thank my creative consultant, Joe Kita, who is an accomplished writer and friend. Joe patiently offered terrific creative and technical suggestions for improvement and was a source of constant encouragement. My thanks also go to Al and George Cuneo and their entire staff at Cuneo Creative in Tallahassee for their assistance in typesetting and laying out the book, helping with the cover design, and developing the website. Thanks to Eric Rinehimer for the excellent job he did in final copyediting. Thanks to two friends of mine, Ken Ross and Jennifer Stalcup, for taking the powerful photographs that I used for the front and back covers.

Finally I would like to thank you, the reader of this book, for reading it in its entirety. I hope by now you know that there is a God and that He loves you and wants to bring joy and peace into your life. He stands at the door and knocks.

Let Him in, won't you?

QUICK ORDER FORM

Email orders: http://www.miracleonluckiestreet.com

Postal orders: Williamson Publishing
1290 NW Honey Lake Road • Greenville Florida 32331

Please send more FREE information on:

❑ Other books ❑ Speaking/Seminars ❑ Mailing lists ❑ Consulting

Name: ______________________________

Address: ______________________________

City: ____________________ State: ________ Zip: ____________

Telephone: ______________________________

Email Address: ______________________________

❑ **$24.95** ❑ **$29.95** Autographed

Preferred Inscription *(if any)*:

____

____

Sales tax: Please add 7.5% for products shipped to Florida addresses.

Shipping by air: **US:** $2.50 for the first book and $2.00 for each aditional book. **International:** $9.00 for the first book and $5.00 for each additional book. *(estimate)*

Payment: ❑ Check or Credit Card: ❑ Visa ❑ MasterCard ❑ AMEX ❑ Discover

Card number: ______________________________

Name on card: ____________________ Exp. date: ____________

Signature: ______________________________

Telephone orders: Call 850-948-9911. Have your credit card ready.

Fax orders: 850-948-5000. *Send this form*